SE

Visual Basic® 2005:
The Complete Reference

Ron Petrusha

McGraw-Hill
New York Chicago San Francisco
Lisbon London Madrid Mexico City
Milan New Delhi San Juan
Seoul Singapore Sydney Toronto

The McGraw·Hill Companies

McGraw-Hill books are available at special quantity discounts to use as premiums and sales promotions, or for use in corporate training programs. For more information, please write to the Director of Special Sales, Professional Publishing, McGraw-Hill, Two Penn Plaza, New York, NY 10121-2298. Or contact your local bookstore.

Visual Basic® 2005: The Complete Reference

1234567890 CUS CUS 019876

ISBN 0-07-226033-5

Sponsoring Editor
Wendy Rinaldi

Editorial Supervisor
Jody McKenzie

Project Editor
Carolyn Welch

Acquisitions Coordinator
Alexander McDonald

Technical Editor
Eric Lippert

Copy Editor
Bob Campbell

Proofreader
Carolyn Welch

Indexer
Claire Splan

Production Supervisor
Jean Bodeaux

Composition
International Typesetting and Composition

Art Director, Cover
Jeff Weeks

Cover Designer
Jeff Weeks

To Vanessa,
for making life worthwhile.

And to the BHGs,
for keeping life interesting.

About the Author

Ron Petrusha has over 30 years of programming
experience, starting with Fortran on the IBM 370
family of mainframe computers, and has been
programming in Visual Basic since version 1.0. Ron
has worked for much of his career as an acquisitions
and development editor and an author. He is the
author and co-author of eight books, including
Inside the Windows 95 Registry and *VBScript in a
Nutshell*, as well as *Access VBA Programming*,
published by McGraw-Hill. He currently works for
Volt Technical Resources as an SDK Writer on
contract to Microsoft Corporation.

Contents

Acknowledgments

This book has turned out to be a far larger project than originally envisioned both in terms of time and the number of pages. I want to thank Wendy Rinaldi and Alex McDonald for their belief in this book, as well as for their commitment to see it through to the end.

I also want to thank Eric Lippert of Microsoft, who served as the book's technical reviewer. This is the second book of mine that Eric has reviewed, and in both cases he's caused me to spend far more time revising my manuscript than I had originally planned. Eric combines a strong talent for writing, a wealth of experience as a language architect and programmer, and a real passion for Visual Basic. He's made an enormous contribution to the quality of this book.

Writing a book of this size is a major endeavor that inevitably reduces the time available for one's family. I am truly blessed that my wife, Vanessa, has constantly been as enthusiastic about this project as I am, and that she was willing to serve as both father and mother to our children while I was preoccupied. I am also thankful for the support of my children Sean, Latina, and Janae. I wish that our four dogs (and especially Dakota, the oldest, who often ignores me for days on end because he feels slighted) had been as supportive.

Introduction

A s its title, *Visual Basic 2005: The Complete Reference*, indicates, this book is intended as a reference guide to the Visual Basic .NET Language. In particular, it has been written to focus on the language elements in Visual Basic .NET's latest release, Visual Basic 2005.

What This Book Is About

The term "reference guide" spans a broad range of works, from dictionaries, which contain brief definitions of individual words, to specialized multivolume encyclopedias that examine relevant aspects of a particular topic in great detail. If you were to locate this book along such a continuum, it would be more like the latter than the former. In fact, succinct references of the former type are readily available online. If you're using Visual Studio .NET 2005 or Visual Basic 2005 Express, both IntelliSense and Object Browser can give you the syntax and basic function of a particular language element, assuming that you know its name. The online documentation provides a more detailed description, often with a code example.

Often when you're programming, though, you need to know some details about a language element that aren't discussed in the documentation. Or you'd like to see an example that doesn't simply display an obvious property value to the system console. Or you'd like to read about a topic that's closely related to a language topic. In this book, you'll find all of these things. For each language entry, you'll typically find a wealth of detail that isn't present in the Visual Basic online help. For example, you may be reading about For…Each next loops not because you don't know their syntax, but because you want to know what you need to do to make your custom container enumerable. The online documentation is silent on that point; this book is not. The book also contains a good deal of sample code—typically, far more than one example per language element. Instead, small code fragments are used to illustrate each theme that's discussed, and longer examples illustrate the usage of the language element as a whole.

As a complete reference to the elements of the Visual Basic language, *Visual Basic 2005: The Complete Reference* is intended to serve as a sourcebook that you can constantly turn to for basic reference documentation, troubleshooting hints, coding techniques, and ideas about how and whether you might use an element.

Because this book is intended as a reference, it is not geared for novice programmers who want to learn the basic details of the language. It does include seven introductory chapters that discuss such topics as the Visual Basic type system, object-oriented programming topics, event-driven programming, and the .NET Framework Class Library. However, these chapters are extremely fast-paced, and assume that you have a basic familiarity with programming topics. Typically, this cryptic approach is suitable for programmers with some prior experience, including those who have developed with other versions of Visual Basic or VBScript, as well as

.NET developers who code in C#. For those who are new to programming and Visual Basic .NET, a more thorough, methodical approach that emphasizes basic programming concepts as well as their implementation in Visual Basic .NET is typically desirable. For such a book, see *Visual Basic 2005 Demystified* by Jeff Kent.

Since we are discussing what this book is and is not, it is important to stress again that this is a reference guide to Visual Basic .NET language elements. That is, it discusses language elements implemented by the Visual Basic compiler, as well as language elements implemented by the core portions of the *Microsoft.VisualBasic.dll* assembly and its Microsoft.VisualBasic namespace. It is not a guide to the .NET Framework Class Library types and their members as a whole. Certainly, framework types and members are discussed frequently in these pages, and often the functionality of a particular language element is compared to similar framework elements. In addition, Appendix G, ".NET Data Type Reference," lists the members of each of the Framework Class Library's primitive data types. So, although the Framework is certainly not neglected or ignored, it is not treated comprehensively or exhaustively.

Whom This Book Is For

Visual Basic 2005: The Complete Reference is written for any advanced novice to advanced programmer who is programming in Visual Basic and can benefit from a core reference and programming sourcebook.

The book focuses most heavily on the needs of Visual Basic programmers, including the many Visual Basic 6.0 and VBScript programmers who are upgrading to Visual Basic .NET for the first time with Visual Basic 2005. For this group, a special VB6 Differences section in Chapter 8 highlights how a particular language feature differs from its Visual Basic 6.0 equivalent. In addition, Chapters 1-7 provide a basic introduction to much of what's new in Visual Basic .NET, and demonstrate that Visual Basic is, at long last, an object-oriented programming language and a first-class language for developing .NET applications and therefore has at its disposal the enormous .NET Framework Class Library.

For Visual Basic programmers who have been developing with the earlier versions of Visual Basic .NET, this reference guide is equally valuable. In addition to its detailed treatment of each language element, it also discusses any differences between a particular Visual Basic 2005 element and its corresponding elements in Visual Basic .NET 2002 and Visual Basic .NET 2003. Appendix A, "What's New in Visual Basic 2005," discusses the new features introduced in Visual Basic 2005.

Increasingly, programmers are beginning to code in multiple languages. For environments that can draw on a comprehensive class library, as does .NET, programming in multiple languages becomes especially easy, since much of the code consists of calls to the members of the class library, and relatively little consists of calls to language elements. Because of the growing emphasis on proficiency in multiple languages, this book is also a useful reference for programmers who work primarily in another .NET language and only occasionally in Visual Basic.

Introduction to Visual Basic 2005

Visual Basic 2005 is the latest version of a programming language and development environment that was originally released in May 1991. Although Visual Basic is relatively new in comparison to many older programming languages such as C and C++, it has changed significantly in its brief history.

Visual Basic 1.0 Through Visual Basic 6.0

When it was released in 1991, some critics described Visual Basic as a "toy" and, because its real point of departure was its support for drag-and-drop placement of interface objects, as a user interface "drawing program." Despite the skeptics, though, the popularity of Visual Basic grew dramatically, and Microsoft continued to improve the product in major ways with each new release. As a result, the number of Visual Basic developers worldwide grew dramatically, eventually making Visual Basic the most widely used programming language in the world.

Visual Basic's success lay precisely in the features that its critics most derided. Visual Basic combined in a single package a programming language with a development environment that focused on creating graphical applications for the Windows environment and that supported drag-and-drop placement of controls. A programmer could design the user interface and then attach code to the events fired by particular controls by simply clicking them. As a result, a very simple "Hello, world!" application for Windows that might require at least 100 lines of code from a C programmer required only three lines of code like the following from a Visual Basic programmer:

```
Private Sub Form_Load()
    Label1.Caption = "Hello, World!"
End Sub
```

Of those three lines of code, the first and the last are the shell of the event handler and were automatically provided by the Visual Basic editor. To create this application, the programmer had to write only a single line of code (and in fact, this application could be created without the programmer writing any lines of code at all). All of the remaining details—creating the window for the application, creating the controls, defining the name and size of the font responsible for displaying the text—were handled automatically by Visual Basic, by the programmer's dragging and dropping items from a toolbox onto the form, or by the programmer's selecting values from or entering values into a property dialog.

Because of the ease with which it could be used to develop complete Windows applications, Visual Basic became one of the first and also the most significant of a new breed of programming tool, the rapid application development (RAD) environment. And as you might surmise from the criticism that Visual Basic was a toy language and a user interface drawing program, it was attacked by its critics precisely because it was a RAD environment, and a highly successful one at that.

Although Visual Basic in Versions 1.0–6.0 had made development of Windows applications and components incredibly easy, it often did so at a price. Rather than requiring the developer to handle such low-level details as defining and creating windows and handling message loops, Visual Basic shielded the developer from much of Windows internals and much of the complexity of Windows. This made it possible for Visual Basic developers to focus on the application to be written and on its business logic. At the same time, however, it often imposed only a thin layer between developers and the Windows environment; programmers who needed control over the low-level features of Windows from their programs generally found that Visual Basic provided them with the "hooks" that allowed them to access the functionality that they needed.

Visual Basic .NET

In 2002, Microsoft introduced a new development platform and runtime execution environment, .NET, and released Visual Basic .NET 2002, a new version of Visual Basic developed to work with the platform. In many respects, Visual Basic .NET is significantly different from its predecessors. As part of the process of developing the new version, individual elements of the Visual Basic language were re-evaluated and the language as a whole streamlined. New features, such as object orientation, were introduced. The basic structure of Visual Basic programs changed.

At the same time, the fact that Visual Basic .NET differs from its predecessors should not obscure the similarities. Visual Basic's early history is important to remember because Visual Basic itself played a major role in changing the way that developers write applications and in many respects set the standard for how applications and components are developed. Regardless of the language that you're using, when you open Visual Studio 2005 today to develop an application or a component for .NET, what you see is a development environment that looks very remarkably similar to and behaves very much like the old Visual Basic integrated development environment, with drag-and-drop placement of controls and user interface objects, easy access to code and especially to event handlers, and an integrated debugging environment. At runtime, .NET provides a managed execution environment that, very much like the old Visual Basic runtime, shields developers from much of the complexity of the underlying platform. In many respects, .NET is a logical continuation of Visual Basic.

At the same time, because it is integrated with .NET, Visual Basic is very much an equal partner in the .NET platform. Because it is a language that conforms to .NET's Common Language Specification, Visual Basic has full access to the features of .NET just as any other .NET-compliant language does. These include a common type system, the availability of an extensive class library, and a managed execution environment.

The Common Type System

Typically, the data types available in a programming language are defined by that programming language's specification or even by an individual language compiler in isolation from other languages. So although two languages may both have a String data type, for example, the actual format of a String value may differ significantly. The result is that language interoperability—the ability of an application or component written in one language to make method calls to components written in another language and to pass data to and receive data back from those components—is often limited.

The .NET platform addresses this issue of language interoperability through the Common Type System. .NET, rather than individual languages or even individual language compiler makers, defines the basic data types available on the platform and makes them available through its class library. An individual language may name these differently, but they nevertheless are the basic types provided by .NET. Visual Basic 2005, for example, retains the data type names of most Visual Basic 6.0 data types. (Of the major Visual Basic 6.0 data types, only Variant and Currency have been eliminated from the language.) But while the names remain the same, the content has changed. An Integer, for instance, is now a 32-bit integer, whereas in Visual Basic 6.0 it was a 16-bit integer. In fact, a new addition to the Visual Basic language (in Visual Basic .NET 2002) is the SystemTypeName function, which returns the name of the .NET type that corresponds to a particular Visual Basic .NET type. For example, the method call

```
Console.WriteLine(SystemTypeName(Long))
```

tells us that the Visual Basic .NET Long data type corresponds to the .NET System.Int64 data type.

The implications of the Common Type System are enormous. As long as an application or component is developed using the Common Type System, it can make method calls to components also developed using the Common Type System. Passing arguments to them and receiving data back becomes seamless. It is even possible to create mixed-language projects in which some of the routines in an assembly (a dynamic link library or executable containing code that the Common Language Runtime can execute) are written in one language, while others are written in another. Appendix E includes a short example that creates a single assembly from Visual Basic and C# code.

The Framework Class Library

The primitive data types defined by .NET themselves are individual types in the .NET Framework Class Library, which is the class library that .NET makes available both at design time (when developers are writing code) and at runtime (when programs are executing). The Framework itself consists of thousands of types organized into *namespaces*. (A namespace is simply a logical name that is used to divide types hierarchically with the aim of preventing naming collisions.) These types contain tens of thousands of members that provide the basic services and core functionality offered by .NET. In addition to data types, the types provided by .NET include exception classes, Windows forms and control classes, web forms and control classes, data classes that are optimized for OLE DB, SQL Server, and Oracle, XML classes, file I/O classes, and classes for interprocess and remote communication, to mention just a few. For somewhat more detail, see Chapter 7.

Along with the fact that it provides extensive functionality in all areas of programming, it is important to note that types defined in the Framework Class Library are available to all languages that support the .NET platform. It is no longer the case, as it was before .NET, that some class libraries were accessible only from C++ projects, while others were primarily available to Visual Basic projects. Any .NET language has equal access to the types defined in the Framework Class Library.

Interestingly, a large part of the Visual Basic language—all of its functions and subroutines other than the conversion functions implemented directly by the compiler—is itself implemented in an assembly, Microsoft.VisualBasic.dll, that is part of the Framework Class Library. This means that not only can these traditionally Visual Basic language elements be called from Visual Basic code, but they can also be called from non–Visual Basic code. The InputBox function, which displays a dialog with a text box and awaits user input, has long been a feature of Visual Basic, but it is typically not available in other languages and is not implemented elsewhere in the Framework Class Library. But it is extremely easy to call the InputBox function from other languages, such as C#.

The extensive functionality that the Framework Class Library makes available means that programming often consists of writing the "glue code" that holds together calls to various Framework Class Library methods, and that most of the actual code consists of framework method calls while very little consists of language glue. It is interesting to note that, in applications where this glue code is fairly minimal, converting between Visual Basic code and C# code, for example, is fairly trivial, and the code often looks more or less identical (except, of course, for the semicolons that C# requires at the end of statements).

The .NET Common Language Runtime

Finally, .NET provides a runtime environment within which code executes. .NET itself handles most resource allocation. It allocates memory when it's needed and deallocates memory when it can be released (a process called garbage collection), and generally manages the lifetime of all resources that are acquired through Framework Class Library method calls. In doing so, it abstracts development from the underlying platform to a far greater degree than previous platforms did.

Visual Basic and Language Independence

What all of this means is that the .NET platform makes the language in which you are writing code far less important than ever before. With .NET, gone are the days when you can be months into a project, only to discover that you chose the wrong language for the application at hand. Far more than any technology that preceded it, .NET realizes the promise of language independence.

What this means for you as a Visual Basic developer is that you can focus on the application you'd like to build, rather than having to also focus on the language that's appropriate to build it. It means that you can code with the language you're comfortable with, which gives you greater freedom to focus on the problems your application needs to solve, and still be able to access all of the resources that .NET makes available. It also means that you can draw on a body of other components and class libraries that, as long as they comply with the Common Language Specification, can be called from your code just as if they were written in Visual Basic.

Many Visual Basic programmers have viewed .NET as a threat. Its introduction coincided with that of a popular new language, C#, which seems to be gaining momentum. It's taken away, or so they believe, much that was distinctive about Visual Basic 6.0. But this rather cynical view harmonizes rather poorly with reality. Through the enhancements introduced in Visual Basic 2005, it is clear that Microsoft not only remains committed to Visual Basic but remains committed to making Visual Basic a great tool for application development. At the same time, Visual Basic now has two basic features that it has always lacked and that in the past have constrained its development: easy interoperability with components and tools written in other languages, and more or less full, open, and equal access to the underlying .NET platform.

I would suggest that rather than being a threat, NET creates an enormous opportunity for Visual Basic developers. It places all of the resources of an enormously sophisticated development environment, a full-featured class library, and a familiar programming language fully at the disposal of the Visual Basic programmer. At the same time, it challenges us to use these resources to create a new generation of great software applications.

Data Types and Variables

T his chapter will begin by examining the intrinsic data types supported by Visual Basic and relating them to their corresponding types available in the .NET Framework's Common Type System. It will then examine the ways in which variables are declared in Visual Basic and discuss variable scope, visibility, and lifetime. The chapter will conclude with a discussion of boxing and unboxing (that is, of converting between value types and reference types).

Visual Basic Data Types

At the center of any development or runtime environment, including Visual Basic and the .NET Common Language Runtime (CLR), is a type system. An individual *type* consists of the following two items:

- A set of values.
- A set of rules to convert every value not in the type into a value in the type. (For these rules, see Appendix F.) Of course, every value of another type cannot always be converted to a value of the type; one of the more common rules in this case is to throw an InvalidCastException, indicating that conversion is not possible.

Scalar or primitive types are types that contain a single value. Visual Basic 2005 supports two basic kinds of scalar or primitive data types: structured data types and reference data types. All data types are inherited from either of two basic types in the .NET Framework Class Library. Reference types are derived from System.Object. Structured data types are derived from the System.ValueType class, which in turn is derived from the System.Object class. Although we will discuss the difference between value types and reference types in greater detail later in this chapter, suffice it to say that the .NET Common Language Infrastructure (CLI) manipulates value types by value and reference types by reference.

To appreciate the difference, consider the following very simple code, which defines a StudentRef class (a reference type) and a StudentVal structure (a value type) to store the name and grade point average of a student, and then creates instances of both:

```
Public Class StudentRef
    Public Name As String
    Public GPA As Double
End Class
```

```
Public Structure StudentVal
    Public Name As String
    Public GPA As Double
End Structure

Public Class Test
    Public Shared Sub Main()
        Dim studentRef1 As New StudentRef()
        Dim studentVal1 As New StudentVal()

        studentRef1.Name = "Jill"
        studentRef1.GPA = 92.3
        studentVal1.Name = "Jill"
        studentVal1.GPA = 92.3

        Dim studentRef2 As StudentRef = studentRef1
        Dim studentVal2 As StudentVal = studentVal1

        studentRef2.GPA += 2
        studentVal2.GPA += 2

        Console.WriteLine("{0}'s GPA is: {1}", studentRef1.Name, studentRef1.GPA)
        Console.WriteLine("{0}'s GPA is: {1}", studentVal1.Name, studentVal1.GPA)
    End Sub
End Class
```

The Main procedure creates an instance of the class, named studentRef1, and an instance of the structure, named studentVal1. The value of studentRef1 is then assigned to a new class instance, studentRef2, and the value of studentVal1 is assigned to a new structure instance, studentVal2. The GPA fields of both studentRef2 and studentVal2 are next incremented by two. Then the GPAs of StudentRef1 and StudentVal1 are displayed to the console. The results are as follows:

```
Jill's GPA is: 94.3
Jill's GPA is: 92.3
```

Note that studentRef1.GPA has changed even though it was studentRef2.GPA that our code modified. That's because studentRef1 and studentRef2 are expressions that both refer to the same instance of the StudentRef class. In contrast, studentVal1.GPA remains unchanged. That's because studentVal1 and studentVal2 are instances of the StudentVal structure, a value type. When we assigned studentVal1 to studentVal2, we assigned studentVal2 the values of the first structure, not a reference to a single set of data.

Table 2-1 lists the data types supported by Visual Basic and shows which are value types and which are reference types.

VB 6 and VB.NET Data Types

Visual Basic .NET supports all but two of the scalar data types supported by COM-based versions of Visual Basic. The Currency type has been eliminated; the Decimal type should be used instead. In addition, the Variant type, the "universal type" of COM-based Visual Basic programming, is no longer supported. Instead, Object is the universal data type in Visual Basic .NET.

VB Type Name	.NET Type Name	Type
Boolean	System.Boolean	Value
Byte	System.Byte	Value
Char	System.Char	Value
Date	System.DateTime	Value
Decimal	System.Decimal	Value
Double	System.Double	Value
Integer	System.Int32	Value
Long	System.Int64	Value
Object	System.Object	Reference
SByte	System.SByte	Value
Short	System.Int16	Value
Single	System.Single	Value
String	System.String	Reference
UInteger	System.UInt32	Value
ULong	System.UInt64	Value
UShort	System.UInt16	Value
user-defined class		Reference
user-defined value type		Value

TABLE 2-1   Visual Basic 2005 Data Types

As we'll see, Visual Basic's intrinsic data types directly correspond to particular .NET data types. Because of this, we'll begin by briefly discussing the .NET Common Type System and the relationship of .NET types to Visual Basic data types. Then we'll turn to each of the intrinsic data types supported by Visual Basic. This chapter provides some basic information about each data type. However, you'll also want to look at Appendix G, which briefly surveys the members (the fields, methods, and properties) of each data type. In addition, since type conversion can be much more important in Visual Basic .NET if Option Strict is set to On (its preferred setting), you may want to examine Appendix F, which lists the methods available to convert any data type into any other data type.

The Common Type System and Shared Functionality

One of the basic features of the .NET platform is the Common Type System. It means that the .NET CLI supplies the data types used by .NET-compliant languages and development environments.

This allows language independence and easy interoperability of components created in different languages. The existence of a common type system has enormous implications for Visual Basic: although Visual Basic .NET, like the COM-based versions of Visual Basic, appears to support a number of "intrinsic" data types, in fact these intrinsic data types are merely wrappers around basic data types defined by the .NET framework. For example, running the following code:

```
Public Class WrappedType
    Public Shared Sub Main()
        Dim intVar As Integer = 100
        Dim intType As Type = intVar.GetType()
        Console.WriteLine(TypeName(intVar) & " = " & intType.FullName)

        Dim stringVar As String = "This is a string."
        Dim stringType As Type = stringVar.GetType()
        Console.WriteLine(TypeName(stringVar) & " = " & stringType. FullName)

        Dim boolVar As Boolean = True
        Dim boolType As Type = boolVar.GetType()
        Console.WriteLine(TypeName(boolVar) & " = " & boolType. FullName)

        Dim singleVar As Single = 3.1417
        Dim singleType As Type = singleVar.GetType()
        Console.WriteLine(TypeName(singleVar) & " = " & singleType. FullName)
    End Sub
End Class
```

produces the following output in a console window:

```
Integer = System.Int32
String = System.String
Boolean = System.Boolean
Single = System.Single
```

This code uses the Visual Basic TypeName function, which returns the name of an "intrinsic" Visual Basic data type, to determine the data type of each variable. It also uses the .NET GetType method to retrieve a Type object representing the data type of a variable. Calling the Type object's FullName method returns the fully qualified name of the data type. The example then uses the Console.WriteLine method to write the results of these two method calls to a command window. As the output shows, the Visual Basic data type name corresponds to a .NET data type name.

Besides language independence, the identity of Visual Basic data types and .NET data types has a major advantage: all .NET types support members (that is, fields, properties, and methods) that are accessible from Visual Basic intrinsic data types. For example, the Visual Basic Date data type wraps the .NET DateTime structure. The following code uses the DateTime structure's constructor to initialize a Date variable, and then calls the DateTime AddMonths method to add five months to the date. Finally, it uses the addition operator (which is equivalent to the DateTime structure's op_Addition method) to add 30 days to the date:

```
Public Class DateMembers
    Public Shared Sub Main()
        Dim dat As Date = New Date(2000, 1, 1)
        Dim ts As New TimeSpan(30, 0, 0, 0)

        Console.WriteLine("The original date is " & dat)
        dat = dat.AddMonths(5)
```

```
      Console.WriteLine("The new date is " & dat)
      dat = dat + ts
      Console.WriteLine("The new date is " & dat)
   End Sub
End Class
```

Appendix E lists the members of each Visual Basic .NET data type.

In the following sections, we'll examine each of Visual Basic's intrinsic data types in greater detail.

Scalar Data Types

Scalar data types are designed to hold a single item of data—a number, a string, a flag, or an indication of state. In this section, we'll examine each of the scalar data types supported by Visual Basic .NET. They are shown in Table 2-2. Note that the literal identifiers are case insensitive; an unsigned long literal, for example, can be identified with a UL, ul, Ul, or uL.

In the remainder of this section, we'll discuss the data types supported by Visual Basic in greater detail.

Boolean

The Boolean type corresponds to the System.Boolean structure and consists of the set {True, False}. An uninitialized Boolean variable is assigned a value of False.

Byte

The Byte data type, which corresponds to the System.Byte structure, holds an eight-bit unsigned integer; its value can range from 0 to 255. (Visual Basic 2005 also adds intrinsic support for a signed byte data type, SByte.) An uninitialized Byte variable is assigned a value of 0.

Char

The Char data type, which corresponds to the System.Char structure, holds a two-byte character code representing a particular UTF-16 Unicode character. Character codes can range from 0 to 65,535. An uninitialized Char variable is assigned a value of character code 0. The Char data type was not supported in Visual Basic 6.0.

When assigning a value of type Char, you can use the literal type character C to treat a literal string as a Char literal. For example, if Option Strict is on, the code

```
Dim ch As Char = "a"
```

produces a compiler error ("Option Strict On disallows implicit conversions from 'String' to 'Char'."). The literal type character defines the data type of the "a" as Char and corrects the error, as the following code illustrates:

```
Dim ch As Char = "a"c
```

Date

The Date data type, which corresponds to the System.DateTime structure, can range from midnight (0:00:00) of January 1, 0001, to 11:59:59 P.M. of December 31, 9999. An uninitialized Date variable is assigned a value of 12:00:00 A.M. on January 1, 0001. Date values occupy eight bytes of memory.

In addition to using the Date constructors, you can also use # characters as literal type characters. For example, the following code initializes a date variable to July 1, 2005:

```
Dim dat As Date = #07/01/2005#
```

Data Type	Type Identifier	Literal Identifier	Range
Boolean	None	None	True, False
Byte	None	None	0 to 255
Char	None	C	UTF-16 character codes from 0 to 65,535
Date	None	#date#	12:00:00 A.M., 1/1/0001 to 11:59:59 P.M., 12/31/9999
Decimal	@	D	−79,228,162,514,264,337,593,543,950,335 to 79,228,162,514,264,337,593,543,950,335. A Decimal value is stored internally as a scaled value, making it far more precise than either the Single or the Double.
Double	#	R	$-1.79769313486231570^{308}$ to $1.79769313486231570^{308}$, as well as positive or negative zero, positive infinity (the result of an operation that exceeds Single.MaxValue or of division of a positive Single value by zero), negative infinity (the result of an operation less than Single.MinValue or of division of a negative Single value by zero), and NaN (not a number), indicating the result of an operation is undefined. A Double value has 15 decimal digits of precision.
Integer	%	I	−2,147,483,648 to 2,147,483,647
Long	&	L	−9,223,372,036,854,775,808 through 9,223,372,036,854,775,807
Object	None	none	Any type
SByte	None	none	−128 to 127
Short	None	S	−32,768 through 32,767
Single	!	F	-3.4028235^{38} to 3.4028235^{38}, as well as positive or negative zero, positive infinity (the result of an operation that exceeds Single.MaxValue or of division of a positive Single value by zero), negative infinity (the result of an operation less than Single.MinValue or of division of a negative Single value by zero), and NaN (not a number), indicating the result of an operation is undefined). A Single value has seven decimal digits of precision).
String	$	Quotation marks	Limited by available memory
UInteger	None	UI	0 to 4,294,967,295
ULong	None	UL	0 to 18,446,744,073,709,551,615
UShort	None	US	0 to 65,535

TABLE 2-2   Scalar Data Types in Visual Basic .NET

In .NET, the Date (or DateTime) type has been substantially enhanced to provide more information about a date (such as the date's time zone) as well as much of the functionality required to work with dates. You can, for instance, convert a Date value to its equivalent FILETIME value (used by the Win32 API) or its equivalent OLE Automation value (a Date value in Visual Basic 6.0). You can also use arithmetic operators to manipulate and compare dates. For details, see the members of the DataTime structure in Appendix G.

Decimal

The Decimal data type, which corresponds to the System.Decimal structure, can be used to hold currency values or values in which rounding error in the most significant fractional digits is unacceptable. (It stores data in a scaled format that minimizes rounding error.) It replaces the Currency data type of Visual Basic 6.0 and earlier versions. The Decimal data type can hold values ranging from –79,228,162,514,264,337,593,543,950,335 to 79,228,162,514,264,337,593,543,950,335. The value of an uninitialized Decimal variable is 0.

You can use the literal type character D to identify a value as a Decimal literal in an assignment statement. For example, if Option Strict is on, attempting to compile code like the following

```
Dim amt As Decimal = 100000
```

may produce a compiler error ("Option Strict On disallows implicit conversions from 'Double' to 'Decimal'."). Instead, you can use the literal type character D to define the value as a decimal. You can also use @ as an identifier type character, which allows you to eliminate "As Decimal" in a decimal's variable declaration. For example:

```
Dim amt As Decimal = 100000D
Dim int@ = .10d
```

Double

The Double data type, which corresponds to the System.Double structure, can contain a double-precision floating point number. It can have a value ranging from $-1.79769313486231570^{308}$ to $1.79769313486231570^{308}$, as well as positive or negative zero, positive infinity, negative infinity, and NaN (not a number). A Double value has 15 decimal digits of precision. Uninitialized Double variables are automatically set equal to 0.

When declaring variables of type Double, you can use # as an identifier type character, which replaces the "As Double" clause in a variable declaration. In assignment statements involving literal values of type Double, you can use the literal type character R to treat a numeric literal as a Double. For example:

```
Dim dist As Double = 10101.3654R
Dim spd# = 68.7931r
```

Integer

The Integer data type, which corresponds to the System.Int32 structure, occupies 32 bits (or four bytes) of memory and can hold values that range from –2,147,483,648 through 2,147,483,647. Uninitialized Integer variables are automatically set equal to 0.

When declaring a variable of type Integer, you can use % as an identifier type character, which substitutes for the clause "As Integer" in a variable declaration. For example:

```
Dim age1% = 43i
```

> **Integers in VB 6 and VB.NET**
>
> In VB 6.0 and earlier versions, the Integer was a 16-bit data type. In contrast, in Visual Basic .NET, the Integer is a 32-bit data type, which means that it is equivalent to the VB 6.0 Long data type. So, if you are making Win32 API calls from .NET code, you should use an Integer whenever a Win32 function argument requires a Long.

You can also use the literal type character *I* to treat a numeric value as an Integer. For example:

```
Dim age2 As Integer = 48I
```

Long

The Long data type is a signed integer that corresponds to the System.Int64 structure. Variables of type Long occupy 64 bits (or eight bytes) of memory and can range in value from –9,223,372,036,854,775,808 through 9,223,372,036,854,775,807. Uninitialized long integers are automatically set equal to 0.

When declaring a variable of type Long, you can use & as an identifier type character, which substitutes for the clause "As Long" in a variable declaration. For example:

```
Dim lng1& = 1800000000001
```

You can also use the literal type character *L* to treat a numeric value as a Long. For example:

```
Dim lng2 As Long = 170000000L
```

Object

The Object data type, which corresponds to the System.Object class, replaces the VB 6.0 (and earlier) Variant as Visual Basic's universal data type. In .NET, Object is a universal data type for another reason: all .NET types other than interfaces are directly or indirectly derived from it. The value of an uninitialized Object variable is Nothing.

You can assign an instance of any reference type or value type to a variable typed as Object. Assigning an instance of a value type to a variable typed as Object incurs a "boxing" operation to convert the value type instance to a reference type instance. We'll discuss boxing and unboxing toward the end of this chapter.

You can determine what kind of data an object variable holds at a particular time by calling the Visual Basic TypeName function, which returns the Visual Basic data type name.

You can also call the object's GetType method, which returns a Type object representing the type of the object instance. Its Name property provides you with the .NET type name, and its

> **Longs in VB 6 and VB.NET**
>
> In VB 6.0 and earlier versions, the Long was a 32-bit data type. In contrast, in Visual Basic .NET, the Long is a 64-bit data type. In other words, VB 6.0 and earlier versions had no equivalent of the Long data type in Visual Basic .NET.

FullName property returns the fully qualified type name (including hierarchical namespaces). For example:

```
Dim o As Object = "This is an object."

Console.Writeline(TypeName(o))          ' Displays String
Console.WriteLine(o.GetType.Name)       ' Displays String
Console.WriteLine(o.GetType.FullName)   ' Displays System.String
```

The Object data type is most convenient when you do not know the precise type of data a variable will hold at runtime. But the use of a variable of type Object to hold other types of data results in a performance penalty as a result of late binding, since only at runtime is the CLR able to perform such functions as member name resolution (determining whether a type actually has a member of a particular name) and argument resolution (determining whether a member has arguments that correspond to those used in a method call). There are numerous benefits as well: strongly typed code is easier to read, easier to optimize, easier to test, easier to debug, and easier to maintain.

You can use early binding in one of two ways:

- By declaring a variable to be a specific type.
- By explicitly converting a variable to the type needed for a particular operation. For conversions, see Appendix F.

The word "object" is used not only to refer to the Object data type, but also to refer generically to any instance of any class. For instance, code such as

```
Dim ht As New System.Collections.Hashtable
```

creates an "object of type Hashtable." Similarly, code such as

```
Public Class Person
End Class
```

defines a class in your own code. You can then instantiate "an object of type Person" or "an object of the Person class" with code like the following:

```
Dim per As Person = New Person()
```

SByte

The SByte data type, which corresponds to the System.SByte structure, holds an eight-bit signed integer; its value can range from –128 through 127. An uninitialized SByte variable is assigned a value of 0. It occupies one byte (eight bits) of memory. The SByte data type is new to Visual Basic 2005.

The SByte data type is not CLS-compliant. This means that to be compliant with the .NET platform, other languages are not required to implement support for a signed byte data type. As a result, although it is safe to use the SByte type internally in your own programs, you may not want to expose it as part of a component's public interface.

Variants in VB 6 and Objects in VB.NET

Instead of defining variables of type Variant as you did in VB 6.0 and earlier versions, you can now define variables to be of type Object. However, you should take a look at the reasons for using Object variables. If you use Visual Basic as a weakly typed language and allow the CLR to determine the precise runtime type of your variables, you might take a more careful look at your code to determine whether the data type of a variable can be more precisely defined. You should use the Object data type only when you legitimately do not know the precise data type of a variable at design time. In addition, when writing methods, take advantage of overloading (a method of the same name can have different signatures) rather than defining a generic Object parameter to allow for values of multiple data types. For example, if a grade report program includes a DisplayResult method that can either display a letter grade, a grade point average, or a numeric grade, rather than having a single method with the signature

```
Private Sub DisplayResult(gradeInfo As Object)
```

you should overload the method as follows to reflect the individual arguments that can be passed to it:

```
Private Sub DisplayResult(letterGrade As String)
Private Sub DisplayResult(gpa As Double)
Private Sub DisplayResult(grade As Integer)
```

Short

The Short is a 16-bit signed integral data type that corresponds to the System.Int16 structure in the .NET Framework Class Library. Values of Short variables can range from –32,768 through 32,767. The Short data type corresponds to the Visual Basic 6.0 Integer data type.

You can use the literal type character s to indicate that a numeric literal is a Short. For example:

```
Dim age1 As Short = 48S
Dim age2 As Short = 43s
```

Single

The Single data type, which corresponds to the System.Single structure, holds a single-precision floating point number that can range from -3.4028235^{38} to 3.4028235^{38}, as well as positive or negative zero, positive infinity, negative infinity, and NaN. A Single value has seven decimal digits of precision. Uninitialized Single variables are automatically set equal to 0.

The Short in VB.NET

VB 6.0 had only two signed integer types: Integer and Long. Visual Basic .NET adds two more, one of which is the Short type. However, since Short is a 16-bit signed integer, it corresponds directly to the Integer data type in the 32-bit versions of Visual Basic from Versions 3.0–6.0. If you are making Win32 API calls from .NET code, you can use a Short whenever a Win32 function argument is an Integer.

When declaring a variable of type Single, you can use *!* (the exclamation mark) as an identifier type character, which substitutes for the clause "As Single" in a variable declaration. When assigning a literal single value, you can use the literal type character *F* to indicate that a literal numeric value is a Single. For example:

```
Dim spd! = 68.7931F
Dim dist As Single = 10101.3654f
```

String

The String data type, which corresponds to the System.String type, is used to store a series of anywhere from 0 to about 2 billion 16-bit (two-byte) UTF-16 Unicode characters. Uninitialized strings are automatically initialized as zero-length strings and can be compared to the Visual Basic VbNullString constant, to an empty string, to the String.Empty field, or to the String.IsNullOrEmpty method. For example:

```
If s = VbNullString Then
    ' Do something
```

or

```
If s = "" Then
    ' Do something
```

or

```
If s = String.Empty Then
    ' Do something
```

or

```
If String.IsNullOrEmpty(s) Then
    ' Do something
```

Since String is a class, an uninitialized string has a value of Nothing. Hence, the following code also tests for an uninitialized string:

```
If s Is Nothing Then
    ' Do something
```

When declaring a variable of type String, you can use *$* as an identifier type character, which substitutes for the clause "As String" in a variable declaration. When initializing or assigning a value to a string variable, Visual Basic treats all text enclosed in quotation marks as the literal string to be assigned to the variable. For example:

```
Dim Name$ = "Gregory of Nyassa"
```

String is a reference type. But because many of the details of working with strings as a reference type are handled by the Visual Basic compiler and the CLR, strings appear to behave as value types. The String type has a second characteristic: it is immutable. That is, once you've initialized a string, neither its length nor its contents can be changed. What appears to be a modified string that results, for example, from concatenating text to a string is actually a new string variable that replaces the old.

One implication of the immutability of strings is that using the String class for code that involves extensive string manipulation involves a major performance penalty. When this is the case, you may choose instead to work with the System.Text.StringBuilder class, which is optimized for string manipulation.

UInteger

The UInteger data type is one of four unsigned integer data types supported by Visual Basic. It corresponds to the System.UInt32 structure and occupies 32 bits (or four bytes) of memory. Values of a UInteger variable can range from 0 to 4,294,967,295. Uninitialized UInteger variables are automatically set equal to 0. The UInteger data type was added to Visual Basic .NET as of Version 2.0.

When initializing a variable of type UInteger, you can also use the literal type character *UI* to treat a numeric literal as a UInteger. For example:

```
Dim age1 As UInteger = 48UI
Dim age2 As UInteger = 43ui
```

The UInteger data type is not CLS-compliant. This means that to be compliant with the .NET platform, other languages are not required to implement support for an unsigned integer data type. As a result, although it is safe to use the UInteger type internally in your own programs, you may choose not to expose it as part of a component's public interface if you care about CLS compliance.

ULong

The ULong data type is an unsigned long integer that corresponds to the System.UInt64 structure. Variables of type ULong occupy 64 bits (or 8 bytes) of memory and can range in value from 0 through 18,446,744,073,709,551,615. Uninitialized unsigned long integers are automatically assigned a value of 0. The ULong data type was added to Visual Basic .NET as of Version 2.0.

When initializing a variable of type ULong, you can also use the literal type character *UL* to treat a numeric literal as a ULong. For example:

```
Dim lng1 As ULong = 170000000UL
Dim lng2 As ULong = 180000000000ul
```

The ULong data type is not CLS-compliant. This means that to be compliant with the .NET platform, other languages are not required to implement support for an unsigned long integer data type. As a result, although it is safe to use the ULong type internally in your own programs, it should not be exposed as part of a component's public interface.

Unsigned Integer Data Types in Visual Basic

Although the .NET Framework provides four unsigned integer types, Visual Basic .NET originally offered intrinsic support for the Byte data type only. However, Visual Basic 2005 added support for UShort (or System.UInt16, a 16-bit unsigned integer), UInteger (or System.UInt32, a 32-bit unsigned integer), and ULong (or System.UInt64, a 64-bit unsigned integer).

UShort

UShort is a 16-bit unsigned integral data type that corresponds to the System.UInt16 structure in the .NET Framework Class Library. Values of UShort variables can range from 0 through 65,535. Uninitialized integers are automatically set equal to 0 by the Visual Basic .NET compiler. The UShort data type was added to Visual Basic .NET as of Version 2.0.

When initializing variables of type UShort, you can use the literal type character *US* to treat a numeric literal as a UShort. For example:

```
Dim age1 As Short = 48US
Dim age2 As Short = 43us
```

Like all the other unsigned data types except for Byte, UShort is not CLS-compliant. Although it is safe to use variables of type UShort internally in your components and applications, you should avoid exposing them as part of a component's public interface, since consumers of your component may not support the UShort or UInt16 data types.

Complex Data Types

Visual Basic .NET also supports two kinds of complex data types: structures (which were called user-defined types in Visual Basic 6.0 and earlier editions) and arrays. In this section, we'll examine these two data types.

Structures

A *structure* is a syntactic element that defines a value type, which is a type derived from System.ValueType. A structure defines a composite data type that must consist of at least one field or one event, but usually consists of multiple fields. When an instance of the value type defined by the structure is declared, each field is set equal to its default value. So in the case of a structure with two integers, each integer would be set equal to 0. For example, the following Structure statement defines a value type named Coordinates that consists of two fields of type Double:

```
Public Structure Coordinates
    Public x As Double
    Public y As Double
End Structure
```

When a variable of type Coordinates is instantiated, the values of both its x and y members are automatically set to 0.0.

Structures are declared using the Structure . . . End Structure construct. For details, see the entry for "Structure . . . End Structure" in Chapter 8. You can then work with the structure as a whole by referring to it by name, or you can work with individual members. The following code shows how you might work with the Coordinates structure:

```
Dim coord As Coordinates       ' The structure as a whole
coord.x = 10.032               ' x member
coord.y = 25.351               ' y member
Console.WriteLine(coord.ToString & ": x=" & coord.x & ", y=" & coord.y)
```

You declare an instance of a structure just as you do any variable, and you access a particular member of a structure by using dot notation, as shown in the preceding code.

Structures and Classes

In .NET, structures are enormously enhanced and have many of the characteristics of classes in previous versions of Visual Basic:

- Each field of a structure can have a different access level (Public, Private, and Friend are allowed, although Protected is not). For example, one field can be public, while another can be private.

- In addition to fields, structures can also have properties, methods, and events. A structure can also have a default property, as long as it is parameterized.

- A structure can implement an interface. However, a structure can't explicitly inherit from a class or from another structure. (All structures implicitly inherit from System.ValueType.)

- A structure can have either parameterized or parameterless constructors.

- A structure can raise an event.

Arrays

An *array* is a reference type that serves as a container for a set of data items that are stored together and are accessed as members of the array. Each element of the array can be identified by its index or ordinal position in the array.

Visual Basic allows you to define arrays in a number of ways. You can declare an array to simply be of type Array:

```
Dim arr As Array
```

This might be termed an untyped array. Each element of the array is capable of holding data of any type, and in fact an array of any type can be assigned to it. For example, the following code assigns an array of Integer to the array:

```
Dim arr As Array
Dim int() As Integer = {12, 16, 20, 24, 28, 32}
arr = CType(int, Array)
```

You can also define a "strong" array, which is an array that will hold data of a defined type. For example:

```
Dim byFours() As Integer = {12, 24, 36, 48}
Dim names() As String = {"Koani", "Saya", "Samuel", "Dakota", "Nikita"}
Dim miscData() As Object = {"this", 12d, 16ui, "a"c}
Dim objArray() As Object
```

Here, byFours is an Integer array; all of its members must be of type Integer, and only an Integer array can be assigned to it. Similarly, names is a String array; all of its members must be of type String, and only a String array can be assigned to it. Finally, miscData and objArray are arrays of type Object; their individual members can be any data type, although only arrays of reference types can be assigned to them. For example, the assignment

```
miscData = names
```

is legal, while

```
miscData = byFours
```

generates a compiler error ("Value of type '1-dimensional array of Integer' cannot be converted to '1-dimensional array of System.Object' because 'Integer' is not a reference type.").

   All arrays have a particular number of dimensions and a particular number of elements in each dimension. Visual Basic supports arrays of up to 32 dimensions, although typical arrays have a single dimension. You define the number of dimensions of an array by indicating the number of members in that dimension. For example, the following code defines a number of one-dimensional arrays:

```
Dim myArray1a() As Integer        ' Uninitialized array
Dim myArray1b As Integer()        ' Uninitialized array
Dim myArray2(10) As Integer       ' 1-dimensional array with 11 elements
```

The following code, on the other hand, defines two two-dimensional arrays:

```
Dim Employees1( , ) As Object     ' Uninitialized 2-D array
Dim Employees(200, 2) As Object   ' 2-D array with 201 and 3 elements
```

The Lower Bounds of an Array

Visual Basic 6.0 allowed you to define a default lower bound for all arrays using the Option Base statement, and to define a default lower bound for a specific array by using syntax like

```
Dim ArrayStartsAt1(1 To 100) As String
```

   In Visual Basic .NET, neither of these methods for defining the lower bound of an array is supported. (Visual Basic 2005 allows you to specify the lower bound of an array, but it must be 0.) However, although non-zero-based arrays are not CLS-compliant, you can explicitly define some other lower bound by calling one of the overloads of the CreateInstance method of the Array class. The following code does this:

```
' Changes lower bound to start at 1
Public Class CArray
    Public Shared Sub Main()
        Dim dims() As Integer = {10}       ' Number of elements in array
        Dim bnds() As Integer = {1}        ' Lower bound of array
        Dim Scores As Array = Array.CreateInstance(GetType(Integer), dims, bnds)
        Console.WriteLine(UBound(Scores))
        Console.WriteLine(LBound(Scores))
    End Sub
End Class
```

   This version of the CreateInstance method has three parameters: a Type object representing the data type of the array, an array of Integer whose elements indicate the number of elements in each dimension (the first element represents the first dimension, and so on), and an array of Integer whose elements indicate the lower bound of each dimension (the first element represents the first dimension, and so on).

The first is an uninitialized two-dimensional array, and the second has 201 elements in the first and three elements in the second dimension.

Notice that the number of elements in each dimension is one greater than the value indicated in the array declaration, since .NET arrays are zero-based; the ordinal position of the first array element is 0, not 1. And the ordinal position of the last element in a dimension of the array is one less than the number of elements in that dimension. Actually, a useful way to think about this is not as an ordinal, but as an *offset*. The array index measures the distance of a particular element from the first element. Thus the element with an index of 1 is not the first element of the array but is one element away from the first element in the array. An array of ten elements has an upper bound of 9 because the last element is nine elements away from the first.

In addition to the standard rectangular or symmetrical arrays, Visual Basic supports jagged arrays—that is, arrays whose second dimension is non-rectangular. Basically, a jagged array is a one-dimensional array each of whose members also contains an array. (Jagged arrays, though, are not CLS-compliant, and so other .NET languages may not be able to handle them.) You can declare a jagged array with code like the following:

```
Dim jagged1(9)() As String
Dim jagged2()() As String = New String(9)() {}
```

All Visual Basic arrays are implicitly derived from the System.Array type in the .NET Framework Class Library. This means that, besides the standard Visual Basic syntax, you can also declare an array as an instance of the Array class, as the following declarations illustrate:

```
Dim myArray1a As Array
Dim myArray2a As Array = Array.CreateInstance(GetType(Integer), 10)
Dim members() As Integer = {3, 10}
Dim myArray3a As Array = Array.CreateInstance(GetType(Integer), members)
```

Because arrays are .NET classes, you can call the members of the .NET Array class when working with Visual Basic arrays. The more important of its instance members are shown in Table 2-3.

Unlike the pre-.NET versions of Visual Basic, which recognized both static and dynamic arrays, all .NET arrays are dynamic. That is, the number of elements in a given dimension can be expanded and contracted dynamically without your having to specify in advance that an array is dynamic. For example, using a dynamic array in Visual Basic 6.0 requires that you declare an uninitialized array, as the following code shows:

```
Dim arr() As Integer, index As Integer

index = 10
ReDim Preserve arr(index)
arr(index) = index ^ 2

index = 20
ReDim Preserve arr(index)
arr(index) = index ^ 2

index = 10
ReDim Preserve arr(index)
MsgBox arr(index)
```

Member	Description
Length property	Returns an Integer indicating the total number of elements in all dimensions of the array.
Rank property	Returns an Integer indicating the number of dimensions in the array.
Clear method	Reinitializes a portion of an array.
GetLength method	Returns an Integer indicating the number of elements in a particular dimension of an array. Its syntax is: *arrVar*.GetLength(*dimension*), where *dimension* is an Integer indicating the zero-based dimension of the array.
GetLowerBound method	Returns an Integer indicating the lower bound of an array. Its syntax is: *arrVar*.GetLowerBound(*dimension*), where *dimension* is an Integer indicating the zero-based dimension of the array.
GetUpperBound method	Returns an Integer indicating the upper bound of an array. Its syntax is: *arrVar*.GetUpperBound(*dimension*), where *dimension* is an Integer indicating the zero-based dimension of the array.
Reverse method	An overloaded method that reverses the order of all or a portion of a one-dimensional array.
Sort method	An overloaded method that sorts a one-dimensional array.

TABLE 2-3   Selected Members of the System.Array Class

In contrast, using Visual Basic .NET, there is no need to declare an uninitialized array. So the preceding VB6 code can be simplified as follows:

```
Dim index As Integer = 10
Dim arr(index) As Integer

arr(index) = CInt(index ^ 2)

index = 20
ReDim Preserve arr(index)
arr(index) = CInt(index ^ 2)

index = 10
ReDim Preserve arr(index)
MsgBox (arr(index))
```

Classes

A *class* is a template from which an object, or an instance of a class, is formed. A class defines a reference type that can be derived directly from some other class and that is derived implicitly from System.Object.

Classes are declared using the Class . . . End Class construct. For details, see the entry for "Class . . . End Class" in Chapter 8. The code between these statements can include the following:

- **Variable or field declarations**   *Fields* are constants or variables that are exposed by the class (they can be publicly available to any client having a reference to the class instance as well as accessible to any client within the assembly in which the class instance resides or to any other class that is derived from the current class) or that are private to the class.

- **Properties**   *Properties* are attributes of the class instance.

- **Methods**   *Public* methods express the functionality that the class makes available, while *private* methods are for internal use within the class. Visual Basic .NET supports two kinds of methods: shared and instance. *Shared* methods do not require that an instance of the class be created in order to call the method (though in Visual Basic, shared methods can be called through class instances, even though this is nonsensical), while *instance* methods must be called through an instance of the class.

- **Constructors**   A *constructor* is automatically invoked when a new instance of the class is created. In Visual Basic code, constructors are defined by methods named New.

- **Events**   *Events* are notifications provided by a class, which is the event source. Event sinks register with the source and receive notification that the event has fired, which causes their event handlers to be invoked. The event itself can be anything of interest, such as a mouse click, a value exceeding or falling below a certain level, or a change to a data item.

In addition to classes defined in your own code, classes can be defined in external libraries that are referenced by your project, such as the .NET Framework Class Library.

Object variables that have been declared but not initialized are assigned a value of Nothing.

Visual Basic Naming Conventions

Visual Basic applies the same set of naming conventions throughout the language. Naming conventions apply to all language elements, including variables, types, and type members.

Visual Basic is a case-insensitive language. The Visual Basic editor attempts to enforce consistency in casing (it attempts to use the same case that was used in a type, member, or variable declaration), but case is ignored by the compiler. This means, of course, that you can't differentiate different program elements by case. Properties, for instance, cannot be assigned proper case names while local variables are assigned identical lowercase names.

- The first character of a name in Visual Basic must be an alphabetic character or an underscore. (Note that underscores are not CLS-compliant. They are often used internally to differentiate local variables from public properties with the same name but no underscore.)

- The remaining characters in a name can consist of alphabetic characters, numeric characters, or underscores.

- The name must not be greater than 1023 characters in length.

- Visual Basic recognizes a number of reserved words, such as Alias, Byte, Date, Default, Friend, Me, and Throw, that the compiler automatically interprets as language elements. If you want to use any of these reserved words to identify program elements in your code, you can indicate to the compiler that the name applies to your program element rather than the Visual Basic language element by enclosing it in brackets. This is called an *escaped name.* For example, to define a Boolean variable named Static (which conflicts with the Static keyword), you use the code:

```
Public [Static] As Boolean = False
```

Any escaped name must also be used together with its brackets subsequently to differentiate the program element from the reserved word. For example, a variable assignment using the Static variable takes the form:

```
[Static] = True
```

Variables in Visual Basic

In this section, we'll examine the rules regarding variable declaration and initialization. The section will also examine variable lifetime and scope.

Variable Declaration

Visual Basic allows you to declare variables of any data type. If you do not declare the precise data type of a variable, it will be of type Object. (This requires, however, that Option Strict be set off, its default value.)

Variables are defined using the Dim keyword or an access modifier. (For details on the access modifiers, see the section "Scope and Accessibility" later in this chapter.) For example,

```
Dim age As Integer
Dim city As String
Dim typ As System.Type
```

You can define multiple variables on the same line of code. So a somewhat unwieldy version of the preceding code is:

```
Dim age As Integer, city As String, typ As System.Type
```

If you define multiple variables on a line but do not specify a data type for each, a single type declaration applies to all of the variables defined to the left of it whose types are not specified. Fore example, the code

```
Dim city, state, zip As String
```

Variable Declaration and Option Explicit

Visual Basic does not actually require that you declare variables in advance. If Option Explicit is set off (by default, it is set on), Visual Basic will create variables dynamically as their names are encountered in code. This, however, is highly undesirable if for no other reason than that variables whose names are misspelled are treated as new variables. For example, the following code reports that an account balance is $30.98 when the correct balance is $254.73, because "balance" is misspelled "balaance" in one assignment statement:

```
Dim balance As Decimal = 200.35
balance -= 169.37
balaance += 223.75
Console.WriteLine("Your current balance is {0}.", FormatCurrency(balance))
```

defines three variables, all of type String. This differs from Visual Basic 6.0 and earlier versions, in which variables whose types were not explicitly declared were created as Variants. In the preceding line of code, for example, Visual Basic 6.0 would have interpreted city and state as Variants and zip as a String.

In Visual Basic .NET, unlike Visual Basic 6.0 and previous versions, you can initialize a variable at the same time as you declare it. For example:

```
Dim age As Integer = 35
Dim city As String = "New York"
Dim typ As System.Type = age.GetType
```

You can initialize multiple variables per line. However, if Option Strict is set on, each must have its own type declaration. For example:

```
Dim age As Integer = 35, weight As Integer = 185
```

You can also create a new class instance at the same time as you declare an object variable by using the New keyword in the declaration. For example:

```
Dim s As New StringBuilder("This is a brand new string.")
```

The New keyword causes the class or structure's constructor to be invoked. That means that you can pass arguments to any parameterized constructor, as in the preceding code fragment.

Variable Initialization

Visual Basic does not require that you explicitly initialize each variable that you declare. Instead, if no initialization is provided by the developer, a default initializer is used. However, it is important to keep in mind that, because class instances are set equal to Nothing if they are not explicitly initialized by the developer, code that expects a valid object reference can throw an exception. (The Visual Basic compiler, however, does produce a warning in this situation.)

Visual Basic and the Set Keyword

Visual Basic 6.0 and earlier versions required that you use the Set keyword when assigning a reference to an object variable. For example:

```
Dim fs As New FileSystemObject
Dim wndFold As Folder

Set wndFold = fs.GetSpecialFolder(WindowsFolder)
```

Since the Set keyword was not necessary in other variable assignments, this requirement was a frequent cause of confusion and error, particularly for inexperienced programmers. In .NET, the Set keyword's use in assigning object references has been eliminated. Set is now used exclusively within the Property . . . End Property construct to assign a value to a property.

Explicit assignment is simply a matter of using the assignment operator in a statement to assign the value of the left side of an expression to the variable on the right. For example:

```
Dim answer As String
answer = "The circumference is " & Circumference(radius) & "."
```

The one qualification is that Visual Basic automatically treats literals as instances of particular data types and generates a compiler error if Option Strict is on and it detects a narrowing conversion. For example, if Option Strict is on, the assignment

```
Dim ch1 As Char
ch1 = "c"
```

generates a compiler error ("Option Strict On disallows implicit conversions from 'String' to 'Char'."). To correct it, you have to explicitly convert the "c" to a Char, as in any of the following statements:

```
ch1 = "c"c
ch1 = CChar("c")
ch1 = Convert.ToChar("c")
```

Variable Scope

All types, type members, and variables have a *scope*, or a set of code to which they are visible without explicit qualification. Visual Basic recognizes five different levels of scope:

- **Global scope**   An element is available to all code without qualification.
- **Namespace scope**   An element is available to all code within the namespace in which it is declared. Types in a namespace are visible to all other types in the namespace without qualification. In addition, the Imports statement makes types in other namespaces available to program elements outside of the namespace.
- **Member scope**   An element is available to all code within the module in which it is declared. A module can include modules defined with the Module . . . End Module construct, classes defined with the Class . . . End Class construct, and structures defined with the Structure . . . End Structure construct.
- **Procedure or local scope**   An element is available to all code within the procedure in which it is declared. A procedure can include a function defined with the Function . . . End Function construct, a subroutine defined with the Sub . . . End Sub construct, or a property defined with the Property . . . End Property construct.
- **Block scope**   An element is available to all code within the code block in which it is declared. Blocks are defined by the Do . . . Loop, For . . . Next, For Each . . . Next, If . . . End If, Select . . . End Select, SyncLock . . . End SyncLock, Try . . . End Try, While . . . End While, and With . . . End With constructs.

In general, a variable should have the smallest scope possible. This helps ensure the variable's integrity by reducing the number of places in which its value can be modified incorrectly or accidentally.

Scope and Accessibility

Visual Basic also includes four keywords (Public, Friend, Protected, and Private) that define the accessibility of a particular type or type member. Accessibility is related to but not identical with scope. *Accessibility* determines whether a program element is visible. *Scope* determines whether it must be qualified to be accessed. For example, a class defined with the Public keyword is globally accessible. However, it has only namespace scope, since it ordinarily can be accessed without using its namespace name only within its own namespace. Types and members with Friend accessibility are visible within the assembly in which they're declared. They have namespace scope to types in the same namespace in the assembly in which they are defined. But since a namespace can be split across multiple assemblies, they are completely inaccessible to types in the same namespace but a different assembly. Types with Protected accessibility have namespace scope to classes that inherit from them in the same namespace, must have their type names qualified to classes that inherit from them in different namespaces, and are not accessible to classes that do not inherit from them and to other types. Types declared with Private accessibility have member scope.

In the following sections, we'll examine each of these levels of scope.

Global Scope

In some cases, publicly available types and type members can be accessed without qualification regardless of the namespace in which they reside. For example, the "intrinsic" methods of classes in the Microsoft.VisualBasic namespace can be referenced without qualification anywhere in Visual Basic code. In Visual Basic, the Global keyword and HideModuleName statements can be used to give program elements global scope.

Namespace Scope

Variables and other elements that are declared as Public are accessible throughout all the types of a namespace, as well as all nested namespaces. If a namespace is not explicitly defined, they are available in all of the classes, modules, and structures in a project.

Member Scope

Member level refers to code that exists outside of any procedure in a class, structure, or module. Variables or other elements defined at member level are defined outside of any function, subroutine, or property belonging to a class, module, or structure. When declared with either the Private or Dim keyword, they are visible to all procedures within the module, but they are not available to any outside of the module.

Procedure Scope

Variables declared within a procedure (which includes a function, a subroutine, or a property procedure) but not inside a block construct are *local* variables. They have scope within that procedure only and are not visible outside of the procedure in which they are declared.

Dim is the only keyword that can be used to declare a variable with procedure scope. Any of the access modifiers (like Private or Protected) in a variable declaration with procedure scope generates a compiler error.

An advantage of local variables (as well as an occasional source of confusion) is that their names can duplicate the names of other variables, which will be effectively hidden by the local variable. The following code illustrates this:

```
Public Class Dog
    Private Name As String

Public Sub New(name As String)
    If name = String.Empty Then
       Dim message As String = "The dog breed must be specified."
       Throw New ArgumentException("message.")
    End If
    ' Parse into an array
    Dim words() As String = Split(name)
    For ctr As Integer = LBound(words, 1) To UBound(words, 1)
        Dim breedname As String = words(ctr)
        If Not Char.IsUpper(breedname, 1) Then
            Dim firstLetter As String = breedname.Substring(0, 1)
            firstLetter = firstLetter.ToUpper
            name = firstLetter & Mid(breedname, 2)
            words(ctr) = breedname
        End If
    Next
    ' return to single string
    name = Join(words)
    Me.name = name
    Console.WriteLine("Created a new record for {0}.", Me.Breed)
    End Sub

    Public ReadOnly Property Breed As String
       Get
           Return Me.Name
       End Get
    End Property
End Class
```

This code declares a class named Dog that has a private variable, name, at the member level to store the value of the Breed property. Its class constructor also has a local variable, name, that is used to validate the string supplied as an argument. However, the two variables are quite independent of one another. Note that in the class constructor, the local name variable hides the private name variable. If we wish to access it, we must preface it with the Me keyword.

Block Scope

In .NET, variables declared inside of a block construct have block scope. That is, they are not visible outside of the block in which they are declared. Block constructs include the following:

- Do . . . Loop
- For . . . Next and For Each . . . Next
- If . . . End If
- Select . . . End Select
- SyncLock . . . End SyncLock
- Try . . . End Try

- While . . . End While

- With . . . End With

The following code declares a variable with block scope, firstChar, to store the first character of a name. This is then used to increment the count of an array element used to track the number of names that begin with that character. The code is

```
Public Class BlockScope
    Public Shared Sub Main()
        Dim maleNames() As String = {"John", "Michael", "Robert", "George", _
                            "Lawrence", "Charles", "James", "Samuel", _
                            "David", "Peter", "Paul", "Thomas", "Steven", _
                            "Abraham", "Isaac", "Joseph", "Ronald", _
                            "Theodore", "William", "Mark", "Luke"}
        Dim startChar(25) As Integer

        ' Find number of names beginning with a letter
        For Each maleName As String in maleNames
            Dim firstChar As Char
            firstChar = CChar(Left(maleName, 1))
            Dim charValue As Integer = AscW(firstChar)
            ' Go to next name if character invalid or unicode character out of range
            If charValue < 65 Or (charValue > 91 And charValue < 97) _
                Or charValue > 123 Then Continue For

            If Char.IsUpper(firstChar) Then
                startChar(Convert.ToInt32(firstChar) - 65) += 1
            ElseIf Char.IsLower(firstChar) Then
                startChar(Convert.ToInt32(startChar) - 97) += 1
            End If
        Next
        Console.WriteLine("Final Count:")
        Dim charCode As Integer = 65
        For Each charCount As Integer in startChar
            Console.WriteLine("Letter " & ChrW(charCode) & " has " & charCount & _
                            " names.")
            charCode += 1
        Next
    End Sub
End Class
```

Dim is the only keyword that can be used to declare a variable with block scope. Using any of the access modifiers (like Private or Protected) in a variable declaration with block scope generates a compiler error.

Visual Basic and Block Scope

Block scope is new to Visual Basic .NET. In Visual Basic 6.0 and earlier versions, variables declared inside a block construct had procedure-level scope; they were visible from the point that they were declared throughout the rest of the procedure.

The lifetime of variables with block scope (see the next section, "Variable Lifetime") is determined by the procedure in which they are declared. This is illustrated by the following code, in which the value of one of the variables with block scope, blockVar, reaches 110,000 in the last iteration of the inner loop:

```
Public Class BlockScope
    Public Shared Sub Main()
        For outerLoop As Integer = 0 to 10000
            For innerLoop As Integer = 0 to 10
                Dim blockVar As Integer
                blockVar += 1
                If blockVar Mod 1000 = 0 Then Console.WriteLine(blockVar)
            Next
        Next
    End Sub
End Class
```

Variable Lifetime

In addition to their scope, variables also have a lifetime, which indicates when during program execution the variable exists. Scope, on the other hand, indicates whether the variables that exist are accessible or not. The difference is most clear in variables with block-level scope: although they are visible only within the block construct within which they are declared, their lifetime is the lifetime of the procedure in which they are declared. Similarly, the lifetime of variables with procedure scope terminates when a procedure ends, but they are visible only when the procedure is actually executing, not when the procedure has in turn called other procedures.

Ordinarily, the lifetime of variables with procedure scope terminates when the procedure ends. However, we can declare variables to be static, in which case their lifetime is the duration of the application, even though they have procedure scope. For example, the following code shows a simple Windows application that tracks the number of times its single interface object, a command button, is clicked:

```
Public Class Form1
    Private Sub cmdClickCtr_Click(ByVal sender As System.Object, _
                                  ByVal e As System.EventArgs) _
                                  Handles cmdClickCtr.Click
        Static ctr As Integer = 1
        MsgBox("Button was clicked " & ctr & " times.")
        ctr += 1
    End Sub
End Class
```

Static in Visual Basic and C#

A possible source of confusion is the use of the static keyword in Visual Basic .NET and C#. In C#, a variable or another program element marked with the static keyword belongs to the type in which it is declared, rather than to an instance of the type. It corresponds to the Shared keyword rather than the Static keyword in Visual Basic .NET.

Ordinarily, the lifetime of the counter variable, ctr, is limited to the duration that the Click event procedure runs. Declaring it as static, however, causes it to exist throughout the lifetime of the application. Hence, it can track the total number of times the button is clicked since the application started. Note that the Static variable declaration, which also initializes the variable ctr to a value of 1, is executed only once. We do not need to be concerned that the value of ctr will be reset to 1 each time the event procedure executes.

Late and Early Binding

Binding refers to the process of member lookup and type checking. Binding can be handled by the compiler in advance at compile time, in which case it is referred to as *early binding*. It can also be handled at runtime by the .NET runtime environment, in which case it is referred to as *late binding*. Early binding occurs whenever an object variable is declared to be a specific object type. In that case, the compiler can perform all necessary type checking in advance.

Late binding occurs whenever any variable is declared to be of type Object; a more specific type of object is subsequently assigned to it, and the Object variable is used to call a member of that more specific object type. In this case, name lookup and type checking must occur at runtime rather than at compile time, which results in a significant performance penalty. Since type checking and member lookup occur only at runtime, it also makes runtime errors more likely, thereby increasing the need for robust error handling.

Reference and Value Type Conversion

In our earlier discussion of data types, we noted that Visual Basic's data types include value types and reference types. The key difference between reference types and value types is that variables hold references to instances of reference types, while they hold copies of instances of value types. In many ways, the difference is the same as the difference between the ByVal and ByRef keywords: when you pass an argument by reference, you're passing the argument itself. When you pass an argument by value, you're passing a copy of your original. So whenever you pass an instance of reference type, the CLR is passing its reference. Whenever you're passing a value type, the CLR is making a copy of the value type and passing that.

This copy operation actually takes two forms:

- When a value type is assigned to a field or variable of the same type, a copy is made.
- When a value type is assigned to a field or variable of type Object, a copy is made, and a process called *boxing* is performed by the CLR. This consists of wrapping a special "box" around that copy. The box is simply a "thin" reference wrapper that holds onto the boxed value so that the called routine that is expecting an instance of a reference type gets one.

Boxing involves a performance penalty. And often, it's a double whammy. When a boxed value is then assigned to a variable or field typed as a value type, the value must be unboxed. This means that another copy has to be made, just as if the value had never been boxed at all.

Visual Basic can perform the process of boxing and unboxing automatically, without the need for the developer to explicitly handle the conversion of value types to reference types and vice versa. However, Visual Basic's automatic boxing and unboxing involves a performance penalty.

There are two major ways to minimize the possible impact on performance that results from Visual Basic's automatic boxing and unboxing:

- Use instances of classes instead of value types to prevent boxing and unboxing. For example, a routine stores instances of a structure to a Visual Basic Collection object. The Collection class expects that each data item assigned to the collection is of type Object. Hence, some performance improvement would result from replacing the structure with a class.

- Rather than allowing Visual Basic to handle unboxing automatically, use the DirectCast operator so that your code handles unboxing. When handling primitive value types (rather than complex value types, such as structures), this saves Visual Basic from having to determine what conversions are possible before performing the unboxing. Instead, DirectCast will only allow you to convert a reference type to the data type of the original value type.

Program Structure

This chapter will examine the basic structure of a Visual Basic .NET program. The chapter will focus on the code needed to get an application to run, on calling functions and subroutines that are available to an application, on writing and invoking event handlers, and on accessing types and type members found in external libraries.

The Application Entry Point

Every executable application must have an entry point, or a routine that the .NET runtime automatically calls in order to begin program execution. Typically, program control both starts and ends with the entry point. In executable applications that run under the .NET Common Language Runtime (that is to say, on console applications and Windows applications), this startup routine is usually named *Main*.

Main must have the following characteristics:

- It must be a routine defined inside of a class or structure.

- It must be a shared routine; that is, running Main should not require that an instance of the class it contains be instantiated.

- It must be a public routine. This differs from Visual Basic 6.0 and earlier versions, in which Main was still accessible if it was private.

- Main can be a sub (and therefore does not have a return value), or it can be a function that returns an Integer. Typically, if Main is a function, the returned Integer is used in a console application to indicate an error condition or provide a status code.

- Main can have zero, one, or more parameters. If one or more parameters are present, the parameter list must be declared to be a string array. The array containing the arguments is then accessible within the Main procedure by using the parameter name, and it is accessible both within and outside the Main procedure by using the Command function, which returns all command-line arguments passed to the Main procedure as a single string that in turn must be parsed to extract individual arguments.

It would appear that more often than not, these requirements are ignored in Visual Basic executables. For instance, the basic structure of many console applications often looks something like the following:

```
Public Module MainModule
    Sub Main()
        ' Do something
    End Sub
End Module
```

Notice that Main is not explicitly declared to be public, nor is it declared to be a shared member of the module. However, if we examine the executable using ILDasm, as Figure 3-1 shows, since we haven't provided an access modifier in our declaration of Main, the Visual Basic compiler has made it public by default. As Figure 3-1 also shows, the compiler has translated our Module . . . End Module construct into a .NET class, and it has made the Main procedure a shared member of the class. (In fact, the compiler defines all public methods of Visual Basic modules as shared.)

Windows applications created with Visual Studio also appear to have no clearly defined entry point other than the Form_Load event procedure. However, if we look at a Windows application's executable file, as Figure 3-2 shows, we see that the My.MyApplication class

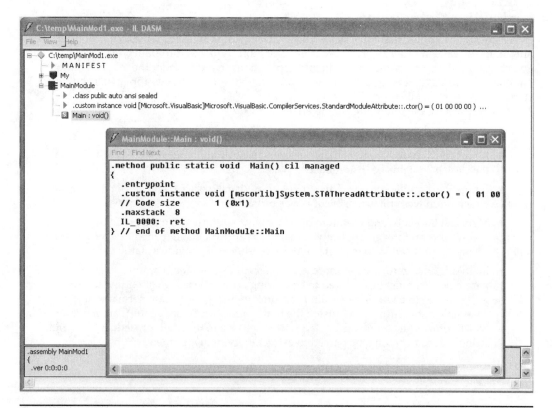

FIGURE 3-1   A console-mode application displayed in ILDasm

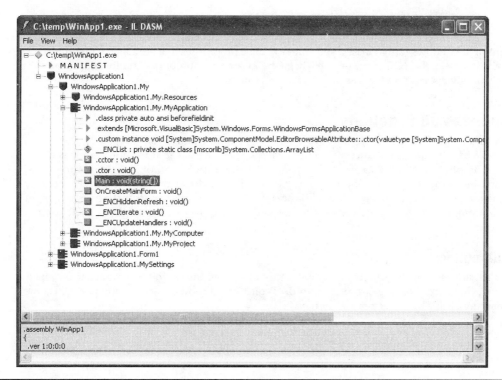

FIGURE 3-2   ILDasm displaying the structure of a Windows application

includes a Main procedure, which serves as the entry point of the application. If we look at the intermediate language generated for the executable (see Figure 3-3), we see that Main's primary responsibility is to call the WindowsFormsApplicationBase.Run method, which starts the Windows Forms component of the application.

```
WindowsApplication1.My.MyApplication::Main : void(string[])
Find  Find Next
.method assembly static void  Main(string[] Args) cil managed
{
  .entrypoint
  .custom instance void [mscorlib]System.STAThreadAttribute::.ctor() = ( 01 00 00 00 )
  .custom instance void [mscorlib]System.Diagnostics.DebuggerHiddenAttribute::.ctor() = ( 01 00 00 00 )
  .custom instance void [System]System.ComponentModel.EditorBrowsableAttribute::.ctor(valuetype [System]System.Compor
  // Code size       14 (0xe)
  .maxstack  8
  IL_0000:  nop
  IL_0001:  call       class WindowsApplication1.My.MyApplication WindowsApplication1.My.MyProject::get_Application()
  IL_0006:  callvirt   instance void [Microsoft.VisualBasic]System.Windows.Forms.WindowsFormsApplicationBase::Run()
  IL_000b:  nop
  IL_000c:  nop
  IL_000d:  ret
} // end of method MyApplication::Main
```

FIGURE 3-3   Intermediate language for the My.MyApplication.Main procedure

Of course, for all but the simplest of applications, you don't want to place all of your code in a single Main procedure. Instead, much as the WindowsFormsApplicationBase.Run method transfers control to Windows forms classes, you want to define procedures that are called either directly by your code or by the .NET runtime. We'll begin by looking at subroutines and functions, and then we'll briefly discuss events and event-driven programming.

Subroutines and Functions

If you're using Visual Basic to develop an executable application, you'll typically want to transfer control to subroutines or functions to perform the specific tasks that the application is designed to accomplish. In other cases, such as if you're developing a library of reusable routines, you want the consumer of your library to be able to call individual routines that provide specific functionality. For this purpose, Visual Basic provides subroutines and functions. We'll begin by examining the difference between subroutines and functions before examining their common features.

Subroutines

A *subroutine* is a procedure that does not return a value to the calling program. (Alternatively, to use C, C++, and C# syntax, it returns **void**.) Typically, subroutines are used to perform some operation. They have the general syntax:

```
<Access Modifier> Sub <Subroutine_Name>(parameter_list)
    ' Subroutine code
End Sub
```

If no access modifier is provided, then the subroutine is public by default. The subroutine name must follow standard Visual Basic naming conventions. Finally, the parameter list, which defines the arguments that a caller passes to the subroutine and assigns the names by which they are referred in the subroutine, is discussed in the section "Constructing Parameter Lists" later in this chapter.

A subroutine can be called using either of the following forms, with the second being the most common:

```
Call object_name.Subroutine_Name(argument_list)
object_name.Subroutine_Name(parameter_list)
```

Here, *object_name* can be omitted if *Subroutine_Name* is a shared member that is being called from another shared member of the same class or structure.

Note that this calling syntax is slightly different from that of Visual Basic 6.0 and earlier versions, where *argument_list* is enclosed in parentheses only if the Call statement is used, or if there is a single argument and the Call statement is not used.

> **The Difference Between Functions and Subroutines**
>
> A function returns a value, while a subroutine does not. But this difference should also reflect a difference in design. A well-designed function shouldn't have a return value that can be safely ignored; functions should be called only for their return values. Subroutines, in contrast, should be called only for their side effects, or for the operations that they perform.

Functions

A *function* is a procedure that returns a value to the caller. That value can be any of the data types recognized by Visual Basic and the .NET platform. Functions have the general syntax:

```
<Access Modifier> Function <Function_Name>(parameter_list) As <return_type>
    ' function code
End Function
```

If no access modifier is provided, then the function is public by default. The function name must follow standard Visual Basic naming conventions (see Chapter 1). The parameter list is discussed in the section "Constructing Parameter Lists" later in this chapter. The As *<return_type>* clause can be omitted if Option Strict is off, in which case the function will return an Object; this, however, is not recommended.

If a function is public and is part of a component or library that might be called from code written in other languages, you should make sure that the return type is CLS-compliant. If it is not, other languages may not be able to correctly handle the return value. You can use the CLSCompliant attribute to generate a compiler warning whenever a non–CLS compliant type is returned by a function; for details, see the Function entry in Chapter 8.

Typically, you call a function and assign the value to a variable, as in the following pseudocode:

```
ret_val = Function_Name(argument_list)
```

or assign it to a property:

```
MyObject.PropertyValue = Function_Name(argument_list)
```

or assign it to a field:

```
MyObject.FieldValue = Function_Name(argument_list)
```

or use it as an expression:

```
If function_name1(argument_list + 3) > function_name2(argument_list -1 ) Then
```

or use it as an argument in another function call:

```
retval = Function_Name1(FunctionName2(arg_list), arg2, arg3)
```

If you're not interested in the function's return value, however, you can call it just as you would a subroutine (although see the sidebar "The Difference Between Functions and Subroutines").

Parameters

Like any structured programming language, Visual Basic allows you to pass parameters to methods. A parameter list takes the following general form, with commas used to separate one parameter from another:

```
(param_name1 As type_name, param_name2 As type_name . . . . )
```

> **Selecting Parameter Names**
>
> Since parameter names may be used by consumers of your classes, you should make sure that the name you assign a parameter reflects use or purpose within the function or subroutine. This makes the code that makes use of named arguments for method calls more readable and self-documenting.

However, you can construct a parameter list in a number of ways, and you can specify whether individual arguments are passed by reference or by value to a function or subroutine. Passing parameters by value and by reference is discussed in the section "Parameters by Reference and by Value," while the various ways to construct a parameter list are discussed in the remaining parts of the "Parameter Lists" section.

When calling functions or subroutines that have parameters, arguments can be passed in either of two ways: positionally or by name. When calling a method using positional arguments, their position must correspond exactly to the order defined by the method's syntax. All Visual Basic methods can be called positionally. For example, the Visual Basic InStr function can be called as follows:

```
pos = InStr(1, targetstring, srchstring)
```

When calling a method by name, the parameter name defined by the method's syntax is followed by a special assignment operator, :=, which is followed by the argument to be passed to the method. Arguments do not have to be passed in the order in which they are defined by the method's syntax, and optional arguments can be skipped. For example, the same call to the InStr function using named arguments might appear as follows:

```
pos = Instr(string1 := targetString, string2 := searchString, start := 1)
```

Not all functions and methods can be called using named arguments (for example, the intrinsic Visual Basic conversion functions cannot).

Parameters by Reference and by Value

Passing a parameter by value means that the .NET runtime makes a copy of a variable, which it then passes to the called procedure. In other words, the called procedure works on a copy of the original, and when the method returns, the original value of the argument is preserved, and any changes made to that value by the called procedure are discarded. In Visual Basic .NET, parameters are passed by value using the ByVal keyword. If it is omitted, Visual Basic .NET passes parameters by value by default.

The following code illustrates passing parameters by value:

```
Public Module modByValue
    Public Sub Main()
        Dim title As String = "Dr."
        Dim lastName As String = "Livingston"
        Dim retVal As String = FormalName(title, lastName)
```

```
        Console.WriteLine(retval)
        ' Displays "Dr."
        Console.WriteLine("Value of title variable: " & title)
        ' Displays "Livingston"
        Console.WriteLine("Value of lastName variable: " & lastName)
    End Sub

    Function FormalName(ByVal title As String, ByVal lastName As String) As
String
        lastName = trim(title & " " & lastName)
        Return lastName
    End Function
End Module
```

Even though the FormalName function has changed the value of the lastName string, the output shows that the change is not reflected in the value of lastName when control returns to the Main subroutine.

On the other hand, passing a parameter by reference means that the .NET runtime does not make a local copy of the data but instead allows the called routine access to the original. The called procedure works on the argument itself, so that when control returns to the calling method, any changes made to the value of the argument by the called method are preserved. Parameters are passed by reference in Visual Basic using the ByRef keyword, as in the following example:

```
Public Module modByValue
    Public Sub Main()
        Dim salary As Decimal = 45000.00d
        Dim reviewPts As Integer = 12
        If ReceiveRaise(salary, reviewPts) Then
          Console.WriteLine("Congratulations, your new salary is " & _
                            FormatCurrency(salary) & ".")
        Else
            Console.WriteLine("Unfortunately, based on your evaluation, " & _
                            "you did not qualify for a raise.")
        End If
    End Sub

    Function ReceiveRaise(ByRef salary As Decimal, ByVal reviewPts As Integer) _
                        As Boolean
        If reviewPts <= 10 Then
          Return False
        Else
          Dim increasePct As Decimal
          increasePct = ((reviewPts - 10) * .005d)
          salary = salary * (1 + increasePct)
          Return True
        End If
    End Function
End Module
```

In this example, the ReceiveRaise function returns a Boolean indicating whether an employee's evaluation was sufficient to merit a raise. The salary parameter is passed to the function by reference, so that when the function returns, it contains the employee's updated salary if he or she has received a raise.

It is important to note that passing a parameter by value does not prevent all changes to values in the case of composite data types. Whether changes are reflected in individual members or elements of a composite data type depends on whether that type is a reference or value type. When a composite reference type (an instance of a class or an array) is passed by value, changes to individual members (such as property values or array elements) made by the called routine are reflected when control returns to the calling routine. When a composite value type (an instance of a structure) is passed by value, changes to individual members made by the called routine are not reflected when control returns to the calling routine. For instance, consider the following code, which passes an instance of a Dog class to two procedures:

```
Public Class Dog
    Private dogBreed As String
    Private dogWeight As Decimal

    Public Sub New(breed As String)
        dogBreed = breed
    End Sub

    Public ReadOnly Property Breed() As String
        Get
            Return dogBreed
        End Get
    End Property

    Public Property Weight() As Decimal
        Get
            Return dogWeight
        End Get
        Set
            dogWeight = CDec(value)
        End Set
    End Property
    Public Sub ShowInfo()
        Console.WriteLine("This " & dogBreed & " weighs " & dogWeight & "
pounds.")
    End Sub
End Class

Public Class testDog
    Public Shared Sub Main()
        Dim td As New testDog
        Dim mal As New Dog("Alaskan Malamute")

        mal.Weight = 130
        td.ChangeDogInfo(mal)
        mal.ShowInfo
```

```
      td.CompletelyChangeDogInfo(mal)
      mal.ShowInfo
   End Sub

   Public Sub ChangeDogInfo(ByVal aDog As Dog)
      aDog.Weight = 125
   End Sub

   Public Sub CompletelyChangeDogInfo(ByVal aDog As Dog)
      Dim newf As New Dog("Newfoundland")
      aDog = newf
   End Sub
End Class
```

The program produces the following output:

```
This Alaskan Malamute weighs 125 pounds.
This Alaskan Malamute weighs 125 pounds.
```

Even though an instance of the Dog class is passed by value to the ChangeDogInfo routine, that routine is able to update the instance's property values and have those changes reflected when control returns to the caller. What passing a class instance by value cannot do (as shown in the return from the CompletelyChangeDogInfo method) is to replace an instance of a class with a completely different instance. This is possible, however, if the class instance is passed to a method by reference, as it is to the ChangeDogReference method in the following code:

```
Public Class testADog
   Public Shared Sub Main()
      Dim td As New testADog
      Dim mal As New Dog("Alaskan Malamute")

      mal.Weight = 130
      td.ChangeDogReference(mal)
      mal.ShowInfo
   End Sub

   Public Sub ChangeDogReference(byRef aDog As Dog)
      Dim newf As New Dog("Newfoundland")
      newf.Weight = 150
      aDog = newf
   End Sub
End Class
```

Here, we pass the method an instance of Dog that's an Alaskan Malamute and receive back an instance of Dog that's a Newfoundland, as shown in the output from the ShowInfo method:

```
This Newfoundland weighs 150 pounds.
```

However, the result is different if we change Dog from a class to a structure. In this case, the code produces the following output:

```
This Alaskan Malamute weights 130 pounds.
This Alaskan Malamute weights 130 pounds.
```

Even though we've modified the property value in the ChangeDogInfo routine, the original value is preserved when control returns to the Main method.

Overriding a ByRef Parameter

There may be times when you don't want to have a called routine modify the value of an argument that's passed to it by reference. You can override the called routine's behavior and instead pass the parameter by value by enclosing it in parentheses. This means that, if a method has a single parameter, enclosing the argument in double parentheses passes it by value to the called procedure.

For example, in the following code, the Square subroutine is passed a parameter by reference and squares its value. In the call to the subroutine from the Main procedure, the argument is instead passed by value so that, when control returns to Main, its value is unchanged:

```
Public Module ByRefOverride
    Public Sub Main()
        Dim sInput As String = InputBox("Enter a number: ")
        Dim inputNumber As Double
        If IsNumeric(sInput) Then
            inputNumber = CDbl(sInput)
            Square( (inputNumber) )
            Console.WriteLine(inputNumber)
        End If
    End Sub

    Public Sub Square(ByRef num As Double)
        num ^= 2
        Console.WriteLine(num)
    End Sub
End Module
```

Constructing Parameter Lists

Ordinarily, how to construct a parameter list for a function or subroutine is clear. In some cases, however, you may find that you want a procedure to accept arguments of various types, or you may want a procedure to accept different numbers of parameters at different times. In this section, we'll look at some of the options open to you in constructing parameter lists.

Untyped Parameters

If you want a procedure to accept a parameter whose data type can vary, you can simply declare the parameter to be of type Object, or you can simply omit the parameter's As clause if Option Strict is off. This allows the procedure to accept an argument of any type.

This approach is often used in the .NET Framework Class Library for defining parameters of methods that can be passed instances of virtually any type. For example, the Object.Equals method has two overloads, one a shared method and one an instance method, both of which define their parameters as type Object:

```
' Instance method of the Object class
Function Equals(obj As Object) As Boolean

' Shared method of the Object class
Shared Function Equals(objA As Object, objB As Object) As Boolean
```

The purpose of the function as it is implemented by the Object class is to determine whether two variables reference the same object instance. However, the parameter allows any type of object to be passed to the method, and therefore defines its parameters as type Object.

Defining parameters of type Object in this manner does have a number of limitations:

- Often, it requires that Option Strict be set off, which means that the Visual Basic compiler will allow implicit narrowing conversions, thereby increasing the possibility of an unhandled runtime exception in your code.

- It requires a good deal more type checking, since your code must ensure that an object of the correct type is passed as an argument to the method.

Optional Parameters

Often, a function or procedure may require a variable number of arguments. One of the ways of handling this scenario is to define optional parameters. *Optional parameters* are preceded by the Optional keyword and include a default value that is provided if the argument is omitted. If a particular parameter is defined as optional, all subsequent parameters in a function or procedure declaration must also be optional. The general syntax of an optional parameter is:

```
Optional parameter_name As type_name = default_value
```

For example, the following function returns the area in square units or cubic units, depending on whether a third optional argument is supplied:

```
Public Function Area(height As Double, width As Double, _
                Optional depth As Double = 1) As Double
    Return height * width * depth
End Function
```

Although they offer an effective solution, optional parameters are not supported by the Common Language Specification, and therefore are not usable in a truly language-independent component.

Parameter Arrays

In some cases, you may not know in advance precisely how many arguments are to be passed to a routine. A statistical routine, for instance, might be expected to work seamlessly with anywhere from one to a virtually unlimited number of data items. In cases such as these, where the number of parameters is not known precisely in advance, a parameter array is an excellent solution.

A *parameter array* is, as its name implies, an array that is defined as a method parameter using the ParamArray keyword. It must be the last parameter in the parameter list and must be passed by value. Finally, although the parameter array is optional, the Optional keyword is not used with it. The syntax of a parameter array is:

```
[ ByVal ] ParamArray method_name() As type_name
```

The following example illustrates the use of the ParamArray keyword:

```
Public Function Mean(ParamArray values() As Integer) As Double
    Dim num As Integer
    Dim total As Double
```

```
    For Each num In values
        total += num
    Next
    Return total / values.Length
End Function
```

Arguments can be passed to the parameter array in either of two ways: as an array, or as a list of comma-separated arguments. Our Mean function in the preceding example, for instance, can be called by providing an array argument, as in the following code:

```
Dim x() As Integer = {12, 16, 101, 104, 103, 12}
Console.WriteLine("The mean is " & Mean(x))
```

or it can be called using a list of scalar arguments, as in the following code:

```
Console.WriteLine("The mean is " & Mean(12, 16, 101, 104, 103, 12))
```

Very much like optional parameters, parameter arrays offer a very effective solution to some programming problems, although they are not supported by the Common Language Specification. Therefore, they should not be used as part of the public interface of a language-independent component.

Overloaded Methods

The final method of defining parameters that we'll discuss, and the one most consistent with an object-oriented programming language and the .NET Framework, is to use *overloaded methods*. Overloading allows you to define multiple versions of a method, each of which has the same name but a different signature than the other similarly named methods. This means that individual methods can have the same name but a different number of parameters and types of parameters. A method's return value is not considered part of its signature; an overloaded method cannot return two different data types.

For example, the following code defines a Person class that uses an overloaded constructor and an overloaded FullName method:

```
Option Strict On

Imports Microsoft.VisualBasic

Public Class Person

    Private ttl As String
    Private fName As String
    Private mName As String
    Private lName As String

    Public Sub New(firstName As String, lastName As String)
        fName = firstName
        lName = lastName
    End Sub
```

```vb
   Public Sub New(firstName As String, middleName As String, _
                  lastName As String)
      fName = firstName
      mName = middleName
      lName = lastName
   End Sub

   Public ReadOnly Property FirstName() As String
      Get
         Return fName
      End Get
   End Property

   Public ReadOnly Property LastName() As String
      Get
         Return lName
      End Get
   End Property

   Public ReadOnly Property MiddleName As String
      Get
         Return mName
      End Get
   End Property

   Public Property Title() As String
      Get
         Return ttl
      End Get
      Set
         ttl = Value
      End Set
   End Property

   Public Function FullName(useTitle As Boolean) As String
      Return FullName(useTitle, True, False)
   End Function

   Public Function FullName(useTitle As Boolean, useFirstName As Boolean) _
                    As String
      Return FullName(useTitle, useFirstName, False)
   End Function

   Public Function FullName(useTitle As Boolean, useFirstName As Boolean, _
                    useMiddleName As Boolean) As String
      Dim outputName As String

      If useTitle Then outputName &= (Trim(Me.ttl) & " ")
      If useFirstName Then outputName &= (Trim(Me.fName) & " ")
      If useMiddleName Then outputName &= (Trim(Me.mName) & " ")
      outputName &= Trim(Me.lName)
```

```
        Return outputName
    End Function

    Public Function FullName() As String
        Return FullName(True, True, False)
    End Function
End Class
```

Two overloaded versions of the constructor are defined in the class, as are three versions of the FullName function. Note that two of the versions of the FullName function don't contain complete code implementations but simply call the third version, passing it the necessary arguments. Except in the simplest of overloaded methods (like our class constructors in this example), you don't want to duplicate code in overloaded methods.

Events

There are two distinct (although not mutually exclusive) models of programming. The first, *procedural programming*, is based on a program flow that is known in advance. Program execution begins with the code in an application's entry point procedure and then proceeds to other procedures that are called by the entry point procedure or its subroutines. Program flow eventually returns to the entry point procedure, and the program terminates.

The second, *event-driven programming*, is based on the execution of event handlers, which are routines that are invoked by the system (in this case, by the .NET runtime) in response to some event. This event can be initiated by the user (a movement of the mouse or a mouse click, for example), the system (the addition of a plug-and-play device), the data processed by the program (the value of an item of data falling below a threshold value), or even the program itself (for instance, if an event fires when a loop has iterated a particular number of times). Once the event occurs and the event handler is executed, code in the event handler can then call functions and subroutines, much as code in a procedural program does.

In Visual Basic .NET, an event handler is simply a subroutine that has a particular signature and that is designated as an event handler. Its general format is:

```
Private Sub handler_name(sender As Object, e As EventArgs) Handles object.event
```

where *handler_name* is the name of the event handler, *sender* is an instance of the class that raised the event, *e* is an instance of the EventArgs class or of a type derived from EventArgs that contains information about the event, and *object.event* designates the event that *handler_name* handles.

The event handler's second parameter, an instance of the EventArgs class or a class derived from it, is not always used to provide additional information about the event. The EventArgs class is derived directly from System.Object, the base class for all .NET classes, to which (starting with .NET 1.1) it adds only a single shared member, Empty.

Naming an Event Handler

Most commonly, the name of the event handler has the format *object_event*. So, for example, an event handler for the Click event of a button named cmdAccept is cmdAccept_Click. However, the use of the Handles clause means that the name of the event handler can be whatever you wish. It also makes it easy for a single procedure to handle multiple events.

Other classes derived from EventArgs, however, may have additional members that provide information about the event. For example, the System.Windows.Forms.Form.Closing event handler receives a CancelEventArgs class instance as an argument. It adds a Boolean Cancel property that indicates whether the Form.Close event should be cancelled; if it is set to True, the form will not close. Similarly, in an ASP.NET application, a System.Web.UI.WebControls.Button.Command event handler, which is executed whenever the button is clicked, receives a CommandEventArgs class instance as an argument. The CommandEventArgs class includes two unique members, CommandName and CommandArgument, which provide the CommandName and CommandArgument properties of the Button control that was clicked.

For additional detail on handling events, including a discussion of delegates and of raising custom events, see Chapter 5.

Windows Forms Events

In a Windows Forms application with a single SDI-form, the order in which code executes is:

1. **The Main procedure**   The application entry point
2. **The form's New constructor**   Fired when the form is instantiated
3. **The form's Load event**   Fired before the form is displayed for the first time
4. **The form's Activated event**   Fired when the form receives the focus
5. **The form's Closing event**   A cancelable event that is fired when the user attempts to close the form
6. **The form's FormClosing event (in .NET 2.0)**   A cancelable event that is fired when the form is about to close
7. **The form's Closed event**   An informational event that is fired as the form closes
8. **The form's FormClosed event (in .NET 2.0)**   An informational event that is fired as the form closes
9. **The Dispose method**   A method called by the .NET runtime to release or free unmanaged resources

In addition, each of the controls on a Windows form generates its own events.

ASP.NET Page Events

In an ASP.NET application, the order in which page events fire is:

1. Page_Init
2. Page_Load
3. Page_DataBind
4. Page_PreRender
5. Page_Unload

Accessing .NET Assemblies

Along with instantiating classes and accessing members defined in your own project, it is important that your code be able to access types found in external libraries, one of the most prominent of which is the .NET Framework Class Library. Making a type available to your project requires that you add a reference to the assembly in which the type is defined. Since types are stored in logical containers called namespaces, you might also want to define the namespaces that the compiler should examine automatically to find your namespaces. In this section, we'll look at the ways in which you add references to your projects and define the namespaces in which the types you use are located.

Adding References to Assemblies

The way in which you add a reference to an assembly depends on the development environment in which you are working:

- When using an ordinary text editor along with the Visual Basic .NET command-line compiler, you define the files containing the assemblies you'd like to reference with the /r compiler switch. For example, the following statement compiles a source code file named *MyProject.vb* and adds references to types contained in System.Drawing.dll, and the Windows Forms library:

```
vbc myproject.vb /r:system.windows.forms.dll,system.drawing.dll
```

- When using Visual Studio and Microsoft Visual Basic 2005 Express, you select the Add Reference option from the Project menu. You then select the .NET assembly to which you'd like to add a reference from the .NET tab of the Add Reference dialog (see Figure 3-4).

- In Microsoft Visual Web Developer 2005 Express, you select the Add Reference option from the Website menu. You then select the assembly to which you'd like to add a reference from the dialog shown in Figure 3-4.

FIGURE 3-4
The Add Reference
dialog in Visual
Studio .NET

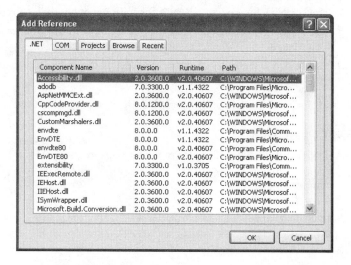

- If you're using a text editor to create ASP.NET pages, you can add a reference to a .NET assembly by adding an <add assembly> tag to the <configuration> section of a *web.config* .file. For example, the following shows the relevant portions of a web.config.file to which a reference to System.Messaging.dll has been added:

```
<configuration xmlns="http://schemas.microsoft.com/.NetConfiguration/v2.0">
  <system.web>
      <compilation debug="false">
       <assemblies>
         <add assembly="System.Messaging, Version=2.0.50727.0,
             Culture=neutral, PublicKeyToken=B03F5F7F11D50A3A"/>
      </assemblies></compilation>
```

Note that these references apply to an ASP.NET project as a whole, rather than to individual pages.

However, depending on the development environment and in some cases the project type, some assemblies are accessed automatically. For instance, if you're using the Visual Basic command-line compiler, you do not need to add references to *mscorlib.dll* or *System.dll*, the two assemblies that contain the types of the System namespaces as well as many of the basic types found in other namespaces, or to *Microsoft.VisualBasic.dll*, the assembly that contains all of the "intrinsic" functions of the Visual Basic language. Similarly, Visual Studio automatically adds the same three references to all but the Empty Project type (which includes references only to *Microsoft.VisualBasic.dll* and *mscorlib.dll*). In addition, for particular project types, Visual Studio adds the additional references shown in Table 3-1. Microsoft Visual Basic 2005 Express also adds the same references for the supported project types listed in Table 3-1. Microsoft Visual Web Developer 2005 Express also automatically adds the references shown in Table 3-1 for the ASP.NET Web Site project type.

Finally, ASP.NET automatically references assemblies stored in the application's *bin* directory; you do not have to explicitly add a reference to these assemblies to an ASP.NET project.

You can see which references are currently defined for a Visual Basic project in Visual Studio 2005 or Visual Basic 2005 Express Edition by either selecting the <ProjectName> Properties option from the Project menu or right-clicking the project name in the Solution Explorer and selecting the Properties option. The upper half of the References tab, which is shown in Figure 3-5, displays the references that have been added to the project.

For ASP.NET projects in Visual Studio 2005 or Visual Web Developer 2005 Express, select the Property Pages option from the View menu, or right-click the project name in the Solution Explorer and select the Property Pages option. The References tab displays the references that have been added to the current project by the developer. (References added automatically by Visual Studio are not shown.)

Namespaces and Qualified Type Names

Once you've made an assembly available to your project, you still have to tell the Visual Basic .NET compiler where in the assembly the type you want to access resides. .NET types are organized into namespaces, which are logical hierarchical groupings of types that allow each type to be uniquely identified by its namespace and type name. Namespace names and type names are separated from one another by a period. So, for instance

```
System.Collections.Hashtable
```

TABLE 3-1
References
Automatically
Added to Selected
Visual Studio .NET
Project Types

Project Type	Reference
ASP.NET Web Service	System.Web.dll System.Web.Services.dll System.Xml.dll
ASP.NET Web Site	System.Web.dll System.Xml.dll
Class Library	System.Data.dll System.Xml.dll
Console Application	System.Data.dll System.Deployment.dll System.Xml.dll
Excel Application	Accessibility.dll Microsoft.Office.Interop.Excel.dll Microsoft.Office.Tools.ActionsPane.dll Microsoft.Office.Tools.Excel.dll Microsoft.Vbe.Interop.dll Microsoft.VisualStudio.OfficeTools.Interop.Runtime.dll Office.dll stdole.dll System.Data.dll System.Drawing.dll System.Windows.Forms.dll System.Xml.dll
Pocket PC 2000 Application	System.Data.dll System.Drawing.dll System.Windows.Forms.dll System.Xml.dll
SQL Server Project	SqlAccess.dll System.Data.dll System.Xml.dll
Web Control Library	System.Data.dll System.Drawing.dll System.Management.dll System.Web.dll System.Xml.dll
Windows Application	System.Deployment.dll System.Drawing.dll System.Windows.Forms.dll
Windows CE Application	System.Data.dll System.Drawing.dll System.Windows.Forms.dll System.Xml.dll

	Project Type	Reference
TABLE 3-1 References Automatically Added to Selected Visual Studio .NET Project Types *(continued)*	Windows Control Library	System.Data System.Drawing.dll System.Windows.Forms.dll System.Xml.dll
	Windows Service	System.Data.dll System.ServiceProcess.dll System.Xml.dll

identifies the Hashtable class in the System.Collections namespace. The combination of a namespace and a type name identifies a type much as the combination of a directory path and a filename uniquely identifies a file system object.

You can, however, designate particular namespaces that the Visual Basic .NET compiler will search when it attempts to resolve type references. This saves you from having to provide a fully qualified type name each time that you refer to a type in code. This means that, rather than always having to refer to the System.Collections.Hashtable class, you can simply refer to the Hashtable class.

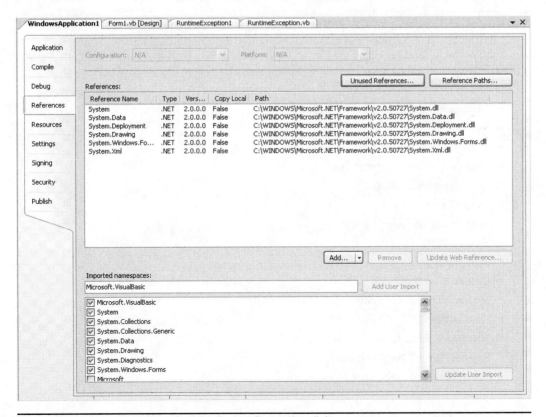

Figure 3-5 The References tab of the Project Properties dialog

When creating non-ASP.NET source code using a text editor or either Visual Studio or Visual Basic .NET 2005 Express, you can use the Imports directive to make a namespace visible without using its fully qualified name. Its syntax is:

```
Imports [aliasname = ] namespace
```

where *namespace* is the fully qualified namespace name, and *aliasname* is an optional alias by which that *namespace* will be referred in code. Typically, *aliasname* is used only if two or more namespaces have types of the same name, and you want to ensure that a type in a particular namespace is used without having to use its fully qualified name. The Imports statement must appear at the beginning of a source code file; it applies to all of the types defined in the file. For details, see the entry for the Imports statement in Chapter 8.

In ASP.NET, you use the @ Import page directive to refer to the types in a namespace without their fully qualified name. Its syntax is:

```
<%@ Import namespace=namespace_name %>
```

The directive must appear at the top of an ASP.NET page and applies to the page in which it appears.

A number of namespaces are imported automatically in the various Visual Basic development environments. The command-line compiler automatically imports the System namespace, as well as the Microsoft.VisualBasic namespace, in which all of the "intrinsic" Visual Basic functions are defined. In non-ASP.NET applications developed using Visual Studio and in Visual Basic .NET 2005 Express, the namespaces that are automatically imported appear in the lower half of the References tab of the Project Properties dialog, as shown earlier in Figure 3-5. In ASP.NET projects in either Visual Studio or Visual Web Developer 2005 Express, the following namespaces are automatically imported:

- Microsoft.VisualBasic
- System
- System.Collections
- System.Collections.Specialized
- System.Configuration
- System.Text
- System.Text.RegularExpressions
- System.Web
- System.Web.Caching
- System.Web.Security
- System.Web.SessionState
- System.Web.UI
- System.Web.UI.HtmlControls
- System.Web.UI.WebControls
- System.Web.UI.WebControls.WebParts

CHAPTER 4

Object-Oriented Programming

From the introduction of Version 4.0 of Visual Basic until the release of Version 6.0, a lively debate raged among developers about whether Visual Basic was or was not an object-oriented programming language. Proponents of the first position could point to Visual Basic's extensive support for objects and interfaces, while advocates of the opposite point of view could point to its lack of inheritance and its overall limited number of object-oriented features. With the release of .NET, however, this debate has become of historical interest only. Visual Basic .NET is clearly an object-oriented language.

Typically, treatments of object-oriented programming begin by discussing the four major characteristics of object-oriented languages: abstraction, encapsulation, inheritance, and polymorphism. This chapter, however, will begin by examining the specific implementation of object-oriented programming features in Visual Basic .NET and the .NET platform.

.NET Types

.NET recognizes six categories of types that can be defined in a namespace:

- *Classes*, which are reference types defined by the Class . . . End Class construct.

- *Arrays*, which are reference types that store objects of another type. The Array class is defined in the System namespace of the .NET Framework Class Library, and array objects can be instantiated in your code; see Chapter 3 for details.

- *Structures*, which are value types defined by the Structure . . . End Structure construct.

- *Interfaces*, which define a contract that implementers must conform to, are defined by the Interface . . . End Interface construct.

- *Delegates*, which are reference types that encapsulate methods with particular signatures. They are defined using the Delegate statement.

- *Enumerations*, which are a collection of related values, defined by the Enum . . . End Enum construct.

TABLE 4-1
The Inheritance
Chain of .NET
Types

Type	Chain of Inheritance
Arrays	System.Object
Classes	System.Object
Structures	System.Object System.ValueType
Delegates	System.Object System.Delegate or System.MulticastDelegate
Enumerations	System.Object System.ValueType System.Enum
Interfaces	none

.NET includes a Type object that can be used to retrieve information about a particular type. The Type object for a type can be retrieved in Visual Basic in either of two ways:

- By using the GetType operator and providing it with the name of the type in which you're interested as an argument. For example,

```
Dim typ As Type = GetType(Integer)
```

returns a Type object with information about the Visual Basic Integer data type.

- By calling the GetType method of an instance of the type. For example, the code:

```
Dim counter As Integer = 10
Dim typ As Type = counter.GetType()
```

returns a Type object with information about the type of the *contents* of the counter variable, which happens to be an Integer. If we had declared the variable to be of type Object, as in the following code, the GetType method would still return a Type object representing the Integer type, which is the variable's runtime type at the time the method is called:

```
Dim counter As Object
counter = 1
Console.WriteLine(counter.GetType().FullName)
```

Ultimately, all .NET types except for interfaces are derived from a single type, System.Object. (That's why Object happens to be .NET's "universal" data type, much as the Variant was in COM-based versions of Visual Basic.) Table 4-1 shows the inheritance chain for each of .NET's six categories of types.

.NET Type Members

Each of the six categories of .NET types can define one or more members. Members define the public interface of a type and either allow you to set or retrieve the data of a .NET type, or provide access to the functionality that a .NET type makes available. Type members include the following:

- *Fields*, which are public constants or variables that allow access to a type's data. Fields can be defined by classes, structures, and enumerations. (In fact, enumerations have only fields.) Since fields allow little opportunity for data validation and offer little protection from inappropriate changes to data values, they are used primarily for read-only data. Often, fields are implemented as constants, which are necessarily read-only, since their value is defined at compile time and cannot be modified in the runtime environment. In other cases, fields are implemented as read-only variables that are, in fact, write-once variables: their values can be defined at runtime by a class constructor but cannot subsequently be modified. For example, field declarations might take the following form:

```
Public Class TestClass
   Public Const Label As String = "Test Class"
   Public ReadOnly CounterStartValue As Integer

   ' Constructor to allow us to assign a value to a read-only variable
   Public Sub New(ctr As Integer)
      CounterStartValue = ctr
   End Sub
End Class
```

- *Properties*, which allow access to the type's data. In Visual Basic .NET, properties can be defined for classes, structures, and interfaces. Most commonly, properties are both readable and writable, although they can also be read-only or write-only (although the latter is rare). Properties are defined with the Property . . . End Property construct. A frequent pattern for assigning and returning property values is shown in the following code, in which the property is responsible for assigning a value to or retrieving a value from a private variable that is otherwise accessible only from within its class:

```
Private annualSalary As Decimal

Public Property Salary() As Decimal
   Get
      Return annualSalary
   End Get
   Set
      annualSalary = Value
   End Set
End Property
```

Some properties may require that you provide an index or key that identifies a particular member of an array or a collection. The Item property of the Visual Basic .NET Collection object, which allows you to retrieve a member of the collection by its key or its ordinal position in the collection, provides an excellent example:

```
Dim states As New Collection
states.Add("California", "CA")
states.Add("Michigan", "MI")
states.Add("New York", "NY")
Dim state As String = CStr(states.Item("CA"))
```

FIGURE 4-1
The .NET
implementation of
properties

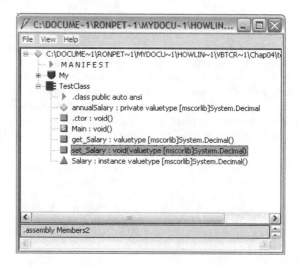

FIGURE 4-1
The .NET
implementation of
properties

Interestingly, properties are actually implemented internally as methods, as Figure 4-1 shows. The Salary property consists of a get accessor method (get_Salary) and a set accessor method (set_Salary), both of which are members of the TestClass class.

- *Methods*, which are the functions (defined by the Function . . . End Function construct) and subroutines (defined by the Sub . . . End Sub construct) that expose the functionality provided by a class, structure, interface, or delegate. Of the major net types, only enumerations cannot have methods. Delegates are a partial exception: although they have methods that they inherit from System.Delegate or System.MulticastDelegate, you cannot define new delegate methods. Functions and subroutines were discussed at length in Chapter 3.

- *Events*, which are function calls from a source to bound delegates that occur in response to some event (such as a mouse click, a press of the keyboard, or a change to the value of a field in a database). Typically, events are passed two parameters: an Object indicating the sender of the event; and an object of type EventArgs or a type derived from it that provides information about the event. Events are discussed in greater detail in Chapter 5.

We'll begin our examination of object-oriented programming with Visual Basic by examining inheritance, since it is the basis of the .NET type system.

Parameterized Properties and CLS Compliance

Parameterized properties are not CLS-compliant. Clients of your components who are using a .NET language that does not support parameterized properties, such as C#, have to use the get_*propertyName*(*index*) or set_*propertyName*(*index*) syntax in order to retrieve or assign a property value. If you want to write CLS-compliant code, you should avoid parameterized properties.

Inheritance

For the most part, the language features that we've covered so far do little to distinguish Visual Basic .NET as a more object-oriented language than its predecessors. There is, however, such a distinguishing feature: *inheritance* is not only the basis of the .NET type system, but the single individual feature that marks Visual Basic .NET as a clearly object-oriented programming language.

Inheritance means that a .NET type is based on, or inherits the members of, the type from which it is derived. If inheritance is not explicitly defined, .NET relies on implicit inheritance; particular types automatically inherit the base types shown earlier in Table 4-1. However, in the case of classes only, inheritance can also be explicit: you can designate a particular class from which a class you're defining derives. Explicit inheritance is indicated by using the Inherits keyword on the line following the class definition. For example:

```
Public Class MyForm
    Inherits System.Windows.Forms.Form
```

.NET supports single inheritance only. That is, a class can inherit directly from only a single other class. In order for a class to inherit from multiple classes, the inheritance must occur in a chain. That is, class D must inherit from class C, which inherits from class B, which inherits from class A.

However, not all classes support explicit inheritance. If a class is *sealed*—which in Visual Basic .NET means that it's marked with the NotInheritable keyword—other classes cannot be derived from it. In an application in which a series of classes are built through inheritance, it is common to mark the final set of inherited classes that the application actually instantiates as sealed, since the application will have no further need to derive classes from them. Often, core classes whose operation is central to an application (or to the system) might also be marked as sealed to prevent the creation of inherited classes with disabled or incorrect functionality.

Conversely, some classes cannot themselves be created (you cannot create an instance of this class using the New keyword) but instead are intended to be used only as a base class from which other classes inherit. Such classes are marked with the MustInherit keyword and are known as *abstract base classes*.

Inheritance automatically makes the attributes and the functionality of a base class available to its derived classes. For example, consider the following code:

```
Public Class EmptyClass
End Class

Public Module modMain
    Public Sub Main()
        Dim ec As New EmptyClass
        Console.WriteLine(ec.ToString())    ' Displays "EmptyClass"
    End Sub
End Module
```

Even though EmptyClass is a class with no members, the Main method is able to call a ToString method, which displays the name of the class. We are able to do this because our seemingly empty class automatically inherits the members of System.Object, the base class for all classes. (For the members of System.Object, see Appendix G.) This functionality of the base class is available for free; we don't have to do anything to get it.

Overriding Members

We don't, however, have to accept all of the data and the behaviors of the base class. In many cases, we can change none, some, or all of them, depending on the needs of the class we're creating. For instance, we might want our class' ToString method to do something other than display its name. In that case, we can override the base class' ToString method by providing a replacement method. This is called *overriding* the base class method, and requires that we use the Overrides keyword when we define our method. For example:

```
Public Class EmptyClass
    Public Overrides Function ToString() As String
        Return "This is an (almost) empty class."
    End Function
End Class

Public Module modMain
    Public Sub Main()
        Dim ec As New EmptyClass
        Console.WriteLine(ec.ToString() )    ' Displays "This is an (almost)
                                            '             empty class."
    End Sub
End Module
```

Very much as you can't inherit from all classes, though, you can't override all base class members. Properties and methods of a base class can be overridden by a derived class only under either of the following two conditions:

- The base class member is marked with the Overridable keyword, which allows you to override it.

- The base class member itself overrides a corresponding member of its base class and is not marked with the NotOverridable keyword.

So, members of base classes are not overridable by default, even if they are not explicitly marked with the NotOverridable keyword. And if a member of a base class can be overridden, that ability to override the member is inherited by derived classes until a particular subclass marks the member as NotOverridable. In other words, unless you have a compelling reason to prevent a class member from being overridden, you should remember to mark it as Overridable.

While there are times when you can't override a member of a class, there are other times when you're required to override a class member. Such members are marked with the MustOverride keyword. Typically, you must override a class member under any of the following conditions:

- The base class provides either no real implementation or a very partial implementation of the method. It relies on derived classes to provide complete implementations.

- The base class itself is an abstract base class—that is, it defines the members that a derived class should have, but it provides no real implementation of them, leaving it to the derived classes to do this.

Overloaded Members

A basic rule of Visual Basic 6.0 and earlier versions was that each member name in a class must be unique, since the Visual Basic compiler relied exclusively on the member name to identify the member. In .NET, that is no longer true. Instead, each member must be uniquely identified by its signature, which includes a combination of its name and the types in its parameter list. (In distinguishing members with the same name, a method's return value or a property type is not part of that member's signature; that is, members with the same name cannot be differentiated by return type alone.)

This makes it possible to *overload* members, which means that multiple members can share the same name but can be distinguished by differing parameter types. In the .NET Framework Class Library, for instance, the Convert.ToString method provides an excellent example of operator overloading; there are 36 different versions of the Convert.ToString method, each of which is distinguished from the other 35 versions by the number and type of its parameters.

Overloading is significant because it allows members to be named in terms of their functionality, rather than the need to find a unique name. And as we saw in Chapter 3, it allows parameter lists to reflect the specific types expected by a method, rather than a weakly typed parameter that can accept an argument of virtually any type.

At the same time, overloading methods in a careless way can lead to a duplication of code, as each of the overloaded methods contains code that performs a more or less identical set of operations. Typically, this problem is solved by performing only the minimum of work that is necessary (typically data conversion and defining default values) before calling the "main" version of the method, where most of the actual work is performed. For example: the Person class in the following code returns an array of Person objects whose name meets the search criteria. The method has three overloads: one that accepts a last name, one that accepts a first and last name, and one that accepts a first, middle, and last name. The first two methods provide a default value for the parameters they don't define and call the third overload.

```
Public Shared Function FindName(lastName As String) As Person()
   Dim middleName As String = String.Empty
   dim firstName As String = String.Empty
   Return FindName(firstName, middleName, lastName)
End Function

Public Shared Function FindName(firstName As String, lastName As String) _
                       As Person()
   Dim middleName As String = String.Empty
   Return FindName(firstName, middleName, lastName)
End Function

Public Shared Function FindName(firstname As String, middleName As String, _
                       lastName As String) As Person()
   ' Query database to return names
   Return matches
End Function
```

Constructors

.NET classes and structures have one or more constructors that can be executed when the class or structure is instantiated. This support for constructors differs in a number of ways from class modules in Visual Basic 6.0 and earlier versions, where a Class_Initialize event procedure appeared to function as a class constructor:

- Constructors are called when the object is instantiated and are executed before any other code belonging to the class. In contrast, the Class_Initialize event was actually fired after the object was created but before it was activated; any code located outside of individual class members that declared and initialized variables was executed first.

- In .NET, constructors can be overloaded; there can be multiple constructors that differ by their parameter list. In contrast, Class_Initialize did not support method arguments.

- .NET constructors can be executed automatically only when an object instance is instantiated, or they can be called from the first line of code in a derived class constructor (a topic that we'll discuss in detail later in this section). In contrast, the Class_Initialize procedure could be called from anywhere in code.

- Structures as well as classes in .NET can have constructors. In contrast, only classes supported the Class_Initialize procedure. (Structures in Visual Basic 6.0 could not have properties or methods.)

In Visual Basic .NET, constructors are subroutines named New, and they can be defined in both classes and structures. Like any method, constructors can have parameter lists and can be overloaded. The overloading of constructors, in fact, is an area of confusion in Visual Basic .NET. If you fail to define any constructors, the Visual Basic .NET compiler automatically implements a parameterless constructor in a class. For example, Figure 4-2 shows the result if we compile the following code and display the resulting assembly in ILDasm:

```
Public Class Animal
    Dim animalName As String

    Public Property Name() As String
        Get
            Return animalName
        End Get
        Set
            animalName = Value
        End Set
    End Property
End Class
```

Note that in addition to the private animalName string variable and the Name property (Name) along with its set (set_Name) and get (get_Name) accessors, ILDasm displays a class constructor (indicated as .ctor) that is a subroutine (it returns void, which means that the method has no return value) with no parameters.

However, if we explicitly define parameterized constructors for a class but fail to define a parameterless constructor, the Visual Basic .NET compiler does not add a parameterless constructor to our class. If we are defining class constructors, we have to remember to include a parameterless constructor if we want one.

In Visual Basic .NET, structures can also have constructors. However, all structure constructors must be parameterized. The Visual Basic .NET compiler does not automatically include a parameterless constructor among a structure's members if you fail to define a parameterized constructor. And the attempt to explicitly define a parameterless constructor generates a compiler error ("Structures cannot declare a non-shared 'Sub New' with no parameters.").

FIGURE 4-2
A compiled class
displayed by
ILDasm

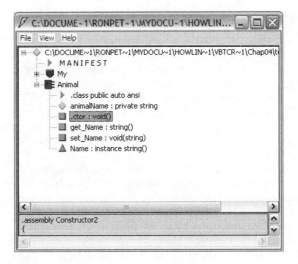

Constructors of derived classes aren't marked with the Overrides keyword. But the constructors of derived classes must call the base class constructor in the first line of the constructor's code, immediately after the constructor's subroutine definition, unless the base class implements a parameterless constructor. In the latter case, the call to the base class constructor can be omitted. To call the base class constructor, the MyBase keyword is used, as the following code illustrates:

```
Public Class BaseClass
    Private _name As String

    Public Sub New(name As String)
        _name = name
    End Sub

    Public ReadOnly Property Name() As String
        Get
            Return _name
        End Get
    End Property
End Class
Public Class DerivedClass
    Inherits BaseClass

    Public Sub New(name As String)
        MyBase.New(name)
    End Sub
End Class
```

Whether or not a call to one of the base class constructors is required it's typically a good idea to include the call, since, unless the documentation explicitly indicates otherwise, the base class constructor may perform some initialization that is important for the proper functioning of the class.

Destructors

Many object-oriented programming languages and runtime environments support both constructors, which execute when a class is instantiated, and destructors, which execute when a class instance is destroyed. .NET, in fact, defines not just one, but two different destructors that execute when an object either is about to be destroyed or is being destroyed.

The need for two destructors stems from the fact that in .NET, garbage collection—the process whereby .NET destroys unused managed objects and releases their resources—is non-deterministic. This means that, although garbage collection will happen sooner or later, there is no guarantee of precisely when a particular object that has gone out of scope or that is no longer needed will actually be destroyed.

When a class or structure instance is destroyed (something that the .NET runtime environment manages without your having to write any code), the object instance often has to perform some cleanup, such as closing files, saving state information, or releasing resources that are not managed by .NET. .NET's non-deterministic destructor for this purpose is named Finalize. Unlike the class constructor, which the compiler creates automatically if it is not explicitly declared, Finalize is not created automatically by the compiler. Since it involves a performance penalty, you should implement it only if there are resources belonging to an object instance that must be released as the object is destroyed. In addition, Finalize must be declared as a Protected method, with the following signature:

```
Protected Sub Finalize()
```

Because it is protected, the Finalize method can be called only from within the class that defines it or from a derived class. Typically, Finalize can also be overridden by a derived class by using the Overrides keyword. However, it cannot be called from client code that instantiates the class.

Because of the non-deterministic garbage collection system and because maintaining unneeded resources can often be expensive, .NET provides a second destructor that can be called at any time both from within a class, from a derived class, and from client code, and that immediately releases resources. This destructor is implemented as an interface (a topic discussed in greater detail in the section "Interfaces" later in this chapter) named IDisposable that has a single method, Dispose. The Dispose method has the following signature:

```
Sub Dispose()
```

However, unlike Finalize, Dispose is not called automatically by .NET. Instead, it should be called by clients of the implementing class or structure.

There are two recommended patterns for implementing Dispose, one for base classes and one for derived classes. The recommended pattern for base classes is:

```
Public Class Base : Implements IDisposable
   Public Overloads Sub Dispose() Implements IDisposable.Dispose
      Dispose(True)
      GC.SuppressFinalize(Me)
   End Sub

   Protected Overridable Overloads Sub Dispose(ByVal disposing As Boolean)
      If disposing Then
         ' Free other state (managed objects).
      End If
```

```
      ' Free your own state (unmanaged objects).
      ' Set large fields to null.
   End Sub
   Protected Overrides Sub Finalize()
      ' Simply call Dispose(False).
      Dispose(False)
   End Sub
End Class
```

Base classes should define two versions of Dispose, one of which implements IDisposable.Dispose and, because it is part of the class or structure's public interface (i.e., it is defined as a Public method), is callable from outside of the class or structure, including by clients of the class. This version of the Dispose method first calls the second version of the Dispose method and passes it a True value as an argument. The argument causes the block of code in the second Dispose method that frees other managed resources to execute. The public version of the Dispose method then calls the GC (garbage collector) object's SuppressFinalize method, which indicates that finalization should not be handled automatically by .NET.

The second version of Dispose is protected, and so can be called only from within the class or by a derived class; it is not accessible to clients that have references to instances of the class. This version of Dispose has a single Boolean parameter. A True indicates a client call, which causes the class to release both managed and unmanaged resources. A False value indicates that the call comes from the class or structure, or from a derived class, and that only unmanaged resources should be released.

Instead of directly calling Dispose from within the class or a derived class, though, Finalize should be called. Finalize in turn calls the protected version of Dispose, passing it a False value that indicates that the call comes from within the class, so that any other managed resources should not be released (since they already have been by the client's call to the public version of Dispose).

The following is the recommended implementation of Dispose and Finalize for derived classes:

```
   Protected Overridable Overloads Sub Dispose(ByVal disposing As Boolean)
         If disposing Then
            ' Free other state (managed objects).
         End If
         ' Free your own state (unmanaged objects).
         ' Set large fields to null.
      End Sub

      Protected Overrides Sub Finalize()
         ' Simply call Dispose(False).
         Dispose(False)
      End Sub
End Class
```

Note that this version implements only the protected version of Dispose, which leaves the base class as the only class with a public implementation of Dispose that implements the public IDisposable.Dispose interface.

Identically Named Variables with Different Scope

It's best to avoid giving variables with different scope identical names, since the practice is unnecessarily confusing. If you give your locals unique names, you won't have to disambiguate them later.

Internal References: Me and MyClass

In Visual Basic .NET, as in Visual Basic 6.0, the Me keyword refers to the instance of the class upon which the method or property that's currently executing was called. (The equivalent in C++ or C# is the **this** object.) Typically, Me is not required, but it can add clarity by calling out that a particular identifier refers to a class member. However, in some situations, using Me is required. This is the case, for example, if there is a local variable or method parameter of the same name as an instance member, as in the following code:

```
Public Class Airplane
    Private seat As New ArrayList

    Public Function AssignSeat(seat As String) As Boolean
        For Each seatAssignment As String In Me.seat
            If seatAssignment = seat Then
                Return False
            End If
        Next
        Me.seat.Add(seat)
        Return True
    End Function
End Class
```

Here, seat represents both an ArrayList variable that holds the locations of assigned seats, as well as the name of the AssignSeat method's single parameter. If we fail to qualify the references to the ArrayList variable named seat with the Me keyword, the .NET compiler will assume in the first case that we want to use the String argument and in the second will generate a compiler error, since the String class does not have an Add member.

Similarly, when a variable is hidden by another identically named variable with more immediate scope (or, to put it another way, when a variable with more restrictive scope *shadows* a variable with broader scope), Me allows you to reference the otherwise hidden variable. For example, consider the following code (which admittedly reflects rather poor programming practice):

```
Public Class Counters
    Dim ctr As Integer

    Public Sub New()
        For ctr = 1 to 20
            DoSomething()
        Next
    End Sub
```

```
    Public Sub DoSomething()
        For ctr As Integer = 0 to 2
            Console.WriteLine("The value of ctr is {0}, but the value of Me.ctr
is {1}.", _
                                ctr, Me.ctr)
        Next
    End Sub
End Class

Public Module modMain
    Public Sub Main()
        Dim obj As New Counters()
    End Sub
End Module
```

Here, a class named Counters has a variable named ctr that is visible throughout the class. A second variable named ctr, however, is local to the For Each . . . Next construct. Nevertheless, we are able to reference the first variable within the For Each . . . Next construct by using the Me keyword.

Finally, Me can be used as an argument in a method call when you need to pass a reference to the current class instance to some method or property outside of the class. This, in fact, is one of its major uses.

Because Me refers to the current instance of a class or structure, it can't be used to access class members within a shared property or method. (Shared members, which do not require that an instance of the class be created in order to execute, are discussed in the section "Shared Members" later in this chapter.)

Closely related to Me is the MyClass keyword. For the most part, MyClass is identical to Me. Its sole difference arises in cases in which the MyClass keyword is used in a base class to call one of its members, and a derived class overrides that member; in that case, the MyClass keyword causes the overridable method to be treated as if it is not overridable, and invokes the base class member. This is reflected in the following code:

```
Public Class BaseClass
    Public Sub MainMethod()
        Console.WriteLine("Calling Me.Method1...")
        Me.Method1()
        Console.WriteLine("Calling MyClass.Method1...")
        MyClass.Method1()
    End Sub
    Public Overridable Sub Method1()
        Console.WriteLine("BaseClass.Method1...")
    End Sub
End Class

Public Class DerivedClass : Inherits BaseClass
    Public Overrides Sub Method1()
        Console.WriteLine("DerivedClass.Method1...")
    End Sub
End Class
```

```
Public Module modMain
    Public Sub Main()
        Console.WriteLine("Invoking BaseClass.MainMethod")
        Dim bc As New BaseClass
        bc.MainMethod()
        Console.WriteLine()
        Console.WriteLine("Invoking DerivedClass.MainMethod")
        Dim dc As New DerivedClass
        dc.MainMethod()
    End Sub
End Module
```

When Method1 is called from an instance of the BaseClass class, there is, of course, only one method that can be called—Method1 in BaseClass. However, when an instance of DerivedClass calls Method1, the Me keyword causes DerivedClass.Method1 to be called, whereas the MyClass keyword causes BaseClass.Method1 to be called, just as if BaseClass.Method1 were marked NotOverridable, and DerivedClass had never been able to override the method.

Referencing the Base Class: MyBase

As we've already noted in the discussion of constructors, the MyBase keyword refers to the base class from which the current class is derived. As we've noted, all classes are derived from another class either implicitly or explicitly, while all structures implicitly derive from System.ValueType. MyBase causes a member of those base classes to be executed.

MyBase.New can be used to call the base class constructor, which is generally a good idea when the base class performs some initialization when it is instantiated. MyBase also can be used to call methods in the base class from a derived class when they are otherwise overridden or inaccessible.

Polymorphism

A general definition of polymorphism is that it describes something that has many different forms. In object-oriented programming, it refers to the ability of callers to call objects that behave differently depending on the type of the callee. It allows for the creation of black box routines that can operate on a range of types but always call the appropriate method of that type. Explanations of polymorphism often tend to be long, laborious, and thoroughly confusing. An example better illustrates the concept. Consider, for instance, the following code, which defines an abstract base class named Mammal, a derived class named Canine, and two derived classes that inherit from Canine named Dog and Wolf:

```
Public MustInherit Class Mammal
    Protected nocturnal As Boolean
    Protected herbivore As Boolean
    Protected carnivore As Boolean
    Protected omnivore As Boolean

    Public Property SleepsAtNight() As Boolean
        Get
            Return nocturnal
        End Get
        Set
            nocturnal = Value
        End Set
    End Property
```

```vbnet
    Public Property IsHerbivore() As Boolean
        Get
            Return herbivore
        End Get
        Set
            herbivore = Value
        End Set
    End Property

    Public Property IsCarnivore() As Boolean
        Get
            Return carnivore
        End Get
        Set
            carnivore = Value
        End Set
    End Property

    Public Property IsOmnivore() As Boolean
        Get
            Return omnivore
        End Get
        Set
            omnivore = Value
        End Set
    End Property

    Public Overridable Function Sound() As String
        Return "This mammal is largely mute."
    End Function
End Class

Public Class Canine : Inherits Mammal
    Public Sub New()
        MyBase.New()
        Me.Carnivore = True
    End Sub

    Public Overrides Function Sound() As String
        Return "Snarl"
    End Function
End Class

Public Class Wolf : Inherits Canine
    Public Overrides Function Sound() As String
        Return "Howl"
    End Function
End Class

Public Class Dog : Inherits Canine
    Public Overrides Function Sound() As String
        Return "Bark"
    End Function
End Class
```

```
Public Module modMammals
    Public Sub Main
        Dim wlf As New Wolf
        Dim dg As New Dog
        DescribeSound(wlf)
        Eats(wlf)

        DescribeSound(dg)
        Eats(dg)
    End Sub

    Private Sub DescribeSound(mamml As Mammal)
        Console.WriteLine("{0} makes a {1}.", mamml.ToString(), mamml.Sound())
    End Sub

    Public Sub Eats(mamml As Mammal)
        If mamml.IsCarnivore Then
            Console.WriteLine("{0} eats meat.", mamml.ToString())
        ElseIf mamml.IsHerbivore Then
            Console.WriteLine("{0} eats plants.", mamml.ToString())
        Else
            Console.WriteLine("{0} eats meat and plants.", mamml.ToString())
        End If
    End Sub
End Module
```

The base class, Mammal, consists of three protected variables, which means that they're accessible within the Mammal class and any classes derived from it. Had we declared the variables to be private, we would not have been able to access them (as we did in the Canine class constructor) from derived classes. Mammal also defines three properties that wrap the three protected variables. Finally, it has a single method, Sound, that simply returns a string indicating that the animal lacks a distinctive sound. Note that the method has been marked Overridable so that classes derived from Mammal can override the function to indicate the animal's sound.

Canine inherits from Mammal and adds a parameterless constructor that sets the value of the Carnivore property to True. (The other properties remain at their default value, which is False for Boolean properties.) It also overrides the Sound method to return the string "Snarl".

The Wolf class inherits from Canine. (It could have inherited from Mammal, but deriving it from Canine eliminates the need to explicitly define the Carnivore property as True, since canines are primarily carnivores, and wolves are canines.) The only code within the Wolf class overrides the Sound method to return the string "Howl".

The Dog class also inherits from Canine and, like the Wolf class, overrides the Sound method, in its case to return the string "Bark".

Finally, the code example includes a module that defines three methods: Main, DescribeSound, and Eats. Main instantiates one Dog object and one Wolf object. Notice that it declares the objects to be of type Mammal and then uses the New keyword to invoke the constructors of the Dog class and the Wolf class and assign a Dog class instance and a Wolf class instance, respectively, to our Mammal variables. We can do this because of polymorphism.

Once the two object variables are instantiated, the code calls the two other methods, once with each object type. DescribeSound accepts an argument of type Mammal (not an argument of type Dog or Wolf) and indicates whether the mammal is a herbivore, a carnivore, or an omnivore.

Sound also accepts an argument of type Mammal and displays a string that describes the sound made by the mammal. Note that in the case of both methods, the single parameter expects an argument of type Mammal, and not an argument of type Dog or Wolf or any other specific mammal.

When the code executes, it produces the following output:

```
Wolf makes a Howl.
Wolf eats meat.
Dog makes a Bark.
Dog eats meat.
```

In this example, the DescribeSound and the Eats methods are polymorphic. They don't care what specific type is passed to them as an argument, as long as that type either is Mammal or is derived from Mammal. Because of inheritance, we can write black box routines that (within limits) don't care about the types passed to them but are nevertheless able to call the correct method and produce the correct result anyway.

Casting Using DirectCast and TryCast

Ordinarily, if you want to convert a variable from one type to another, you use the CType function or one of the other conversion functions implemented by the compiler (like CStr, CInt, CDbl, etc.). However, Visual Basic has two other casting or conversion operators, DirectCast and TryCast, which are designed to handle conversions between types that are related to one another through inheritance or implementation (a topic discussed later, in the section "Interfaces"). Although DirectCast was introduced in .NET 1.0, TryCast is new to Visual Basic 2005. Both have the same syntax as CType:

```
ConvertedType = DirectCast(variable_name, type_name)
Convertedtype = TryCast(variable_name, type_name)
```

DirectCast will fail under either of two conditions:

- The object reference to be converted is not related to *type_name* through a relationship based on inheritance or interface implementation. In this case, Visual Basic generates a compiler error.

- The cast is a narrowing conversion that fails. In this case, the .NET runtime generates an InvalidCastException. .NET considers a narrowing conversion to be any conversion from a base class instance to a derived class, while it considers a widening conversion to be any conversion from a derived class to a base class or interface. For example, the conversion from an instance of the Wolf or Dog class to the Mammal class is a widening conversion. On the other hand, the conversion of an instance of the Mammal class to either the Wolf or Dog class is a narrowing conversion. For instance, the following code instantiates a Dog instance and then calls the DirectCast conversion function twice:

```
Dim dg As New Dog
' Cast Dog instance to Mammal
Dim objMammal As Mammal = DirectCast(dg, Mammal)
' Cast Mammal instance to Wolf
Dim objWolf As Wolf = DirectCast(objMammal, Wolf)
```

The conversion from Dog to Mammal always succeeds because it is a widening conversion: every Dog is a Mammal. The conversion from Mammal to Wolf fails (it throws an InvalidCastException) because the original variable before its conversion was of type Dog, and a Dog is not a Wolf. The attempt to convert a Dog to a Wolf in this case violates the IS A relationship.

When using DirectCast, you have two options for dealing with potential errors. The first is to use rigorous type checking before the conversion to prevent the exception. For instance, in our preceding code fragment, we might have checked the Mammal variable as follows before performing the conversion:

```
If TypeOf objD Is Wolf Then Dim objMD As Wolf = DirectCast(objD, Wolf)
```

The second is to use exception handling, as illustrated in the following code:

```
Dim objD As Mammal = DirectCast(dg, Mammal)
Try
   Dim objMD As Wolf = DirectCast(objD, Wolf)
Catch e As InvalidCastException
   Console.WriteLine("Can't cast from " & TypeName(objD) & " to " _
                     & TypeName(objMW) & " here.")
End Try
```

Handling exceptions, however, has a serious impact on a program's performance. To eliminate the need for handling an exception (and even to save yourself from having to examine object types before converting them), you can use the TryCast function instead of DirectCast. Like DirectCast, TryCast performs conversions between two types that are related through either inheritance or interface implementation. Unlike DirectCast, however, TryCast doesn't raise an exception if the conversion fails; it simply returns Nothing. As a result, if you use TryCast, you should always check its return value after attempting the conversion.

Shadowing

In the discussion of the Me keyword, we noted that a variable with more restrictive scope shadows an identically named variable with less restrictive scope, so that the former hides the latter while the former is in scope. Shadowing also applies to any program element declared in a type that is derived from a base type. It means that, when members of the derived type are accessed through a variable of the derived type, the derived type members shadow the base type members.

To use a simple example, the following code defines a class with a ToString member:

```
Public Class ShadowClass
   Private value As String

   Public Sub New(value As String)
      Me.value = value
   End Sub

   Public Shadows Function ToString() As String
      Return "Value of " & Me.GetType.Name & ": " & Me.value
   End Function
End Class
```

This version of ToString is declared with the Shadows keyword, which indicates that it shadows the ToString method found in System.Object, the class from which ShadowClass implicitly inherits. If we declare and then instantiate a variable of type ShadowClass, as in the following code:

```
Dim sc As ShadowClass = New ShadowClass("The Shadow")
Console.WriteLine(sc.ToString())
```

the program's output displays the class name along with the value of its private value variable:

```
Value of ShadowClass: The Shadow
```

However, if we declare the variable to be of type Object and instantiate it using the ShadowClass constructor, as the following code shows:

```
Dim obj As Object = New ShadowClass("The Shadow")
Console.WriteLine(obj.ToString())
```

the result is very different:

```
ShadowClass
```

Because in the first example we've called the ToString method through an instance of ShadowClass, the ShadowClass implementation of ToString shadows the implementation of ToString in the System.Object class. But when we call ToString in a variable declared to be of the base class type, the shadowed base class implementation becomes visible and is executed.

Shadowing is somewhat different that overriding. Any base class member can be shadowed, including those that are not overridable. Second, shadowing is based exclusively on name, and not on signature. Thus, a derived class property can shadow a base class method, for instance, or a derived class constant can shadow a base class property.

Interfaces

Visual Basic 6.0 and its earlier 32-bit versions implemented polymorphism through the use of interfaces, and they continue to be very important in Visual Basic .NET. An interface defines a contract that implementers of the contract must fulfill. Interfaces define a set of public members but have no implementation code; the implementation code is provided by the implementers of the interface. Interfaces are defined using the Interface . . . End Interface construct, as follows:

```
<access_modififer> Interface <interface_name>
End Interface
```

Member declarations within the interface cannot have access modifiers because all members are necessarily public. (The purpose of an interface is precisely to define a set of public members that types must define to properly implement that interface.) In addition, they contain no code, and even omit the terminating End statement. The interface can define methods, properties, and events as members, but it cannot define constructors or destructors.

For example, the following code defines an interface named IBreed (the names of interfaces traditionally begin with the letter "I"):

```
Public Interface IBreed
    Property BreedName As String
    Property Group As String
    Function IsBreedInAmericanKennelClub() As Boolean
End Interface
```

Interfaces are used for a variety of purposes:

- To define a particular service or functionality that is common to a range of classes. In .NET, this is probably the most common use of interfaces. For instance, two interfaces, IEnumerable and IEnumerator, allow you to use the For Each . . . Next loop to iterate various container objects like arrays and collections. The IComparer interface allows two objects to be compared and determines whether they are equal, or whether one is "less than" or "greater than" the other. If you were defining an Automobile class, you might implement the IComparer interface to consider the car that provided the better mileage per gallon of fuel as the "greater" one.

- To apply a particular service or functionality that is common to only a subset of the members of a class. For instance, although all dogs have a breed, IBreed is intended primarily to provide information about purebred dogs.

- To support multiple inheritance in environments (like .NET) that support only single inheritance, or in environments (like Visual Basic 6.0 and earlier versions) that don't support inheritance. This is not a good use of interfaces.

- As a substitute for classes. Again, this is not a good use of interfaces.

As this list suggests, when used properly, interfaces express a "can do" or a "has a" relationship with its implementers: types that implement an interface CAN DO something (such as compare objects using the IComparer interface) or HAVE something (such as a dog's breed, as recognized by the American Kennel Club in the United States and Canada). This differs from the IS A relationship that results when a derived class inherits from a base class. (For example, a Dog is a Mammal.)

Client classes that implement interfaces use the Implements statement on the line following the class definition, or on the line following the Inherits statement. Classes can implement multiple interfaces (hence the tendency to use "interface inheritance" as a work-around for single inheritance); in this case, interface names are separated from one another by commas. In addition, each member that implements an interface member includes the Implements keyword and the name of the interface and member it implements, separated by a dot or period, on the same line as the method definition. The signature of implemented members must conform to the signature defined in the interface.

For example, the following code provides a redefinition of the Dog class we presented earlier to implement the IBreed interface:

```
Public Class Dog : Inherits Canine
    Implements IBreed

    Private IsRecognizedAsBreed As Boolean
    Private Breed As String
    Private BreedGroup As String
```

```
    Public Sub New(breedName As String, breedGroup As String, _
                isRecognizedAsBreed As Boolean)
        MyBase.New()
        Me.Carnivore = True
        Me.Breed = breedName
        Me.BreedGroup = breedGroup
        Me.IsRecognizedAsBreed = isRecognizedAsBreed
    End Sub

    Public Overrides Function Sound() As String
        Return "Bark"
    End Function

    Public Property BreedName As String   Implements IBreed.BreedName
        Get
            Return Me.Breed
        End  Get
        Set
            Me.Breed = Value
        End Set
    End Property

    Public Property Group As String   Implements IBreed.Group
        Get
            Return Me.BreedGroup
        End Get
        Set
            Me.BreedGroup = Value
        End Set
    End Property

    Public Function IsAKC() As Boolean  _
                    Implements IBreed.IsBreedInAmericanKennelClub
        Return Me.IsRecognizedAsBreed
    End Function
End Class
```

Once we've implemented the interface members in our class, we can instantiate the class and access the implemented members just as we would any other member of the class, as the following code illustrates:

```
Public Sub Main
    Dim malamute As New Dog("Malamute", "Working", True)
    Console.WriteLine(malamute.Group)
    Console.WriteLine(malamute.IsAKC)
End Sub
```

We can, however, require that the interface members be accessed only through an instance of the interface itself. We do this by implementing the interface members as private members of the implementing class, as the following code illustrates:

```
Public Class Dog : Inherits Canine
    Implements IBreed
```

```
    Private IsRecognizedAsBreed As Boolean
    Private Breed As String
    Private BreedGroup As String

    Public Sub New(breedName As String, breedGroup As String, _
                isRecognizedAsBreed As Boolean)
        MyBase.New()
        Me.Carnivore = True
        Me.Breed = breedName
        Me.BreedGroup = breedGroup
        Me.IsRecognizedAsBreed = isRecognizedAsBreed
    End Sub

    Public Overrides Function Sound() As String
        Return "Bark"
    End Function

    Private Property BreedName As String   Implements IBreed.BreedName
        Get
            Return Me.Breed
        End  Get
        Set
            Me.Breed = Value
        End Set
    End Property

    Private Property Group As String   Implements IBreed.Group
        Get
            Return Me.BreedGroup
        End Get
        Set
            Me.BreedGroup = Value
        End Set
    End Property

    Private Function IsAKC() As Boolean  _
                    Implements IBreed.IsBreedInAmericanKennelClub
        Return Me.IsRecognizedAsBreed
    End Function
End Class
```

Because the BreedName and Group properties and the IsAKC method are now private, we can no longer access them through an instance of the Dog class. Instead, we must instantiate an object of the interface type, assign the instance of the Dog class to it, and then access the implemented members. The following code illustrates this:

```
Public Sub Main
    Dim malamute As New Dog("Malamute", "Working", True)
    Dim breed As IBreed = malamute

    Console.WriteLine(breed.Group)
    Console.WriteLine(breed.IsBreedInAmericanKennelClub)
End Sub
```

Note that, because we are accessing the IBreed interface, rather than accessing the IBreed interface members through the Dog class, we cannot access the method that implements IsBreedInAmericanKennelClub by the name we've assigned to it, IsAKC. Instead, we must access it by the name assigned to it in the interface definition, IsBreedInAmericanKennelClub.

Shared Members

In discussing the object-oriented features of classes, we've focused on defining and instantiating classes, and using the object reference to access the class members. In .NET, these are termed *instance members*; in order to access them in code, they require that an instance of the class or structure be created, and each instance of the class has its own set of members with their own values. However, some class members can be accessed or invoked without instantiating an instance of the class. These are *shared members* (in C++ and C#, they're known as static members), and they maintain a single set of values for an application as a whole. In Visual Basic .NET, they're defined using the Shared keyword. Fields, properties, and methods can all be declared as shared.

The System.Math class provides an excellent example of shared members. You can calculate the circumference of a circle, for example, with code like the following:

```
Dim radius As Single = 2
Dim circum As Single = Math.Pi * radius ^ 2
```

Here, we've accessed the shared Pi field of the Math class to compute the circumference. We could also find the absolute value of a number by using the shared Abs method of the Math class:

```
Dim num As Integer = -12
Dim absNum As Integer = Math.Abs(num)
```

In comparison to C#, Visual Basic .NET is somewhat unusual in that you can access shared members either through an instance variable or by specifying the name of the type. For example:

```
Dim mth As System.Math
Dim circum As Single = mth.Pi * radius ^ 2
Dim absNum As Integer = mth.Abs(num)
```

The major restriction when defining shared members is that they can't access instance member of their class. Doing so produces the compiler error, "Cannot refer to an instance member of a class from within a shared method or shared member initializer without an explicit instance of the class." If you want to call an instance method or retrieve the value of an instance property of the class that has the shared member, you have to instantiate an instance of that class. This is a common problem in console applications or executables that have an explicitly defined Sub Main. For example:

```
Public Class SharedClass
    Public Shared Sub Main()
        ' DoSomething()    '-- produces compiler error

        Dim sc As New SharedClass
        sc.DoSomething()
        End Sub
```

```
    Public Sub DoSomething
        ' Code in an instance method
    End Sub
End Class
```

In addition to using the Shared keyword to define members whose values are shared on an application-wide basis, it is also possible to define members whose values are shared on a per-thread basis. This is done using the System.ThreadStaticAttribute class. (An attribute is a class that serves as a label in code to modify the behavior of the compiler at compile time, Visual Studio or some other environment at design time, or the .NET runtime at runtime.) For example, in the following code, the application's main thread and a secondary thread make repeated calls to the IncrementCounter subroutine, which increments a shared per-thread counter:

```
Imports System.Threading

Public Class SharedByThread

    <ThreadStatic> Private Shared Count As Integer

    Public Shared Sub Main()
        Dim secondThread As New thread(AddressOf Thread2Proc)
        secondThread.Start()
        count = 100
For ctr As Integer = 0 to 10
    Console.WriteLine("The value of count in the main thread is {0}.", _
                    count)
    IncrementCounter(200)
Next
    End Sub

    Public Shared Sub Thread2Proc()
        count = 0
For ctr As Integer = 0 to 10
    Console.WriteLine("The value of count in the second thread is " & _
                    "{0}.", count)
    IncrementCounter(250)
Next
    End Sub

    Public Shared Sub IncrementCounter(delay As Integer)
        count +=1
        Thread.Sleep(delay)
    End Sub
End Class
```

When run, the code produces the following output, which shows that the counter has been incremented separately for each thread:

```
The value of count in the main thread is 100.
The value of count in the second thread is 0.
The value of count in the main thread is 101.
The value of count in the second thread is 1.
```

```
The value of count in the main thread is 102.
The value of count in the second thread is 2.
The value of count in the main thread is 103.
The value of count in the second thread is 3.
The value of count in the main thread is 104.
The value of count in the main thread is 105.
The value of count in the second thread is 4.
The value of count in the main thread is 106.
The value of count in the second thread is 5.
The value of count in the main thread is 107.
The value of count in the second thread is 6.
The value of count in the main thread is 108.
The value of count in the second thread is 7.
The value of count in the main thread is 109.
The value of count in the second thread is 8.
The value of count in the main thread is 110.
The value of count in the second thread is 9.
The value of count in the second thread is 10.
```

Event-Driven Programming

An *event* is a function call from a source to zero, one, or more sinks that have registered themselves with the source. The source can be Windows, the .NET runtime, or any application or component, and the event provides the source with a means of notifying its sinks that something has occurred. What that something is may vary—a movement of the mouse, a change to a record in a dataset, a decline in a stock price below a certain level, the completion of an external process, or the termination of a worker thread. The assumption is that the event may be significant and that clients of the component tracking the event may wish to know about it.

Handling events introduces an element of unpredictability in code execution. At any given time, we cannot be sure what code is being executed. This differs markedly from classical procedural programming, in which the path of code execution (except for branches resulting from the evaluation of conditional statements) was always known in advance. For users, this has made computer applications more intuitive and more accessible. For developers, it's added a level of complexity at the same time as it's encouraged the development of more responsive, higher-quality software.

Given the significance of events and handling events for all event-driven programming, this overview would not be complete without a chapter that discusses handling events as well as defining events that can be raised in your own code.

Handling Events

If we create a very simple WinForms application using Visual Studio, include a button, and define some code to execute when the button is clicked, it appears that Visual Basic and .NET automatically know to execute our event handler. If we look behind the scenes, though, there's nothing automatic about it; the Visual Studio forms designer provides a single line of code that makes it all work.

```
Friend WithEvents btnOK As System.Windows.Forms.Button
```

Our event handler's procedure declaration provides the rest:

```
Private Sub btnOK_Click(ByVal sender As System.Object, _
                        ByVal e As System.EventArgs) Handles btnOK.Click
```

The point here is that there's really nothing magical, automatic, or mysterious about event handlers; you have to decide whether or not you want to handle particular events, and provide the code to do it. Broadly, Visual Basic provides two methods for doing this. You can define your event handlers at design time, or you can define them dynamically at runtime. We'll begin by looking at these two methods.

Defining Event Handlers at Design Time

Assuming that a source exposes its events, there are two requirements for handling them:

- An object must indicate that it wants to subscribe to event notifications.
- An object must provide event handlers for those events in which it is interested.

In this section, we'll examine how this is done for event handlers that are static. That is, they are written and defined as event handlers at design time. And the binding between an event source and an event sink as defined by the WithEvents and Handles keywords remains in effect from the time the sink is instantiated until either the source object is no longer in the member variable to which the sink is sinked or until the sink itself is destroyed.

Subscribing to Event Notifications

In order to receive event notifications, an application or component has to indicate to the source that it wants them in the first place. In Visual Basic, this is done by using the WithEvents keyword in a variable declaration. WithEvents means that the Me object of every instance of the class is a listener of the events sourced by the instance of the object stored in the member variable defined using the WithEvents keyword. In other words, if the statement

```
Friend WithEvents btnOK As System.Windows.Forms.Button
```

is found in a Windows form, it indicates that the Form object is a listener for any events sourced by the Button object. The object variable defined WithEvents is the event source; the object variable's container (the type in which it is defined) is the event sink.

The following rules apply to the use of the WithEvents keyword:

- The variable declaration must declare the object variable as a specific type. A variable of type Object cannot serve as an event source. The container of the source variable must know what kinds of events it will sink to at runtime, and therefore the type of the event source must be known at compile time. This means that the following declaration is illegal:

  ```
  Private WithEvents btnOK As Object        ' Illegal
  ```

  In addition, the sink needs to be able to sink events on a single unique named object source. Because of this, the object representing the event source must be a single object; it cannot be an array of objects. For this reason, the following is also illegal:

  ```
  Private WithEvents btnOK() As Button        ' Illegal
  ```

- Structures do not support static event handling. As a result, the WithEvents keyword cannot be used when declaring an instance of a structure.

- The variable declaration must be at the module or class level; that is, it cannot be local to a procedure, function, or property.

- You can both declare and instantiate a variable that will serve as the reference to the event source in the same line of code. The following, for example, is legal:

  ```
  Dim WithEvents btn As Button = New Button()
  ```

> **Derived Classes and Events**
>
> Derived classes don't have to do anything to subscribe to the events raised by their base classes. They simply have to provide event handlers for them, a topic discussed in the following section "Defining an Event Handler."

The following two lines of code, for example, each define a variable named btnOK, an instance of a command button that can receive event notifications:

```
Protected WithEvents btnOK As Button
Protected WithEvents btnOK As New Button
```

Defining an Event Handler

In Visual Basic 6.0 and earlier versions, event handlers appeared to execute automatically, as long as they were properly named. An event handler's name had to take the form *variableName_eventName*.

Visual Basic .NET, on the other hand, defines event handlers using the Handles clause, which must appear on the same line of code as the subroutine definition. The Handles clause is followed by the events that it handles, with the variable name separated from the event name by a period. For example, the code

```
Private Sub OKButtonClicked(ByVal sender As System.Object, _
ByVal e As System.EventArgs) Handles Button1.Click
```

defines an event handler for the Button1.Click event, while the code

```
Private Sub Form1_Load(ByVal sender As System.Object, _
ByVal e As System.EventArgs) Handles MyBase.Load
```

defines an event handler for the Form.Load event. In this case, since Form1_Load is an event handler for an event raised by Form1's base class, the Handles clause indicates that the procedure handles MyBase.Load, the Load event of the Form1's base class.

The use of the Handles clause has two distinct advantages:

- It allows the event handler to be named something other than *objectName_eventName*.

- It allows a single event handler to be associated with multiple events. The Handles clause can be followed by multiple event names, each of which must be separated with a comma. This differs markedly from Visual Basic 6.0 and earlier versions, in which a control array was the only method for defining an event handler that could handle the events of multiple objects. A control array was capable of handling the events of only a single control type.

An event handler for multiple objects can determine which object raised the event by examining the arguments passed to the handler by the .NET runtime. Although an event handler can have any signature, the recommended one (and the one used throughout the .NET Framework Class Library) takes the form:

```
procedureName(sender As Object, e As EventArgs)
```

Here, *sender* is the object that raised the event, while *e* is an object of type EventArgs or of a type derived from it. By examining the *sender* argument, the event handler can determine which object raised the event. For example, the following code shows a single event handler for three command buttons, btnOK, btnCancel, and btnQuit, that makes use of the *sender* parameter to determine which button was clicked to fire the event:

```
Private Sub ButtonClicked(ByVal sender As System.Object, _
ByVal e As System.EventArgs) _
Handles btnOK.Click, btnCancel.Click, btnQuit.Click
    If TypeOf sender Is Button Then
        Dim btn As Button = DirectCast(sender, Button)
        If btn.Name = "btnOK" Then
            ' do whatever selecting OK indicates
        ElseIf btn.Name = "btnCancel" Then
            ' perhaps perform cleanup
            Exit Sub
        Else                  ' The Quit button
            Me.Close()
        End If
    Else
        Throw New ArgumentException( _
        "The event was raised by an invalid object.")
    End If
End Sub
```

The instance of EventArgs or one of its derived classes can be used to provide the event handler with information about the event. The EventArgs class itself provides no useful information and, in addition to its parameterless constructor, adds only a shared field, Empty, that is to be passed as an argument (rather than instantiating an EventArgs object using the New keyword) when raising events. However, its derived classes do provide useful information about events. For example, an argument of type MouseEventArgs is passed to many mouse form and control events (MouseClick, MouseDoubleClick, MouseDown, MouseMove, MouseUp, and MouseWheel). MouseEventArgs, which is derived from EventArgs, adds the following properties, which provide information about the mouse event:

- **Button** A member of the MouseButtons enumeration that indicates which mouse button was pressed when the event was raised
- **Clicks** The number of times the mouse button was clicked when the event was raised
- **Delta** A signed count of the number of mouse wheel rotations that occurred when the event was raised
- **Location** A Point structure (with two Integer values, X and Y) indicating the position of the mouse cursor when the event was raised

Handling Events Dynamically

In addition to defining event handlers at design time, it is also possible to define event handlers dynamically at runtime. This is an excellent alternative for applications or components in which the code that should handle an event is based on conditions that can be determined only at runtime.

Event handlers are added at runtime in Visual Basic .NET using the AddHandler statement. Its syntax is:

```
AddHandler event, AddressOf eventHandler
```

Delegates

Delegates are a new type category introduced in .NET that represent a method reference and that derive from either of two abstract base classes. The first class is System.Delegate; its subclasses represent single invocation delegates (that is, the delegate is able to hold a reference to a single method). The second is System.MulticastDelegate; its subclasses represent combinable delegates (that is, the delegate is able to invoke multiple methods). Delegates can refer to both static and instance methods, and they know the signature of the method to which they refer.

Although the Visual Basic compiler creates delegates for its event handlers behind the scenes, Visual Basic shields developers from the details of using delegates directly. However, a delegate is useful in any case in which it is useful to separate the method invocation from the particular method to be invoked—that is, whenever you want the flexibility to use the same object (represented by a delegate) to be able to invoke a method that is selected on the basis of conditions at runtime.

For additional details about delegates, see the entry for the Delegate statement in Chapter 8.

where *event* is the event to handle in the form *objectName.eventName*, and *eventHandler* is the procedure that handles the event. *eventHandler* has to have the appropriate signature to handle the event, or a compiler error results.

An event handler assigned with the AddHander statement can be deactivated with the RemoveHandler statement. Its syntax is identical to that of AddHandler:

```
RemoveHandler event, AddressOf eventHandler
```

For example, an application might want to write data input by the user into a central database if the user is connected to the network, but into a temporary file if the user is not. The following code checks whether the user is connected to a network and defines an event handler for a command button's Click event accordingly:

```
Private Sub Form1_Load(ByVal sender As System.Object, _
ByVal e As System.EventArgs) Handles MyBase.Load
    If My.Computer.Network.IsAvailable Then
        AddHandler btnOK.Click, AddressOf SaveToDB
    Else
        AddHandler btnOK.Click, AddressOf SaveLocally
    End If
End Sub
```

Defining Events

In addition to handling events raised by objects that your code consumes, you can also define and raise events that can be handled by clients of your classes. A custom event that you define can be anything that either a derived class or a consumer of your class needs to know about and needs to write code to respond to. Defining a custom event requires that you declare the event and, at the appropriate point in your code, raise the event.

Declaring an Event

You declare an event in Visual Basic .NET by using the Event statement inside a class module (a class definition that uses the Class . . . End Class construct). The most common form of the Event statement has the syntax:

```
[<attributes>] [accessModifier] [shadows] Event eventName(argList) _
          [Implements implementsList]
```

where *attributes* is a list of attributes, if any, that are to be applied to the event, *accessModifier* is one of the keywords (Public, Private, Protected, Friend, and Protected Friend) that determines the accessibility of the event, *shadows* is the Shadows keyword, which indicates that the event hides a base class event with the same name, *eventName* is the name of the event (and must follow standard Visual Basic .NET naming conventions), *argList* is the event's argument list, and, if the event is a member of a class implementing one or more interfaces, *implementsList* lists the events defined in those interfaces that *eventName* implements. Each of these elements is optional except for *eventName* and *argList*. (For full details on the syntax of the Event statement, see the entry for Event Statement in Chapter 8.)

If *accessModifier* is omitted, the event is public by default. *argumentList* can take any form that you want, except that optional parameters (indicated using the Optional keyword) and parameter arrays (indicated using the ParamArray keyword or the <ParamArray> attribute) are not permitted. However, in declaring an event, it is strongly recommended that you adopt the general signature used by .NET events, which is:

```
sender As Object, e As EventArgs
```

The EventArgs class is the base class for all event arguments. You should either use EventArgs in raising events, use a derived class in the .NET framework that is suitable for the event you want to raise, or define your own class derived from EventArgs that provides consumers of your events the information they need to handle the event effectively.

A second syntax for defining an event takes the form:

```
[<attributes>] [accessModifier] [shadows] Event eventName As delegateName _
          [Implements implementsList]
```

which defines an event and gives it the same signature as the delegate *delegateName*. The .NET Framework Class Library includes numerous delegates that can be used to define events. For example, the System.EventHandler delegate represents an event that provides no event data. The System.Data.DataRowChangeEventHandler delegate can be used to represent the RowChanging, RowChanged, RowDeleting, and RowDeleted events of a DataTable object. The System.Windows.Forms.MouseEventHandler delegate can be used to represent the MouseDown, MouseUp, or MouseMove events in a Windows form application.

Raising an Event

Once you declare an event, you can raise the event by using the RaiseEvent statement. Its syntax is:

```
RaiseEvent eventName(argumentList)
```

where *eventName* is the name of the event as it is assigned in the Event statement, and *argumentList* is the argument list defined in the Event statement. If *argumentList* doesn't correspond to the argument list defined in the Event statement, an error results.

Defining an Event: An Example

The following code defines an event, named AccountBalanceWarningEvent, whenever an account balance falls below a level set when the Account object is created. A custom event argument class, AccountBalanceWarningEventArgs, is used to provide information about the warning level and the current balance when the event is fired. A delegate, AccountBalanceWarningEventHandler, is used to define the event's signature.

```
Public Class AccountBalanceWarningEventArgs : Inherits EventArgs
    Private level As Decimal
    Private current As Decimal

    Public Sub New(warningLevel As Decimal, currentBalance As Decimal)
        Me.level = warningLevel
        Me.current = currentBalance
    End Sub

    Public ReadOnly Property WarningLevel As Decimal
        Get
            Return level
        End Get
    End Property

    Public ReadOnly Property Balance As Decimal
        Get
            Return current
        End Get
    End Property
End Class

Public Delegate Sub AccountBalanceWarningEventHandler(sender As Object, _
                e As AccountBalanceWarningEventArgs)

Public Class Account
    Private warningLevel As Decimal
    Private balance As Decimal

    Public Event AccountBalanceWarningEvent _
                As AccountBalanceWarningEventHandler

    Public Sub New(warningLevel As Decimal)
        Me.warningLevel = warningLevel
    End Sub

    Public Function Deposit(amount As Decimal) As Decimal
        balance += amount
        If balance < warningLevel Then
            RaiseEvent AccountBalanceWarningEvent(Me, New _
                    AccountBalanceWarningEventArgs( _
                    warningLevel, balance))
        End If
        Return balance
    End Function
```

```
    Public Function Debit(amount As Decimal) As Decimal
        balance -= amount
        If balance < warningLevel Then
            RaiseEvent AccountBalanceWarningEvent(Me, New _
                    AccountBalanceWarningEventArgs( _
                    warningLevel, balance))
        End If
        Return balance
    End Function
End Class
```

Handling an Event with a Delegate: An Example

Rather than using the Handles keyword to define an event handler, we can use a delegate. This makes it possible to use the WithEvents keyword to handle events statically but still define multiple possible event handlers and determine the precise one to execute at runtime. The following code instantiates a delegate of type AccountBalanceWarningEventHandler, which is defined in the preceding code example:

```
Public Class TestAcct
    Dim WithEvents acct As Account

    Dim warning As AccountBalanceWarningEventHandler = _
            AddressOf acct_AccountBalanceWarning

    Public Shared Sub Main()
        Dim ta As New TestAcct()
        ta.UseAccount()
    End Sub

    Private Sub UseAccount()
        Dim bal As Decimal
        acct = New Account(200.00d)
        bal = acct.Deposit(500.00d)
        Console.WriteLine("Deposited {0} to bring my balance to {1}.", _
                    bal, 500.00d)
        bal = acct.Debit(400.00d)
        Console.WriteLine("Wrote a check for {0} to
        bring my balance to {1}.", _
                    bal, 400.00d)
        bal = acct.Debit(50.00d)
        Console.WriteLine("Wrote a check for {0} to
        bring my balance to {1}.", _
                    bal, 50.00d)
    End Sub

    Friend Sub acct_AccountBalanceWarning(sender As Object, _
            e As AccountBalanceWarningEventArgs)
        Console.WriteLine("Warning: The balance of {0} " & _
                    "has fallen below {1}.", _
                    e.balance, e.WarningLevel)
    End Sub
End Class
```

Exception Handling

Regardless of our best efforts, errors will always exist in program code. Visual Studio provides a rich development environment that makes it easy to detect and correct both compile-time and runtime errors. However, since they are not implemented as Visual Basic .NET language features, we will not survey them here.

Instead, we will examine the language elements present in Visual Basic .NET that support error detection and exception handling. Then we will examine Visual Basic .NET's facilities for handling and generating exceptions.

Controlling the Character of Visual Basic

From its earliest version, Visual Basic has emphasized ease of use and has aimed at handling many of the details of programming that other languages, like C and C++, leave to developers. Although historically this had made Visual Basic an easy-to-learn language that has allowed even inexperienced programmers to become productive quickly, it also tends to make it easy for programmers to introduce a variety of design errors and runtime errors in their code. Visual Basic provides two statements—Option Explicit and Option Strict—that allow you to control how much work the compiler does on your behalf and that you can set to make particular kinds of errors less likely.

The Option Explicit Statement

Visual Basic can be a dynamically typed language in which variables have a compile-time type of Object but whose runtime types can vary. But the Visual Basic compiler can go one step further: it can automatically declare a variable when its name is first encountered in code, as if the developer had included a variable declaration statement. For example, in the code

```
Option Explicit Off

Module Explicit
   Public Sub Main()
      For ctr As Integer = 0 to 100
         ' Do something
         result = cntr
      Next
```

```
        Console.WriteLine("The counter reached " & result & ".")
    End Sub
End Module
```

the variable *cntr* is the result of a typographical error (it should appear as *ctr*). The result is that the highest value reached by the loop counter is inaccurately reported as 0 when the Console.WriteLine method call executes.

Errors of this kind—which can be difficult to detect, especially since our eyes are often trained to see what we want to see—can be mitigated by setting Option Explicit on. (That is, incidentally, its default setting.)

Option Explicit requires that variables be declared before they are used. It does not, however, require that variable declarations explicitly assign variables a type; all variables not explicitly assigned a type are automatically declared to be of type Object.

To set Option Explicit on for all projects in the Visual Studio interface, select Tools | Options. In the Options dialog, expand the Projects and Solutions node, select the VB Defaults tab, and select On in the Option Explicit drop-down list box, as shown in Figure 6-1. If you're entering the statement manually in code, it must appear at the top of a code module, before any statements other than Option Strict and Option Compare.

On the other hand, with Option Explicit set on, Visual Studio readily identifies a number of errors (see Figure 6-2) and fails to successfully compile our code. As Figure 6-2 shows, Visual Basic identifies two undeclared variables, *cntr* and *result*.

By default, Option Explicit is on in all Visual Basic projects, whether they are developed in Visual Studio or using the command-line compiler. This means that although you should be aware of the setting, you do not have to change it. And although you can set Option Explicit on or off on a per-module basis, there is not really any need to ever do so.

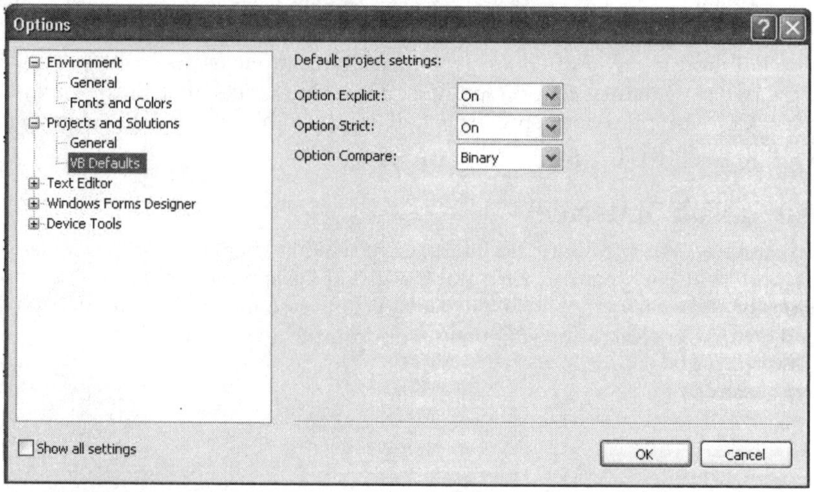

FIGURE 6-1   The VB Defaults tab of the Options dialog

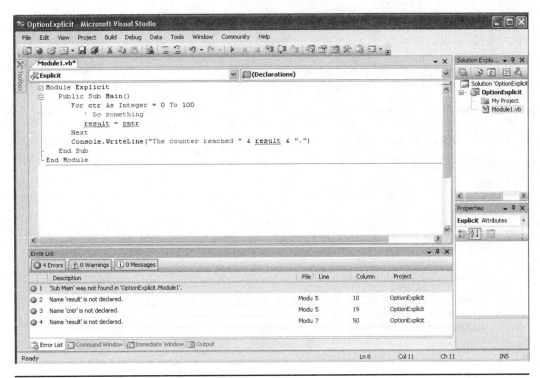

FIGURE 6-2   Compiler errors with Option Strict set on

Where Is the Option Explicit Statement?

In Visual Basic 6.0, checking a Require Variable Declaration box in the Editor tab of the Options dialog caused the Option Explicit On statement to be inserted at the beginning of every code module added to a Visual Basic project after the setting was turned on. This meant that, if the Require Variable Declaration box was turned on after some of a project's code modules had already been created, those modules would be compiled with Option Explicit set off.

In projects developed using Visual Studio 2005, you won't find any Option Explicit statements. If you attempt to enter one in a code window, it will seemingly disappear. Instead, in Visual Basic projects developed using Visual Studio, the Option Explicit setting is controlled by the VB project (.vbproj) file, an XML file that contains many of a project's settings. Since Option Explicit is on by default, an <OptionExplicit> tag appears in the file only if Option Explicit is set to off for the project. This also means that the entire project is always compiled with a single Option Explicit setting.

The Option Strict Statement

Visual Basic is capable of being a dynamically typed language, in which data is stored in variables of type Object and automatically converted from one specific data type to another at runtime as needed. Using Visual Basic as a dynamically typed language, however, makes two types of runtime error more likely:

- **Invalid type conversions** The variable may contain a value that cannot be converted from its current runtime type to the data type required by a particular method.

- **Loss of data** Narrowing conversions (such as a conversion from a Long to an Integer or a Byte to an SByte) can result in a loss of data.

A language feature that partially helps prevent these runtime errors is the Option Strict statement. By default, Option Strict is set off. However, by setting it on, the Visual Basic compiler enforces the following rules:

- The types of all variables must be declared in advance. With Option Strict set on, Visual Basic becomes more like a statically typed language in which the precise type of a variable is known at compile time and never changes at runtime. (Dynamic typing is still permitted, though, since it is still possible to declare a variable of type Object.)

- Visual Basic will not perform implicit narrowing conversions. All narrowing conversions must be explicitly handled by a call to a conversion method. (For the conversion methods available in Visual Basic .NET and in the .NET Framework, see Appendix F.) Visual Basic can continue to handle widening conversions automatically, however.

- Late binding is not allowed. The use of variables of type Object will in most instances result in a compiler error.

Although by default Option Strict is off, setting it on forces you, rather than Visual Basic, to control the behavior of your code, and is therefore highly recommended. To set it on for all projects in the Visual Studio interface, select Tools | Options. In the Options dialog, expand the Projects and Solutions node, select the VB Defaults tab, and select On in the Option Strict drop-down list box, as shown earlier in Figure 6-1.

You can also set Option Strict on in Visual Studio on a project-by-project basis. To do this, select the project in the Solution Explorer, right-click and select Properties from the pop-up menu, and select the Compile tab, which is shown in Figure 6-3. The Option Strict drop-down list box controls the Option Strict setting for the project.

If you're using an editor other than that provided by the Visual Studio IDE for entering code, the Option Strict statement must appear at the start of a code module, before any statements other than Option Explicit and Option Compare.

Where Is the Option Strict Statement?

If you've set Option Strict on but don't see the statement in your code, that's because the project-wide setting is stored in the VB project (.vbproj) file, an XML file that contains many of a project's settings. Since Option Strict is off by default, an <OptionStrict> tag appears in the file only if Option Strict is set on for the project as a whole.

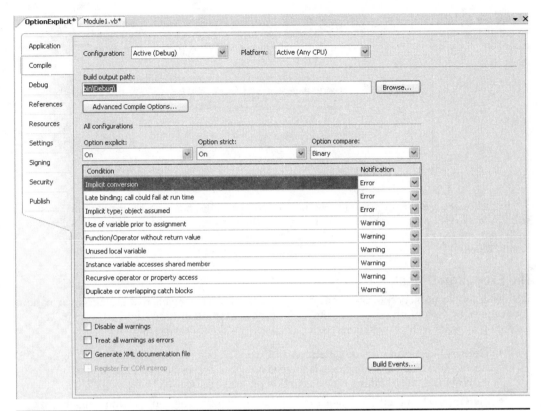

FIGURE 6-3   A project's Option Strict box

Structured Exception Handling

Despite extensive debugging and testing, runtime errors will inevitably occur in our code. In fact, some exceptions will occur at runtime regardless of debugging and testing. Network connections fail and required resources become inaccessible, required files are inadvertently deleted, and users sometimes do not have adequate permission for the files an application needs to access.

When exceptions do occur, the CLR by default will handle them rather inelegantly. For example, Figure 6-4 shows the result when the user enters invalid data into an input box. When the user selects the No button, the program will terminate abruptly. To prevent such scenarios, exception handling is a must.

Exception Handling vs. "Die in Flames"

In some cases, you may not be able to do much better than the dialog box in Figure 6-4. Many exceptions indicate a fatal error condition from which your application cannot recover. If that is the case, the best you can do is create a more friendly and informative alternative to the error dialog shown in Figure 6-4.

FIGURE 6-4
An unhandled
exception

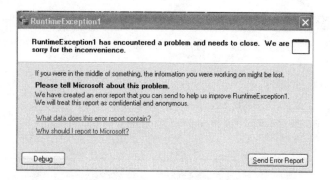

In contrast to VB 6.0 and earlier versions, Visual Basic .NET has a new error handling system, structured exception handling (SEH), to handle runtime errors. In the remainder of this chapter, we'll examine the Exception object and structured exception handling using Try . . . Catch . . . Finally blocks.

The Exception Object

Whenever an exception occurs, .NET makes an exception object available that contains information about the error. Exception objects are objects of type Exception or types derived from it. The Exception class, as well as most of its derived classes, has the following members:

- **GetBaseException method**   Returns an Exception object representing the first exception thrown in a chain of exceptions. If there is only one exception in the chain, it returns the current exception, and the InnerException property returns Nothing.

- **GetObjectData method**   Called by the CLR serializer when an exception hits the application domain boundary on the call stack. GetObjectData permits exception information to be serialized so that an exception can be thrown across an application domain boundary, thereby making it available to its host.

Error Handling with the On Error Statement

Visual Basic continues to support error handling with the On Error Goto and On Error Resume Next statements. However, in comparison to structured exception handling, it has a number of disadvantages:

- The traditional Visual Basic error handling system is an additional layer built on top of the structured exception handling system. In areas where the integration is weak and the translation of exception object to error object is not seamless, it becomes very difficult for developers using other languages to make use of your components.

- It tends to produce unstructured code that can make it difficult to follow program flow and sometimes even to determine whether an error handler is active or not. As a result, debugging is more difficult. (Structured exception handling is also subject to the same criticism, although it's a bit better in this regard.)

- The On Error Resume Next statement offers inferior performance when it serves as the error handler for long code blocks containing 20 or more statements.

- **ToString method**   Returns a String that includes the name of the exception object, the value of its Message property, and the name of the instance member in which the exception was thrown. Its implementation can be overridden in custom derived classes.

- **Data property**   A read-only IDictionary instance containing custom key/value pairs that provide additional information about the exception. If no custom data is provided, the property returns an IDictionary collection with no members. Items can be added to the collection using the IDictionary.Add method. Its syntax is

```
IDictionary.Add(key As Object, value As Object)
```

where *key* is the data item's key, and *value* is the data itself. The property is new to .NET 2.0.

- **HelpLink property**   A String containing the uniform resource name (URN) or uniform resource locator (URL) of a help file that provides information about the exception.

- **HResult property**   Gets or sets an HRESULT, which is an Integer value representing a COM error code that corresponds to an exception. Note that the property is protected.

- **InnerException property**   Returns the previous exception object in a chain of nested exceptions. The inner exception is defined as a parameter to one of the Exception object's overloaded constructors. The InnerException property is extremely useful when developing components, for example, and passing exceptions back to clients. They allow you to wrap exceptions thrown by components or subsystems that your component uses, while retaining information about the root cause of the exception. For example, a customizable menu component might store custom menu information in a system file. If the attempt to read the file throws a FileNotFoundException, it could be wrapped in a MenuGenerationException and passed to the client. The outer exception would provide information about why the menu component cannot behave as expected, while the inner exception contains information about the root cause.

- **Message property**   A read-only String containing the Exception object's error message. Its value can be assigned using one of the overloaded constructors of the Exception class when a class instance is created.

- **Source property**   A String that indicates the name of the application, component, or object that caused the error. If its value is not set explicitly, it defaults to the name of the assembly in which the exception occurred.

- **StackTrace property**   A read-only String that provides a list of the methods on the call stack when the current exception was thrown. Its value is automatically supplied by the .NET runtime when the exception is thrown.

- **TargetSite property**   A read-only MethodBase object representing the method in which the current exception was thrown.

The Exception class is the base class for all exception classes. It should be the base class used for custom exceptions unless you derive from an existing exception class that provides additional members with more detailed information about the type of exception you are handling.

Table 6-1 lists the exceptions defined in the System namespace and shows the classes from which they are derived.

Most of the classes that inherit from Exception or one of its derived classes do not implement any additional members. They differ from the Exception class only in name and in property values. The Comments column of Table 6-1 notes which exception types implement additional members.

Exception Class	Derived From	Comments
Exception		The base class for all exceptions.
ApplicationException	Exception	A deprecated base class for application exceptions (see the sidebar "Deriving from ApplicationException" later in this chapter).
SystemException	Exception	The base class for all system exceptions found in the System namespace.
AccessViolationException	SystemException	An attempt was made to read or write to protected memory.
AppDomainUnloadedException	SystemException	An attempt was made to access an unloaded application domain.
ArgumentException	SystemException	A method argument is invalid. The ParamName property contains the name of the invalid parameter.
ArgumentNullException	ArgumentException	An invalid Null was passed as a method argument.
ArgumentOutOfRangeException	ArgumentException	The value of an argument is outside its valid range. The invalid valid is contained in the ActualValue property.
ArithmeticException	SystemException	An error in arithmetic, casting, or conversion has occurred.
ArrayTypeMismatchException	SystemException	An attempt was made to store an element of the wrong type to an array.
BadImageFormatException	SystemException	A DLL or EXE image is invalid. Its filename is indicated by the FileName property, while the FusionLog property contains a string from the log file indicating why the attempt to load the file failed.
CannotUnloadAppDomainException	SystemException	An attempt to unload an application domain has failed.
DataMisalignedException	SystemException	Data is not aligned as expected.
DivideByZeroException	ArithmeticException	A division by zero error has occurred.
DllNotFoundException	TypeLoadException	A DLL cannot be found.
DuplicateWaitObjectException	ArgumentException	An object appears multiple times in an array of synchronization objects.

TABLE 6-1   Some Exception Classes in the System Namespace and Their Base Classes

Exception Class	Derived From	Comments
EntryPointNotFoundException	TypeLoadException	The attempt to load a class has failed because of a missing entry point. The TypeName property contains the name of the type whose entry point was not found.
ExecutionEngineException	SystemException	An internal error has occurred in the .NET Common Language Runtime.
FieldAccessException	MemberAccessException	An attempt was made to access a class' private or protected field.
FormatException	SystemException	The format of an argument is invalid.
IndexOutOfRangeException	SystemException	An array index is out of bounds.
InvalidCastException	SystemException	A cast or explicit conversion is invalid.
InvalidDataException	SystemException	Data to be compressed is in an invalid format.
InvalidOperationException	SystemException	A method call is invalid in an object's current state.
InvalidProgramException	SystemException	A program contains invalid MSIL or metadata.
MemberAccessException	SystemException	An attempt to access the member of a class or structure has failed.
MethodAccessException	MemberAccessException	An attempt was made to access a class' private or protected method.
MissingFieldException	MissingMemberException	An attempt was made to access a field that does not exist.
MissingMemberException	SystemException	An attempt was made to access a class member that does not exist.
MissingMethodException	SystemException	An attempt was made to access a method that does not exist.
MulticastNotSupportedException	SystemException	An attempt was made to combine instances of a non-combinable delegate type.
NonCancelableException	SystemException	An operation could not be canceled. The exception is new to .NET 2.0.
NoteFiniteNumberException	ArithmeticException	A floating point operation was attempted with a positive infinity, negative infinity, or NaN (not a number) value. The OffendingNumber property contains the invalid number.

TABLE 6-1   Some Exception Classes in the System Namespace and Their Base Classes *(continued)*

Exception Class	Derived From	Comments
NotImplementedException	SystemException	The requested operation or member is not implemented.
NotSupportedException	SystemException	The requested member or operation is not supported.
NullReferenceException	SystemException	An attempt was made to dereference a null object reference. (Applications should use ArgumentNullException instead.)
ObjectDisposedException	InvalidOperationException	An operation on a disposed object was attempted. The ObjectName property indicates the name of the disposed object.
OperationCanceledException	SystemException	The operation that a thread was performing was cancelled. The exception is new to .NET 2.0.
OutOfMemoryException	SystemException	Insufficient memory is available for program execution to continue.
OverflowException	ArithmeticException	A narrowing conversion has resulted in a loss of data.
PlatformNotSupportedException	NotSupportedException	An attempt was made to access a feature that is not supported on this platform.
RankException	SystemException	An array with the wrong number of dimensions has been passed to a method.
StackOverflowException	SystemException	The stack has overflowed because of too many nested method calls.
SystemException	Exception	The base class for most system-related exceptions. It adds a Data property that returns a collection of key/value pairs providing additional information about the exception.
TimeoutException	SystemException	The time allotted for a process or operation has expired.
TypeInitializationException	SystemException	An attempt to initialize an instance of a type has failed. The InnerException property holds the underlying exception thrown by the class initializer, while the TypeName property indicates the name of the type that could not be initialized.

TABLE 6-1   Some Exception Classes in the System Namespace and Their Base Classes *(continued)*

Exception Class	Derived From	Comments
TypeLoadException	SystemException	The attempt to load a type has failed. Its TypeName property contains the name of the type that caused the exception.
TypeUnloadedException	SystemException	An attempt was made to access an unloaded instance of a type.
UnauthorizedAccessException	SystemException	Access is denied by the operating system because of an I/O error or a security issue.
UriFormatException	FormatException	The formatting of a uniform resource identifier (URI) is invalid.

TABLE 6-1 Some Exception Classes in the System Namespace and Their Base Classes *(continued)*

Try . . . Catch . . . Finally Blocks

Visual Basic's implementation of structured exception handling uses the Try . . . Catch . . . Finally . . . End Try construct to handle exceptions.

The Try block contains the code for which the Catch block handles exceptions.

The Catch block contains one or more handlers for specific or general exceptions. The syntax of the Catch statement is

```
Catch [ exception [ As type ] ] [ When expression ]
```

Here, *exception* represents the Exception object that is passed to the Catch block by the .NET runtime. Its use is optional, but without it, the exception handler would have no information about the type of exception that occurred. Hence, the minimum useful exception handler takes the form

```
Try
    ' Code to execute
Catch e
    ' Exception handler
End Try
```

The As *type* and When *expression* clauses are exception filters. The As *type* clause determines the specific exception type that the Catch block handles. If an exception occurs and *type* corresponds to the type of the thrown exception or to one of its base classes, the block executes. This means that a Catch block like the following:

```
Try
    ' Code to execute
Catch e As Exception
    ' Exception handler
End Try
```

will catch all exceptions, since Exception is the base class for all exception types.

The When *expression* clause, if it is present, causes the Catch block to execute only if *expression* is true. For example, the following code handles exceptions that are thrown in the course of two divisions:

```
Public Module modFilteredException
    Public Sub Main

        Dim dividendStr, divisorStr1, divisorStr2 As String
        Dim dividend, divisor1, divisor2 As Integer
        Dim quotient1, quotient2 As Integer

        Try
            dividendStr = InputBox("Enter the dividend: ")
            divisorStr1 = InputBox("Enter the first divisor: ")

            divisor1 = CInt(divisorStr1)
            dividend= CInt(dividendStr)

            Console.WriteLine("First Quotient: ")
            quotient1 = dividend\divisor1
            Console.WriteLine("The result of the division is " & quotient1)

            divisorStr2 = InputBox("Enter the second divisor: ")
            divisor2 = CInt(divisorStr2)

            Console.WriteLine("Second Quotient:")
            quotient2 = quotient1\divisor2
            Console.WriteLine("The result of the division is " & quotient2)
        Catch e As DivideByZeroException When divisor1 = 0
            Console.WriteLine("Division by zero error: " & _
                            "the first divisor must not be zero.")
        Catch e As DivideByZeroException When divisor2 = 0
            Console.WriteLine("Division by zero error: " & _
                            "the second divisor must not be zero.")
        Catch e As Exception
            Console.WriteLine("Error: " & e.Message)
        End Try
    End Sub
End Module
```

One Catch block uses the When clause to handle division by zero errors in the first divisor, while a second Catch block uses the When clause to handle division by zero errors in the second divisor.

Along with the Try block, there must always be at least one Catch block or one Finally block in an exception handler. Of course, a Try block with only a Finally block really isn't an exception handler; although the Finally block will execute when an exception is thrown, it also executes when an exception is not thrown.

As the previous example shows, there can be multiple Catch blocks. However, since the As *type* exception filter catches exceptions for a particular exception class and any of its base classes, it is important that multiple Catch blocks be ordered from most specific to most general exception type. For example, if we had reorganized our previous Catch blocks to appear as follows:

```
Catch e As Exception
    Console.WriteLine("Error: " & e.Message)
Catch e As DivideByZeroException When divisor1 = 0
    Console.WriteLine("Division by zero error: " & _
                    "the first divisor must not be zero.")
Catch e As DivideByZeroException When divisor2 = 0
    Console.WriteLine("Division by zero error: " & _
                    "the second divisor must not be zero.")
End Try
```

the two handlers that trap DivideByZeroExceptions would never execute, since the Exception filter would necessarily handle all exceptions, including DivideByZeroExceptions.

The Finally block executes whether or not an error occurs. That is, the Finally block of an exception handler executes after the Try block if no exception occurs, and after the Catch block if an exception is thrown. The Finally block always executes, even if the Catch block itself throws an exception. Typically, the Finally block is used to perform any necessary cleanup operations.

Variables declared within each block of the Try . . . Catch . . . Finally construct are local to that block. In other words, if you want a variable to be visible both to the Try and the Finally blocks, for instance, it must be declared outside of the Try . . . Catch . . . Finally construct.

The following code illustrates a pattern that is commonly used with resources, such as files, streams, or database connection objects, that should be closed once they are opened. The Finally block is the appropriate place to do this, since the resource will be closed and any contents stored in a buffer will be written whether or not there is an error.

```
Private Sub WriteUserInput(filename As String)
    Dim sw As StreamWriter
    Dim inputString As String
    Try
        sw = New StreamWriter(filename, True)
        Do
            inputString = GetUserInput()
            If Not String.IsNullOrEmpty(inputString) Then sw.WriteLine(inputString)
        Loop While inputString <> String.Empty
    Catch e As FileNotFoundException
        Console.WriteLine("The file you specified, {0}, cannot be found.", filename)
    Catch e As Exception
        Console.WriteLine(e.Message)
    Finally
        If sw IsNot Nothing Then sw.Close()
    End Try
End Sub
```

Several points are worth noting about this pattern:

- In this example, in order to close the StreamWriter object in the Finally block, we have to declare it outside of the Try . . . Catch . . . Finally construct. If we declare it inside the Try block, the object would have block-level scope and be accessible only within the Try block.

- We cannot unconditionally call the StreamWriter object's Close method in the Finally block, since we don't know whether the code in the Try block executed without throwing an exception, whether an exception was thrown after the stream was opened, or whether an exception was thrown before the stream was opened. In the last case, calling the Close method generates a NullReferenceException, since the StreamWriter object has been declared but not instantiated. Therefore, we must test to determine whether the object is Nothing.

Nested Exceptions

An exception handler remains active from the time that the Try statement is encountered until the End Try statement is encountered. If program flow passes to another method, the exception handler will be invoked if an exception occurs in the called method that the method's own exception handlers are unable to handle. In this way, exception handlers can be nested. Consider, for example, the following very simplistic example:

```
Public Module modException
    Public Sub Main()
        Try
            RoutineA()
        Catch e As Exception
            Console.WriteLIne("Main exception handler: " & e.Message)
        End Try
    End Sub

    Private Sub RoutineA()
        Try
            Throw New ApplicationException
        Catch e As ApplicationException
            Console.WriteLine("Exception in RoutineA: " & e.Message)
        End Try

        Try
            Throw New ArgumentException
        Catch e As ApplicationException
            Console.WriteLine("Exception in RoutineA: " & e.Message)
        End Try

        Console.WriteLine("About to exit RoutineA.")
    End Sub
End Module
```

Executing this code produces the following output:

```
Exception in RoutineA: Error in the application.
Main exception handler: Value does not fall within the expected range.
```

In this code, two exceptions are thrown in the RoutineA procedure. The first, an ApplicationException, occurs within a Try . . . Catch construct and is handled by its exception handler. The second, an ArgumentException, is not, since the handler within which it occurs recognizes only ApplicationException. Because this exception handler cannot be invoked, .NET checks the call stack for another active exception handler and finds the handler in the

Main procedure. Control then returns to the exception handler in the Main procedure, and when it has finished, the program terminates. Note that control does not return to RoutineA after the exception handler executes.

Raising Exceptions

Particularly if you're developing components or reusable code libraries, you frequently have to throw exceptions to pass back to the application or component that is consuming your component. You do this by using the Throw statement to throw either a custom exception or an exception that's predefined in the .NET Class Library.

The Throw Statement

To throw an exception that is sent back to the caller, Visual Basic .NET uses the Throw statement. Its syntax is

```
Throw
```

or

```
Throw exception
```

The first version of the Throw statement, with no argument, must be in a Catch block. It simply rethrows the original exception that caused the Catch block to execute. The second version can appear anywhere in code and throws an exception of a specified type.

If you're using the second version of the Throw statement, you can throw an exception of a type that's predefined in the .NET Framework Class Library, or you can throw an exception based on a custom exception class that you define.

Raising an Application-Defined Exception

If you choose to define an exception type for your component or application, in most cases you should create a class derived from System.Exception, which is the base class for all exceptions. Hence, the code for a custom exception class might be something like the following:

```
Public Class CustomException
   Inherits System.Exception

   Public Sub New()
      Me.New("An error occurred in the component.", Nothing)
   End Sub

   Public Sub New(message As String)
      Me.New(message, Nothing)
   End Sub

   Public Sub New(message As String, innerException As Exception)
      MyBase.New(message, innerException)
      Source = "My_Custom_Component"
   End Sub
```

> ### Deriving from ApplicationException
> In .NET 1.0 and 1.1, developers were urged to derive custom application exception classes from the ApplicationException class rather than the Exception class. In .NET 2.0, however, developers are urged to derive directly from Exception and not use ApplicationException. The reason is that ApplicationException adds unnecessary depth to the object model without adding any useful exception information, while the overall design of the exception classes does not provide a programmatic scenario for catching ApplicationException.

```
' Protected constructor for derived classes to handle
   ' serialization/deserialization
   Protected Sub New(info As SerializationInfo, context As StreamingContext)
      MyBase.New(info, context)
   End Sub
End Class
```

Since Visual Basic .NET automatically provides only a parameterless constructor for derived classes, our custom exception class includes a complete set of constructors that match those of the Exception class. Aside from providing constructors, we merely need to override any unwanted values that are provided by the Exception class by default. These include the Message property, whose default value is "Exception of type 'System.Exception' was thrown.", and the Source property, whose default value is String.Empty.

The constructors of an exception object take three major forms:

- A parameterless constructor, which you can use if you are willing to accept the defaults (and particularly the default error message) provided by a predefined or custom exception class.

- A constructor that accepts a String argument. This string is assigned to the object's Message property.

- A constructor that accepts two arguments, one of type String and the other of type Exception. This is the constructor that you'd most likely want to use if you throw an exception from within a Catch block (that is, if you throw an exception from an exception handler) to return to a client of a component. The String argument is assigned to the exception object's Message property, while the Exception argument is assigned to the exception object's InnerException property. This allows you to pass the original exception (or exceptions) that invoked the exception handler back to the client.

The .NET Framework
Class Library

Although the introduction of .NET has brought sweeping changes to the Visual Basic language, nevertheless for Visual Basic programmers, the greatest innovation in .NET does not concern changes to the language or its new features, but rather the fact that .NET now comes with an extensive and comprehensive class library. The presence of the .NET Framework Class Library has a number of implications for Visual Basic programming:

- Decreased reliance on the Win32 API. Although it still cannot be entirely dispensed with, the .NET class library wraps significant portions of the Win32 API that Visual Basic programmers had to call. For instance, the .NET class library incorporates a complete set of registry functions that can replace calls to the registry functions in the Win32 API.

- Visual Basic has full access to the .NET Framework Class Library, which comes very close to realizing the goal of language independence. In .NET, Visual Basic is an equal player along with every other .NET language.

- A popular paradigm for end-user programming is to write programs that glue together existing objects, thereby reusing the work of others. The vast number of types and the diverse functionality implemented by the .NET Framework Class Library make this paradigm realizable.

The .NET Framework Class Library itself is enormous, consisting of nearly 200 namespaces with thousands of types and tens of thousands of members. This means that, in a short chapter such as this, even a very unsystematic and eclectic tour of the class library could hardly do it justice. Instead, this chapter will focus on a handful of the more useful or interesting features of the .NET Framework Class Library, in the hope that it will motivate you to explore the class library further. The selection of topics (which focus on getting file system information, working with weakly and strongly typed collections, using reflection to dynamically gather information about .NET types, manipulating string data, and accessing the system registry) are necessarily arbitrary and incomplete. Needless to say, many other topics (like multithreaded programming, using streams for input and output, networking, configuring applications with configuration files, and data access, just to mention a few) might have been included. Nevertheless, it is our hope that this chapter offers a solid foothold from which you can begin exploring the .NET Framework Class Library.

Getting File System Information

The Microsoft Scripting Runtime, which was included with Visual Basic 6.0, featured a FileSystemObject object that had a wealth of methods to make gathering information about the file system easier. In .NET, most of this functionality resides in the new My.Computer.FileSystem object, as well as in various informational classes (like DriveInfo, FileSystemInfo, etc.) in the System.IO namespace.

In Visual Basic 6.0, you had to instantiate an instance of the FileSystemObject class in order to gain access to the file system. Although in a few cases you could then directly access the file system resource in which you were interested, in most cases you had to navigate the file system object model in order to reach a particular resource. In contrast, the combination of the Visual Basic and the .NET Framework Class Library in many cases allows you to directly access the file system resource about which you'd like information. At the same time, if your interest is in the file system as a whole, Visual Basic allows you to navigate an object model to assemble information about multiple file system resources, although in a slightly easier way than Visual Basic 6.0.

My Computer and the FileSystemObject Object

The FilesystemObject object of the Microsoft Scripting Runtime has been in part replaced with the My.Computer.FileSystem object, which is an intrinsic object that is new to Visual Basic 2005. Unlike the FileSystemObject object, the FileSystem object doesn't require instantiation; it is in essence a shared class whose members are always available to you. The My.Computer.FileSystem object serves as a bridge that returns .NET types and eases integration with the .NET framework for the Visual Basic programmer.

Navigating the File System

One of the most common starting points for navigating the file system is, of course, to determine the drives that are available on it. This information is available from the Drives property of the My.Computer.FileSystem, which returns a strongly typed System.Collections.ObjectModel .ReadOnlyCollection of System.IO.DriveInfo objects.

However, you're not required to start navigating the file system by enumerating its available drives. If you know the directory in which you'd like to start, you can retrieve its subdirectories by calling the My.Computer.FileSystem.GetDirectories method and passing it the fully qualified path of the directory from which you want to start. (If you've previously enumerated drives and now want to enumerate directories on a drive, you can pass it the value of the DriveInfo object's Name property.) It returns a strongly typed ReadOnlyCollection collection of strings, in which each string contains the fully qualified path of a subdirectory. If you're interested in more than just the name of the subdirectory, you can then pass its name to the DirectoryInfo class constructor. The DirectoryInfo class is discussed later in this section. The following code illustrates this:

```
Dim dirs As ReadOnlyCollection(Of String) = _
          My.Computer.FileSystem.GetDirectories(dirPath)
For Each dir As String In dirs
   Dim dirInfo As DirectoryInfo = New DirectoryInfo(dir)
   Console.WriteLine("{0} : Created {1}", dirinfo.Name, _
                  dirInfo.CreationTime)
Next
```

Finally, if you're interested in the files in a particular directory, you can retrieve their names by calling the My.Computer.FileSystem.GetFiles method, which returns a strongly typed System.Collections.ObjectModel.ReadOnlyCollection of strings. Again, if you're interested in more than just the file's name, you can pass a string containing the path and name of a file to the FileInfo class constructor.

Retrieving Information about One File System Object

If you're not interested in enumerating drives, folders, or files but know the drive, directory, or file that you want to work with, you can access it directly using My.Computer.FileSystem as follows:

- For a single drive, call the GetDrive method and pass it the name of the drive. It returns a System.IO.DriveInfo object representing that drive.
- For a single directory, call the GetDirectory method and pass it the fully qualified path of the directory. The method returns a System.IO.DriveInfo object representing that directory.
- For a single file, call the GetFile method and pass it the fully qualified path and name of the file. The method returns a System.IO.FileInfo object representing that directory.

A major problem with retrieving information on directories and files, though, is that many of the most important directories are virtual and have no fixed physical location in the file system. The Windows and Windows system directories, as well as the My Documents, My Music, and My Photo directories, are examples of this.

The paths of some of these virtual directories are available from the SpecialDirectoriesProxy object, which is returned by the My.Computer.FileSystem object's SpecialDirectories property. Each property (listed in Table 7-1) of the SpecialPropertiesProxy object returns a string containing the path to a particular Windows shell folder.

Since the number of special folders whose location can be determined by the SpecialDirectoriesProxy object is rather limited, an alternative is to call the shared GetFolderPath method of the System.Environment class. It takes a single argument, a member of the

Property	Description
AllUsersApplicationData	Returns the path to the application data directory for all users
CurrentUserApplicationData	Returns the path to the application directory for the current user
Desktop	Returns the path to the directory representing the user's desktop
MyDocuments	Returns the path to the user's MyDocuments folder
MyMusic	Returns the path to the user's MyMusic folder
MyPictures	Returns the path to the user's MyPictures folder
Programs	Returns the path to the folder that contains the items to be displayed when the user selects the Programs menu item from the system's Start Menu
Temp	Returns the path to the user's directory for temporary files

TABLE 7-1   Properties of the SpecialDirectoriesProxy Object

System.Environment.SpecialFolder enumeration, and returns the path to that particular system directory. For the enumeration members and the virtual directories whose locations they return, see the entry for the My.Computer.FileSystem.SpecialDirectories property in Chapter 9.

The .NET File Information Classes

Once you're retrieved a reference to a DriveInfo, DirectoryInfo, or FileInfo object, you can gather the information you want, as well as use the properties of the object to navigate further into the file system.

In the case of a DriveInfo object, you can determine such things as the amount of available free space on the drive (its AvailableFreeSpace property returns a Long), the total size of the drive (its TotalSize property returns a Long), and whether or not the drive is ready (the Boolean IsReady property). The last of these properties is particularly useful whenever you are working with drives; it helps to prevent the substantial delay that results when any programmatic operation is attempted on a drive that is not ready. Finally, a DriveInfo object's RootDirectory property returns a DirectoryInfo object representing the root directory of that drive. From the root, you can navigate throughout the drive's directory structure.

The DirectoryInfo and FileInfo objects share a number of properties. The Attributes property, for example, allows you to retrieve or set a file or directory's attributes. Its value consists of one or more members of the FileAttributes enumeration, which means that to display a file or directory's individual attributes, you need merely call the ToString method on the value returned by the property. For example, the following code fragment:

```
Dim docPath As String = _
    My.Computer.FileSystem.SpecialDirectories.MyDocuments
For Each fn As String In My.Computer.FileSystem.GetFiles(docPath)
    Dim fi As FileInfo = New FileInfo(fn)
    Console.WriteLine("{0}: {1}", fi.Name, fi.Attributes.ToString())
Next
```

produces output that resembles the following:

```
test4.rtf: Archive, Compressed
test5.rtf: Archive, Compressed
test6.rtf: Archive, Compressed
test7.rtf: Archive, Compressed
test8.rtf: Archive, Compressed
test9.rtf: Archive, Compressed
testrtf1.rtf: Archive, Compressed
testrtf2.rtf: Archive, Compressed
testrtf3.rtf: Archive, Compressed
```

The CreationTime, CreationTimeUtc, LastAccessTime, LastAccessTimeUtc, LastWriteTime, and LastWriteTimeUtc properties of the DirectoryInfo and FileInfo classes allow you to read or to set the time that the file or directory was created, last accessed, or last modified, respectively. Both classes have a read-only Extension property that allows you to examine a file or folder's extension. The FullName property of each class returns the fully qualified path to the file or directory, while its Name property returns its name with an extension, if one is present, but without any part of the path. Both classes have a property that allows you to retrieve the object's parent. In the case of a DirectoryInfo object, the Parent property returns a DirectoryInfo object representing its parent directory. In the case of a FileInfo object, the Directory property returns a DirectoryInfo object representing the directory containing that file, while the DirectoryName property returns the fully qualified path of the directory containing the file.

The DirectoryInfo object also allows you to retrieve its subdirectories by calling the GetDirectories method, which returns an array of DirectoryInfo objects, one for each file in the directory. Its GetFiles method returns an array of FileInfo objects, one for each subdirectory.

The FileInfo class also has some additional members that are relevant only to files. The IsReadOnly property indicates whether the file is read-only, while the Length property returns a Long indicating the total size of the file in bytes.

Collection Classes and Data Structures

Visual Basic 6.0 included an intrinsic Collection class, along with the very similar Dictionary class in the Microsoft Scripting Runtime. While the Collection class remains a part of Visual Basic (it is defined in the Microsoft.VisualBasic namespace), .NET as a whole includes a number of collection objects and specialized data structures in the System.Collections and System.Collections.Specialized namespaces, as well as the System.Collections.Generic namespace discussed in the section "Strongly Typed Collections and Generics" later in this chapter. In this section, we'll examine a few of these classes.

The ArrayList Class

Once you've initially established the upper bounds of an array, Visual Basic requires that you must explicitly resize it using the ReDim statement whenever you want to add or remove elements. On the other hand, the ArrayList class, which is located in the System.Collections namespace, automatically handles the process of resizing. Because the .NET runtime, rather than your code, is responsible for managing the size of the array, the ArrayList class works somewhat differently than standard arrays:

- Rather than adding data by assigning it to an array element, you call the ArrayList object's Add method, passing it the data you'd like to add as the method's single argument. The method places the data at the end of the array and returns an Integer indicating the zero-based ordinal position of the newly added item. You can also insert an element at a specific position by calling the ArrayList object's Insert method, passing it the position at which you'd like the element inserted along with the data to insert.

- You retrieve items from the ArrayList object with its Item property, and supply the index of the item you'd like to retrieve. You can also determine whether an item already exists in the ArrayList object by calling its Contains method, and you can locate the first occurrence of a value by calling its IndexOf and LastIndexOf methods.

- While deleting elements from an array is cumbersome, you can easily delete items from the ArrayList object by calling its Remove method and passing the data you'd like to remove, by calling its RemoveAt method and passing the index of the element you'd like to remove, or by calling its RemoveRange method and passing the starting index and the number of elements to remove.

- You can manage the ArrayList object's Capacity property, which provides the .NET runtime with a hint about how many elements the ArrayList object will hold. The .NET runtime then uses this value to prevent unnecessary reallocations of memory as the array grows, thus improving overall performance. You can set its capacity either by providing an integer argument to the constructor (an ArrayList object's default capacity is 16) or by explicitly setting the Capacity property. You can also call the TrimToSize method, which sets the ArrayList object's capacity to its current number of elements. You cannot, however, shrink an ArrayList object by setting its capacity to less than its number of elements.

The Hashtable Class

Very much like the Collection and Dictionary objects, the Hashtable class allows you to store a collection of name/value pairs. The hash table is intended to support efficient storage and retrieval of the data it holds; members are stored internally based on a hashing function that is computed from the member's key. Because of this, the Hashtable class does not allow you to access values by index number.

You add elements to the hash table by calling its Add method and passing two arguments, the first an Object (usually a string) containing the key, and the second an Object representing the data. The key must be unique or an ArgumentException exception is thrown. You can determine whether a key already exists in a hash table by calling either its Contains or its ContainsKey method; both return True if the key exists in the hash table. The data need not be unique, and in fact it can even be null (i.e., Nothing).

You can retrieve data from the hash table in a number of ways. If you know the key of the data item you want, you can use the Item property, which has a single parameter, the key of the member you want to retrieve. You can also use the Keys property to retrieve an ICollection object containing all of the hash table's keys, and you can use the Values property to retrieve and ICollection object containing all of the hash table's data items. An ICollection object can be iterated using the For Each . . . Next construct, or its CopyTo method can be called to copy its data to an array (designated by the method's first argument) starting at a particular index position (designated by the method's second argument).

You can delete a hash table member by calling the Hashtable object's Remove method and passing it the key of the member you'd like to remove. You can also remove all members by calling the Clear method.

The following code creates a Hashtable object consisting of airport codes and their corresponding names, retrieves a single member by key, retrieves all key values and displays them in sorted order, and finally retrieves all values and displays them in sorted order:

```
Imports System.Collections

Public Module modMain
    Public Sub Main()
        ' Store airport codes and names to hashtable
        Dim airports As New Hashtable
        airports.Add("JFK", "John F. Kennedy, New York")
        airports.Add("LAX", "Los Angeles International, Los Angeles")
        airports.Add("ORD", "O'Hare International, Chicago")
        airports.Add("LHR", "Heathrow Airport, London")
        airports.Add("ORY", "Orly Airport, Paris")
        airports.Add("SVO", "Sheremetyevo, Moscow")
        airports.Add("NRT", "Narita Airport, Tokyo")
        airports.Add("SFO", "San Francisco International, San Francisco")
        airports.Add("MEX", "Benito Juarez International, Mexico City")

        ' Retrieve single airport by key
        Console.WriteLine(airports.Item("JFK"))

        ' Retrieve all keys, sort and iterate
        Dim keys As ICollection = airports.Keys
        Dim keysArray(airports.Count - 1) As String
        keys.CopyTo(keysArray, 0)
```

```
        Array.Sort(keysArray)
        Console.WriteLine()
        Console.WriteLine("Displaying airport codes alphabetically:")
        For Each key As String in KeysArray
            Console.WriteLine("{0} is {1}", key, airports(key))
        Next

        ' Retrieve airport names
        Dim values As ICollection = airports.Values
        Dim valuesArray(airports.Count - 1) As String
        values.CopyTo(valuesArray, 0)
        Array.Sort(valuesArray)
        Console.WriteLine()
        Console.WriteLine("Displaying airport names alphabetically:")
        For Each value As String in valuesArray
            Console.WriteLine(value)
        Next
        End Sub
End Module
```

The Queue Class

Among its advanced data structures, the System.Collections namespace includes a Queue class, which is a first in, first out (FIFO) structure. That is, the first item to be placed in the queue should be the first item removed. In contrast, a stack (represented in the System.Collections namespace by the Stack class, which we won't examine in this chapter) is a last in, first out (LIFO) structure.

At any time, you can determine how many items are in the queue by examining the queue object's Count property. Items are placed on the queue using the Enqueue method, whose only parameter is an Object representing the data to be placed on the queue. Calling the Enqueue method also increases the Count property by one. Items are removed from the queue by calling the Dequeue method, which has no parameters. It returns an Object containing the data removed from the queue and decrements the Count property by one. It is also possible to examine the first item in the queue without removing it by calling the Queue object's Peek method. It returns an object containing the data but leaves both the queue and the Count property unchanged.

The contents of the queue can also be copied to an array by calling the Queue Object's ToArray method, which returns a one-dimensional array containing the queue's data. You can also use the Queue object's CopyTo method to copy the queue's data to an array starting with a particular element of the array. The method's first argument is the name of the array, while the second is the starting index position in the array. The array must be properly sized before the call to the CopyTo method.

A queue can be used to model a business process in which a dispatcher responds to customers on a first-come, first-serve basis. Figure 7-1 shows a form from a Windows application for such a business, a taxi service.

The following is the form's code:

```
Imports System.Collections

Public Class frmQueue

    Private waitingPassengers As New Queue
```

FIGURE 7-1
A taxi dispatcher's
application that
uses the Queue
class

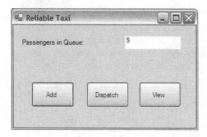

```vb
Private Sub frmQueue_Load(ByVal sender As System.Object, _
                     ByVal e As System.EventArgs) _
                     Handles MyBase.Load
    lblPassengers.Text = CStr(waitingPassengers.Count)
End Sub

Private Sub btnAdd_Click(ByVal sender As System.Object, _
                     ByVal e As System.EventArgs) _
                     Handles btnAdd.Click
    Dim passenger As String = InputBox( _
                     "Enter name and address of passenger: ")
    If passenger = String.Empty Then Exit Sub

    waitingPassengers.Enqueue(passenger)
    lblPassengers.Text = CStr(waitingPassengers.Count)
End Sub

Private Sub btnDispatch_Click(ByVal sender As System.Object, _
                  ByVal e As System.EventArgs) Handles btnDispatch.Click
    Dim available As String = InputBox("How many taxis are available?")
    If available = String.Empty Then Exit Sub
    If Not IsNumeric(available) Then
        MsgBox("You must enter a number")
        Exit Sub
    End If
    If CInt(available) <= 0 Then
        MsgBox("You failed to enter a positive number") : Exit Sub
    End If
    Dim taxis As Integer
    If CInt(available) > waitingPassengers.Count Then
        MsgBox("There are more taxis than passengers.")
        taxis = waitingPassengers.Count
    Else
        taxis = CInt(available)
    End If
    For ctr As Integer = 1 To taxis
        Dim passenger As String = CStr(waitingPassengers.Dequeue())
        lblPassengers.Text = CStr(waitingPassengers.Count)
        MsgBox("Passenger " & ctr & ": " & passenger)
    Next
End Sub
```

```
Private Sub btnView_Click(ByVal sender As System.Object, _
            ByVal e As System.EventArgs) Handles btnView.Click
    Dim toView As String = InputBox( _
                    "How many customers would you like to view?")
    If toView = String.Empty Then Exit Sub
    If Not IsNumeric(toView) Then
        MsgBox("You must enter a number") : Exit Sub
    End If
    If CInt(toView) <= 0 Then
        MsgBox("You failed to enter a positive number") : Exit Sub
    End If
    Dim views As Integer = CInt(toView)
    If views > waitingPassengers.Count Then _
        views = waitingPassengers.Count
    Dim msg As String = ""

    If views = 1 Then
        msg = "Passenger 1: " & CStr(waitingPassengers.Peek())
    Else
        Dim inQueue(waitingPassengers.Count) As Object
        waitingPassengers.CopyTo(inQueue, 1)
        For ctr As Integer = 1 To views
            msg += "Passenger " & ctr & ": " & CStr(inQueue(ctr)) & vbCrLf
        Next
    End If
    MsgBox(msg)
End Sub
End Class
```

The use of the Queue class in this example is fairly straightforward. Clicking the Add button displays an input box, then adds the information entered by the dispatcher into the queue by calling the Queue object's Enqueue method, and updates the label that displays the number of customers waiting for a taxi. Clicking the Dispatch button displays an input box asking the dispatcher how many taxis are available. The button's event handler calls the Queue object's Dequeue method as many times as there are taxis, displays the name and address of each customer in a message box, and updates the label that displays the number of customers still waiting for a taxi. Clicking the View button also displays an input box asking the dispatcher how many taxis are available. If the dispatcher only wants to see the name and address of the next customer, the Queue object's Peek method is used to display the data. Otherwise, the Queue object's CopyTo method is used to copy the contents of the queue to an array, starting at the second position in the array (that is, the element in ordinal position 1 in the array), and the contents of the array are displayed in a message box.

Strongly Typed Collections and Generics

One of the problems with using the standard collection objects and data structures provided by Visual Basic and the .NET Framework Class Library is that they are dynamically typed—they are designed to hold data of type Object. Typically, however, applications use collection objects to hold data of a specific type. This requires developers to do extensive type checking and casting whenever using collection objects, or risk runtime errors.

The Systems.Collections namespace offers two major solutions to this problem. The first involves implementing a custom collection class by inheriting from the CollectionBase or the DictionaryBase class, two abstract base types designed especially to allow strongly typed collections of indexed members and key/value pairs, respectively. Second, if your collection consists of strings or your keys and values are both strings, you can use the StringCollection and StringDictionary classes in the System.Collections.Specialized namespace.

.NET 2.0, however, offers a more flexible solution called *generic classes,* which allows you to define a collection object as strongly typed when you declare and instantiate it. For the most part, generic classes belong to the System.Collections.Generic namespace. The Visual Basic Collection class does not support generics.

Strongly typing a collection object is simply a matter of providing a type argument when the collection object is declared. The declaration takes this general form:

```
Dim varName As className(Of typeName)
Dim varName = New className(Of typeName)()
```

or for objects declared and instantiated on a single line of code:

```
Dim varName As New className(Of typeName)()
```

where *varName* is the name of the variable being declared, *className* is the name of the class to which *varName* belongs, and *typeName* is the name of the data type of *varName*'s members. Notice that the type definition is preceded by the Of keyword and includes one or more type names. (Some collection types require that you specify multiple type names. The generic Dictionary class, for example, requires that you provide separate type names to define the type of the collection's key and its value.) This in turn is followed by the remaining arguments to the class constructor, enclosed in a second set of parentheses. If there are no arguments, this second set of parentheses can be omitted.

The following example illustrates the use of two generic classes, Dictionary, a collection of name/value pairs, and KeyValuePair, which represents a single name/value pair stored in the Dictionary object:

```
Imports System.Collections.Generic

Public Module modMain
    Private employees As Dictionary(Of String, Employee)

    Public Sub Main()
        employees = New Dictionary(Of String, Employee)
```

```vb
        AddToDictionary("John Bond", "001")
        AddToDictionary("Jane Bond", "002")
        AddToDictionary("Janet Bond", "003")
        AddtoDictionary("Janice Bond", "004")
        AddToDictionary("Joe Bond", "005")
        AddToDictionary("James Bond", "007")

        Console.WriteLine("There are {0} employees now on file. They are:", _
                    employees.Count)
        For Each pair As KeyValuePair(Of String, Employee) In Employees
            Console.WriteLine("   {0}: {1}", pair.Key, pair.Value.Name)
        Next
        End Sub

    Private Sub AddToDictionary(name As String, id As String)
        Dim emp As New Employee(name, id)
        employees.Add(emp.ID, emp)
    End Sub
End Module

Public Class Employee
    Private empName As String
    Private empID As String

    Public Sub New(name As String, ID As String)
        Me.empName = name
        Me.empID = ID
    End Sub

    Public Property Name() As String
        Get
            Return Me.empName
        End Get
        Set
            Me.empName = Value
        End Set
    End Property

    Public Property ID As String
        Get
            return Me.empID
        End Get
        Set
            Me.empID = Value
        End Set
    End Property
End Class
```

Besides classes, structures, interfaces, delegates, and methods can also be generic. For instance, the standard Array class provides a number of shared generic methods that allow you to do such things as search or iterate a strongly typed array.

You can also implement your own generic classes by using the Of keyword along with a type parameter. For example:

```
Public Class MyGenericClass(Of itemType)
```

where *itemType* is the type parameter. You can then use *itemType* as a placeholder for the collection's strong data type in your code. For example:

```
Public Sub add(ByVal item As itemType)
```

Strings and StringBuilder

In .NET, strings are immutable; once initialized and assigned a value, they cannot be changed. Although it appears that an assignment statement such as

```
Dim chars() As Char = {"T"c,"h"c,"i"c,"s"c," "c,"i"c,"s"c," "c,"a"c,"n"c, _
                       " "c,"a"c,"r"c,"r"c,"a"c, "y"c," "c,"o"c,"f"c, _
                       " "c,"C"c,"h"c,"a"c,"r"c,"s"c}
Dim convertedChars As String = String.Empty
For Each ch As Char in chars
   convertedChars += ch
Next
```

simply appends characters one at a time to an existing string, in fact behind the scenes the .NET runtime is destroying the existing convertedChars variable and creating a new one that is one character longer than the previous one. This can result in a substantial performance penalty in routines that perform extensive string manipulation.

In contrast, instances of the StringBuilder class in the System.Text namespace represent mutable strings, which makes them more suitable for use in string concatenation. The instance methods of the StringBuilder class allow you to append data to the end of a StringBuilder object, to insert data into an existing StringBuilder instance, to replace a portion of text, and to remove portions of text.

A StringBuilder object, however, is not a string. So once you've finished manipulating a StringBuilder string, it's generally a good idea to convert it to a string by calling the StringBuilder object's ToString method.

The following code illustrates the use of the StringBuilder class to append elements of a character array to a string, and also calls the StringBuilder.ToString method to convert the StringBuilder object to a string once string concatenation has been completed:

```
Imports System.Text

Public Module modMain
   Public Sub Main()
      Dim chars() As Char = {"T"c,"h"c,"i"c,"s"c," "c,"i"c,"s"c, _
                             " "c,"a"c,"n"c," "c,"a"c,"r"c,"r"c,"a"c, _
                             "y"c," "c,"o"c,"f"c," "c,"C"c,"h"c, _
                             "a"c,"r"c,"s"c}
      Dim convertedChars As New StringBuilder
      For Each ch As Char in chars
         convertedChars.Append(ch)
      Next
```

```
        Dim displayString As String = convertedChars.ToString()
        Console.WriteLine(displayString)
    End Sub
End Module
```

Registry Access

From Visual Basic 4.0 through Visual Basic 6.0, Visual Basic programmers who wanted to use the registry could use Visual Basic's intrinsic language elements for registry/initialization file access, which included DeleteSetting, GetAllSettings, GetSetting, and SaveSetting; or they could use the registry functions in the Win32 API. The former were inflexible and underpowered (see the discussion of each of these language elements in Chapter 8, *Visual Basic Language Reference*), while many Visual Basic programmers found the latter to be intimidating and complex.

In contrast, the .NET Framework Class Library offers a convenient, simple set of methods that allows you to write from and read to the registry. The registry classes are found in the Microsoft.Win32 namespace and consist of the following:

- The Registry class, whose static fields provide access to the top-level registry keys, like HKEY_CLASSES_ROOT, HKEY_CURRENT_USER, or HKEY_LOCAL_MACHINE.

- The RegistryKey class, which allows you to access particular registry subkeys, as well as their default value and named values.

If you simply want to read or write a single registry value, you can call the static GetValue and SetValue methods, respectively, of the Registry class; you don't have to navigate the registry's hierarchical system of keys and subkeys, nor do you need to handle opening and closing registry keys. The code to read a value is as follows:

```
Dim appTextFiles As String = _
CStr(Registry.GetValue("HKEY_CLASSES_ROOT\txtfile\shell\open\command", _
    "", String.Empty))
appTextFiles = Left(appTextFiles, InStr(1, appTextFiles, "%") - 1)
Console.WriteLine("Text files are handled by {0}.", appTextFiles.Trim())
```

The static GetValue method takes the fully qualified registry key name as its first argument, the value name as its second (a key's default value is designated as an empty string), and the default value that the method should return if the value entry does not exist. GetValue returns an Object, which here is converted to a String.

Calling the SetValue method is equally easy. For instance, the following code writes four bytes of binary data to a registry value named BinData in the Software\MyCompany\MyApp key of HKEY_LOCAL_MACHINE. If we use RegEdit to examine the registry afterward, as Figure 7-2 shows, we find that that data has been written successfully.

```
Dim regData As Byte() = {&HF0, &HFF, &H20, &H00}
Dim regTopKey As String = "HKEY_LOCAL_MACHINE"
Dim regPath As String = "\Software\MyCompany\MyApp"
Registry.SetValue(regTopKey & regPath, "BinData", regData, _
                RegistryValueKind.Binary)
```

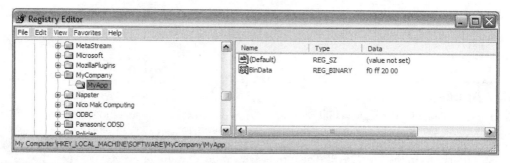

FIGURE 7-2   RegEdit showing the BinData value entry

If you want to perform a series of registry operations using a single key, though, you'll want to use the instance methods of the RegistryKey class. To do this, you retrieve a reference to a RegistryKey object representing a top-level key, and you call its OpenSubKey method to open one of its subkeys, as the following code shows:

```
Dim regKey As RegistryKey = _
  Registry.LocalMachine.OpenSubKey("Software\MyCompany\MyApp", _
  True)
```

If you want to be able to write to as well as read from the key's values, you have to call the overloaded version of the OpenSubKey method that has two parameters. You assign the second argument a value of True to indicate that the key should be writable.

Once you've opened a key, you can perform any of the following operations:

- Count the number of subkeys the key has by retrieving the value of its SubKeyCount property. This is particularly useful if you want to enumerate a key's subkeys.

- Retrieve an array of the names of all the current key's subkeys by calling its GetSubKeyNames method.

- Open a subkey and return a RegistryKey object representing the open key.

- Count the number of value entries the key has by retrieving the value of its ValueCount property. This is particularly useful if you want to enumerate a key's values. A key's default value is included in the count only if it is not null (i.e., String.Empty).

- Retrieve an array of the key's value names by calling its GetValueNames method. The array includes an empty string if the key's default value is present.

- Create a subkey by calling the CreateSubKey method.

- Delete a subkey that has no subkeys by calling the DeleteSubKey method, or delete a subkey with all of its child subkeys by calling the DeleteSubKeyTree method.

- Determine the data type (as defined by the RegistryValueKind enumeration) of a particular registry value by calling the GetValueKind method.

- Retrieve a value entry's data by calling the GetValue method.

- Store a value entry's data by calling the SetValue method.

For example, the following code creates a subkey named HKEY_CURRENT_USER\Software\ MyCompany\MyApp; creates four value entries and assigns values to them; and then retrieves the names of all the value entries, determines their data types, and retrieves their values:

```
Dim regKey As RegistryKey
Dim keyTop As RegistryKey = Registry.CurrentUser
regKey = KeyTop.OpenSubkey("Software\MyCompany\MyApp", True)
If regKey Is Nothing Then
    regKey = keyTop.CreateSubKey("Software\MyCompany\MyApp")
End If
' Write an integer, string, binary, and null-terminated array
Dim binValue As Byte() = {&HF0, &HFF, &H12, &HE0, &H43, &HAC}
Dim strngValue As String() = {"Client", "Service", _
                              Professional Services", "Fee"}

regKey.SetValue("WindowState", 0, RegistryValueKind.DWord)
regKey.SetValue("CustomWindowCaption", "Client Contact Management", _
            RegistryValueKind.String)
regKey.SetValue("CustomPosition", binValue, RegistryValueKind.Binary)
regKey.SetValue("CustomLabels", strngValue, RegistryValueKind.MultiString)


' Retrieve names of values
Dim valueNames As String() = regKey.GetValueNames()
For Each valueName As String In valueNames
    ' Determine data type
    Dim regType As RegistryValueKind = regKey.GetValueKind(valueName)
    ' Retrieve data
    Select Case regType
       Case RegistryValueKind.String
           Dim displayName As String = ValueName
           If ValueName = String.Empty Then displayName = "<Default Value>"
           Console.WriteLine("{0} has a value of {1}.", displayName, _
                            regKey.GetValue(ValueName))
       Case RegistryValueKind.MultiString
           Dim stringArray() As String = CType(regKey.GetValue(ValueName), _
                                         String())
           Dim strngLine As String = String.Empty
           For Each strng As String In stringArray
              strngLine += (strng & "  ")
           Next
           Console.WriteLine("{0} has a value of: {1}", ValueName, strngLine)
       Case RegistryValueKind.DWord
           Console.WriteLine("{0} has a value of {1}.", ValueName, _
                            CStr(regKey.GetValue(ValueName)))
       Case RegistryValueKind.Binary
           Dim bytData() As Byte = CType(regKey.GetValue(ValueName), Byte())
           Dim bytLine As String = String.Empty
           For Each byt As Byte In bytData
              bytLine += ("&H" & Hex(byt) & " ")
           Next
           Console.WriteLine("{0} has a value of {1:X2}", ValueName, bytLine)
    End Select
Next
```

Notice that the GetValue method handles the conversion between registry data types and .NET data types fairly seamlessly. As long as we call the GetValueKind method to determine a value's data type, we know whether to assign the value to a string (for RegistryValueKind.String and RegistryValueKind.ExpandString data), an Integer (for RegistryValueKind.DWord data), a Long (for RegistryValueKind.QWord data), a Byte array (for RegistryValueKind.Binary data), or a String array (for RegistryValueKind.MultiString data).

Reflection

In .NET, every type in an assembly is described by the metadata stored in that assembly. This makes .NET types self-describing and allows us to retrieve information about .NET types at any time, including in the runtime environment. This ability to gather information by examining .NET assemblies is termed *reflection*. Reflection can be an enormous aid in preparing documentation, in debugging and troubleshooting software, and in deepening your understanding of .NET. This section attempts to provide a very hasty introduction to using reflection to extract information about .NET code.

There are two points of entry for using reflection: an assembly, represented by the Assembly class, and a .NET type (a class, a structure, an interface, a delegate, or an enumeration), represented by the Type class. Frequently, the real focus of reflection is the examination of one or more .NET types. But often, a .NET assembly provides the best means to get at the Type object. So we'll begin by examining the Assembly class and the ways in which you commonly instantiate an Assembly object.

Retrieving an Assembly Object

You can retrieve a reference to the particular assembly in which you're interested (usually because it contains the .NET type or types in which you're interested) by doing the following:

- If you're interested in the assembly whose code is executing (the assembly from which the method call to retrieve an Assembly object is made), you can call the Assembly class' shared GetExecutingAssembly method, which takes no parameters and returns an Assembly object representing the currently executing assembly.

- If you're interested in an assembly that's already loaded, you can call the Assembly class' static GetAssembly method, which takes a Type object representing a type defined in that assembly as an argument. The method returns an Assembly object representing the assembly in which that type is defined. You can be sure the assembly is loaded if you've instantiated a type defined in that assembly.

- If you're interested in assembly that is not loaded, you can call the Assembly class' static LoadFile method and pass it the path and name of the file you'd like to load.

Instantiating a Type Object

Typically, once you have a reference to an assembly, you can proceed to work with the types it contains. If you're interested in multiple types in an assembly, you can call its GetTypes method, which returns an array of Type objects, one for each type defined in the assembly. You can then iterate the array using a For Each . . . Next construct until you've found the types you want.

If you're interested in a single type, you can retrieve a reference to its Type object by calling the Assembly object's overloaded GetType method. Of the four overloads, three are of interest to us. One accepts a single argument, the fully qualified name of the type (the complete path to the namespace, along with the type name). The second argument of the remaining two overloads is

Interfaces and GetType

You can call GetType to retrieve the type object corresponding to an object instance because GetType is a member inherited from the System.Object class, the base class of .NET types. However, interfaces don't inherit from System.Object (they don't implicitly inherit from any other .NET type) and therefore don't support the GetType method. In order to retrieve the Type object corresponding to an interface object, you can cast the interface to an object using code like the following:

```
Dim cl As New AnyClass("This is a class")
Dim int As IAnyInterface = cl
Dim interfaceType As Type = CObj(int).GetType()
```

a Boolean that defines whether the method call should throw an exception if it can't find the type you're looking for. (By default, it will throw an exception.) The third argument of the third overload is a Boolean that determines whether the type name in the first argument is case sensitive. By default, the comparison is case sensitive.

In many cases, though, you don't need to work with an Assembly object in order to instantiate a Type object. If you're interested in a Type object that corresponds to a variable (such as an instance of a class, structure, or delegate) or an enumerated value used in your code, you can call that object's GetType method, which returns a Type object representing its type.

Alternatively, if there isn't a variable of the specified type but its assembly is referenced by the current project, you can use Visual Basic's GetType statement, which takes as a single argument the name of the type. For example, the statement

```
Dim dataType As Type = GetType(Integer)
```

returns a Type object for the System.Int32 type, the 32-bit integer type in the .NET Framework Class Library.

Describing a Type

The Type object's members provide a wealth of information about the type it represents. This information includes:

- The fully qualified name of the type, including its namespace, which is returned by the FullName property. A string containing the type's namespace only is returned by the Namespace property. The type's name only is returned by the Name property.

- Whether the type is a reference type or a value type, which is indicated by the value of the IsValueType property.

- The category (class, structure, etc.) to which the type belongs, which is indicated by the IsValueType, IsClass, IsInterface, and IsEnum properties, all of which return a Boolean. The IsGenericType property indicates whether the type is a generic type, while the IsGenericTypeDefinition property indicates whether the type provides a generic type definition from which other generic types can be constructed.

- The type's accessibility, which is available from the IsPublic and IsNotPublic properties.

- Individual attributes of the type, all defined by properties with Boolean values. These include whether the class is an abstract type marked with the MustOverride keyword (the Boolean IsAbstract property); whether it is sealed or marked with the NonInheritable keyword, as indicated by the IsSealed property; whether it is an intrinsic type (String, Integer, etc.), as indicated by the IsPrimitive property; and whether it is public, as indicated by the IsPublic property.

- The assembly in which the type is defined. A reference to this Assembly object is returned by the Type object's Assembly property.

- The base type from which the type is directly derived. A reference to this Type object is returned by the BaseType property. If the type does not directly inherit from any type, the property returns a Type object representing the most immediate type to which the type implicitly inherits. You can also determine whether the type inherits from a specific type by calling the IsSubclassOf method and passing it a Type object representing the possible base class.

- The interfaces implemented by the type. They are returned as an array of Type objects by the GetInterfaces method.

- Any child objects (nested types) that are instantiated by the type. They are returned as an array of Type objects by the GetNestedTypes method.

- Any custom attributes applied to the type. (For attributes, see the section "Attributes.") They are returned as an array of Type objects by the GetAttributes method.

Describing a Type's Members

Besides retrieving information about the type itself, you can call Type object methods to retrieve information about the type's members. Most of the general methods that return an array of objects (including the GetNestedTypes method, which was mentioned in the preceding section) are overloaded. The first overload has no parameters and simply returns information about every appropriate member (or, in the case of GetNestedTypes, about every type). The second overload has a single parameter of type BindingFlags that defines the precise information to be included in the array. Some of the more commonly used members of the BindingFlags enumeration are shown in Table 7-2. In order for the methods to return any member information, you must supply at least one value of BindingFlags.Instance or BindingFlags.Static, and you must supply at least one value of BindingFlags.Public or BindingFlags.NonPublic. For example, the following code stores MemberInfo objects representing the public instance members of the Array class to an array and then displays the number of elements in the array to the console:

```
Const path As String =
"C:\WINDOWS\Microsoft.NET\Framework\v2.0.50215\mscorlib.dll"
Dim ass As Assembly = Assembly.LoadFrom(path)
Dim typ As Type = ass.GetType("System.Array")
Dim members As MemberInfo() = typ.GetMembers(BindingFlags.Instance _
                                    Or BindingFlags.Public)
Console.WriteLine(members.Length)
```

Member	Description
DeclaredOnly	Specifies that only unique members of the type, and not its inherited members, should be included
Instance	Specifies that instance members should be included
NonPublic	Specifies that non-public (private, protected, and friend) members should be included
Public	Specifies that public members should be included
Static	Specifies that static members should be included

TABLE 7-2   Some Members of the BindingFlags Enumeration

Once you've retrieved a Type object representing a particular type, you can retrieve the following:

- Information on all type members. Calling the GetMember method and providing the name of a member returns a MemberInfo object representing that member, if it exists. Calling the GetMembers method returns an array of MemberInfo objects.

- Information on all constructors. Calling the GetConstructor method with an array of Type objects returns a ConstructorInfo object whose signature matches the order of those Type objects, if there is one. Calling the GetConstructors method returns an array of ConstructorInfo objects.

- Information on all fields. Calling the GetField method and providing the name of a field returns a FieldInfo object representing that field, if it exists. Calling the GetFields method returns an array of FieldInfo objects.

- Information on all properties. Calling the GetProperty method and providing the name of a property returns a PropertyInfo object representing that property, if it exists. Calling the GetProperties method returns an array of PropertyInfo objects.

- Information on all methods. Calling the GetMethod method and providing the name of a method returns a MethodInfo object representing that method, if it exists. Calling the GetMethods method returns an array of MethodInfo objects.

- Information on all events. Calling the GetEvent method and providing the name of an event returns an EventInfo object representing that event, if it exists. Calling the GetEvents method returns an array of EventInfo objects.

MemberInfo is the base class for all of the reflection classes that relate to type members. The EventInfo, FieldInfo, PropertyInfo, and MethodBase classes, and even the Type class, inherit from it directly, while the MethodInfo and ConstructorInfo classes inherit from it indirectly (both are directly derived from MethodBase). Its read-only MemberType property returns a member of the MemberTypes enumeration that indicates what type of member (constructor, event, field, method, property) the object represents. The GetCustomAttributes method returns an array of attributes applied to the member.

The derived member type classes provide greater detail about specific member types, although we won't discuss them in detail in this brief introduction. From them, you can learn the types and names of parameters and whether they are passed by reference, whether any attributes are applied to the member, and what the return type of a method or the data type of a property or field is.

Attributes

One of the more novel features of .NET is its support for attributes, which are classes that can be used by a language compiler, a development environment, the .NET Common Language Runtime, or a specialized tool or utility to perform some special, customized handling. The .NET Framework Class Library includes several hundred attributes distributed among most of its namespaces.

Several examples will give some sense of the power of attributes. In Chapter 4 we saw an example in which the ThreadStaticAttribute class was used to modify the way in which shared members were used. Because the ThreadStaticAttribute class was applied to a field, the .NET runtime knew that it should maintain that field's value for each thread, rather than for the application as a whole. Visual Basic itself includes a number of attributes, one of which is the VbFixedArrayAttribute class. Unlike arrays in Visual Basic 6.0, all .NET arrays are dynamic. However, this creates difficulties for a number of traditional Visual Basic file create and read functions and for some Win32 API calls, both of which require fixed-length arrays. The VbFixedArrayAttribute class solves this problem by allowing arrays to behave more like the fixed-length arrays of VB 6.0. In fact, many language features of Visual Basic .NET, like default values (defined by the Default keyword) and parameter arrays (defined by the ParamArray keyword) are actually translated by the Visual Basic compiler into a corresponding .NET attribute.

An attribute is a class derived from an abstract base class named System.Attribute. By convention, the end of the class' name ends in "Attribute" (for instance, WebMethodAttribute, VbFixedStringAttribute). Often, an attribute class adds a parameterized constructor, which allows the attribute's custom properties to be set. (Attribute properties are typically read-only.)

An attribute is included in code by enclosing it within angle brackets (< and >). The shorted attribute name (like <WebMethod> instead of <WebMethodAttribute>, though the latter is perfectly legal) is followed by parentheses and any arguments that are passed to the attribute constructor. If no arguments are present, the parentheses can be eliminated.

Although some attributes take no arguments, others have both required and optional arguments. Required arguments are defined by the attribute class constructor; required arguments must be passed positionally (and not as named arguments) in the order defined by the attribute class constructor. Optional arguments, which correspond to attribute class properties, can be passed as named arguments.

Attributes are applied to the language element that they modify, and must be on the same line of code as the element to which they are applied. (If they are on separate physical lines, the line continuation character—a space followed by an underscore—must be used.) Specific attributes can be applied to one or more of the following:

- **Assemblies**   Attributes that apply to assemblies must be located at the beginning of a source code file (immediately following any Option and Imports statements) and be prefaced with the Assembly: keyword. For example:

```
Imports System.Reflection

<Assembly:AssemblyTitle("A Collection of Useful Utilities")>
Public Class Utility
```

- **Modules**   Attributes that apply to modules must also be located at the beginning of a source code file and be prefaced with the Module keyword. For example:

```
<Module:CLSCompliant(True)>

Public Module modMain
```

- **Classes, Delegates, Enums, Events, Interfaces, and Structures**   The following example shows the placement of an attribute when applied to one of these elements:

```
<StructLayout(LayoutKind.Explicit)> Public Structure ApiStruct
```

- **Constructors, Fields, Methods, and Properties**   The following example shows the placement of an attribute when applied to one of these elements:

```
<Obsolete> Public Function IsAnError() As Boolean
```

- **Parameters**   Notice that in the following example, ParamArray is a Visual Basic keyword, so we've enclosed it in brackets as well:

```
Public Function ComputeMean(<[ParamArray]> Rainfall() As Double) _
                        As Double
```

- **Return values**   For example:

```
Public Function PublicInterface() As <CLSCompliant(True)> SByte
```

One very useful attribute is <Flags>, which changes the way in which an enumeration is viewed. Ordinarily, an enumeration is treated as a set of mutually exclusive values. The <Flags> attribute, on the other hand, allows individual Enumeration members to be ORed together and treated as individual elements of a bitmask. The following code illustrates the use of the <Flags> attribute:

```
<Flags> Public Enum ComputerStatus As Integer
    Online   = 1
    DVDReady = 2
    CDReady  = 4
    SoundOn  = 8
End Enum

Public Module modMain
    Public Sub Main()
        Dim Computer1 As ComputerStatus = ComputerStatus.Online _
                                Or ComputerStatus.DVDReady
        Console.WriteLine(Computer1.ToString())
        End Sub
End Module
```

The program's output is:

```
Online, DVDReady
```

In contrast, had we not used the <Flags> attribute, the program would simply have output the value 3, since it views enumeration member names as representing mutually exclusive values and has no name to correspond to the value 3.

Language Reference

This language reference is an extremely long chapter that documents each of the current language elements in the Visual Basic .NET language. Each of the following elements is presented:

- Directives, which provide instructions for special handling in a design-time or compile-time environment but are not included in a project's final executable. They can be used for such purposes as defining expandable and collapsible blocks of code in the Visual Studio editor or defining compile-time constants that allow special versions of an executable to be generated.

- Statements, which are stand-alone language elements recognized by the Visual Basic .NET compiler. For example, Dim, Class, and Do are all language statements in Visual Basic .NET.

- Keywords, which are typically language elements that modify a language statement and are also recognized by the Visual Basic .NET compiler. For example, ByVal, Handles, and Shared are all language keywords in Visual Basic .NET.

- "Intrinsic" classes and objects. These consist of several attributes (such as VbFixedStringAttribute) and several objects (like the Collection object and the Err object) all defined in the Microsoft.VisualBasic namespace.

- "Intrinsic" functions, procedures, and properties. Many of these are a traditional part of the Visual Basic language dating to version 1.0, such as the Len and Instr functions. Others are traditionally a part of VBScript, such as the FormatCurrency function or the ScriptEngine property. All of these language elements are currently implemented as shared, global members of various classes in the Microsoft.VisualBasic namespace. In addition, a number of conversion functions (like CInt, CStr, CType, and DirectCast) are actually implemented by the Visual Basic compiler and are not defined in any .NET class library.

> ### Additional Language Elements
> Other language elements, such as data types, constants, and operators, are documented in individual appendixes to this book.

Each language element follows a more or less standard format, depending on the particular nature of that element. In most cases, this standardized treatment includes the following individual items:

- A brief description of the language element.
- For functions, procedures, and properties, the namespace and class in which the element is defined.
- The syntax of the language element.
- Comments about the language element. These comments tend to be very diverse and include a wealth of detail that you need to know to use that particular language element effectively. For example, the discussion of the Visual Basic Collection class, along with providing basic information about using the Collection class, also includes discussions of implementing your own customized collection classes and using the new generic collection classes introduced in Visual Basic 2005.
- A code example that shows how the element is used. Most language elements except keywords are typically accompanied by a code example.
- Changes in the implementation of the language element in the three versions of the .NET platform that have been released to date.
- Differences in the implementation of the language element from that of Visual Basic 6.0.
- A list of related language elements.

It's also important to emphasize what this language reference does not cover. Although it discusses individual classes and members of the .NET Framework Class Library, particularly in the Comments section of individual Visual Basic .NET language entries, it does not document the classes or members of the Framework Class Library. It confines itself to documenting those portions of the framework that are found in the Microsoft.VisualBasic assembly and the Microsoft.VisualBasic namespace.

#Const Directive

Defines a conditional compiler constant.

Syntax

```
#Const constname = expression
```

Element	Description
constname	The name of the constant, which must follow standard Visual Basic naming conventions.
expression	The value to assign to *constname*.

Comments

Conditional compiler constants defined with the #Const directive are evaluated at compile time with the #If . . . Then . . . #Else compiler directive. Compiler constants affect which blocks of code are included in the executable and therefore are used to produce different versions of an executable. For example, the directives can be used to produce separate debug and release versions of an executable, separate platform versions (e.g., one version that runs under Windows 95, 98, and ME, and another for Windows NT and XP), localized versions, or separate vertical market versions.

A conditional compiler constant differs from a constant defined with the Const statement in two major ways:

- Const makes a constant value available to a program at runtime; #Const defines a value that determines what code is compiled into the final executable and is not available at runtime.

- Information about constants defined with Const is stored with the metadata in the .NET assembly. Conditional compiler constants, on the other hand, are available only at compile time, and no information about them is preserved in the compiled assembly.

The conditional compiler constant defined by #Const has scope only in the file in which it is declared, and is visible from the point at which it is declared to the end of the file. It is possible, however, to define global conditional compiler constants that apply to all the files in a project by using the Visual Studio project properties dialog or the command-line compiler's /define switch. (This latter topic is discussed in the next three items.)

expression has a compile-time data type and can be a Boolean, any of the intrinsic numeric data types, String, or Char. The compiler will generate compiler errors for some illegal type conversion operations, such as string to double or string to Boolean. Conversion between data types in *expression* is not affected by the setting of Option Strict.

expression can consist of literals, other conditional compiler constants that have been defined previously in the file, and arithmetic and logical operators. In addition, any of the conversion functions implemented by the compiler (such as CInt, CStr, CType, etc.) other than CObj can be used. It *cannot* include runtime types such as variables and objects.

Although the compiler will detect some errors in #Const statements, others may go undetected. This means that if you use the #Const statement to define a conditional compiler constant in which *expression* is anything other than a simple literal, you should make sure that the #If directive evaluates the constant in the way that you intend.

#Const can not only be used to define a constant, but it can also be used to undefine one. To undefine a constant in code, set it equal to Nothing. For example:

```
#Const flag = True
' code
#If flag Then
    ' code to compile
#End If
#Const flag = Nothing                          ' undefines flag
#If flag Then
    ' code not included in executable
#End If
```

The chief advantage of the #If . . . Then . . . #Else directive is that it permits multiple versions of an executable to be generated without requiring a modification of source code. Using the

#Const directive in code partly defeats this purpose, however, since source code must be modified to reflect the value of the conditional compiler constant. Because of this, both Visual Studio and the Visual Basic .NET command-line compiler provide an alternate way to define global conditional compilation constants (that is, conditional compiler constants that apply to a project as a whole).

To define a conditional compiler constant in Visual Studio, open the Project Properties dialog and select the Compile tab. Then click the Advanced Compile Options button. This opens the Advanced Compiler Settings dialog shown in Figure 8-1. You can define a conditional compiler constant in the Custom constants text box by indicating the constant name and its value, just as if you were using the #Const directive in code (without the #Const keyword, however). For example,

```
debug=true,platform="xp"
```

defines two conditional compiler constants, debug (whose value is True) and platform (whose value is "xp").

Global conditional compiler constants are defined with the /define or /d switch when using the Visual Basic .NET command-line compiler. For example,

```
/define:debug=true,platform="xp"
```

defines two conditional compiler constants, debug (with a value of True) and platform (with a value of "xp"). For details on using the command-line compiler, see Appendix E.

Like all other Visual Basic language elements, conditional compiler constants are not case sensitive. In particular, the name of the compiler constant that you declare when using the command-line compiler or the project's Properties dialog need not match the case of the conditional compiler constant as it appears in #If . . . Then . . . #Else directives.

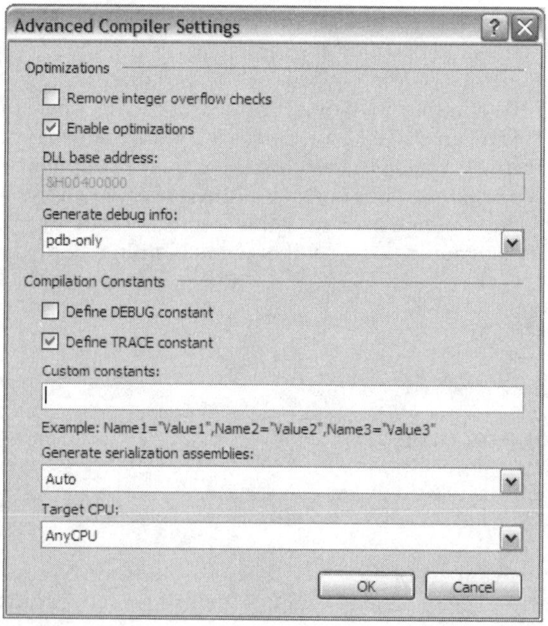

FIGURE 8-1
The Advanced Compiler Settings dialog

A number of conditional compiler constants either are predefined or have special meaning to the compiler. All are new to the Visual Basic 2005 compiler. They are shown in the following table:

#Const Constant	Description
CONFIG	A String indicating a configuration defined in the Visual Studio Configuration Manager. This constant is automatically recognized in the Visual Studio environment only.
DEBUG	A Boolean that defines whether calls to Debug class methods are included in the build. By default, in both Visual Studio .NET and the command-line compiler, it is set to False. To change this setting in Visual Studio .NET, check the Define DEBUG constant box shown in Figure 8-1. To change it for the command-line compiler, use the following Const directive: `#Const Debug = True`
TARGET	A String indicating the output type of the build. Possible values are **winexe** (a Windows executable), **exe** (a console-mode application), **library** (a .NET assembly), and **module** (a .NET module).
TRACE	A Boolean that defines whether calls to Trace class methods are included in the build. By default, in Visual Studio .NET, it is set to True. To change this setting, uncheck the Define TRACE constant box shown in Figure 8-1. By default, the Visual Basic .NET command-line compiler sets it to False. To change this setting, use the following #Const directive: `#Const TRACE = True`

VBC_VER	A Double indicating the version of the Visual Basic compiler. (The value of VBC_VER for Visual Basic 2005 is 8.0.) Earlier versions of the Visual Basic .NET compiler do not recognize the constant. Note that, when using VBC_VER, you typically test for a baseline version, as in `#If VBC_VER >= 8.0 Then`
	`    ' Code to include in output`
	`#End If`

Example

The following is a simple example that shows how a conditional compiler constant might be used to produce different error message in debug and release versions.

```
#Const debug = True

Public Class TestCondConst
   Public Shared Sub Main
      Try
         Throw New ApplicationException("This is an application exception.")
      Catch e As Exception
         #If debug Then
            MsgBox(e.Message & ": " & vbCrLf & e.StackTrace)
```

```
            #Else
                MsgBox("Application error: terminating application.")
            #End If
        End Try
    End Sub
End Class
```

VB.NET Changes

CONFIG, DEBUG, TARGET, and TRACE, the four conditional compiler constants automatically recognized by the Visual Basic compiler, are new to Visual Basic 2005.

VB6 Differences

Although their use was undocumented, the expressions used to define conditional compiler constant definitions in Visual Basic 6.0 included selected functions such as Int. In Visual Basic .NET, calls to those functions generate compiler errors; only the conversion functions implemented directly by the compiler can be used.

See Also

#If . . . Then . . . #Else Directive

#ExternalSource Directive

Maps specific lines of source code indicated by the #ExternalSource block construct to text in an external file.

Syntax

```
#ExternalSource(StringLiteral, IntLiteral)
    [ Visual Basic .NET code ]
#End ExternalSource
```

Element	Description
StringLiteral	The path and name of the external source file.
IntLiteral	The line number of the first line in the external source to which the #ExternalSource code block maps.

Comments

The #ExternalSource directive is used by the compiler to attribute an error in Visual Basic source code to lines in an external file. When a compiler error occurs, it is attributed to the external file named *StringLiteral*. The line reported to be in error is defined by *IntLiteral* plus the zero-based offset of the line on which the error actually occurred.

The #ExternalSource directive is not the equivalent of the C/C++ #Include preprocessor directive.

The compiler does not actually check that the file defined by *StringLiteral* exists or that it has a line number *IntLiteral*. It simply attributes errors to that file, and numbers its line starting with *IntLiteral*. The file in fact need not exist.

The #ExternalSource directive is used extensively by the ASP.NET engine so that, for example, a compiler error in the Visual Basic .NET code-behind file can be attributed to the control for which the code is written.

Code blocks marked with the #ExternalSource directive cannot be nested.

Example

The following is one of those simple "do nothing" examples that simply illustrates the operation of the #ExternalSource directive. The following code, which is in a source code file named ExternalSource1.vb, defines a SqlConnection object but fails to import the System.Data .SqlConnection namespace:

```
Public Sub Main()
    #ExternalSource("DataAccess.vb", 9)
        Dim connect As New SqlConnection
        connect.ConnectionString = "not a real connection string"
        connect.Open
        ' To do: write code to use connection
        connect.Close
    #End ExternalSource
End Sub
```

Attempting to compile the source code using the Visual Basic .NET command-line compiler produces the following output, which indicates that the compiler error occurred on line 9 of a source code file named DataAccess.vb:

```
DataAccess.vb(9) : error BC30002: Type 'SqlConnection' is not defined.

        Dim connect As New SqlConnection
                           ~~~~~~~~~~~~~
```

VB.NET Changes

The #ExternalSource directive is new to Visual Basic .NET as of .NET 1.1.

VB6 Differences

The #ExternalSource directive is new to Visual Basic .NET and did not exist in Visual Basic 6.0.

#If . . . Then . . . #End If Directive

Evaluates a conditional compiler constant and, if true, includes the following code block in the compiled application.

Syntax

```
#If expression Then
        statements
[ #ElseIf expression Then
    [ statements ] ]
. . .
```

```
[ #ElseIf expression Then
   [ statements ] ]
[ #Else
   [ statements ] ]
#End If
```

Element	Description
expression	An expression that evaluates a conditional compiler constant defined using the #Const directive.

Comments

Syntactically, the #If directive is very similar to the If statement (for details, see the entry for the If statement), except that the former is evaluated at compile time to determine what code is included in the final executable, while the latter is evaluated at runtime. Using the #If directive allows you to create separate versions of your application, such as debug and production versions, localized versions, vertical market versions, etc.

expression must include at least one conditional compiler constant. It can also include literal values, as well as logical and comparison operators. *expression* can also be a compound expression that evaluates multiple conditional compiler constants. For example:

```
#If VBC_VER >= 8.0 And ConditionFlag Then
   ' code to compile if both conditions are true
#End If
```

You can use all of the conversion functions implemented by the compiler except for CObj to convert conditional compiler constant values to the necessary data type. For example:

```
#If CInt(VBC_VER) = 8 Then
```

If a conditional compiler constant evaluated in an #If directive has not been defined, the compiler does not issue an warning or error. Instead, the expression simply evaluates to False.

String comparisons in #If directives are case sensitive. Comparisons are not affected by the setting of Option Compare.

The #If . . . Then . . . #End If directive is a block construct, which means that if #If is used within a block construct, the entire directive must be contained within that construct. It also means that if any other block constructs (such as For . . . Next, If . . . Then . . . End If, or Try . . . Catch . . . End Try) begin within the #If . . . Then . . . #End If directive, they must be entirely contained within it. In practice, the compiler enforces this requirement and generates an error only if the evaluation of *expression* would result in the exclusion of some portion of a block construct.

Although conditional compiler constants defined by the #Const statement have a data type, they are not .NET types, and you cannot call .NET type members.

The use of an #If directive requires, at a minimum, a closing #End If. Unlike the If statement, the #If directive does not support a one-line version.

Example

See the example for the #Const Directive.

VB6 Differences

In Visual Basic 6.0, string comparisons made in *expression* were case insensitive, whereas in Visual Basic .NET they are case sensitive. In neither case, however, is the comparison affected by the setting of Option Compare.

See Also

#Const Directive, If . . . Then . . . End If Statement

#Region Directive

Defines a block of code for special handling in a design-time environment.

Syntax

```
#Region "identifier_string"
    ' Visual Basic .NET code
#End Region
```

Element	Description
identifier_string	A string describing the code block that is displayed when the block is collapsed.

Comments

The #Region . . . #End Region construct is used by Visual Studio to mark blocks of code that can be collapsed (so that only *identifier_string* is visible) and expanded. It is an extremely useful feature that can make large source code files much more manageable.

identifier_string can contain embedded spaces.

Code blocks defined by the #Region directive can be nested.

The #Region directive cannot appear within the body of a method. It can appear, however, in a property definition, but only outside of the individual property Get and Set blocks.

As a block statement, the #Region directive must entirely contain or entirely be contained by any other block construct. Practically, this requirement has little effect, since most block constructs (such as Try . . . Catch . . . End Try, Do . . . Loop, or If . . . End If) occur within method bodies, where the #Region directive is not supported. Interestingly, however, the #Region directive need not nest or be nested by an #If . . . #End If directive.

Example

The following code illustrates the use of the #Region directive. When all but an outer code block are collapsed in a Visual Studio code window, the window appears as shown in Figure 8-2.

```
Public Class Form1
#Region "API Constants Definitions"
' Const statements go here
#End Region
#Region "Win32 API Definitions"
' Declare statements go here
#End Region
#Region "Variable Declaration"
```

FIGURE 8-2
The Visual Studio
.NET code window
hiding code blocks

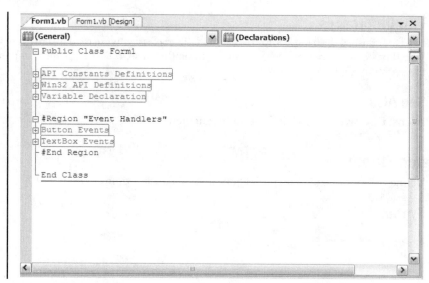

```
' Variable declarations go here
#End Region

#Region "Event Handlers"
#Region "Button Events"
' Button event handlers go here
#End Region
#Region "TextBox Events"
#End Region
#End Region
End Class
```

VB6 Differences

The #Region directive is new to Visual Basic .NET.

AddHandler Statement

Dynamically associates an event with an event handler.

Syntax

```
AddHandler event, AddressOf eventhandler
```

Element	Description
event	The name of an event, in the form *className.event*.
eventhandler	The name of the procedure responsible for handling *event*.

Comments

An event handler defined with AddHandler can be removed using the RemoveHandler statement.

In contrast to the Handles statement, which allows you connect an event with an event handler for the lifetime of an application, AddHandler allows you to define an event handler dynamically for a duration of your choice. This is an excellent alternative for applications or components in which the code that should handle an event is based on conditions that can only be determined at runtime.

Although structures can raise events, the WithEvents keyword cannot be used to define event handlers to respond to them. The AddHandler statement provides the only way in which a client can handle events raised by a structure.

Custom events defined using the Custom keyword in the Event statement (see the entry for the Event Statement) require that the AddHandler statement be used.

The Visual Basic .NET compiler implements the event handler added by the AddHandler statement as a delegate, as Figure 8-3 shows.

Example

The example program illustrates the use of the AddHandler and RemoveHandler statements to handle the events raised by a structure. The example prompts the user for a baby's name and then tracks the individual's age by asking the user whether the age should be increased by one year.

FIGURE 8-3
Implementing the event handler added by AddHandler as a delegate

The program then uses events to indicate that two milestones, adulthood and retirement, have been reached.

```vbnet
Public Module TrackAge
    Private indiv As Person

    Public Sub Main()
        ' Prompt user for baby name
        Dim name As String = InputBox("Enter name of newborn: ", "Baby's Name")
        If name = String.Empty Then Exit Sub

        indiv = New Person(name)

        ' Add event handlers
        AddHandler indiv.ReachedAdulthood, AddressOf ReachedAdulthood
        AddHandler indiv.ReachedRetirement, AddressOf ReachedRetirement

        ' Track individual's age while response to messagebox is MsgBoxResult.Yes
        Do While Not indiv.Name = String.Empty
            Dim result As MsgBoxResult
            result = MsgBox("Increase " & indiv.Name & "'s age by one year? ", _
                    MsgBoxStyle.Question Or MsgBoxStyle.YesNoCancel, "A Year Older?")
            Select Case result
                Case MsgBoxResult.Cancel
                    Exit Sub
                Case MsgBoxResult.No
                    Console.WriteLine("We lose track of " & indiv.Name & " at age " _
                                & indiv.Age)
                    indiv = Nothing
                Case MsgBoxResult.Yes
                    indiv.IncreaseAge()
                    Console.WriteLine(indiv.Name & " is now " & indiv.Age & ".")
            End Select
        Loop
        ' Remove event handlers on exit
        RemoveHandler indiv.ReachedAdulthood, AddressOf ReachedAdulthood
        RemoveHandler indiv.ReachedRetirement, AddressOf ReachedRetirement
    End Sub

    ' Event handler for child reaching adulthood
    Public Sub ReachedAdultHood(sender As Object, e As EventArgs)
        Dim per As Person = Nothing
        If TypeOf sender Is Person Then
            per = DirectCast(sender, Person)
            Console.WriteLine("{0} is now {1} and has reached adulthood.", _
                            per.Name, per.Age)
        End If
    End Sub

    ' Event handler for adult beginning retirement
    Public Sub ReachedRetirement(sender As Object, e As EventArgs)
        Dim per As Person = Nothing
        If TypeOf sender Is Person Then
            per = DirectCast(sender, Person)
            Console.WriteLine("{0} is now {1} and has reached retirement.", _
                            per.Name, per.Age)
```

```
            End If
        End Sub
End Module

' Person class used by life milestone tracker
Public Structure Person
    Private Const AgeOfMajority As Integer = 21
    Private Const AgeOfRetirement As Integer = 65

    Private _name As String
    Private _age As Integer

    Public Event ReachedAdulthood(sender As Object, e As EventArgs)
    Public Event ReachedRetirement(sender As Object, e As EventArgs)

    Public Sub New(name As String)
        Me._name = name
    End Sub

    Public ReadOnly Property Name() As String
        Get
            Return Me._name
        End Get
    End Property

    Public Property Age() As Integer
        Get
            Return Me._age
        End Get
        Set
            Me._age = Value
            TestForAgeEvent(Me._age)
        End Set
    End Property

    ' Increment age by one
    Public Function IncreaseAge() As Integer
        Me._age += 1
        TestForAgeEvent(Me._age)
        Return Me._age
    End Function

    ' Helper routine to test age and raise event
    Private Sub TestForAgeEvent(age As Integer)
        If age = AgeOfMajority Then
            RaiseEvent ReachedAdulthood(Me, EventArgs.Empty)
        ElseIf age = AgeOfRetirement Then
            RaiseEvent ReachedRetirement(Me, EventArgs.Empty)
        End If
    End Sub
End Structure
```

VB6 Differences

The AddHandler statement does not exist in VB 6.0. Its closest equivalent is the ConnectObject method of the WScript object in Windows Script Host.

See Also
Event Statement, Handles Statement, RemoveHandler Statement, WithEvents Keyword

---

Alias Keyword

Used in the Declare statement to define the actual name of a procedure in a Windows dynamic link library when that name differs from the name by which the routine will be invoked in code.

Syntax

```
Alias name
or
Alias "#ordinalNumber"
```

Element	Description
name	The name of the external routine as it is defined in its dynamic link library
ordinalNumber	The ordinal position of the routine in its dynamic link library

Comments

If *name* is used, the procedure name defined by the Alias keyword is case sensitive. It must exactly match the case of the procedure name as it is defined in the DLL.

There are two closely related reasons for using the Alias keyword when defining an external DLL routine, particularly one in the Win32 API:

- By convention, the function name itself is aliased. This is common in the Win32 API, where functions with string parameters have two versions: an ANSI (non-wide-string) version; and a wide-string (or Unicode) version. For instance, what is conventionally called the Win32 GetSystemDirectory function is actually two different functions, GetSystemDirectoryA and GetSystemDirectoryW. The Alias keyword allows you to specify the name by which the procedure is actually called, while allowing you to call it by its conventional name. For example, calling GetSystemDirectory requires the following Declare statement:

```
Private Declare Function GetSystemDirectory Lib "kernel32.dll" _
Alias "GetSystemDirectoryA" _
(ByVal lpBuffer As String, ByVal nSize As Integer) As Integer
```

The procedure can then be called with a code fragment like the following:

```
Dim buffer As String = Space(256)
Dim result As Integer = GetSystemDirectory(buffer, Len(buffer))
Console.WriteLine("System directory: {0}.", Left(buffer, result))
```

The function is typically referred to by a name other than its official name. For example, the CopyMemory function, which is used to directly access memory, is really not named CopyMemory at all, as its Declare statement shows:

```
Private Declare Sub CopyMemory Lib "kernel32.dll" _
Alias "RtlMoveMemory" _
(ByRef Destination As Any, ByRef Source As Any, _
ByVal Length As Integer)
```

- The Alias clause can also be used to identify the ordinal position of a procedure in its DLL. The DumpBin utility can be used to determine the ordinal position of a DLL's exports by using the syntax:

```
dumpbin dllname /exports
```

where *dllname* is the dynamic link library's filename. This produces output like the following for user32.dll, for instance:

```
ordinal hint RVA        name
      1    0 0001ECDD ActivateKeyboardLayout
      2    1 00021118 AdjustWindowRect
      3    2 000105A2 AdjustWindowRectEx
      4    3 0005D098 AlignRects
      5    4 000460AC AllowForegroundActivation
      6    5 0001B8D0 AllowSetForegroundWindow
      7    6 0001BBE6 AnimateWindow
      8    7 000597E7 AnyPopup
      9    8 00021ADF AppendMenuA
     10    9 0001CD4A AppendMenuW
     11    A 00045BDE ArrangeIconicWindows
     12    B 00021E23 AttachThreadInput
```

If the Auto keyword is used in the Declare statement, it is not necessary to use the Alias clause to specify the mangled name of an external routine. The .NET runtime will resolve the call dynamically based on the host system.

VB6 Comparison

The utility of the Alias keyword has declined somewhat not only because the Declare statement is less important in Visual Basic .NET than it was in Visual Basic 6.0, but also because two of the reasons for using it no longer apply. In Visual Basic 6.0, the Alias keyword was used to call procedures whose names contained illegal characters (such as the file manipulation functions in Kernel32.dll like _lcreat, _lopen, _lwrite, and _lclose). In Visual Basic .NET, these can be called without the Alias keyword. It was also used to call procedures (like the GetObject function in Gdi32.dll) whose names were the same as Visual Basic reserved words. However, in Visual Basic .NET, when a name conflicts with a reserved word, it need merely be placed in brackets to be recognized as a programming element other than the reserved word.

See Also

Auto Keyword, Declare Statement

Ansi Keyword

Used in the Declare statement to indicate that the .NET runtime should marshal any strings passed from .NET code to an external function from Unicode to ANSI, and should marshal strings returned by external function calls from ANSI to Unicode.

Syntax

See the syntax for the Declare statement.

Comments

Ansi is the default behavior. Alternatives to it are Unicode (all strings are marshaled as Unicode strings) and Auto (selection of the method name and string marshalling is resolved dynamically at runtime based on whether the system is ANSI or Unicode).

Ansi corresponds to setting the CharSet property of the DllImport attribute to CharSet.Ansi.

If the Ansi keyword is used either explicitly or as the default setting, the Declare statement must exactly specify the name of the external DLL routine to be called either in the Lib clause or in the body of the Declare statement itself. Calling a routine that has a mangled name only by its unmangled alias produces a runtime exception in Visual Basic .NET. This differs from the behavior of C#, in which the ExactSpelling property of the DllImport attribute is False by default so that the .NET runtime first attempts to locate an unmangled version of an ANSI function (such as MessageBox), followed by a mangled version (such as MessageBoxA).

There tends to be a good deal of confusion about the use of the Ansi keyword. In particular, it does not allow you to call wide-character versions of functions and convert the results back to ANSI. Because Ansi is the default, this means that you must use either the Unicode or Auto keyword with the Declare statement if you want to call a Unicode function.

Example

The code example consists of two short routines. The first is a standard call to the ANSI version of two functions in the Win32 API, GetSystemDirectory and MessageBox. In both cases, the Alias clause specifies the mangled name of the function as it exists in the DLL. The following code uses the Declare statement very much like the previous versions of Visual Basic:

```
Public Module AnsiTest

    Public Declare Ansi Function MessageBox Lib "User32.dll" _
          Alias "MessageBoxA" _
          (ByVal hWnd As IntPtr, ByVal lpText As String, _
          byVal lpCaption As String, ByVal uType As UShort) As Short

    Private Declare Ansi Function GetSystemDirectory Lib "kernel32.dll" _
          Alias "GetSystemDirectoryA" _
          (ByVal lpBuffer As String, ByVal nSize As Integer) As Integer

    Private Const MB_OK As Integer = &H0&
    Private Const MAX_LEN As Integer = 256

    Public Sub Main()
       Dim caption As String = "System Directory"
       Dim message As String
       Dim buffer As String = Space(MAX_LEN)
       Dim retChars As Integer

       retChars = GetSystemDirectory(buffer, Len(buffer))
       message = Left(buffer, retChars)

       MessageBox(Nothing, message, caption, MB_OK)
    End Sub
End Module
```

In contrast, the following code uses the <DllImport> attribute rather than the Declare statement to provide the .NET runtime with details about the two Win32 routines, and sets the attribute's ExactSpelling property to False so that .NET resolves the precise name of the function to be called at runtime:

```
Imports System.Runtime.InteropServices
Imports System.Text

Public Module AnsiTest

    <DllImport("User32.dll", EntryPoint:="MessageBox", ExactSpelling:=False)> _
    Private Function MessageBox(ByVal hWnd As IntPtr, ByVal lpText As String, _
            byVal lpCaption As String, ByVal uType As UShort) As Short
    End Function

    <DllImport("Kernel32.dll", EntryPoint:="GetSystemDirectory",
ExactSpelling:=False)> _
    Private Function GetSystemDirectory(ByVal lpBuffer As StringBuilder, _
            ByVal nSize As Integer) As Integer
    End Function

    Const MB_OK As Integer = &H0
    Const MAX_PATH As Integer = 260

    Public Sub Main()
        Dim caption As String = "System Directory"
        Dim buffer As New StringBuilder(MAX_PATH)

        GetSystemDirectory(buffer, MAX_PATH)
        MessageBox(Nothing, buffer.ToString(), caption, MB_OK)
    End Sub
End Module
```

VB6 Differences

The Ansi keyword is new to Visual Basic .NET.

See Also

Auto Keyword, Declare Statement, Unicode Keyword

AppActivate Subroutine

Gives the focus to a particular application window.

Namespace

Microsoft.VisualBasic.Interaction

Syntax

```
AppActivate(Title)
AppActivate(ProcessId)
```

Element	Description
Title	A String containing all or part of a window caption.
ProcessId	A Win32 process ID number.

Comments

If *Title* is supplied as an argument, the Visual Basic runtime performs a substring comparison of *Title* with the beginning of the captions of active windows.

If *Title* matches the caption of more than one open window, one of the windows is arbitrarily activated.

Title is not case sensitive.

AppActivate merely activates (or gives the focus to) an application window; it does not change its window state (for example, by maximizing a window that was previously minimized).

If no window has a caption beginning with *Title* or a process ID of *ProcessID*, AppActivate throws an ArgumentException.

AppActivate activates top-level windows only. It does not activate child windows or MDI windows.

If an application is launched using the Visual Basic Shell function, it can be activated by passing the process ID returned by the Shell function to the AppActivate subroutine. However, this technique does not always work reliably. For example, the code

```
Dim pid1, pid2 As Integer
Dim proc As Process

pid1 = Shell("Notepad.exe", vbNormalNoFocus)
proc = Process.GetProcessById(pid1)
If proc Is Nothing Then Exit Sub
pid2 = Shell("mspaint.exe", vbNormalFocus)
proc.WaitForInputIdle()
proc.Refresh
AppActivate(pid1)
```

fails to activate the Notepad window.

VB6 Differences

The AppActivate statement in Visual Basic 6.0 included a second parameter, *wait*, that determined whether the calling application had to have the focus before it could activate the window. This parameter is absent in Visual Basic .NET.

Some documentation for previous versions of Visual Basic described the return value of the Shell function and the numeric parameter of the AppActivate subroutine as the task ID and implied that it was different from the process ID. However, this was incorrect. The Shell function returned the process ID, and the AppActivate subroutine allows a window to be activated based on its process ID.

See Also

Shell Function

As Keyword

Begins an As clause, which constrains the legal types that may be stored in a variable or argument, returned by a function or property, or used as a generic type parameter.

Syntax

See the syntax for each of the respective statements that use the As keyword.

Comments

Since As is used in two very different ways, the following sections will discuss each usage separately.

As for Type Definition

The As keyword begins a clause defining a data type in the following statements:

- Const statement
- Declare statement
- Delegate statement
- Dim statement
- Enum statement
- Event statement
- For . . . Next statement
- For Each . . . Next statement
- Function statement
- Operator statement
- Property statement
- Structure statement
- Sub statement
- Try . . . Catch . . . Finally statement

Constraints

In Visual Basic 2005, you use the As clause to define constraints in generic parameter type lists when you are defining your own generic types. Constraints define the precise requirements that a type must meet in order to instantiate a parameterized type. For example, the statement

```
Public Class GenericArrayList(Of someType {As IEnumerable})
```

requires that the type that is supplied using the Of clause when instantiating GenericArrayList must implement the IEnumerable interface.

For the precise use of As in each of these cases, see the entry for the individual statement that uses As.

The general syntax of As when used for type definition is illustrated in the following Function statement, which defines the System.Data.OleDb.OleDbCommand class constructor:

```
Public Sub New(ByVal cmdText As String, _
            ByVal connection As OleDbConnection)
```

The As keyword is used twice here, once to define a parameter of type String, an intrinsic Visual Basic .NET type, and the second time to define a parameter of type OleDbConnection, a non-intrinsic type also defined in the System.Data.OleDb namespace.

In general, the As *type* clause can define any of the types listed in the following table:

Type	Description
Boolean	True/False, corresponding to System.Boolean.
Byte	An 8-bit unsigned integer, corresponding to System.Byte.
Char	A single character, corresponding to System.Char.
Date	For dates and times, corresponds to System.DateTime.
Decimal	A floating point (decimal) number, corresponding to System.Decimal.
Double	A double-precision floating point number, corresponding to System.Double.
Integer	A 32-bit signed integer, corresponding to System.Int32.
Long	A 64-bit signed integer, corresponding to System.Int64.
Object	A generic object reference type, the "universal" data type in .NET.
SByte	An 8-bit signed integer, corresponding to System.Sbyte.
Short	A 16-bit signed integer, corresponding to System.Int16.
Single	A single-precision floating point number, corresponding to System.Single.
String	A string, corresponding to System.String.
UInteger	A 32-bit unsigned integer, corresponding to System.UInt32.
ULong	A 64-bit unsigned integer, corresponding to System.UInt64.
UShort	A 16-bit unsigned integer, corresponding to System.UInt16.
<enum>	An enumeration, which is a named set of constants derived indirectly from the System.Enum class. In Visual Basic, such value types are defined with the Enum . . . End Enum construct.
<object>	A specific reference type derived directly or indirectly from System.Object. In Visual Basic, such types are defined with the Class . . . End Class, Interface . . . End Interface, and Delegate constructs.
<structure>	A specific value type derived indirectly from the System.ValueType class. In Visual Basic, such value types are defined with the Structure . . . End Structure construct.

As for Constraint Definition

The As keyword is used to introduce a constraint on a generic type parameter in the following statements:

- Class statement
- Delegate statement
- Interface statement

The general syntax for As when defining a constraint is:

```
Of(parameterName As constraintlist)
```

If there is a single constraint, it simply appears after the As keyword. For example:

```
Public Class GenericArray(Of value As IEnumerable)
```

This statement defines a class named GenericArray whose defined type (the type that can be supplied using the Of keyword when instantiating the generic type) must implement the IEnumerable interface.

If there are multiple constraints, they are enclosed in brackets and separated from one another by commas. For example:

```
Public Class GenericArray2(Of value As {IEnumerable, Class})
```

This statement defines a class named GenericArray2 whose defined type must be a reference type that implements the IEnumerable interface.

The following constraints can be applied to a generic type parameter:

- The names of the interface or interfaces that the defined type must implement. Practically, there is no limit to the number of interfaces that can be required.
- The name of a single class that the defined type must be derived from.
- The New keyword, indicating that the defined type must have a public parameterless constructor.
- The Class keyword, indicating that the defined type must be a reference type. (If you include the Class keyword, you can't include the Structure keyword.)
- The Structure keyword, indicating that the defined type must be a value type. (If you include the Structure keyword, you can't include the Class keyword.)

The Example provides some code that illustrates the use of the As keyword in a generic class definition.

Example

The example is a very simple one that defines a generic class, GenericArray, to wrap the ArrayList class. The generic class imposes two restraints on its type parameter: it must implement IEnumerable, and it must be a reference type. Later, we attempt to instantiate our generic class with a String data type; the String class is a reference type that implements IEnumerable. Had we attempted to use a Char as the defining type, however, the Visual Basic compiler would have generated an error and displayed the message, "'Char' does not inherit from or implement the constraint type 'System.Collections.IEnumerable'."

```vb
Imports System.Collections

Public Class GenericArray(Of refType As {IEnumerable, Class})
    Implements IEnumerable

    Private aList as New ArrayList

    Public Sub Add(item As reftype)
        aList.Add(item)
    End Sub

    Public Function Item(ByVal index As Integer) As refType
        Return DirectCast(aList.Item(index), refType)
    End Function

    Public Sub Sort()
        aList.Sort()
    End Sub

    Public Function GetEnumerator() As IEnumerator _
        Implements IEnumerable.GetEnumerator
        Return aList.GetEnumerator
    End Function
End Class

Public Module modMain
    Public Sub Main()
        Dim arr As New GenericArray(Of String)
        arr.Add("Toyota")
        arr.Add("Ford")
        arr.Add("Honda")
        arr.Add("Volvo")
        arr.Add("BMW")
        arr.Add("Saab")
        arr.Add("Kia")
        arr.Sort()
        For Each car As String In arr
            Console.WriteLine(car)
        Next
    End Sub
End Module
```

VB.NET Changes

The use of the As keyword to introduce constraints on generic type parameters is new as of Visual Basic 2005.

Visual Basic 2005 introduces several new intrinsic data types, including SByte, UInt16, UInt32, and UInt64. Previously, they could only be instantiated as types in the .NET class library.

VB6 Differences

Visual Basic 6.0 did not support generic parameters and so did not support the As keyword as a constraint on generic type parameters.

Visual Basic 6.0 supported an As Any type declaration with the Declare statement that allowed an argument of any type to be passed to a property, function, or subroutine. This syntax is not supported in Visual Basic .NET; instead, method overloading is the preferred (and type-safe) method of allowing a single method to accept arguments of different types.

Two Visual Basic data types (Variant, Currency) declared with the As keyword are not supported in Visual Basic .NET. The Variant data type as the "universal" data type of Visual Basic 6.0 has been replaced with the Object, and the Decimal data type should be used instead of Currency.

Visual Basic .NET adds a range of unsigned (UShort, UInteger, ULong) and signed (SByte) data types, along with the Char data type, that were not supported in Visual Basic 6.0.

See Also

Dim Statement, Function Statement, Of Keyword, Property Statement, Sub Statement

Asc, AscW Functions

Returns the character code that represents a character.

Member Of

Microsoft.VisualBasic.Strings

Syntax

For the Asc function:

```
Asc(string As String)
Asc(string As Char)
```

For the AscW function:

```
AscW(string As String)
AscW(string As Char)
```

Element	Description
string	Any String or Char expression.

Return Value

An integer containing the character code represented by *string*.

Comments

If *string* is an expression of type String, the function returns the character code of the first character in the string.

If *string* is an empty string, an ArgumentException is thrown.

Since Visual Basic .NET is a Unicode system, the AscW function is preferable to Asc.

As an alternative to calling the Asc and AscW functions, you can pass a Char to the Framework Class Library's Convert.ToInt32 function.

The Asc or AscW function was often used in Visual Basic 6.0 to determine if a particular character in a string was uppercase or lowercase. The function would return the numeric value of the character, which was then compared to the numeric range of uppercase (65–90) or lowercase (97–122) characters. For example, Visual Basic 6 code might look like the following:

```
Dim c As String
Dim ascVal As Integer

c = InputBox("Enter a letter: ")
ascVal = Asc(c)
If ascVal >= 65 And ascVal <= 90 Then
    Debug.Print "The character is uppercase."
Else
    If ascVal >= 97 And ascVal <= 122 Then
        Debug.Print "The character is lowercase."
    End If
End If
```

The shared IsUpper and IsLower methods of the Char class accomplish the same purpose, with the added advantage that they work on Unicode characters, whereas the preceding code just works on A–Z and a–z.

In some cases, alphanumeric character strings are stored in binary format. This is sometimes the case in the Windows registry, for example, if strings are stored as data of type REG_BINARY instead of type REG_SZ. In such cases, the ASC and ASCW were typically used for iterating each character of a string, which would then be converted to its binary representation and added to the appropriate position in a Byte array. In .NET, however, these operations are performed far more efficiently in a single method call by calling the GetBytes method of one of the character encoding classes (such as System.Text.UTF32Encoding, which encodes a string into four-byte characters, or System.Text .UnicodeEncoding, which encodes a string into two-byte characters, or UTF8Encoding, which encodes a string into one-byte characters). For example:

```
Dim encode16 As New UnicodeEncoding
Dim textToConvert As String = "This is a string."
Dim binaryValues() As Byte = encode16.GetBytes(textToConvert)
```

VB6 Differences

Visual Basic 6.0 included the AscB function, which accepted a one-byte character as an argument. It is no longer supported in Visual Basic .NET.

See Also

Chr, ChrW Functions

Assembly Keyword

Indicates that an attribute applies to an entire assembly, rather than to an individual programming element within it.

Syntax

```
<Assembly:attribute(arglist)>
```

Element	Description
attribute	The attribute to be applied to the assembly.
arglist	The attribute's optional argument list.

Comments

Ordinarily, attributes are placed immediately before the language element to which they apply. Since there is no assembly element, the Assembly keyword is used to indicate that the attribute applies to an assembly.

The Assembly keyword must precede any declarations in a program file; that is, it must precede any Namespace, Class, Module, Structure, Interface, and Enumeration statements. It must immediately follow any Option and Imports statements. It can either proceed or follow the Module keyword.

If multiple attributes are to be applied to an assembly or module, you can place them all in a single statement (i.e., a single set of < and > brackets). However, each attribute that applies to the assembly must be preceded by the Assembly keyword. For example:

```
<Assembly: AssemblyTitle("Assembly1"), _
Assembly: AssemblyDescription("Illustrates the Assembly keyword")>
```

If you're using Visual Studio, you can also place attributes that apply to an entire assembly in the AssemblyInfo.vb file. Figure 8-4 shows a portion of an AssemblyInfo.vb file with the assembly-level attributes that Visual Studio automatically applies to any project.

FIGURE 8-4

A portion of an AssemblyInfo.vb file

```
Imports System
Imports System.Reflection
Imports System.Runtime.InteropServices

' General Information about an assembly is controlled through the following
' set of attributes. Change these attribute values to modify the information
' associated with an assembly.

' Review the values of the assembly attributes

<Assembly: AssemblyTitle("ConsoleApplication1")>
<Assembly: AssemblyDescription("")>
<Assembly: AssemblyCompany("")>
<Assembly: AssemblyProduct("ConsoleApplication1")>
<Assembly: AssemblyCopyright("Copyright @  2004")>
<Assembly: AssemblyTrademark("")>

<Assembly: ComVisible(False)>

'The following GUID is for the ID of the typelib if this project is exposed to COM
<Assembly: Guid("1527f2a8-3feb-4516-991b-24c4117d4178")>

' Version information for an assembly consists of the following four values:
'
'       Major Version
'       Minor Version
'       Build Number
'       Revision
'
' You can specify all the values or you can default the Build and Revision Numbers
' by using the '*' as shown below:
' <Assembly: AssemblyVersion("1.0.*")>

<Assembly: AssemblyVersion("1.0.0.0")>
<Assembly: AssemblyFileVersion("1.0.0.0")>
```

The CLSCompliant attribute is commonly applied using the Assembly keyword. The attribute has a single required parameter, *isCompliant,* a Boolean that indicates whether the compiler should enforce compliance with the Common Language Specification. You can use the attribute to ensure that your code is CLS-compliant using code something like the following:

```
<Assembly:CLSCompliant(True)>

Public Class AssemblyClass
    ' code for class
End Class
```

Because Assembly is both a Visual Basic keyword and the name of a .NET class (in the System.Reflection namespace), attempting to define an Assembly object may produce a compiler error. In that case, simply bracket the variable type, as follows:

```
Dim assem As [Assembly]
```

Example

The following code fragment illustrates the placement of the Assembly keyword in a file:

```
' Comments can go anywhere
Option Strict On

Imports System.Collections

<Assembly:ClsCompliant(True)>
Namespace Utilities
    Public Class UtilLib
```

VB6 Differences

The Assembly keyword is new to Visual Basic .NET. Visual Basic 6.0 did not support assemblies or attributes.

See Also

Module Keyword

Auto Keyword

Used with the Declare statement to resolve an external function or subroutine name at runtime.

Syntax

See the syntax for the Declare statement.

Comments

The Auto keyword can be used instead of the Ansi or Unicode keywords. If none is used, Ansi is the default.

Auto is a partial substitute for the Lib clause in the Declare statement, as the example shows. It allows .NET to dynamically invoke the Unicode or Ansi version of an external routine, depending on the platform on which the code is running.

Ordinarily, the name of the routine that an application calls is determined by the string provided as an argument to the Alias clause or, if none is present, by the name of the function or subroutine. If the Auto keyword is present, the exact routine that the .NET runtime attempts to invoke depends on the platform on which the code is running. On ANSI platforms (like Windows 95, Windows 98, and Windows ME), the .NET runtime first attempts to execute the procedure by its name and, if that fails, then appends an "A" to the end of its name and attempts to execute a procedure with that name. On Unicode platforms (Windows NT, Windows 2000, and Windows XP), it first appends a "W" to the end of the procedure name and attempts to locate a procedure with that name. If the attempt fails, it then attempts to execute the routine by its original name.

The Auto keyword also means that the case is ignored when attempting to identify the name of the function or subroutine. This differs from the typical behavior of the Declare statement, in which declared function or subroutine names must correspond exactly to the case of functions or subroutines as they are defined in their dynamic link library.

Example

Typically, the Alias clause is used to specify the Ansi or Unicode version of a procedure with string parameters. For example, in calling the Win32 GetSystemDirectory function, the following customary Declare statement indicates that the name by which the function is to be called in code is GetSystemDirectory, and the Alias clause indicates that the routine that is actually to be executed in the kernel32.dll dynamic link library is GetSystemDirectoryA:

```
Private Declare Function GetSystemDirectory Lib "kernel32.dll" _
        Alias "GetSystemDirectoryA" _
        (ByVal lpBuffer As String, ByVal nSize As Integer) As Integer
```

However, by using the Auto keyword, we can dispense with the Alias clause and have .NET runtime attempt to invoke GetSystemDirectory and either GetSystemDirectoryA or GetSystemDirectoryW, depending on the host platform. For example:

```
Public Module modTestAuto

    Private Declare Auto Function GetSystemDirectory Lib "kernel32.dll" _
            (ByVal lpBuffer As String, ByVal nSize As Integer) As Integer

    Public Sub Main()
        Dim buffer As String = Space(1024)
        Dim retString As Integer = GetSystemDirectory(buffer, Len(buffer))
        buffer = Left(buffer, retString)
        Console.WriteLine("The Windows system directory is {0}.", buffer)
    End Sub
End Module
```

Despite the failure of the Declare statement to specify the precise name of the procedure in the DLL, the .NET runtime is able to resolve the function and produces output like the following:

```
The Windows system directory is C:\WINDOWS\system32.
```

VB6 Differences

The Auto keyword is new to Visual Basic .NET.

See Also

Ansi Keyword, Declare Statement, Lib Keyword, Unicode Keyword

Beep Subroutine

Sounds a tone on the computer's speaker.

Namespace

Microsoft.VisualBasic.Interaction

Syntax

```
Beep()
```

Comments

The exact frequency and duration of the tone depend on the individual computer system.

As even low-end computers have become excellent multimedia platforms, the ability of Beep to communicate information to users has diminished. Its use is appropriate in either of the following situations:

- The system does not have multimedia support. (To determine whether sound is supported, see the next item.)

- You want to use sound to respond to an event for which Windows would ordinarily play its Default Beep sound. Even in this case, however, you can't be certain that the beep corresponds to the sound that the individual system produces in response to the Default Beep event.

You can determine whether sound is supported on a system at runtime by calling the Win32 mixerGetNumDevs function. Its syntax is:

```
Private Declare Function mixerGetNumDevs Lib "winmm.dll" () As Integer
```

It returns the number of sound devices present on a system. Note that some documentation suggests that you use the Win32 auxGetNumDevs function for this purpose. However, auxGetNumDevs is a "legacy" function developed for an older generation of multimedia hardware and will generally report the absence of sound support on most Windows systems.

A far better method of using sound to communicate with the user is to select an appropriate one of the system sounds defined on the user's system. (System sounds are played by the system in response to specific events, such as a Windows or an application program closing or a warning dialog appearing. They are defined on the System Sounds tab of the Sounds and Audio Devices applet in Control Panel.) The code example (as well as the next comment) illustrates how to use a system sound in version 2.0 of the .NET framework.

Version 2.0 of the .NET framework includes a System.Media.SystemSounds class that returns any of five system sounds (Asterisk, Default Beep, Exclamation, Hand, Question), each of which is represented by a System.Media.SystemSound object. A static property of the SystemSounds class with the same name as the system sound returns that sound. The SystemSound class' Play method then plays that sound. For example:

```
' Operation not permitted
SystemSounds.Hand.Play()
```

Example

The example program defines a utility class named SoundUtil that determines whether a system has sound capabilities in its class constructor. When its PlayWarning message is called, it can then play the Hand system sound if sound is supported or beep if it is not.

```
Imports System.Media

Public Class SoundUtil
    Private Declare Function mixerGetNumDevs Lib "winmm.dll" () As Integer

    Private soundEnabled As Boolean = False

    Public Sub New()
        If mixerGetNumDevs > 0 Then soundEnabled = True
    End Sub

    Public Sub PlayWarning
        If soundEnabled Then
            Dim hand As SystemSound = SystemSounds.Hand
            hand.Play()
        Else
            Beep
        End If
    End Sub
End Class
```

See Also

My.Computer.Audio Property

ByRef and ByVal Keywords

Indicate that an argument is passed by reference or by value, respectively, to a called method.

Syntax

```
ByRef | ByVal parameterName [As type]
```

Element	Description
parameterName	The name of the parameter. It can be used as a named argument when calling the method.
type	The parameter's data type. It is required if Option Strict is on; otherwise, it is optional but highly recommended. If Option Strict is off and type is omitted, it is an Object by default.

Comments

The ByRef and ByVal keywords are used in parameter lists with the Declare, Delegate, Event, Function, Property, Set, and Sub statements.

ByRef means that *parameterName* is an alias for the argument passed to the member. Therefore, any modifications that might be made to *parameterName* persist when control returns to the calling routine. The following is a simple example:

```
Public Module modMain
    Public Sub Main()
        Dim number As Integer = 10
        If Cube(number) Then Console.WriteLine(number)
    End Sub

    Private Function Cube(ByRef value As Integer) As Boolean
        Try
            value = CInt(value ^ 3)
            Return True
        Catch
            Return False
        End Try
    End Function
End Module
```

After the call to the Cube function, the value of number is 1000 rather than 10 because number is cubed in the cube function, and this value persists when control returns to the calling routine because number is passed to the Cube function by reference rather than by value.

ByVal means that a copy of the data, rather than a reference to the data, is passed as an argument. Therefore, any modifications that might be made to *parameterName* are discarded when control returns to the calling routine. The following is a simple example:

```
Public Module modMain
    Public Sub Main()
        Dim number As Integer = 100
        Console.WriteLine("Before the function call, the value of number is {0}.", _
                          number)
        Console.WriteLine("The value returned by Increment() is {0}.", _
                          Increment(number))
        Console.WriteLine("After the function call, the value of number is {0}.", _
                          number)
    End Sub

    Public Function Increment(ByVal value As Integer) As Integer
        value += 1
        Return value
    End Function
End Module
```

Here, even though the value of number is increased by one in the Increment function, its value remains unchanged when control returns to the module's Main procedure because it is passed by value rather than by reference.

A read-only variable, field, or property value can be passed to method by reference without generating a runtime exception. However, the variable, field, or property is effectively passed by value; when control returns to the caller, its value is unchanged.

In designing method parameters, you should carefully consider whether it is necessary to pass a parameter by reference, since it leaves method arguments exposed to accidental or unintended change.

There is some confusion between reference types and by reference parameters. Reference types can be passed both by reference and by value. When a reference type other than a string is passed by value, changes to type members nevertheless persist. For example, the following code defines a class, Automobile, that has two properties, Year and Model. Values for these properties are provided in the class constructor, and the properties can also be changed individually. The code for the automobile class is:

```
Public Class Automobile
    Private modelName As String
    Private modelYear As Integer

    Public Sub New(name As String, year As Integer)
        MyBase.New
        Me.modelName = name
        Me.modelYear = year
    End Sub

    Public Property Year() As Integer
        Get
            Return Me.modelYear
        End Get
        Set
            Me.modelYear = value
        End Set
    End Property

    Public ReadOnly Property Model() As String
        Get
            Return modelName
        End Get
    End Property
End Class
```

The module that instantiates the Automobile class also includes the following methods to change the automobile's year (the ChangeAutomobileYear method) and to replace the existing Automobile object with a different one (the ChangeAutomobileValue method):

```
Private Sub ChangeAutomobileYear(ByVal auto As Automobile)
    auto.year = auto.year + 3
End Sub

Private Sub ChangeAutomobileValue(ByVal auto As Automobile)
    Dim newAuto As New Automobile("Accord", 2003)
    auto = newAuto
End Sub
```

Note that in both cases, the Automobile instance is passed by value to the method. When the following code executes and calls these methods:

```
Dim auto As New Automobile("Corolla", 2002)
Console.WriteLine("Automobile year before change: {0}", auto.Year)
ChangeAutomobileYear(auto)
Console.WriteLine("Automobile year after change: {0}", auto.Year)
ChangeAutomobileValue(auto)
Console.WriteLine("Automobile is a {0} {1}", auto.Year, auto.Model)
```

the output to the console window is:

```
Automobile year before change: 2002
Automobile year after change: 2005
Automobile is a 2005 Corolla
```

In other words, changes to the Automobile object's Year property persisted even though the Automobile object was passed to the procedure by reference. More generally, even though an object is passed by value when calling a function or procedure, changes to its properties and public writable fields persist when control returns to the caller. The ChangeAutomobileValue procedure also receives an Automobile object by value, but it doesn't change an individual property value; it attempts to replace the Automobile object passed to it as an argument with a completely different Automobile object that is declared and instantiated within the subroutine. When control returns to the caller, however, this change is lost, and the Automobile object in the caller is the original one.

In contrast, consider the following variation of the ChangeAutomobileValue subroutine, which instead accepts the Automobile object instance passed to it by reference rather than by value:

```
Private Sub ChangeAutomobile(ByRef auto As Automobile)
    Dim newAuto As New Automobile("Accord", 2003)
    auto = newAuto
End Sub
```

When the Automobile object from the preceding code is passed to this method, the output produced is:

```
Automobile is a 2003 Accord
```

Here, one Automobile object instance has been replaced by another, different Automobile object instance. This makes the meaning of passing values of reference types by value and by reference clear. Passing a variable of a reference type by value allows individual member values to be changed. It does not, however, allow the reference itself to be changed or replaced with another reference. Passing a reference type by reference, on the other hand, allows the reference itself to be replaced with another reference.

There is a difference between a value type and a parameter passed by value. The behavior of value types passed by value differs from that of reference types that are passed by value. For example, to modify the code used in the previous Automobile class, the following class defines an Automotible structure (a value type):

```
Public Structure Automobile
    Private modelName As String
    Private modelYear As Integer
```

```vb
    Public Sub New(name As String, year As Integer)
        Me.modelName = name
        Me.modelYear = year
    End Sub

    Public Property Year() As Integer
        Get
            Return Me.modelYear
        End Get
        Set
            Me.modelYear = value
        End Set
    End Property

    Public ReadOnly Property Model() As String
        Get
            Return modelName
        End Get
    End Property
End Structure
```

The following code creates an Automobile instance, attempts to change a property value, and then twice attempts to replace the existing Automobile instance with a new Automobile instance:

```vb
Public Module modMain
    Public Sub Main()
        Dim auto As New Automobile("Corolla", 2002)
        Console.WriteLine("Automobile year before change: {0}", auto.Year)
        ChangeAutomobileYear(auto)
        Console.WriteLine("Automobile year after change: {0}", auto.Year)
        ChangeAutomobileValue(auto)
        Console.WriteLine("Automobile is a {0} {1}", auto.Year, auto.Model)
        Dim oldAuto As Automobile = auto
        ChangeAutomobile(auto)
        Console.WriteLine("Automobile is a {0} {1}", auto.Year, auto.Model)
    End Sub

    Private Sub ChangeAutomobileYear(ByVal auto As Automobile)
        auto.year = auto.year + 3
    End Sub

    Private Sub ChangeAutomobileValue(ByVal auto As Automobile)
        Dim newAuto As New Automobile("Accord", 2003)
        auto = newAuto
    End Sub

    Private Sub ChangeAutomobile(ByRef auto As Automobile)
        auto.Year = 2006
    End Sub
End Module
```

The program produces the following output:

```
Automobile year before change: 2002
Automobile year after change: 2002
Automobile is a 2002 Corolla
Automobile is a 2006 Corolla
```

This code and its output clarify the meaning of passing a value type by value and by reference. Because Automobile here is a value type, and the first two method calls pass an Automobile instance by value, the modifications to Automobile object values do not persist when control returns to the caller because the called routines have been modifying a copy of the original object, rather than the original object itself. In the final method call, Automobile is passed by value, which means that the called subroutine receives a reference to the Automobile instance. In this case, the result of passing a value type by reference is comparable to passing a reference type by value; modifications to individual property values persist.

The ByRef keyword can be overridden and an argument instead passed by value by enclosing the argument in an extra set of parentheses in the method call. For example, the following code defines a method, Increment, that has a by reference parameter. Despite this, number is passed to it by value because it is enclosed in an extra set of parentheses:

```
Public Module modMain
    Public Sub Main()
        Dim number As Integer = 10
        Increment(number)
        Console.WriteLine("Number after call to increment: {0}", number)
        Increment((number))
        Console.WriteLine("Number after parens around argument: {0}", number)
    End Sub

    Public Sub Increment(ByRef value As Integer)
        value += 1
    End Sub
End Module
```

VB6 Differences

In Visual Basic 6.0, parameters were passed by reference by default, and the use of the ByRef keyword was optional. In Visual Basic .NET, parameters are passed by value by default, and ByRef must be used to pass a parameter by reference.

In Visual Basic 6.0, parentheses were not used to invoke subroutines called without the Call keyword. Parentheses could be used with a single argument, however, to pass it by value instead of by reference. In Visual Basic .NET, parentheses are required to surround the argument list when calling subroutines. As a result, the following code,

```
' Code in Main() routine
Dim stringValue As String
stringValue = "Original String"
ChangeString (stringValue)
MsgBox ("stringValue: " & stringValue)

Private Sub ChangeString(ByRef strng As String)
    strng = "New Value"
End Sub
```

passes stringValue by value in Visual Basic 6.0 but by reference in Visual Basic .NET.

In Visual Basic 6.0, it was possible to override the default method of passing an argument to a parameter defined as type As Any by specifying the ByVal keyword in the function call. (The As Any clause could be used with the Declare statement only.) In Visual Basic .NET, the As Any clause is not supported, and the ability to define a by-value argument in the method call is not supported.

In Visual Basic 6.0, object properties and fields were always passed by value regardless of whether the called method defined its parameter as by value or by reference. In Visual Basic .NET, object properties and fields can be passed either by value or by reference just as any non-object variable can.

See Also

Declare Statement, Delegate Statement, Event Statement, FunctionStatement, Property Statement, Sub Statement

Call Statement

Calls a function, subroutine, class method, or external dynamic link library routine.

Syntax

```
Call ProcedureName[(ArgumentList)]
```

Element	Description
ProcedureName	The name of the function, subroutine, or external DLL routine.
ArgumentList	Zero, one, or more arguments to pass to *ProcedureName*, separated by commas. If any arguments are present, *ArgumentList* must be enclosed in parentheses; otherwise, parentheses can be omitted. For details on the syntax of *ArgumentList*, see the entry for the Sub statement.

Comments

The Call statement is obsolete. Subroutines, functions, methods, and external DLL routines can all be called without using the Call statement.

If the Call statement is used to call a function or a method that returns a value, that return value is always discarded.

If an argument is passed by reference to a method, you can override this behavior in the function call and instead pass the argument by value by enclosing it in an extra set of parentheses. For example, the following function has two parameters passed to it by reference, which it then doubles:

```
Private Function DoubleSumTwoNums(ByRef num1 As Integer, ByRef num2 As Integer) _
                        As Integer
    num1 = num1 * 2
    num2 = num2 * 2
    Return num1 * num2
End Function
```

However, if the function is invoked as follows, only the second argument is passed by value:

```
Call DoubleSumTwoNums(sum1, (sum2))
```

The Call statement cannot be used to access a property value.

Arguments can be passed to a called function or subroutine either positionally or using named arguments. The name of a particular arguments corresponds to the name assigned to it in the documentation or the name displayed using a reflection tool such as ILDasm. For example, the following code illustrates a call to the FileOpen function using positional arguments:

```
Call FileOpen(fileNo, filename, OpenMode.Append)
```

The following is the equivalent function call using named arguments:

```
Call FileOpen(fileNumber := fileNo, mode = OpenMode.Append, fileName := filename)
```

Note that named arguments to not have to appear in a particular order, while positional arguments do.

VB6 Differences

Visual Basic 6.0 allowed you to override the method by which an argument was passed by specifying ByVal or ByRef before the argument when the function or procedure was called. This is not supported in Visual Basic .NET. However, you can still pass an argument by value instead of by reference by enclosing it in an extra set of parentheses.

See Also

Function Statement, Sub Statement, Declare Statement

CallByName Function

Invokes a method or accesses a property's set or get accessor dynamically at runtime.

Member Of

Microsoft.VisualBasic.Interaction class

Syntax

```
CallByName(ByVal ObjectRef As Object, ByVal ProcName As String, _
    ByVal UseCallType As CallType, ByVal Args() As Object)
```

Element	Description
ObjectRef	A reference to the object whose method or property is being called.
ProcName	The name of the property or method being called.
UseCallType	A member of the CallType enumeration indicating the type of procedure call. Possible values are CallType.Method (a method call), CallType.Get (a property get accessor), or CallType.Set (a property set accessor).
Args()	A parameter array containing the arguments to pass to *ProcName*.

Return Value

For methods with a return value and property get accessors, CallByName returns an Object whose runtime type is that of the return value of *ProcName*. For methods with no return value and property set accessors, the CallByName function returns Nothing.

Comments

The CallByName method is intended for calling an object member at runtime when either its name or the class it belongs to is not known at design time.

In addition to invoking methods and assigning and retrieving property values, you can also retrieve field values and, if they are not read-only, assign them as well. (Fields are public variables of a class.) To do this, you use the CallByName method as if you were retrieving or setting a property value, and use the CallType.Get enumerated value for the *UseCallType* parameter to retrieve a field value and the CallType.Set enumerated value to set a field value.

Since *Args()* is a parameter array, you have considerable flexibility in passing arguments to the method being called. If it has no arguments, you can pass Nothing as the value of *Args()*, or you can simply omit *Args()*. For instance, the following code retrieves the value of the Count property of an ArrayList object:

```
Dim alist As New ArrayList
CallByName(alist, "Add", CallType.Method, "MethodCall")
Dim count As Integer = CInt(CallByName(alist, "Count", CallType.Get))
```

If the method takes a single parameter, you can either package it in an array or simply include it as the fourth argument to the CallByName function, as in the previous late-bound call to the ArrayList object's Add method. If the method being called has multiple parameters, you can pass the arguments in an array, as in the following call to the Hashtable object's Add method:

```
Dim htable As New Hashtable
Dim args() As String = {"WA", "Washington"}
CallByName(htable, "Add", CallType.Method, args)
```

Alternatively, you can simply include multiple arguments at the end of the CallByName argument list, separating each with a comma, as in the following call to the Hashtable object's Add method:

```
CallByName(htable, "Add", CallType.Method, "NY", "New York")
```

Whether you use an array or list the arguments serially, they must appear in the order required by the method's syntax.

You cannot call a shared method by specifying *ObjectRef* as a type. For example, the following call to the shared String.IsNullOrEmpty method generates a rather misleading error message ("'Of' required when specifying type arguments for a generic type or method."):

```
If DirectCast(CallByName(String, "IsNullOrEmpty", CallType.Method, _
                    msg), Boolean) Then
```

Fortunately, Visual Basic .NET allows you to invoke shared members either by using the name of the type whose shared member you care calling or by using the name of an instance object of that type. The following code successfully uses CallByName to invoke the static String.Clear method:

```
Public Sub Main()
    Dim stringArray() As String = {"Integer", "Byte", "Long", _
                                   "Short", "Double", "Single"}
    Dim params() As Object = {stringArray, 0, stringArray.Length}

    CallByName(stringArray, "Clear", CallType.Method, params)
    Console.WriteLine("Contents of String array after call to Clear method: ")
For ctr As Integer = stringArray.GetLowerBound(0) To _
                     stringArray.GetUpperBound(0)
    Console.WriteLine("{0}. {1}", ctr, stringArray(ctr))
    Next
End Sub
```

CallByName cannot be used to invoke methods in Visual Basic .NET code modules (methods inside a Module . . . End Module construct). However, they are available using reflection. The following, for example, is a module that contains a very simple function we'd like to call at runtime:

```
Public Module MathLib
    Public Function Square(x As Integer) As Long
        Return x ^ 2
    End Function
End Module
```

The following code loads the module dynamically and invokes its Square method using reflection:

```
Public Module TestReflection
    Public Sub Main()
        Dim modAssem As [Assembly] = [Assembly].LoadFrom("MathLib.dll")
        Dim typ As Type = modAssem.GetType("MathLib")
        dim method As MethodInfo = typ.GetMethod("Square")
        Dim parms() As Object = {4}
        Console.WriteLine(method.Invoke(typ, parms))
    End Sub
End Module
```

Although endless variations on this code are possible, the basic steps are the same: loading an assembly dynamically, retrieving a reference to the Type object whose method is to be called from it, retrieving a MethodInfo object representing the method to be called from its Type object, and invoking the method.

The CallByName function also allows arguments to be passed only by value to called methods. This means that, if a method ordinarily receives an argument passed by reference and modifies its value, that changed value is not reflected when control returns to the caller. The work-around, once again, is reflection: the type can be retrieved from its assembly, an instance of the type can be instantiated dynamically, the MethodInfo object representing the method we'd like to call can be retrieved from the Type object, and the method can be invoked dynamically by calling the MethodInfo object's Invoke method and passing it an instance of the type whose method we are invoking and an array of Objects containing the method arguments. (Note that we could also call a shared method in the same way, except that we can pass Nothing in place of the instance of the type as the first parameter to the Invoke method.) The following code illustrates a correct early-bound function call, two late-bound calls using CallByName in which the argument passed by reference is not updated by the called method, and a method call using the MethodInfo object's Invoke method in which the by reference argument is modified by the called routine:

```
Imports System.Reflection

Public Module modMain
    Public Sub Main()
        Dim rm As New RefMethod
        Dim param As Integer = 3
        Dim params() As Object = {param}

        ' Call method ordinarily
        If rm.Increment(param) Then _
            Console.WriteLine("Calling method ordinarily: {0}", param)

        ' Call method using array as final argument
        params(0) = 3
        If CBool(CallByName(rm, "Increment", CallType.Method, params)) = True Then
            Console.WriteLine("Calling method with array argument: {0}", params(0))
        End If

        ' Call method using integer as final argument
        param = 3
        If CBool(CallByName(rm, "Increment", CallType.Method, param)) = True Then
            Console.WriteLine("Calling method with integer argument: {0}", param)
        End If

        ' Call method using reflection
        params(0) = 3
        Dim assem As [Assembly] = [Assembly].GetExecutingAssembly()
        Dim typ As Type = assem.GetType("RefMethod")
        Dim targetObj As Object = assem.CreateInstance("RefMethod")
        Dim method As MethodInfo = typ.GetMethod("Increment")
        If CBool(method.Invoke(targetObj, params)) Then
            Console.WriteLine("Calling method using reflection: {0}", CInt(params(0)))
        End If
    End Sub
End Module

Public Class RefMethod
    Public Function Increment(ByRef value As Integer) As Boolean
        Try
            value += 1
            Return True
        Catch
            Return False
        End Try
    End Function
End Class
```

Since the name of the method or property being called is not known at runtime, CallByName results in a late-bound method call. This means that, for performance reasons, you don't want to call CallByName as a matter of routine, but only when you genuinely don't know the name of the property or method to call at design time.

If you need to use late-bound calls to properties or methods, the reflection classes in the .NET framework offer far greater flexibility, reliability, and robustness than the CallByName function.

See Also

Call Statement

Case Keyword

Used with the Select Case statement to define the individual values against which the statement's test expression is to be evaluated.

Syntax

```
Case expressionList
Case Else
```

Element	Description
expressionList	One or more expressions whose value matches a possible value of the Select Case statement's test expression.

Comments

Each expression in *expressionList* is compared with the test expression until one is found to be true.

Each expression in *expressionList* must be of the same type as the Select Case statement's test expression, which can be elementary data type (Boolean, Byte, Char, Date, etc.). If it is not, the Visual Basic compiler will attempt to perform an implicit conversion. If Option Strict is on, narrowing conversions will generate compiler errors.

expressionList can be one or more of the following:

- A single expression. For example, if the Select Case statement's test expression is an integer, a valid Case clause is:

  ```
  Case 1
  ```

- An inclusive range of values. For example, the following clause is executed if the test expression is an integer between 2 and 6:

  ```
  Case 2 To 6
  ```

- An explicit comparison. This clause takes the form

  ```
  [Is] comparisonOperator expression
  ```

  where *comparisonOperator* is any comparison operator (=, <>, <, <=, >, >=). For example:

  ```
  Case Is < 0
  ```

Note that a logical operator cannot be included. The following, for example, is illegal:

```
Case (Is < 0) Or (Is > 100)          ' Illegal
```

Multiple expressions can be evaluated by a single Case clause if they are separated with commas. For example:

```
Case Is < 0, Is > 12
```

The code following the Case Else clause is executed if none of the Case clauses evaluates to True.

See Also

Select Case Statement, If . . . Then . . . End If Statement

Catch Keyword

Used with the Try statement to introduce a code block that executes if an exception is thrown.

Syntax

```
Catch [exceptionVar [ As exceptionType ] ] [ When expression ]
```

Element	Description
exceptionVar	The name by which the Exception object will be referenced in the code block.
exceptionType	The type of exception to be handled.
expression	Any expression that evaluates to a Boolean. If *expression* evaluates the value of any variables, they must not have been defined in the previous Try block.

Comments

The *exceptionVar* clause is optional. If it is omitted, the block will handle all exceptions. However, your code has no access to the Exception object that was created at the time the exception was raised.

The Catch block will be executed if the exception is of type *exceptionType* or of a type derived from *exceptionType*.

Multiple catch blocks can appear within a single Try . . . Catch . . . Finally . . . End Try construct. However, only the first applicable Catch block is executed if an exception is thrown. This means that Catch blocks should be ordered from most specific to most general. If they are not, the Visual Basic .NET compiler generates a warning.

The following code illustrates a correctly structured set of Catch blocks that handles exceptions from most specific to most generic:

```
Catch ex As ArgumentNullException
   ' Code to handle exception
Catch ex As ArgumentException
   ' Code to handle exception
Catch ex As ApplicationException
   ' Code to handle exception
Catch ex As Exception
   ' Code to handle exception
End Try
```

Only one Catch block can be executed because, just before exiting the code block, the Visual Basic compiler calls the shared ClearProjectError method of the Microsoft.VisualBasic. CompilerServices.ProjectData class.

Example

See the example for the Try . . . Catch . . . Finally Statement.

VB6 Differences

The Catch keyword is new to Visual Basic .NET.

See Also

Try . . . Catch . . . Finally Statement

CBool Function

Converts an expression to a Boolean.

Syntax

```
CBool(expression)
```

Element	Description
expression	An expression to be converted to a Boolean.

Return Value

A Boolean

Comments

CBool supports the conversions listed in the following table:

Type of *expression*	Conversion	Comments
Boolean		Returns *expression* unchanged.
integral types (Byte, SByte, Short, UShort, etc.)	Narrowing	Non-zero values convert to True, zero values convert to False.
floating point types (Decimal, Double, and Single)	Narrowing	Non-zero values convert to True, zero values convert to False.
Object	Depends on runtime type of *expression*	*expression* must be a supported type (a valid string, an integer or floating point number, or a Boolean) or a null object reference (objects that equal Nothing convert to False).
String	Narrowing	Strings equal to a case-insensitive version of Boolean .TrueString convert to True, and of Boolean.FalseString to False. For string representations of numbers, CBool converts the string to a number before performing the conversion. All other strings cause an InvalidCastException to be thrown.

Note that the narrowing conversions can be handled implicitly by the compiler only if Option Strict is off. If Option Strict is on, they require an explicit conversion using CBool or another conversion function.

Conversion of Char and Date expressions to Boolean is not supported.

All of the conversions performed by CBool can also be performed by the shared System.Convert.ToBoolean method. The only difference is that the latter is more restrictive in converting strings; in order for ToBoolean to not throw a FormatException, the string passed to the ToBoolean method must be a case-insensitive version of either Boolean.TrueString or Boolean.FalseString. In contrast, CBool converts string representations of numbers to numeric values before performing the conversion to Boolean.

Care should be taken in how the compiler interprets what you assume are Boolean values if Option Strict is off. (The best way to avoid this problem of misinterpretation, of course, is by setting Option Strict on.) Since the compiler will automatically convert an integer to a Boolean, the If statement in the following code evaluates to True:

```
Dim intVar As Integer = 101
' more code
If intVar Then                      ' Evaluates to True
```

The If statement in the following code also evaluates to True:

```
Dim dblVar As Double = .000000001
' more code
If dblVar Then                      ' Evaluates to true
```

However, if we combine these two expressions into what we might think is a single compound expression, it evaluates to False:

```
If intVar And dblVar Then                      ' Evaluates to true
```

This occurs because the And is not interpreted by the Visual Basic compiler as a logical operator that evaluates two Booleans, but as a bitwise operator that performs logical conjunction on two numbers. The result of this logical conjunction is 0, which the compiler then converts to a Boolean value of False.

Typically, an unsuccessful conversion throws an InvalidCastException.

Like all of the intrinsic Visual Basic conversion functions, the CBool function is not defined in the Microsoft.VisualBasic namespace but instead is implemented directly by the compiler. This differs from Visual Basic 6.0, where CBool was a member of the Conversion class in the VBA library.

See Also

CObj Function, CType Function

CByte Function

Converts an expression to a Byte.

Syntax

CByte(*expression*)

Element	Description
expression	An expression to be converted to a Byte.

Return Value

A Byte

Comments

CByte supports the conversions listed in the following table:

Type of *expression*	Conversion	Comments
Boolean	Narrowing	Converts True to 255 (the unsigned equivalent of –1), False to 0.
Byte		Returns *expression* unchanged.
SByte	Narrowing	The numeric ranges of SByte (–128 to 127) and Byte (0 to 255) only partially overlap. Where they do not, an OverflowException is thrown.
All integral types other than Byte and SByte	Narrowing	The numeric ranges of all other integer types are supersets of the Byte range. Where a narrowing conversion results in loss of data, an OverflowException is thrown.
Floating point types (Decimal, Double, and Single)	Narrowing	The floating point value is rounded to the nearest integer before conversion.
Object	Depends on runtime type of *expression*	*expression* must be a supported type (a numeric string, any integer other than an SByte, a floating point number, or a Boolean) or a null object reference (objects that equal Nothing convert to 0).
String	Narrowing	Converts the string representation of a number to a byte if it is in the range of the Byte type; otherwise, an OverflowException is thrown. An empty string is converted to 0. If the string does not represent a number, an InvalidCastException is thrown.

Note that the narrowing conversions can be handled implicitly by the compiler only if Option Strict is off. If Option Strict is on, they require an explicit conversion using CByte or another conversion function.

All of the conversions performed by CByte can also be performed by the shared System.Convert.ToByte method. The sole difference in return value is that System.Convert .ToByte converts a Boolean value of False to 1, whereas CByte converts it to 255.

Conversion of Char and Date expressions to Boolean is not supported by CByte. System.Convert .ToByte does support Char-to-Byte conversion; it is identical in function to the Visual Basic AscW function.

Like all of the intrinsic Visual Basic conversion functions, the CByte function is not defined in the Microsoft.VisualBasic namespace but instead is implemented directly by the compiler. This differs from Visual Basic 6.0, where CByte was a member of the Conversion class in the VBA library.

See Also

CObj Function, CSByte Function, CType Function

CChar Function

Converts an expression to a Char.

Syntax

```
CChar(expression)
```

Element	Description
expression	An expression to be converted to a Char.

Return Value

A Char

Comments

CChar supports the conversions listed in the following table:

Type of *expression*	Conversion	Comments
Char		Returns *expression* unchanged.
Object	Depends on runtime type of *expression*	*expression* must be a supported type (a Char or a string) or a null object reference (objects that equal Nothing convert to a null character).
String	Narrowing	Converts the first character of a string to a Char. The string can be of any length.

Note that the narrowing conversions can be handled implicitly by the compiler only if Option Strict is off. If Option Strict is on, they require an explicit conversion using CChar or another conversion function.

Conversion of Boolean, Byte, Date, Decimal, Double, and Single expressions to Char is not supported. In addition, conversion of any of the integral types, both signed and unsigned, is not supported by the CChar function.

To convert an integer value to a Char, you can use the Visual Basic .NET Chr and ChrW functions, which interpret the integer as a character code. In all cases except Byte, this is a narrowing conversion. The Convert.ToChar function, when passed any integral type, performs the same conversion.

Like the CChar function, the Convert.ToChar method can also be used to convert a String to a Char. However, unlike CChar, it requires that the string be one character in length; otherwise, a FormatException is thrown.

Like all of the intrinsic Visual Basic conversion functions, CChar is not defined in the Microsoft.VisualBasic namespace but instead is implemented directly by the compiler.

VB6 Differences

The CChar function is new to Visual Basic .NET. (The Char data type did not exist in Visual Basic 6.0.)

See Also

CObj Function, CType Function

CDate Function

Converts an expression to a Date.

Syntax

```
CDate(expression)
```

Element	Description
expression	An expression to be converted to a Date.

Return Value

A Date

Comments

CDate supports the conversions listed in the following table:

Type of *expression*	Conversion	Comments
Date		Returns *expression* unchanged.
Object	Depends on runtime type of *expression*	At runtime, *expression* must be a supported type (a Date or the string representation of a date) or a null object reference (objects that equal Nothing convert to 1/1/0001 at 12:00:00 AM.).
String	Narrowing	The string must be a string representation of a date; otherwise, an InvalidCastException is thrown.

Note that the narrowing conversions can be handled implicitly by the compiler only if Option Strict is off. If Option Strict is on, they require an explicit conversion using CDate or another conversion function.

Conversion of all numeric types, as well as Boolean and Char, is not supported.

To prevent an InvalidCastException resulting from passing a string that does not contain a valid date representation to the CDate function, you can call the IsDate function beforehand. It returns True if the expression passed to it can be converted to a valid date. For example:

```
Dim dateThen As Date
If IsDate(dateString) Then
    dateThen = CDate(dateString)
End If
```

If *expression* is a string representation of a date, it must be localized; that is, it must take the form of the date format recognized on the local computer. Otherwise, an InvalidCastException is thrown.

If *expression* is a string representation of a time, it can be in either 12-hour or 24-hour format in order to be successfully converted to a Date value.

The CDate function recognizes a number of date and time delimiters, depending on the system's regional settings. For example, for U.S. English, the slash, hyphen, and comma characters are acceptable in dates, while only the colon is acceptable as a delimiter for times.

The CDate function adds a time component to dates that it converts from a date string only, and it adds a date component to all strings that it converts from a time string only. In the former case, it adds a time of 12:00:00 AM; in the latter, a date of 1/1/0001.

All of the conversions performed by CDate can also be performed by the shared System.Convert .ToDateTime method. The two methods are largely identical in operation and return value, except for two differences:

- The Convert.ToDateTime method adds the current date when it converts a string that consists of only a time component, whereas CDate adds a date of 1/1/0001.

- The Convert.ToDateTime method throws a FormatException if expression is not a localized representation of a date, whereas CDate throws an InvalidCastException.

To convert between a Visual Basic 6.0 Date data type (an OLE Automation Date) and a .NET Date data type, you can use the System.DateTime.ToOADate and System.DateTime.FromOADate methods. The former is an instance method (it's called from a Date expression) with the syntax

```
dateTime.ToOADate()
```

that returns a Double representing the Date value in OLE Automation format. The latter is s shared method with the syntax

```
DateTime.FromOADate(d)
```

where *d* is a Double whose value is an OLE Automation Date value.

Like all of the intrinsic Visual Basic conversion functions, the CDate function is not defined in the Microsoft.VisualBasic namespace but instead is implemented directly by the compiler. This differs from Visual Basic 6.0, where CDate was a member of the Conversion class in the VBA library.

Example

The following is a simple program that allows you to enter a string containing a possible date or time. The routine then determines whether the IsDate function validates it as date and displays the date converted by CDate and Convert.ToDateTime or, if either of these methods fails, the exception that was thrown. To terminate the program, click the OK or Cancel button of the input box when nothing has been entered into the text InputBox function's text box.

```
Public Module modMain
    Public Sub Main()
        Dim inputDate As String = String.Empty
        Dim convertedDate As Date

        Do While True
            inputDate = InputBox("Enter a date or time: ")
            If inputDate = String.Empty Then Exit Sub

            If IsDate(inputDate) Then
                Console.WriteLine("The expression {0} is a valid date or time.", _
                            inputDate)
            Else
                Console.WriteLine("The expression {0} is not a valid date or time.", _
                            inputDate)
            End If

            Try
                convertedDate = CDate(inputDate)
                Console.WriteLine("The result of calling the CDate function is {0}", _
                            convertedDate)
            Catch ex As Exception
                Console.WriteLine("The conversion of {0} with CDate resulted in an {1} exception.", _
                            inputDate, ex.GetType.Name)
            End Try

Try
    convertedDate = Convert.ToDateTime(inputDate)
    Console.WriteLine("The result of calling the Convert.ToDateTime method is {0}.", _
                convertedDate)
Catch ex As Exception
    Console.WriteLine("Using Convert.ToDateTime with {0} threw an {1} exception.", _
                inputDate, ex.GetType().Name)
End Try
        Console.WriteLine()
    Loop
    End Sub
End Module
```

VB6 Differences

The CDate function in Visual Basic 6.0 interpreted an integer value as the number of days before or after December 30, 1899. (Both negative and positive integers could be passed to the CDate function.) In Visual Basic .NET, conversion of integers to dates is not supported.

The CDate function in Visual Basic 6.0 converted a fractional value to time units after 12:00:00 AM. Again, both positive and negative floating point values were allowed, although negative floating point values were converted to positive floating point values before conversion. In Visual Basic .NET, conversion of expressions including floating point values to times is not supported.

See Also

CObj Function, CType Function, DateValue Function, IsDate Function

CDbl Function

Converts an expression to a Double.

Syntax

```
CDbl(expression)
```

Element	Description
expression	An expression to be converted to a Double.

Return Value

A Double

Comments

CDbl supports the conversions listed in the following table:

Type of *expression*	Conversion	Comments
Boolean	Widening	Converts False to 0, True to –1.
All integral types (Byte, Integer, Long, SByte, UShort, etc.)	Widening	Conversions from Long and ULong may involve a loss of precision.
Floating point types (Decimal and Single)	Widening	Conversions from Decimal may involve a loss of precision.
Double		Returns the original Double value unchanged.
Object	Depends on runtime type of *expression*	At runtime, *expression* must be a supported type (a Boolean, integer, floating point, or string representation of a number) or a null object reference (objects that equal Nothing convert to 0). Otherwise, it throws an InvalidCastException.
String	Narrowing	The string must be a string representation of a number; otherwise, an InvalidCastException is thrown.

Note that the narrowing conversions can be handled implicitly by the compiler only if Option Strict is off. If Option Strict is on, they require an explicit conversion using CDbl or another conversion function.

Conversion from Char and Date to Double using CDbl is not supported.

To prevent a non-numeric string from throwing an InvalidCastException when passing a string to the CDbl function, you can call the IsNumeric function beforehand. For example:

```
Dim convertedDouble As Double
If IsNumeric(inputString) Then
    convertedDouble = CDbl(inputString)
End If
```

CDbl can successfully convert strings that include the localized thousands separator. However, it cannot convert strings that include currency symbols.

The conversions performed by CDbl can also be performed by the shared System.Convert .ToDouble method. The only difference in operation is that ToDouble converts a Boolean True to 1, whereas CDbl converts it to –1.

Like all of the intrinsic Visual Basic conversion functions, the CDbl function is not defined in the Microsoft.VisualBasic namespace but instead is implemented directly by the compiler. This differs from Visual Basic 6.0, where CDbl was a member of the Conversion class in the VBA library.

VB6 Differences

In Visual Basic 6.0, the CDbl function could be used to convert a Date to a Double; the integral component of the Double returned represented the number of days since December 30, 1899, and the fractional component represented the elapsed time since midnight. In Visual Basic .NET, Date-to-Double conversion using CDbl is not supported.

See Also

CDec Function, CObj Function, CSng Function, CType Function, IsNumeric Function

---

CDec Function

Converts an expression to a Decimal.

Syntax

```
CDec(expression)
```

Element	Description
expression	An expression to be converted to a Decimal.

Return Value

A Decimal

Comments

CDec supports the conversions listed in the following table:

Type of *expression*	Conversion	Comments
Boolean	Widening	Converts False to 0, True to –1.
All integral types (Byte, Integer, Long, SByte, UShort, etc.)	Widening	
Floating point types (Double, Single)	Widening	
Decimal		Returns the original Decimal value unchanged.
Object	Depends on runtime type of *expression*	At runtime, *expression* must be a supported type (a Boolean, integer, floating point, or string representation of a number) or a null object reference (objects that equal Nothing convert to 0). Otherwise, it throws an InvalidCastException.
String	Narrowing	The string must be a string representation of a number; otherwise, an InvalidCastException is thrown.

Note that the narrowing conversion from String to Decimal can be handled implicitly by the compiler only if Option Strict is off. If Option Strict is on, the conversion of a String to a Decimal requires an explicit conversion using CDec or another conversion function.

Conversion from Char and Date to Decimal using CDec is not supported.

To prevent a non-numeric string from throwing an InvalidCastException when passing a string to the CDec function, you can call the IsNumeric function beforehand. For example:

```
Dim convertedDecimal As Decimal
If IsNumeric(inputString) Then
    convertedDecimal = CDec(inputString)
End If
```

When declaring and instantiating a Decimal, the compiler will often produce the error message, "Option Strict On disallows implicit conversions from 'Double' to 'Decimal'." in response to code such as

```
Dim decToConvert As Decimal = 1234.315
```

if Option Strict is set on. One way to prevent this error is by using the CDec function in the variable assignment:

```
Dim decToConvert1 As Decimal = CDec(1234.315)
```

A second method is to use the Decimal type identifier, d or D, in the variable assignment:

```
Dim decToConvert As Decimal = 1234.315d
```

CDec can successfully convert strings that include both the localized thousands separator and the localized currency symbol.

Because it offers superior precision, the Decimal data type is intended as a replacement for the Visual Basic 6.0 Currency data type, which is not supported by the .NET Common Type System.

The System.Decimal structure, however, includes two members for Currency-Decimal conversion. System.Decimal.ToOACurrency is a shared method that has a single parameter, *d*, the Decimal value to be converted; it returns a Long containing the OLE Automation Currency value. System.Decimal.FromOACurrency is also a shared method whose single parameter, *cy*, is a Long that contains an OLE Automation Currency value; it returns the Decimal value that corresponds to *cy*.

The conversions performed by CDec can also be performed by the shared System.Convert.ToDecimal method, with two differences. First, ToDecimal converts a Boolean True to 1, whereas CDec converts it to –1. Second, ToDecimal throws an InvalidFormatException if *expression* is a string that includes a currency symbol; CDec, on the other hand, is able to successfully perform the conversion.

Like all of the intrinsic Visual Basic conversion functions, the CDec function is not defined in the Microsoft.VisualBasic namespace but instead is implemented directly by the compiler. This differs from Visual Basic 6.0, where CDec was a member of the Conversion class in the VBA library.

VB.NET Changes

In Visual Basic 6.0, the Decimal was a Variant whose runtime type was Decimal. As a result, because syntax like

```
Dim dollarAmount As Decimal
```

was illegal, the CDec function offered the only method to define a Decimal data type. In Visual Basic .NET, the Decimal is an "intrinsic" data type that can be defined using the Dim statement.

In Visual Basic 6.0, the CDec function could be used to convert a Date to a Decimal; the integral component of the returned Decimal represented the number of days since December 30, 1899, and the fractional component represented the elapsed time since midnight. In Visual Basic .NET, Date-to-Decimal conversion using CDec is not supported.

See Also

CDec Function, CObj Function, CSng Function, CType Function, IsNumeric Function

ChDir Subroutine

Changes the current directory.

Member Of

Microsoft.VisualBasic.FileSystem

Syntax

```
ChDir(ByVal path As String)
```

Element	Description
path	The name and path to the new current directory.

Comments

path is not case sensitive.

path must describe a valid path. If it does not, the subroutine can throw any of a number of exceptions (an IOException for an invalid network path, an ArgumentException for invalid characters or white space, an ArgumentNullException for an empty string, a PathTooLongException for a path that exceeds 247 characters, or a FileNotFoundException for a local path that could not be found).

The path can be either absolute or relative. A relative path defines the location of the new directory in relationship to the present directory. An absolute path defines the location of the new directory in relationship to some absolute starting point, which is either a drive or the root directory of a drive.

Relative paths can be indicated in any of three ways:

- By using the . symbol, which indicates the current directory. This defines a path from the current directory to the new current directory.

- By using the .. symbol, which indicates the parent of the current directory. This defines a path from the parent of the current directory to the new current directory. If the current directory is the root directory, .. is ignored, and *path* describes a path from the current directory to the new current directory.

- By beginning *path* with no path separator character. This defines a path from a child of the current directory to the new current directory.

Absolute paths can be indicated in either of two ways:

- By beginning *path* with a drive designator (e.g., "C:\"). This defines a path from the root directory of the designated drive to the new current directory.

- By beginning path with the path separator symbol (e.g., "\"). This defines a path from the root directory of the current drive to the new current directory.

The ChDir subroutine does not accept UNC paths as arguments, although it will accept mapped network drives as the beginning of the absolute path. Attempting to provide a UNC path throws an IOException.

If you need to determine what the current drive is before changing it so that you can restore it later, you can call the CurDir function before calling ChDir.

Each local or mapped drive on a system has a current directory.

The CurDir subroutine merely wraps a call to the shared SetCurrentDirectory method of the System.IO.Directory class. Its syntax is:

```
Directory.SetCurrentDirectory(path)
```

Each Windows process has its own current directory. Changing an application's current directory has no effect outside of the application. Changing the current directory in a console-mode application affects the current directory of that application only. In addition, the console process has a current directory, which is completely separate from the current directory of any particular console application.

If your application gives users interactive access to the file system (using the Windows forms OpenFileDialog or SaveFileDialog classes, for instance), you should carefully consider the effect of changing the current directory once the user has accessed a file. It's not a bad idea to provide a basic application configuration setting (stored in either a configuration file or the registry) that allows users to determine whether the current directory should become the directory in which they've last opened a file. You can implement this functionality easily using the new My.Settings class in Visual Basic 2005.

See Also

ChDrive Function, CurDir Function, My.Computer.FileSystem.CurrentDirectory Property

ChDrive Subroutine

Changes the current drive.

Member Of

Microsoft.VisualBasic.FileSystem

Syntax

```
ChDrive(ByVal Drive As String)
ChDrive(ByVal Drive As Char)
```

Element	Description
Drive	The local or mapped drive to make the current drive.

Comments

Drive is not case sensitive.

Drive must represent a valid drive name, or an IOException is thrown.

If *Drive* is a multicharacter string, all but the first character of the string is ignored.

You can determine what drives are available on a system at runtime by calling the shared GetDrives method of the System.IO.DriveInfo object. Its syntax is:

```
Public Function GetDrives() As DriveInfo()
```

You can then iterate the returned array of DriveInfo objects to determine the drives (including the mapped network drives) installed on a system. For example:

```
' Get drive information using DriveInfo
Dim drives() As DriveInfo = DriveInfo.GetDrives()
For each drive As DriveInfo In Drives
    Console.WriteLine(drive.Name)      ' Displays "C:\", etc.,
Next
```

You could also create a simple DriveExists function to test whether a particular drive letter represents a valid drive: Ordinarily, this should simply be a matter of passing a drive letter to the DriveInfo class constructor and returning True if the constructor succeeds in instantiating a DriveInfo object, and returning False otherwise. However, since there appears to be a bug in the class constructor, it is necessary to iterate the collection:

```
Public Overloads Function DriveExists(DriveLetter As Char) As Boolean
    Return DriveExists(DriveLetter.ToString())
End Function

Public Overloads Function DriveExists(DriveLetter As String) As Boolean

    ' Retrieve collection of valid DriveInfo objects
    Dim Drives As DriveInfo() = DriveInfo.GetDrives()

    ' Make sure DriveLetter is valid
    If DriveLetter = String.Empty Then Return False
    If DriveLetter.Length > 1 Then DriveLetter = Left(DriveLetter, 1)

    ' Format DriveLetter to end with ":\" like DriveInfo.Name
    DriveLetter += ":\"
    DriveLetter = DriveLetter.ToUpper

    ' Iterate DriveInfo array
    For Each drive As DriveInfo In Drives
        If DriveLetter.ToUpper = drive.Name.ToUpper Then
            ' If there's a match, no need to continue iterating
            Return True
        End If
    Next
    ' Array iterated with no match: return False
    Return False
End Function
```

If your code will make a removable device the current drive, you should check to ensure that it is ready before calling the ChDrive subroutine. The example illustrates how to do this.

Visual Basic lacks a CurDrive function comparable to the CurDir function. The following code implements a CurDrive method that allows you to determine what the current drive is before calling ChDrive:

```
Public Function CurDrive() As Char
    Return CChar(Left(CurDir(), 1))
End Function
```

Example

The example code uses the DriveInfo object's DriveType and IsReady properties to determine whether a drive is removable and, if so, whether it is ready before changing the current drive. It assumes that the drive letter passed to the subroutine represents the name of a valid drive.

```
Public Overloads Sub ChangeDrive(driveName As Char)
    ChangeDrive(driveName.ToString())
End Sub

Public Overloads Sub ChangeDrive(driveName As String)
    If driveName = String.Empty Then Exit Sub
    If driveName.Length > 1 Then driveName = Left(driveName, 1)
    Dim drive As New DriveInfo(driveName)
    If drive.DriveType = DriveType.Removable Or drive.DriveType = DriveType.CDRom Then
```

```
   If Not drive.IsReady Then
      Dim choice as MsgBoxResult
      Do While Not drive.IsReady
         choice = MsgBox("Is Drive " & drive.Name & " ready now?", _
                  MsgBoxStyle.YesNoCancel Or MsgBoxStyle.Question, _
                  "Drive Not Ready")
         If choice = MsgBoxResult.Cancel Then Exit Sub
      Loop
      End If
   End If
   ChDrive(driveName)
End Sub
```

See Also

ChDir Subroutine, CurDir Function

Choose Function

Returns one of many values based on an index value.

Member Of

Microsoft.VisualBasic.Interaction

Syntax

```
Choose(Index, Choice() )
```

Element	Description
Index	A Double whose value is an index indicating which item in Choice() to return.
Choice()	A parameter array of possible values to return.

Return Value

An Object whose value is the item in *Choice*() at position *Index*.

Comments

Choose is a lookup function. It looks up and returns the item at a particular ordinal position in a list. *Choice*() can take either of two forms. It can be an array, as the following code illustrates:

```
Dim choice() As String = {"Chocolate Mousse", "Blackberry Torte", _
                          "Peach Cobbler", "Key Lime Pie"}
Console.WriteLine(Choose(index, choice))
```

or it can be a comma-delimited list of expressions, as the following code illustrates:

```
Console.WriteLine(Choose(index, "Chocolate Mousse", "Blackberry Torte", _
                         "Peach Cobbler", "Key Lime Pie"))
```

That it can be an array means that the options from which index chooses can be defined at runtime, rather than in the design-time environment.

Index is one-based; that is, one (and not zero) returns the first item in the list, two returns the second, etc. However, if *Index* is zero or negative, it is simply ignored, and the function returns Nothing.

If *Index* has a fractional component, it is truncated before the call to the Choose method.

The elements of *Choice* can consist not only of literals and variables, but also of any expression, including expressions that call functions. However, when the Choose function is called, each expression in *Choice* is evaluated, whether or not it is the expression in the *Index* position. As a result, calls to the Choose function can produce bugs and unintended side effects that are difficult to track down and correct, since these function calls can modify values in other parts of the program unexpectedly, as well as throw exceptions.

In Visual Basic 6.0, the Choose function was especially useful in handling values from control arrays of radio buttons. However, its utility has diminished somewhat, since Visual Basic .NET does not support control arrays.

Choose can produce clearer, more concise, more readable code when compared with long Select Case statements in particular.

The Choose function is very similar to a simple array assignment like the following:

```
Dim index As Integer = 3
Dim animals() As String = {"Cats", "Dogs", "Elephants", "Lions", "Bears"}
retVal = arrArray(index)
```

The Choose function, however, executes significantly more slowly, which suggests that it should be used judiciously.

The Choose function is superficially like the Switch function. The former selects an item according to its position in a list. The latter returns a value according to whether an expression associated with it evaluates to True.

VB6 Differences

In Visual Basic 6.0, if *Index* was negative, 0, or greater than the number of elements in *Choice*, the Choose function returned a Null. In Visual Basic .NET, Null is not supported as a runtime data type, and Choose instead returns Nothing.

In Visual Basic 6.0, Choose had to be a list of elements, rather than an array. For example, in Visual Basic 6.0, the code

```
Dim choices() As Variant, retVal As Variant
choices = Array("Pie", "Cake", "Candy")
Dim index As Double
index = InputBox("Enter the number of your choice: ")
retVal = Choose(index, choices)
```

returned a variant array with three items if *index* is 1, and returns Null otherwise. In contrast, comparable code in Visual Basic .NET returns "Pie" if index is 1, "Cake" if index is 2, etc. One implication of this is that the *Choice* values had to be build statically at design time in Visual Basic 6.0, while they can be build dynamically at runtime in Visual Basic .NET.

See Also

If . . . Then . . . Else Statement, IIf Function, Select Case Statement, Switch Function

Chr, ChrW Functions

Returns the character that corresponds to a character code.

Member Of

Microsoft.VisualBasic.Strings

Syntax

```
Chr(ByVal CharCode As Integer) As Char

ChrW(ByVal CharCode As Integer) As Char
```

Element	Description
CharCode	An integer representing a character code.

Return Value

A Char whose character code is *CharCode*

Comments

Legal values of *CharCode* depend on whether the Chr or ChrW function is called, as well as on the code page of the thread from which the function is invoked. The following comments should help to make this clear.

ChrW always returns the Char value whose Unicode character code is *CharCode*. The value of *CharCode* must range from –32768 to 65535, as the documentation indicates.

That *CharCode* may be negative may seem strange at first glance. This was done to preserve compatibility with Visual Basic 6.0, which also allowed *CharCode* to be a negative integer from –32768 to –1. But it particularly allows signed integers that are neither Long nor Integer to be passed to the function. In these cases, negative values are interpreted as their signed hexadecimal equivalents. For example, the following table lists some negative Short and SByte values and their unsigned Integer equivalents:

SByte Value	Short Value	Hexadecimal Value	Integer Equivalent
	–32768	&H8000	32768
	–1024	&HFC00	64512
	–128	&HFF80	65408
–128		&H80	128
–100		&H9C	156
–50		&HCE	206
–1		&HFF	255
	–1	&HFFFF	65535

The negative range of the SByte type is –1 to –128; the Chr and ChrW functions interpret these values as integers ranging from 255 to 128. The negative range of the Short type is –1 to –32,768; the Chr and ChrW functions interpret these values as integers ranging from 65535 to 32768. Finally, Integers ranging from –1 to –32,768 are treated as if they were Shorts with the same value.

The Chr function interprets *CharCode* as the character code that corresponds to the current thread's code page. An integer indicating the code page can be retrieved from the static CurrentCulture property of the CultureInfo class as follows:

```
System.Globalization.CultureInfo.CurrentCulture.TextInfo.ANSICodePage
```

If *CharCode* is out of the range of a valid character for the current code page, an ArgumentException is thrown.

In some cases, character data is stored in binary format, as a collection of bytes whose character codes represent string characters. This is sometimes true, for instance, of most recently used (MRU) lists in the registry. The Chr or ChrW functions can be used to convert this binary data to string data, as the example illustrates.

If you find the rule about embedding quotation marks in a string confusing, you can simply use Chr(34). For example, instead of using embedded quotation marks to define the query string SELECT * FROM CUSTTABLE WHERE STATE = "CA", as in the following code:

```
queryString = "SELECT * FROM CUSTTABLE WHERE STATE = ""CA"""
```

the Chr function can be used:

```
queryString = "SELECT * FROM CUSTTABLE WHERE STATE = " & Chr(34) & "CA" & Chr(34)
```

The following table lists some *CharCode* values used to produce special characters:

CharCode Value	Constant or Enum Member	Description
Chr(0)	vbNullChar, ControlChars.NullChar	A null character, often used to terminate C language strings
Chr(8)	vbBack, ControlChars.Back	Backspace
Chr(9)	vbTab, ControlChars.Tab	Horizontal tab
Chr(10)	vbLf, ControlChars.Lf	Linefeed
Chr(11)	ControlChars.VerticalTab	Vertical tab
Chr(12)	ControlChars.FormFeed	Formfeed
Chr(13)	vbCr, ControlChars.Cr	Carriage return
Chr(13) + Chr(10)	vbCrLf, ControlChars.CrLf, ControlChars.NewLine	Carriage return + linefeed
Chr(32)		Space
Chr(34)	ControlChars.Quote	Quotation mark

Example

The example retrieves the Windows Explorer's most recently used (MRU) list from the
HKEY_CURRENT_USER\Software\Microsoft\Windows\CurrentVersion\Explorer\RecentDocs
key of the registry. A value entry named MRUListEx contains formatted binary (REG_BINARY)
data: each consecutive four bytes form an integer whose string representation is the name of a
value entry whose value is the filename of a most recently used file. This example retrieves this
binary data and stores it in a byte array, which is enumerated four bytes at a time. An unsigned
integer is formed from each set of four bytes, and this unsigned integer is then converted to a string
that represents the name of a value entry whose value is a most recently used filename. This is also
stored as binary (REG_BINARY) data, so the example retrieves the data and assigns it to a byte
array. It iterates this array, uses the Chr function to convert every two bytes to their string
equivalent, and displays the resulting filename to the console window.

```
Imports Microsoft.Win32

Public Class ConvertToString
    Public Shared Sub Main
        ' Open MRU key as read-only
        Dim key As RegistryKey = Registry.CurrentUser.OpenSubKey( _
            "Software\Microsoft\Windows\CurrentVersion\Explorer\RecentDocs")
        If key Is Nothing Then Exit Sub

        ' Get the ordered list of files from the MRUListEx value entry
        ' Get its data type: should be REG_BINARY for this to work
        If key.GetValueKind("MRUListEx") <> RegistryValueKind.Binary Then
            Console.WriteLine("Registry data is not in expected format.")
            Exit Sub
        ' Data is in acceptable format: extract names of MRU keys from MRUList
        Else
            Dim ptr As Integer = 0                  ' Pointer into MRUList
            Dim MRUList() As Byte = CType(key.GetValue("MRUListEx"), Byte())
            ' Retrieve sets of 4 bytes from MRUList
            Do While ptr <= MRUList.Length - 1
                Dim numListItem As UInteger = 0
                ' Form integer from 4 bytes
                For ctr As Integer = 0 To 3
                    numListItem += CUInt(MruList(ctr + ptr)) << (ctr * 8)
                    ' Exit Do if &HFFFFFFFF (end of stream) encountered
                    If numListItem = UInteger.MaxValue Then Exit Do
                Next
                ptr += 4
                ' Convert integer value to string (name of list item)
                Dim listItem As String = CStr(numListItem)
                ' Retrieve bytes containing MRU filename
```

```
        Dim MRUName() As Byte = CType(key.GetValue(listItem), Byte())
        ' Define string to eventually hold filename
        Dim fileName As String = String.Empty
        Dim letter As Integer
        ' Iterate byte array and convert to strings
        For ctr As Integer = 0 to MRUName.Length - 1 Step 2
            letter = MRUName(ctr) + MRUName(ctr + 1) * 255
            ' Exit when Chr(0) -- end of filename -- encountered
            If letter = 0 Then Exit For
            fileName += Chr(letter)
        Next
        ' Output filename
        Console.WriteLine(fileName)
      Loop
    End If
  End Sub
End Class
```

VB6 Differences

In Visual Basic 6.0, the Chr and ChrW functions returned a one-character String (or, in fact, a variant whose runtime type was a String); in Visual Basic .NET, they return a Char.

Visual Basic 6.0 included "string" versions (Chr$, ChrB$, and ChrW$ functions) of the Chr, ChrB, and ChrW functions. The former returned strings, while the latter returned variants whose runtime time was a string. In Visual Basic .NET, the "string" versions are not supported.

Visual Basic 6.0 included the ChrB function to convert a byte to its character equivalent. In Visual Basic .NET, ChrB is not supported.

See Also

Asc, AscW Functions, CStr Function, Str Function. Val Function

CInt Function

Converts an expression to an Integer.

Syntax

```
CInt(expression)
```

Element	Description
expression	An expression to be converted to an Integer.

Return Value

An Integer

Comments

CInt supports the conversions listed in the following table:

Type of *expression*	Conversion	Comments
Boolean	Narrowing	Converts False to 0, True to -1.
Byte, SByte	Widening	The numeric ranges of the Byte (0 to 255) and SByte (–128 to 127) data types constitute a subset of the numeric range of the Integer data type.
floating point types (Decimal, Double, Single)	Narrowing	The range of all floating point types exceeds the range of an Integer. Fractional components are rounded before conversion.
Integer		Returns *expression* unchanged.
Long, ULong	Narrowing	The numeric range of the Long (–9,223,372,036,854,775,808 to 9,223,372,036,854,775,807) and ULong (0 to 18,446,744,073,709,551,615) data types exceeds the range of an Integer.
Object	Depends on the runtime type of *expression*	*expression* must be a supported type (a valid string, an integer or floating point number, or a Boolean) or a null object reference (objects that equal Nothing convert to 0).
Short, UShort	Widening	The numeric ranges of the Short (–32,768 to 32,767) and UShort (0 to 65,535) data types is a subset of the numeric range of an Integer.
String	Narrowing	Converts the string representation of a number to an Integer if it is in the range of the Integer data type; otherwise, an OverflowException is thrown. An empty string is converted to 0. If the string does not represent a number, an InvalidCastException is thrown.
UInteger	Narrowing	The numeric range of the UInteger data type (0 to 4,294,967,295) only partially overlaps the range of an Integer.

Note that the narrowing conversions can be handled implicitly by the compiler only if Option Strict is off. If Option Strict is on, they require an explicit conversion using CInt or another conversion function.

The CInt function is able to handle strings containing localized currency symbols and thousands separators without generating an error.

Conversion of Char and Date expressions to Integer is not supported and throws an InvalidCastException. However, the shared Convert.ToInt32 method can be used to convert a Char to an Integer that represents its character code.

All of the conversions performed by CInt can also be performed by the shared System.Convert. ToInt32 method. When converting a Boolean to an Integer, however, ToInt32 converts True to 1, while CInt converts it to –1.

Like all of the intrinsic Visual Basic conversion functions, the CInt function is not defined in the Microsoft.VisualBasic namespace but instead is implemented directly by the compiler. This differs from Visual Basic 6.0, where CInt was a member of the Conversion class in the VBA library.

See Also

CObj Function, CType Function, CUInt Function

Class Keyword

Constrains a generic type parameter by requiring that the argument passed to it be a reference type (a string, array, interface, delegate, or class instance). For details, see the discussion of the As keyword.

Syntax

See the syntax of the As keyword.

Comments

A generic parameter can be constrained by reference type by using the Class keyword or by value type by using the Structure keyword. If neither keyword is used, the generic parameter is not constrained by type.

The Class keyword is unrelated to the Class statement.

Example

See the example for the As Keyword.

VB.NET Changes

The Class keyword is new as of Visual Basic 2005.

VB6 Differences

The Class keyword is new to Visual Basic .NET; Visual Basic 6.0 did not support generic types.

See Also

As Keyword, Structure Keyword

Class Statement

Defines a class.

Syntax

```
[ <attrlist> ] [ accessModifier ] [ Shadows ] [ inheritability ] [ Partial ] _
Class name [( Of typelist )]
```

```
    [ Inherits classname ]
    [ Implements interfacenames ]
    [ statements ]
End Class
```

Element	Description
attrlist	The attributes that can be applied to a class. Only attributes whose AttributeUsage attribute is AttributeTargets.All or AttributeTargets.Class can be applied to a class
accessModifier	The accessibility of the class. Possible keywords are Public, Private, Friend, and Protected. (A fifth access modifier, Protected Friend, is available for class members, but not for a class itself.) If *accessModifier* is not specified, the class has Friend access; it is accessible only within the assembly in which it is defined. For details, see the entry for each of the access modifiers.
Shadows	Indicates that the current class hides an identically named programming element or a set of overloaded elements in a base class. For details, see the entry for the Shadows Keyword.
inheritability	Either MustInherit (for an abstract base class) or NotInheritable (for a sealed class). See the entries for the MustInherit and NotInheritable keywords. If these keywords are omitted, the class is inheritable and concrete.
Partial	Indicates that this Class . . . End Class construct contains a partial definition of the class, and that the remaining class definition is to be found in one or more other Class . . . End Class constructs.
name	The name of the class. It must be unique within the namespace in which the class is defined.
typelist	The list of parameters for the class. *typelist* is used when defining a generic class and takes the general form `(Of value [As constraintlist])` where *value* is a placeholder for the runtime type of the generic class, and *constraintlist* is a one or more predefined conditions that the runtime type of the generic class must satisfy. For details, see the entry for the As Keyword.
classname	The name of a class from which the current class inherits.
interfacenames	The name of one or more interfaces implemented by the current class.
statements	The code that defines the class' state and functionality. This can include variables and constants with different levels of accessibility (including fields, or public variables), properties, methods (that is, procedures and functions), as well as other types (enumerations, nested classes, structures, delegates, and interfaces).

Comments

The Class . . . End Class construct defines a .NET class, which is a reference type. In contrast, the Structure . . . End Structure construct defines a .NET structure, which is a value type. For some of the additional differences between classes and structures, see the sidebar "Classes and Structures" for this entry.

The optional Inherits statement indicates the class from which this class directly inherits. If present, the Inherits statement must immediately follow the Class statement. Unless the current class provides an implementation, members of the base classes can be called as if they belong to the current class.

Visual Basic .NET supports single inheritance: only a single class can be listed using the Inherits clause. If the Inherits statement is not used, the class implicitly inherits from the System.Object class, the base class for all classes.

As a work-around for .NET's support for single rather than multiple inheritance, it is possible to establish an inheritance hierarchy. For example, instead of class C inheriting from both Class A and Class B, Class C can inherit from Class B, which in turn inherits from Class A.

Classes and Structures

In Visual Basic .NET, classes and structures are very similar. Both can include constructors, fields, properties, and methods, and both can raise events. There are, however, a number of important differences:

- Classes are reference types. Structures are value types.

- Classes can inherit explicitly from any class other than System.ValueType (as long as that class is not NotInheritable). Structures can only inherit implicitly from System.ValueType and cannot inherit explicitly from any class or structure.

- Unsealed classes (classes not marked with the NotInheritable keyword) are inheritable (that is, other classes can inherit from these classes); structures are never inheritable. As a consequence of this, structure members cannot be declared with Protected accessibility.

- Structures must contain at least one instance variable or member. Classes can be completely empty.

- Variables declarations in structures cannot include initializers, nor can they define sizes of arrays. In classes, variable declarations can also initialize variables and define array sizes.

- Classes require constructors. (If you don't supply a constructor for a class, the compiler creates a parameterless one.) Structures, although they can have constructors, do not require them. (And as a result, structures cannot have explicitly defined parameterless constructors.)

- All members of structures are public by default. In contrast, class variables and constants are private by default, while the remaining class members are public by default.

- A structure's event handler must be shared and must be defined dynamically, using the AddHandler statement. In contrast, a class' event handlers can be defined either statically (using the Handles clause) or dynamically (using the AddHandler statement).

- Structures are not garbage collected, so the .NET Garbage Collection can never call their Finalize methods, if they are implemented. Classes are garbage collected, and the Garbage Collection will call class Finalize methods when it detects that there are no valid references to a class instance.

statements can consist of any of the following program elements:

- Constructors, which are invoked whenever an instance of the class is created. Constructors are a particular kind of subroutine
- Variables (fields) with varying levels of accessibility
- Constants, which are read-only fields
- Properties
- Methods (functions and subroutines)
- Events
- Event handlers, which are also a particular kind of subroutine
- Nested types, such as classes, structures, and enumerations

Constructors can be parameterized (arguments are passed to them by the code that instantiates the class) or parameterless. Constructors are subroutines (sub procedures) that in Visual Basic have the name New.

If no constructors are defined in the class' *statement* block, the Visual Basic .NET compiler will automatically supply a default (parameterless) constructor with the following form:

```
Public Sub New()
    MyBase.New()
End Sub
```

A derived class does not inherit any constructors from its base class. Instead, the class must define its own constructors and must invoke the appropriate base class constructor from its class constructor. The Visual Basic .NET compiler will automatically supply this code for a default or parameterless constructor in the derived class if the base class also has a default constructor. This would appear as follows if you supplied the constructor in your own code:

```
Public Sub New()
    MyBase.New()
End Sub
```

A class can implement a finalizer that is called by the Common Language Runtime just before the object is released. It takes the form:

```
Public Sub Finalize()
```

Typically, Finalize is used to release unmanaged resources (i.e., resources not managed by the Common Language Runtime, such as objects with handles). The execution of the Finalize method is non-deterministic; that is, exactly when Finalize will be called once an object reference is no longer valid cannot be determined in advance. To allow immediate release of unmanaged resources under an application or component's programmatic control, .NET also supports a disposer, Dispose, that can be called from the client of a class. Its syntax is:

```
Public Sub Dispose()
```

Within the class itself, rather than in a client of the class, Dispose must be implemented by implementing the IDisposable interface, which has a single method, Dispose. To implement Dispose, do the following:

- Add a protected member to the class that keeps track of whether Dispose has been called and unmanaged objects already disposed of:

```
Protected disposed As Boolean = False
```

- Supply the actual code for the disposer, which can only be called from within the class or from a derived class:

```
Protected Overridable Sub Dispose(ByVal disposing As Boolean)
    If Not Me.disposed Then      ' execute only if Dispose not called already
        If disposing
            ' add code to free unmanaged resources
        End If
        ' add code to free shared resources
    End If
    Me.disposed = True
End Sub
```

- Add the implementation of Dispose required by the IDisposable interface, which can be called from client code:

```
Public Sub Dispose() Implements IDisposable.Dispose
    Dispose(True)
    GC.SuppressFinalize(Me)
End Sub
```

- Provide an override of Finalize with the following code:

```
Public Overrides Sub Finalize()
    Dispose(False)
    MyBase.Finalize()
End Sub
```

In a derived class, the implementation of Dispose should call to the base class definition. The derived class implementation of Dispose should conform to the following pattern:

```
Protected Overrides Sub Dispose(ByVal disposing As Boolean)
    If Not Me.disposed Then      ' execute only if Dispose not called already
        If disposing
            ' add code to free unmanaged resources
        End If
        ' add code to free shared resources
    End If
    MyBase.Disposed(disposing)
End Sub
```

In addition to whatever members it inherits from its base class, the current class inherits the following members from the Object class:

- **Equals method**   Returns a Boolean indicating whether two object variables reference the same object instance. The method is overloaded as follows:

```
Equals(obj As Object)
Equals(objA As Object, objB As Object)
```

  The first variation is identical to the ReferenceEquals method, except that it is an instance method rather than a shared method. Equals can be overridden, and in fact value types generally override Equals to indicate equality of values rather than references.

- **GetHashCode method**   Returns a hash code used by a Hashtable object to store and retrieve instances of the class. The GetHashCode method can be overridden, and should return an integer that is based on the value of one or more of the object's instance members and that serves to distinguish the object from similar objects with different values. While the hash code does not have to uniquely identify a particular object, it must have the property that a small change in the value of the instance members on which the hash code is based produces a large change in the hash code value.

- **GetType method**   Returns a Type object that represents the current class. The GetType method cannot be overridden.

- **ReferenceEquals method**   A shared method that returns a Boolean indicating whether two object variables reference the same object instance. The method cannot be overridden. Its syntax is:

```
ReferenceEquals(objA As Object, objB As Object)
```

- **ToString method**   Returns a String containing the fully qualified name of the class. The ToString method can be, and in fact often is, overridden. For instance, in the case of intrinsic Visual Basic value types (such as Boolean or Integer), it returns a string containing the instance's value.

The Implements statement must immediately follow the Inherits statement, if it is present, or must immediately follow the Class statement, if the Inherits statement is not present. The names of multiple interfaces can be specified, separated by a comma. If the class does implement any interfaces, it must provide an implementation for each interface member. (See the Interface Statement for details.)

A class can include both shared and instance members. Shared members belong to the class as a whole, rather than to individual class instances. A shared variable, for example, has a single value across all instances of a class in an application. Instance members, on the other hand, belong to individual instances of a class. An instance variable, for example, can have a different value in each class instance in a particular application.

Classes can be declared and instantiated either at the same time or in separate lines of code. In either case, the New keyword is used to create a new class. The following statement, for example, declares a new instance of the Hashtable class and sets its initial capacity to 55 elements in a single line of code:

```
Dim hashtbl As Hashtable = New Hashtable(55)
```

This can also be written more succinctly:

```
Dim hashtbl1 As New Hashtable(55)
```

It is also possible to declare a class variable and instantiate it separately. For example:

```
Dim hashtbl As Hashtable
hashtbl = New Hashtable(55)
```

Often, whether a variable is declared and instantiated simultaneously or whether this is done in separate lines of code is a matter of programming style. In some cases, however, separating the declaration from the instantiation of a class allows the class to be instantiated and its parameterized constructor called using values gathered at runtime, and also permits the class instance to take advantage of polymorphism, as the following code illustrates:

```
Public Class Vehicle
    Private numWheels As Integer

    Public Property Wheels As Integer
        Get
            Return numWheels
        End Get
        Set
            numWheels = value
        End Set
    End Property
End Class

Public Class Bicycle : Inherits Vehicle
    Private gears As Integer

    Public Property Speed As Integer    ' e.g., 10-speed
        Get
            Return gears
        End Get
        Set
            gears = value
        End Set
    End Property
End Class

Public Class Automobile : Inherits Vehicle
    Private numCylinders As Integer

    Public Property Cylinders As Integer
        Get
            Return numCylinders
        End Get
        Set
            numCylinders = value
        End Set
    End Property
End Class

Public Module modVehicle
    Public Sub Main
        ' Instantiate vehicle
```

```
      Dim vehicle As Vehicle
      If MsgBox("Is your vehicle a bicycle? ", _
              MsgBoxStyle.Question Or MsgBoxStyle.YesNo, _
              "Bicycle") = MsgBoxResult.Yes Then
         vehicle = New Bicycle
         vehicle.Wheels = 2
         DirectCast(vehicle, Bicycle).Speed = 10
      ElseIf MsgBox("Is your vehicle an automobile? ", _
                MsgBoxStyle.Question Or MsgBoxStyle.YesNo, _
                "Bicycle") = MsgBoxResult.Yes Then
         vehicle = New Automobile
         vehicle.Wheels = 4
         DirectCast(vehicle, Automobile).Cylinders = 6
      Else
         If vehicle Is Nothing Then Exit Sub
      End If
      DisplayVehicleInfo(vehicle)
   End Sub

   Private Sub DisplayVehicleInfo(vehicle As Vehicle)
      ' Display vehicle information
      Console.WriteLine("Your vehicle has {0} wheels.", vehicle.Wheels)
      If TypeOf vehicle Is Bicycle Then
         Dim bicycle As Bicycle = DirectCast(vehicle, Bicycle)
         Console.WriteLine("You have a {0}-speed {1}.", bicycle.Speed, _
                         bicycle.GetType.Name)
      ElseIf TypeOf vehicle Is Automobile Then
         Dim auto As Automobile = DirectCast(vehicle, Automobile)
         Console.WriteLine("You have a {0}-cylinder {1}.", _
                         auto.Cylinders, auto.GetType.Name)
      End If
   End Sub
End Module
```

The example defines a base class, Vehicle, and two derived classes, Bicycle and Automobile. A variable of type Vehicle is declared, and it is instantiated as either a Bicycle or an Automobile, depending on which type the user has. The DirectCast function is used to convert from Vehicle to either Bicycle or Automobile, depending on which vehicle the user has chosen.

Shared members of a class can be accessed without instantiating that class. For example, the following code defines a class named Greeting with a shared method named SayHello:

```
Public Class Greeting
   Public Shared Function SayHello() As String
      Return "And a top of the morning to you!"
   End Function
End Class
```

VB6 Differences

In relationship to VB6, the Class . . . End Class construct is new. Classes were supported in Visual Basic 6.0, but they were stored in a separate .cls file, so that no language element was necessary to define them.

VBScript, which didn't recognize the division of program structures into separate files, did recognize the Class . . . End Class construct.

Although Visual Studio creates separate .vb files for each non-nested class, this is not a requirement either of the Visual Basic .NET compiler or of the .NET platform. Instead, multiple non-nested classes can be defined in a single file.

See Also

As Keyword, Module Statement, Partial Keyword, Structure Statement

CLng Function

Converts an expression to a Long.

Syntax

```
CLng(expression)
```

Element	Description
expression	An expression to be converted to a Long.

Return Value

A Long

Comments

CLng supports the conversions listed in the following table:

Type of *expression*	Conversion	Comments
Boolean	Narrowing	Converts False to 0, True to –1.
Byte, SByte	Widening	The numeric ranges of the Byte (0 to 255) and SByte (–128 to 127) data types is a subset of the numeric range of the Long data type.
floating point types (Decimal, Double, Single)	Narrowing	The range of all floating point types exceeds the range of a Long. Fractional components are rounded before conversion.
Integer, UInteger	Widening	The numeric range of the Integer (–2,147,483,648 to 2,147,483,647) and UInteger (0 to 4,294,967,295) data types is a subset of the numeric range of the Long data type.
Long		Returns *expression* unchanged.
Object	Depends on the runtime type of *expression*	*expression* must be a supported type (a valid string, an integer or floating point number, or a Boolean) or a null object reference (objects that equal Nothing convert to 0).

Type of *expression*	Conversion	Comments
Short, UShort	Widening	The numeric ranges of the Short (–32,768 to 32,767) and UShort (0 to 65,535) data types is a subset of the numeric range of a Long.
String	Narrowing	Converts the string representation of a number to a Long if it is in the range of the Long data type; otherwise, an OverflowException is thrown. An empty string is converted to 0. If the string does not represent a number, an InvalidCastException is thrown.
ULong	Narrowing	The numeric range of the ULong data type (0 to 18,446,744,073,709,551,615) only partially overlaps the range of a Long.

Note that the narrowing conversions can be handled implicitly by the compiler only if Option Strict is off. If Option Strict is on, they require an explicit conversion using CLng or another conversion function.

The CLng function is able to handle strings containing localized currency symbols and thousands separators without generating an error.

Conversion of Char and Date expressions to Long is not supported and causes an InvalidCastException to be thrown. However, the shared Convert.ToInt64 method can be used to convert a Char to a Long that represents its character code.

All of the conversions performed by CLng can also be performed by the shared System.Convert. ToInt64 method. When converting a Boolean to a Long, however, ToInt64 converts True to 1, while CLng converts it to –1.

Like all of the intrinsic Visual Basic conversion functions, the CLng function is not defined in the Microsoft.VisualBasic namespace but instead is implemented directly by the compiler. This differs from Visual Basic 6.0, where CLng was a member of the Conversion class in the VBA library.

See Also

CObj Function, CType Function, CULng Function

CObj Function

Converts an expression to an Object data type.

Syntax

```
CObj(expression)
```

Element	Description
expression	Any expression.

Returns

expression converted to an Object data type.

Comments

Since all .NET types other than interfaces are ultimately derived from the Object class, *expression* can evaluate to any data type.

Since interfaces do not derive from the Object class, some of the members (such as GetType and ToString) that you ordinarily expect to be use with any data type are unavailable. The *CObj* function can be used to convert an interface variable to an Object so that these members are available. This is illustrated by the example.

The Visual Basic compiler treats a conversion from a derived class to a base class as a widening conversion. This means that simple assignment can be used in place of the CObj function for any type that is directly or indirectly derived from System.Object. For instance, the call to the CObj function in the example code could be replaced with the following assignment statement:

```
objectVariable = interfaceVariable
```

Like the other Visual Basic .NET conversion functions, CObj is implemented directly by the compiler, rather than in a .NET class library such as Microsoft.VisualBasic.dll.

CObj is the only conversion function implemented by the compiler that cannot be used in defining a conditional compiler constant with the #Const statement.

Example

The example program illustrates the use of the CObj function to convert an interface variable, ISomeInterface, to an object so that the ToString and GetType methods can be called.

```
Public Interface ISomeInterface
   Sub AMethod(name As String)
End Interface

Public Class SomeClass : Implements ISomeInterface
   Public Sub AMethod(name As String) Implements ISomeInterface.AMethod
      Console.WriteLine(name)
   End Sub
End Class

Public Module modMain
   Public Sub Main()
      Dim interfaceVariable As ISomeInterface = New SomeClass()
      Dim objectVariable As Object
      interfaceVariable.AMethod("a string")
      ' Console.WriteLine(interfaceVariable.ToString)    ' GENERATES COMPILER ERROR
      objectVariable = CObj(interfaceVariable)
      Console.WriteLine(objectVariable.GetType().Name)
      Console.WriteLine(objectVariable.ToString)
   End Sub
End Module
```

VB6 Differences

The CObj function is new to Visual Basic .NET. Its closest equivalent in Visual Basic 6.0 is the CVar function, which converts a non-object data type to a Variant, Visual Basic 6.0's "universal" data type.

See Also

CType Function, DirectCast Function, TryCast Function

Collection Class

Serves as a container that allows items to be stored and retrieved using a unique key. In other words, each item stored by a Collection object consists of a value and its name. The Collection class is similar to an associative array in languages, such as Perl, that support this feature.

Namespace

```
Microsoft.VisualBasic
```

Syntax

```
Dim objectVar As New Collection()
```

or

```
Dim objectVar As Collection
objectVar = New Collection()
```

Comments

Although the Collection object serves as a container that holds name/value pairs, there is no formal requirement that the members of the collection be named; it is possible to add a value without supplying a name. In this case, the Collection object becomes a simple container whose members can be retrieved either sequentially or by ordinal position, but not by key.

You can iterate a collection using either a For or a For Each construct.

Collection objects are one-based. That is, if you iterate the collection using either the For construct or retrieve a member by its ordinal position using the Item property, the first element in the collection is found at position 1, not position 0.

The Collection class is a weakly typed collection object. That is, it can be used to store objects of any type, and objects stored to it do not all have to be of the same type. Visual Basic .NET does not provide a generic (strongly typed) Collection object.

The Collection class constructor has no parameters, so that members cannot be added to a collection when it is instantiated. To add members, use the Collection class' Add method.

If you want your collection class to be strongly typed but don't need to add any customization features to it, the best method to use is a generic class, which was introduced in .NET Version 2.0. Generic classes are located primarily in the System.Collections.Generic namespace. The generic Dictionary class roughly corresponds to the Visual Basic Collection class, since it stores data as name/value pairs. The following code uses the generic Dictionary class to store codes abbreviations for educational degrees and their corresponding descriptions:

```
Public Class GenericTest
  Public Shared Sub Main()
    Dim education As New Dictionary(Of String, String)
    education.Add("BA", "Bachelor of Arts")
    education.Add("BS", "Bachelor of Science")
```

```
        education.Add("MA", "Master of Arts")
        education.Add("MS", "Master of Science")
        education.Add("MPhil", "Master of Philosophy")
        education.Add("PhD", "Doctor of Philosophy")

        Console.WriteLine(education.Item("BS"))
        Console.WriteLine()
        For Each pair As KeyValuePair(Of String, String) In education
            Console.WriteLine(pair.Value)
        Next
    End Sub
End Class
```

If you want your collection class to be strongly typed and you also want to add customization features to it, the best technique is to derive a class from either the .NET Framework's System .Collections.CollectionBase class or the .NET Framework's System.Collections.DictionaryBase class. CollectionBase is not a Visual Basic–like collection; it does not serve as a container for name/value pairs, but only for unnamed data items. DictionaryBase, in contrast, allows the storage of name/value pairs. Note that you cannot inherit from the Visual Basic Collection class, since it is marked as non-inheritable. For example, the following code inherits from the CollectionBase class to define a customized collection class that can maintain a sorted collection of strings:

```
Imports System
Imports System.Collections

Public Class SortedStrings
    Inherits CollectionBase

  Public Function Add(ByVal value As String) As Integer
      MyBase.List.Add(value)
  End Function

  Default Public Property Item(ByVal index As Integer) As String
      Get
          Return DirectCast(MyBase.List.Item(index), String)
      End Get
      Set(ByVal value As String)
         MyBase.List.Item(index) = value
      End Set
  End Property

  Public Function Sort
      ' Copy collection to an array and sort it
      Dim sArr(Me.Count - 1) As String
      Dim IColl As ICollection = Me
      IColl.CopyTo(sArr,0)
      Array.Sort(sArr)

      ' Clear the collection
      Me.Clear

      ' Write strings back to the collection
      For Each s As String In sArr
```

```
        Me.List.Add(s)
      Next
    End Function
End Class
```

The following code inherits from the DictionaryBase class to define a customized collection class that stores name/value pairs whose value is an array:

```
Imports System
Imports System.Collections
Imports Microsoft.VisualBasic

Public Class StateInfo
   Inherits DictionaryBase

   Public Function Add(ByVal key As String, value() As String) As Integer
      MyBase.Dictionary.Add(key, value)
   End Function

   Default Public Property Item(ByVal key As String) As String()
      Get
         Return MyBase.Dictionary.Item(key)
      End Get
      Set(ByVal value As String())
         MyBase.Dictionary.Item(key) = value
      End Set
   End Property

   Public Function Contains(ByVal key As String) As Boolean
      Return MyBase.Dictionary.Contains(key)
   End Function
End Class
```

Example

The example code illustrates the process of creating a collection, adding members to it, and iterating it. Note that each iteration of the For Each . . . Next loop returns the collection item's data, rather than its key.

```
Imports Microsoft.VisualBasic
Imports System
Imports System.Collections

Public Class Collect
   Public Shared Sub Main()
      Dim sta As New Collection

      sta.Add("New York", "NY")
      sta.Add("Michigan", "MI")
      sta.Add("New Jersey", "NJ")
      sta.Add("Massachusetts", "MA")
```

```
        For Each stcode As String In sta
            Console.WriteLine(stcode)
        Next
    End Sub
End Class
```

Members

The properties and methods of the Collection class allow you to determine how many members a Collection object has, to add and remove members, to enumerate the collection's members, and to retrieve individual members from it.

New Method (class constructor)

Called when a member of the class is instantiated. Its syntax is:

```
New()
```

The parameterless constructor means that a newly instantiated Collection object has no elements.

Add Method

Adds a name/value pair to the collection. By default, unless either the *Before* or *After* argument is specified, members are stored in the collection in the order in which they are added. The method's syntax is:

```
Add(Item[, Key][, Before][, After])
```

Its parameters are shown in the following table:

Parameter	Description
Item	An Object representing the data to be added to the collection. It can be of any data type.
Key	An optional String containing the key name. *Key* must be unique among members of the collection, or an ArgumentException is thrown. (The comparison of *Key* with keys assigned to collection members is case insensitive and not affected by the setting of Option Compare.) If *Key* is omitted, members of the collection can be accessed directly only by numeric index or enumerated by using For Each . . . Next.
Before	An Object indicating the relative position in the collection before which the new member is to be added. It can contain either the ordinal position or the key of the item in front of which the new item is to be added. Both *Before* and *After* arguments cannot be specified, or an ArgumentException is thrown. An ArgumentException also is thrown if *Before* does not identify a valid member of the collection. Adding a member to a collection using the *Before* argument can change the ordinal position of existing members of the collection.
After	An Object indicating the relative position in the collection after which the new member is to be added. It can contain either the ordinal position or the key of the item after which the new item is to be added. Both *Before* and *After* arguments cannot be specified, or an ArgumentException is thrown. An ArgumentException also is thrown if *After* does not identify a valid member of the collection. Adding a member to a collection using the *After* argument can change the ordinal position of existing members of the collection.

Clear Method

Removes all items from the collection. Its syntax is:

```
Clear()
```

If Clear is called on a Collection object that has been declared but not instantiated, a NullReferenceException is thrown. If Clear is called on an empty collection (i.e., a properly instantiated collection that has no members), the method has no effect.

Contains Method

Returns a Boolean indicating whether a specific key exists in the collection. Its syntax is:

```
Contains(ByVal Key As String)
```

where *Key* is the key string to locate in the collection. The search for *Key* is case insensitive and is not affected by the setting of Option Compare. Contains searches keys only; it does not search values, nor can it determine whether an item added without a key already exists in the collection.

Since attempting to add a key that already exists in the collection throws an exception, the Contains method is useful for checking whether a key already exists in the collection before calling the Add method. For example:

```
If Not weights.Contains("kg") Then _
    weights.Add("kilograms", "KG")
```

Count Property

A read-only Integer that indicates the number of items in the collection. Its syntax is:

```
Public ReadOnly Property Count() As Integer
```

GetEnumerator Method

Returns an enumerator that can iterate the members of a Collection instance. Its syntax is:

```
IEnumerable = Collection.GetEnumerator()
```

IEnumerable.MoveNext can then be called to iterate the members of the collection. The following code illustrates the use of the GetEnumerator method to enumerate the items in a Collection object:

```
Imports System.Collections

Public Class Enumerate
    Public Shared Sub Main()
        Dim weights As New Collection
        Dim iterator As IEnumerator

        weights.Add("ounces", "oz")
        weights.Add("pounds", "lbs")
        weights.Add("kilograms", "kg")
        weights.Add("milligrams", "mg")
```

```
       iterator = weights.GetEnumerator
       Do While iterator.MoveNext
           Console.WriteLine(iterator.Current)
       Loop
    End Sub
End Class
```

However, iterating the collection can be performed much more elegantly using the For Each . . . Next construct, which wraps the calls to GetEnumerator and MoveNext. Explicit use of the GetEnumerator method can be confined to cases in which you want to begin enumerating the members of a collection, save your place in the collection, do something else for a while, and then return to the same place in the collection. You can use the GetEnumerator method to have as many of these "bookmarks" as you want in a particular collection.

Item Property
Retrieves a particular member from the collection. Its syntax is:

```
Collection.Item(Index As Integer)
Collection.Item(Key As String)
Collection.Item(Object As Object)
```

These three overloaded versions of the Item property provide two ways of retrieving a member of the collection:

- By ordinal position in the collection. *Index* and *Object* can be Integer expressions that indicate which item to retrieve from the collection based on its ordinal position. The Collection class is one-based, so *Index* or *Object* must evaluate to an Integer whose value ranges from 1 to Collection.Count. If *Index* or *Object* is outside of this range, an IndexOutOfRangeException is thrown.

- By name. The property returns the member whose key corresponds to the *Key* argument. If *Key* does not exist in the collection, an ArgumentException is thrown.

Item is the default member of the Collection class. That means that the Item property does not have to be referenced explicitly when retrieving a member using the Item property. The following two statements, which retrieve the third member of a Collection object, are functionally identical:

```
Dim weight As String = weights.Item(3)
Dim weight As String = weights(3)
```

Similarly, the following two statements both retrieve the member of the collection whose key is "lbs":

```
Dim weight As String = weights.Item("lbs")
Dim weight As String = weights("lbs")
```

Remove Method
Deletes a member of the collection. Its syntax is:

```
Collection.Remove(Index As Integer)
Collection.Remove(Key As String)
```

where *Index* is the one-based ordinal position in the collection of the item to be deleted, and *Key* is the key of the member to be deleted. Deleting collection members changes the ordinal position of the remaining members whose ordinal positions were greater than the deleted member. Therefore, if deleting multiple members by ordinal position, the members with the highest ordinal position should be deleted first. The following code fragment illustrates this by deleting all members of the collection individually based on ordinal position starting with the last one and ending with the first one:

```
Dim weights As New Collection

weights.Add("ounces", "oz")
weights.Add("pounds", "lbs")
weights.Add("kilograms", "kg")
weights.Add("milligrams", "mg")

' Delete all members from last ordinal position to first
For ordinal As Integer = weights.Count To 1 Step -1
    weights.Remove(ordinal)
Next
Console.WriteLine("The collection now has {0} items.", weights.Count)
```

VB.NET Changes

The Clear and Contains members were added to the Collection object as of Visual Basic 2005.

VB6 Comparison

The GetEnumerator method was not supported in Visual Basic 6.0. In .NET, GetEnumerator is the single member of the IEnumerable interface, which is used to create enumerable container objects such as collection objects and arrays.

See Also

Default Keyword, For Each . . . Next Statement

ComClass Attribute

Instructs the Visual Basic .NET compiler that a class is to be exposed as a COM object.

Namespace

Microsoft.VisualBasic

Syntax

The constructor of the ComClassAttribute class is overloaded, which permits the attributes to take any one of the following three forms:

```
<ComClass(_ClassID As String)>
<ComClass(_ClassID As String, _InterfaceID As String)>
<ComClass(_ClassID As String, _InterfaceID As String, _EventID As String)>
```

Element	Description
_ClassID	A GUID representing the class identifier, or the name of a constant that contains the class identifier. The _ClassID argument is assigned to the ComClassAttribute object's ClassID property.
_InterfaceID	A GUID representing the interface identifier for the class' default interface, or the name of a constant that contains the interface identifier. The _InterfaceID argument is assigned to the ComClassAttribute object's InterfaceID property. You class should register an interface identifier only if it includes public instance members.
_EventID	A GUID representing the event identifier, or the name of a constant that contains the event identifier. The _EventID argument is assigned to the ComClassAttribute object's EventID property. Your class only needs to register an event identifier if it raises events.

Comments

The ComClass attribute simplifies the process of creating and registering a COM component by assigning it a class identifier (ClassId), an interface identifier (IId), and an event identifier.

The presence of the _ClassID, _InterfaceID, and _EventID arguments indicates to the compiler that the respective identifier is defined and should be used when registering the COM component. The string provided as the argument can either consist of the GUID itself or of the name of the constant that defines the GUID. For example, the following code provides GUIDs for the class and interface identifiers to the ComClassAttribute class constructor:

```
<COMClass("AF20CF46-2196-471f-8ADB-CA7DE0200DB5", _
          "732E94D5-FCA6-4bcb-B3E3-7F1006BEE5EC")> _
Public Class COMLib
```

On the other hand, the following code indicates that the GUIDs are defined as constants named ClassID and InterfaceID within the COMLib class itself:

```
<COMClass(COMLib.ClassID, COMLib.InterfaceID)> Public Class COMLib

    Friend Const ClassID As String = "AF20CF46-2196-471f-8ADB-CA7DE0200DB5"
    Friend Const InterfaceID As String = "732E94D5-FCA6-4bcb-B3E3-7F1006BEE5EC"
```

Note that the constant definition takes the general form

```
className.constantName
```

If constants are used to define GUIDs, the constant statements must have access modifiers that make the GUID accessible outside of the class (since the attribute is defined outside of the class). In other words, the constants cannot be private (in which case they are accessible only inside of the class) or protected (in which case they are accessible only to derived classes). The most restrictive access modifier that can be used is Friend.

The class identifier, interface identifier, and event identifier are all globally unique identifiers (GUIDs), strings that represent 128-bit (or 16-byte) hexadecimal values that are guaranteed to be globally unique. In order to register the component at compile time, the GUIDs must be predefined, rather than assigned dynamically at runtime using the Guid.NewGuid method. (This also ensures

FIGURE 8-5
The Create GUID dialog

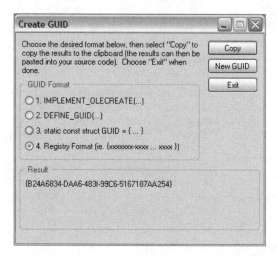

that the component retains the same GUIDs when it is recompiled.) The best way to do this is to use the GUIDGen utility, GUIDGen.exe, which is included with the .NET Framework 2.0 SDK and is shown in Figure 8-5. Select the Registry Format button, then click the Copy button to copy the GUID shown in the Result group box to the Clipboard. You can then paste it into your code. To generate each subsequent GUID, click the New GUID button, then again click the Copy button to copy the new GUID to the Clipboard.

When you copy the GUID into your code, it has the format

```
{91D36006-8316-40c5-A53D-657C2517F802}
```

To place it in the format required by the ComClass attribute, you need to remove the opening and closing braces in the constant declaration that defines the GUID. For example:

```
Private Const ClassID As String = "91D36006-8316-40c5-A53D-657C2517F802"
```

COM classes created with .NET require a parameterless class constructor.

To expose a class as a COM object, you must compile the project with the Register for COM Interop option selected in the Build section of the Configuration Properties dialog.

The ComClass attribute can only be applied to a class. (Its AttributeUsage attribute has a value of AttributeTargets.Class.)

Members

All properties are assigned by supplying arguments in the attribute statement. Positional arguments correspond to parameters defined by the class constructor. All other arguments must be supplied as named arguments.

New Method (class constructor)

Called when the attribute is used. The class constructor's parameters correspond to required arguments of the ComClass attribute. For details, see the Syntax section.

ClassID Property

A String that defines the class identifier (CLSID) of the COM component. It corresponds to the class constructor's _ClassID_ parameter.

EventID Property

A String that defines the event identifier of the COM component. It corresponds to the class constructor's _EventID_ parameter.

InterfaceID Property

A String that defines the interface identifier of the COM component. It corresponds to the class constructor's _InterfaceID_ parameter.

InterfaceShadows Property

A Boolean that indicates whether the COM interface name shadows another member of this class or a base class. Its default value is False. It can be set by using a named argument in the ComClass attribute.

VB6 Differences

The ComClass attribute is new to Visual Basic .NET; Visual Basic 6.0 is a COM-based development environment that automatically assigns class and interface interfaces to components and registers them in the system registry.

Command Function

Returns any command-line arguments used to launch a Visual Basic executable.

Member Of

Microsoft.VisualBasic.Interaction

Syntax

```
Command()
```

Return Value

A String containing all command-line arguments.

Comments

The Command function returns the entire command line, without the name of the executable, in a single string. For example, if an application is invoked from the command line as follows:

```
vbapp myfavoritefile.txt /a
```

the Command function returns the string

```
myfavoritefile.txt /a
```

If no command-line arguments were provided when the executable was launched, the function returns a null string. You can compare it with the String.Empty value, as the following code shows:

```
If arguments = String.Empty Then
    Console.WriteLine("An empty string.")
Else
    ' handle command line argument(s)
End If
```

Programs that support command-line arguments expect arguments in a particular position, require arguments to have a particular syntax, or both. For example, Notepad accepts a single argument, the name of the file to be opened (along with its optional path). Often, command-line switches are used as syntax elements to indicate a particular argument's purpose. Windows Explorer, for example, expects arguments to be separated by commas, and expects each argument to be preceded by a slash. It recognizes the following arguments, as shown in this table:

Argument	Description
/n	Opens a new single-paned window.
/e	Opens a new window in Explorer (two-paned) view.
/root,<object>	Defines the root level of the Explorer window's view. By default, the root is the desktop.
/select,<sub object>	The folder or file to receive the initial focus.

Similarly, the Visual Basic .NET compiler has a syntax that is documented in Appendix E. The point here is that, if your application is to accept command-line arguments, you must decide in advance what they are and what syntax they have.

Once you've established the possible arguments that can be provided on the command line and their syntax, using the Command function to extract command-line arguments requires the following steps:

- Extracting individual arguments from the single string returned by the Command function.
- Taking the appropriate action based on an argument.

Typically, extracting individual command-line arguments from the string returned by the Command function requires that you parse the string in some form. However, no parsing is necessary if the program accepts a single argument. For example, since Notepad accepts only a single argument, the name of the file to open or create, it has no difficulty handling a command line like the following, which includes embedded spaces, as Figure 8-6 shows.

```
Notepad My favorite text file.txt
```

Code like the following (which assumes that the contents of a text file are displayed in a text box named txtFileViewer) is all that is needed to handle the possible command-line argument:

FIGURE 8-6
Notepad handling
embedded spaces
in a filename

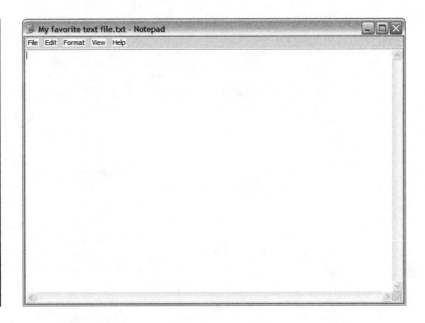

```vb
Private Sub Form1_Load(ByVal sender As System.Object, _
                       ByVal e As System.EventArgs) Handles MyBase.Load
    filename = Command()
    If Not filename = String.Empty Then
        Dim fi As New FileInfo(filename)

        If Not fi.Exists Then
            If MsgBox("File " & filename & " does not exist. Create it?", _
                    MsgBoxStyle.Question Or MsgBoxStyle.YesNo, _
                    "Create File") = MsgBoxResult.No Then Exit Sub
            File.Create(filename)
        Else
            Dim sw As StreamReader = New StreamReader(filename)
            Me.txtFileViewer.Text = sw.ReadToEnd
            sw.Close()
        End If
    End If
End Sub
```

If a program does accept multiple arguments, parsing the command line typically requires that some delimiter be used to separate one argument from another. Often, spaces are used as delimiters. However, your code has to be particularly careful about treating paths and filenames with embedded spaces as a single argument. Typically, to avoid confusion, these must be enclosed in quotation marks. For example, the following code parses a command line that can include any number of arguments delimited with quotation marks as well as of ordinary arguments delimited with spaces:

```vb
Private Function GetCommandLineArguments(cmdLine As String) _
                                    As ReadOnlyCollection(Of String)
    If cmdLine = String.Empty Then Return Nothing
```

```
    Dim argList As New List(Of String)
    Dim pos As Integer = 1              ' position of pointer
    Dim startPos, quotePos, quoteCtr As Integer
    ' Count occurrences of quotation marks
    Do
        pos = Instr(pos, cmdLine, Chr(34))
        If pos > 0 Then
            quoteCtr += 1
            pos += 1
        End If
    Loop While pos > 0
    ' Make sure number of quotation marks is even
    If quoteCtr Mod 2 = 1 Then quoteCtr += 1

    pos = 1
    Do
        startPos = pos
        ' Get first quotation mark
        If quoteCtr > 0 Then quotePos = InStr(startPos, cmdLine, Chr(34))

         pos = InStr(startPos, cmdLine, " ")
        ' quotations are next on command line
        If quoteCtr > 0 And ((pos > quotePos) Or (pos = 0)) Then
            Dim endQuotePos As Integer = Instr(quotePos + 1, cmdLine, Chr(34))
            ' If no end quote, take rest of string
            If endQuotePos = 0 Then endQuotePos = Len(cmdLine)
            argList.Add(Mid(cmdLine, quotePos, endQuotePos - quotePos + 1))
            If endQuotePos < Len(cmdLine) Then
                pos = endQuotePos + 2
            Else
                pos = 0
            End If
            quoteCtr -= 2
        ' quotations are not next
        Else
            If pos = 0 Then pos = Len(cmdLine)
            argList.Add(Mid(cmdLine, startPos, pos - startPos + 1))
            If pos < Len(cmdLine) Then
                pos += 1
            Else
                pos = 0
            End If
        End If
    Loop While pos > 0
    Return New ReadOnlyCollection(Of String)(argList)
End Function
```

Rather than writing the code to parse the command line returned by the Command function yourself, you can use one of the methods discussed later in this section that parses the command line for you.

You can use command-line arguments during debugging by selecting the Debug tab of the Project Properties dialog and entering the command-line arguments in the **Command line arguments** text box, as Figure 8-7 shows.

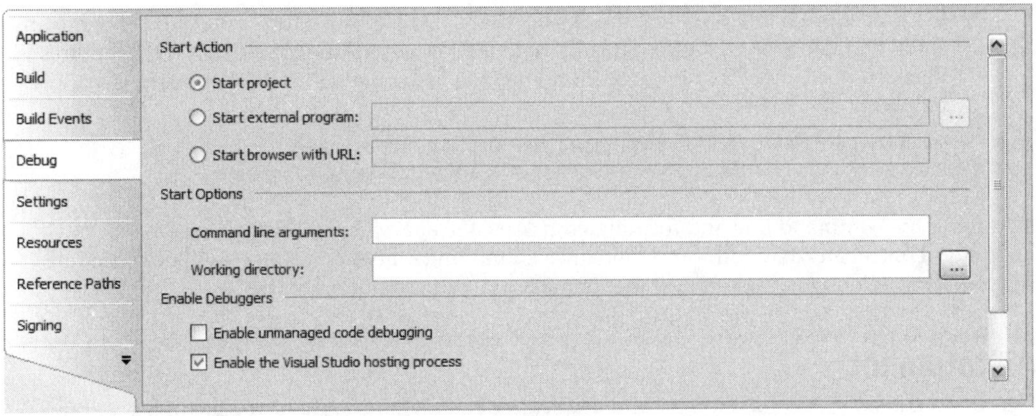

FIGURE 8-7   The Debug tab of the Project Properties dialog

You can supply command-line arguments to an executable in a number of ways:

- If the application is launched by the user directly from the command line, the user can be responsible for entering the correct command-line arguments.

- The application can be launched from a batch file, which provides the correct arguments when launching the program.

- The application can be launched from a shortcut. Command-line arguments should follow the name of the executable file and be placed outside of the closing quotation mark that terminates the executable path and filename. For example:

```
"c:\program files\consoleapp\paramapp.exe" <command-line arguments>
```

If the application handles a particular file type, the registry (the default value of the HKEY_CLASSES_ROOT\<*application_identifier*>\shell\open\command key) can be used to pass arguments to the executable. For example, a value of

```
c:\program files\consoleapp\paramapp.exe %1 /t"
```

passes two arguments to the application: %1, the path and name of the file on which the user double-clicked in an Explorer window; and /t, a hard-coded switch supplied by the registry value.

There are a number of alternate methods for retrieving the command-line arguments passed to an application:

- The static Environment.CommandLine() method, very much like the Command function, returns a single string containing all command-line arguments. However, it includes the name of the executable in the string, along with the command-line arguments.

- The Microsoft.VisualBasic.ApplicationServices.ConsoleApplicationBase class includes a CommandLineArgs property that returns a ReadOnlyCollection(Of String) collection, with each member of the collection representing one command-line argument. The CommandLineArgs property of the ConsoleApplicationBase class corresponds to the My.Application.CommandLineArgs property.

- If a procedure named Main is the application's startup procedure, you can designate an array variable that will automatically hold all command-line arguments. This requires that you implement a Main procedure that has the general syntax of either one of the following statements:

```
Public Sub Main(ByVal cmdArgs() As String)
Public Function Main(ByVal cmdArgs() As String) As Integer
```

In parsing the command line and forming cmdArgs, the space character is considered a delimiter. This means that paths and filenames containing embedded spaces will be placed in separate array elements, even if they are demarcated with quotation marks.

Const Statement

Declares a constant. A constant is a value that cannot change throughout the life of a program.

Syntax

```
[AttributeList] [AccessModifiers] [Shadows] Const constantList
```

Element	Description
AttributeList	Attributes to apply to this constant. Only attributes whose AttributeUsage attribute is AttributeTargets.All or AttributeTargets.Field can be applied to a constant.
AccessModifiers	Any one of the Public, Private, Protected, Friend, or Protected Friend access modifiers, which can be used only with module-level constants. If the access modifier is omitted, constants in classes or modules are private by default, and constants in structures are public by default.
Shadows	The constant hides an identically named language element in a base class. For details, see the entry for the Shadows Keyword. If Shadows is used, the Const statement can only declare a single constant. Shadows can only be used for module-level constants.
constantList	The definition of one or more constants, including their values and optionally their data types. If multiple constants are declared, constant definitions are delimited from one another with commas. constantList takes the form: `constantName [ As dataType ] = initializer` where constantName is the name of the constant, which must follow standard Visual Basic naming conventions, dataType is the constant's data type, and initializer is an expression that defines the value to be assigned to constantName. dataType is optional if Option Strict is off, and all three elements are required if Option Strict is on.

Comments

The major advantage of a constant is that it makes code more readable (and makes errors less likely) by replacing a value or an expression with a self-documenting label.

The second advantage of a constant that's typically cited—that it allows a value to be defined in a single place, so that if the value subsequently changes, the code needs to be modified in only a single place—is highly problematic. Since it requires that an application or library be recompiled and the new executables distributed, it is a valid argument only for beta releases or for a production executable that runs only on your system and only under your direct control. The classic example of such a constant is the sales tax. Yet, imagine if the sales tax is coded as a constant: whenever the sales tax changes (as it tends to do in some areas with some regularity), all users of an application must received new executables just as the sales tax changes, or they end up charging their customers too little sales tax. Rather than coding such relatively stable value as constants, they should be read-only variables whose values are read from a configuration file.

Constants can be defined in any class (a construct defined by the Class . . . End Class statements), module (a construct defined by the Module . . . End Module statements), or structure (a construct defined by the Structure . . . End Structure statements). Since static members cannot be defined as members of interface, constants cannot be defined inside of interfaces (constructs defined by the Interface . . . End Interface statements). Nor can they be defined as members of enumerations (constructs defined by the Enum . . . End Enum statements).

Constants can be declared at the *member level* (inside a class, structure, or module definition, but outside of properties or methods) but not as local values (inside of properties, methods, and event handlers). Access modifiers, attributes, and the Shadows keyword can be used in the former case, but not in the latter.

Constants can be of any intrinsic Visual Basic .NET data type (Boolean, Byte, Char, etc.) or any enumerated type (including user-defined enumerations). The instance members of that data type can be called from the constant. For example:

```
Const pastDate As Date = #07/28/1993#
Console.WriteLine(pastDate.AddDays(30).ToString)
```

If Option Strict is off and a data type is not explicitly defined, the data type of a constant is the data type of *initializer*. If *initializer* is a literal value whose type is not explicitly identified (as would be the case if a type identifier such as % or c is not provided), integers are initialized as Objects whose runtime type is Integer for integers, Double for floating point values, and String for strings of any length.

initializer can be an expression and need not be only a literal value. There are, however, some restrictions about the use of expressions or non-literal values to define the value of constants:

- For local constants (constants defined within type members), a constant whose value is assigned to another constant must be defined before the other constant.

- For all constants, any part of *initializer* must be a constant or literal value. This includes the return value of some pure functions (that is, functions whose output depends wholly on its arguments) whose arguments are constants or literals (which are constant values as well). For this reason, the statement

  ```
  Const quote As String = Chr(34)
  ```

  is valid.

By definition, constants are shared, and read-only. However, these keywords cannot be used when defining constants.

FIGURE 8-8

Information on constants displayed by ILDasm

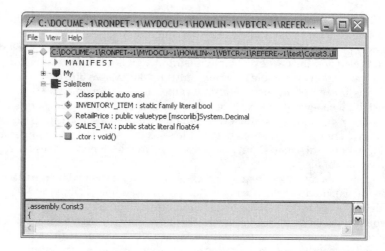

Constants appear to be identical to read-only properties, since neither allows a value to be assigned to it at runtime. They differ, however, in one major respect: the value of a read-only property can be dynamically assigned in its class constructor as well as when it is declared, whereas the value of a constant must be assigned when it is declared.

It is generally believed that constants are replaced with their values at compile time, so that no trace of the constant remains in the final executable. However, this is not true of constants in .NET. For example, the following very simple code defines a class that has two constants and one field:

```
Public Class SaleItem
    Public Const SALES_TAX As Double = .0725
    Protected Const INVENTORY_ITEM As Boolean = True
    Public RetailPrice As Decimal
End Class
```

Examining the class using ILDasm indicates that information on the two module-level constants is stored with the assembly's metadata, as Figure 8-8 shows, and therefore is available at runtime. Double-clicking on either of the constants provides us with additional information about it. For example, ILDasm reports the following information about the SALES_TAX constant:

```
.field public static literal float64 SALES_TAX = float64(7.2499999999999995e-002)
```

Since information about module-level constants is stored with the assembly's metadata, it is dynamically available at runtime using reflection. For example, the following code, assuming that it is located in a module in the same assembly as the definition of the SaleItem class, successfully extracts information about both the public constant and the protected constant in SaleItem:

```
Public Sub Main()
    Dim si As New SaleItem

    Dim Flags As BindingFlags = BindingFlags.Instance Or BindingFlags.Static _
                        Or BindingFlags.NonPublic Or BindingFlags.Public
    Dim ass As [Assembly] = Assembly.GetExecutingAssembly()
```

```
    Dim typ As Type = ass.GetType("SaleItem")
    Dim flds() As FieldInfo = typ.GetFields(Flags)
    Console.WriteLine("{0} has {1} fields:", typ.Name, flds.Length)
    For Each fld As FieldInfo In flds
        Console.WriteLine("   {0}", fld.Name)
        Console.WriteLine("        Data Type: {0}", fld.FieldType.Name)
        If fld.IsStatic Then
            Console.WriteLine("        Value: {0}", fld.GetValue(Nothing).ToString)
        Else
            Console.WriteLine("        Value: {0}", fld.GetValue(si).ToString)
        End If
    Next
End Sub
```

The routine produces the following output to a console window:

```
SaleItem has 3 fields:
    RetailPrice
        Data Type: Decimal
        Value: 0
    SALES_TAX
        Data Type: Double
        Value: 0.0725
    INVENTORY_ITEM
        Data Type: Boolean
        Value: True
```

In Visual Basic .NET, module-level constants (depending on their access modifiers) are inherited by derived classes. For example, the following code defines a base class, ConstantBase, which includes a single constant, and a derived class, ConstantDerived, with no members:

```
Public Class ConstantBase
    Public Const GENERATION As Integer = 1
End Class

Public Class ConstantDerived : Inherits ConstantBase
End Class

Public Class classMain
    Public Shared Sub Main()
        Dim cd As New ConstantDerived
        Console.WriteLine(cd.GENERATION)
    End Sub
End Class
```

When the code is compiled and run, we are able to access the Generation constant through the ConstantDerived class, even though it is defined in the base ConstantBase class.

VB6 Differences

Visual Basic 6.0 permitted module-level constants to be declared only with the Public and Private access modifiers. Visual Basic .NET adds the Friend modifier (which was supported in Visual Basic 6.0, though not with constants) and the Protected modifier (which is new to Visual Basic .NET).

Visual Basic 6.0 did not permit constants to be defined inside of user-defined types, the rough equivalent of structures in Visual Basic .NET. Visual Basic .NET, on the other hand, supports this usage and makes constants in structures public by default.

Visual Basic 6.0 did not allow constants defined in a class module (the equivalent of the Visual Basic .NET Class . . . End Class construct) to be public. In Visual Basic .NET, although constants defined in a class are private by default, they can be declared as public.

Visual Basic 6 required that a constant whose value was used in an expression or assignment to define the value of another constant be defined before the other constant. Visual Basic .NET enforces this requirement for local constants only. The order in which module-level constants that are defined in terms of the value of other module-level constants are declared is unimportant.

Visual Basic 6 allowed public constants to be defined with the Global keyword as well as the Public keyword. Visual Basic .NET does not support the Global keyword.

See Also

Dim Statement, Friend Statement, Private Statement, Protected Statement, Public Statement, Shadows Keyword

Continue Statement

Transfers control from within a looping structure to the beginning of a loop.

Syntax

```
Continue { Do | For | While }
```

Comments

The Continue For statement works with both the For . . . Next construct and the For Each . . . Next construct, as well as with the Do . . . Loop and While . . . End While constructs.

To exit from a loop, you use the Exit Do, Exit For, or Exit While statement. In contrast, Continue Do, Continue For, and Continue While skip the remaining code to the end of the loop and resume execution at the beginning of the loop.

In the case of nested loops of the same type (such as nested For . . . Next loops), the Continue statement transfers control to the beginning of the inner loop.

In the case of nested loops of different types, the keyword that follows Continue specifies whether control should transfer to the inner or the outer loop. The example program illustrates this.

The Continue statement cannot transfer control outside of a Try . . . Catch . . . Finally block.

VB.NET Changes

The Continue statement is new to Visual Basic 2005 and .NET 2.0.

VB6 Differences

The Continue statement was not supported in Visual Basic 6.0 and earlier versions. To skip a portion of a looping construct and continue execution at the top of the loop, If . . . EndIf statements were used, or a label was placed at the top of the loop and the GoTo statement was used to transfer program execution to it.

See Also

Exit Statement

CreateObject Function

Creates a COM object and returns a reference to it.

Member Of

Microsoft.VisualBasic.Interaction

Syntax

```
CreateObject(ByVal ProgId As String, Optional ByVal ServerName As String = "") _
        As Object
```

Element	Description
ProgId	The programmatic identifier of the COM class
ServerName	For applications based on distributed COM (DCOM), the network computer on which the object will reside.

Return Value

A reference to an instance of the COM class

Comments

ProgId is a string found in the system registry that often takes the general form *libraryName.className* (although it in fact can be any string whose value is unique). It is the name of a subkey of the HKEY_CLASSES_ROOT key, and it in turn contains a subkey named CLSID. The default value of the CLSID key is the class identifier, which is a GUID (a globally unique identifier) that theoretically uniquely identifies the COM object across time and space. The HKEY_CLASSES_ROOT\CLSID*<class_identifier>* key in turn provides the necessary information on where the class is defined and how it should be instantiated.

Except for single-instance objects (see the next item), the CreateObject function creates a new instance of a COM object; to retrieve a reference to an existing instance, use the GetObject function.

If an application is registered as single-instance, the CreateObject function creates a new instance if one does not already exist. If one does exist, however, it returns a reference to that single instance.

Since .NET creatable .NET classes are not assigned programmatic identifiers, the CreateObject function cannot be used to instantiate .NET types unless they are explicitly exposed as COM objects.

In addition to the CreateObject function, COM objects can be instantiated using the same syntax as .NET objects:

```
Dim objectVar As typeName
objectVar = New typeName
```

or

```
Dim objectVar As typeName = New typeName
```

As long as *typeName* is not Object, early binding can be used to bind to the object at compile time rather than at runtime. In contrast, because they rely on the registry, objects instantiated with the CreateObject function always are late-bound; binding occurs at runtime rather than at compile time.

In order to use early binding, you must add a reference to the COM object to your project in the Visual Studio environment. To do this, select the COM tab of the Add Reference dialog, and select the COM library you'd like to add to your project. The compiler will look for a primary interop assembly (PIA), a .NET library that marshals calls to and from the COM library. If one is not found, Visual Studio creates a temporary .NET interoperability assembly. The net result is that you will be able to use the COM library as if it were a .NET assembly. If you're using the Visual Basic .NET command-line compiler, you can only use the /r switch to reference a PIA; attempting to reference a COM library generates a syntax error. This means that, in the absence of a PIA, you have to use late binding and the CreateObject function.

Example

The following code uses the CreateObject function to instantiate a Dictionary object from scrrun.dll, the Microsoft Scripting Runtime:

```
Option Strict Off

Public Module modMain

    Public Sub Main()
        Dim dict As Object
        dict = CreateObject("Scripting.Dictionary")
        dict.Add("CA", "California")
        dict.Add("MI", "Michigan")
        dict.Add("NY", "New York")

        For Each stateName As String In dict
            Console.WriteLine(stateName)
        Next
    End Sub

End Module
```

See Also

GetObject Function

CSByte Function

Converts an expression to an SByte, or signed byte, data type.

Syntax

```
CSByte(expression)
```

Element	Description
expression	An expression to be converted to a SByte.

Return Value

An SByte

Comments

CSByte supports the conversions listed in the following table:

Type of *expression*	Conversion	Comments
Boolean	Narrowing	Converts True to –1, False to 0.
Byte	Narrowing	The numeric ranges of Byte (0 to 255) and SByte (–128 to 127) only partially overlap. Where they do, CSByte returns the Byte value unchanged. Where they do not, an OverflowException is thrown.
SByte		Returns *expression* unchanged.
All integral types other than Byte and SByte	Narrowing	The numeric ranges of all other integer types are supersets of the Byte range. Where a narrowing conversion results in loss of data, an OverflowException is thrown.
Floating point types (Decimal, Double, and Single)	Narrowing	The floating point value is rounded to the nearest integer before conversion.
Object	Depends on runtime type of *expression*	*expression* must be a supported type (a numeric string, any integer, a floating point number, or a Boolean) or a null object reference (objects that equal Nothing convert to 0).
String	Narrowing	Converts the string representation of a number to an SByte if it is in the range of the SByte type; otherwise, an OverflowException results. An empty string is converted to 0. If the string does not represent a number, an InvalidCastException results.

Note that the narrowing conversions can be handled implicitly by the compiler only if Option Strict is off. If Option Strict is on, they require an explicit conversion using CByte or another conversion function.

The .NET type that SByte wraps is System.SByte.

All of the conversions performed by CByte can also be performed by the shared System.Convert. ToSByte method. The sole difference in return value is that System.Convert.ToSByte converts a Boolean value of False to 1, whereas CSByte converts it to –1.

Conversion of Char and Date expressions to Boolean is not supported by CSByte. System.Convert.ToSByte does support Char-to-SByte conversion; it is identical in function to the Visual Basic AscW function.

Like all of the intrinsic Visual Basic conversion functions, the CSByte function is not defined in the Microsoft.VisualBasic namespace but instead is implemented directly by the compiler.

VB.NET Changes

The CSByte function was introduced for the first time in Visual Basic 2005. In previous versions of Visual Basic .NET, the function was absent. This is because the SByte type, although it existed in the .NET Framework Class Library's System namespace, did not become an "intrinsic" Visual Basic data type until Visual Basic 2005.

VB6 Differences

Visual Basic 6.0 did not recognize the signed byte as a data type and therefore had no need for a CSByte conversion function.

See Also

CByte Function, CObj Function, CType Function

CShort Function

Converts an expression to a Short (a 16-bit integer).

Syntax

```
CShort(expression)
```

Element	Description
expression	An expression to be converted to a Short.

Return Value

A Short (System.UInt16)

Comments

CShort supports the conversions listed in the following table:

Type of *expression*	Conversion	Comments
Boolean	Narrowing	Converts False to 0, True to –1.
Byte, SByte	Widening	The numeric ranges of the Byte (0 to 255) and SByte (–128 to 127) data types is a subset of the numeric range of the Short data type.

Type of *expression*	Conversion	Comments
floating point types (Decimal, Double, Single)	Narrowing	The range of all floating point types exceeds the range of a Short. Fractional components are rounded before conversion.
Integer, UInteger	Narrowing	The numeric range of the Integer (−2,147,483,648 to 2,147,483,647) and UInteger (0 to 4,294,967,295) data types exceeds the range of a Short.
Long, ULong	Narrowing	The numeric range of the Long (−9,223,372,036,854,775,808 to 9,223,372,036,854,775,807) and ULong (0 to 18,446,744,073,709,551,615) data types exceeds the range of a Short.
Object	Depends on the runtime type of *expression*	*expression* must be a supported type (a valid string, an integer or floating point number, or a Boolean) or a null object reference (objects that equal Nothing convert to 0).
Short		Returns *expression* unchanged.
String	Narrowing	Converts the string representation of a number to a Short if it is in the range of the Short data type; otherwise, an OverflowException is thrown. If the string represents a number with a fractional component, it is rounded before conversion. An empty string is converted to 0. If the string does not represent a number, an InvalidCastException results.
UShort	Narrowing	The numeric range of the UShort data type (0 to 35,535) only partially overlaps the range of a Short.

Note that the narrowing conversions can be handled implicitly by the compiler only if Option Strict is off. If Option Strict is on, they require an explicit conversion using CShort or another conversion function.

The CShort function is able to handle strings containing localized currency symbols and thousands separators without generating an error.

Conversion of Char and Date expressions to Short is not supported and throws an InvalidCastException. However, the shared Convert.ToInt16 method can be used to convert a Char to a Short that represents its character code.

All of the conversions performed by CShort can also be performed by the shared System.Convert.ToInt16 method. When converting a Boolean to a Short, however, ToInt16 converts True to 1, while CShort converts it to −1.

Like all of the intrinsic Visual Basic conversion functions, the CShort function is not defined in the Microsoft.VisualBasic namespace but instead is implemented directly by the compiler.

VB6 Differences

Although the CShort function itself is new to Visual Basic .NET, it is equivalent to the CInt function in Visual Basic 6.0. (In Visual Basic 6.0, the Integer was a 16-bit integral data types; in Visual Basic .NET, the Short is a 16-bit integral data type.)

See Also

CObj Function, CType Function, CUShort Function

CSng Function

Converts an expression to a Single.

Syntax

```
CSng(expression)
```

Element	Description
expression	An expression to be converted to a Single.

Return Value

A Single

Comments

CSng supports the conversions listed in the following table:

Type of *expression*	Conversion	Comments
Boolean	Narrowing	Converts False to 0, True to −1.
All integral types (Byte, Integer, Long, SByte, UShort, etc.)	Widening	Conversions from Integer, Long, Uinteger, and ULong may involve a loss of precision.
Decimal	Widening	Conversions from Decimal may involve a loss of precision.
Double	Narrowing	The valid range of the Single data type (Single.MinValue to Single.MaxValue) only partially overlaps the valid range of the Double data type (Double.MinValue to Double.MaxValue).
Object	Depends on runtime type of *expression*	At runtime, *expression* must be a supported type (a Boolean, integer, floating point, or string representation of a number) or a null object reference (objects that equal Nothing convert to 0). Otherwise, it throws an InvalidCastException.
Single		Returns *expression* unchanged.
String	Narrowing	The string must be a string representation of a number; otherwise, an InvalidCastException is thrown.

Note that the narrowing conversions can be handled implicitly by the compiler only if Option Strict is off. If Option Strict is on, they require an explicit conversion using CSng or another conversion function.

Conversion from Char and Date to Single using CSng is not supported.

To prevent a non-numeric string from throwing an InvalidCastException when passing a string to the CSng function, you can call the IsNumeric function beforehand. For example:

```
Dim convertedDouble As Double
If IsNumeric(inputString) Then
    convertedDouble = CSng(inputString)
End If
```

The CSng function is able to handle strings containing localized currency symbols and thousands separators without generating an error.

The conversions performed by CSng can also be performed by the shared System.Convert. ToSingle method. The only difference in operation is that ToSingle converts a Boolean True to 1, whereas CSng converts it to –1. In addition, Decimal-to-Single conversions can be performed by the shared Decimal.ToSingle method.

Like all of the intrinsic Visual Basic conversion functions, the CSng function is not defined in the Microsoft.VisualBasic namespace but instead is implemented directly by the compiler. This differs from Visual Basic 6.0, where CSng was a member of the Conversion class in the VBA library.

Example

The example contains an overloaded CanConvertToSingle method that can be called before performing a narrowing conversion to a Single. The function returns True if the conversion is legal and will not result in data loss, and False otherwise. The example also illustrates calls to the CSng function if CanConvertToSingle returns True.

```
Public Class SingleUtil

Public Shared Sub Main()
    Dim value As Double = Double.MaxValue
    If CanConvertToSingle(value) Then
        Console.WriteLine("Can convert: {0}", CSng(value))
    Else
        Console.WriteLine("Cannot convert {0}", value)
    End If

    Dim strng As String = Nothing
    If CanConvertToSingle(strng) Then
        Console.WriteLine("Can convert: {0}", CSng(strng))
    Else
        Console.WriteLine("Cannot convert {0}", strng)
    End If

    Dim emptyStrng As String = ""
    If CanConvertToSingle(emptyStrng) Then
        Console.WriteLine("Can convert: {0}", CSng(emptyStrng))
    Else
        Console.WriteLine("Cannot convert {0}", emptyStrng)
    End If
End Sub
```

```
Private Overloads Shared Function CanConvertToSingle(value As Double) As Boolean
    Console.WriteLine("Double version")
    Dim sng As Single = 0
    If value > sng.MaxValue Or value < sng.MinValue Then
        Return False
    Else
        Return True
    End If
End Function

Private Overloads Shared Function CanConvertToSingle(value As String) As Boolean
    If value = "" And (Not value Is Nothing) Then
        Return False
    Else
        Return CanConvertToSingle(CObj(value))
    End If
End Function

Private Overloads Shared Function CanConvertToSingle(value As Object) As Boolean
    If value Is Nothing Then
        Return True
    ElseIf Not IsNumeric(value) Then
        Return False
    Else
        Return CanConvertToSingle(CDbl(value))
    End If
End Function
End Class
```

VB6 Differences

In Visual Basic 6.0, the CSng function could be used to convert a Date to a Single; the integral component of the returned Single represented the number of days since December 30, 1899, and the fractional component represented the elapsed time since midnight. In Visual Basic .NET, Date-to-Single conversion using CSng is not supported.

See Also

CObj Function, CType Function

CStr Function

Converts an expression to a String.

Syntax

```
CStr(expression)
```

Element	Description
expression	An expression to be converted to a string.

Return Value

A String

Comments

As the following table shows, the CStr function is able to perform most conversions:

Type of *expression*	Comments
Boolean	Converts False to the value of Boolean.FalseString, True to the value of Boolean.TrueString.
Char	Converts the Char value to a one-character String.
Date	Converts a date or time to its string representation using the local system's Short Date format or Time format, as defined by the Control Panel's Regional and Language Options applet. "Neutral" date and time values are suppressed (see the note in the Comments section).
floating point types (Decimal, Double, Single)	Converts the floating point value to its string representation.
integer types (Byte, SByte, Integer, UInteger, etc.)	Converts the integer value to its string representation.
Object	The runtime type of *expression* must be an intrinsic Visual Basic .NET data type. Objects of other types, including objects whose value is Nothing, (a valid string, an integer or floating point number, or a Boolean) or a null object reference (objects that equal Nothing convert to 0).
String	Returns expression unchanged.

Although expressions of the types listed in the previous table can be assigned to a String if Option Strict is set off, all require the use of a conversion operator if Option Strict is set on, or a compiler error results.

Although a value of type Date always contains both a date and a time component, CStr sometimes returns only a date or only a time. If it considers either the date or the time to be a neutral value, it includes only the value that is not neutral in the returned string. The neutral date is January 1, 0001 C.E., and the neutral time is 00:00:00 (midnight). (These are, incidentally, the date and time values of an uninitialized Date variable.) For purposes of type conversion, Visual Basic .NET considers 1/1/1 (January 1 of the year 1) to be a neutral value for the date, and 00:00:00 (midnight) to be a neutral value for the time.

If the CStr function is called to convert a null object reference (an object that equals Nothing), a NullReferenceException is thrown.

If the CStr function is called to convert an object instance that is not an intrinsic Visual Basic .NET data type, an InvalidCastException is thrown. For class or structure instances, call the ToString method, which typically returns the name of the class or structure.

Instead of using the CStr function, it is also possible to call the shared Convert.ToString method to perform each of the conversions listed in the previous table. In addition, each of the intrinsic Visual Basic .NET types has a ToString method that returns a string. CStr, Convert.ToString, and ToString all produce identical results.

Like all of the intrinsic Visual Basic conversion functions, the CSng function is not defined in the Microsoft.VisualBasic namespace but instead is implemented directly by the compiler. This differs from Visual Basic 6.0, where CSng was a member of the Conversion class in the VBA library.

The CStr function merely wraps a call to the shared overloaded Microsoft.VisualBasic. CompilerServices.Conversions.ToString method.

See Also

CObj Function, CType Function

CType Function

Converts one .NET type to another.

Syntax

```
CType(expression, type)
```

Element	Description
expression	An expression that evaluates to an instance of a value or reference type.
type	The type to which to convert *expression*.

Returns

expression converted to *type*.

Comments

type can be any intrinsic Visual Basic data type, as well as a class, structure, interface, or enumeration.

expression must evaluate to an object or structure instance that derives directly or indirectly from *type* (if type is a class), implements *type* (if type is an interface), is a base class to *type*, or supports a defined conversion to *type*.

A defined conversion exists if either of the following cases:

- A conversion is defined by a member of the Conversions class in the Microsoft.VisualBasic namespace. These are conversions from one intrinsic type to another and are the same conversions defined for the conversion functions with a single target type, such as CBool, CByte, etc.

- A custom conversion operator is defined for expression if it is a custom class or structure. The example illustrates such a conversion.

CType is a kind of super-conversion operator that combines the CBool, CByte, CChar, CDate, CDbl, CDec, CInt, Cng, CObj, CSByte, CShort, CSng, CStr, CUInt, CULng, CUShort, and DirectCast functions into a single function.

CType recognizes implicit inheritance relationships. You can, for instance, use CType to convert an Integer to an Object and vice versa, or to convert a Long to a System.ValueType.

CType can be used to convert an integral type to an enumerated value, which is a narrowing conversion that must be explicitly handled if Option Strict is on. For example, the code

```
Dim x As Integer = 1
Dim mr As MsgBoxResult = CType(x, MsgBoxResult)
Console.WriteLine(mr.ToString)
```

displays "OK" to the console. If the conversion fails, however, CType does not raise an exception but instead assigns the original integer value to the enumeration variable. For example, the code

```
x = 39341
mr = CType(x, MsgBoxResult)
Console.WriteLine(mr.ToString)
```

displays the value "39341" to the console.

Like the other Visual Basic .NET conversion functions, CType is implemented directly by the compiler, rather than in a .NET class library like Microsoft.VisualBasic.dll.

A conversion can fail for either of two reasons:

No conversion between the type of *expression* and *type* is defined. In that case, CType throws an InvalidCastException.

The conversion is a narrowing one that results in a loss of information. In that case, CType throws an OverflowException.

Before converting a reference type using CType, it is always wise to use the TypeOf . . . Is construct to check the runtime type of the expression being converted to determine whether it is likely to raise an exception. For example, we could use code like the following to convert MyBaseClass to MyDerivedClass:

```
If TypeOf myBaseClass1 Is myDerivedClass Then
    myDerivedClass1 = DirectCast(myBaseClass1, MyDerivedClass)
Else
    ' Do something to handle inability to perform conversion
End If
```

Generally, it is argued that DirectCast offers significantly improved performance over CType when converting from base to derived types. It is unclear, however, whether the difference in performance is significant.

Example

The example defines a Dog class that includes a custom conversion operator to convert instances of Dog to a string. The conversion operator simply returns a string containing the dog's breed (or the more generic word "dog" if no value is assigned to the Dog.Breed property) and name.

```
Public Module TestCType
    Public Sub Main()
        Dim myDog As New Dog("Dakota")
        myDog.Breed = "Alaskan Malamute"
        Dim dogInfo As String = CType(myDog, String)
        Console.WriteLine(dogInfo)
    End Sub
End Module
```

```
Public Class Dog
   Private dogName As String
   Private dogBreed As String

   Public Sub New(name As String)
      Me.dogName = name
   End Sub

   Public Property Breed() As String
      Get
         Return dogBreed
      End Get
      Set
         dogBreed = Value
      End Set
   End Property

   Public Shared Narrowing Operator CType(dogInst As Dog) As String
      If dogInst.dogBreed = String.Empty Then dogInst.dogBreed = "dog"
      Return "A " & dogInst.dogBreed & " named " & dogInst.dogName & "."
   End Operator
End Class
```

Note the use of the Operator statement to define a custom conversion function. All operators must be Shared. The CType keyword indicates that this is a conversion operator, dogInst as Dog indicates the expression to be converted, and String indicates the target data type of the conversion. Conversion defined in this manner can be performed only with CType; DirectCast, TryCast, and the other Visual Basic .NET conversion functions will not work.

VB6 Differences

The CType function was not supported by Visual Basic 6.0.

See Also

CObj Function, CType Function, DirectCast Function, Operator Statement, Option Strict Statement, TryCast Function

CUInt Function

Converts an expression to a UInteger (System.UInt32) data type.

Syntax

```
CInt(expression)
```

Element	Description
expression	An expression to be converted to a UInteger.

Return Value

A UInteger

Comments

CUInt supports the conversions listed in the following table:

Type of *expression*	Conversion	Comments
Boolean	Narrowing	Converts False to 0, True to 4,294,967,295 (which is equal to UInteger.MaxValue, and also has the same bit pattern as a signed integer equal to –1).
Byte	Widening	The numeric range of the Byte data type (0 to 255) is a subset of the numeric range of the UInteger data type.
floating point types (Decimal, Double, Single)	Narrowing	The range of all floating point types exceeds the range of a UInteger. Fractional components are rounded before conversion.
Integer	Narrowing	The numeric range of the Integer data type (–2,147,483,648 to 2,147,483,647) only partially overlaps the range of a UInteger (0 to 4,294,967,295).
Long, ULong	Narrowing	The numeric range of the Long (–9,223,372,036,854,775,808 to 9,223,372,036,854,775,807) and ULong (0 to 18,446,744,073,709,551,615) data types exceeds the range of a UInteger.
Object	Depends on the runtime type of *expression*	*expression* must be a supported type (a valid string, an integer or floating point number, or a Boolean) or a null object reference (objects that equal Nothing convert to 0).
Short	Narrowing	The numeric range of the Short data type (–32,768 to 32,767) only partially overlaps the numeric range of a UInteger data type.
SByte	Narrowing	The numeric range of the signed byte data type (–128 to 127) only partially overlaps that of the UInteger data type.
String	Narrowing	Converts the string representation of a number to a UInteger if it is in the range of the Integer data type; otherwise, an OverflowException results. If the string represents a number with a fractional component, it is rounded before conversion. An empty string is converted to 0. If the string does not represent a number, an InvalidCastException results.
UInteger		Returns *expression* unchanged.
UShort	Widening	The numeric range of the UShort data type (0 to 65,535) is a subset of the numeric range of a UInteger.

Note that the narrowing conversions can be handled implicitly by the compiler only if Option Strict is off. If Option Strict is on, they require an explicit conversion using CUInt or another conversion function.

The CUInt function is able to handle strings containing localized currency symbols and thousands separators without generating an error.

Conversion of Char and Date expressions to UInteger is not supported and throws an InvalidCastException. However, the shared Convert.ToUInt32 method can be used to convert a Char to an Integer that represents its character code.

In performing arithmetic operations with numeric literals and UInteger types, Visual Basic may generate compiler errors if Option Strict is on. For example, the code

```
Dim unsigned As UInteger = 132
unsigned *= 2
```

generates a compiler error because implicit Long-to-UInteger conversions are disallowed by Option Strict, and the numeric literal 2 is interpreted by the Visual Basic .NET compiler as a Long. The problem can be fixed either by using a type identifier (the type identifier for a UInteger is UI or ui):

```
unsigned *= 2ui
```

or it can be fixed by using the CUInteger conversion function:

```
unsigned *= CUInt(2)
```

All of the conversions performed by CUInt can also be performed by the shared System.Convert. ToUInt32 method. When converting a Boolean to an Integer, however, ToUInt32 converts True to 1, while CUInt converts it to 4,294,967,295.

Like all of the intrinsic Visual Basic conversion functions, the CUInt function is not defined in the Microsoft.VisualBasic namespace but instead is implemented directly by the compiler.

VB.NET Changes

The CUInt function is new to Visual Basic 2005, which for the first time supports the UInteger as an intrinsic Visual Basic data type.

VB6 Differences

Visual Basic 6.0 did not support the CUInt data type, nor did it include an unsigned integer data type other than the Byte.

See Also

CInt Function, CObj Function, CType Function

CULng Function

Converts an expression to a ULong data type.

Syntax

CULng(expression)

Element	Description
expression	An expression to be converted to a Ulong.

Return Value

A ULong

Comments

CULng supports the conversions listed in the following table:

Type of *expression*	Conversion	Comments
Boolean	Narrowing	Converts False to 0, True to 18,446,744,073,709,551,615 (which is equal to ULong.MaxValue, and also has the same bit pattern as a signed integer equal to –1).
Byte	Widening	The numeric range of the Byte data type (0 to 255) is a subset of the numeric range of the UInteger data type.
floating point types (Decimal, Double, Single)	Narrowing	The range of all floating point types exceeds the range of a UInteger. Fractional components are rounded before conversion.
signed integral data types	Narrowing	The numeric range of the SByte (–128 to 127), Short (–32,768 to 32,767), Integer (–2,147,483,648 to 2,147,483,647), and Long (–9,223,372,036,854,775,808 to 9,223,372,036,854,775,807) data types only partially overlaps that of the ULong data type.
ULong		Returns *expression* unchanged.
other unsigned data types (Byte, UShort, UInteger)	Widening	The numeric range of the ULong exceeds that of the Byte (0 to 255), UShort (0 to 65,535), and UInteger (4,294,967,295) data types.
Object	Depends on the runtime type of *expression*	*expression* must be a supported type (a valid string, an integer or floating point number, or a Boolean) or a null object reference (objects that equal Nothing convert to 0).
String	Narrowing	Converts the string representation of a number to a UInteger if it is in the range of the Integer data type; otherwise, an OverflowException results. If the string represents a number with a fractional component, it is rounded before conversion. An empty string is converted to 0. If the string does not represent a number, an InvalidCastException results.

Note that the narrowing conversions can be handled implicitly by the compiler only if Option Strict is off. If Option Strict is on, they require an explicit conversion using CULng or another conversion function.

The CULng function is able to handle strings containing localized currency symbols and thousands separators without generating an error.

Conversion of Char and Date expressions to ULong is not supported and throws an InvalidCastException. However, the shared Convert.ToUInt64 method can be used to convert a Char to a ULong that represents its character code.

In performing arithmetic operations with numeric literals and ULong types, Visual Basic may generate compiler errors if Option Strict is on. For example, the code

```
Dim number As ULong = 132
number \= 2
```

generates a compiler error because the literal 2 is interpreted as a Long, and implicit Long-to-ULong conversions are narrowing conversions disallowed by Option Strict. The problem can be fixed either by using a type identifier (the type identifier for a ULong is UL or ul):

```
number \= 2ul
```

or it can be fixed by using the CULng conversion function:

```
number \= CULng(2)
```

All of the conversions performed by CULng can also be performed by the shared System.Convert.ToUInt64 method. When converting a Boolean to a Long, however, ToInt64 converts True to 1, while CULng converts it to 18,446,744,073,709,551,615.

Like all of the intrinsic Visual Basic conversion functions, the CULng function is not defined in the Microsoft.VisualBasic namespace but instead is implemented directly by the compiler.

VB.NET Changes

The CULng function is new to Visual Basic 2005, which for the first time supports the ULong as an intrinsic Visual Basic data type.

VB6 Differences

The function is not supported in Visual Basic 6.0, which did not include an unsigned data type other than Byte.

See Also

CLng Function, CObj Function, CType Function

CUShort Function

Converts an expression to a UShort data type.

Syntax

```
CUShort(expression)
```

Element	Description
expression	An expression to be converted to a Ushort.

Return Value

A UShort

Comments

CUShort supports the conversions listed in the following table:

Type of *expression*	Conversion	Comments
Boolean	Narrowing	Converts False to 0, True to 65,535 (which is equal to ULong.MaxValue, and also has the same bit pattern as a signed integer equal to –1).
Byte	Widening	The numeric ranges of the Byte (0 to 255) data types lies entirely within the numeric range of the UShort data type.
floating point types (Decimal, Double, Single)	Narrowing	The range of all floating point types exceeds the range of a Short. Fractional components are rounded before conversion.
rightall signed integer types	Narrowing	The numeric ranges of the SByte (–128 to 127), Short (–32,768 to 32,767), Integer (–2,147,483,648 to 2,147,483,647), and Long (–9,223,372,036,854,775,808 to 9,223,372,036,854,775,807) data type only partially overlaps that of a UShort.
Object	Depends on the runtime type of *expression*	*expression* must be a supported type (a valid string, an integer or floating point number, or a Boolean) or a null object reference (objects that equal Nothing convert to 0).
String	Narrowing	Converts the string representation of a number to a UShort if it is in the range of the UShort data type; otherwise, an OverflowException results. If the string represents a number with a fractional component, it is rounded before conversion. An empty string is converted to 0. If the string does not represent a number, an InvalidCastException results.
UInteger and ULong	Narrowing	The numeric range of the UInteger (0 to 4,294,967,295) and ULong (0 to 18,446,744,073,709,551,615) data types exceeds the numeric range of a UShort.
UShort		Returns expression unchanged.

Note that the narrowing conversions can be handled implicitly by the compiler only if Option Strict is off. If Option Strict is on, they require an explicit conversion using CUShort or another conversion function.

The CUShort function is able to handle strings containing localized currency symbols and thousands separators without generating an error.

Conversion of Char and Date expressions to UShort is not supported and throws an InvalidCastException. However, the shared Convert.ToUInt16 method can be used to convert a Char to a UShort that represents its character code.

The use of conversion operators applies not only to variable assignment, but also to assigning literals and the result of arithmetic operations to a UShort as well. For example, the addition in following code generates a compiler error if Option Strict is on:

```
Dim number As UShort = 264
number += 132
```

The reason is that the compiler interprets the literal 132 as an Integer, and implicit Integer-to-UShort conversions are narrowing conversions disallowed by Option Strict. The problem can be fixed either by using a type identifier (the type identifier for a UShort is US or us):

```
number += 132us
```

or by using the CUShort conversion function:

```
number += CUShort(132)
```

All of the conversions performed by CShort can also be performed by the shared System.Convert.ToUInt16 method. When converting a Boolean to a UShort, however, ToUInt16 converts True to 1, while CUShort converts it to 65,535.

Like all of the intrinsic Visual Basic conversion functions, the CUShort function is not defined in the Microsoft.VisualBasic namespace but instead is implemented directly by the compiler.

VB.NET Changes

The CUShort function is new to Visual Basic 2005, which for the first time supports UShort as an intrinsic Visual Basic data type.

VB6 Differences

The function is not supported in Visual Basic 6.0, which did not include an unsigned data type other than Byte.

See Also

CObj Function, CShort Function, CType Function

CurDir Function

Returns the current directory of a particular drive or of the application's default drive.

Member Of

Microsoft.VisualBasic.FileSystem

Syntax

```
CurDir(drive)
CurDir()
```

Element	Description
drive	A Char representing the drive whose directory is to be returned.

Return Value

A String containing the path to the current directory.

Comments

The function returns the complete absolute path to the current directory starting from the drive.

The overloaded version of the CurDir function that accepts no arguments returns the current directory of the current or default drive.

According to the documentation, if an empty string is passed to the function, it returns the current directory of the default drive. In fact, it throws an ArgumentException.

Note that the data type of the *drive* argument is a Char. Typically, this means that if Option Strict is on, you must convert a String to a Char before calling the function. This in turn has two additional implications:

- *drive* must be the letter of a drive without a colon. However, converting a multicharacter string to a character discards all but the first letter of the string, which presumably is the drive letter.

- Although *drive* can be the name of a mapped network drive (e.g., z), it cannot be the UNC path to a network drive.

If *drive* is the letter of a drive with removable media but none present, CurDir simply returns the path to the drive's root directory; it does not first attempt to determine whether the drive is ready.

If drive is not a valid drive on the local system, the function throws an IOException. To prevent this, you can call the GetDrives method of the System.IO.DriveInfo class; the method returns a collection of DriveInfo objects representing all valid drives on the local system. This allows you to implement an IsValidDrive function like the following:

```
Public Shared Function IsDriveValid(drive As Char) As Boolean
    Dim drives As DriveInfo() = DriveInfo.GetDrives()
    For Each dr As DriveInfo In drives
        If drive = CChar(dr.Name) Then Return True
    Next
    Return False
End Function
```

Visual Basic .NET lacks a CurDrive function that corresponds to CurDir and returns the name of the current drive. However, you can easily implement one as follows:

```
Public Shared Function CurDrive() As Char
    Return CChar(CurDir())
End Function
```

The function returns a Char indicating the current drive. It works because the CurDir function returns the complete drive and filename of the current directory, and CChar extracts and converts only the first character of the string passed to it. Note that the Convert.ToChar method could not have been used for this purpose, since it requires that a one-character String be passed to it for conversion.

You can also get the current directory from the shared Environment.CurrentDirectory property. Like the CurDir function, it returns a string containing the complete absolute path from the drive to the current directory. Unlike CurDir, it returns the current directory only for the current drive. In addition, as of Visual Basic 2005, you can use the shared CurrentDirectory property of the Microsoft.VisualBasic.FileIO.FileSystem class, or its equivalent, the My.Computer.FileSystem .CurrentDirectory property. The following code illustrates calls to the properties to retrieve the current directory:

```
Console.WriteLine(Environment.CurrentDirectory)

Console.WriteLine(FileIO.FileSystem.CurrentDirectory)
Console.Writeline(My.Computer.FileSystem.CurrentDirectory)
```

VB6 Differences

In Visual Basic 6.0, it was legal to pass the CurDir function an uninitialized string or an empty string (a string whose value is ""). In Visual Basic .NET, however, this throws an ArgumentException.

See Also

ChDir Subroutine, ChDrive Subroutine, MkDir Subroutine, RmDir Subroutine

---

Custom Keyword

Used with an Event statement to indicate the presence of custom code that executes when an event handler is added or removed or when an event is raised.

Syntax

See the syntax of the Event statement.

Comments

If the Custom keyword is present, the Event statement must be in the form of an Event . . . End Event construct that includes the following:

- Code that executes when the consumer of a class adds an event handler using either the Handles statement or the AddHandler statement. It is defined by the AddHandler . . . End AddHandler construct.

- Code that executes when a consumer of the class removes an event handler using the RemoveHandler statement. It is defined by the RemoveHandler . . . End Removehandler construct.

- Code that executes when the event is raised. It is defined by the RaiseEvent . . . End RaiseEvent construct.

Ordinarily, the Event statement can define the event handler's syntax either explicitly or by using a delegate. However, when the Custom keyword is used, it must define the event using an explicit delegate type.

Both the AddHandler and RemoveHandler constructs have a single parameter, a delegate representing the event handler to be added. Their signatures are:

```
AddHandler(ByVal value As delegatename)
AddHandler(ByVal value As delegatename)
```

The RemoveHandler construct must specify the signature of the delegate that handles the events. The delegate itself cannot be used. For example, a statement such as

```
RaiseEvent(e As EventHandler)
```

generates a compiler error, while its rough equivalent

```
RaiseEvent(sender As Object, e AS EventArgs)
```

does not.

Ordinarily, event notification occurs through a single multicast delegate that executes synchronously. This means that if there are multiple event handlers, they execute in succession, with one event handler executing after the previous one. This also means that an event handler that takes a particularly long time to process its event can block the other handlers until it completes its processing. Custom event processing using the Custom keyword can be used to define asynchronous event handlers. The Example section illustrates such a scenario and provides the code that implements a custom event handler.

Custom event processing can be used to reduce the amount of memory consumed in handling events. The Visual Basic document contains an example, entitled "How to: Declare Events that Conserve Memory Use," that provides an explanation along with sample code.

Example

Some event notifications are critical. In a real-time event system, synchronous processing of events is highly undesirable. It is even possible, that if an unhandled exception occurs in an event handler, that a subsequent event handler might never be invoked. In such situations, defining an asynchronous event handler is important.

One such scenario might involve a temperature monitoring system. The following code provides a very simple implementation that monitors temperature, allows a warning level to be set, fires an event when the temperature reaches or exceeds that warning level that passes a custom WarningEventArgs instance rather than the standard EventArgs interest, and executes any client event handlers asynchronously.

The following class defines such a custom temperature monitor. A threshold temperature that fires a warning event is defined when the Monitor class is instantiated. Thereafter, when a new temperature reading (reflected in an assignment to the object's Temperature property) is greater than or equal to the threshold temperature, the Warning event is fired.

When clients instantiate the class and define an event handler, the code in the AddHandler construct executes, and reference to the event handler's delegate is added to an ArrayList named eventHandlers. If an event handler is removed, a reference to its delegate is passed to the RemoveHandler construct, which simply passes it to the ArrayList object's Remove method to remove it from the eventHandlers ArrayList. When the temperature threshold is reached or exceeded, the event is raised, which in turn causes the code in the RaiseEvent construct to execute.

This iterates the eventHandler ArrayList and uses the BeginInvoke method to asynchronously invoke each delegate.

```vb
Imports System.Collections

Namespace TemperatureWarningSystem

    ' Define delegate with event handler signature
    Public Delegate Sub WarningEventHandler(sender As Object, e As WarningEventArgs)

    ' Define custom EventArgs class to pass to event with extra information
    Public Class WarningEventArgs : Inherits EventArgs

        Private temp As Decimal

        Public Sub New(temperature As Decimal)
            MyBase.New()
            Me.temp = temperature
        End Sub

        Public ReadOnly Property Temperature() As Decimal
            Get
                Return Me.temp
            End Get
        End Property
    End Class


    ' Define monitor class that notifies listeners if temperature passes threshold
    Public Class Monitor

        Private temp As Decimal
        Private warningTemp As Decimal
        Private eventHandlers As New ArrayList()

        Public Custom Event Warning As WarningEventHandler
            AddHandler(ByVal e As WarningEventHandler)
                eventHandlers.Add(e)
            End AddHandler

            RemoveHandler(ByVal e As WarningEventHandler)
                eventHandlers.Remove(e)
            End RemoveHandler

            RaiseEvent(ByVal sender As Object, ByVal e As WarningEventArgs)
                For Each eventHandler As WarningEventHandler In eventHandlers
                    Try
                        eventHandler.BeginInvoke(sender, e, Nothing, Nothing)
                    Catch
                        ' handle exception
                    End Try
                Next

            End RaiseEvent
        End Event
```

```
    Public Sub New(warning As Decimal)
        Me.warningTemp = warning
    End Sub

    Public Property Temperature() As Decimal
        Get
            Return Me.temp
        End Get
        Set
            Me.temp = Value
            If Me.Temp >= warningTemp Then
                RaiseEvent Warning(Me, New WarningEventArgs(Me.temp))
            End If
        End Set
    End Property
    End Class
End Namespace
```

VB.NET Changes

The Custom keyword is new in Visual Basic 2005.

VB6 Differences

The Custom keyword is not supported in Visual Basic 6.0.

See Also

AddHandler Statement, Event Statement, Handles Keyword, RaiseEvent Statement, RemoveHandler Statement

---

DateAdd Function

Adds a number of date or time units to a date.

Member Of

Microsoft.VisualBasic.DateAndTime

Syntax

```
DateAdd(ByVal Interval As DateInterval, ByVal Number As Double, _
        ByVal DateValue As DateTime) As DateTime
DateAdd(ByVal Interval As String, ByVal Number As Double, _
        ByVal DateValue As Object) As DateTime
```

Element	Description
Interval	Indicates the date or time unit represented by *Number*, and therefore the unit by which *DateValue* is to be incremented or decremented. Its value can be either a string or its corresponding DateInterval enumeration member, both of which are as shown in Table 8-1.
Number	A floating point expression that indicates the number of *Interval* time units to add to (if its value is positive) or to subtract from (if its value is negative) DateValue.
DateValue	A Date expression representing the date to which *Number* is to be added or subtracted. It is passed by value to the function.

String	DateInterval Member	Description
d	DateInterval.Day	Days
y	DayInterval.DayOfYear	Days
h	DateInterval.Hour	Hours
n	DateInterval.Minute	Minutes
m	DateInterval.Month	Months
q	DateInterval.Quarter	Quarters
s	DateInterval.Second	Seconds
w	DateInterval.Weekday	Day of the week
ww	DateInterval.WeekOfYear	Weeks
yyyy	DateInterval.Year	Years

Return Value

A date representing the Date equivalent of *DateValue* incremented or decremented by *Number*.

Comments

DateAdd is an "intelligent" function that automatically takes into account such factors as leap years and the different number of days in each month of the year when performing date calculations.

When used with the DateAdd function, "d". "y", and "w" (or the equivalent enumerated values DateInterval.Day, DateInterval.DayOfYear, and DateInterval.Weekday) all function identically: they add or subtract a designated number of days from a date.

Using a member of the DateInterval enumeration instead of a string as the argument for *Interval* makes the function call far more self-documenting.

According to the documentation, any fractional component of *Number* is ignored except in date addition or subtraction involving time units (hours, minutes, or seconds). In fact, any fractional component of *Number* is always ignored regardless of the value of *Interval*.

The documentation implies that the *Number* must lie within a range of values if particular intervals are used. For instance, it mentions that "d" represents the number of days in a month (ranging from 0 to 31), and "y" the number of days in a year, and "w" the number of days in the week. This is not accurate, however; *Number* simply cannot be a value that, when added or subtracted from *DateValue*, results in a date outside the bounds of the DateTime value. The range of the resulting Date must lie between 12:00:00 midnight, January 1, 0001 C.E., and 11:59:59 P.M., December 31, 9999 C.E.

DateValue must be a Date or a string representation of a Date, or an InvalidCastException is thrown when the function attempts to convert *DateValue* to a date. To prevent this, you can use the IsDate function to check that *DateValue* is a valid date representation.

The Date data type and the .NET Framework Class Library support a number of ways for doing date/time arithmetic. None, however, are quite as simple as the DateAdd function. These include:

- Date addition and subtraction, in which a TimeSpan object defining a time period is added to or subtracted from a Date. The time period is defined by the arguments supplied to the TimeSpan object's overloaded constructor, which has the following syntax:

```
TimeSpan(ticks)
TimeSpan(hours, minutes, seconds)
TimeSpan(days, hours, minutes, seconds)
TimeSpan(days, hours, minutes, seconds, milliseconds)
```

where ticks is a time period measured in 100-nanosecond units, and the remaining parameters are self-explanatory. For example, the following code subtracts one day and 12 hours to the current time and displays the result:

```
Console.WriteLine(Date.Now - New TimeSpan(1, 12, 0, 0))
```

- The Add method, which adds the time interval indicated by a TimeSpan object to a Date instance. Code adding the same 36-hour interval as in the previous example appears as follows:

```
Console.WriteLine(Date.Now.Add( New TimeSpan(1, 12, 0, 0)))
```

Example

The following code illustrates the use of the DateAdd function to add and subtract 36 hours from the current date and time:

```
Console.WriteLine(DateAdd(DateInterval.Hour, 36, Date.Now))
Console.WriteLine(DateAdd(DateInterval.Hour, -36, Date.Now))
```

VB6 Differences

Visual Basic 6.0 accepted only the String values shown in Table 8-1 as the *Interval* argument. Visual Basic .NET also accepts a member of the DateInterval enumeration.

The range of the Date data type in Visual Basic 6.0 began at 1 January 100 C.E., one hundred years later than the beginning range of the Date data type in Visual Basic .NET.

See Also

DateDiff Function

DateDiff Function

Indicates the time interval between two date values.

Member Of

Microsoft.VisualBasic.DateAndTime

Syntax

The DateDiff function is overloaded:

```
DateDiff(ByVal Interval As DateInterval, ByVal Date1 As Date, _
        ByVal Date2 As Date, _
        Optional ByVal DayOfWeek As FirstDayOfWeek = FirstDayOfWeek.Sunday, _
        Optional ByVal WeekOfYear As FirstWeekOfYear = FirstWeekOfYear.Jan1)
```

```
DateDiff(ByVal Interval As String, ByVal Date1 As Object, _
        ByVal Date2 As Object, _
        Optional ByVal DayOfWeek As FirstDayOfWeek = FirstDayOfWeek.Sunday, _
        Optional ByVal WeekOfYear As FirstWeekOfYear = FirstWeekOfYear.Jan1)
```

Element	Description
Interval	A string or a member of the DateInterval enumeration that defines what date interval between Date1 and Date2 is to be calculated. Valid values are the same as those for the Interval argument of the DateAdd function and were shown earlier in Table 8-1.
Date1	A Date expression to subtract from Date2.
Date2	A Date expression.
DayOfWeek	An optional member of the FirstDayOfWeek enumeration, as shown in Table 8-2.
WeekOfYear	An optional member of the FirstWeekOfYear enumeration, as shown in Table 8-3.

Return Value

A Long indicating the interval between the two dates.

Comments

The DateDiff function returns the result of the expression

```
Date2 - Date1
```

in time units defined by *Interval*. If *Date1* is later than *Date2*, the result is negative; if *Date1* is earlier than *Date2*, the result is positive.

Both DateInterval.Day (or "d") and DateInterval.DayOfYear (or "y") calculate the number of days between two dates and return identical results.

TABLE 8-2
Members of the
FirstDayOfWeek
Enumeration

FirstDayOfWeek Member	Description
System	Use the first day of the week specified by the system settings in Control Panel.
Sunday	Sunday; this is the default value.
Monday	
Tuesday	
Wednesday	
Thursday	
Friday	
Saturday	

FirstWeekOfYear Member	Description
System	Use the system definition of the first week of the year.
Jan1	Consider the first week of the year as the week on which January 1 falls. This is the default value.
FirstFourDays	Consider the first week of the year as the first week of the new year that has four full days.
FirstFullWeek	Consider the first week of the year as the first week of the new year that has seven full days.

DateInterval.WeekOfYear (or "ww") calculates the number of weeks between the first day of the week on which *Date2* falls and the first day of the week on which *Date1* falls. (The *DayOfWeek* argument determines when that first day of the week is.) In contrast, the DateInterval.Weekday (or "w") argument calculates the number of full seven-day periods between the two dates.

In calculating intervals of DateInterval.Month (or "m"), the DateDiff function simply considers the month number of *Date1* and *Date2* along with the year. For example, the DateDiff function returns a value of 1 if DateInterval.Month is chosen as the Interval Value, *Date1* is set equal to 12/31/2005, and *Date2* is set equal to 1/1/2006, because the two dates fall on different months, even though they are only a day apart.

In calculating quarter intervals (DateInterval.Quarter, or "q"), the function considers the number of quarters between the beginning of the quarter on which *Date2* falls and the beginning of the quarter on which *Date1* falls.

In calculating year intervals (DateInterval.Year, or "yyyy"), DateDiff merely subtracts the year value of *Date1* from the year value of *Date2*. Because of this, the function is able to report that the difference between January 1, 2006, and December 31, 2005, is one year, even though they are only one day apart.

If the *Interval* is specified as a String argument rather than a DateInterval enumeration member, *Date1* and *Date2* can both be strings in Date format, and the function will convert them to dates before calculating the time interval between dates. If the conversion cannot be performed at runtime, an InvalidCastExeption exception occurs. To prevent this, the IsDate function can be used to check that the strings can be successfully converted to dates.

You can also use the members of the Date data type to calculate the different between two dates. In particular, the Date data type supports date/time subtraction both as an arithmetic operation (one date/time value is subtracted from another using the subtraction operator) and by calling the Subtract method (a date is subtracted from the Date instance whose method is called). In either case, the return value is a TimeSpan object that represents the resulting time interval, which can be translated into a desired time interval by calling one of the TimeSpan object's members. A number of these (TotalDays, TotalHours, TotalMinutes, and TotalSeconds) return a value that is identical to the DateDiff function's return value when called with a corresponding member of the DateInterval enumeration. However, the TimeSpan object does not allow you to readily express time in terms of years, quarters, months, or week, as the DateDiff function does.

Supplying a DateInterval enumeration member rather than a string as the *Interval* argument makes the DateDiff function far more self-documenting.

Example

The example shows a number of calls to the DateDiff function and, for each call, shows a corresponding call to the Date data type's Subtract method and the result of Date subtraction:

```
Public Module DateDiffTest
    Public Const dat1 As Date = #12/10/2005#
    Public Const dat2 As Date = #1/2/2006 01:00:00PM#

    Public Sub Main()
        ' Perform subtraction and return days: all return 23
        Console.WriteLine(DateDiff(DateInterval.Day, dat1, dat2))
        Console.WriteLine((dat2 - dat1).Days)
        Console.WriteLine(dat2.Subtract(dat1).Days)

        ' Perform subtraction and return hours: all return 565
        Console.WriteLine(DateDiff(DateInterval.Hour, dat1, dat2))
        Console.WriteLine((dat2 - dat1).TotalHours)
        Console.WriteLine(dat2.Subtract(dat1).TotalHours)

        ' Perform subtraction and return minutes: all return 33,900
        Console.WriteLine(DateDiff(DateInterval.Minute, dat1, dat2))
        Console.WriteLine((dat2 - dat1).TotalMinutes)
        Console.WriteLine(dat2.Subtract(dat1).TotalMinutes)

        ' Perform subtraction and return seconds: all return 2,034,000
        Console.WriteLine(DateDiff(DateInterval.Second, dat1, dat2))
        Console.WriteLine((dat2 - dat1).TotalSeconds)
        Console.WriteLine(dat2.Subtract(dat1).TotalSeconds)
    End Sub
End Module
```

VB6 Differences

Visual Basic 6.0 accepted only the String values shown earlier in Table 8-1 as the *Interval* argument. Visual Basic .NET also accepts a member of the DateInterval enumeration.

See Also

DateAdd Function

DatePart Function

Extracts a particular component from a date or time.

Member Of

Microsoft.VisualBasic.DateAndTime

Syntax

The function is overloaded as follows:

```
DatePart(ByVal Interval As DateInterval, ByVal DateValue As DateTime, _
    Optional ByVal FirstDayOfWeekValue As FirstDayOfWeek = VbSunday, _
    Optional ByVal FirstWeekOfYearValue As FirstWeekOfYear = VbFirstJan1)

DatePart(ByVal Interval As String, ByVal DateValue As Object, _
    Optional ByVal DayOfWeek As FirstDayOfWeek = FirstDayOfWeek.Sunday,
    Optional ByVal WeekOfYear As FirstWeekOfYear = FirstWeekOfYear.Jan1)
```

Element	Description
Interval	A String or a member of the DateInterval enumeration that defines the date/time unit the function is to return. Valid values for Interval are shown in Table 8-1.
DateValue	A Date value, or a String capable of conversion to a Date value.
FirstDayOfWeekValue or *DayOfWeek*	An optional member of the FirstDayOfWeek enumeration (see Table 8-2).
FirstWeekOfYearValue or *WeekOfYear*	An optional member of the FirstWeekOfYear enumeration (see Table 8-3).

Return Value

An Integer representing the time unit specified by *Interval*.

Comments

For the most part, the function simply extracts the time element defined by *Interval* from *DateValue*. For example, if DateValue is #8/18/2006#, the function returns 8 for an *Interval* value of DateInterval.Month, 18 for DateInterval.Day, 2006 for DateInterval.Year, etc. It combines into a single function the functionality offered by functions such as Day, Hour, Minute, Month, Second, Weekday, and Year.

DateInterval.Day (or "d") and DateInterval.DayOfYear (or "y") when used with DatePart yield very different results. The former simply extracts the number representing the day from *DateValue,* while the latter calculates the numerical position of *DateValue* in the current year of either 365 or 366 days.

If Interval is set equal to DateInterval.Weekday (or "w"), the function returns the ordinal position of the *DateValue* day in the week that starts with *DayOfWeek*. To make this clear, May 10, 2006, was a Wednesday. If the function is called as follows:

```
DateDiff(DateInterval.Weekday, #5/10/2006#)
```

it returns 4, because Wednesday is the fourth day of a week that begins with Sunday. However, the following function call:

```
DateDiff(DateInterval.Weekday, #5/10/2006#, FirstDayOfWeek.Monday)
```

returns 3, because Wednesday is the third day of a week that begins with Monday.

If *Interval* equals DateInterval.Week, the function returns the position of *DateValue* in a year of 52 or 53 weeks. In calculating which week of the year *DateValue* falls in, it considers both the values of *DayOfWeek* and *WeekOfYear*.

The function's second overload allows *DateValue* to be either a String or a Date. In the former instance, the function converts it to a date before returning a date/time component. If the conversion fails, an InvalidCastExeption exception occurs. To prevent this, the IsDate function can be used to check that the string can be successfully converted a date.

Supplying a DateInterval enumeration member rather than a string as the *Interval* argument makes the DatePart function more self-documenting.

Much of the functionality provided by the DatePart function is available from the members of the Date data type. The example illustrates a function call to DatePart and the equivalent use of a Date property to retrieve the same result. All of the values returned by the DatePart function can also be retrieved from Date properties except for the quarter on which a date falls and the week of the year on which a date falls.

Example

The following example calls the DatePart function four times and also illustrates the use of a DateTime property to retrieve an identical value.

```
Public Sub Main()
    Dim DateValue As Date = #05/10/2006 11:36:05AM#

    ' Display month number: Both return 5
    Console.WriteLine(DatePart(DateInterval.Month, DateValue))
    Console.WriteLine(DateValue.Month)

    ' Display day number: Both return 10
    Console.WriteLine(DatePart(DateInterval.Day, DateValue))
    Console.WriteLine(DateValue.Day)

    ' Diaplay day of week: Return 4 and Wednesday
    Console.WriteLine(DatePart(DateInterval.Weekday, DateValue))
    Console.WriteLine(DateValue.DayOfWeek.ToString)

    ' Display day of year: Both return 130
    Console.WriteLine(DatePart(DateInterval.DayOfYear, DateValue))
    Console.WriteLine(DateValue.DayOfYear)
End Sub
```

VB6 Differences

Visual Basic 6.0 accepted only the String values shown earlier in Table 8-1 as the *Interval* argument. Visual Basic .NET also accepts a member of the DateInterval enumeration.

See Also

DateValue Function, Day Function, Hour Function, Minute Function, Month Function, Second Function, Weekday Function, and Year Function

DateSerial Function

Forms a date out of individual date components.

Member Of

Microsoft.VisualBasic.DateAndTime

Syntax

```
DateSerial(ByVal Year As Integer, ByVal Month As Integer, ByVal Day As Integer) _
        As Date
```

Element	Description
Year	An integer expression from 1 through 9999 representing a year.
Month	An integer expression from 1 to 12 representing a month.
Day	An integer expression from 1 to 31 representing a day of the month.

Return Value

A Date value

Comments

As a means of assigning a Date value, the following three statements are all equivalent:

```
Dim dateValue As Date = DateSerial(2006, 8, 18)
Dim dateValue As Date = #8/18/2006#
Dim dateValue As Date = CDate("8/18/2006")
Dim dateValue As Date = New DateTime(2006, 8, 18)
```

The advantage of DateSerial (although this is true as well of CDate and the Date constructor) is that it can evaluate dynamic expressions or variables, whereas the middle assignment statement requires a literal expression. Interestingly, the syntax of DateSerial and the overloaded constructor of the Date data type used here are identical.

The DateSerial function interprets values for *Year* that range from 0 to 29 as representing the years 2000–2029, and it interprets values for *Year* from 30 to 99 as representing the years 1930–1999. Probably the reason for this is compatibility with Visual Basic 6.0, since the earliest year that a Date type could represent was 100 C.E.

This means that the time period from 1/1/0001 C.E. to 12/31/0099 C.E. is out of the normal range of the DateSerial function. To return a date in that range, *Year* must be a negative value that, when subtracted from the current year, yields the desired year. For example, if the current year is 2006, the following statement returns the date 7/8/0070 C.E.:

```
Dim DateValue As Date = DateSerial(-1935, 07, 08)
```

The function handles negative arguments as follows:

- *Year* is subtracted from the current system year.
- *Month* is decremented by one and subtracted from January (e.g., 0 is equivalent to December, –1 to November, etc.)
- *Day* is decremented by one and subtracted from the first of *Month* (e.g., 0 returns the last date in the previous month).

More generally, if an argument is outside of its normal range, DateSerial uses date addition or subtraction to adjust the date accordingly. For instance, if *Days* exceeds the number of days in a month, the *Month* component of the date is incremented accordingly.

If the result of date addition and subtraction performed by the function produces a date outside the range of the Date data type, an ArgumentOutOfRangeException is thrown.

An excellent use of the DateSerial function is to assemble a date value when not all components of the date are constant, but some recur on a regular interval. For example, the following code stores four dates representing the beginning of each quarter of a particular year to an array:

```
Private Function GetStartOfQuarters(year As Integer) As Date()
   Dim qtrs(3) As Date
   For qtr As Integer = 0 To 3
      qtrs(qtr) = DateSerial(year, qtr * 3 + 1, 1)
   Next
   Return qtrs
End Function
```

VB6 Differences

In Visual Basic 6.0, a negative *Year* value was subtracted from 2000 to form the returned date's year component; in Visual Basic .NET, it's subtracted from the current year.

See Also

CDate Function, TimeSerial Function

DateString Property

Gets or sets the current system date.

Member Of

Microsoft.VisualBasic.DateAndTime

Syntax

```
DateString
```

Property Value

The string representation of a current date

Comments

The function returns the date in a string with an invariant format of MM-DD-YYYY (such as 10-01-2005).

The date can be set using a string whose format must be "M-d-yyyy", "M-d-y", "M/d/yyyy", and "M/d/y". These formats are not affected by the system's regional settings. Any other format causes an InvalidCastException to be thrown.

You should consider carefully whether it's actually necessary to set the system date.

You can retrieve the date from the more culturally sensitive members of the Date data type, including Date.Now (which returns the current system date and time) and Date.Today (which returns the current system date).

VB6 Differences

The function is new to Visual Basic .NET; it replaces the Visual Basic 6.0 Date$ property (which returned a string representation of the current system date) and Date statement (which allowed the date to be set).

See Also

TimeString Property

DateValue Function

Converts the formatted string representation of a date to a Date value.

Member Of

Microsoft.VisualBasic.DateAndTime

Syntax

```
DateValue(ByVal StringDate As String)
```

Element	Description
StringDate	A string representation of a date.

Return Value

A Date value

Comments

If StringDate includes a time component, DateValue fails to convert it to a time; instead, the date returned by the function always has a time of midnight (12:00:00 AM), which represents an uninitialized time value.

Even though DateValue discards the time component of *StringDate,* it throws an InvalidCastException if an invalid time component is present and is invalid.

DateValue is capable of converting any date for which the IsDate function returns True, and is capable of recognizing months in long name, abbreviated name, and numeric formats (e.g., December, Dec, and 12). However, if *StringDate* consists of only numbers and date delimiters (for example, 20/11/05), the function interprets *StringDate* according to the short date format defined in the local system's regional settings.

If *StringDate* includes only day and month but not year information, the function uses the current year, as defined by the system calendar.

See Also

CDate Function

Day Function

Extracts the numerical day of the month from a particular date value.

Member Of

Microsoft.VisualBasic.DateAndTime

Syntax

```
Day(ByVal DateValue As Date)
```

Element	Description
DateValue	A Date value.

Return Value

An Integer ranging from 1 to 31 indicating the day of the month

Comments

If Option Strict is off, the function throws an InvalidCastException if you pass *DateValue* a string that cannot be cast to a date. (If Option Strict is on, the conversion must be performed before calling the function.)

In attempting to compile code that includes a call to the Day function, you may receive the compiler error, "'Day' is a type and cannot be used as an expression.," This is because you have used the Imports statement to import a namespace that defines a type named Day. Most likely, this is the Day enumeration in the System.Windows.Forms namespace. You can resolve this problem in several ways:

- Since Day is a shared function, you can preface the call to the Day function with the name of the type (DateAndTime) of which it is a member.

- You can provide a fully qualified path to the Day function (Microsoft.VisualBasic. DateAndTime.Day or, just in the event that you've declared a variable named Microsoft in your code, Global.Microsoft.VisualBasic.DateAndTime.Day) to eliminate any ambiguity.

- You can use an alias for the System.Windows.Forms namespace. See the entry for the Namespace Statement for details.

The Day function is equivalent to calling a Date object's Day method, or to calling the DatePart function with an *Interval* argument of DayInterval.Day (or "d").

See Also

DatePart Function, WeekdayName Function

DDB Function

Calculates the depreciation of an asset for a specific time period.

Member Of

Microsoft.VisualBasic.Financial

Syntax

```
DDB( ByVal Cost As Double, ByVal Salvage As Double, ByVal Life As Double, _
       ByVal Period As Double, Optional ByVal Factor As Double = 2.0)
```

Element	Description
Cost	The initial value of the asset.
Salvage	The value of the asset at the end of its useful life.
Life	The useful life of the asset.
Period	The period for which depreciation is calculated.
Factor	The rate of depreciation. The default value of 2 represents the double-declining depreciation method.

Return Value

A Double indicating the amount of depreciation of an asset.

Comments

Three major depreciation methods are available:

- The straight-line method, which depreciates an asset by a constant value in each period. The straight-line method is performed by the SLN function and is not supported by the DDB method.

- The single-declining balance method, which assumes a constant rate of depreciation of an asset in each period. The single-declining balance method is performed by supplying a value of 1 for the *Factor* argument of the DDB function.

- The double-declining balance method, which uses a variable rate of acceleration that varies inversely with year. In other words, the rate of depreciation is greater in the early period of an asset's useful life than in the later period. The double-declining balance method is performed by supplying a value of 2 for the *Factor* argument of the DDB function.

The formula used for calculating the depreciation in a period by the DDB function is:

```
Depreciation / Period = ((Cost - Salvage) * Factor) / Life
```

Life and *Period* must represent the same time unit. For instance, if an asset's life is measured in years, depreciation must be measured in years as well.

Factor must be positive, or an ArgumentException is thrown. Of positive numeric values, only 1 are 2 are meaningful, although the DDB function makes no attempt to enforce this restriction. However, the value returned by the function if *Factor* is greater than 2 is unlikely to conform to standard accounting practice.

Example

The following procedure displays a depreciation table that lists the amount of depreciation and the remaining value of an asset for each year of its useful life.

```
Public Sub DepreciateAsset(cost As Double, salvage As Double, _
                        life As Double, factor As Double)
    Dim depreciation As Double = 0
    Dim currentValue As Double = cost
    Dim period As Double = 0

    Console.WriteLine("Period       Depreciation       Value of Asset")
    Console.WriteLine()
    Console.WriteLine("{0,5}.         {1,10:C}            {2,10:C}", _
                    period, depreciation, currentValue)
    For period = 1 to life
        depreciation = DDB(cost, salvage, life, period, factor)
        currentValue -= depreciation
        Console.WriteLine("{0,5}.         {1,10:C}            {2,10:C}", _
                    period, depreciation, currentValue)
    Next
End Sub
```

See Also

SLN Function, SYD Function

Declare Statement

Defines an external routine located in a Windows dynamic link library.

Syntax

```
[ <attrlist> ] [ accessModifier ] [ Shadows ] _
Declare [ Ansi | Unicode | Auto ] [ Sub ] name Lib "libname" _
[ Alias "aliasName" ] [([ arglist ])]
```

or

```
[ <attrlist> ] [ accessModifier ] [ Shadows ] _
Declare [ Ansi | Unicode | Auto ] [ Function ] name Lib "libname" _
[ Alias "aliasName" ] [([ arglist ])] [ As type ]
```

Element	Description
<attrlist>	An attribute that can be applied to a function or subroutine. Only attributes whose AttributeUsage attribute is AttributeTargets.All or AttributeTargets.Method can be applied to a Declare statement.
accessModifier	The accessibility of the function or subroutine. Possible keywords are Public, Private, Friend, and Protected, and Protected Friend. For details, see the entry for each of the access modifiers. If *accessModifier* is not specified, the class has Public access; it is accessible not only within the class, but by any application that can reference the assembly in which the class resides.

Element	Description
Shadows	Indicates that the routine hides an identically named programming element in a base class. For details, see the Shadows keyword.
ANSI, UNICODE, or AUTO	Defines how string arguments are marshaled. For details, see the entries for the Ansi Keyword, Auto Keyword, and Unicode Keyword.
name	If *aliasName* is present, the name by which the function or procedure will be called in code. If *aliasName* is not present, both the name by which the function or procedure will be called in code and the name of the function or procedure as it is defined in its external library. In the latter case, name is case sensitive; its case must match that of the routine as it is defined in its external library.
libname	The name of the Windows dynamic link library in which *name* or, if it is present, *aliasName* resides. The file extension (.dll) can be omitted if the library is loaded (as the major Windows system libraries are). For additional detail, see the entry for the Lib keyword.
aliasName	The name of the function or subroutine as it is found in *libname*. There are a number of reasons for calling the routine by one name when it is defined by another name in its external DLL. In addition, *aliasName* can also begin with a # symbol and define the ordinal position of the function or subroutine in the external DLL. For a complete discussion, see the entry for the Alias Keyword.
arglist	The function or subroutine's parameter list, which defines its signature. The parameters must be replaced with arguments when calling the routine.
type	For functions, the data type of the return value. The return value can be any intrinsic Visual Basic .NET data type (Boolean, Byte, Char, etc.), as well as any enumeration, structure, class, or interface.

The syntax of *arglist* is:

```
[ByVal | ByRef[ paramName[()] [As Type]
```

Element	Description
ByVal I ByRef	Indicates whether the argument is passed by value or by reference to the called routine. If the keyword is omitted, the argument is passed by value.
paramName	The parameter name. It is a simple placeholder.
As *Type*	The parameter's data type. It is required if Option Strict is on. If Option Strict is off and the clause is omitted, the argument type defaults to Object.

Comments

The Declare statement can be used to define procedures in Windows dynamic link libraries only. It cannot be used to define procedures in such files as .NET assemblies, Microsoft Foundation Class (MFC) class libraries, or Component Object Model (COM) libraries. To access members in COM libraries, use the CreateObject function.

Declare statements appear at the member level in classes, structures, and modules. The Declare statement cannot appear in an interface.

It's important to explicitly assign an access modifier that reflects the accessibility that you want the external routine to have. In particular, routines that are marked as public or that have no access modifier become part of a type's public interface and therefore can be invoked from any code that has access to the type in which they're defined.

Although you can't use the Overloads keyword with the Declare statement, Declare statements can be overloaded; you can use the same function or procedure name to define multiple functions or procedures, as long as they have unique signatures. This is an attractive alternative when an external routine can accept one of several data types as an argument. For example, many Win32 API functions accept a pointer to a string buffer but expect a null pointer if one is not supplied. This can be handled by defining two separate versions of the function, one that passes the string by value, the other than passes an integer whose value is 0 to the function.

The Visual Basic compiler performs no type checking of Declare statements at compile time; it merely checks them for valid syntax. Each time that an external routine is called at runtime, the .NET runtime checks that .NET types can be marshaled to and, if necessary, from the external routine. If not, a MarshalDirectiveException results.

Typically, errors in syntax or in passing arguments to external routines generate runtime exceptions. Errors in the API calls themselves, however, may or may not generate exceptions. If an API call fails, error information is sometimes available from the LastDLLError property of the Err object.

The importance of the Declare statement has declined, as much of the functionality of the Win32 API has been incorporated into the .NET Framework Class Library. In such areas as networking, registry access, and gathering system information, it is often far simpler and easier to call a member of the .NET Framework Class Library than it is to call an external DLL routine.

Example

The following code illustrates a call to the Win32 GetKeyboardType function, which can indicate the type of keyboard and the number of keyboard function keys available on a system keyboard. In addition to illustrating the use of the Declare statement, the example also defines enumerations to enhance the readability of the function's single parameter and of the return values when the function returns information about a keyboard's type.

```
Module Module1
    Private Enum KeyboardFlagType As Short
        KeyboardType = 0
        KeyboardSubtype = 1          ' return values are manufacturer-defined
        FunctionKeys = 2
    End Enum

    Private Enum KeyboardReturnType As Short
        XtOrCompatible = 1
        OlivettiIco = 2
        AtOrCompatible = 3
        IBMEnhanced = 4
        Nokia1050Family = 5
        Nokia9140Family = 6
        Japanese = 7
        UsbKeyboard = 81
    End Enum
```

```
    Private Declare Function GetKeyboardType Lib "user32" _
                (ByVal nTypeFlag As Short) As Short

   Sub Main()
     Dim returnValue As Short = _
         GetKeyboardType(KeyboardFlagType.FunctionKeys)
     If returnValue <> 0 Then
       Console.WriteLine("The keyboard has {0} function keys.", _
                         returnValue)
     End If
     returnValue = GetKeyboardType(KeyboardFlagType.KeyboardType)
     If returnValue > 0 Then
       If [Enum].IsDefined(GetType(KeyboardReturnType), returnValue) Then
         Console.WriteLine("The keyboard type is {0}.", _
                           [Enum].GetName(GetType(KeyboardReturnType), _
                           returnValue))

       Else
         Console.WriteLine("The keyboard type is {0}.", _
                           CStr(returnValue))

       End If
     End If
   End Sub
End Module
```

VB6 Differences

Visual Basic 6.0 allowed different combinations of arguments to be passed to external procedures by using the As Any clause, which allowed the argument to be of any data type and suspended type checking by the compiler. This usage is not supported by Visual Basic .NET, which instead relies on method overloading.

In Visual Basic 6.0, it is possible to override the method by which an argument is passed to the called routine in the call itself by using the ByRef or ByVal keyword. In Visual Basic .NET, this usage is not permitted.

Visual Basic .NET adds the Ansi, Auto, and Uncode keywords, which determine how strings are marshaled when calling external routines. The keywords are not supported by Visual Basic 6.0.

In Visual Basic 6.0, if the ByRef or ByVal keyword was not specified with an argument, it was passed by reference; in Visual Basic .NET, it is passed by value.

In Visual Basic 6.0, a Declare statement placed in the declarations section of a class module had to be private; only Declare statements in code modules could have different levels of access. In Visual Basic .NET, however, a Declare statement can have one of five levels of accessibility.

The standard integer data types used in calling Win32 API functions have changed in the Visual Basic .NET. In both the Win32 API and Visual Basic 6.0, an Integer is a 16-bit data type and corresponds to a Visual Basic .NET Short, and a Long is a 32-bit data type that corresponds to a Visual Basic .NET Integer.

See Also

Alias Keyword, Ansi Keyword, Auto Keyword, Lib Keyword, Unicode Keyword

Default Keyword

Identifies a property as the default property of a class.

Syntax

See the syntax for the Property statement.

Comments

A *default property* is a property value whose value can be assigned or retrieved when an instance of the class to which it belongs, rather than the property itself, is referenced. For example, the first line of code following the last call to the breeds Collection object's Add method retrieves the value of an item from the Item collection by explicitly referencing the Items property:

```
Dim breeds As New Collection
breeds.Add("Alaskan Malamute", "mal")
breeds.Add("Siberian Husky", "husky")
breeds.Add("Newfoundland", "newf")
breeds.Add("Golden Retriever", "golden")
Console.WriteLine(breeds.Item("mal"))
Console.WriteLine(breeds("newf"))
```

However, the line of code following it also retrieves an item from the Item collection but doesn't explicitly reference the Item property. This is because Item is the default property of the Collection class.

Default properties must be parameterized (that is, they must include a parameter list). In fact, it is the presence of an argument that allows the compiler to distinguish between references to the object and references to the property of the object. Typically, this means that the value of a default property must be an array, an array-like data type (such as an ArrayList), a Collection object, or some other container object. For example, the following class definition includes a default property named Date that stores a series of dates in an ArrayList object internally:

```
Imports System.Collections

Public Class EventTracker
    Private eventDates As ArrayList

    Public Sub New()
        MyBase.New()
        eventDates = New ArrayList()
    End Sub

    Public Sub AddDate(eventDate As Date)
        Me.eventDates.Add(eventDate)
    End Sub

    Public Default ReadOnly Property [Date](index As Integer) As Date
        Get
            Return CDate(eventDates(index))
        End Get
    End Property
End Class
```

An instance of the class can then be created and the default property accessed as follows:

```
Public Sub Main()
    Dim et As New EventTracker()
    et.AddDate(#5/10/1993#)          ' birthday of older BHG
    et.AddDate(#1/2/1995#)           ' birthday of younger BHG
    Console.WriteLine(et(1))
End Sub
```

Default properties are a convenience feature and are resolved at compile time. For example, the Visual Basic compiler translates the previous code that explicitly references the Item property and that references it as the default property into identical IL:

```
  IL_004f:  ldstr       "mal"
  IL_0054:  callvirt    instance object
[Microsoft.VisualBasic]Microsoft.VisualBasic.Collection::get_Item(string)
  IL_0059:  call        object
[mscorlib]System.Runtime.CompilerServices.RuntimeHelpers::GetObjectValue(object)
  IL_005e:  call        void [mscorlib]System.Console::WriteLine(object)
  IL_0063:  ldloc.0
  IL_0064:  ldstr       "newf"
  IL_0069:  callvirt    instance object
[Microsoft.VisualBasic]Microsoft.VisualBasic.Collection::get_Item(string)
  IL_006e:  call        object
[mscorlib]System.Runtime.CompilerServices.RuntimeHelpers::GetObjectValue(object)
  IL_0073:  call        void [mscorlib]System.Console::WriteLine(object)
  IL_0078:  ret
```

As Figure 8-9 shows, the Visual Basic compiler translates the Default keyword into the <DefaultMember> attribute. This attribute defines a default member (a field, property, method, or constructor) that is to be invoked when the InvokeMember method of the Type object is passed Nothing as the value of the method's *name* argument. The name of the default member is provided as an argument to the attribute. This means that the EventTracker class could be rewritten as follows:

```
<DefaultMember("Date")> _
Public Class EventTracker
    Private eventDates As ArrayList

    Public Sub New()
        eventDates = New ArrayList()
    End Sub

    Public Sub AddDate(eventDate As Date)
        Me.eventDates.Add(eventDate)
    End Sub

    Public ReadOnly Property [Date](index As Integer) As Date
        Get
            Return CDate(eventDates(index))
        End Get
    End Property
End Class
```

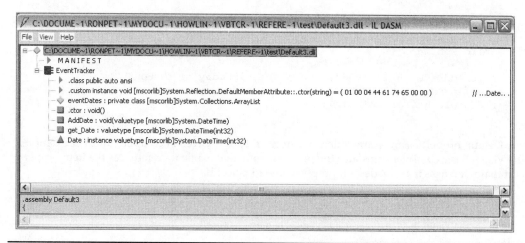

FIGURE 8-9   The compiler's translation of the Default keyword

The major restriction is that the class must be compiled separately from client code that uses the class, which must be compiled using a reference to the library that contains the class. Otherwise, the Visual Basic compiler will detect the absence of the Default keyword and generate a compiler error.

VB6 Differences

The Default keyword is new to Visual Basic .NET. However, VBScript supported the use of the Default keyword to designate a default property.

Although Visual Basic 6.0 supported the use of default properties, it did not allow you to designate default properties for your own classes.

In Visual Basic 6.0, a property did not have to be parameterized to be a default property. For example, the Text property was the default property of the TextBox control. Visual Basic .NET only allows parameterized properties to be designated as default properties.

VB.NET Differences

Visual Basic 7.0 produced a compiler error if both the Default keyword and the <DefaultMember> attribute were applied to the same class. From Visual Basic 7.1 onward, the use of both the attribute and the keyword is permitted, as long as they both reference the same member.

See Also

Property Statement

Delegate Statement

Defines a delegate, an object that allows you to encapsulate a function call into an object which can be passed around and invoked at will.

Syntax

```
[ <attrlist> ] [ accessmodifier ] [ Shadows ] Delegate [ Sub | Function ] _
    name [( Of typeparamlist )] [([ arglist ])] [ As type ]
```

Element	Description
attrlist	Any attributes that apply to the delegate. An attribute can be applied to a delegate if it has an AttributeTargets value of AttributeTargets.All or AttributeTargets.Delegate.
accessmodifier	Any one of the following keywords, which define the accessibility of the delegate: Private, Friend, Protected, Protected Friend, and Public.
Shadows	Indicates that the delegate hides an identically named program element in a base class. For details, see the entry for the Shadows keyword.
Sub | Function	Indicates whether the delegate can reference a subroutine or a function. Either Sub or Function must be specified. If Function is specified, the As *type* clause must also be present.
name	The name of the delegate. It must conform to standard Visual Basic .NET naming conventions.
Of *typeparamlist*	The type parameter list of delegates that accept generic parameters.
arglist	The optional list of arguments that are passed to the delegate when it is invoked. It must correspond to the argument list of the methods to which an instance of the delegate will refer. *arglist* has the same form as the argument list of a function or procedure; for details, see the entries for Function Statement and Sub Statement.
As *type*	The delegate return type. It is required if the delegate references a function.

Comments

A delegate is a reference type that refers to a method and has a particular signature and return type. You create an instance of that delegate by assigning the address of a shared method of a class or the instance method of a class instance that has the same signature and return type to an instance of the delegate.

The Delegate statement can appear within a namespace, class, module, or structure. Delegates cannot, however, be declared within class, module, or structure members.

A delegate's constructor takes the form

```
New name(AddressOf [<expression>.]<methodname>)
```

where *name* is the name of the delegate, *expression* is the name of a structure, class, or interface instance that contains *methodname*, and *methodname* is the name of the method that the delegate will reference. *methodname* must have the same signature and return type as the delegate. *expression* can be omitted if *methodname* is a member of the class in which the delegate is instantiated. For example:

```
Dim eventhandler As New EventProc(AddressOf cmdOKButton.Click)
```

Like any other type, delegates have a number of members. Some of the more interesting or more useful of these include the following:

Member	Method Syntax	Description
BeginInvoke method	*name*.BeginInvoke(*arglist*, DelegateCallBack As System.AsyncCallBack, DelegateAsyncState As Object) As System.IAsyncResult	Asynchronously executes the method that the delegate references.
DynamicInvoke	*name*.DynamicInvoke(*arglist*)	Same as Invoke.
EndInvoke method	*name*.EndInvoke(DelegateAsyncResult As System.IAsyncResult	End the asynchronous execution of the method begun by the BeginInvoke method.
GetInvocationList method	*name*.GetInvocationList() As Delegate()	Returns an array of Delegate instances that represent the delegate's invocation list. For single-cast delegates (delegates that are derived from System.Delegate and can invoke only one method), it returns an array with one element, a reference to the delegate itself. For multicast delegates (delegates derived from System.MulticastDelegate), it returns an array of all delegates to be invoked by the current delegate.
Invoke method	*name*.Invoke(*arglist*)	Synchronously executes the method that the delegate references.
Method property		Returns a MethodInfo object with information about the method reference by the delegate.

Since a delegate is a type, a delegate instance can be passed as an argument to a function. This makes it possible to determine based on runtime conditions what operation a particular function should perform, and to pass it a delegate that points to code that can perform that function. The example provides an illustration.

Ordinary method calls are synchronous. Often, this is undesirable. For example, when multiple consumers of a class instance are receiving event notifications, each of them is notified of the event and their event handlers are executed in sequence, which sometimes leads to poor performance. Delegates, however, make asynchronous method calls quite easy; for an example, see the Example section of the Custom keyword.

Example

A simple two-function calculator that performs either addition or subtraction could be implemented so that a single routine, PerformOperation, performs the addition or subtraction requested by the user and returns the result. However, whether to perform addition or subtraction is known only at runtime, when the user clicks either the add button or the subtract button. To call the PerformOperation function and have it either add or subtract as appropriate, we can call it from each button's event handler and pass it a delegate in addition to the two numbers to be added or subtracted. The delegate then contains a reference to the function to be executed.

The code for the simple two-function Windows calculator is as follows:

```
Public Delegate Function MathOperation(ByVal num1 As Integer, _
                                 ByVal num2 As Integer) As Integer

Public Class Calculator

    Private Sub cmdAdd_Click(ByVal sender As System.Object, _
                         ByVal e As System.EventArgs) Handles cmdAdd.Click
        Dim op As MathOperation = New MathOperation(AddressOf Add)
        Dim result As Integer = PerformOperation(op, CInt(txtNumber1.Text), _
                                       CInt(txtNumber2.Text))
        txtResult.Text = CStr(result)
    End Sub

    Private Sub cmdSubtract_Click(ByVal sender As System.Object, _
                         ByVal e As System.EventArgs) _
                         Handles cmdSubtract.Click
        txtResult.Text = PerformOperation(New MathOperation(AddressOf Subtract), _
                    CInt(txtNumber1.Text), CInt(txtNumber2.Text)).ToString
    End Sub

    Public Function PerformOperation(ByVal op As MathOperation, _
                                 ByVal num1 As Integer, _
                                 ByVal num2 As Integer) As Integer
        Return op.Invoke(num1, num2)
    End Function

    Public Function Add(ByVal num1 As Integer, ByVal num2 As Integer) As Integer
        Return num1 + num2
    End Function

    Public Function Subtract(ByVal num1 As Integer, ByVal num2 As Integer) _
                        As Integer
        Return num1 - num2
    End Function

End Class
```

VB.NET Changes

Visual Basic .NET supports type parameters with delegates only as of Visual Basic 2005.

VB6 Differences

The Delegate statement is new to Visual Basic .NET; delegates are not implemented in Visual Basic 6.0.

See Also

AddHandler Statement, Custom Keyword, RemoveHandler Statement, Handles Keyword, WithEvents Keyword

DeleteSetting Subroutine

Deletes a key or named value from the registry.

Member Of

Microsoft.VisualBasic.Interaction

Syntax

```
DeleteSetting(ByVal AppName As String, _
    Optional ByVal Section As String = Nothing, _
    Optional ByVal Key As String = Nothing)
```

Element	Description
AppName	A string describing a relative registry path from HKEY_CURRENT_USER\Software\VB and VBA Program Settings to the key named *section*.
Section	A string describing a relative registry path from the *AppName* key to the key that contains *Key* (which is, incidentally, not a key).
Key	A named value whose fully qualified path is HKEY_CURRENT_USER\Software\VB and VBA Program Settings*AppName**Section*.

Comments

The DeleteSetting function was introduced in Visual Basic 4.0 and worked with both the 16- and 32-bit versions of Visual Basic. In the 16-bit version, it deleted portions of an initialization file; in the 32-bit version, it deleted a key or value from the registry. The result is a confusing use of parameter names that reflects a usage more appropriate for initialization files than the registry. For instance, the *Key* parameter specifies not the name of a registry key, as one might naturally suppose, but a named value.

Like the other registry settings that are a part of the Visual Basic language, DeleteSetting does not work with the entire registry, but only with the subkeys of HKEY_CURRENT_USER\Software\VB and VBA Program Settings. The function is not intended as a general-purpose registry value or key removal utility. Instead, it is intended to be used by an application to delete the keys and values that the application itself has written to the registry.

AppName is described in the documentation as "the name of the application or project to which the section or key setting applies." This assumes that there is a single registry key named *AppName*, and that its name corresponds to the name of a Visual Basic project or application. There is nothing, however, to enforce this rule. In fact, *AppName* can consist of one or more registry keys.

Section is described in the documentation as "the name of the section in which the key setting is being saved." The phrase "section," when applied to the registry, however, has no meaning. In fact, *Section* can consist of one or more registry keys.

AppName and *Section* in fact together describe a relative path that begins with HKEY_CURRENT_USER\Software\VB and VBA Program Settings and ends with the key that has a named value named *Key*. Neither begins with the registry path delimiter. For example, if the program is to delete a value named WindowState in the HKEY_CURRENT_USER\Software \VB and VBA Program Settings\MyCompany\MyApplication\UserSettings\Windows key, *AppName* and *Section* have any of the following values:

AppName	Section
MyCompany	MyApplication\UserSettings\Windows
MyCompany\MyApplication	UserSettings\Windows
MyCompany\MyApplication\UserSettings	Windows

If *AppName*, *Section*, or *Key* does not exist, the function throws an ArgumentException.

If *Key* is specified along with AppName and Section, the function attempts to delete the *Key* named value from the registry key whose fully qualified path is HKEY_CURRENT_USER\ Software\VB and VBA Program Settings*AppName**Section.*

The DeleteSetting function can only be used to delete a named value; it cannot be used to delete a key's default (or unnamed) value (other than by deleting the key to which the default value belongs).

If *Key* is not specified but *AppName* and *Section* are, the function attempts to delete the last key specified in the absolute path HKEY_CURRENT_USER\Software\VB and VBA Program Settings*AppName**Section.*

If *Key* and *Section* are not specified, the function attempts to delete the last key specified in the absolute path HKEY_CURRENT_USER\Software\VB and VBA Program Settings*AppName.*

The Visual Basic registry functions are badly underpowered and of very limited utility. Rather than use them, you should use either the registry classes in the Microsoft.Win32 namespace or the My.Computer.Registry object. For example, the following code uses the RegistryKey class in the Microsoft.Win32 namespace to create a registry key named HKEY_LOCAL_MACHINE\Software\MyCompany\MyApp\Installation\FilePaths or to open it if it already exists. It then writes a series of values (including integer and binary values) to the key before it deletes the default value, a named value, the subkey, and finally the entire registry tree that it had just added.

```
Imports Microsoft.Win32

Module Module1
    Sub Main()
        ' Create key if it doesn't exist and write some data
        Dim regPath As String = "Software\MyCompany\MyApp\Installation\FilePaths"
        Dim regKey As RegistryKey = Registry.LocalMachine.CreateSubKey(regPath)

        ' Define some data to be written
        Dim binData As Byte() = {1, 1}
        Dim engineVersion As Long = 2
        Dim dlls As String = "C:\Program Files\My Company\My App\Libraries"
        Dim exe As String = "C:\Program Files\My Company\My App"
```

```
    ' Write (or overwrite) data
    regKey.SetValue("InstallDate", CStr(Date.Now))
    ' Since blnData is a Byte array, registry type will be REG_BINARY
    regKey.SetValue("Authorization", binData)
    ' Specify createion of DWORD value
    regKey.SetValue("Version", engineVersion, RegistryValueKind.DWord)
    regKey.SetValue("", "Completed")                  ' Default value

    ' Delete default value
    regKey.DeleteValue("")
    ' Delete one named value
    regKey.DeleteValue("Version")
    ' Close registry key
    regKey.Close()

    ' Delete Libraries key
    Registry.LocalMachine.DeleteSubKey(regPath)

    ' Delete entire MyCompany tree
    Registry.LocalMachine.DeleteSubKeyTree("Software\MyCompany")
  End Sub
End Module
```

VB6 Differences

In Visual Basic 6.0, the behavior of the DeleteSetting function differed on the two major Windows platforms. On the Windows 9*x* family, if *Key* was not present, DeleteSetting deleted the last registry key specified by *AppName* or *Section*, as well as any of its subkeys. On the Windows NT family, if Key was not present, DeleteSetting deleted the last registry key specified by *AppName* or *Section* only if it had no child keys. In Visual Basic .NET, the last key specified by *AppName* or *Section* and all of its subkeys are deleted.

See Also

GetAllSettings Function, GetSetting Function, SaveSetting Function, My.Computer.Registry Class

Dim Statement

Declares one or more variables.

Syntax

```
[ <attributelist> ] [ accessmodifier ] _
[[ Shared ] [ Shadows ] | [ Static ]] [ ReadOnly ]
Dim [ WithEvents ] variablelist
```

Element	Description
attributelist	An attribute that can be applied to a variable. Only attributes whose AttributeUsage attribute is AttributeTargets.All or AttributeTargets.Field can be applied to a Dim statement Attributes can only be applied to member variables (that is, to variables defined at module level).
accessmodifier	The variable's accessibility. Possible keywords are Public, Private, Friend, and Protected, and Protected Friend. For details, see the entry for each of the access modifiers. *acccessModifier* can only appear in member variable definitions; local variables (variables defined in property, procedure, or function statements) cannot have access modifier. If *accessModifier* is not specified at the member level, the variable is Public by default if it is defined in a structure, and Private by default if it is defined in a class or module.
Shared	Indicates that the variable exists on a per-application rather than a per-instance basis. A shared variable has a single value across all class instances. For additional detail, see the entry for the Shared keyword. Shared cannot be combined with the Static keyword. (To avoid confusion, it's worth mentioning here that the Visual Basic .NET Shared keyword is equivalent to the C# **static** keyword. Shared cannot be used in a local variable declaration.)
Shadows	Indicates that the routine hides an identically named programming element in a base class. Shadows cannot be used in a local variable declaration. For additional detail on Shadows, see the Shadows keyword.
Static	Indicates that the variable preserves its value between invocations of the routine in which it is defined. Static can only be used in local variable declarations, and not in member variable declarations. Static cannot be used along with Shared, Shadows, or ReadOnly.
ReadOnly	Indicates that the variable is read-only. ReadOnly and Static cannot be used together, and ReadOnly can only be used in module-level declaration.
WithEvents	Indicates an object variable that is an instance of a class that raises events, and that the variable is to receive event notifications. WithEvents can only be used in module-level declarations. Arrays cannot be declared using WithEvents. For details, see the entry for the WithEvents keyword.
variablelist	A comma-delimited list of variables, if multiple variables are defined by the same Dim statement.

Each variable defined in *variablelist* has the syntax:

```
variablename[ ( [ boundslist ] ) ] [ As [ New ] datatype ] [ = initializer ]
```

Element	Description
variablename	The name of the variable; it must follow standard Visual Basic naming conventions.

boundlist	Defines the variable as an array and indicates the array's upper bounds in a particular dimension. Array bounds are specified as positive integers, one integer for each dimension, with the integers separated by commas. Since arrays are typically zero-based, the actual number of elements is one greater than the upper bound. For example:
	
	`myArray(10)`
	
	defines an 11-element array, and
	
	`thisArray(10,2)`
	
	defines a two-dimensional array with 11 elements in the first dimension and three in the second. *boundlist* can also include the lower bound of an array, although this form is rarely used, since Visual Basic .NET only allows you to declare arrays whose lower bound is 0. The following are equivalent to the two previous statements:
	
	`myArray(0 To 10)`
	`thisArray(0 To 10, 0 To 2)`
	
	An array can have up to 32 dimensions, although it's rare to encounter an array with more than 2.

New	Creates a new instance of a class or structure and invokes its constructor.
datatype	The variable's data type. If Option Strict is on, the As *datatype* clause must be present (although a single As datatype clause at the end of the Dim statement can apply to all variables defined in the statement; see the Comments section for additional detail). If Option Strict is off (but Option Explicit is on), it is optional; any variable whose data type is not explicitly declared and cannot be determined by *initializer* is an Object by default. *datatype* can be any intrinsic Visual Basic .NET data type (or its corresponding .NET Framework Class Library equivalent), as well as a class, a structure, an interface, a delegate, or an enumeration.
initializer	An expression whose value is assigned to the variable. If New is present, *intializer* must not be present; otherwise, it is optional.

Comments

Since the syntax and usage of the Dim statement depends on the particular kind of variable it is used to declare, the following sections separately discuss each of the major kinds of variables you can create with the Dim statement.

General Syntax

For member variables, the Dim keyword is optional if Friend, Private, Protected, Protected Friend, or Public are present. For example, the following two Dim statements are equivalent:

```
Public counter1 As Integer
Public Dim counter2 As Integer
```

If the WithEvents keyword is used, the As *datatype* clause must be present, and *variablename* must be the data type whose events it is handling; it cannot be declared as an Object.

The following rules apply to multiple variables defined by a single Dim statement:

- If each variable declaration is self-contained, and each declaration is separated from other declarations by a comma, you can define as many variables as you want using a single Dim statement (though this does not, of course, contribute to code readability). For example:

```
Dim obj1 As New Hashtable, obj2 As New Collection, _
    int1 As Integer = 6, ch As Char = "a"c
```

- If multiple variables are defined without As *datatype* clauses, New keywords, or initializers, the data type of all the variables is defined by the rightmost As *datatype* clause, and the variable whose declaration includes the As *datatype* clause cannot have an initializer. For example, in the statement

```
Dim var1, var2 As Integer, var3 As String = "A short string."
```

the data type of both var1 and var2 is Integer.

- If either the New keyword or *initializer* are present, the variable's declaration must be self-contained, although it can be separated from other self-contained variable declarations by a comma.

Type Definition and Default Initialization

If *datatype* is not present but *initializer* is, the compiler assigns the variable the data type of *initializer*.

If you are assigning a literal value to a variable in the Dim statement, you can in many cases use a literal identifier to define the data type of the literal value. The literal identifiers are: Char, **C** or **c**; Date, #<dateValue>#, Decimal, **D** or **d**; Double, **R** or **r**; Integer, **I** or **i**; Long, **L** or **l**; Short, **S** or **s**; Single, **F** or **f**; UInteger, **UI** or **ui**; ULong, **UL** or **ul**; UShort, **US** or **us**. The Byte, Boolean, Object, SByte, and String types have no literal identifiers.

The compiler must be able to convert *initializer* to a value of type *datatype*. Moreover, if Option Strict is on, this must be a widening conversion or a compiler error results. In order to fix it, you can do any of the following:

- Use a literal type identifier, if one exists and you are assigning a literal value to the variable.
- Cast the initializer using one of the Visual Basic .NET conversion functions.
- Use the New keyword to invoke a constructor that performs initialization. You can do this particularly with Date and Decimal data types.

For example, if Option Strict is on, the code

```
Dim letter As String = "a"
Dim character As Char = letter
```

generates a compiler error (error BC30512: "Option Strict On disallows implicit conversions from 'String' to 'Char'"). You can correct it using a conversion function as follows:

```
Dim character As Char = CChar(letter)
```

Rather than allow the compiler to decide the data type of a variable, it's preferable to define its type yourself. Option Strict should be set on so that your code, rather than the compiler, handles variable typing and conversion.

If the Dim statement is used only to declare a variable and not to initialize it, it takes on a default value until it is initialized. For reference types, uninitialized strings have a value of String.Empty or Nothing, and uninstantiated objects are equal to Nothing. For value types, the integral and floating point types are equal to 0, Booleans are False, Dates are equal to 01/01/0001 C.E. at 12:00:00 AM, and Char variables are equal to Chr(-1). For structures, each field is initialized to its default value. For an array, each element of an array is initialized to its default value (unless the array itself is uninitialized; see the first comment in the Arrays subsection).

Static Variables

Static and shared variables should not be confused. Shared variables are module-level variables that have a single value across all class instances in an application. Static variables are local variables with a separate value instance that persists through invocations of the methods in which they are declared.

Some programming languages that support static variables require you to prevent the statement that declares the variable from executing if it has already been declared; otherwise, the variable is reinitialized, its value is lost, and the purpose of having a static variable in the first place is defeated. This is not true of Visual Basic .NET: the Dim statement that declares a static variable executes only the first time a routine executes, and not subsequently. For example, the following code successfully initializes and increments the static variable *ctr* each of the ten times the Invocations function executes:

```
Public Module staticVar
    Public Sub Main()
        For loopCtr As Integer = 1 to 10
            Console.WriteLine(Invocations())
        Next
    End Sub

    Private Function Invocations() As Integer
        Static ctr As Integer
        ctr += 1
        Return ctr
    End Function
End Module
```

If your code needs to initialize a static variable to something other than its default value, you should to that in the variable declaration. While the Dim statement that declares the variable executes only the first time the routine that contains the variable executes, a separate initialization statement executes on each invocation and thus resets the value of the static variable.

Arrays

Along with declaring an array with a particular number of elements, you can declare an uninitialized array of a particular number of dimensions. In this case, because an array is a reference type, the value of the array is Nothing until it is assigned an array having the same number of dimensions. You do this by using the *boundlist* format without supplying any actual numbers for the upper bounds of each dimension. For example:

```
Dim oneD() As String
Dim twoD(,) As Integer
```

Array declarations that also initialize the array (see the next comment) also must take this form.

Arrays can be initialized at the same time they are declared by declaring an array without explicit bound values and providing an *initializer* in which the expressions that define the value of individual elements are enclosed in braces and delimited from one another by commas. For example:

```
Dim numArray() As Integer = {12, 10, 8, 14, 16}
Dim D2Array(,) As Char = { {"a"c, "b"c, "d"c}, _
                           {"x"c, "y"c, "z"c} }
```

In the second case, the elements of the first dimension are specified first, followed by the elements of the second. If we iterate the second array with nested For loops, as follows:

```
For d2OuterCtr As Integer = D2Array.GetLowerBound(0) To D2Array.GetUpperBound(0)
   For d2InnerCtr As Integer = D2Array.GetLowerBound(1) To _
                              D2Array.GetUpperBound(1)
      Console.WriteLine(D2Array(d2OuterCtr, d2InnerCtr))
   Next
Next
```

the output to the console window is:

```
a
b
d
x
y
z
```

In fact, array declaration has almost a bewildering array (no pun intended) of syntaxes. The following are all valid ways to declare and in some cases to initialize a one-dimensional array:

```
' No size, array is Nothing
Dim array1() As String

' No size, array is Nothing
Dim array2() As String = New String() {}

' Initial size, default initialization
Dim array3(10) As String

' Initial size, default initialization
Dim array4() As String = New String(10) {}
```

```
' Initial size determined by initialization
Dim array5() As String = {"zero", "one", "two", "three", "four", "five", _
                          "six", "seven", "eight", "nine", "ten"}

Dim array6() As String = New String(10) {"zero", "one", "two", "three", _
                          "four", "five", "six", "seven", _
                          "eight", "nine", "ten"}
```

You can declare an array that has a lower bound other than zero. This requires that you call one of the overloads of the shared CreateInstance method of the Array class. Its syntax is:

```
CreateInstance(ByVal elementType As Type, ByVal lengths() As Integer, _
        ByVal lowerBounds() As Integer) As Array
```

where *elementType* is a Type object representing the type of the array, *lengths* is an array that indicates the number of elements to in each dimension, and *lowerBounds* is an array that defines the lower bound of each dimension. The index number of the element in both *lengths* and *lowerbounds* defines the dimension whose number of elements and lower bound is declared. For example, the following code creates a ten-element string array whose lower bound is 1, then outputs the index number of each array element to the console:

```
Public Sub Main()
    Dim elements() As Integer = {10}
    Dim lower() As Integer = {1}
    Dim arr() As String = DirectCast(Array.CreateInstance(GetType(String), _
                        elements, lower), String())

    For ctr As Integer = arr.GetLowerBound(0) To arr.GetUpperBound(0)
        Console.WriteLine(ctr)
    Next
End Sub
```

The program's output indicates that the new array has 10 elements with a lower bound of 1 and an upper bound of 10.

You can also define arrays by including *boundlist* after *datatype* rather than after *variablename*. For example, the following array declarations:

```
Dim arr1() As String
Dim arr3(,) As Integer
Dim arr5() As String = {"this", "that", "the other"}
```

can also be expressed as:

```
Dim arr1 As String()
Dim arr3 As Integer(,)
Dim arr5 As String() = {"this", "that", "the other"}
```

This syntax, however, does not permit you to explicitly set the upper bound of the array.

If you attempt to access an array that has been declared but not initialized, a NullReferenceException generally is thrown, as the following code illustrates:

```
Dim nullArray() As String
For Each element As String In nullArray        ' Generates exception
   Console.WriteLine(element)
Next
```

Besides checking for a value of Nothing before iterating the array, you could also initialize the array with a value of –1 for *boundlist*, as illustrated in the following code:

```
Dim emptyArray(-1) As String
For Each element As String In emptyArray
   Console.WriteLine(element)
Next
```

This creates a zero-length array that nevertheless is a valid object reference.

Visual Basic .NET supports *jagged arrays*. A jagged array is an array whose elements are arrays, with each subarray possibly having a different number of elements. When using jagged arrays, declaration and initialization are typically separate steps. You declare a jagged array using the syntax:

```
Dim arrayName As typename(boundlist)()
```

You then populate each element of the array with its array:

```
arrayName(0) = New typeName() { values }
```

The following code declares a jagged array, subsequently initializes it, and then iterates it:

```
Public Module Jagged
   Public Sub Main()
      Dim dogs(4)() As String      ' Create jagged array with 5 elements
      dogs(0) = New String() {"Dakota", "Malamute", "100 lbs."}
      dogs(1) = New String() {"Samuel", "Malamute", "130 lbs."}
      dogs(2) = New String() {"Koani", "Husky", "90 lbs."}
      dogs(3) = New String() {"Mr. Widda", "Black Labrador"}
      dogs(4) = New String() {"Sayatika Nerve", "Welsh Corgi"}

      For ctr As Integer = dogs.GetLowerBound(0) To Dogs.GetUpperBound(0)
         Dim innerArray() As String = dogs(ctr)
         For Each element As String in innerArray
            Console.Write("{0}    ", element)
         Next
         Console.WriteLine
      Next
   End Sub
End Module
```

It is also possible to declare and initialize a jagged array in the Dim statement that declares the array. The following code shows the preceding example rewritten to do this:

```
Public Module Jagged
   Public Sub Main()
      Dim dogs()() As String  = { New String() {"Dakota", "Malamute", "100 lbs."} ,
```

—

```
                              New String() {"Samuel", "Malamute", "130 lbs."} ,
                              New String() {"Koani", "Husky", "90 lbs."}, _
                              New String() {"Mr. Widda", "Black Labrador"}, _
                              New String() {"Sayatika Nerve", "Welsh Corgi"} }

        For ctr As Integer = dogs.GetLowerBound(0) To Dogs.GetUpperBound(0)
            Dim innerArray() As String = dogs(ctr)
            For Each element As String in innerArray
                Console.Write("{0}      ", element)
            Next
            Console.WriteLine
        Next
    End Sub
End Module
```

Generic Types

Visual Basic .NET allows you to instantiate classes that accept generic parameters. This means that instead of the traditional container object that ordinarily must accept weakly typed object variables, you can provide arguments to a generic class constructor that allows a generic class instance to accept only object instances of a particular type. Generic parameters are indicated by the Of keyword preceding the constructor's parameter list. For example, the definition of the generic Dictionary class constructor is:

```
Public Sub New(Of TKey, TValue)
```

where *TKey* and *TValue* are the names of the types that will be supplied as arguments for Dictionary keys and Dictionary values, respectively.

The following code illustrates the instantiation and use of the generic List class, which is a generic equivalent to the ArrayList class:

```
Imports System.Collections.Generic

Public Module GenericList
    Public Sub Main()
        Dim ducks As New List(Of String)
        ducks.Add("mallard")
        ducks.Add("American black duck")
        ducks.Add("northern shoveler ")
        ducks.Add("green-winged teal")
        ducks.Add("mottled duck")
        ducks.Sort()
        For Each duck As String In ducks
            Console.WriteLine(duck)                 ' Display in sorted order
        Next
    End Sub
End Module
```

Ordinarily, the syntax

```
Dim variableName As typename = New typename(argumentList)
```

can be used to instantiate a class and invoke its constructor. However, when generic classes are instantiated, this syntax is illegal and generates a compiler error. Instead, the call to the constructor must have the form

```
Dim variablename As New genericClassName(Of argumentList)
```

Constructors and New

You can instantiate a type and invoke its constructor apart from the Dim statement. Typically, you do this when you are passing a newly instantiated object as an argument to a method call and don't wish to preserve the object instance within your program. Raising an exception provides a good example of this. For example, the following code defines a class with a method, AlwaysExceptional, that always throws an exception and also falsely reports an OutOfMemoryException as its inner exception:

```
Public Class AlwaysExceptional
    Public Function ThrowAnException(param As Integer) As Integer
        Throw New ArgumentException("The parameter is invalid", "param", _
                                New OutOfMemoryException)
    End Function
End Class
```

The method instantiates and invokes the class constructors of two exception classes, but both objects are created without using the Dim statement.

All .NET types other than interfaces have constructors, and you can in fact use the New keyword whenever you declare any variable other than a variable of an interface type. For example, rather than declaring an integer as

```
Dim counter As Integer
```

you can also use the code

```
Dim counter As New Integer
```

The drawback is that you cannot provide *initializer* if New is present. So although

```
Dim counter As Integer = 10
```

is a legal statement,

```
Dim counter As New Integer = 10
```

is not. But the real power of New with value types comes when those value types define a non-default constructor. The Date data type, for instance, has 11 overloaded parameterized constructors that make it easy to initialize date and time values. These include the following:

```
Dim dateVar As New Date(ticks)
Dim dateVar As New Date(year, month, day)
Dim dateVar As New Date(year, month, day, hour, minute, second)
```

Similarly, the Decimal data type has seven overloaded parameterized constructors, including:

```
Dim decimalVar As New Decimal(Value As Double)
Dim decimalVar As New Decimal(Value As Single)
Dim decimalVar As New Decimal(Value As Integer)
```

A constructor can be invoked in a separate initialization statement apart from the variable declaration. For example, while

```
Dim ht As New Hashtable
```

combines variable declaration and initialization, the following separates them:

```
Dim ht As Hashtable
ht = New HashTable()
```

The type of the constructor need not be the same type as in the original variable declaration, as long as the former is derived from the latter. In this case, we can instantiate an object of a base class as an instance of a derived class (although we may have to cast the former to the latter). For example, the following code declares an Account instance and invokes the constructor of the Customer class, which is derived from Account:

```
Public Class Account
    Private acctName As String

    Public Property Name() As String
        Get
            Return Me.acctName
        End Get
        Set
            Me.acctName = Value
        End Set
    End Property
End Class

Public Class Customer : Inherits Account
    Private custBalance As Decimal

    Public Sub New(name As String, openingBalance As Decimal)
        MyBase.New()
        Me.Name = name
        Me.Balance = openingBalance
    End Sub

    Public Property Balance() As Decimal
        Get
            Return Me.custBalance
        End Get
        Set
            custBalance = Value
        End Set
    End Property
End Class
```

```
Public Module modTest
    Public Sub Main()
        Dim acct As Account = New Customer("Extraordinary Widgets", 1000.23d)
        Dim cust As Customer = DirectCast(acct, Customer)
        Console.WriteLine(cust.Balance)
    End Sub
End Module
```

Miscellaneous Comments

Local variables are of two types: those with procedure-level scope, and those with block-level scope. Block-level scope applies to variables defined within such programming structures as For . . . Next, If . . . End If, and Try . . . End Try.

In addition to defining the counter of a For loop or the container iterator of a For Each loop outside of the loop, you can also define it along with the For or For Each statement using the syntax

```
For <varname> As <datatype> = <initialvalue> To <upperlimit> Step <increment>
```

or

```
For Each <varname> As <datatype> In <containerobject>
```

This creates a local variable that has visibility only within the For or For Each construct. This is appropriate, since in most cases these variables are never used outside of these constructs.

In addition to being able to declare a variable as a member of an enumeration, as in the code

```
Dim retval As MsgBoxResult = MsgBoxResult.OK
```

it is also possible to declare and instantiate a variable of the enumerated type. For example:

```
Dim enumResult As New MsgBoxResult
```

The chief advantage of instantiating an enumeration is that the members of the Enum structure, which the enumeration inherits, can now be called from the enumeration instance, or a Type object representing that enumeration can be passed to a shared Enum method. For details, as well as a list of members of the Enum structure, see the entry for the Enum Statement.

The Dim statement, if it is used to declare a variable, is not an executable statement, and so it is not executed repeatedly if it is inside of a loop. For example, the following looping structure executes successfully without creating an endless loop even though ctr is a local variable with block-level scope that is declared at the very beginning of the loop:

```
Do While True
    Dim ctr As Integer
    ctr += 1
    If ctr Mod 100 = 0 Then
        Console.WriteLine("ctr at {0}", ctr)
        If ctr = 1000000 Then Exit Do
    End If
Loop
```

However, if Dim is used not only to declare a variable but also to initialize it, the variable initialization is performed at each pass through the loop. This means that the following code, which is identical to the previous code except that it explicitly sets the value of ctr to 0 in the Dim statement, does cause an endless loop:

```
Do While True
   Dim ctr As Integer = 0
   ctr += 1
   If ctr Mod 100 = 0 Then
      Console.WriteLine("ctr at {0}", ctr)
      If ctr = 1000000 Then Exit Do
   End If
Loop
```

VB.NET Changes

Beginning with .NET 1.1, Visual Basic permits the counters in For loops and the iterators in For Each statements to be declared as part of the For statement or the For Each statement. Previously, even though the variables were almost always used only within the looping construct, they had to be declared outside of the loop.

Beginning with Visual Basic 2005, you can instantiate container classes with generic parameters so that the container is able to accept only objects of a particular type.

VB6 Differences

The Global keyword, which was found in the earliest versions of Visual Basic, was undocumented but still supported in Visual Basic 6.0; it could be used in a code module only and was synonymous with the Public keyword. In Visual Basic .NET, it is not supported. In addition, the Protected and Protected Friend keywords are new to Visual Basic .NET and were not supported in Visual Basic 6.0.

Aside from creating a new variable using the New keyword, Visual Basic strictly separated variable declaration and initialization; variables were declared in the Dim statement and initialized in a separate line of code. Although this is still legal under Visual Basic .NET, variable declaration and initialization also can be combined in a single line of code.

In Visual Basic 6.0, the default data type is Variant; in Visual Basic .NET, only those variables whose types can't be determined either by an explicit data type or by their initializers are Objects, and the Visual Basic 6.0 Variant data type no longer is supported.

In Visual Basic 6.0, if multiple variables were declared in a single line of code and some lacked explicit data types, they defaulted to Variant. In Visual Basic .NET, they all share the data type of the last variable whose type is defined. For example, in Visual Basic 6.0, the code

```
Dim i1, i2, i3, i4 As Integer
```

creates one integer (i4) and three variants (i1, i2, and i3), while in Visual Basic .NET it creates four integers.

Although both Visual Basic 6.0 and Visual Basic .NET support the use of the To clause in array declarations, as in

```
Dim arr(0 To 9) As Integer
```

Visual Basic .NET only allows you to declare 0 as the lower bound of the array, whereas Visual Basic 6.0 allowed you to set another lower bound.

By default, if the lower bound of an array was not specified in a variable declaration, Visual Basic 6.0 created an array whose lower bound was defined by the Option Base statement, which allowed you to set the default lower bound of an arrays as either 1 or 0. Visual Basic .NET does not support the Option Base statement.

In Visual Basic 6.0, a variable defined in a procedure was local through that procedure, regardless of where it was defined. This means that a variable could be defined in a For loop, for example, and be used subsequently below that loop. Visual Basic .NET, on the other hand, introduces local variables with block-level scope; the variables are visible only within the programming construct within which they are defined. This means that a variable declared in a For loop is visible only within that For loop, and that an attempt to access it after the For loop completes will generate an exception.

In Visual Basic 6.0, you could declare a fixed-length string using the syntax

```
Dim name As String * length
```

In Visual Basic .NET, this syntax is not supported.

In Visual Basic 6.0, if an object is instantiated using the New keyword as part of the Dim statement, a subsequent test for the validity of the object reference in the form

```
If object Is Nothing
```

always returns False, since it causes Visual Basic to reinstantiate the object if it is equal to Nothing. This is no longer the case in Visual Basic .NET, and there is very little difference between invoking an object's constructor as part of the Dim statement or as part of a subsequent assignment.

See Also

Friend Keyword, Option Strict, Private Keyword, Protected Keyword, Public Keyword, ReDim Statement

Dir Function

Returns the name of a file system object with a particular file specification or that possesses particular file system attributes.

Member Of

Microsoft.VisualBasic.FileSystem

Syntax

```
Dir() As String
```

or

```
Dir(Optional ByVal Pathname As String, _
    Optional ByVal Attributes As FileAttribute = FileAttribute.Normal _
) As String
```

Element	Description
Pathname	An optional path and a filename specification. It can include the standard wildcard characters * and ?.
Attributes	One or more file attributes that a file must possess to meet the search criteria. Possible values are shown in Table 8-4.

Return Value

The name of a file, directory, or volume label, or String.Empty if no file system object meets the search criteria.

Comments

Because Dir is a function that is intended to return multiple file system names, it remembers its state between invocations. Hence, arguments are passed to Dir when it is first called, but subsequent invocations call the parameterless version of the function to return file system objects that match the same search criteria. This can continue until Dir returns String.Empty, indicating that no more file system objects meet the search criteria, or a search using a new set of criteria is desired. The basic "template" for using the Dir function to retrieve a set of files is:

```
Dim filename As String
filename = Dir("*.*", FileAttribute.Normal)
Do While Not filename = String.Empty
   Console.WriteLine(filename)
   filename = Dir()
Loop
```

Note that a downside to the stateful design of the Dir function is that the code in this pattern must not call out to any other code that might change the stored state, either by changing the query or iterating unexpectedly.

Visual Basic Constant	FileAttribute Member	Description
vbNormal	Normal	The file has no attribute set.
vbReadOnly	ReadOnly	The file is read-only.
vbHidden	Hidden	The file is hidden.
vbSystem	System	The file is a system file.
vbArchive	Archive	The file has changed since the last backup operation.
vbDirectory	Directory	A directory.
vbVolume	Volume	A disk volume label.

TABLE 8-4   Possible Values for the *Attributes* Argument

In addition to returning the names of drives and directories, Dir can also return the volume label of a drive or mountable device. To do this, *Pathname* must at a minimum specify the name of the drive; as long as the drive name is at the beginning of *Pathname*, the function will extract it. Since there is only one volume label, a subsequent call to Dir with no new arguments throws an ArgumentException. The following code illustrates a call to the Dir function to retrieve a drive's volume label:

```
Dim volName As String = Dir("C:\Windows", FileAttribute.Volume)
If volName = String.Empty Then
    Console.WriteLine("Drive {0} has no volume name.", driveName)
Else
    Console.WriteLine("The volume name of drive {0} is {1}", driveName, volName)
End If
```

It's particularly important to check for an empty string before using the value returned by the function, since many, if not most, drives lack a volume label.

Pathname must unambiguously indicate whether it is to retrieve drives or directories, this specification must correspond to *Attributes* for the function to return the expected results. For example, the function call

```
filename = Dir("C:\Windows", FileAttributes.Normal)
```

probably will fail to return any files, since the function looks for a file named Windows in the root directory of drive C:. On the other hand, either

```
filename = Dir("C:\Windows\", FileAttributes.Normal)
```

or

```
filename = Dir("C:\Windows\*.*", FileAttributes.Normal)
```

unambiguously identifies files in the Windows directory as the target of the function's search.

The FileAttribute enumeration is marked with the Flags attribute, which means that its members are not mutually exclusive. That means that you can Or them when supplying them as arguments to the Dir function. For example:

```
filename = Dir(pathname, FileAttribute.Hidden Or FileAttribute.System)
```

FileAttribute.Normal, however, indicates the absence of a flag (its integer value is 0, which means that it does not set correspond to a bit that is set on). So there is no point in including it in the expression.

The Dir function returns the names of file system objects in case-insensitive ascending alphabetical order (Aa–Zz). Unless you prefer some other sort order, you do not have to store the names of the objects returned by the function to an object that implements the IComparer interface in order to subsequently sort them.

The particular set of file system objects returned by the Dir function if *Attributes* is supplied tends to be somewhat confusing. The following are the types of files returned (based on their file attributes) for the various combinations of file attributes:

Attributes Value	Returns
FileAttribute.Normal	Files with no attribute set, or with their Archive attribute set and/or their read-only attribute set.
FileAttribute.Archive	Files with no attribute set, plus all files with the Archive attribute set, even if the any of the Hidden, System, and ReadOnly attributes is set.
FileAttribute.ReadOnly	Files with no attribute set, files with just the Archive attribute set, and files with the ReadOnly attribute set, including read-only files marked Hidden and System.
FileAttribute.Hidden	Files with no attribute set, files with just the Archive attribute set, files with the ReadOnly attribute set, and files with the Hidden attribute set, including files marked both Hidden and System.
FileAttribute.System	Files with no attribute set, files with just the Archive attribute set, files with the ReadOnly attribute set, and files with the System attribute set, including files marked both Hidden and System.
FileAttribute.Directory	Files with no attribute set, files with just the Archive attribute set, files with the ReadOnly attribute set, and Directories without any special attributes set.
FileAttribute.Directory and FileAttribute.Hidden	Files with no attribute set, files with just the Archive attribute set, files with the ReadOnly attribute set, and Directories without any special attributes set and with the Hidden attribute set.

In other words, Dir returns as broad a subset of file system objects as possible, and each flag added to *Attributes* tends to increase rather than decrease the number of names returned.

Interestingly, given that it retrieves file system object names based in part on their attributes, the Dir function does not provide information about the attributes of the files it returns. If you want to discover the attributes of the file returned by the Dir function, you can use the GetAttr function. See the example for the GetAttr function.

If you want to set or modify the attributes of the files whose names are returned by the Dir function, you can use the SetAttr function.

Particularly before the release of Visual Basic 6.0, the Dir function was used to check whether a particular file or directory existed. In Visual Basic 6.0, the FileSystemObject object in the Microsoft Scripting Runtime (*scrrun.dll*) made this functionality directly accessible through the FileSystemObject.FileExists and FileSystemObject.FolderExists methods. In Visual Basic .NET, Visual Basic makes this a simple function call using the My.Computer.FileSystem.FileExists and My.Computer.FileSystem.DirectoryExists methods, while the .NET Framework Class Library includes the shared Exists methods of the System.IO.Directory and System.IO.File classes.

The Dir function's remembering its state between invocations is critical to its ability to retrieve the names of all the files or directories in a particular directory that meet a particular *pathname* specification. Because of this, using the function to recursively iterate the objects in a file system is simply not practical, since Dir would lose its state each time that it navigates to a child directory. To iterate a file system, the functions in the Framework Class Library are much more suitable.

Although the Dir function has the nice feature of supporting wildcard characters, its use of attributes has always made it confusing and fairly obscure. The .NET Framework Class Library offer several alternative methods to retrieve the names of files and directories in a particular directory, including the shared GetDirectories and GetFiles methods of the System.IO.Directory class. The most

methods that most resemble the Dir function, however, are the shared GetDirectories and GetFiles methods of the Visual Basic My.Computer.FileSystem object. Both return a generic ReadOnlyCollection(Of String) object containing the path and filenames of all directories, and files, respectively, in a particular directory. Both methods are overloaded to support wildcard searches, as well as to return the names of files and directories in subfolders. The syntax of GetDirectories is:

```
Function GetDirectories(ByVal directory As String) _
        As ReadOnlyCollection(Of String)

Function GetDirectories(ByVal directory As String, _
        ByVal searchType As SearchOption,
        ByVal ParamArray wildCards() As String) As ReadOnlyCollection(Of String)
```

The syntax of GetFiles is identical:

```
Function GetFiles(ByVal directory As String) As ReadOnlyCollection(Of String)

Function GetFiles(ByVal directory As String, ByVal searchType As SearchOption, _
        ByVal ParamArray wildCards() As String) As ReadOnlyCollection(Of String)
```

The parameters are:

Element	Description
directory	The path to the directory whose directory or file information is to be returned.
searchType	A member of the SearchOption enumeration that defines whether only *directory* is searched for files or directories, or whether subdirectories are searched as well. Possible values are SearchOption.SearchAllSubDirectories or SearchOption.SearchTopLevelOnly.
wildCards	A parameter array (see the entry for the ParamArray keyword) of strings that contain wildcard specifications.

For example, the following code calls the My.Computer.FileSystem.GetFiles method to retrieve all files in a directory that have extensions of either *.exe or *.vb and lists them to the console:

```
Imports Microsoft.VisualBasic.FileIO
Imports System.Collections.ObjectModel

Public Module modFileSystem
    Public Sub Main()
        ListFiles("C:\temp")
    End Sub

    Public Sub ListFiles(ByVal path As String)
        Dim files As ReadOnlyCollection(Of String)
        Dim fileSpec() As String = {"*.vb", "*.exe"}
```

```
        files = My.Computer.FileSystem.GetFiles(path, _
            SearchOption.SearchTopLevelOnly, filespec)
        For Each filename As String In files
            Console.WriteLine(filename)
        Next
    End Sub
End Module
```

VB6 Differences

In versions of Visual Basic before 6.0, Dir returned file system objects in the order in which they were listed in the file allocation table. From Visual Basic 6.0 onward, they were returned in ascending case-insensitive alphabetical order.

In addition to the weakly typed version of the function, Visual Basic 6.0 supported a strongly typed Dir$ function that took a string rather than a variant as the argument for *pathname*. In Visual Basic .NET, the Dir function is strongly typed, but Dir$ is not supported.

See Also

GetAttr Function, My.Computer.GetDirectoryInfo, SetAttr Function

DirectCast Function

Performs type conversion based on inheritance or interface implementation.

Syntax

DirectCast(*expression*, *type*)

Element	Description
expression	An expression that evaluates to an instance of a value or reference type.
type	The type to which to convert *expression*.

Returns

expression converted to *type*.

Comments

expression must evaluate to an object or structure instance that derives from *type* (if type is a class) or implements *type* (if type is an interface), or is a base class to *type* or an interface that *type* implants.

DirectCast recognizes implicit inheritance relationships. You can, for instance, use DirectCast to convert an Integer to an Object and vice versa, or to convert a Long to a System.ValueType.

Like the other Visual Basic .NET conversion functions, DirectCast is implemented directly by the compiler, rather than in a .NET class library like Microsoft.VisualBasic.dll.

Interestingly, at compile time, the compiler may replace your call to DirectCast with a call to a conversion function that it considers more appropriate. For example, if you use DirectCast to convert an object to an integer, the compiler will substitute a call to the CInt function.

If the conversion fails, DirectCast throws an InvalidCastException. The conversion itself can fail for either of two reasons. The first is that the object instance and the target type are not related to each other through inheritance or interface implementation. The second is that the operation requires a narrowing conversion (a conversion from a base type to a derived type) that would result in a loss of information.

In many cases, the call to the DirectCast function generates a compiler error if it is apparent at compile time that no conversion to type *exists*. For example, the statement

```
Dim lng As Long = DirectCast(int, Long)
```

where int is an Integer, generates a compiler error because an Integer and a Long are unrelated to one another through inheritance or implementation. Note that DirectCast is not affected by the presence or absence of a defined implicit or explicit conversion operator.

Before performing a conversion using DirectCast, it is always wise to use the TypeOf . . . Is construct to check the runtime type of the expression being converted to determine whether it is likely to raise an exception. For example, we could use code like the following to convert MyBaseClass to MyDerivedClass:

```
If TypeOf myBaseClass1 Is myDerivedClass Then
    myDerivedClass1 = DirectCast(myBaseClass1, MyDerivedClass)
End If
```

The TryCast function is very similar to DirectCast, except that it returns Nothing rather than raising an error if the conversion fails.

Although DirectCast can be used for widening conversions (conversions from a derived type to a base type or from an instance of a class implementing an interface to an interface), these conversions can also be performed without using a conversion function. It is most useful for narrowing conversions (conversions from a base type to a derived type or from an interface to a type implementing that interface), particularly since, if Option Strict is on, such conversions cannot be made implicitly.

Some .NET Framework functions return an Array instance, which is not an intrinsic .NET data type. However, the compiler views an attempt to assign an Array type to a String or Integer, for instance, as a narrowing conversion and, if Option Strict is on, generates a compiler error. You can use DirectCast (as well as CType) to perform the conversion. For example:

```
Dim lengths() As Integer = {50}
Dim bounds() As Integer = {1}
Dim states As String() = DirectCast(Array.CreateInstance(GetType(String), _
                         lengths, bounds), String())
```

Although the conversion from an enumerated value to an integer is a widening conversion, the conversion from an integer to an enumerated value is a narrowing conversion that generates a compiler error if Option Strict is on. DirectCast can also be used to perform this conversion. For example:

```
Dim choice As Integer = MsgBox("Continue?", MsgBoxStyle.YesNo)
Dim result As MsgBoxResult = DirectCast(choice, MsgBoxResult)
Console.WriteLine(result.ToString)
```

DirectCast is usually recommended over the CType function for its superior performance. It is unclear, however, whether it actually yields a significant performance improvement.

VB6 Differences

The DirectCast function is new to Visual Basic .NET.

See Also

CObj Function, CType Function, Option Strict Statement, TryCast Function

---

Do . . . Loop Statement

Repeats a block of statements while an expression is true or until it becomes true.

Syntax

```
Do { While | Until } condition
    [ statements ]
[ Continue ]
[ Exit Do ]
    [ statements ]
Loop
```

or

```
Do
    [ statements ]
[ Continue Do ]
[ Exit Do ]
    [ statements ]
Loop { While | Until } condition
```

Element	Description
While	Causes the loop to execute while *condition* is True. While and Until are mutually exclusive.
Until	Causes the loop to execute until *condition* becomes True. Until and While are mutually exclusive.
condition	An expression that evaluates to a Boolean.
statements	Statements that are repeated while *condition* is True or until *condition* becomes True.
Continue Do	Statement that causes program flow to return to the top of the loop.
Exit Do	Statement that causes program flow to exit the loop regardless of *condition*.

Comments

The combination of Do While and Do Until allow the creation of four different looping structures, depending on when the condition is evaluated and whether the condition must be True or False for the loop to continue:

- Do While . . . Loop evaluates *condition*. If *condition* is False at the outset, the loop never executes. If it is True, *condition* is evaluated again each time at the beginning of the loop, and execution proceeds to the statement after the Loop statement once it is False.

- Do Until . . . Loop evaluates *condition*. If *condition* is True at the outset, the loop never executes. If it is False, *condition* is evaluated again each time at the beginning of the loop, and execution proceeds to the statement after the Loop statement once it is True.

- Do . . . Loop While executes the loop. When program flow reaches the bottom of the loop, *condition* is evaluated. If *condition* is False at the outset, the loop executes this single time. If it is True, *condition* is evaluated again each time at the end of the loop, and execution proceeds to the statement after the Loop While statement once it is False.

- Do . . . Loop Until executes the loop. When program flow reaches the bottom of the loop, *condition* is evaluated. If *condition* is True at the outset, the loop executes this single time. If it is False, *condition* is evaluated again each time at the end of the loop, and execution proceeds to the statement after the Loop Until statement once it is True.

The Exit Do statement causes an unconditional transfer of control from the loop. When Exit Do is encountered, program flow jumps to the first statement immediately after the Loop statement.

The Continue statement causes an unconditional transfer of control to the beginning of the loop. In the case of a Do While or a Do Until loop, this causes condition to be re-evaluated. In the case of a Do . . . Loop While or Do . . . Loop Until loop, it causes the evaluation to be skipped.

There can be multiple Exit Do and Continue statements within the body of a loop. Typically, they are statements within If . . . End If or Select Case constructs that redirect program flow if some condition is True or False.

Once program flow enters the Do While or Do Until Loop, and once *condition* evaluates to True in a Do . . . Loop While loop or to False in a Do . . . Loop Until loop, some code must exist within the body of the loop that either changes *condition* or causes program flow to leave the loop. Most commonly, the value of *condition* changes. In a While loop, *condition* changes from True to False, and in an Until loop, *condition* changes from False to True. However, as the next comment illustrates, control over the number of iterations of the loop may result from a condition evaluated within the loop and not by the formal *condition* expression that is evaluated either at the beginning or the end of the loop.

In some cases, the use of an infinite loop is deliberate. For example, the looping structures

```
Do While True
    [ statements ]
Loop
```

and

```
Do
    [ statements ]
Loop
```

don't evaluate a condition at all but simply loop endlessly. They depend, however, on a conditional branch using an If statement to terminate the loop. This endless loop is in fact a good choice to test code modules that accept user input:

```
Private Sub HandleUserInput()
    Dim input As String
    Do While True
        input = InputBox("Enter the data:")
        If input = String.Empty Then Exit Sub
        ' Handle user input
        ' loop back for more input
    Loop
End Sub
```

Although the Continue Do statement adds greater flexibility to the Do . . . Loop construct, it also provides one more tool that can be used to build an endless loop. The following code provides a very simplified version of the problem:

```
Public Sub Main()
    Dim counter As Integer = 0
    Dim flag As Boolean = True
    Do
        ' do something

        ' evaluate a condition
        If flag = True Then Continue Do
        counter += 1

    Loop Until counter > 40
End Sub
```

The problem is most likely to occur in a Do . . . Loop Until or Do . . . Loop While construct, when the Continue Do statement sends control back to the beginning of the loop, which prevents the evaluation of the conditional expression at the bottom of the loop.

The Do While . . . End While statement is identical to the Do While . . . Loop statement: both evaluate a conditional expression and loop as long as it is True. If the condition is not true when the expression is first encountered, the loop does not execute. Do While . . . End While, however, has no counterpart to the Do Until . . . Loop, Do . . . Loop While, or Do . . . Loop Until constructs.

Typically, you use one of the Do . . . Loop constructs or the For Each . . . Next construct when you don't know in advance (that is, at design time or compile time) the precise number of iterations that the loop will make. If the number is known, a For . . . Next construct is more appropriate. In many situations, however, whether to use a Do loop, a For loop, or a For Each loop is a matter of personal preference.

Example

Reading data from a database or file often involves using a Do . . . Loop structure, since typically the precise amount of data to be read is not known in advance, but the program should continue reading all the data until there is no more. The following code reads the contents of a text file named FileToRead.txt until all of its lines have been displayed to the console:

```
Public Sub Main()
    Dim streamOpen As Boolean = False
    Dim sr As StreamReader
    Try
        sr = New StreamReader("FileToReadTR.txt")
        streamOpen = True

        Dim output As String = String.Empty
        Do
            output = sr.ReadLine()
            If Not output = String.Empty Then
                Console.WriteLine(output)
            End If
        Loop Until output = String.Empty
    Catch e As Exception
        Console.WriteLine(e.GetType().Name & ": " & e.Message)
    Finally
        if streamOpen Then sr.Close()
    End Try
End Sub
```

This example loops *while* the StreamReader object is still finding new lines of text to retrieve. However, we could easily change the code so that the StreamReader object loops *until* it finds no more data:

```
Public Sub Main()
    Dim sr As StreamReader
    Dim streamOpen As Boolean = False
    Try
        sr = New StreamReader("FileToRead.txt")
        streamOpen = True

        Dim output As String = String.Empty
        Do
            output = sr.ReadLine()
            If Not output = String.Empty Then
                Console.WriteLine(output)
            End If
        Loop Until output = String.Empty
    Catch e As Exception
        Console.WriteLine(e.GetType().Name & ": " & e.Message)
    Finally
        if streamOpen Then sr.Close()
    End Try
End Sub
```

Both the Do . . . Loop While and Do . . . Loop Until constructs attempt to read a line and then check to make sure that it contains valid text before outputting it to the console. The result is that there are actually two checks to ensure that the line is valid: one testing whether the string buffer can be written to the console, and one testing the looping condition. This code can be streamlined with a Do While loop:

```
Public Sub Main()
    Dim sr As StreamReader
    Dim streamOpen As Boolean = False
    Try
        sr = New StreamReader("FileToRead.txt")
        streamOpen = True
        Dim output As String = sr.ReadLine()
        Do While Not output = String.Empty
           Console.WriteLine(output)
           output = sr.ReadLine()
        Loop
    Catch e As Exception
        Console.WriteLine(e.GetType().Name & ": " & e.Message)
    Finally
        if streamOpen Then sr.Close()
    End Try
End Sub
```

Here, the first ReadLine operation occurs outside of the loop, so that the variable can be tested for valid data when the loop is first entered. If it does not contain valid data, the loop is never entered; otherwise, subsequent ReadLine operations occur in the loop, and tests for valid data occur at the beginning of the loop.

This code, of course, can easily be rewritten to read text until there is no valid data:

```
Public Sub Main()
    Dim sr As StreamReader
    Dim streamOpen As Boolean = False
    Try
        Dim sr As New StreamReader("FileToRead.txt")
        Dim output As String = sr.ReadLine()
        Do Until output = String.Empty
           Console.WriteLine(output)
           output = sr.ReadLine()
        Loop
    Catch e As Exception
        Console.WriteLine(e.GetType().Name & ": " & e.Message)
    Finally
        if streamOpen Then sr.Close()
    End Try
End Sub
```

VB.NET Changes

Visual Basic 2005 added support for the Continue Do statement, which causes program flow to jump to the beginning of the loop.

See Also

Continue Statement, End Do Statement, Exit Do Statement, While . . . End While Statement

End Statement

Abruptly terminates program execution.

Syntax

```
End
```

Comments

The compiler implements the End statement as a call to the EndApp method of the Microsoft .VisualBasic.CompilerServices.ProjectData class. EndApp in turn closes all files opened by calls from the assembly in which the End statement was invoked; it then calls the System.Environment .Exit method. This in its turn calls the Win32 process termination function to terminate the application. In doing this, it bypasses the .NET destructors. In addition, other than files opened using Visual Basic statements, the End statement does not free unmanaged resources (and may retard the process of freeing managed ones, as well).

The End statement by itself terminates a program rather abruptly, while bypassing the ordinary methods of terminating a process. Because of this, the End statement should certainly not be used as a means of routinely terminating a Visual Basic .NET application. Moreover, it is difficult to conceive of the circumstances in which it might be used as an extraordinary means of programmatically terminating a program.

End *<codeblock>* Statement

Marks the end of a code block begun with a Visual Basic language statement.

Syntax

```
End AddHandler        ' ends AddHandler statement
End Class             ' ends Class definition
End Enum              ' ends Enum definition
End Event             ' ends Event statement
End Function          ' ends Function statement
End Get               ' ends property Get statement
End If                ' ends If structure
End Interface         ' ends Interface definition
End Module            ' ends Module statement
End Namespace         ' ends Namespace statement
End Operator          ' ends Operator statement
End Property          ' ends Property statement
End RaiseEvent        ' ends RaiseEvent statement
End RemoveHandler     ' ends RemoveHandler statement
End Select            ' ends Select statement
End Set               ' ends property Set statement
End Structure         ' ends Structure definition
End Sub               ' ends Sub statement
End SyncLock          ' ends SyncLock statement
End Try               ' ends Try exception handling block
End Using             ' ends Using block to handle resource disposal
End While             ' ends While statement
End With              ' ends With statement
```

VB.NET Changes

A number of the End statements are new to Visual Basic 2005:

- The End AddHandler statement
- The End Event statement
- The End Operator statement, which supports operator overloading
- The End RaiseEvent statement
- The End RemoveHandler statement

VB6 Differences

The Property Set . . . End Property and Property Let . . . End Property statements have been replaced by the Set . . . End Set construct within a Property . . . End Property statement, while Property Get . . . End Get has been replaced by the Get . . . End Get construct within a Property . . . End Property statement.

The Type . . . End type statement has been replaced by the Structure . . . End Structure statement.

The While . . . Wend construct has been replaced by the While . . . End While construct.

Although Visual Basic 6.0 had both classes and code modules, it stored them in separate files. A class was a file with an extension of .cls; a module was a file with an extension of .mod. In Visual Basic .NET, this one-to-one relationship no longer hold. Instead, the Class . . . End Class construct is used to define a class, and the Module . . . End Module construct is used to define a code module.

See Also

Exit Statement

Enum Statement

Declares an enumeration and defines its members.

Syntax

```
[ < attributes > ] [ access_modifier ]   [ Shadows ] _
Enum enumeration_name [ As data_type ]
    member_list
End Enum
```

Element	Description
attributes	Any attributes that are to be applied to the enumeration. Only attributes whose AttributeUsage attribute is AttributeTargets.All or AttributeTargets.Enum can be applied to an enumeration. <Flags> is the attribute most commonly used with enumerations.
access_modifier	One of the standard access modifiers (Private, Protected, Friend, Protected Friend, or Public) that defines the accessibility of the enumeration. By default, enumerations defined at the namespace level are Private, while nested enumerations are Public (which means that they have the accessibility of the type in which they are defined).

Element	Description
Shadows	Indicates that the enumeration redeclares an identically named programming element in a base class. Shadows can only be used with a nested enumeration.
enumeration_name	The name of the enumeration. It must follow standard Visual Basic naming conventions.
data_type	The data type of each member of the enumeration. It can be any of the integral data types (SByte, Byte, Short, UShort, Integer, UInteger, Long, ULong). If Option Strict is on, data_type is required.
member_list	The members of the enumeration. Each member must appear on a separate line.

Each member defined in *member_list* has the syntax:

```
member_name [ = initializer ]
```

Element	Description
member_name	Name of the enumeration member. It must conform to standard Visual Basic naming conventions.
initializer	An optional value to be assigned to the member. If *initializer* is not used, the value of the first member of the enumeration is 0, and the value of each successive member is incremented by 1.

Comments

An enumeration is a value type that is derived directly from System.Enum, which in turn is derived from System.ValueType. Like a class, structure, interface, or delegate, an enumeration is a basic .NET type. In addition to the fact that it is a type, the enumeration in turn has an underlying type, which in .NET can be any of the integral types. It also has one or more constant fields, or *members,* that return literal values of the enumeration's underlying type.

A less formal way of defining an enumeration is as a related set of constants of a particular integral type that are bundled together in a container. Like constants, enumeration members are shared and read-only, although the Shared and ReadOnly keywords cannot be used in an enumeration definition

An enumeration can be defined at the namespace level, apart from any other type, or it can be nested within a class or structure. If it is nested, it must be defined at the member level; it cannot be nested in the code for a type member.

initializer, which defines the value of an enumeration member, is resolved at compile time and stored in the assembly manifest as the value of the member. This means that although *initializer* can be an expression, it must evaluate at compile time to a literal value that does not rely on the value of any instance variables, external function calls, etc. If *initializer* is an expression, it can include literal numeric values, operators, other enumeration members, and calls to functions implemented by the compiler, such as CInt or CLng.

You can define variables whose type is that of an enumeration. You can also assign the value of a member of an enumeration to a variable. To reference a member of an enumeration, you must include the name of the enumeration as well as the name of the member. For example, the following code defines a variable named *result* that is of type MsgBoxResult, the enumerated value returned by the MsgBox function. The following If . . . Else . . . End If construct then determines which button the user clicked to close the dialog:

```
Dim result As MsgBoxResult
result = MsgBox("Do you wish to continue?", MsgBoxStyle.YesNoCancel)
If result = MsgBoxResult.Yes Then
    Console.WriteLine("You closed the dialog by clicking Yes . . . ")
ElseIf result = MsgBoxResult.No Then
    Console.WriteLine("You closed the dialog by clicking No . . . ")
Else
    Console.WriteLine("You closed the dialog by clicking Cancel . . . ")
End If
```

You can avoid having to avoid explicitly referencing the enumeration type along with its member by importing it, which allows you to reference only the enumeration only. The full name of the enumeration (including the complete path to its namespace) must be used. For example, if the following two Imports statements are used:

```
Imports Microsoft.VisualBasic.MsgBoxResult
Imports Microsoft.VisualBasic.MsgBoxStyle
```

the preceding code fragment can be rewritten as follows:

```
Dim result As MsgBoxResult
result = MsgBox("Do you wish to continue?", YesNoCancel)
If result = Yes Then
    Console.WriteLine("You closed the dialog by clicking Yes...")
ElseIf result = No Then
    Console.WriteLine("You closed the dialog by clicking No...")
Else
    Console.WriteLine("You closed the dialog by clicking Cancel...")
End If
```

An enumeration can be used as a parameter type and as the return value of a function.

Although the conversion of an enumerated value to an integer is a widening conversion that can be handled implicitly by the compiler, the conversion of an integer to an enumerated value is a narrowing conversion. A compiler error will result if Option Strict is on and an explicit conversion operator (CType, DirectCast, and TryCast) is not used.

Enumerations are not type safe, in particular because the .NET runtime does not do bounds checking on variables of enumeration types. For example, the following code defines a variable, myPet, as an enumerated type but then passes it a value that does not correspond to any member of an enumeration:

```
Enum Pets As Integer
    Dogs = 1
    Cats = 2
    Birds = 3
```

```
      Fish = 4
      Lizards = 5
      Frogs = 6
      Other = 7
End Enum

Public Module TestEnum
    Public Sub Main()
        Dim myPet As Pets = 12
        Console.WriteLine(myPet.ToString)
    End Sub
End Module
```

If Option Strict is on, the code will fail to compile because of an implicit narrowing conversion from an Integer to a value of type Pets. However, once the offending line is replaced with the statement

```
Dim myPet As Pets = CType(12, Pets)
```

the code compiles. The call to the ToString method then displays the value 12 to the console, even though it isn't a valid member of the enumeration.

Typically, the .NET runtime interprets enumeration members as mutually exclusive. For instance, it is clear that the enumeration

```
    Enum OnOffState As Integer
       OffSwitch = 0
       OnSwitch = 1
       Indeterminate = -1
    End Enum
```

is meant to indicate whether something is either off or on, or its state cannot be determined. Because of this, an assignment like the following, which combines enumerated values, makes no sense (irrespective of the fact that OnOffState.OffSwitch is 0, so that it contributes nothing to the value of the state variable):

```
Dim state As OnOffState = OnOffState.OffSwitch Or OnOffState.OnSwitch
```

You can use the <Flags> attribute to indicate that an enumeration consists of members that are not mutually exclusive, so that enumerated values can be combined. The attribute has no arguments. For example:

```
<Flags> Enum Activities As Integer
    Shopping = 1
    Dining = 2
    Sports = 4
    Pets = 8
    Walking = 16
End Enum
```

A particular variable can then be assigned multiple members of the enumeration by ORing them together (or adding them together). For example:

```
Dim pastimes As Activities = Activities.Shopping Or Activities.Dining
```

In defining an enumeration whose members are not mutually exclusive, two principles apply:

- A member of the enumeration should not be assigned the value 0. For example, if an enumeration, BadEnumeration, has a member, Value0, whose value is 0, then the expression

  ```
  BadEnumeration.Value0 Or BadEnumeration.Value1
  ```

  produces the same result as BadEnumeration.Value1 alone, and the presence of BadEnumeration.Value0 cannot be detected.

- Each member of the enumeration should be assigned a value with a unique bit pattern. For example, the enumeration

  ```
  <Flags> Public Enum BadEnum As Integer
     Value0 = 0
     Value1 = 1
     Value2 = 2
     Value3 = 3
  End Enum
  ```

  is problematic because the runtime cannot differentiate between BadEnum.Value3 and (BadEnum.Value1 Or BadEnum.Value2). The following code correctly defines the enumeration so that each of its members can be uniquely identified:

  ```
  <Flags> Public Enum GoodEnum As Integer
     Value0 = 1
     Value1 = 2
     Value2 = 4
     Value3 = 8
  End Enum
  ```

If the <Flags> attribute is used, the Visual Basic compiler does not enforce these requirements. (And if the <Flags> attribute is absent, the compiler does not disallow a logical Or operation on two enumerated values.) Instead, the only effect of using the <Flags> enumeration is that the runtime attempts to display each member of an enumeration when an enumerated value's ToString method is called. For example, the code

```
Dim good As GoodEnum = GoodEnum.Value1 Or GoodEnum.Value2
Console.WriteLine(good.ToString)
```

produces the output

```
Value1, Value2
```

Enumerations derive directly from the System.Enum structure, which provides the following members that can be used in working with enumerations:

Member	Method Syntax	Description
Format method	```Format(enumType As Type, _ value As Object, _ format As String) As String```	A shared method that converts an enumerated value to a string representation defined by the *format* argument. *enumType* is a Type object representing the enumeration, *value* is the enumeration member, and *format* defines the string format to output. *format* can be "G" or "g" to output the name of the enumerated value, "X" or "x" to output its hexadecimal equivalent, and "D" or "d" to output its decimal equivalent.
GetName method	```GetName(enumType As Type, _ value As Object) As String```	A shared method that returns the name of an enumeration member that corresponds to an integer value. *enumType* is a Type object representing the enumeration, and *value* is the underlying value of an enumerated constant.
GetNames method	```GetNames(enumType As Type) _ As String()```	A shared method that returns an array containing the names of the members of an enumeration. *enumType* is a Type object that represents the enumeration.
GetValues method	```GetValues(enumType As Type) _ As Array```	A shared method that returns an array containing the underlying values of each enumeration member. *enumType* is a Type object that represents the enumeration.
IsDefined method	```IsDefined(enumType As Type, _ value As Object) As Boolean```	A shared method that indicates whether an integral value corresponds to a member of an enumeration. *enumType* is a Type object that represents the enumeration; *value* is an integral value.
Parse method	```Parse(enumType As Type, _ value As String) As Object``` or ```Parse(enumType As Type, _ value As String, _ ignoreCase As Boolean) _ As Object```	A shared method that converts the string representation of an enumeration member name or value to an enumeration member. The enumeration is defined by *enumType*, the representation of its value by *value*. The first overload is case sensitive; the second allows you to supply a Boolean, *ignoreCase*, that determines whether *value*, if it is a name, must match the name of the enumerated value in case.

Member	Method Syntax	Description

ToString method	`ToString() As String`
	
	or
	
	`ToString(format As String) _`
	`   As String`
		Converts an inumerated member to a string representing its name, or if that fails, to a string representation of its integral value. The second overload has a *format* argument that allows you to define the output format; it can have the values listed for the Enum.Format method. Note that this is an instance method, not a shared method; it can be called from a member of an enumeration.

You may at times need to enumerate the members of an enumeration. The following code shows how to do it:

```
Public Module Enumerations
    Public Sub Main()
        Dim firstday As FirstDayOfWeek
        EnumerateMembers(firstday)
    End Sub

    Public Sub EnumerateMembers(fd As FirstDayOfWeek)
        ' Iterate strings representing names
        For Each member As String In [Enum].GetNames(fd.GetType)
            Console.WriteLine(member)
            ' Convert string to enum member
            Console.WriteLine("Member {0} of enumeration {1} has a value of {2}", _
                [Enum].Parse(fd.GetType, member).ToString, _
                fd.GetType.Name, _
                [Enum].Format(fd.GetType, _
                DirectCast([Enum].Parse(fd.GetType, member), FirstDayOfWeek), "D"))
        Next
    End Sub
End Module
```

The code makes extensive use of the shared members of the Enum structure. First, it retrieves an array of names of the enumeration. For each name, it calls the Enum.Parse method to convert the string name back to an enumerated value, and then it displays both its name (which is once again converts back to a string) and its integral value.

VB6 Differences

In Visual Basic 6.0, an enumeration was simply a loose collection of constants. You referenced an enumerated value by its name, without its enumeration. In Visual Basic .NET, enumerated values can only be referenced as members of their enumeration.

The members of enumerations in Visual Basic 6.0 were Long. In Visual Basic .NET, they can be any integral value.

In Visual Basic 6.0, it was possible to prevent a particular member of an enumeration from being displayed in the Object Browser by prefacing its name with an underscore character. This technique has no effect in Visual Basic .NET.

See Also

Const Statement

Environ Function

Returns the value of an operating system environment variable.

Member Of

Microsoft.VisualBasic.Interaction

Syntax

The Environ function is overloaded as follows:

```
Environ(ByVal Expression As Integer) As String
```

or

```
Environ(ByVal Expression As String) As String
```

Element	Description
Expression	A string indicating the name of the environment variable whose value is to be returned, or an Integer indicating the one-based ordinal position of the value to return from the environment table.

Return Value

A String indicating the value of the environment variable, or String.Empty if *Expression* does not specify an entry that is present in the environment table.

Comments

Values are stored in the environment table as named values in the format *name=value*. The overloaded string version of the function returns only the value whose name is indicated by *Expression*. The overloaded integer version of the function, on the other hand, returns a string that includes the entire environment table entry.

If the second overload of the function is called, *Expression* must be an Integer whose value ranges from 1 to 255, or an ArgumentException is thrown.

If you retrieve environment variables by their ordinal position, you then have to parse the returned string to extract the environment variable's name from its value. The following code does that and displays the results to the console:

```
Dim envVar As String
Dim ctr As Integer = 0
```

```
Do
    ctr += 1
    envVar = Environ(ctr)
    If Not envVar = String.Empty Then
        ' Determine where equals sign is in string
        Dim pos As Integer = Instr(envvar, "=")
        Console.WriteLine("{0} = {1}", Left(envVar, pos - 1), Mid(envVar, pos + 1))
    End If
Loop While Not envVar = String.Empty
```

Windows creates a separate set of environment variables for each process running on a system. Environment variables are defined for the process by per-user and per-machine registry keys (in the former case, HKEY_CURRENT_USER\Environment; in the latter, HKEY_LOCAL_MACHINE\SYSTEM\CurrentControlSet\Control\Session Manager\ Environment), by Autoexec.bat and any batch files it runs, by any other batch file run during startup, and by the user entering a SET command in a console during a session. The set of active environment variables for a process is held in the process environment table.

The .NET Framework Class Library includes two methods for retrieving environment variables that also provide enhanced functionality. The first, the shared Environment .GetEnvironmentVariable method, is overloaded as follows:

```
Environment.GetEnvironmentVariable(variable As String)
Environment.GetEnvironmentVariable(variable As String, _
    target As EnvironmentVariableTarget)
```

The first overload of the GetEnvironmentVariable method is identical in operation to the second overload of the Environ function; it looks in the process environment table for a variable named *variable*. The second overload returns a particular environment variable, *variable*, either from the process environment table (if the value of *target* is EnvironmentVariableTarget.Process), from the user key of the registry (if *target* is EnvironmentVariableTarget.User), or from the machine key of the registry (if target is EnvironmentVariableTarget.Machine). The second method, the shared Environment.GetEnvironmentVariables method, returns an IDictionary object that contains a collection of environment variables. It is overloaded as follows:

```
Environment.GetEnvironmentVariables()
Environment.GetEnvironmentVariables(target As EnvironmentVariableTarget)
```

The first overload retrieves variables from the process environment table, the second from the location specified by *target*, which is a member of the EnvironmentTarget enumeration whose values discussed earlier. Very much like the Dictionary object in the Microsoft Scripting Runtime included with Visual Basic 6.0, the IDictionary object is a collection object that stores name-value or key-value pairs. The following code uses the GetEnvironmentVariables method to retrieve and iterate environment variables from the environment process table:

```
Imports System.Collections
Imports System.IO

Public Module modEnviron

    Public Sub Main()
        Dim sw As StreamWriter = New StreamWriter("C:\temp\environment.txt")
```

```
        ' Get process environment variables
        Dim dict As IDictionary = _
Environment.GetEnvironmentVariables(EnvironmentVariableTarget.Process)
        Console.WriteLine("Writing Process variables")
        sw.WriteLine("Process Variables")
        sw.WriteLine("-----------------")
        For Each entry As DictionaryEntry In dict
            sw.WriteLine("        {0} = {1}", entry.Key, entry.Value)
        Next
        sw.WriteLine()
        sw.Close()
    End Sub
End Module
```

The values of environment variables themselves often contain substrings that include environment variables (for example,

```
Fonts=%windir%\fonts
```

includes the windir environment variable). If any embedded environment variables are included in a value, Environ, Environment.GetEnvironmentVariable, and Environment.GetEnvironmentVariables all expand them either by calling the Win32 API ExpandEnvironmentStrings function or by calling the .NET Environment.ExpandEnvironmentVariables function before returning their values.

You can set environment variables by calling the shared Environment.SetEnvironmentVariable method, which is overloaded as follows:

```
Environment.SetEnvironmentVariable(variable As String, value As String)
Environment.SetEnvironmentVariable(variable As String, value As String, _
            target As EnvironmentVariableTarget)
```

where *variable* is the name of the environment variable, *value* is its value, and *target* indicates whether the environment variable will be defined in the process table, the user branch of the registry, or the machine branch of the registry.

VB6 Differences

Visual Basic 6.0 included two similar functions, Environ and Environ$. The former returned a Variant, the latter a String. In Visual Basic .NET, the Environ$ function has been discontinued, and the Environ function returns a String.

See Also

Command Function

EOF Function

Indicates whether the end of a file opened for random or sequential input has been reached.

Member Of

Microsoft.VisualBasic.FileSystem

Syntax

```
EOF(ByVal FileNumber As Integer) As Boolean
```

Element	Description
FileNumber	The file number of a binary, random, or sequential file opened input.

Return Value

A Boolean indicating whether the file pointer is at the end of the file.

Comments

When using Visual Basic's file input/output functions to read a file, the file pointer advances to the end of the data read after every operation. You use the EOF function to make sure that you haven't already read all the data and that more data remains to be read. Attempting to read past the end of the file throws an exception.

The EOF function can be used when reading from a sequential file to detect whether all data has been read. For example, the following code opens a text file, reads one line at a time until it reaches the end of the file, and displays the output to the screen:

```
Private Sub ReadTextFile()
    Dim fileOpened As Boolean = False
    ' Get filename and file number
    Dim fileName As String = "c:\temp\SeqFile.txt"
    Dim fileNumber As Integer = FreeFile()
    Try
        ' Open file
        FileOpen(fileNumber, fileName, OpenMode.Input)
        fileOpened = True
        ' Iterate until no more lines
        Do While Not EOF(fileNumber)
            Console.WriteLine(LineInput(fileNumber))
        Loop
    Catch e As Exception
        Console.WriteLine(e.GetType.Name & ": " & e.Message)
    Finally
        If fileOpened Then FileClose(fileNumber)
    End Try
End Sub
```

The EOF function can be used when reading from a binary file to determine whether all bytes have been read. For example, the following code opens a .jpeg file, reads it one byte at a time, and stores the byte in an array. When it reaches the end of the file, it closes the file and displays the number of bytes it read to the console.

```
Private Sub ReadBinaryFile()
    Dim fileOpened As Boolean = False
    Try
        ' Get filename, file number, and file size
        Dim fileName As String = "C:\temp\Blue hills.jpg"
```

```
        Dim fileNumber As Integer = FreeFile()
        Dim fileLength As Long = FileLen(fileName)
        ' Create array to hold bytes of binary file
        Dim binArray(CInt(fileLength - 1)) As Byte
        ' Define position index
        Dim ctr As Integer = 0
        ' Open file
        FileOpen(fileNumber, fileName, OpenMode.Binary)
        fileOpened = True
        ' Read file byte by byte
        Do While Not EOF(fileNumber)
            ctr += 1
            FileGet(FileNumber, binArray(ctr - 1), ctr)
        Loop
        Console.WriteLine("Read {0} bytes . . . ", ctr)
    Catch e As Exception
        Console.WriteLine("Error reading file {0}: {1}", _
                          fileName, e.Message)
    Finally
        if fileOpened Then FileClose(fileNumber)
    End Try
End Sub
```

In the preceding code example, the FileGet procedure, rather than the Input or InputString procedure, is used to read the file. If the latter procedures are used for reading a binary file, the LOF and Loc functions should be used instead of the EOF function.

The EOF function can be used when reading from a random access file to determine whether all records have been read. For example, the following code opens a file named mailinglist.dat that consists of contact records whose structure is defined by the Contact structure.

```
Public Structure Contact
    <VBFixedString(25)> Public Name As String
    <VBFixedString(28)> Public Address As String
    <VBFixedString(24)> Public CityState As String
    <VBFixedString(3)> Private EndOfRecord As String
End Structure

Private Sub ReadRandomFile()
    Dim fileOpened As Boolean = False
    Try
        Dim mailContact As New Contact
        Dim recLength As Integer = 80
        Dim filename As String = "C:\temp\mailinglist.dat"
        Dim fileNumber As Integer = FreeFile()
        Dim recCtr As Integer = 1
        ' Open file
        FileOpen(fileNumber, fileName, OpenMode.Random, OpenAccess.Read, _
                 ,recLength)
        fileOpened = True
        ' Iterate until no more lines
        Seek(fileNumber, recCtr)
```

```
      Do While Not EOF(fileNumber)
          FileGet(fileNumber, mailContact, recCtr)
          Console.WriteLine("{0} lives at {1} in {2}", Trim(mailContact.Name), _
                      Trim(mailContact.Address), Trim(mailContact.CityState))
          recCtr += 1
          Seek(fileNumber, recCtr)
      Loop
   Catch e As Exception
      Console.WriteLine("Error reading file {0}: {1}", _
                      fileName, e.Message)
   Finally
      if fileOpened Then FileClose(fileNumber)
   End Try
End Sub
```

It then reads one record at a time, displaying the results to the console for each record read, until the end of file is reached. Note that Option Strict must be set off for this code to work successfully, since we have to allow Visual Basic compiler to handle a narrowing conversion from System.ValueType to Contact when the record is returned by the FileGet function call.

If a FileGet statement is unable to read a complete record from a random access file, the end of file marker is automatically set to True.

Typically, if you open a file to write to it (that is, the open mode is OpenMode.Write or OpenMode.Append), there's no need to check for the end of file marker, since the file pointer is automatically positioned at the end of the file.

The EOF function is one of a number of interrelated file input/output functions that Visual Basic .NET inherited from previous versions of Visual Basic. For new code, it's far preferable to use the file input/output services available in the .NET Framework Class Library. For a description of some of these, see the comments for the FileOpen Subroutine as well as for each of the file read and write functions.

See Also

FileOpen Subroutine, LOF Function

Erase Statement

Erases array variables and releases their memory.

Syntax

Erase *arrays*

Element	Description
arrays	The name of an array, or a comma-delimited list of array names.

Comments

Erase does not merely "clear out" an array, it is equivalent to setting the array variable to Nothing. In order to use the array again, you must reinitialize it with the ReDim statement.

If you use ReDim to redeclare an array that you've set to Nothing with the Erase statement, you cannot change its type or number of dimensions.

VB6 Differences

Visual Basic .NET allows you to declare an array using the Dim statement, erase it using Erase, and then redimension it using ReDim. In contrast, Visual Basic 6.0 does not allow you to reuse the array that was cleared using the Erase statement unless it was declared using the ReDim statement rather than the Dim statement.

See Also

Nothing Keyword, ReDim Statement

Erl Function

Returns the line number on which an error occurred.

Member Of

Microsoft.VisualBasic.ErrObject and Microsoft.VisualBasic.Information

Syntax

```
Function Erl() As Integer
```

Return Value

The number of the line on which the error or exception occurred, or 0 if lines were not numbered.

Comments

The Erl function works with both structured and unstructured exception handling.

The successful operation of the Erl function requires that lines be numbered. Otherwise, Erl simply returns a 0.

Lines are numbered in Visual Basic .NET by assigning a numeric label followed by a colon to them. Line numbers do not have to be sequential, nor do all lines have to be numbered. The only requirement is that they be unique within the member in which they appear.

Example

The code example illustrates the how lines are numbered and uses the Erl function with structured exception handling.

```
Public Sub Main()
    Try
        Dim int As Integer = 10
    1:  int += 1
    2:  Console.WriteLine(int)
    3:  Throw New SystemException
        MsgBox("Message should never appear.")
    Catch
        Console.WriteLine("Exception on line {0}", Erl)
    End Try
End Sub
```

VB6 Differences

The Erl function was a method of the Information class in Visual Basic for Applications, but it was marked as hidden in the VBA type library and was undocumented.

In Visual Basic 6.0, line numbers are simply numbers that appear at the beginning of a line of Visual Basic code. In Visual Basic .NET, line numbers are labels that must be followed by a colon.

See Also

Err Object

Err Function

Provides access to the Err object, which provides error information when using unstructured exception handling.

Member Of

Microsoft.VisualBasic.Information

Syntax

```
Function Err() As ErrObject
```

Return Value

An instance of the ErrObject class, commonly known as the Err object.

Comments

Strangely, this is a virtually undocumented function. But it explains what was defined as the ErrObject class in the Visual Basic 6.0 type library and as the ErrObject class in the Microsoft.VisualBasic.dll assembly, can be called the Err object in the documentation and referenced as the Err object in code: Err is a shared Visual Basic method that returns an ErrObject instance. This ErrObject instance can be retrieved and its reference saved, as in:

```
Dim errObj As ErrObject = Err
```

or, since there is only one ErrObject object per application (and it is not externally creatable), it can be referenced directly through the function that returns it.

Example

The example illustrates the fact that the ErrObject object is an instance of the ErrObject class, and that Err is simply the member that returns the ErrObject:

```
Public Module modErr
    Dim exc As ErrObject
```

```
Public Sub Main()
    On Error GoTo ErrHandler:
    Err.Raise(5)

    Exit Sub
ErrHandler:
    exc = Err
    Console.WriteLine(exc.Description)
End Sub

End Module
```

See Also

Err Object

Err Object

Provides information about errors if unstructured exception handling is used.

Type

Microsoft.VisualBasic.ErrObject

Comments

The Err object (which is actually an instance of the ErrObject class, making it an ErrObject object) is returned by the shared Err method of the Microsoft.VisualBasic.Information class. Only one ErrObject instance can exist per application, and a class instance cannot be created by client code.

The Err object is always available, whether or not an error has occurred. Only if an error has occurred or the previous error has not been cleared, however, does it contain useful information. You can determine whether the Err object has useful error information by testing for a non-zero value of the Number property.

The Err object is used in unstructured exception handling. Unless you're porting legacy code to Visual Basic .NET, this book instead recommends that you use structured exception handling with the Try . . . Catch . . . End Try statement.

The Err object reports information about a single error. In contrast, an exception object in structured exception handling has an InnerException property that allows it to nest information about a virtually unlimited number of exceptions.

If you're building class libraries that will be accessed from other programming languages, the .NET runtime will translate errors into .NET exceptions when they're passed on to clients by the Err.Raise method. Table 8-5 lists some predefined Visual Basic errors (which, incidentally, are the error codes that Bill Gates and Paul Allen used for Altair BASIC) and their corresponding .NET exceptions. Note that the runtime translates a number of specific errors (like 57, Device I/O error, and 58, File already exists error) into more general .NET exceptions (IOException). Moreover, the .NET runtime is inconsistent in migrating the Err.Description property to the exception object's Message property. This means that clients of your code using different languages are going to have less specific error information available to them than clients using Visual Basic. That alone is a powerful argument to adopt structured exception handling over unstructured exception handling.

TABLE 8-5
Visual Basic
Err.Number Values
and Their
Corresponding
.NET Exceptions

Error Number(s)	Exception Name
3	InvalidOperationException
5	ArgumentException
6	OverflowException
7, 14	OutOfMemoryException
9	IndexOutOfRangeException
11	DivideByZeroException
13	InvalidCastException
20	InvalidOperationException
28	StackOverflowException
48	TypeLoadException
52, 54–54, 57–59, 61, 63, 67–68, 70–71, 74–75	IOException
53, 76	FileNotFoundException
62	EndOfStreamException
91	NullReferenceException
94, 100	InvalidOperationException

Members

The members of the Err object provide information about the error being handled, as well as allow errors to be raised and error information to be cleared. Note that all of the properties of the Err object are read-write.

Clear Method

Clears the Err object of all existing error information and resets its properties to their default values. Its syntax is:

```
Err.Clear()
```

The method is called by the runtime whenever an Exit Function, Exit Sub, or Exit Property statement is encountered. It is also a good idea to call it in code after handling an error in an error handler.

Description Property

A String that provides a textual description of the error. For custom errors, this property can be populated by supplying a *Description* argument to the Raise method.

GetException Method

Returns an Exception object that corresponds to the current error, or Nothing if there is no error. The method was added to Visual Basic in .NET version 1.0. Its syntax is:

```
Function GetException() As Exception
```

If you do continue to use unstructured exception handling, the method can be used to document the exceptions raised by a component or class library when they are instantiated by an application that uses structured exception handling.

HelpContext Property

An Integer containing the context ID of a topic related to the error in a help file. For custom errors, this property can be populated by supplying a *HelpContext* argument to the Raise method. For errors that correspond to standard Visual Basic error numbers, the property should be assigned the appropriate help context identifier.

HelpFile Property

A String that contains the fully qualified path of a Windows help file. For custom errors, this property can be populated by supplying a *HelpFile* argument to the Raise method. For errors that correspond to standard Visual Basic error numbers, the property should be assigned the name and path of the Visual Basic help file.

LastDLLError Property

An Integer that contains an error code that can be used to retrieve error information about an unsuccessful Win32 API call. The error code can in turn be used to call the FormatMessage function to display a text message rather than an error number. The behavior of the LastDLLError property in the event of failed Win32 API calls tends to be unpredictable; in many cases, it provides no error information even though an API call has failed.

Number Property

The number of the error. In order that custom errors not duplicate standard Visual Basic error numbers, custom error numbers should be formed by adding an error number to the vbObjectErr constant. The Number property can be populated by supplying a *Number* argument to the Raise method.

Raise Method

Raises an error. This method is used in a class to force the consuming class to handle the error. If the client code is Visual Basic, it can be handled using either unstructured exception handling or structured exception handling; if the client code is not Visual Basic code, it can be handled using structured exception handling. The method syntax is:

```
Raise(ByVal Number As Integer, Optional ByVal Source As Object, _
    Optional ByVal Description As Object, Optional ByVal HelpFile As Object, _
    Optional ByVal HelpContext As Object)
```

Source Property

The String that indicates the name of the application or object in which the error occurred. For custom errors, this property can be populated by supplying a *Source* argument to the Raise method.

See Also

Err Function, Try Statement

Error Statement

Raises an error.

Syntax

```
Error errornumber
```

Element	Description
errornumber	The number of the error to be raised.

Comments

Using the Error statement sets the Err object's Number property to *errornumber*. If *errornumber* is a standard Visual Basic error number, it also sets the Err object's Description property to the description corresponding to that error number and sets the Err object's Source property to the name of the application or component in which the Error statement was called.

The Error statement is a legacy of the early days of Visual Basic. If you're using unstructured exception handling in code, call the Err.Raise method. But preferably, use structured exception handling and raise exceptions with the Throw statement.

See Also

Err Object, Throw Statement

ErrorToString Function

Converts a standard Visual Basic error number to its corresponding error message.

Member Of

Microsoft.VisualBasic.Conversion

Syntax

```
Function ErrorToString(ByVal ErrorNumber As Integer) As String
```

Element	Description
ErrorNumber	A standard Visual Basic error number. If *ErrorNumber* is out of range, an ArgumentException is thrown.

Return Value

A String representing the error message that corresponds to *ErrorNumber,* or the string, "Application-defined or object-defined error." if *ErrorNumber* does not correspond to a standard Visual Basic error.

Comments

The ErrorToString method simply returns the Description property that corresponds to a particular Err object Number property.

VB6 Differences

The ErrorToString function is new to Visual Basic .NET. It was probably intended as a way of providing familiar error messages to Visual Basic 6.0 programmers while throwing exceptions, as the following code fragment illustrates:

```
If Not TypeOf(arg) Is String Then
    Throw New ArgumentException(ErrorToString(5))
End If
```

Event Statement

Defines an event.

Syntax

```
[ < attributes > ] [ access_modifier ] [ Shadows ] Event eventname[(arglist)] _
[ Implements implementsList ]
```

or

```
[ < attributes > ] [ access_modifier ] [ Shadows ] Event eventname As delegatename _
[ Implements implementsList ]
```

or

```
[ < attributes > ] [ access_modifier ] [ Shadows ] Custom Event eventname _
        As delegatename [ Implements implementsList ]
    [ <attrlist> ] AddHandler(ByVal value As delegatename)
        [ statements ]
    End AddHandler
    [ <attrlist> ] RemoveHandler(ByVal value As delegatename)
        [ statements ]
    End RemoveHandler
    [ <attrlist> ] RaiseEvent(delegatesignature)
        [ statements ]
    End RaiseEvent
End Event
```

Element	Description
attributes	Any attributes that are to be applied to the event. Only attributes whose AttributeUsage attribute is AttributeTargets.All or AttributeTargets.Event can be applied to an event.

Element	Description
access_modifier	One of the standard access modifiers (Private, Protected, Friend, Protected Friend, or Public) that defines the event's accessibility. The accessibility of an event determines from what code the event can be fired. If *access_modifier* is not present, the event is Public by default. *access_modifier* cannot be used for events defined in interfaces, since all interface members are public anyway.
Shadows	Indicates that the event redeclares and hides an identically named program element in a base class.
eventname	The name of the event. It must follow standard Visual Basic naming conventions.
arglist	The list of arguments to be supplied when an event is raised. The argument list must be enclosed in parentheses, with each argument separated from other arguments by a comma. Each argument in *arglist* takes the form: `[ByVal	ByRef] argname[()] [As type]` where *argname* is the name of the argument and *type* is its data type, which is required if Option Strict is on.
implementsList	Indicates the event or events in an interface that this event implements. If multiple events are implemented, they are separated by commas. Each implemented event has the form *interfacename.eventname*. This clause is equivalent to the Handles clause for a method.
delegatename	The name of a delegate whose signature defines the event's argument list.
Custom	Defines a custom event. A custom event is one that provides code that executes when an event handler is added and removed and when an event is raised. See the entry for the Custom Keyword for additional detail.
attrlist	Any attributes to be applied to the custom event procedure. Only attributes whose AttributeUsage attribute is AttributeTargets.All or AttributeTargets.Method can be applied to a custom event procedure.
AddHandler . . . End AddHandler	The code block that executes when an event handler is added to receive event notifications. Its syntax includes the delegate type that defines the event's argument list, as well as the name by which the delegate instance will be known in the procedure. For example: `AddHandler(ByVal ev As EventHandler)` It is required if the Custom keyword is used.
RemoveHandler . . . End RemoveHandler	The code block that executes when an event handler no longer is to receive event notifications. Like that of the AddHandler . . . EndAddHandler code block, its syntax includes the delegate type that defines the event's argument list, along with the name by which the delegate instance will be referenced in the procedure. It is required if the Custom keyword is used.
RaiseEvent . . . End RaiseEvent	The code block that executes when the event is raised. Its syntax includes a formal parameter list that must match that of the delegates in the AddHandler . . . EndHandler and RemoveHandler . . . End RemoveHandler constructs. For example: `RemoveHandler(sender As Object, e As EventArgs)`

Comments

Events are type members; they can be defined as members of classes, structures, and interfaces.

If the event implements an event defined in an interface, its name does not have to be the same as the interface name. A nice feature of the Implements keyword is that it frees the event from the requirement that it have the same name as the event that it implements.

The event statement both declares an event and defines its signature. The event handler itself is implemented as a procedure rather than a function and can have an argument list very much like any Visual Basic .NET function or subroutine, except that it cannot make use of optional parameters or parameter arrays (and as a result cannot use the Optional or ParamArray keywords). The RaiseEvent statement and the event handler also cannot use named arguments.

Although an event can have any signature, by convention. .NET events have the following signature:

```
eventname(ByVal sender As Object, ByVal e As EventArgs)
```

where *sender* is a reference to the object raising the event, and *e* is a class instance derived from System.EventArgs that can provide information about the event. Adopting this basic signature and either using EventArgs or defining a custom class derived from it makes it far easier for consumers of your classes to handle events.

The only unique member of the EventArgs class that is not inherited from System.Object is EventArgs.Empty. EventArgs, in other words, provide no information about an event other than the fact that it occurred.

By default, event notifications are synchronous. That is, when an event is raised, control returns to the object instance that raised the event only after all event handlers have executed. This makes it possible to use events to as warning indicators of some operation that can be canceled, or as a means of receiving data back from client code handling the event, as the following comment illustrates.

Often, you want clients who are receiving event notifications to have the ability to respond to an event that allows them to cancel some pending operation. For example, before a Windows form is about to close, it fires a Closing event that passes a CancelEventArgs object to clients handling the event. The CancelEventArgs object includes a property, Cancel, that is False by default but if set to True cancels the closing operation. A feature such as this is easy to implement, as the following code shows:

```
Public Class CancelEventArgs
    Inherits EventArgs

    Private flagCancel As Boolean = False

    Public Property Cancel As Boolean
        Get
            Return flagCancel
        End Get
        Set
            flagCancel = Value
        End Set
    End Property
End Class
```

```vb
Public Class classCtr
    Public Event Resetting(sender As Object, e As CancelEventArgs)

    Public Function GetCounter() As Integer
        Return GetCounter(False)
    End Function

    Private Function GetCounter(reset As Boolean) As Integer
        Static ctr As Integer
        If reset Then
            ctr = 0
        Else
            ctr += 1
        End If
        Return ctr
    End Function

    Public Sub ResetCounter()
        Dim e As New CancelEventArgs()
        RaiseEvent Resetting(Me, e)
        If e.Cancel = True Then
            Console.WriteLine("Reset event canceled")
        Else
            Console.WriteLine("Counter reset . . . ")
            GetCounter(True)
        End If
    End Sub
End Class

Public Class TestEvent
    Private WithEvents ctr1, ctr2 As classCtr
    Private te As TestEvent

    Public Shared Sub Main()
        Dim te As New TestEvent
        te.HandleEvents()
    End Sub

    Private Sub HandleEvents
        ctr1 = New classCtr
        Console.WriteLine("ctrl1: " & ctr1.GetCounter)
        Console.WriteLine("ctrl1: " & ctr1.GetCounter)
        ctr2 = New classCtr

        Console.WriteLine("ctrl2: " & ctr2.GetCounter)
        Console.WriteLine("ctrl2: " & ctr2.GetCounter)
        Console.WriteLine("Calling ctrl1.ResetCounter")
        ctr1.ResetCounter()
        Console.WriteLine("ctrl1: " & ctr1.GetCounter)
        Console.WriteLine("ctrl2: " & ctr2.GetCounter)
        Console.WriteLine("Calling ctrl1.ResetCounter")
        ctr2.ResetCounter()
        Console.WriteLine("ctrl1: " & ctr1.GetCounter)
        Console.WriteLine("ctrl2: " & ctr2.GetCounter)
    End Sub
```

```
Private Sub ResettingCtr(sender As Object, e As CancelEventArgs) _
                    Handles ctr1.Resetting, ctr2.Resetting
   If MsgBox("OK to reset counter?", MsgBoxStyle.YesNo) = MsgBoxResult.No Then
      e.Cancel = True
   End If
   Console.WriteLine("Cancel is {0}", e.Cancel)
   End Sub
End Class
```

This code defines a class, CancelEventArgs, that inherits from EventArgs and adds a single property, Cancel. (Note that an identical class exists in the .NET Framework Class Library. It's defined here simply to illustrate how to define your own event arguments class.) The code also defines a second class, classCtr, that has three members: GetCounter, an overloaded method that maintains a static Integer variable that returns a count of the number of times it has been called; and ResetCounter, a method that passes a value of True to one of the overloads of the GetCounter method to reinitialize the counter to 0; and Resetting, an event raised before the counter is reset that passes the class instance and a CancelEventArgs instance to the client receiving event notifications. When the ResetCounter method is called, it raises the Resetting event to notify the client of the class that the counter will be reset. If the client sets the Cancel property to True, when control returns to the ResetCounter method the value of the Cancel property can be retrieved and the reset operation canceled.

If we use ILDasm to look at the code for the compiled executable from the preceding example (see Figure 8-10), we can see that Visual Basic has implemented our event handler as a multicast delegate.

Typically, the first version of the Event statement, in which the event's parameter list is specified exactly, is the one most commonly used by Visual Basic programmers. A delegate, however, could be used instead. This requires that we define a delegate either at the namespace

FIGURE 8-10
A class declaring an event viewed in ILDasm

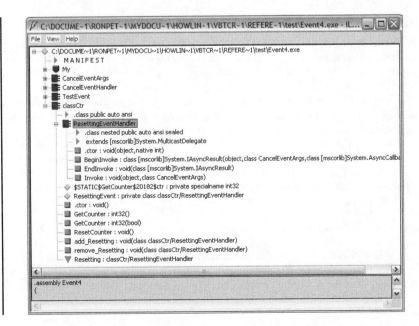

level (especially if it is a delegate that we wish to reuse) or as a class member. The following code does that (again by defining an existing delegate):

```
Public Delegate Sub CancelEventHandler(sender As Object, e As CancelEventArgs)
```

Then we can declare our event as having that delegate's signature, as the following code does:

```
Public Class classCtr
  Public Event Resetting As CancelEventHandler
  ' the rest of the class definition
```

Client code is unaffected by this change.

You can also define an event using the Custom keyword, which requires that you provide code that executes whenever an event handler is added or removed, as well as whenever an event handler executes. This allows you to do such things as execute handlers asynchronously or execute multiple event handlers in response to a single event. For details, see the Custom keyword.

Once an event is declared, it can be raised by using the RaiseEvent statement. RaiseEvent can be called not only by code within the class in which the event is defined, but by any consumer of the class to which the event is accessible.

Example

See the example for the Custom Keyword for an example of an event that's defined using the Custom keyword.

VB.NET Changes

The Custom keyword, as well as the AddHandler . . . End AddHandler, RemoveHandler . . . End RemoveHandler, and RaiseEvent . . . End RaiseEvent constructs are new to Visual Basic 2005.

VB6 Differences

In Visual Basic 6.0, events defined using the Event statement were necessarily public, either because an access modifier was omitted (events were public by default) or because the Public keyword was present; either of the two other access modifiers (Private or Friend) generated a compiler error. In Visual Basic .NET, all access modifiers are allowed. This in turn means that if an event is to be handled in Visual Basic 6.0, it must be handled by clients of the class. In Visual Basic .NET, the event handler can be included as a part of the class implementation, and an event can be declared Private so that it is visible only within the class itself.

Although Visual Basic 6.0 permitted interfaces to define events, they were not a part of the interface's public interface. As a result, implementing classes were not required to implement the event.

In Visual Basic .NET, arguments were passed by reference in an event handler to allow clients of a class to perform operations such as canceling a pending operation. For example, the Form_QueryUnload event had the signature:

```
QueryUnload(Cancel As Integer, UnloadMode As Integer)
```

Here, Cancel and UnloadMode are passed by reference, since Visual Basic 6.0 passes arguments by reference by default. In Visual Basic .NET, if an EventArgs object or an object derived from it is passed to event handlers, there is no need to pass arguments by reference.

See Also

Custom Keyword, Handles Keyword, RaiseEvent Statement, WithEvents Keyword

Exit Statement

Prematurely exits a Visual Basic programming construct.

Syntax

```
Exit { Do | For | Function | Property | Select | Sub | Try | While }
```

Element	Description
Do	Unconditionally exits a Do While . . . Loop, Do Until . . . Loop, Do . . . Loop While, or Do . . . Loop Until construct before the looping condition is evaluated. Program flow continues with the line of code following the Loop statement.
For	Unconditionally exits a For . . . Next or For Each . . . Next construct before the For condition is evaluated. Program flow continues with the line of code following the Next statement.
Function	Exits a Function . . . End Function construct before all code in the function has executed, and returns control to the caller.
Property	Exits a property set or get procedure before the end of the procedure is encountered and returns control to the caller.
Select	Immediately exists the Case block of the Select Case statement in which it appears. Program flow continues with the line of code following the End Select statement.
Sub	Exits a Sub . . . End Sub construct before all code in the subroutine has executed and returns control to the caller.
Try	Immediately exits the try or Catch block of a Try . . . Catch . . . Finally . . . End Try construct. (Exit Try cannot appear in the Finally block.) Program flow proceeds to the Finally block, if one is present, then continues with the line of code following the End Try statement.
While	Unconditionally exits a While . . . End While loop before the looping condition is evaluated. Program flow continues with the line of code following the End While statement.

Comments

Typically, Exit statements are placed within If statements so that they immediately and prematurely exit a looping or other construct if some condition is met.

In the case of the Exit Function, Exit Sub, and Exit Property statements, if the Exit statement is found inside either a Try block or a Catch block of a Try . . . Catch . . . Finally . . . End Try construct, the Finally block is executed before control returns to the caller.

The Return statement is analogous to the Exit Sub, Exit Function, and Exit Property statements: it causes execution of any remaining code to be skipped and control to return immediately to the caller.

If an Exit statement is encountered within nested programming constructs (such as an Exit For statement encountered within a set of nested For . . . Next constructs), the inner loop is exited immediately, and program flow proceeds to the first statement after the inner loop's Next statement.

Exit statements are also used in unstructured exception handling to prevent the exception handler from being executed. For example:

```
Public Sub ReadFile(filename As String)
   On Error GoTo errHandler:

   Dim fileNo As Integer = FreeFile()
   FileOpen(fileNo, filename, OpenMode.Input)
   ' Read File
   FileClose(fileNo)
   Exit Sub
errHandler:
   Console.WriteLine(err.Description)
End Sub
```

Often, the Exit For, Exit Do, or Exit While statement is used when iterating members of a collection or array to find the first member or element that meets a particular condition. For example, the following routine iterates a collection to find the first word that begins with the substring "Br":

```
Public Function FindWord(stringArray As String(), startString As String, _
                      insensitive As Boolean) As Integer
   Dim index As Integer
   Dim comparison As StringComparison
   If insensitive Then
      comparison = StringComparison.CurrentCultureIgnoreCase
   Else
      comparison = StringComparison.CurrentCulture
   End If
   For ctr As Integer = stringArray.GetLowerBound(0) To _
                      stringArray.GetUpperBound(0)
      If stringArray(ctr).StartsWith(startString, comparison) Then
         index = ctr              ' could also (preferably) use Return here
         Exit For
      End If
   Next
   If index = stringArray.Length Then index = -1
   FindWord = index
End Function
```

Example

The example illustrates the use of the Exit statement both to prevent program flow from falling into an event handler and to prematurely exit a looping construct:

```
Public Sub ExitErrHandler
   On Error GoTo ErrHand:
   Dim fn As String = InputBox("Enter file to open:")
   If fn = "" Then Exit Sub
   Dim sr As StreamReader = New StreamReader(fn)
```

```
    Do While Not sr.EndOfStream
        Console.WriteLine(sr.ReadLine)
    Loop
    Exit Sub
ErrHand:
    MsgBox("The following error occurred: " & vbCrLf & Err.Description)
End Sub
```

VB6 Differences

The Exit Select, Exit Try, and Exit While statements are new to Visual Basic .NET.

See Also

Do . . . Loop Statement, End Statement, For Each . . . Next Construct, For . . . Next Construct, Function Statement, Get Statement, Return Statement, Select Case Statement, Set Statement, Sub Statement, Try . . . Catch . . . Finally Construct, While . . . End While Construct

FileAttr Function

Indicates the file mode in which a file was opened by the FileOpen subroutine.

Member Of

Microsoft.VisualBasic.FileSystem

Syntax

```
FileAttr(ByVal FileNumber As Integer) As OpenMode
```

Element	Description
FileNumber	The file number used in the call to the FileOpen subroutine.

Return Value

One of the following members of the OpenMode enumeration:

OpenMode Member	Value	Description
OpenMode.Input	1	The file was opened for reading.
OpenMode.Output	2	The file was opened for writing.
OpenMode.Random	4	The file was opened as a random-access file with fixed-length records.
OpenMode.Append	8	The file was opened for writing at the end of the file.
OpenMode.Binary	32	The file is a binary file.

Comments

FileAttr works only with files opened using the FileOpen subroutine.

The FileAttr function is one of a number of interrelated file input/output functions that Visual Basic .NET inherited from previous versions of Visual Basic. There is little reason to use FileAttr in new code written expressly for Visual Basic .NET.

VB6 Differences

In Visual Basic 6.0, the function returned a Long rather than an intrinsic constant or enumeration member. Possible values are indicated in the Return Value section.

Visual Basic 6.0 included an optional *returntype* parameter whose value, if it was present, had to be 1. The parameter was inherited from 16-bit versions of Visual Basic, when the function, if passed a value of 2, returned the file system handle for the file. (This also explains the rather unusual name of the function given its limited functionality in Visual Basic .NET.) In Visual Basic .NET, this parameter has been eliminated.

See Also

FileOpen Subroutine, FreeFile Function

FileClose Subroutine

Closes one or more files opened using the FileOpen subroutine.

Member Of

Microsoft.VisualBasic.FileSystem

Syntax

```
FileClose([ParamArray FileNumbers() As Integer])
```

Element	Description
FileNumbers	The number or numbers of the file(s) opened using the FileOpen subroutine.

Comments

FileClose works only with files opened using the FileOpen subroutine.

If *FileNumbers* is not present, the FileClose subroutine closes all files opened with the FileOpen subroutine.

When the FileClose subroutine is encountered, any data in the buffer of files opened in output or append mode is written to the file and the file is closed.

Once the FileClose subroutine is called, any subsequent attempt to access the files using a file number passed to FileClose either explicitly or implicitly throws an IOException.

If you use Fileclose in your code, you should put it in the Finally block of an exception handler so that the file is closed whether or not an exception is thrown. This requires the following pattern:

```
Dim fileOpened As Boolean        ' flag to indicate whether file was opened
Try
    FileOpen(fileNo, filename)
    fileOpened = True
    ' perform file operations
Catch e As Exception
    ' handle exceptions
Finally
    If fileOpened Then FileClose(fileNo)
End Try
```

The FileClose subroutine is one of a number of interrelated file input/output functions that Visual Basic .NET inherited from previous versions of Visual Basic. There is little reason to use these in new code written expressly for Visual Basic .NET.

VB6 Differences

FileClose is new to Visual Basic .NET. It replaces the Close (or Close #) statement in Visual Basic 6.0.

In Visual Basic 6.0, if *FileNumbers* represents multiple file numbers, they must be delimited by commas. In Visual Basic .NET, since *FileNumbers* is a parameter array, multiple file numbers can either be delimited by commas or passed as a single array.

See Also

FileOpen Subroutine, FreeFile Function, Reset Subroutine

FileCopy Subroutine

Copies a file.

Member Of

Microsoft.VisualBasic.FileSystem

Syntax

```
FileCopy(ByVal Source As String, ByVal Destination As String)
```

Element	Description
Source	The name of the file to be copied, along with an optional path.
Destination	The name of the copy of *Source*, along with an optional path.

Comments

If no path is specified in either *Source* or *Destination*, the subroutine attempts to copy a file in the current directory to a file named *Destination* in the current directory. If a path is provided for either *Source* and/or *Destination*, it can be an absolute path (starting from a drive and navigating to the source or destination directory) or a relative path (starting from the current directory and navigating to the source or destination directory).

Neither *Source* nor *Destination* is case-sensitive.

If *Destination* already exists, it is overwritten without warning. To prevent this, you could use the My.Computer.FileSystem.FileExists method to determine whether the file exists before calling the FileCopy subroutine. For example:

```
Public Sub AttemptFileCopy(source As String, target As String)
    Dim copyFlag As Boolean = True
    Try
        If My.Computer.FileSystem.FileExists(target) Then
            If MsgBox("File already exists. Overwrite it?", _
                    MsgBoxStyle.YesNo Or MsgBoxStyle.Question, _
                    "Overwrite File") = MsgBoxResult.No Then copyFlag = False
        End If
        If copyFlag Then
            FileCopy(source, target)
        End If
        ' copy failed: rethrow exception
    Catch e As Exception
        Throw e
    End Try
End Sub
```

The FileCopy subroutine is intended to copy a single file at a time. It does not accept wildcard characters.

According to the documentation, if you attempt to use FileCopy to copy an open file, an IOException is thrown. This appears to be true, however, only if the file was opened using the FileOpen subroutine. For most if not all other open files, the copy operation completes without generating an exception. (Given that portions of the open file may be stored in memory, however, this copy operation may not create an accurate copy of the source file.) However, if *Destination* exists and is open, an IOException is thrown regardless of how the file has been opened

A number of more flexible methods are available for copying files:

- The My.Computer.FileSystem class includes an overloaded CopyFile method that, like FileCopy, allows you to specify a source and destination. In addition to this basic version, however, other overloads allow you to specify whether the target file should be overwritten if it already exists, whether user interface elements should be used to show the copy operation's progress, and how the method should behave if the user attempts to cancel the copy operation.

- The shared, overloaded System.IO.File.Copy method, which allows you to specify a source and destination file, as well as whether the destination file is to be overwritten if it already exists.

See Also

Kill Subroutine, MkDir Subroutine, My.Computer.FileSystem.CopyFile Method, RmDir Subroutine, Rename Subroutine

FileDateTime Function

Indicates the date and time when a file was created or last modified.

Member Of

Microsoft.VisualBasic.FileSystem

Syntax

```
FileDateTime(ByVal PathName As String) As DateTime
```

Element	Description
PathName	The filename, along with an optional path.

Return Value

A Date value indicating when the file was created or last modified, whichever is later.

Comments

If a path is not included in *PathName,* the function looks in the current directory. If a path is provided, it may be an absolute path or a path relative to the current directory.

If *PathName* does not specify a valid path and filename, a FileNotFoundException is thrown. To prevent this, you can check whether the file exists before calling the FileDateTime function by using either the My.Computer.FileSystem.FileExists method or the shared System.IO.File.Exists method.

Since the interpretation of the function's return value may be problematic, you can instead use the instance System.IO.FileInfo.CreationTime property if you would like to retrieve what is definitely the file creation date, or you can use the instance System.IO.FileInfo.LastWriteTime property if you would like to retrieve what is definitely the date the file was last modified. You can retrieve a FileInfo object for the file in which you are interested by calling the My.Computer .FileSystem.GetFileInfo method. The method takes a single argument, the path and name of the file for which you would like to instantiate a FileInfo object. For an example, see the entry for the My.Computer.FileSystem.GetFileInfo method.

See Also

My.Computer.FileSystem.GetFileInfo Method

FileGet, FileGetObject Subroutines

Reads data from an open file into a variable.

Member Of

Microsoft.VisualBasic.FileSystem

Syntax

```
FileGet(ByVal FileNumber As Integer, ByRef Value As [type], _
        Optional RecordNumber As Integer = -1)
```

```
FileGetObject(ByVal FileNumber As Integer, ByRef Value As [type], _
         Optional RecordNumber As Integer = -1)
```

Element	Description
FileNumber	The file number used in the call to the FileOpen subroutine.
Value	The variable to which the data read from the file is to be assigned.
[type]	The data type of the variable to which the data is to be assigned. Possible values are: Array, Boolean, Byte, Date, Decimal, Double, Integer, Object, Short, Single, and String.
RecordNumber	For random files, the record number to read; for binary files, the byte position at which to start reading. A value of −1 indicates the current position.
ArrayIsDynamic	For random files, indicates whether arrays are to be dynamic and are to have descriptors written to describe their length (the value is True) or whether they are static or their size is to be handled by code rather than by data stored with the array (the value is False). By default, its value is False.
StringIsFixedLength	For random files, indicates whether strings have a fixed length (the value is True) or whether they are written with two-byte descriptors that indicate their length (the value is False). By default, its value is False.

Comments

FileGet and FileGetObject work only with files opened using the FileOpen subroutine.

FileGet and FileGetObject are typically used to read data from files written with FilePut and FilePutObject, respectively, although they can be used to read from any binary or random access file.

When you open a random file to read from it, it you should always use the same *RecordLength* value in the FileOpen call that was used to write to it.

FileGet and FileGetObject allow you to read all of the scalar Visual Basic .NET data types. However, if you attempt to define a structure that includes the SByte, UShort, UInteger, or ULong types, Visual Basic throws an exception at runtime.

When the file is first opened, the file pointer for a binary file points to position 0 (the value of the file pointer is one-based), and the record pointer for a random file points to record 1. For a binary file, each subsequent read operation automatically advances the file pointer by the number of bytes read (see the next comment). For a random file with fixed-length records, each subsequent read operation automatically advances the record pointer by *RecordLength* bytes, as defined in the FileOpen subroutine. This should position the pointer at the beginning of the next record to be read. You have to explicitly position the record file or record pointer by supplying a value for the *RecordNumber* argument only if you are not reading data sequentially.

For a binary file, each read operation advances the file pointer by the number of bytes read, which is equivalent to the length (or size) of *Value.*

Often, binary files are used to store small amounts of data, such as the next record number for a transactional document or some basic user configuration settings. In this case, your code can simply read the necessary settings from the file without having to check whether the file pointer is at the end of the file. For instance, the following example writes six items of various data types and then simply reads them in the order in which they were written:

```
Public Module modMain
    Public Sub Main()
        ' Define data to be written to binary file
        Dim fileNo As Integer
        Dim uint As Integer = 120
        Dim int As Integer = -1604
        Dim ch As Char = "r"c
        Dim strng As String = "EndOfData"
        Dim fileOpened As Boolean = False

        Try
            ' Open file and write data
            fileNo = FreeFile
            FileOpen(fileNo, "UserData.bin", OpenMode.Binary, OpenAccess.Write)
            fileOpened = True

            FilePut(fileNo,uint)
            FilePut(fileNo, int)
            FilePut(fileNo, ch)
            FilePut(fileNo, strng)
            FileClose(fileNo)
            fileOpened = False

            ' Reopen file and read data
            fileNo = FreeFile
            FileOpen(fileNo, "UserData.bin", OpenMode.Binary, OpenAccess.Read)
            fileOpened = True
            FileGet(fileNo, uint)
            Console.WriteLine(uint)
            FileGet(fileNo, int)
            Console.WriteLine(int)
            FileGet(fileNo, ch)
            Console.WriteLine(ch)
            FileGet(fileNo, strng)
            Console.WriteLine(strng)
        Catch
            Console.WriteLine(e.GetType.Name & ": " & e.Message)
        Finally
            If fileOpened Then FileClose(fileNo)
        End Try
    End Sub
End Module
```

Along with reading scalar data types, you can also read and write structures. For example, the following code defines a structure, Point, very much like the one defined in System.Drawing. It writes the data from three instances of the Point structure to a file and then retrieves and displays them:

```
Public Structure Point
    Dim x As Integer
    Dim y As Integer
```

```vb
    Public Sub New(x As Integer, y As Integer)
        Me.x = x
        Me.y = y
    End Sub
End Structure

Public Module modMain
    Public Sub Main()
        Dim pt1 As New Point(110,130)
        Dim pt2 As New Point(90, 140)
        Dim pt3 As New Point(70, 150)
        Dim fileOpened, fileWritten As Boolean

        Try
            Dim fileNo As Integer = FreeFile()
            FileOpen(fileNo, "StructFile.bin", OpenMode.Binary, OpenAccess.Write)
            fileOpened = True
            FilePut(fileNo,pt1)
            FilePut(fileNo, pt2)
            FilePut(fileNo, pt3)
            fileWritten = True
        Catch e As Exception
            Console.WriteLine(e.GetType.Name & ": " & e.Message)
        Finally
            If fileOpened Then FileClose(fileNo)
        End Try

        If fileWritten Then ReadFile()
    End Sub

    Sub ReadFile()
        Dim pt As New Point
        Dim fileNo As Integer = FreeFile()
        Dim fileOpened As Boolean = False

        Try
            FileOpen(fileNo, "StructFile.bin", OpenMode.Binary, OpenAccess.Read)
            fileOpened = True
            FileGet(fileNo, pt)
            Console.WriteLine("Coordinates: {0}, {1}", pt.x, pt.y)
            FileGet(fileNo, pt)
            Console.WriteLine("Coordinates: {0}, {1}", pt.x, pt.y)
            FileGet(fileNo, pt)
            Console.WriteLine("Coordinates: {0}, {1}", pt.x, pt.y)
        Catch e As Exception
            Console.WriteLine(e.GetType().Name & ": " & e.Message)
        Finally
            If fileOpened Then FileClose(fileNo)
        End Try
    End Sub
End Module
```

In most cases when reading from a binary file, you must check the position of the file pointer to make sure that it hasn't reached the end of the file. There are two techniques to do this. The first simply examines the value returned by the EOF function to determine if the pointer is at the end of the file. The second compares the position of the file pointer, as reported by the Loc function, with the number of bytes in the file, as reported by the Lof function. For example:

```
Do While Lof(fileNo) < Loc(fileNo)
```

When reading strings from a binary file, the *StringIsFixedLength* argument has no effect. Instead, the number of bytes read and assigned to a string variable always equals the number of bytes assigned to *Value* when it is passed to the FileGet or FileGetObject subroutine. This is admittedly inconvenient, since often the exact content and size of strings is determined only at runtime. However, there is a work-around: you can provide the descriptor yourself when writing a string, and then read it before calling the FileGet or FileGetObject subroutine to retrieve the string value. The following code illustrates this:

```
Public Class StringDescriptors
    Private Const FILENAME As String = "FileGetStrings.bin"

    Public Shared Sub Main()
      Dim ops As New FileOperations
      ops.WriteStrings()
      ops.ReadStrings()
    End Sub

    Private Sub WriteStrings()
      Dim fileOpened As Boolean = False
      Try
         Dim fileNo As Integer = FreeFile
         FileOpen(fileNo, FILENAME, OpenMode.Binary, OpenAccess.Write)
         fileOpened = True
         Do
            Dim strng As String = InputBox("Enter a string to write to " & _
                                  FILENAME & ": ")
            If strng = String.Empty Then Exit Do
            FilePut(fileNo, CShort(strng.Length))
            FilePut(fileNo, strng,)
         Loop
      Catch e As Exception
         Console.WriteLine(e.GetType().Name & ": " & e.Message)
      Finally
         If fileOpened Then FileClose(fileNo)
      End Try
    End Sub

    Private Sub ReadStrings()
      Dim fileOpened As Boolean = False
      Try
         Dim fileNo As Integer = FreeFile()
         FileOpen(fileNo, FILENAME, OpenMode.Binary, OpenAccess.Read)
         Dim strngRead As New String(" "c, 20)
```

```
        Do
            Dim descriptor As Short
            FileGet(fileNo, descriptor)
            Dim stringToRead As New String(" "c, descriptor)
            FileGet(fileNo, stringToRead,, False)
            Console.WriteLine(stringToRead)
        Loop While Not EOF(FileNo)
    Catch e As Exception
        Console.WriteLine(e.GetType().Name & ": " & e.Message)
    Finally
        If fileOpened Then FileClose(fileNo)
    End Try
End Sub
End Class
```

The FileGet and FileGetObject subroutines, along with the corresponding FilePut and FilePut object subroutines, remain useful for reading and writing data in binary files, particularly small binary files. For virtually all random files, but particularly random files with a large number of records, a far better choice is a database management system.

VB.NET Changes
The ArrayIsDynamic and StringIsFixedLength parameters were introduced to Visual Basic .NET Version 1.1.

VB6 Differences
The FileGet and FileGetObject subroutines are new to Visual Basic .NET. They replace the Visual Basic 6.0 Get and Get # statements.

See Also
FileClose Subroutine, FileOpen Subroutine, FilePut, FilePutObject Subroutine

---

FileLen Function
Indicates the size of a file in bytes.

Member Of
Microsoft.VisualBasic.FileSystem

Syntax

```
FileLen(ByVal PathName As String) As Long
```

Element	Description
PathName	The name and optional path of the file.

Return Value
The number of bytes in the file.

Comments

If a path is not included as part of *PathName,* .NET looks in the current directory for the file. If *PathName* includes a path component, it can be either an absolute or a relative path.

If the file specified in *PathName* does not exist, the function throws a FileNotFoundException. To prevent this, you can verify that the file exists beforehand by using either the shared System.FileIO.File.Exists method or the My.Computer.FileSystem.FileExists method. Both take a single argument, a string containing an optional path along with the filename, which can then be passed to the FileLen function.

Since the FileLen function returns a signed long integer, it is able to accurately report file sizes from 0 to 9,223,372,036,854,775,807 bytes, which makes it capable of reporting virtually any file size.

In the case of binary and random files, rather than reporting their current size, the FileLen function reports the size of open files at the time they were opened. For sequential files, on the other hand, it reports their current size. For files opened with the FileOpen subroutine, the LOF function can be used instead of FileLen to determine the size of the file.

You can also determine the size of a file from the Length property of a FileInfo object, which is returned by the My.Computer.FileSystem.GetFileInfo method. The method's single argument is the same as *PathName*: the name and optionally the path to the file whose length is to be reported.

VB6 Differences

Although the return value of the FileLen function in both Visual Basic 6.0 and Visual Basic .NET is a Long, the Long in Visual Basic 6.0 is a 32-bit integer, whereas it is a 64-bit integer in Visual Basic .NET. This means that in Visual Basic 6.0, the function reported file sizes in the range of 2,147,483,648 to 4,294,967,295 bytes as negative numbers, and that it subtracted whatever multiple of 4,294,967,295 was necessary to prevent an overflow when reporting a file size larger than 4,294,967,295 bytes. In Visual Basic .NET, the positive range of a Long is sufficiently large (approximately 10 quintillion) to handle all files.

See Also

LOF Function, My.Computer.FileSystem.GetFileInfo Method

FileOpen Subroutine

Opens a binary, random, or sequential file for input or output.

Member Of

Microsoft.VisualBasic.FileSystem

Syntax

```
FileOpen(ByVal FileNumber As Integer, ByVal FileName As String, _
    ByVal Mode As OpenMode, _
    Optional ByVal Access As OpenAccess = OpenAccess.Default, _
    Optional ByVal Share As OpenShare = OpenShare.Default, _
    Optional ByVal RecordLength As Integer = -1)
```

Element	Description
FileNumber	The number by which the open file will be referenced in subsequent file operations.
FileName	An optional path, along with the name of the file to be opened.
Mode	A member of the OpenMode enumeration that indicates the type of file to open and, for sequential files, why it is being opened. Possible values are OpenMode.Random for a random access file (that is, a file with fixed-length records) and OpenMode.Binary for a binary file. For sequential files (files whose contents must be accessed in a linear fashion, from some starting point to some end point), possible values are OpenMode.Input for a file that will be read, OpenMode.Ouput for a file that will be written to starting at the beginning of the file, and OpenMode.Append for a file that will be written to starting at the end of the existing file. Note that the Visual Studio documentation confuses OpenMode.Input and OpenMode.Output.
Access	A member of the OpenAccess enumeration indicating the access mode in which the file is opened. Possible values are OpenAccess.Default, which is the default value; OpenAccess.Read; OpenAccess.ReadWrite; and OpenAccess.Write. If no argument is provided, *Access* defaults to OpenAccess.Default, which opens binary and random files for read-write access, sequential files opened with OpenMode.Append or OpenMode.Output for write access, and sequential files opened with OpenMode.Input for read access.
Share	Defines the operations permitted on *FileName* by other processes or threads. Possible values are OpenShare.Default, which is the same as OpenShare.LockReadWrite; OpenShare.LockRead, which prevents others from reading from the file; OpenShare.LockReadWrite, which prevents others from reading from or writing to the file; OpenShare.LockWrite, which prevents other processes from writing to the file; and OpenShare.Shared, which allows other processes to both read from and write to the file.
RecordLength	For random files, the record length in bytes. For sequential files, the size of the file buffer for read or write operations in bytes. Its value can range from 1 to 32,767.

Comments

FileOpen is one of a series of "native" Visual Basic procedures that support file access. In order to use any of these procedures, you must open the file with which you're working with FileOpen, since it not only opens the file but also associates it with *FileNumber*. The remaining procedures then refer to the file by *FileNumber* rather than by its path and name.

FileOpen and its related file manipulation functions and subroutines allow you to work with the following kinds of files:

- Sequential files, which are text files that typically are read from beginning to end, or which are written from the beginning to the end of the file.

- Binary files, which are files in which each byte can be accessed independently of one another.

- Random files, which are structured files that contain records of a particular length.

Function or Subroutine	Binary	Random	Sequential
EOF function	X	X	X
FileAttr function	X	X	X
FileClose subroutine	X	X	X
FileGet, FileGetObject subroutine	X	X	
FilePut, FilePutObject subroutine	X	X	
FileWidth subroutine			X
FreeFile function	X	X	X
Input subroutine			X
InputString function	X		X
LineInput function			X
Loc function	X	X	X
Lock subroutine		X	
LOF function	X	X	X
Print, PrintLine subroutine			X
Reset subroutine	X	X	X
Seek subroutine	X	X	
SPC function			X
Tab function			X
Unlock subroutine		X	
Write, WriteLine subroutine			X

TABLE 8-6   File Access Functions and Subroutines That Use *FileNumber*

Table 8-6 lists the Visual Basic file access functions and subroutines that perform an operation on *FileNumber* and show the file types with which they work:

To ensure that *FileNumber* is not already in use, you can retrieve its value by first calling the FreeFile function. For example:

```
fileNumber = FreeFile()
FileOpen(filenumber, "SourceDoc.Doc", OpenMode.Input)
```

If *FileName* does not include path information, .NET looks for the file in the current directory. If path information is provided, it can be either relative (in relation to the current directory) or absolute.

If *FileName* does not exist but FileOpen attempts to open it for input as a sequential file, a FileNotFoundException is thrown. In order to prevent this, you can call the shared System .IO.File.Exists function or the My.Computer.FileSystem.FileExists method. In all other cases, the call to the FileOpen subroutine creates a zero-length file named *FileName* if it does not already exist.

In the case of sequential files, the *Mode* and *Access* arguments are not mutually exclusive. If *Access* is present, its value must be consistent with the *Mode* argument or an ArgumentException results at runtime. If *Mode* is OpenMode.Input, valid values are OpenAccess.Default or OpenAccess.Read. If *Mode* is OpenMode.Output or OpenMode.Append, valid values of *Access* are OpenAccess.Default or OpenAccess.Write.

If you are creating a random-access file, you don't necessarily have to supply a value for the *RecordLength* property; the compiler will supply a default value. This may not be an efficient value, and it may result in an inefficient use of available storage for large files. If no value is supplied for *RecordLength* when creating the file, subsequent calls to FileOpen to read from and write to the file should also rely on the compiler's supplying a default record length.

When you open a random file to read from it, it you should always use the same *RecordLength* value that was used when writing to it.

Although the FileOpen subroutine itself is new to Visual Basic .NET (see the VB6 Differences section), it is one of a series of interrelated compatibility functions that is rarely used in new Visual Basic .NET code. The functions for sequential file access have been replaced by the members of the TextReader and TextWriter classes, and the functions for binary and random file access have been replaced by members of the FileStream class. In addition, the easy availability of database management systems such as Microsoft Access, Microsoft SQL Server Desktop Edition (MSDE), and Microsoft SQL Server has meant that database tables have increasingly replaced stand-alone random files for data storage, and that ADO.NET has increasingly replaced the random access functions and procedures as the preferred way to access record-based data.

Example

See the example for the FileClose subroutine.

VB6 Differences

FileOpen corresponds more or less directly to the Visual Basic 6.0 Open statement, which had the syntax:

```
Open pathname For mode [Access access] [lock] As [#]fileNumber [Len = reclength]
```

The order of arguments is somewhat different. In addition, Visual Basic 6.0 supported a number of keywords for mode, access, and lock that were implemented by the compiler but in Visual Basic 6.0 are enumerated constants.

See Also

FreeFile Function, FileClose Subroutine, Reset Subroutine

FilePut, FilePutObject Subroutines

Writes data from a variable to an open file.

Member Of

Microsoft.VisualBasic.FileSystem

Syntax

```
FilePutObject(FileNumber As Integer, Value As Object, _
            RecordNumber As Integer = -1)

FilePut(FileNumber As Integer, Value As [type], _
        Optional RecordNumber As Integer = -1)

FilePutObject(FileNumber As Integer, Value As [type], _
            Optional RecordNumber As Integer = -1)

FilePut(FileNumber As Integer, Value As System.Array, _
        Optional RecordNumber As Integer = -1, _
        Optional ArrayIsDynamic As Boolean = False)

FilePutObject(FileNumber As Integer, Value As System.Array, _
            Optional RecordNumber As Integer = -1, _
            Optional ArrayIsDynamic As Boolean = False)

FilePut(FileNumber As Integer, Value As String, _
        Optional RecordNumber As Integer = -1, _
        Optional StringIsFixedLength As Boolean = False)

FilePutObject(FileNumber As Integer, Value As String, _
            Optional RecordNumber As Integer = -1, _
            Optional StringIsFixedLength as Boolean = False)
```

Element	Description
FileNumber	The file number used in the call to the FileOpen subroutine.
Value	The variable whose value is to be written to the data file. A value of –1 indicates the current position.
[type]	The data type of the variable containing the data. Possible values are: Array, Boolean, Byte, Date, Decimal, Double, Integer, Short, Single, and String.
RecordNumber	For random files, the record number to read; for binary files, the byte position at which to start reading. A value of –1 indicates the current position.
ArrayIsDynamic	Indicates whether the array is dynamic, so that an array descriptor describing its length should be included.
StringIsFixedLength	For random files, indicates whether strings have a fixed length (the value is True) or whether they are written with two-byte descriptors that indicate their length (the value is False). By default, its value is False.

Comments

FilePut and FilePutObject work only with files opened using the FileOpen subroutine.

FilePut and FilePutObject are typically used to write data to files that will subsequently be read with FileGet and FileGetObject. For examples of reading and writing to binary and random files, see the comments for the FilePut and FilePutObject subroutines.

FilePut and FilePutObject allow you to write all of the scalar Visual Basic .NET data types. However, if you attempt to write a structure that includes a field of type SByte, UShort, UInteger, or ULong, Visual Basic generates a runtime exception.

When a file is first opened using FileOpen, the file pointer in binary files points by byte 0 (immediately before the first byte), and the record pointer in random files points to the beginning of the first record. After each FilePut or FilePutObject operation, the file pointer for binary files advances by the number of bytes written, and the record pointer for random files advances to the beginning of the next record. If this behavior is satisfactory, you do not have to explicitly set the position of the pointer by supplying a *RecordNumber* argument.

When you are finished writing to a file, it is particularly important to call the FileClose subroutine, since this closes the file after flushing the buffer used to write to and read from the open file. Failure to call FileClose may result in data loss.

VB.NET Changes

The ArrayIsDynamic and StringIsFixedLength parameters were introduced in Visual Basic .NET Version 1.1.

VB6 Differences

The FilePut and FilePutObject subroutines are new to Visual Basic .NET. They replace the Visual Basic 6.0 Put and Put # statements.

See Also

FileClose Subroutine, FileOpen Subroutine, FileGet, FileGetObject Subroutine

FileWidth Subroutine

Defines the maximum size of a line when writing to a sequential file.

Member Of

Microsoft.VisualBasic.FileSystem

Syntax

```
FileWidth(FileNumber As Integer, RecordWidth As Integer)
```

Element	Description
FileNumber	The file number used in the call to the FileOpen subroutine.
RecordWidth	The maximum line length. A value of 0 indicates no maximum line length.

Comments

The FileWidth subroutine applies only to write operations to sequential files. It does not apply to reads from a sequential file, or to attempts to access binary and random files.

The FileWidth subroutine applies only to data written using the Print subroutine. It does not apply to PrintLine (which automatically inserts a carriage return/line feed character at the end of its data) or to the Write and WriteLine subroutines.

If writing a single item of data would cause the length of that line to exceed *RecordWidth*, that data is written on a new line.

VB6 Differences

The FileWidth subroutine is new to Visual Basic .NET.

See Also

FileOpen Subroutine, Print Subroutine, SPC Function, Tab Function

Filter Function

Returns a filtered string array whose elements match a particular substring search criterion.

Member Of

Microsoft.VisualBasic.Strings

Syntax

```
Filter(ByVal Source() As { Object | String }, ByVal Match As String, _
       Optional ByVal Include As Boolean = True, _
       Optional ByVal Compare As CompareMethod = CompareMethod.Binary) _
       As String()
```

Element	Description
Source	An array containing the values to search.
Match	A substring to search for in each element of *Source*.
Include	A flag indicating whether the function is to return values that contain or do not contain *Match*. If omitted, its default value is True; the function returns values that contain the substring *Match*.
Compare	A CompareMethod value indicating whether the comparison is case-sensitive (CompareMethod.Binary) or case-insentitive (CompareMethod.Text). If *Compare* is not specified, searches are case-sensitive.

Return Value

A filtered string array containing the elements of *Source* that meet the search criterion.

Comments

Filter performs a substring comparison; that is, in any part of an element in *Source* contains *Match* and *Include* is True, or if any element in *Source* does not include *Match*, that element is included in the array returned by the function.

If *Match* is not found in any of the elements of *Source*, the function returns an empty string. You can test for this by examining its length (If source.Length > 0, then at least one match was found) or by comparing it to Nothing (If Not source Is Nothing, then at least one match was found).

Source can be an array whose individual elements are of any scalar data type and that is declared to be type Object. Before performing the comparison, the function converts the elements of *Source* to their string representations; it then performs the substring comparison. For example, the code

```
Public Sub Main()
    Dim dat1 As Date = CDate("12/25/06")
    Dim dat2 As Date = #7/04/1776#
    Dim arr() As Object = {dat1, dat2, True, 16.753d, 17.02312d}
    Dim result() As String = Filter(arr, "12")
    If result.Length = 0 Then
        Console.WriteLine("No results found . . . ")
    Else
        Console.WriteLine("Found {0} matches:", result.Length)
        For Each word As String In result
            Console.WriteLine("   {0}", word)
        Next
    End If
End Sub
```

produces the following output:

```
Found 2 matches:
    12/25/2006
    17.02312
```

If *Compare* is omitted, the comparison of *Source* with *Match* is controlled by the setting of the Option Compare statement. If the Option Compare statement is not present, the comparison is case-sensitive by default.

The Filter function does not recognize string conversions for classes or structures that are defined using the Operator statement. As a result, *Source* can consist only of scalar types.

The generic FindAll method of the Array class offers similar functionality to the Filter function. Its arguments are a strongly typed array and an instance of a generic predicate delegate. The syntax of the latter is:

```
Public Delegate Function Predicate(Of T)( ByVal obj As T) As Boolean
```

where *obj* is an element in the strongly typed array. The FindAll method iterates each element in the array, which it passes to the Predicate delegate instance. If the delegate instance returns True, the element is added to the array returned by the method. The following code illustrates the use of the FindAll method to return the objects of an array whose Name property starts with a substring that is entered by the user at runtime:

```
Public Class Person
    Private personName As String

    Public Sub New(name As String)
        personName = name
    End Sub
```

```
    Public ReadOnly Property Name() As String
        Get
            Return personName
        End Get
    End Property
End Class

Public Module TestFilter
    Public Sub Main
        Dim people() As Person = { New Person("Bob"), New Person("Bill"), _
                               New Person("Jack"), New Person("Boris"), _
                               New Person("Will"), New Person("Seymour")}
        Dim substring As String = InputBox("Enter first part of name to find: ")
        If substring = String.Empty Then Exit Sub

        PeopleFinder.StartOfName = substring
        Dim matchingPeople() As Person = Array.FindAll(people, _
                                 AddressOf PeopleFinder.FindAll)
        For Each person As Person In matchingPeople
            Console.WriteLine(person.Name)
        Next
    End Sub
End Module

Public Class PeopleFinder
    Private Shared substring As String

    Public Shared Property StartOfName() As String
        Get
            Return substring
        End Get
        Set
            substring = Value.ToUpper()
        End Set
    End Property

    Public Shared Function FindAll(individual As Person) As Boolean
        Return individual.Name.ToUpper.StartsWith(substring)
    End Function
End Class
```

The example defines a class, Person, which has a single property, Name. The example uses the generic FindAll method to return an array of Person objects whose names begin with a substring entered by the user. This substring is assigned to the shared StartOfName property of a class, PeopleFinder, whose only other member is a method, FindAll, the address of which is passed to the Array.FindAll method to instantiate the delegate. At runtime, if the user enters the letter "B" into the input box, the program produces the following result:

```
Bob
Bill
Boris
```

Example

The example performs a case-insensitive search for the substring "to" on an array containing the words from the beginning of Hamlet's "To be or not to be" soliloquy.

```
Public Sub Main()
    Dim quotation As String = "To be or not to be, that is the question: " & _
                              "Whether 'tis nobler in the mind to suffer " & _
                              "The slings and arrows of outrageous fortune, " & _
                              "Or to take arms against a sea of troubles, " & _
                              "And by opposing end them?"
    Dim stringArray() As String = Split(quotation, " ")
    Dim result() As String = Filter(stringArray, "To", True, CompareMethod.Text)
    If result Is Nothing Then
        Console.WriteLine("No results found...")
    Else
        Console.WriteLine("Found {0} words:", result.Length)
        For Each word As String In result
            Console.WriteLine("    {0}", word)
        Next
    End If
End Sub
```

Fix Function

Returns the integer portion of a number.

Member Of

Microsoft.VisualBasic.Conversion

Syntax

```
Fix(ByVal Number As Double) As Double
Fix(ByVal Number As Integer) As Integer
Fix(ByVal Number As Long) As Long
Fix(ByVal Number As Object) As Object
Fix(ByVal Number As Short) As Short
Fix(ByVal Number As Single) As Single
Fix(ByVal Number As Decimal) As Decimal
```

Element	Description
Number	A numeric expression whose integer value is to be extracted.

Return Value

An integral value of the same data type as *Number*.

Comments

Fix is often categorized as a conversion function. However, it is actually a math function, since it operates on the value of the argument passed to it without modifying its data type.

If *Number* is Nothing, the Fix function throws an ArgumentNullException.

Fix is very similar in operation to the Visual Basic Int function, which also returns the integer portion of a number. Both functions return a value of the same data that was passed to them as an argument. And both simply truncate the value of the number passed to them as an argument. If that number is positive or zero, they return an identical result. The difference lies in their handling of negative numbers: Fix returns the integer greater that its argument, while Int returns an integer smaller than its argument. For example, if passed the value –.01, Fix returns 0 (because 0 > –.01), while Int returns –1 (because –1 < –.01).

Fix differs from the family of integer conversion functions (CInt, CLng, CUInt, CULng, etc.), which convert their argument to an integral data type. While Fix truncates values, the conversion functions round them before converting them to integral types.

If you wish to round rather than to truncate a value, you call the shared Round method of the System.Math class. The method is overloaded to accept either a Double or a Decimal as arguments and returns a rounded value of the data type passed to it as an argument. Other overloads allow you to specify the numeric position to which the argument is rounded, and whether midpoint values are rounded toward the closest even number or away from zero. The Decimal data type also supports a Round method with similar overloads.

Example

The example code defines an array that has four values, two positive and two negative, and calls the Fix and Int functions with each of them:

```
Public Sub Main()
   Dim arr() As Decimal = {12.6d, 12.1d, -12.1d, -12.6d}
   For Each num As Decimal In arr
      Console.WriteLine("Fix({0}): {1}", num, Fix(num))
      Console.WriteLine("Int({0}): {1}", num, Int(num))
      Console.WriteLine()
   Next
End Sub
```

The output illustrates the difference between Fix and Int:

```
Fix(12.6): 12
Int(12.6): 12

Fix(12.1): 12
Int(12.1): 12

Fix(-12.1): -12
Int(-12.1): -13

Fix(-12.6): -12
Int(-12.6): -13
```

See Also

CInt Function, Int Function, Round Function

For . . . Next Statement

Executes a series of statements a number of times that depends on the value of a loop counter.

Syntax

```
For counter [ As datatype ] = start To end [ Step step ]
      [ statements ]
[ Continue For ]
[ Exit For ]
      [ statements ]
Next [ counter ]
```

Element	Description
counter	The loop counter, which controls how many times the loop executes. In a normal loop, counter is initially assigned a value of start, is incremented by step with each subsequent iteration of the loop, and is compared with end to determine whether iteration of the loop should continue.
datatype	The data type of counter, if it is not previously defined in code. Typically, counter is a variable of any numeric data type. (See the Comments section for additional details.)
start	The value to assign to counter for the first iteration of the loop.
end	The value with which counter is compared to determine whether the loop should terminate. If step is positive, the loop terminates if counter > end. If step is negative, the loop terminates if counter < end.
step	Determines by how much counter is incremented or decremented after each iteration of the loop. If the Step construct is omitted, the value of step defaults to 1. See the entry for the Step Keyword.

Comments

The For . . . Next loop is used when you know in advance how many iterations of a loop should occur. If you don't know how many iterations of the loop should occur, use a Do . . . Loop or While . . . End While construct.

With each iteration of the loop, counter is automatically incremented by step. Accordingly, you should not modify the value of counter within the loop.

Although counter is usually numeric, it can be any data type that supports the >=, <=, +, and – operators.

Although start, end, and step are usually numeric, if Option Strict is on, they can be any data type that supports an automatic widening conversion to counter. If Option Strict is off, they can be any data type that defines a narrowing conversion to counter as well.

The values of start, end, and step are read only once, before the first iteration of the loop. As a result, modifying their values within the body of the loop has no effect on the execution of the loop.

Any number of Continue For statements can appear within the For . . . Next construct to transfer control to the beginning of the For loop. Typically, the Continue For statement appears within a conditional statement, such as an If . . . End If construct; if some condition is met so that further processing during the current iteration of the loop is not necessary, the counter can be incremented and control can return to the beginning of the looping structure, where the looping condition is once again evaluated.

Any number of Exit For statements can appear within the For Each . . . Next construct. Typically, these are used within a conditional statement to prematurely stop iterating the loop if some condition is met. Note that the Exit For statement is unconditional; it causes program flow to exit the For . . . Next loop regardless of the evaluation of the looping expression.

It is possible for the loop to not execute; see the comments for the Step Keyword for details.

You can iterate the elements of an array using either the For . . . Next construct or the For Each . . . Next construct. However, if you use the For . . . Next construct to iterate all of the elements of an array, you should set *start* equal to *array*.GetLowerBound(*dimension*) and end equal to *array*.GetUpperBound(*dimension*) if *step* is positive, and reverse these if *step* is negative. This prevents your code from having to make any assumptions about the size of the array, and allows your code to deal with an array whose lower bound in a particular dimension is something other than 0.

For . . . Next statements can be nested. In fact, nested For . . . Next constructs are often used to iterate multidimensional arrays. For example, the following code uses nested For . . . Next constructs to iterate a two-dimensional array:

```
Public Module ForLoop
    Public Sub Main()
        Dim items(,) As String = {{"reading", "book", "magazine", "newspaper"}, _
                                   {"writing", "letter", "note", "article"}, _
                                   {"arithmetic", "reconciling bank account", _
                                    "computing salary", "calculating expenses"}}
        For outerCtr As Integer = items.GetLowerBound(0) To items.GetUpperBound(0)
            Console.WriteLine(items(outerCtr, 0) & ": ")
            For innerCtr As Integer = items.GetLowerBound(1) + 1 To _
                                      items.GetUpperBound(1)
                Console.WriteLine("    " & items(outerCtr, innerCtr))
            Next innerCtr
        Next outerCtr
    End Sub
End Module
```

The code produces the following output to the console:

```
reading:
    book
    magazine
    newspaper
writing:
    letter
    note
    article
arithmetic:
    reconciling bank account
    computing salary
    calculating expenses
```

In the preceding code example, note the use of the counter variable after the Next keyword to clarify which loop a particular Next statement refers to. The use the counter variable is strictly optional, but it can enhance code readability. It is most useful as a documentation tool, however, when used with nested loops. Note, though, that if *counter* is used with the Next statement, inner counters must precede outer counters or a compiler error results.

Sometimes, For . . . Next loops (and even nested For . . . Next loops) are used to introduce timing delays. This, however, is a very poor use of the For . . . Next construct for a number of reasons, including that the exact delay attributable to the loop depends on processor speed and that it prevents other threads or processes from running, thus preventing the operating system from doing useful work. A much better technique is to call the shared Sleep method of the Thread class. The method is overloaded as follows:

```
Thread.Sleep(millisecondsTimeout As Integer)
Thread.Sleep(timeout As TimeSpan)
```

where *millisecondsTimeout* is the number of milliseconds to pause, and *timeout* is a TimeSpan instance indicating how long to pause. For example, the following code causes the executing thread to pause for 10 seconds:

```
Dim pause As Integer = 10000
Thread.Sleep(pause)
```

VB.NET Changes

The Continue For statement was added to VB.NET as of Version 2.0. Previously, returning control to the top of the loop required a sometimes long If . . . End If construct that allowed the remaining code in the loop to be skipped and execution to return to the beginning of the loop.

Before Visual Basic 2005, *counter, start, end,* and *step* all had to be numeric values. This is no longer the case as of Visual Basic 2005. *counter* must have addition, subtraction, and two comparison operators defined, while the remaining arguments must have a defined (preferably widening) conversion to the data type of *counter*.

See Also

Do . . . Loop Statement, For Each . . . Next Statement, Step Keyword, While . . . End While Statement

For Each . . . Next Statement

Executes a series of statements for each member of an array or a collection.

Syntax

```
For Each element [As datatype] In collection
    [ statements to execute ]
[ Continue For]
[ Exit For ]
    [ statements to execute ]
Next [ element ]
```

Element	Description
element	A variable representing an element of the array or a member of the collection.
datatype	The data type of *element*, if it is not previously defined in code. *element* can be a variable of any data type capable of being stored in an array or collection.
collection	An array or collection variable.

Comments

The elements of the collection or array can be of any data type. When enumerating these elements, VB.NET automatically attempts to convert them to the data type of *element*.

If *collection* is an uninitialized or undimensioned array, or if *collection* is a collection object that has not been instantiated, attempting to iterate *collection* throws a NullReferenceException.

If *collection* is an empty collection, the statements contained within the For Each . . . Next construct do not execute.

The As *datatype* clause is can be used only if *element* has not been previously defined or is not currently in scope.

Any number of Continue For statements can appear within the For Each . . . Next construct to transfer control to the beginning of the For Each . . . Next loop so that the next element in *collection* is iterated. Typically, the Continue For statement appears within a conditional statement, such as an If . . . End If construct; if an array or collection member meets some condition so that further processing is not necessary, control can return to the beginning of the looping structure and the next element of the array or collection can be iterated.

Any number of Exit For statements can appear within the For Each . . . Next construct. Typically, these are used within a conditional statement to prematurely stop iterating the collection or array if some condition is met. This is illustrated in the example, where the For Each . . . Next construct is used to search an array for a specified string. If the string is found, the Exit For statement is used to stop iterating the array.

In order for its members to be enumerated using the For Each . . . Next construct, *collection* must be an object that implements that IEnumerable interface. All arrays and all of the collection classes in the System.Collections, System.Collections.Generic, and System.Collections.Specialized namespaces implement IEnumerable, as does the intrinsic VB.NET Collection class.

If you're implementing a custom container for your object and want to be able to iterate it using the For Each . . . Next construct, you must implement the GetEnumerator method of the IEnumerable interface, as well as the Current, MoveNext, and Reset members of the IEnumerator interface. If you're developing a custom generic container, you must implement the GetEnumerator method of the generic System.Collections.Generic.IEnumerable interface, as well as the Current property of the generic System.Collections.Generic.IEnumerator interface. The following code, for instance, defines a simple collection class, NameContainer, that implements the IEnumerable and IEnumerator interfaces, and that therefore can be iterated using For Each . . . Next:

```
Public Class NameContainer
    Implements IEnumerator
    Implements IEnumerable

    Dim iCurrent As Integer = 0
    Dim sName(10) As String
    Dim ptr As Integer = -1
    Dim upperbnd As Integer = 0

    Public Sub Add(Value As String)
        If upperbnd > UBound(sName) Then
            ReDim Preserve sName(Ubound(sName) + 10)
        End If
        sName(upperbnd) = Value
        upperbnd += 1
    End Sub
```

```
    Public ReadOnly Property Current() As Object _
        Implements IEnumerator.Current
      Get
        Return sName(ptr)
      End Get
    End Property

    Public Function MoveNext() As Boolean _
        Implements IEnumerator.MoveNext
      ptr += 1
      If ptr < upperbnd Then Return True
    End Function

    Public Sub Reset()  Implements IEnumerator.Reset
      ptr = -1
    End Sub

    Public Function GetEnumerator() As IEnumerator _
            Implements IEnumerable.GetEnumerator
      Return Me
    End Function
End Class

Public Class TestCollec
    Public Shared Sub Main()
      Dim na As New NameContainer
      na.Add("Alaskan Malamute")
      na.Add("Siberian Husky")
      na.Add("Keeshound")
      na.Add("Chinook")

      For Each s As String In na
        Console.WriteLine(s)
      Next
    End Sub

End Class
```

Notice that the IEnumerator interface works by defining a record pointer to a particular element of an array or collection. When the enumerator is created by the call to the GetEnumerator method, MoveNext is called automatically to position the pointer to the first element of the collection. Hence, the pointer must be initialized to point to one position before the first element of the array or collection. In the case of a zero-based array, this means the pointer must be initialized to have a value of –1.

When iterating arrays, the compiler translates the For Each . . . Next construct into code like the following:

```
Dim arr() As Integer = {1, 2, 3, 4, 5}
For ctr As Integer = 0 to arr.Length - 1
   Console.WriteLine(arr(ctr))
Next
```

On the other hand, For Each . . . Next constructs that iterate collection objects are translated as follows:

```
Dim list As New ArrayList
list.Add(1)
List.Add(2)
List.Add(3)
List.Add(4)
List.Add(5)
Try
    Dim iEnum As IEnumerator = list.GetEnumerator()
    Do While iEnum.MoveNext
        Console.WriteLine(iEnum.Current)
    Loop
Catch
    If list Is IDisposable Then
        Dim iDisp As IDisposable = list
        iDisp.Dispose()
End Try
```

While the For Each . . . Next construct is executing, you should ensure that the array or collection is not modified by adding to or deleting from its existing elements. If elements are added or deleted, an InvalidOperationException is thrown.

Because *element* is a value returned by an array or collection's IEnumerator.Current method, its value cannot be modified inside the For Each . . . Next loop. For example, the code:

```
Dim names() As String = {"Jon", "John", "Jonathan", "Jack", "Jake"}

For Each s As String In names
    If s = "Jake" Then s = "Jacob"
    Exit For
Next

For Each s As String In names
    Console.WriteLine(s)
Next
```

produces the following output, which indicates that the string "Jake" has not been modified in the original array:

```
Jon
John
Jonathan
Jack
Jake
```

collection is examined only once, when the loop is first entered. Accordingly, a change to the *collection* object reference while *collection* is being enumerated has no effect. You can, however, change the value of *element* inside the loop. However, neither modification is recommended, and both can needlessly complicate testing and debugging.

The order in which the *members* of collection are enumerated depends entirely on the implementation of the IEnumerator interface. Accordingly, unless you've implemented the

IEnumerator interface for a custom container, your code should make no assumptions about the order in which particular members are returned.

VB.NET Changes

The As *datatype* construct was added to VB.NET as of Version 1.1.

The Continue For statement was added to VB.NET as of Version 2.0. Previously, returning control to the top of the loop required a sometimes long If . . . End If construct that allowed the remaining code in the loop to be skipped and execution to return to the beginning of the loop.

VB6 Differences

VB6 does not support the As datatype clause, which allows the variable containing the member of the collection or array to be defined dynamically.

In VB6, *element* had to be of type Variant. In VB.NET, on the other hand, it can be any data type, including Object, VB.NET's "universal" data type, as well as a strongly typed data type.

VB6 does not support the Continue For statement, which immediately begins the next iteration of the loop.

Example

The example illustrates the use of the For Each . . . Next construct to identify the first element of an array that matches a string. The example also uses the Exit For statement to exit the loop without iterating any remaining array elements once a match has been found.

```
' FindName Function
'
' Searches an array for a string
' Returns the index of the element in which the string is first found
'
Private Function FindName(arr() As String, search As String) As Integer
    Dim Ctr As Integer
    FindName = -1
    For Each n As String In arr
        If n = search Then
            FindName = Ctr
            Exit For
        End If
        Ctr += 1
    Next
End Function
```

See Also

Continue For Statement, Exit For Statement, For . . . Next Statement

Format Function

Returns a formatted string.

Member Of

Microsoft.VisualBasic.Strings

Syntax

```
Format(ByVal Expression As Object, Optional ByVal Style As String = "") _
     As String
```

Element	Description
Expression	The expression to be formatted and returned as a string.
Style	A predefined or user-defined format string that defines how Expression is to be formatted. The format string depends on the data type of Style, as discussed in the comments section.

Return Value

A string formatted according to *Style.*

Comments

If the Format function is invoked without a *Style* argument, its behavior is identical to calling the Visual Basic CStr function or the instance's own ToString method; it returns the string representation of the argument passed to it.

When invoked without a *Style* argument, the behavior of the Format function is similar to that of the Visual Basic Str function, with two differences. First, Format is internationally aware, whereas Str is not. Second, when converting a positive number to a string, the Str function returns a string with a leading space (representing the plus sign), whereas Format does not.

The functionality of the Format function is also available in the .NET Framework Class Library. The most common method for converting a numeric or data/time value to a formatted string is the overloaded ToString method. The parameterless version of the function

```
objectVar.ToString()
```

converts a scalar Visual Basic data type to its string representation, just as calling the Format function with no arguments does. A second overload

```
objectVar.ToString(format As String)
```

accepts a *format* argument whose syntax is identical to that of the single-character format strings accepted by the Visual Basic Format function. A third overload

```
objectVar.ToString(provider As IFormatProvider)
```

accepts an object that implements the IFormatProvider interface as an argument. IFormatProvider provides culture-specific formatting information and thus provides finer control over the string returned by the ToString method than do either the previous two overloads of the ToString method or the Visual Basic Format function.

The Format method of the String class and the Write and WriteLine methods of the Console class also can take format specifiers as arguments. They allow you to place indexed placeholders in literal text that, at runtime, are replaced by formatted values. The indexed placeholders are enclosed in brackets and numbered consecutively starting at 0, and correspond to output expressions that appear after the format string. For example, in the format string:

```
Console.WriteLine("The range of a {0} is from {1} to {2}.", _
              dblNum.GetType().Name, dblNum.MinValue, dblNum.MaxValue)
```

there are three index placeholders (also called *index components* or *parameter specifiers*) numbered from 0 to 2, which correspond to three output expressions. The complete syntax of the format item is:

```
{index, [,alignment][:formatString]}
```

where *alignment* is an optional *alignment component* containing a signed integer that indicates the field width that the corresponding expression is to occupy in the output string. The number must be greater than the total length of the output expression, or it is ignored. If alignment is positive, it indicates that the output expression is right-aligned in the format string, and if it is negative, the output expression is left-aligned in the output string. *formatString* is a standard or custom formatting string; these are the same as the formatting strings used with the Visual Basic Format function, which are shown in subsequent tables.

Date and Time Values

If *Expression* is a Date, *Style* can be one of the predefined strings shown in Table 8-7. The predefined multicharacter formatting codes (such as `General Date` or `Long Date`) are case insensitive, while the single-character ones are case sensitive.

Several methods of the Date data type output a formatted string, thus replicating the functionality of the Format function when passed particular predefined formats. These are:

- ToLongDateString, which outputs a Date value as "Monday, January 01, 2007", for example. It is equivalent to calling the Format function which a *Style* argument of "Long Date", "Medium Date", or "D".

- ToLongTimeString, which outputs a Date value as "12:00:00 AM". It is equivalent to calling the Format function which a *Style* argument of "Long Time", "Medium Time", or "T".

- ToShortDateString, which outputs a Date value as "1/1/2007". It is equivalent to calling the Format function which a *Style* argument of "Short Date" or "d".

- ToShortTimeString, which outputs a Date value as "12:00 AM". It is equivalent to calling the Format function which a *Style* argument of "Short Time" or "t".

It is also possible to supply a user-defined date format string as the *Style* argument. This allows you to work with the individual components of a date and time to format them as you desire, or to add additional components, such as the era (only AD is supported) or the strings AM or PM. The supported symbols that can compose a custom user-defined date format string are shown in Table 8-8. The strings shown in Table 8-8 are case-sensitive. Any other character that appears in the *Style* argument is interpreted as a character literal and is output untranslated nto the formatted string.

Some of the user-defined format strings duplicate the functionality of Visual Basic date and time functions while converting the returned value to a string at the same time. For example:

```
Public Sub Main()
    Dim dat As Date = #06/09/2003 08:16:03 AM#
    Console.WriteLine(CStr(Day(dat)))        ' Displays 9
    Console.WriteLine(Format(dat, "%d"))     ' Displays 9
```

```
        Console.WriteLine(CStr(Month(dat)))      ' Displays 6
        Console.WriteLine(Format(dat, "%M"))     ' Displays 6

        Console.WriteLine(CStr(Second(dat)))     ' Displays 3
        Console.WriteLine(Format(dat, "%s"))     ' Displays 3
    End Sub
```

Style Value	Outputs
General Date G	A general date and time format based on the system's locale ID. For example, "1/1/2007 11:00:00 AM".
Long Date Medium Date D	A long date format based on the system's locale ID. For example, "Monday, January 01, 2007".
Short Date d	A short date format based on the system's locale ID. For example, "1/1/2007".
Long Time Medium Time T	A long time format based on the system's locale ID. For example, "12:00:00 AM".
Short Time t	A short time format based on the system's locale ID. For example, "12:00 AM".
F	A long date, long time format based on the system's locale ID. For example, "Monday, January 1, 2007 12:00:00 AM".
f	A long date, short time format based on the system's locale ID. For example, "Monday, January 1, 2007 12:00 AM".
g	A short date, short time format based on the system's locale ID. For example, "1/1/2007 12:00 AM".
M m	The month and the day. For example, "January 1".
R r	The date and time in GMT format. For example, "Mon, 1 Jan 2005 00:00:00 GMT".
U	The long date and long time in GMT format. For example, "Monday, January 1, 2007 7:00:00 AM".
s	A sortable string representation of a date and time. For Example, "2005-01-01T00:00:00".
u	A sortable string representation of a date and time in GMT format. For example, "2007-01-01 00:00:00Z". (The Z stands for Zulu, another international symbol for UTC.)
Y y	The year and month. For example, "January, 2007".

TABLE 8-7   Predefined Date and Time Style Strings

Custom Date Format Substring	Outputs:
:	The time separator, used to delimit hours, minutes, and seconds. It is replaced with the localized time separator in the output string.
/	The date separator, used to delimit months, days, and years. It is replaced with the localized date separator in the output string.
%	Indicates that the following letter is a single-character user-defined date format.
d	The day as a number without a leading zero if it is less than 10. If d is the only character in a user-defined format string, it should be preceded by a % character to differentiate it from the predefined short date format string. For example, Format(#01/03/2007#, "%d") returns "3".
dd	The day as a number with a leading zero if it is less than 10.
ddd	The abbreviated name of the day (e.g., Sun, Mon, etc.).
dddd	The full name of the day (e.g., Sunday, Monday, etc.).
M	The number of the month without a leading zero if it is less than 10. If M is the only character in a user-defined format string, it should be preceded by a % character to differentiate it from the predefined format string. For example, Format(#01/03/2007#, "%M") returns "1".
MM	The month as a number with a leading zero if the month is less than 10.
MMM	The abbreviated name of the month (e.g., Jan, Feb, etc.).
MMMM	The full name of the month (e.g,, January, February, etc.).
gg	The era associated with the date. It appears as A.D. (anno Domini), rather than C.E. (common era). Only the common era is within the range of the Date data type.
h	The hour without a leading zero if it is less than 10 using the 12-hour clock. If h is the only character in a user-defined format string, it should be preceded by the % character to prevent a FormatException.
hh	The hour with a leading zero if it is less than 10 using the 12-hour clock.
H	The hour without a leading zero if it is less than 10 using the 24-hour clock. If H is the only character in a user-defined format string, it should be preceded by the % character to prevent a FormatException.
HH	The hour with a leading zero if it is less than 10 using the 24-hour clock.
m	The minute without a leading zero if it is less than 10. If m is the only character in a user-defined format string, it should be preceded by the % character to differentiate it from the m predefined format string.

TABLE 8-8   Custom Date Format Symbols for User-Defined Date Formats

Custom Date Format Substring	Outputs:
mm	The minute with a leading zero if it is less than 10.
s	The number of seconds without a leading zero if it is less than 10. If s is the only character in a user-defined format string, it should be preceded by the % character to differentiate it from the s predefined format string.
ss	The number of seconds with a leading zero if it is less than 10.
f	Fractions of a second. A single f outputs tenths of a second, two output hundredths of a second, etc. Up to seven f custom format characters can be used. If f is the only character in a user-defined format string, it should be preceded by the % character to differentiate it from the f predefined format string.
t	Used with a 12-hour clock to output "A" if the time is between midnight and 11:59 A.M., and "P" if the time is between noon and 11:59 P.M. If t is the only character in a user-defined format string, it should be preceded by the % character to differentiate it from the t predefined format string.
tt	Used with a 12-hour clock to output "AM" if the time is between midnight and 11:59 A.M., and "PM" if the time is between noon and 11:59 P.M.
y	The rightmost digit of the year. If y is the only character in a user-defined format string, it should be preceded by the % character to differentiate it from the y predefined format string.
yy	The two rightmost digits of the year.
yyy	The year as a three-digit number if it ranges from 0 to 999; otherwise, a four-digit year.
yyyy	The year as a four-digit number.
z	The time zone offset (the difference between the local time and Greenwich Mean Time) without a leading 0 if the difference is less than ten. If z is the only character in a user-defined format string, it should be preceded by the % character to prevent a FormatException.
zz	The time zone offset (the difference between the local time and Greenwich Mean Time) with a leading 0 if the difference is less than ten.
zzz	The full time zone offset (the difference between the local time and Greenwich Mean Time) in hours and minutes.

TABLE 8-8   Custom Date Format Symbols for User-Defined Date Formats *(continued)*

Numeric Values

If *Expression* is a date or the string representation of a date/time value, *Style* can be one of the predefined strings shown in Table 8-9. The predefined multicharacter formatting codes (such as General Date or Long Date) are case insensitive.

Style Value	Outputs
General Number G g	A number with no thousands separator.
Fixed F f	A number with no thousands separator and at least one digit to the left and two digits to the right of the decimal point.
Standard N n	A number with a thousands separator, at least one digit to the left and two digits to the right of the decimal point.
Currency C c	A number with a thousands separator, two digits to the right of the decimal separator, and a localized currency symbol.
Percent	A number multiplied by 100 and with a percent sign immediately to the right. Two digits to the right of the decimal point are always displayed. No thousands separators are used.
P p	A number multiplied by 100, with a space and a percent sign to the right of the number. Two digits to the right of the decimal point are always displayed, and a thousands separator is output if the number is large enough.
Scientific	A number in standard scientific notation with two significant digits. For example, 1034.768 is output as 1.03E+03.
E e	A number in standard scientific notation with six significant digits. For example, 1034.768 is output as 1.034768E+003.
D d	A number in decimal format with no thousands separator and no decimal point. *Expression* must be an integral value (Byte, SByte, Short, UShort, etc.) or a FormatException is thrown.
X x	A number in hexadecimal format. *Expression* must be an integral value (Byte, SByte, Short, UShort, etc.) or a FormatException is thrown.
Yes/No	Yes for any non-zero numeric value, and No for any value equal to zero.
True/False	True for any non-zero numeric value, and False for any value equal to zero.

TABLE 8-9   Predefined Numeric Style Strings

In a few cases, a predefined numeric formatting strings causes the Format function to return the same value as other standard Visual Basic functions. For example, the X and x strings are equivalent to calling the Hex function, while True/False is equivalent to the expression:

```
CStr(CBool(numericValue))
```

The *Style* argument also allows you to provide a user-defined numeric format string. However, unlike predefined data and numeric format strings and user-defined date strings, which can consist of only a single part, user-defined numeric format strings can consist of three parts, which are separated from one another by semicolons. The range of applicability of the format string depends on how many parts are present:

- If there is one part, it applies to all values.
- If there are two parts, the first applies to numbers that are zero or greater, and the second applies to negative numbers.
- If there are three parts, the first applies to positive numbers, the second to negative numbers, and the third to zero.
- If a part is missing, as in

```
Console.WriteLine(Format(number, "#.0;;zero"))
```

the format for the positive value is used instead.

The supported substrings that can compose a custom user-defined date format string are shown in Table 8-10.

Example

The example illustrates the use of each of the user-defined numeric format strings. The Main procedure defines a series of numeric expressions and format styles and then calls the

Style Value	Outputs
0	Digit placeholder. Displays a digit or, if there are too few digits, a zero in that digit's position. If there are fewer digits than there are 0 placeholders either to the left of the decimal point or to the right of the decimal point, a 0 appears at that position in the output string. Any additional digits to the left of the decimal point for which there are no digit placeholders will appear in the output string, while any additional digits to the right of the decimal point for which there are no placeholders will not appear; instead, the number in the output string will be rounded to the number of positions specified by the digit placeholders.
#	Digit placeholder. Displays a digit or nothing, if there are fewer digits than there are placeholders. If there are more digits to the left of the decimal point than there are placeholders, they will appear in the output. If there are more digits to the right of the decimal point than there are placeholders, they will not appear; instead, the result will be rounded to the number of positions specified by the digit placeholders.
E+ e+ E- e-	Scientific format. *Style* must also include at least one digit placeholder (a # or 0) to the left of E+, e+, E-, or e-, or they will be interpreted as literal characters. It should also include at least one digit placeholder to the right of the scientific format symbols. E- and e- indicate that a minus sign should be placed next to negative exponents. E+ and e+ indicate that a minus sign should be placed next to negative exponents and a plus sign next to positive exponents.
.	The decimal placeholder, used to delimit the integral from the fractional part of a number. It is replaced with the localized decimal placeholder in the output string.

TABLE 8-10   Custom Symbols for User-Defined Numeric Formats

Style Value	Outputs

,	The thousands separator. It is replaced with the localized thousands separator in the output string. Note that the thousands separator does not have to appear in every position that it normally would in *Style*. To indicate that a thousands separator should appear in the output, it should be surrounded by digit placeholders, as in the strings
	
	`"0,0"`
	
	and
	
	`"#,#.0"`
	
	If the thousands separator is immediately to the left of the decimal placeholder, or if it is the leftmost character of *Style* because the position of the decimal placeholder is assumed, the thousands separator indicates that *Expression* should be divided by 1000 and rounded if necessary. This allows large values to be scaled for output in tables and charts, for example.

%	Percent placeholder. Multiples *Expression* by 100 and add the percent sign in the position in which it appears in the format string.
– + $ ( )	Literal characters that appear in the output exactly as they are defined in the format string.
\	Literal symbol indicator, which defines the symbol that follows it as a literal character to be included without translation in the output. Although it can be used to indicate any literal character, it has to be used only to differentiate a literal character that might be misinterpreted as a formatting symbol, such as d, g, n, and t. If a backslash is to appear in the output string, it should appear as \\ in *Style*.
" "	Literal string indicator. Any string enclosed within quotation marks within *Style* is included without translation in the output. In order to include the quotation marks within the string, use the Chr function, as the example shows.

TABLE 8-10 Custom Symbols for User-Defined Numeric Formats *(continued)*

DisplayNumber function, which in turn calls the Format function and displays the resulting string to the console. The output from the function is shown in the comment immediately following the DisplayNumber function call.

```
Public Module modMain
    Public Sub Main()
        ' 0 as digit placeholder
        Console.WriteLine("0 As Digit Placeholder")
        DisplayNumber(1503789000, "000,000.0000")        ' Displays 1,503,789,000.0000
        DisplayNumber(9000, "000,000.0000")              ' Displays 009,000.0000
        DisplayNumber(9000.039178, "00,000,000.00000000")
```

```
                   ' Displays 00,009,000.03917800
     DisplayNumber(9000.039178, "000.00")              ' Displays 9000.04
     Console.WriteLine()


     ' # as digit placeholder
     Console.WriteLine("# As Digit Placeholder")
     DisplayNumber(1503789000, "###,###.#")             ' Displays 1,503,789,000
     DisplayNumber(9000, "#,###.###")                   ' Displays 9,000
     DisplayNumber(9000.039178, "##,###,###.########")  ' Displays 9,000.039178
     DisplayNumber(9000.039178, "#,#.########")          ' Displays 9,000.039178
     DisplayNumber(9000.039178, "###.##")               ' Displays 9000.04
     Console.WriteLine()


     ' . decimal placeholder
     Console.WriteLine(". As Decimal Placeholder")
     DisplayNumber(.349, "0.##")                        ' Displays 0.35
     DisplayNumber(.349, "#.##")                        ' Displays .35
     Console.WriteLine()


     ' Scientific format
     Console.WriteLine("Scientific Format")
     DisplayNumber(1503789000, "##.#0E+##")             ' Displays 1503789000.00E+
     DisplayNumber(1.039830, "#0.##e-00")               ' Displays 10.4e-01
     Console.WriteLine()


     ' , as thousands delimiter
     Console.WriteLine(", As Thousands Separator")
     DisplayNumber(1503789000, "0,")                    ' Displays 1503789
     DisplayNumber(1503789000, "0,0")                   ' Displays 1,503,789,000
     DisplayNumber(1503789000, "#,")                    ' Displays 1503789
     DisplayNumber(1503789000, "#,#.#")                 ' Displays 1,503,789,000
     Console.WriteLine()


     ' Percent placeholder
     Console.WriteLine("% As Percent Placeholder")
     DisplayNumber(.667, "0.###%")                      ' Displays 66.7%
     DisplayNumber(.333, "0.00 %")                      ' Displays 33.30 %
     Console.WriteLine()


     ' Literal characters
     Console.WriteLine("Literal symbols")
     DisplayNumber(16.45, "$ #,0.#0")                   ' Displays $ 16.45
     DisplayNumber(-.45, "+0.##;(0.##);0.0")            ' Displays (0.45)
     DisplayNumber(56.03, Chr(34) & "****" & Chr(34) & "$#.00" & Chr(34) _
                    & "****" & Chr(34) )   ' Displays ****$56.03****
  End Sub

  Private Sub DisplayNumber(num As Double, style As String)
     Try
        Console.WriteLine("{0} with {1} produces the output: {2}", _
                    style, num, Format(num, style))
     Catch e As Exception
        Console.WriteLine("{0}", e.GetType.Name)
     End Try
  End Sub
End Module
```

VB6 Differences

The Visual Basic 6.0 version of the Format function included two additional parameters, dayofweek and weekofyear, that applied to Date values and specified the first day of the week and the first week of the year for strings that were to contain information on the day of the week and the week of the year. In Visual Basic .NET, this functionality is provided by other members of the DateTime structure and the Visual Basic DateAndTime class and is not supported.

Visual Basic 6.0 included a Format$ function that required Style to be a String rather than a Variant. In Visual Basic .NET, this version of the function is not supported.

Both the predefined and user-defined Date format strings in Visual Basic 6.0 could operate on both a Date value and the string representation of a date/time value. In Visual Basic .NET, however, they can only operate on Date values.

A number of Visual Basic 6.0 date/time format strings are no longer supported in Visual Basic .NET. These include q (to output the quarter of the year), n and nn (to output the minutes in a time value), AM/PM, am/pm, A/P, and a/p (to output a variously formatted AM/PM indicator in a twelve-hour time value), ww (to output the number of the week of a particular date), w (to indicate the weekday of a particular date).

Some Visual Basic 6.0 date/time format strings function differently in Visual Basic .NET than they did in Visual Basic 6.0. In Visual Basic 6.0, ddddd output the date in short date format; in Visual Basic .NET, it outputs the weekday name of the date. In Visual Basic 6.0, y output the ordinal position of a date in a particular year; in Visual Basic .NET, it outputs the rightmost digit of the year.

Both the predefined and user-defined numeric format strings in Visual Basic 6.0 could operate on both a numeric value and its string representation. In Visual Basic .NET, however, they can only operate on numeric values.

Visual Basic 6.0 supported a number of symbols (@, &, <, >, and !) to format string expressions. In Visual Basic .NET, however, the use of the Format function to format string expressions is not supported.

See Also

FormatCurrency Function, FormatDateTime Function, FormatNumber Function, FormatPercent Function

FormatCurrency, FormatNumber, and FormatPercent Functions

Return string-formatted numeric strings.

Member Of

Microsoft.VisualBasic.Strings

Syntax

```
FormatCurrency(ByVal Expression As Object,_
    Optional ByVal NumDigitsAfterDecimal As Integer = -1, _
    Optional ByVal IncludeLeadingDigit As TriState = TriState.UseDefault, _
    Optional ByVal UseParensForNegativeNumbers As TriState = TriState.UseDefault, _
    Optional ByVal GroupDigits As TriState = TriState.UseDefault _
) As String
```

```
FormatNumber(ByVal Expression As Object,_
    Optional ByVal NumDigitsAfterDecimal As Integer = -1, _
    Optional ByVal IncludeLeadingDigit As TriState = TriState.UseDefault, _
    Optional ByVal UseParensForNegativeNumbers As TriState = TriState.UseDefault, _
    Optional ByVal GroupDigits As TriState = TriState.UseDefault _
) As String

FormatPercent(ByVal Expression As Object,_
    Optional ByVal NumDigitsAfterDecimal As Integer = -1, _
    Optional ByVal IncludeLeadingDigit As TriState = TriState.UseDefault, _
    Optional ByVal UseParensForNegativeNumbers As TriState = TriState.UseDefault, _
    Optional ByVal GroupDigits As TriState = TriState.UseDefault _
) As String
```

Element	Description
Expression	An expression that evaluates to an integral or floating point value, or the string representation of an integral or floating point value.
NumDigitsAfterDecimal	A value ranging from −1 to 99 that indicates the number of digits to display after the decimal point. −1 (the default) uses the value defined by the computer's regional settings.
IncludeLeadingDigit	Indicates whether a zero should appear to the left of the decimal point for values less than 1. The default value is TriState.Default; the system's regional settings will be used.
UseParensForNegativeNumbers	Indicates whether a negative value is represented by parentheses or a minus sign. The default value is TriState.Default; the system's regional settings will be used.
GroupDigits	Indicates whether a thousands separator should be used for values greater than 999. The default value is TriState.Default; the system's regional settings will be used.

Return Value

A string representation of a number with currency, numeric, or percentage formatting, depending on the method called.

Comments

These three functions, along with FormatDateTime, are "lightweight" formatting functions that were first introduced in VBScript Version 2.0 and then were added to Visual Basic 6.0. They offer more intuitive, easy-to-use versions of the Format function with a *Style* argument of Currency, C, or c, and a range of user-defined formatting strings.

Each function returns the string representation of a number, with optional localized thousands separators, zeros before fractional numbers, and parentheses or minus signs to signify negative numbers. While FormatNumber simply returns a formatted number only, FormatCurrency returns a formatted number with a localized currency symbol, and FormatPercent multiplies its argument by 100 and displays it with a percent sign.

Regardless of the setting of Option Strict, all three functions can handle either integral or floating point numbers or string representations of numbers. If *Expression* cannot be converted to the string representation of a number with currency formatting, an InvalidCastException is thrown.

You can call the IsNumeric function to determine whether *Expression* can be converted to the string representation of a number before calling the respective formatting function.

The final three parameters of these three functions are of type TriState. Possible values are TriState.True, TriState.False, and TriState.UseDefault (use the value from the system's regional settings).

The FormatCurrency function does not allow the position of the currency symbol to be positioned in the returned string; instead, its position is defined by the system's regional settings.

Although these three formatting functions derive their default settings for such things as the currency symbol, the decimal point, and the thousands separator from the system's regional settings, these can be overridden. The system's regional settings are automatically assigned to each thread at startup. However, the culture of each individual thread can be changed by assigning a different CultureInfo object representing a specific language and country/region to the thread's CurrentCulture property. The example illustrates how to do this for the current thread.

Example

The example illustrates changing the culture of the current thread so that the formatting functions can output strings that are localized for regions other than the one defined by the local system's regional settings.

```
Imports System.Globalization
Imports System.Threading

Public Module modMain

    Private thrd As Thread

    Public Sub Main()
        ' Get current thread
        thrd = Thread.CurrentThread()

        ' Format as en-gb
        thrd.CurrentCulture = New CultureInfo("en-gb")
        DisplayFormattedOutput()

        ' Format as fr-FR
        thrd.CurrentCulture = New CultureInfo("fr-FR")
        DisplayFormattedOutput()
        ' Format as ru-RU
        thrd.CurrentCulture = New CultureInfo("ru-RU")
        DisplayFormattedOutput()
    End Sub

    Private Sub DisplayFormattedOutput()
        Dim dat As Date = #03/01/2006 1:46:00 PM#

        Console.WriteLine(thrd.CurrentCulture.Name)
        Console.WriteLine("    {0}", FormatCurrency(12045.035, 2,,,TriState.True))
        Console.WriteLine("    {0}", FormatNumber(1063942.98377, 3,,, TriState.True))
        Console.WriteLine("    {0} {1}", FormatDateTime(dat, DateFormat.LongDate), _
                          FormatDateTime(dat, DateFormat.LongTime))
        Console.WriteLine("    {0}", FormatPercent(.3333, 2, TriState.True, _
                          TriState.True, TriState.True))
    End Sub
End Module
```

See Also

Format Function, FormatDateTime Function, Format Number Function, FormatPercent Function

FormatDateTime Function

Returns a formatted string representation of a date/time value.

Member Of

Microsoft.VisualBasic.Strings

Syntax

```
FormatDateTime(ByVal Expression As DateTime, _
    Optional ByVal NamedFormat As DateFormat = DateFormat.GeneralDate _
) As String
```

Element	Description
Expression	An expression that evaluates to a Date data type (a date or a time).
NamedFormat	A member of the DateFormat enumeration indicating how to format *Expression*. See the Comments section for additional details.

Return Value

A formatted string representation of a Date value.

Comments

FormatDateTime is a "lightweight" formatting function that was first introduced in VBScript Version 2.0 and then was added to Visual Basic 6.0 as an alternative to the Format function.

If Option Strict is off, *Expression* can be either a Date or the string representation of a date. If Option Strict is on, *Expression* must evaluate to a Date value.

If you are passing a date literal directly to the function, you should ensure that it is in #mm/dd/yyyy# format, since the FormatDateTime function always interprets an *Expression* argument that is a Date literal as a date in English (US) format.

NameFormat is a member of the DateFormat enumeration that determines how the date is formatted in the string returned by the function. Possible values, well as the equivalent argument to the Format function, are:

DateFormat Member	Description	Comparable Format Function *Style* Argument
GeneralDate	Outputs a date and time in short date format and a long time format. GeneralDate is the default value.	General Date G
LongDate	Outputs a date in long date format.	Long Date Medium Date D

DateFormat Member	Description	Comparable Format Function *Style* Argument
ShortDate	Outputs a date in short date format.	Short Date d
LongTime	Outputs a time in long time format.	Long Time Medium Time T
ShortTime	Outputs a time in short time format.	"HH:MM"

In determining whether to include date values, time values, or both in the returned string, the FormatDateTime function automatically excludes dates and times that it considers to be "neutral" (i.e., default date or time values that have likely not been assigned a meaningful value). The neutral date value is 1/1/0001; the neutral time value is midnight (00:00:00).

Although the FormatDateTime function derives its default settings from the system's regional settings, these can be overridden. For sample code, se the example for the FormatCurrency, FormatNumber, and FormatPercent functions.

Example

The example prompts the user to input a date and then calls the FormatDateTime function once for each value in the DateFormat enumeration. In order to iterate the members of the enumeration, the example uses the static Enum.GetNames method to retrieve a string array containing the names of the enumeration members. When calling the FormatDateTime function, which requires an enumeration member rather than an enumeration member name as an argument, the static Enum.Parse method is used to convert an enumeration member's name back to its value.

```
Imports System.Reflection

Public Module modMain
    Public Sub Main()
        ' A type object of the DateFormat enum
        Dim dateFormatType As Type = GetType(DateFormat)
        ' An array of strings with the names of DateFormat members
        Dim formats() As String = [Enum].GetNames(dateFormatType)
        ' Get input from user
        Dim dateString As String = InputBox("Enter a Date and Time: ")
        Dim dat As Date

        If dateString = String.Empty Then Exit Sub
        If Not IsDate(dateString) Then
            MsgBox("The input cannot be converted to a date/time value.")
            Exit Sub
        End If
        dat = CDate(dateString)

        Console.WriteLine("The input date: {0}", dateString)
        For Each dateFmt As String In formats
            Console.WriteLine(" Date with format {0}: {1}", dateFmt, _
            FormatDateTime(dat, _
            DirectCast([Enum].Parse(dateFormatType, dateFmt), DateFormat)))
        Next
    End Sub
End Module
```

See Also

CDate Function, Format Function, FormatDateTime Function

FreeFile Function

Returns the next available file number for use with the FileOpen subroutine.

Member Of

Microsoft.VisualBasic.FileSystem

Syntax

```
FreeFile() As Integer
```

Return Value

An Integer representing an unused file number.

Comments

The FileOpen subroutine has a required *FileNumber* parameter that is used to assign a file number to the file being opened. Thereafter, in calls to Visual Basic's intrinsic file input and output functions, you use this number to identify the file with which you wish to work. Therefore, this number must uniquely identify the file within your process. You can assign the number yourself in code (and risk assigning a number already in use, which will either create confusion or generate a runtime exception), or you can use FreeFile to return the next free number.

You should not call FreeFile repeatedly without opening a file using the value returned by FreeFile. Otherwise, FreeFile returns the same number. For example, if you call FreeFile twice with the intention of retrieving two different unique file numbers that you subsequently can use to call FileOpen twice, FreeFile will return the same number, which will eventually cause .NET to throw a FileIOException and report that the file is already open.

If you're using the intrinsic Visual Basic file input/output functions, you should make a call to FreeFile a standard part of assigning a number to the file you're accessing.

The Visual Basic file input/output functions are legacy language elements. For new code, it's far better to use the file input/output services available in the .NET Framework Class Library. For a description of some of these, see the comments for the FileOpen Subroutine.

Example

See the examples for the EOF Function and the FileOpen Subroutine.

See Also

FileOpen Subroutine, FileClose Subroutine

Friend Keyword

Limits the accessibility of a programming element to the assembly in which it is declared.

Syntax

The Friend keyword can be used with the following Visual Basic language elements:

- Type declarations: the Class, Delegate, Enum, Interface, Module, and Structure statements.
- Member declarations: the Const, Declare, Dim, Event, Function, Property, and Sub statements.

For syntax, see the entry for the respective language element that the Friend keyword modifies.

Comments

Friend can be used as an access modifier only at the namespace and member levels. In other words, it can apply to the following language elements:

- Classes
- Structures
- Modules
- Interfaces
- Delegates
- Enumerations
- Events
- Properties
- Methods
- Constants
- Fields

According to the documentation, classes, modules, structures, and interfaces are given Friend access by default if they are not explicitly assigned an access modifier. Using ILDasm (see Figure 8-11) to examine the assembly produced by compiling the following code, however, indicates that all of these programming elements are marked private:

```
Module FriendlyModule
    Public Sub DoSomething()
    End Sub
End Module


Class FriendlyClass
    Public Function ReturnAString() As String
        Return "Friendly"
    End Function
End Class


Friend Class AnotherFriendlyClass
    Public Function SayHello() As String
        Return "Hello!"
    End Function
End Class
```

```
Interface FriendlyInterface
    Sub BeFriendly()
End Interface

Structure FriendlyStruct
    Dim number As Integer
End Structure
```

However, the single class declared using the Friend access modifier is also marked private in the assembly. This evident contradiction is explained by the fact that these types are private to the assembly in which they are defined—which is precisely what friend access means.

Giving a program element Friend access makes it accessible throughout the assembly in which it is declared, but does not make it a part of a component or application's public interface; therefore, it leaves it inaccessible to code that references the assembly.

Even though program elements with Friend access are not accessible outside the assembly in which they are defined, information about them can be retrieved using reflection (as Figure 8-11 shows). In addition, if these private program elements are exposed by an assembly's public interface (as would happen, for instance, if a method in a public class returns an instance of a class declared with Friend access), they can be accessed outside of the assembly in which they are defined.

Programming elements that can be declared with Friend access can also be declared with Protected Friend access. Many developers assume that, aside from Private, this is the most restrictive access possible. In fact, this is not the case. Protected Friend programming elements are visible both within the assembly in which they are declared and to types that derive from them.

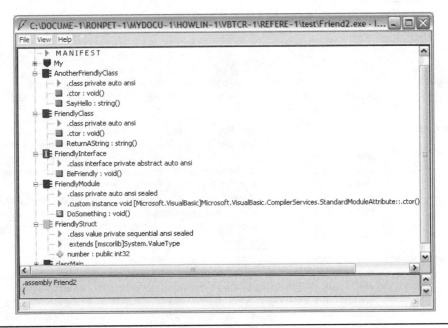

FIGURE 8-11   ILDasm depicting Friend access

VB6 Differences

In Visual Basic 6.0, Friend access could only be applied to program elements, such as module-level variables, functions, and subroutines, defined in a class module (.cls file) or form module (.frm file). It could not be applied to types. In contrast, Visual Basic .NET allows Friend access to be applied to a broader number of programming elements, including the basic categories of .NET types.

See Also

Dim Statement, Private Keyword, Protected Keyword, Public Keyword

Function Statement

Defines a procedure that returns a value.

Syntax

```
[ <attributelist> ] [ accessmodifier ] [ proceduremodifiers ] _
[ Shared ] [ Shadows ] Function name [ (Of typeparamlist) ] _
[ ( parameterlist) ] [ As returntype ] _
[ Implements implementsList ]
        [ statements ]
        [ Exit Function ]
        [ statements ]
        [ name = returnvalue  | Return returnvalue ]
[ End Function ]
```

Element	Description
attributelist	A list of attributes to be applied to the function. Only attributes whose AttributeUsage attribute is AttributeTargets.All or AttributeTargets.Method can be applied to a function.
accessmodifier	The function's accessibility. Possible keywords are Public (the function is accessible to any code that can access the type in which it is defined), Private (the function is only accessible from the type in which it is defined), Friend (the function is only accessible from the assembly in which it is defined), Protected (the function is only accessible in classes that derive from the class in which it is defined), and Protected Friend. For details, see the entry for each of the access modifiers. If *accessModifier* is not specified, the function is Public by default. If the function statement appears in an interface definition, *accessmodifier* cannot be used, since functions defined in interfaces must be public.
proceduremodifiers	One or more of the following modifiers: Overloads, which indicates this is one of two or more identically named functions with different signatures; Overrides, which indicates that this function overrides an identically named programming element in a base class; Overridable, which indicates that this function can be overridden by an identically named function in a derived class; NotOverridable, which indicates that a derived class cannot override this function; and MustOverride, which indicates that a derived class must override the function. By default, functions are NotOverridable.

Element	Description
Shared	Indicates that the function can be called without creating an instance of the type in which it is defined. The Shared keyword cannot be used with the Function statement in interface definitions (since interfaces by definition define public instance members) or in modules (since they can only define shared members). Shared cannot be used with the Overrides, Overridable, NotOverridable, and MustOverride keywords.
Shadows	Indicates that the function hides an identically named programming element in a base class. For details, see the entry for the Shadows Keyword. Shadows cannot be used along with Overloads.
name	The name of the function. It must follow standard Visual Basic naming conventions.
typeparamlist	A list of type parameters for a generic function. For details, see the entry for the Of Keyword.
paramlist	The function's parameter list, which can consist of zero or more parameters. If multiple parameters are present, they are separated from one another with commas. At runtime, the arguments passed to the function can be referenced by their parameter names. The syntax of a single parameter is shown at the end of the Syntax section.
returntype	The data type returned by the function. If Option Strict is on, *returntype* is required. If Option Strict is off and *returntype* is not specified, the function returns a value of type Object. If *returntype* is an array, it includes parentheses around the type name. For example, the following function returns a string array: `Function GetNames() As String()`
implementsList	A comma-separated list of interface methods, in the form *interfacename.methodname* . . . , which defines the function as implementing a particular interface method. If *implementsList* is present, the function's containing class, structure, or interface must also implement that interface (it must have an Implements statement), and the function must have the same signature as the interface member for which it provides an implementation.

A single parameter in *paramlist* has the syntax:

```
[ <attribute_list> ] [ Optional ] [{ ByVal | ByRef }] [ ParamArray ] _
argument_name[( )] [ As argument_type ] [ = default_value ]
```

Element	Description
attribute_list	A comma-separated list of attributes that apply to the parameter. Only attributes whose AttributeUsage attribute is AttributeTargets.All or AttributeTargets.Parameter can be applied to a function parameter.
Optional	Indicates that an argument need not be supplied when calling the function. All parameters that follow an optional parameter must also be optional or a compiler error results. For details on optional arguments, see the entry for the Optional keyword.

Element	Description
ByVal	Indicates that the argument is passed by value to the function. When control returns to the caller, the value of its original argument is not modified. If ByVal or ByRef is not explicitly specified, the argument is passed to the function by value.
ByRef	Indicates that the argument is passed by reference to the function. When control returns to the caller, any modifications to the value of the argument made by the function are reflected in the value of the argument.
ParamArray	Indicates that the argument is an optional parameter array whose size is not known at design time. If present, it must be the last parameter is *paramlist*. For details on the user of parameter arrays, see the entry for the ParamArray Keyword.
argument_name	The name of the parameter. The argument passed to the function by the caller is referenced by this name within the function.
argument_type	The data type of the argument. It can be any data type recognized by the .NET framework.
default_value	The default value to be assigned to optional arguments.

Comments

Functions are useful only to the degree that your code can call them. Therefore, separate sections discuss declaring a function and calling it.

Declaring Functions

The Function statement can be used to define a function (that is, a procedure that returns a value) in a class, structure, interface, or module. However, a function cannot be defined within a member of any of those types. In addition, the Function statement can be used with the Delegate statement to define the signature of the delegate. The Function statement, however, cannot be used to handle events, since they do not return a value. The Handles keyword, therefore, cannot be used with the Function statement.

The Overrides keyword cannot be used with a function defined in an interface (because interfaces provide no code implementation) or in a module (because it cannot be used with shared members, only with instance members).

Unless they are explicitly declared otherwise, functions in base classes are not overridable, which in turn means that the attempt to override them using the Overrides keyword generates a compiler error (error BC31086: "'Public Overrides Function <function signature>' cannot override 'Public Function <function signature>' because it is not declared 'Overridable'"). As a result, if there is any possibility that your class can legitimately be used as a base class from which other classes derive, you should define its methods as Overridable. (And if there isn't, you should seal the class by declaring it NotInheritable.)

The Overloads keyword cannot be used with a function defined in a module, since Overloads cannot be used with shared members.

If the MustOverride keyword is used in the function definition, the function block consists only of the Function statement without implementation code or the End Function statement.

Generally, the End Function construct is used to end the function definition. However, functions that provide no code implementation but simply define signatures do not have an End Function statement. This is true of the functions defined using the Delegate statement, as well as functions defined in interfaces and external DLL routines.

A function implementation (that is, a function statement that is not merely a declaration, as in an interface, a delegate, or an external DLL) can return a value in either of two ways:

- By using the Return statement along with the value to be returned by the function. For example, the following function, GetTaxRate, uses the Return statement to return the tax rate that corresponds to a particular income level:

```
Public Function GetTaxRate(income As Integer) As Decimal
   For ctr As Integer = Me.Income.GetLowerBound(0) To Me.Income.GetUpperBound(0)
      ' iterated all: this is the top top tax bracket
      If ctr = Me.Income.GetUpperBound(0) Then
         Return TaxRate(ctr)
      Else
         If  income <= Me.Income(ctr) Then
            Return TaxRate(ctr)
         End If
      End If
   Next
End Function
```

- By assigning the return value to a variable whose name is the same as that of the function. For example, the following is an equivalent implementation of the GetTaxRate function that assigns the return value of the function to a variable named GetTaxRate:

```
Public Function GetTaxRate(income As Integer) As Decimal
   For ctr As Integer = Me.Income.GetLowerBound(0) To Me.Income.GetUpperBound(0)
      GetTaxRate = TaxRate(Ctr)
      If income < Me.Income(ctr) then
         Exit Function
      End If
   Next
End Function
```

The *implementsList* syntax effectively frees you from having to assign a function the same name as the interface methods that it implements. However, you'll find that it is still helpful (and self-documenting) to give the function a name that is reasonably close to that of the interface method it implements.

Use self-documenting names that describe the purpose of the parameter. Not only will the function signature appear in Object Browser and IntelliSense, but callers of the function can more easily call it using named arguments.

Any number of Exit Function statements can occur within the body of a Function . . . End Function construct to exit the function body prematurely. Typically, the Exit Function statement is placed within an If statement to transfer control outside of the function body if some condition exists. The GetTaxRate function shown earlier in this section illustrates the use of the Exit Function statement to exit the function construct prematurely.

It is important to ensure that all code paths in a function return a value that you've assigned. If you do not explicitly assign a return value to a function, the function returns the default uninitialized value of its return type (0 for integral and floating types, False for Booleans, String.Empty for strings, etc.). It is especially important that a function that returns an object instance does not inadvertently return Nothing, and that a valid return value of Nothing be documented. A common error made by clients of a class method, and one often attributable to poor coding or inadequate documentation in the consumed class, is the failure to test that the returned value is a valid object instance.

Calling Functions

If a function has a parameter list, arguments can usually be passed to the function either positionally (by specifying the argument in the order in which it occurs in the function declaration) or by name (by assigning the parameter name the value of the argument). For example, if a class named Person is defined in part as follows:

```
Public Class Person

    Private firstName As String
    Private middleName As String
    Private lastName As String

    Public Sub New(firstName As String, middleName As String , lastName As String)
        Me.firstName = firstName
        Me.middleName = middleName
        me.lastName = lastName
    End Sub
End Class
```

its constructor can be invoked using positional arguments as follows:

```
Dim person2 As New Person("John", "J.", "Smith")
```

or it can be invoked using named arguments as follows:

```
Dim person1 As New Person(firstName := "John", lastName := "Smith", _
                          middleName := "J.")
```

Named arguments can be passed to the function in any order.

If a function takes an argument by reference and you would prefer that the value not be modified, you can do any of three things. For example, the following function, SquareIt, returns the square of a number that is passed to it by reference. It also increments the number passed to it as an argument by one.

```
Function SquareIt(ByRef number As Integer) As Long
    Dim square As Long = CLng(number ^ 2)
    number += 1
    Return square
End Function
```

Ordinarily, you would call the function as follows:

```
Dim number As Integer = 12
Dim square As Long = SquareIt(number)
Console.WriteLine("The value of number is now {0}", number)
```

However, to pass an argument by value rather than by reference, you can do the following:

- Override the by-reference argument by enclosing it in parentheses. If it is the only argument to the function, enclose it in double parentheses. For example, the following code passes its argument to the SquareIt function by value rather than by reference:

  ```
  square = SquareIt((number))
  ```

The result is that *number* is unchanged when the function completes and control returns to the caller.

- Pass a literal value to the function. For example:

```
square = SquareIt(12)
```

  Often, this is not possible, since the literal value to pass to the function is not known at design time.

- Make a copy of the variable that you can then pass to the function. For example, in the following code, a new variable, *duplicateNumber,* is assigned the value of *number* and then passed as an argument to the function:

```
Dim duplicateNumber As Integer = number
square= SquareIt(duplicateNumber)
```

This value can then be discarded when control returns to the caller. This method works only for value types, however. For reference types, you can make a copy of a class instance by calling the MemberwiseClone method if you are calling a function from within the class itself or one of its derived classes. (MethodwiseClone is a protected method.)

Passing an argument to a function by value does not necessarily mean that it cannot be modified by the function. If the argument is a reference type, property and field values can be modified, and if the argument is an array (which is also a reference type), individual array elements can be modified. For details, see the entry for the ByRef Keyword.

VB.NET Changes

The use of the Of *typeparamlist* clause to support a generic parameter list is new to Visual Basic 2005.

VB6 Differences

Probably the most significant difference between Visual Basic 6.0 functions and Visual Basic .NET functions is that the default method of passing arguments to the former is by reference, and to the latter is by value.

In Visual Basic 6.0, methods had to be named after the interface members that they implemented. In Visual Basic .NET, the Implements *implementsList* clause removes this requirement and leaves you free to name interfaces as you choose.

In Visual Basic 6.0, parameter arrays had to be of type Variant, whereas in Visual Basic .NET they can be strongly typed. In addition, the argument supplied to the parameter array parameter had to be an array, whereas in Visual Basic .NET it can also be a list of comma-separated values.

In Visual Basic 6.0, optional parameters defined using the Optional keyword could have a default value, although it was not required. When a function was called, it was usually possible to detect omitted arguments by using the IsMissing function. In Visual Basic .NET, a default value is required, and the IsMissing function is not supported.

In Visual Basic 6.0, the only way for a function to return a value to the caller was to assign the function's return value to an automatically instantiated variable whose name was the same as that of the function. Although Visual Basic .NET supports this syntax, it adds the Return statement.

In Visual Basic 6.0, a function could be called by assigning its return value to a variable (or using it in an expression) and by enclosing its argument list in parentheses. If you were uninterested in the function's return value, however, you could simply call the function and provide the argument list without parentheses. In Visual Basic .NET, regardless of whether you are using or discarding the function's return value, its argument list, if one is present, must be enclosed in parentheses.

See Also

Delegate Statement, Exit Statement, MustOverride Keyword, NotOverridable Keyword, Optional Keyword, Overloads Keyword, Overridable Keyword, Overrides Keyword, ParamArray Keyword, Return Statement, Shadows Keyword, Shared Keyword, Sub Statement

FV Function

Calculates the future value of an annuity based on periodic fixed payments and a fixed interest rate.

Member Of

Microsoft.VisualBasic.Financial

Syntax

```
FV(ByVal Rate As Double, ByVal NPer As Double, ByVal Pmt As Double, _
    Optional ByVal PV As Double = 0, _
    Optional ByVal Due As DueDate = DueDate.EndOfPeriod) As Double
```

Element	Description
Rate	The interest rate per period.
NPer	The number of payment periods in the annuity.
Pmt	The payment to be made each period.
PV	The present value of a series of future payments. Its default value is 0.
Due	A DueDate enumeration member that specifies when payments are due. Possible values are either DueDate.BegOfPeriod (payments are due at the beginning of the period) or DueDate.EndOfPeriod (payments are due at the end of the period). If not specified, Due defaults to DueDate.EndOfPeriod.

Return Value

A Double indicating the value of the annuity after *NPer* periods.

Comments

An *annuity* is a series of equal payments or receipts (a level stream of cash inflow or outflow) that occurs at evenly spaced intervals for a fixed period of time. Mortgage payments, lease payments, and rental payments are all examples of annuities. Typically, for an ordinary annuity, the payments or receipts occur at the end of each period, while for an annuity due they occur at the beginning of each period.

Rate, *NPer,* and *Pmt* must be expressed in the same time unit for the value returned by the function to make sense. For example, if the rate is 5.75 percent per year for fixed payments of $1,458.93 per month for 30 years, the three arguments must either be expressed in terms of years (in which case the fixed payment would have to be changed to $17,507.16) or of months (in which case the rate would have to be changed to .4792 percent and the number of payments would have to be changed to 360).

Rate is expressed as a fraction. For example, an interest rate of 1 percent per month is expressed as .01.

Typically, the *PV* argument is used in the case of loans to indicate the initial loan amount.

Arguments that represent cash paid out are expressed with negative numbers; arguments that represent cash received are expressed with positive numbers.

Example

The following code fragment calculates the future value of an annual $5,000 investment made at the end of the year that accumulates interest at 6 percent annually:

```
Dim rate As Double = .06
Dim NPer As Double = 5
Dim Pmt As Double = 5000
Dim PV As Double = 0
Dim Due As DueDate = DueDate.EndOfPeriod
Dim FValue As Double = FV(rate, nPer, -Pmt, PV, Due)
Console.WriteLine(Format(FValue, "C"))
```

See Also

IPmt Function, IRR Function, MIRR Function, NPer Function, NPV Function, Pmt Function, PV Function, Rate Function

Get Statement

Defines a property get accessor, which is used to retrieve the value of a property.

Syntax

```
[ <attrlist> ] [<accessmodifier>] Get()
    [ statements ]
    [ Exit Property ]
    [ statements ]
End Get
```

Element	Description
attrlist	A list of attributes to be applied to the property get accessor. Only attributes whose AttributeUsage attribute is AttributeTargets.All or AttributeTargets.Property can be applied to a Get statement.
accessmodifier	An optional access modifier (possible values are Private, Friend, Protected, or Protected Friend) if access to the property get accessor is less restrictive than the access defined in the Property statement.
statements	The code that executes when the property value is retrieved.

Comments

The Property Get statement is contained within a Property . . . End Property statement that defines the name of the property, its return type, its parameter list (if it has one) and whether it is the default property, and whether it is read-write, read-only, or write-only (in which case a Get statement is not allowed).

The Get statement returns a property value either by using the Return statement or by assigning the property value to be returned to a variable whose name is the same as that of the property.

The property get accessor can have a different access level than the property construct as a whole. (Where access levels differ, though, the property set accessor is more likely to have the more restrictive access.)

Typically, the Property Get statement returns a private variable that is used to hold the property value, or it returns a computed value. The purpose of the Property construct then becomes to provide a single access point to otherwise protected data, which allows the property accessors to be used for such things as data validation or checking user credentials. The example illustrates this pattern of using a property get accessor to provide access to private instance data.

Example

The example defines a class, Book, that consists of two private variables, authorName and bookTitle. Their values can be set by the class constructor, as well as by a property set accessor, and they can be retrieved only by a property get accessor. Because they are private, the variables themselves are inaccessible except to code within the Book class.

```
Public Class Book
    Private authorName As String
    Private bookTitle As String

    Public Sub New(author As String, title As String)
        Me.authorName = author
        Me.bookTitle = title
    End Sub

    Public Property Author() As String
        Get
            Return Me.authorName
        End Get
        Set
            Me.authorName = Value
        End Set
    End Property

    Public Property Title() As String
        Get
            Return Me.bookTitle
        End Get
        Set
            Me.bookTitle = Value
        End Set
    End Property
End Class
```

VB.NET Changes

As of Visual Basic 2005, a property can have mixed access levels. The Property . . . End Property construct defines either the least restrictive access or the access level that applies to the property get and property set accessors, if both are present. The Get statement (or the Set statement) can then define a different, more restrictive access level.

VB6 Differences

Visual Basic 6.0 supported separate Property Get, Property Let, and Property Set statements. In contrast, Visual Basic .NET supports a single Property . . . End Property statement, which in turn can contain a Get statement and a Set statement. The functionality of both the Property Let and the Property Set statement has been merged into the single Set statement, leaving the Property Let statement with no equivalent in Visual Basic .NET. Overall, the syntax of the Property statement in Visual Basic .NET is far more straightforward than its Visual Basic 6.0 counterpart.

See Also

Property Statement, Return Statement, Set Statement

GetAllSettings Function

Retrieves all the values belonging to a designated registry key.

Member Of

Microsoft.VisualBasic.Interaction

Syntax

```
GetAllSettings(ByVal AppName As String, ByVal Section As String) As String(,)
```

Element	Description
AppName	A string describing a relative registry path from HKEY_CURRENT_USER \Software\VB and VBA Program Settings to the key named Section.
Section	A string describing a relative registry path from the AppName key to the key whose named values are to be read.

Return Value

A two-dimensional array containing name/value pairs, where index, 0 contains the value name, and index, 1 contains its value.

Comments

The GetAllSettings function was introduced in Visual Basic 4.0 and worked with both the 16- and 32-bit versions of Visual Basic. In the 16-bit version, it deleted portions of an initialization file; in the 32-bit version, it deleted a key or value from the registry. Even though the 16-bit version of Visual Basic is long gone, its spirit lives in the GetAllSettings function and in its documentation. Such terms as "key settings" and "section whose key settings are requested" are not standard ways of describing the registry and make this (as well as the other registry access functions in Visual Basic .NET) more confusing than they need be.

Like the other registry settings that are a part of the Visual Basic language, GetAllSettings does not work with the entire registry, but only with the subkeys of HKEY_CURRENT_USER\Software\VB and VBA Program Settings. The function is not intended as a general-purpose registry value retrieval utility. Instead, it is intended to be used by an application to retrieve the values of registry keys that the application itself has written to the registry using the SaveSetting subroutine.

AppName is described in the documentation as "the name of the application or project whose key settings are requested." This assumes that there is a single registry key named *AppName*, and that its name corresponds to the name of a Visual Basic project or application. There is nothing, however, to enforce this rule. In fact, *AppName* can consist of one or more registry keys.

Section is described in the documentation as "the name of the section whose key settings are requested." Neither the phrase "section" nor the phrase "key settings," when applied to the registry, however, have meaning. In fact, *Section* can consist of one or more registry keys.

AppName and *Section* in fact together describe a relative path that begins with a subkey of HKEY_CURRENT_USER\Software\VB and VBA Program Settings and ends with the key whose named values are to be retrieved. Neither begins with the registry path delimiter. For example, if the program is to retrieve the values of the HKEY_CURRENT_USER\Software\VB and VBA Program Settings\MyCompany\MyApplication\UserSettings\Windows key, *AppName* and *Section* have any of the following values:

AppName	Section
MyCompany	MyApplication\UserSettings\Windows
MyCompany\MyApplication	UserSettings\Windows
MyCompany\MyApplication\UserSettings	Windows

The only real requirements are that *AppName* and *Section* describe a valid registry path, and that neither argument be a null string.

If *AppName* or *Section* does not exist, the function returns an uninitialized array. Before attempting to access the array's members, you should test whether it is a valid object reference.

Interestingly, given that the SaveSetting subroutine is capable of writing only string data and is unable to save a registry key's default (or unnamed) value, the GetAllSettings function populates the array it returns with information on all value entries, including the default value. For REG_SZ and REG_EXPAND_SZ data (that is to say, for string data and string data with embedded macros), an array element contains the name of the value entry at index 0 and its data at index 1. (An empty string is used as the name of the default value.) REG_EXPAND_SZ strings are also correctly handled: the macros in them are expanded to their full strings. The other major data types supported by the registry (REG_DWORD, REG_BINARY, and REG_MULTI_SZ) are not supported by the GetAllSettings function, which instead includes only the name of the value entry at index 0 and an empty string at index 1. Before attempting to use the data, you should first compare it to String.Empty to make sure that it is valid.

The Visual Basic registry functions are badly underpowered and of very limited utility. Rather than use them, you should use either the registry classes in the Microsoft.Win32 namespace or the My.Computer.Registry object. For example, the following code uses the RegistryKey class in the Microsoft.Win32 namespace to open a registry key and read its value entries. It first iterates retrieves an array containing the names of the value entries. It determines the data type of each data entry and then retrieves and displays its data.

```vbnet
Imports Microsoft.Win32

Public Module modMain
    Public Sub Main()
        Dim opened As Boolean = False
        Dim regKey As RegistryKey
        ' Retrieve existing key
        Dim regPath As String = "Software\MyCompany\MyApp"
        Try
            regKey = Registry.CurrentUser.OpenSubKey(regPath)
            If regKey IsNot Nothing Then opened = True
            ' Determine number of value entries
            If regKey.ValueCount > 0 Then
                ' Retrieve names of value entries
                Dim valueNames() As String = regKey.GetValueNames()
                ' iterate names array to determine data type of each value entry
                For Each valueName As String In valueNames
                    Select Case regKey.GetValueKind(valueName)
                        Case RegistryValueKind.String, RegistryValueKind.ExpandString
                            Dim value As String = _
                                DirectCast(regKey.GetValue(valueName), String)
                            Dim namedValue As String = valueName
                            If namedValue = String.Empty Then _
                                    namedValue = "<Default Value>"
                            Console.WriteLine("{0} (string data): {1}", valueName, value)
                        Case RegistryValueKind.Binary
                            Dim byt() As Byte = DirectCast(regKey.GetValue(valueName), _
                                            Byte())
                            Console.Write("{0} (binary data): ", valuename)
                            For Each bytData As Byte In byt
                                Console.Write("&H{0} ", Format(bytData, "X"))
                            Next
                            Console.WriteLine()
                        Case RegistryValueKind.MultiString
                            Dim strings() As String = _
                                DirectCast(regKey.GetValue(valueName), String())
                            Console.WriteLine("{0} (string array data):", valuename)
                            For Each strng As String In strings
                                Console.WriteLine("   {0}", strng)
                            Next
                        Case RegistryValueKind.DWord
                            Dim value As Integer = _
                                DirectCast(regKey.GetValue(valueName), Integer)
                    End Select
                Next
            Else
                Console.WriteLine("{0} contains no value entries.", regKey.Name)
            End If
        Catch e As Exception
            Console.WriteLine("Registry Access Error: {0} ({1} Exception", _
                        e.Message, e.GetType.Name)
        Finally
            If opened Then regKey.Close()
        End Try
    End Sub
End Module
```

VB6 Differences

In Visual Basic 6.0, GetAllSettings did not return data from a registry key's default value. In contrast, Visual Basic .NET does.

In Visual Basic 6.0, GetAllSettings raised an error if it encountered non-string data in a registry key; it assumed that the Visual Basic application (or another Visual Basic application) had sole control of the key and its values. In contrast, Visual Basic .NET retrieves the name of the key, but not its data.

See Also

DeleteSetting Subroutine, GetSetting Function, SaveSetting Subroutine

GetAttr Function

Retrieves information about a file system object's attributes.

Member Of

Microsoft.VisualBasic.FileSystem

Syntax

```
GetAttr(ByVal PathName As String) As FileAttribute
```

Element	Description
PathName	The name, and the optional drive and path, of a file or directory.

Return Value

A FileAttribute value indicating which attributes have been set.

Comments

Along with a filename, *PathName* can include either a relative or an absolute path. If a path is not provided, the function looks in the current directory for the file named *PathName.*

The FileAttribute enumeration is a bitmask rather than a set of mutually exclusive flags. This means that multiple attributes can be set in the function's return value.

Possible values of the FileAttribute enumeration that can be returned by the GetAttr function are as follows:

Enumeration Member	Description
Normal	No attributes are set.
ReadOnly	The file system object is read-only.
Hidden	The file system object is hidden.
System	The file system object is for system use.
Directory	The file system object is a directory rather than a file.
Archive	The file system object has been created or modified since the last backup.

Note that FileAttribute.Normal indicates not that the Normal flag is set, but rather that no flags are set. (The integer value of the FileAttribute.Normal constant is 0.)

To determine whether a particular attribute is set, you use the And operator to perform a bitwise comparison of the function's return value with the attribute in which you're interested. For example, the following expression evaluates to True if the file named *filename* has its System attribute set:

```
If (GetAttr(filename) And FileAttribute.System) <> 0 Then
```

To examine the attributes of multiple files, you could use a combination of the Dir function to retrieve the files and the GetAttr function to display information about their attributes. However, the difficulties of using the *attributes* argument of the Dir function makes it far easier to use either the overloaded My.Computer.FileSystem.GetFiles method or a comparable method from the .NET Framework Class Library, such as the shared GetFiles method of the System.IO.Directory class. The first overload of the former method has a single parameter, *directory*, that defines the directory to be searched for files. (The second overload allows you to specify whether subdirectories are searched as well and to provide a wildcard specification that determines which files the method should search for.) It returns a generic read-only collection of String containing the complete names of files. The example illustrates the use of the GetFiles method along with the GetAttr function.

Instead of the GetAttr function, you can use the read-write Attributes property of the System.IO.FileInfo class. The property's get accessor returns a System.IO.FileAttributes enumerated value that, like the value returned by the GetAttr function, is a flag that indicates which, if any, attributes are set for the file. Possible values include FileAttributes.Normal (no flags set), FileAttributes.Archive (the file has been modified since the last backup), FileAttributes.Compressed (the file is compressed), FileAttributes.Directory (the file system object is a directory), FileAttributes.Encrypted (the file or directory is encrypted), FileAttributes.Hidden (the file is hidden), FileAttributes.Offline (the file is stored offline and its content is not immediately available), FileAttributes.ReadOnly (the file is read-only), FileAttributes.System (the file is reserved for system use), and FileAttributes.Temporary (the file is a temporary file).

Example

The example uses the My.Computer.FileSystem.GetFiles method to retrieve all of the files in the current directory, then iterates them and retrieves information about their file attributes. It then displays this information to the system console.

```
Imports System.IO

Public Module fileAttributes
    Public Sub Main()
        For Each filename As String In My.Computer.FileSystem.GetFiles(".")
            Dim flags as String
            ' Get file's attributes
            Dim attributes As FileAttribute = GetAttr(filename)
            ' Determine if no attributes are set
            If attributes = FileAttribute.Normal Then
                flags = "N"
                ' No point in iterating everything else
                Continue For
            Else
                flags = " "
            End If
```

```
            If (attributes Or FileAttribute.Archive) = FileAttribute.Archive Then
                flags += "A"
            Else
                flags += " "
            End If
            ' Determine if file is R/O
            If (attributes  And FileAttribute.ReadOnly) = FileAttribute.ReadOnly Then
                flags += "R"
            Else
                flags += " "
            End If
            ' Determine if file is system
            If (attributes  and FileAttribute.System) = FileAttribute.System Then
                flags += "S"
            Else
                flags += " "
            End If
            ' Determine if file is hidden
            If (attributes  And FileAttribute.System) = FileAttribute.System Then
                flags += "H"
            Else
                flags += " "
            End If
            ' Display file information
            Console.WriteLine("{0,-30}:      {1}", Path.GetFileName(filename), flags)
        Next
    End Sub
End Module
```

See Also

Dir Function, SetAttr Subroutine

GetChar Function

Retreives a Char representing a single character from a string.

Member Of

Microsoft.VisualBasic.Strings

Syntax

```
GetChar(ByVal str As String, ByVal Index As Integer) As Char
```

Element	Description
str	The string from which to extract the single character.
Index	The one-based position in *str* of the character to extract.

Return Value

A Char representing the character at position *Index*.

Comments

If *str* is empty, or if *Index* is negative or it exceeds the length of *str*, an ArgumentException is thrown.

On the one hand, GetChar in part duplicates the functionality of the Left, Mid, and Right functions, which can return single-character as well as multicharacter strings according to their ordinal position in a larger string. On the other hand, GetChar is unusual among Visual Basic string handling functions, since it returns a Char rather than a one-character String.

GetChar is useful if you want to use the methods of the Char class to work with a single character in a string. For example, the following code determines whether the first letter of a word is a letter or digit:

```
Public Shared Function StartsWithLetterOrDigit(s As String) As Boolean
    Return Char.IsLetterOrDigit(GetChar(s, 1))
End Function
```

VB6 Differences

The GetChar function is new to Visual Basic .NET.

See Also

Instr Function, Left Function, Mid Function, Right Function

GetObject Function

Returns a reference to a COM object.

Member Of

Microsoft.VisualBasic.Interaction

Syntax

```
Public Function GetObject(Optional ByVal PathName As String = Nothing, _
                          Optional ByVal Class As String = Nothing) As Object
```

Element	Description
PathName	The full path and name of the file containing the COM object. If *Class* is omitted, PathName is required.
Class	The programmatic identifier (ProgID) of the object class. If *PathName* is omitted, *Class* is required.

Return Value

An instance of a COM object.

Comments

GetObject returns a late-bound object. If possible, you might want to consider adding a reference to the COM component to your project and allowing .NET to create a runtime callable wrapper (RCW) to creating a COM wrapper to marshal calls between the runtime and the COM component.

Confusingly, GetObject is a function that serves three different purposes: it creates an object from a moniker (when *PathName* is a path, for example, it is a moniker that allows you to "launch" a data file and returns a reference to the COM object that corresponds to that data file); it allows you to retrieve a reference to an existing COM object that is currently open in the Windows environment (*PathName* is omitted); and it creates a new object (*PathName* is String.Empty or ""). In the latter case, its functionality is identical to that of CreateObject.

Creating an Object from a Moniker

A *moniker* is simply a name that represents an object without indicating how that object should be instantiated. The path of a data file, for example, can serve as a moniker, since its file extension provides information on how it can be instantiated. Some other common monikers are IIS (which identifies the IIS metabase), JAVA (a Java object), SCRIPT (a Windows Script component), and QUEUE (a COM+ component).

If you are using *PathName* as a moniker to identify a data file, you should always provide the fully qualified path of the data file. If you use a relative path, the host application capable of handling the file interprets the relative path. While this may produce the behavior you want, it is more likely to result in a FileNotFoundException or a general Exception with the error message, "Cannot create ActiveX object."

If *PathName* is provided as a moniker, the GetObject function first uses the registry to determine the application responsible for handling a data file with that file extension or a moniker with that name. If an application is registered, it loads that application, which in turn opens the data file. The application does not have to be open on the desktop for it to load the data file.

The GetObject method returns a reference to the data type that it opened. This means, for example, that if you use the GetObject function to open an Excel spreadsheet, the function returns a Workbook object, not an Excel.Application object. If you need to retrieve the top-level or application-level object, you often can find an upward navigation property in the object model. For example, in Microsoft Word, the Document object's Application property returns a reference to the Word Application object.

Typically, when the application is launched and opens the data file, the application window remains hidden. You may wish to show it, as well as to work with the COM object's object model, by using the object reference returned by the GetObject function.

Some applications recognize subobjects within data files. To open the data file and return a reference to that particular object type, you use an exclamation point (!) to separate the data file's path and name from the subobject type.

In some case, a single data file can contain more than one type of COM object. In that case, you can designate the particular kind of object you would like the GetObject function to return by providing a value for the *Class* argument. For details on the *Class* argument, see the following section.

Retreiving a Reference to an Existing COM Object

The second version of the GetObject function, in which the optional *PathName* argument is omitted and only the *Class* argument is supplied, returns a reference to an existing object.

Although *Class* is an arbitrary string that is defined in the HKEY_CLASSES_ROOT branch of the registry, it often takes the form *Application_Name.ClassName* or *LibraryName.ObjectName*. Examples are Excel.Application, Word.Document, or Scripting.Dictionary.

If the .NET runtime cannot retrieve a reference to the object either because *Class* is invalid or because the application is not already open, the GetObject function throws an Exception and returns the error message, "Cannot create ActiveX component."

To create an object rather than retrieve a reference to an existing one, use the CreateObject function, or set *PathName* to an empty string (see the next section).

Creating a New Object

You can specify a *PathName* of either String.Empty or "".

    Class does not have to be the programmatic identifier of an application; it can also be the programmatic identifier of a data object (such as a Microsoft Word document or a Microsoft Excel workbook).

See Also

ComClass Attribute, CreateObject Function

GetSetting Function

Retrieves a value from the registry.

Member Of

Microsoft.VisualBasic.Interaction

Syntax

```
GetSetting(ByVal AppName As String, ByVal Section As String, _
          ByVal Key As String, Optional ByVal Default As String = "" _
          ) As String
```

Element	Description
AppName	A string describing a relative registry path from HKEY_CURRENT_USER\Software\VB and VBA Program Settings to the key named *Section*.
Section	A string describing a relative registry path from the *AppName* key to the key whose named values are to be read.
Key	Tbe named value entry whose value is to be retrieved.
Default	The value to return if the path to the registry key specified by *AppName* plus *Section* does not exist, or if the value entry named *Key* does not exist.

Return Value

A string containing the value of the value entry, or *Default* if the value entry cannot be found.

Comments

The GetSetting function was introduced in Visual Basic 4.0 and worked with both the 16- and 32-bit versions of Visual Basic. In the 16-bit version, it deleted portions of an initialization file; in the 32-bit version, it deleted a key or value from the registry. Unfortunately, five versions afterward, the documentation has still not been revised sufficiently to accurately reflect the terminology used to describe the registry. Such terms as "key setting" and "name of the section in which the key setting is found" are just plan incorrect.

    Like the other registry settings that are a part of the Visual Basic language, SaveSetting does not work with the entire registry, but only with the subkeys of HKEY_CURRENT_USER\Software\VB and VBA Program Settings. The function is not intended as a general-purpose registry value retrieval utility. Instead, it is intended to be used by an application to retrieve the value of a registry key that the application itself has written to the registry using the SaveSetting subroutine.

As is true of the other registry access functions, *AppName* and *Section* together describe a relative path that begins with a subkey of HKEY_CURRENT_USER\Software\VB and VBA Program Settings and ends with the key whose named values are to be retrieved. Neither begins with the registry path delimiter. For example, if the program is to retrieve the values of the HKEY_CURRENT_USER\Software\VB and VBA Program Settings\MyCompany \MyApplication\UserSettings\Windows key, *AppName* and *Section* have any of the following values:

AppName	Section
MyCompany	MyApplication\UserSettings\Windows
MyCompany\MyApplication	UserSettings\Windows
MyCompany\MyApplication\UserSettings	Windows

The only real requirement is that neither *AppName* nor *Section* be a null string. (This throws an ArgumentException.)

GetSetting is unable to retrieve the default or unnamed value of a registry key. Attempting to retrieve it throws an ArgumentException with the error message, "Argument 'path' is missing or empty."

The GetSetting function is able to retrieve only string (REG_SZ) and macro or environmental string (REG_EXPAND_SZ) data from the registry. It also expands environmental strings before returning them. However, the attempt to retrieve string array (REG_MULTI_SZ) data from the registry throws an ArgumentException, as does the attempt to read binary (REG_BINARY) data. Finally, when attempting to read integer (REG_DWORD) data, the GetSetting function returns an empty string.

The Visual Basic registry functions are badly underpowered and of very limited utility. Rather than use them, you should use either the registry classes in the Microsoft.Win32 namespace or the My.Computer.Registry object. For an example of using RegistryKey class in the Microsoft.Win32 namespace to read a registry key's value entries, see the GetAllSettings function.

See Also

DeleteSetting Subroutine, GetAllSettings Function, SaveSetting Subroutine

GoTo Statement

Unconditionally transfers control to a label within a function or subroutine.

Syntax

```
GoTo label
```

Element	Description
label	A line label.

Comments

A line label is a numeric, alphabetic, or alphanumeric string ending in a colon (:) that is placed at the beginning of a line. For example, in the following code, 5: and NoChange2: are labels:

```
       If x = 10 Then GoTo 5
       x = 20
5:     Console.WriteLine(x)
       GoTo NoChange2
       x = 30
NoChange2:
       Console.WriteLine(x)
```

The GoTo statement cannot be used to transfer control outside of the function or subroutine in which it is found.

The GoTo statement cannot be used to transfer control from outside any of the following programming constructs to a label inside of them:

- For . . . Next.
- For Each . . . Next
- SyncLock . . . End SyncLock
- Try . . . Catch . . . Finally
- With . . . End With

GoTo can be used to transfer control from a Try block to one of its corresponding Catch blocks, from a Catch block to its Try block, or from a Try or Catch block to outside of the Try . . . Catch . . . Finally construct.

GoTo is also used with the On Error statement to direct program flow in the event of an error.

VB6 Differences

In Visual Basic 6.0, the GoTo statement could transfer control either to a line number or to a line label. In Visual Basic .NET, the GoTo statement can only be used with line labels.

See Also

On Error Statement

Global Keyword

Qualifies a .NET Framework Class Library reference to make it unambiguous.

Comments

Naming conflicts can make it impossible for the Visual Basic .NET compiler to resolve references to portions of the .NET Framework Class Library. When this happens, the Global keyword can be prepended to the .NET Framework Class Library namespace name to provide a fully qualified, unambiguous reference.

The Global keyword can be used whenever a qualified namespace reference is used. This includes the Class, Const, Declare, Delegate, Dim, Enum, Event, For . . . Next, For Each . . . Next, Function, Interface, Operator, Property, Structure, Sub, Try . . . Catch . . . Finally, and Using statements.

Most commonly, it is used in the As clause to define a type, or in the Of clause to define a generic parameter list.

The Global keyword cannot be used with the Imports statement. It can only be used to qualify individual type definitions.

Example

The following code generates repeated compiler errors (error BC30456) because the compiler attempts to resolve the references to Console and AppDomain as members of the String class, rather than as classes in the System namespace:

```
Interface ISysInfo
    ReadOnly Property System As String
    ReadOnly Property AppDomain As String
End Interface

Public Class MyInfo
    Implements ISysInfo

    Public ReadOnly Property System As String _
        Implements ISysInfo.System
        Get
            Return My.Application.Info.Version.Major
        End Get
    End Property

    Public ReadOnly Property AppDomain As String _
        Implements ISysInfo.AppDomain
        Get
            System.Console.WriteLine(System.AppDomain.CurrentDomain.FriendlyName)
            Return System.AppDomain.CurrentDomain.FriendlyName
        End Get
    End Property
End Class
```

The problem stems from the fact that we've had to implement a property named System that is of type String, so the compiler interprets subsequent occurrences of System as referring to this property when in fact they refer to the System namespace. The Global keyword can be used in this situation to create unambiguous references to the System namespace:

```
Interface ISysInfo
    ReadOnly Property System As String
    ReadOnly Property AppDomain As String
End Interface

Public Class MyInfo
    Implements ISysInfo

    Public ReadOnly Property System As String _
        Implements ISysInfo.System
        Get
            Return My.Application.Info.Version.Major
        End Get
    End Property
```

```
     Public ReadOnly Property AppDomain As String _
        Implements ISysInfo.AppDomain
        Get
           Global.System.Console.WriteLine( _
                  Global.System.AppDomain.CurrentDomain.FriendlyName)
           Return Global.System.AppDomain.CurrentDomain.FriendlyName
        End Get
     End Property
  End Class
```

VB.NET Changes

The Global keyword was introduced in Visual Basic 2005.

VB6 Differences

In Visual Basic 6.0, although it was deprecated, the Global keyword was synonymous with the Public access modifier. This usage is completely unrelated to that of Visual Basic .NET, where the Global keyword is used to provide unambiguous namespace references.

See Also

Imports Statement, Namespace Statement

Handles Keyword

Used in a Sub statement to indicates that the procedure handles one or more events raised by an object.

Syntax

```
Handles objectName.event[, ...]
```

Element	Description
objectName	The name of the object whose event is being handled by the procedure.
event	The name of the event handled by the procedure.

Comments

The Handles keyword is used exclusively with the Sub statement to define that subroutine as an event handler. (The Function statement cannot be used to define an event handler.) The Handles keyword must appear on the same code line as the Sub statement. For example:

```
Private Sub Button1_Click(ByVal sender As System.Object, _
                     ByVal e As System.EventArgs) Handles Button1.Click
```

If a class handles its own event, the Handles clause takes the form:

```
Handles Me.eventName
```

For example, the following code illustrates an event handler in a checking account class that has a single method, Deposit. If the amount of a deposit is greater than $10,000, a warning is displayed that the check will take extra time to clear:

```
Public Class CheckingAccount
    Private balance As Decimal
    Event TimeToClear(sender As Object, e As EventArgs)

    Public Sub Deposit(amount As Decimal)
        If amount > 10000 Then
            RaiseEvent TimeToClear(Me, New EventArgs)
        End If
        balance += amount
    End Sub

    Friend Sub TimeAlert(sender As Object, e As EventArgs) Handles Me.TimeToClear
        Console.WriteLine("This check will take extra time to clear.")
    End Sub
End Class
```

If a derived class handles an event of its base class, the Handles clause takes the form

```
Handles MyBase.eventName
```

This example provides an illustration both of a derived class handling an event raised by its base class and an instance of a derived class handling an event raised by the base class.

The event or events for which a class instance receives notifications can be defined by the class or by one of its base classes. In either case, the object instance must be declared using the WithEvents keywords to indicate that it receives event notifications.

The event that the Handles clause designates must have the same signature as the subroutine or a compiler error occurs.

The name of an event handler is usually some combination of the name of the object and the name of the handled event (for example, SubmitButton_Click). However, you can use the Handles clause to make a subroutine into an event handler regardless of its name. This is especially important for event handlers that handle the events of more than one object.

The combination of WithEvents and Handles allows you to define static event handlers. That is, from the time that an object is instantiated until it goes out of scope, the event handler defined by the Handles keyword is executed if the event is fired. In contrast, the AddHandler . . . RemoveHandler statements allow you to define events dynamically, so that the code handling an object's event need not be known at the time that that object is instantiated.

It is possible for a single event to have multiple handlers, each of which executes synchronously when the event is fired. (The same object, for instance, can be represented by multiple object instances, each of which receives notification when the event fires.) This means that event handlers should execute quickly and exit immediately if at all possible, since lengthy processes can degrade performance disproportionately.

Example

The following code illustrates the use of the Handles keyword to handle an event fired by the base class. It defines a base class, Animal, that raises an Eating event when its Eat method is called, and a derived class, Person, that in this case has no unique members. A custom event handler, FoodEventArgs, is also defined to provide information about the Eating event. Note that the format and syntax of the Handles clause is the same whether the object receiving event notification is handling its own event or that of its base class.

```
Public Class FoodEventArgs : Inherits EventArgs
    Private instFood As String

    Public Sub New(food As String)
        Me.instfood = food
    End Sub

    Public ReadOnly Property Food() As String
        Get
            Return Me.instFood
        End Get
    End Property
End Class

Public Class Animal
    Public Event Eating(sender As Object, e As FoodEventArgs)

    Public Sub Eat(food As String)
        RaiseEvent Eating(Me, New FoodEventArgs(food))
    End Sub
End Class

Public Class Person : Inherits Animal
End Class

Public Module HandleEvent
    Dim WithEvents per As New Person()

    Public Sub Main()
        per.Eat("Eggplant")
    End Sub

    Private Sub Eating(sender As Object, e As FoodEventArgs) Handles per.Eating
        Console.WriteLine("Umm . . . Eating " & e.Food)
    End Sub
End Module
```

In this case, the event is raised by the base class but is handled by an instance of the derived class. However, it can also be handled by the derived class, in which case the MyBase keyword replaces the reference to the name of the class instance, as the following code illustrates. The only changes are to the derived Person class, as well as to the Main routine:

```
Public Class Person : Inherits Animal
    Private Sub Dining(sender As Object, e As FoodEventArgs) Handles MyBase.Eating
        Console.WriteLine("Umm...Dining on " & e.Food)
    End Sub
End Class

Public Module HandleEvent
    Dim WithEvents per As New Person()
```

```
Public Sub Main()
    per.Eat("Eggplant")
End Sub
End Module
```

VB.NET Changes

As of Visual Basic 2005, the Handles keyword can list multiple events, allowing a single event handler to handle events raised by multiple objects or to handle multiple events raised by the same object.

VB6 Differences

In Visual Basic 6.0, the Handles keyword did not exist, and as a result, event handlers necessarily had to have the same name as the object whose event they handled. In contrast, the Handles keyword allows event handlers to have different names than the events they handle.

In Visual Basic 6.0, an event handler could handle multiple events only for a control array. (A *control array* was an array of controls of the same type.) The event handler could determine which control fired the event by the *Index* argument passed to the handler. In contrast, Visual Basic .NET does not support control arrays. Instead, a reference to the object that raises an event is available from the *Sender* argument.

See Also

AddHandler Statement, RemoveHandler Statement, RaiseEvent Statement, Sub Statement, WithEvents Keyword

Hex Function

Returns a string representing the hexadecimal value of a number.

Member Of

Microsoft.VisualBasic.Conversion

Syntax

```
Hex(ByVal Number As { Byte | SByte | Short | UShort |
    Integer | UInteger | Long | ULong | Object } ) As String
```

Element	Description
Number	Any numeric or string expression.

Return Value

A string containing the hexadecimal representation of a number.

Comments

If *Number* is the string representation of a number, the Hex function must be able to successfully convert it to a numeric value before converting it to hexadecimal or an InvalidCastException is thrown. To prevent this, you can pass a string to the IsNumeric function beforehand to ensure that it can be successfully converted.

If *Number* is a floating point number (a Double, Single, or Decimal), the Hex function rounds it before converting it to a string. All positive floating point values of .5 and lower are rounded down, while positive values ending in .5 are rounded using banker's rounding. All negative floating point values greater than .5 are rounded up. Negative floating point values ending in .5 are rounded using banker's rounding.

If a string already contains the hexadecimal representation of a number, the Hex function merely returns that string unchanged, except that it strips off its identifying &H characters. For example:

```
Console.WriteLine(Hex("&HE0F1"))        ' Displays "E0F1"
Console.WriteLine(Hex("&HFFFF"))        ' Displays "FFFF"
```

This means, ironically, that if you immediately pass the string returned by the Hex function back to the Hex function, an InvalidCastException is thrown.

To convert the string representation of a hexadecimal number to a decimal number, you just have to pass it to an integer conversion function. For example:

```
Dim convertedHex As Integer = CInt("&H75FF")
Console.WriteLine(convertedHex)                  ' writes 30207
```

Note, however, that the conversion functions always interpret hexadecimal strings as positive values. This means that they have difficulty handling the conversion of string representations of hexadecimal values with the high-order bit of their high-order word set if the number is the same size (byte, short, integer, or long) as the hexadecimal value. For example, the code:

```
Dim hexValue As String = "&HF0"
Console.WriteLine("CSByte: " & CSByte(hexValue))
```

throws an OverflowException. This behavior is by design, since the interpretation of the sign bit as a negative number depends on the size of the number; interpreting a hexadecimal string as a positive numeric value is less likely to be a source of error, even if it does raise an occasional exception. But this does mean that attempts at hexadecimal-to-numeric conversion should include exception handling. An alternative is the use of the TryParse method, which assigns a value of 0 to the target variable if the conversion fails. A call to the TryParse method appears as follows:

```
Dim sbyt As SByte = SByte.TryParse(hexValue, sbyt)
```

You can assign hexadecimal values to numeric variables directly by using the &H symbols in front of the hexadecimal numbers. For example:

```
Dim maxValue As Byte = &HFF
Dim posValue As UInteger = &HF034
Dim negValue As Integer = &HF034
```

See Also

Oct Function

HideModuleName Attribute

Allows a member of a module to be accessed without referring to its containing module.

Namespace

Microsoft.VisualBasic

Syntax

```
<HideModuleName> Module moduleName
```

Element	Description
moduleName	The name of the module defined by the Module . . . End Module statement.

Comments

Ordinarily, to access a member of a module defined with the Module . . . End Module statement from outside of that module, you have to reference the module name as well as the member name. For example, since the AttributeUsage attribute of the HideModuleName attribute has a value of AttributeTargets.Class, it can be applied to either a class (defined with the Class . . . End Class statement) or a module (defined with the Module . . . End Module statement). However, it has no effect when applied to a class.

The HideModuleName attribute allows you to access members of a module very much as you can access members of the classes that reside in the Microsoft.VisualBasic namespace. For example, although you could call the IsDate function, because it resides in the Microsoft .VisualBasic namespace and is a member of the Information class, can be called using the "proper" syntax

```
Console.WriteLine(Microsoft.VisualBasic.Information.IsDate(dateNow))
```

But because of functionality very much like that of the HideModuleName attribute, it is not necessary to reference the Information class in order to access its IsDate member:

```
Console.WriteLine(Microsoft.VisualBasic.IsDate(dateNow))
```

If the HideModuleName attribute is applied to more than one module in a particular namespace, there must be no duplication of member names, or a compiler error results. In other words, HideModuleName eliminates the module name as an element in producing a unique, unambiguous reference, and requires that each name be unique in its namespace.

If the Microsoft.VisualBasic namespace is imported, then you don't have to reference it to access the IsDate method either:

```
Console.WriteLine(IsDate(dateNow))
```

Example

The following code defines a module, Utilities, that in this case has a single routine, IsOdd, which reports whether the number passed to it as an argument is odd:

```
<HideModuleName()> Public Module Utilities
    ' Determines whether a number is odd or even
    Public Function IsOdd(number As Long) As Boolean
        If (number And 1) = 1 Then Return True
    End Function
End Module
```

The function can be called as follows, either with out without its module name:

```
Public Sub Main
    Console.WriteLine(IsOdd(12))
    Console.WriteLine(IsOdd(1))
    Console.WriteLine(Utilities.IsOdd(-16))
End Sub
```

In addition, as Figure 8-12 shows, Visual Studio displays IntelliSense for the IsOdd function without displaying its member name. It is listed just as if it were an "intrinsic" Visual Basic .NET function.

VB.NET Changes

The HideModuleName attribute is new to Visual Basic 2005.

VB6 Differences

Although the HideModuleName attribute did not exist in Visual Basic 6.0, it causes the members of a module to behave very much like the Globals of a COM object model (such as the global Word or Excel objects) in Visual Basic 6.0. That is, they are globally available without the need to access them through the class or an instance of the class to which they belong.

See Also

Module Statement

FIGURE 8-12
IntelliSense for a member of a module with the HideMemberName attribute

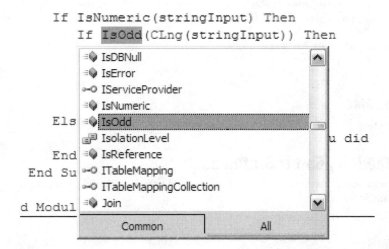

Hour Function

Returns the hour component of a time value based on a 24-hour clock.

Member Of

Microsoft.VisualBasic.DateAndTime

Syntax

```
Hour(ByVal TimeValue As DateTime) As Integer
```

Element	Description
TimeValue	An expression that evaluates to a Date value.

Return Value

An integer ranging from 0 to 23 representing the hour component of *TimeValue*.

Comments

If *TimeValue* is an uninitialized variable of type Date (or System.DateTime), or if *TimeValue* is a date value with an uninitialized time component, the Hour function returns 0, representing 12:00 AM.

If Option Strict is off, the Hour function will attempt to convert the string representation of a date and time to a Date value before extracting its hour component. If it is unable to do this, it throws an InvalidCastException. To prevent this, you can call the IsDate function to test that the string contains a valid date before calling the Hour function.

Calling the Hour function returns identical results to calling the DatePart function with the syntax:

```
DatePart(DateInterval.Hour, timeValue)
```

You can also retrieve the hour component of a Date value from its Hour property, which returns identical results to the Visual Basic .NET Hour function. For example:

```
Dim timeValue As Date = Date.Now
Console.WriteLine(Hour(timeValue))
Console.WriteLine(timeValue.Hour)
```

See Also

DatePart Function, IsDate Function, Minute Function, Second Function

If . . . Then . . . End If Statement

Conditionally executes a block of statements based on the evaluation of a logical (True or False) condition.

Syntax

The syntax of the multiline version of the If statement is:

```
If condition [ Then ]
    [ statements ]
[ ElseIf elseifcondition [ Then ]
    [ elseifstatements ] ]
[ Else
    [ elseStatements ] ]
End If
```

The syntax of its one-line version is:

```
If condition Then [ statements ] [ Else [ elseStatements ] ]
```

Element	Description
condition	An expression that must result in a Boolean or a data type that can be converted to a Boolean.
statements	One or more statements to be executed if condition is True.
Then	An optional keyword in the multiline form of the If statement; a required keyword in the single-line form.
elseifcondition	An expression that is evaluated if an optional ElseIf clause is present and all prior If or ElseIf clauses have evaluated to False. Like condition, it must result in a Boolean or a data type that can be converted to a Boolean.
elseifstatements	One or more statements to be executed if elseifcondition is True.
Else	An optional keyword beginning a code block to be executed if none of the previous If and ElseIf expressions are True.
elseStatements	Statements to execute if all previous If and ElseIf code blocks are False.

Comments

Aside from its one-line variation, the If statement has three major variations:

- The If . . . End If block alone, which executes if *condition* is True.
- The If . . . block with one or more ElseIf blocks. The code belonging to the first block whose conditional expression evaluates to True is executed. All previous blocks are skipped because their conditions evaluate to False, while all subsequent blocks are skipped regardless of the resulting value of their expression.
- The If block, possibly with one or more ElseIf blocks, and with an Else block. The code in the first block of the If and ElseIf blocks whose condition evaluates to True executes. If none are True, the code in the Else block executes.

There can be multiple ElseIf statements in an If . . . End If construct. Each ElseIf block must follow the If block and precede the Else block, if one is present. All multiline If statements must terminate with an End If statement.

Although there can be a virtually unlimited number of ElseIf statements in an If . . . End If construct, they can tend to make code less readable. If the ElseIf statements merely evaluate values returned by the same expression, a better alternative in terms of readability and clarity is the Select Case statement.

If *condition* or *elseifcondition* is Nothing, an InvalidCastException is thrown.

condition and *elseifcondition* can contain multiple Boolean expressions that are joined by the And, AndAlso, Or, and OrElse operators. And and AndAlso are identical, except that the latter operator performs short-circuiting. For example, in the statement

```
If Func1() And Func2()
```

both Func1 and Func2 are always called as part of evaluating the compound expression. In the statement

```
If Func1() AndAlso Func2()
```

Func1 is called, and Func2 is called only if Func1 is True. If Func1 is False, there is no need to call Func2, since the result of the expression is already known (it is False). The Or and OrElse operators work similarly. In the statement

```
If Func1() Or Func2()
```

both Func1 and Func2 are always called when evaluating the compound expression. In the statement

```
If Func1() OrElse Func2()
```

Func1 is always called, and Func2 is called only if Func1 is False. If Func1 is True, there is no need to call Func2, since the result of the expression is already known (it is True).

If statements can be nested. Nested If statements are only evaluated if their containing If statements evaluate to True.

It is possible to execute multiple statements in the single-line form of the If statement by using the Visual Basic line separator symbol, the colon (:). For example:

```
Dim condition As Boolean
Dim x, y As Integer
If condition Then x = 10 : y = 20 Else x = 5 : y = 10
```

An If statement is often used to test the type of object variable. For example:

- If tests whether a variable contains a valid object reference, as in the following code fragments:

```
If instClass1 Is Nothing Then
```

```
If Not instClass1 Is Nothing Then
```

```
If instClass1 IsNot Nothing Then
```

- If tests whether an object variable is of a particular type, as in the following code fragment:

  ```
  If TypeOf instClass2 Is CustomClass Then
  ```

- If tests whether an two object variables reference the same object, as in the following code fragment:

  ```
  If instClass1 Is instClass2 Then
  ```

VB6 Differences

In Visual Basic 6.0, the Then keyword was always required on lines containing the If clause. In Visual Basic .NET, it is optional except on single-line If statements.

In Visual Basic 6.0, short-circuiting operators were not supported in compound conditional expressions, and each part of the expression was evaluated. In Visual Basic .NET, this is true only of compound conditional expressions that use the And and Or logical operators.

See Also

#If . . . Then . . . #End If Directive, Choose Function, IIf Function, Select Case Statement, Switch Function

---

IIf Function

Evaluates either of two expressions and returns the result, depending on whether a conditional expression is True or False.

Member Of

Microsoft.VisualBasic.Interaction

Syntax

```
IIf(ByVal Expression As Boolean, ByVal TruePart As Object, _
    ByVal FalsePart As Object) As Object
```

Element	Description
Expression	An expression to be evaluated.
TruePart	The expression or value to return if *Expression* is True.
FalsePart	The expression or value to return if *Expression* is False.

Return Value

TruePart if *expression* is True; *FalsePart* otherwise.

Comments

Regardless of whether *Expression* is True or False, both *TruePart* and *FalsePart* are evaluated. This means that any methods called by both *TruePart* and *FalsePart* are executed. If these method calls are time-consuming, the performance of the IIf function degrades accordingly. In addition, these method calls can have undesirable side effects (and also limit the utility of the function). For instance, the seemingly innocuous code

```
Dim result As Integer = CInt(IIf(x > 0, y \ x, 0))
```

is designed to prevent a division by zero error. But if x is 0, a DivideByZeroException always is thrown, because the expression in *TruePart* is always evaluated (and the division by zero performed) whether or not x is 0.

The IIf function is really just a shorthand form of the If . . . Else . . . End If construct. For example, the IIf function in the previous comment could be written using an If statement as follows:

```
Dim result As Integer
If x > 0 Then
    result = y \ x
Else
    result = 0
End If
```

See Also

If . . . Then . . . End If Statement

Implements Keyword

Indicates that a particular member of a class or structure provides the concrete implementation of a particular interface member.

Syntax

```
Implements implementsList
```

Element	Description
implementsList	A comma-separated list of interface members that the member implements. Each member in the list takes the form *interfaceName.memberName*.

Comments

The Implements keyword is used with a Function, Sub, Property, or Event statement to indicate that the particular type member provides the implementation for an interface member.

The Implements clause must appear on the same line as the Event, Function, Property, or Sub statement that it applies to. For example, if a class implements the ICustomFormatter interface, it might have a Format method that is defined as follows:

```
Public Function Format(fmt As String, arg As Object,
                formatProvider as IFormatProvider) As String _
                Implements ICustomFormatter.Format
```

The Implements keyword requires that the Implements statement be used with the member's containing class or structure to define the interface that the class or structure implements.

The signature of the member implementing the interface must be the same as that of the interface member it implements.

The Implements keyword removes the limitation that the name of the implemented member be the same as the member that it implements.

A derived class can reimplement the interfaces defined by its base class. This involves the following steps:

- Using the Implements statement to define the interfaces that the derived class is reimplementing (along with any other interfaces it is implementing).

- Use the Implements keyword for each interface member that the derived class is reimplementing. Method implementations in the base class do not have to be explicitly marked Overridable to be overridden as part of the interface reimplementation. The derived class does not have to provide a new implementation of every interface method, only of those that it wishes to reimplement; it inherits the base class implementation of all remaining interface implementations.

If the implemented member is declared Private, it can only be accessed through a variable of the interface type, rather than of the class instance implementing the interface. For example, the following example defines an interface, IAnimalSound, that has a single method, MakeSound, intended to return a string indicating an animal sound. The Dog class implements MakeSound as a private method, but it can still be called when the Dog class instance is cast to an interface object:

```
Public Interface IAnimalSound
    Function MakeSound() As String
End Interface

Public Class Dog : Implements IAnimalSound
    Private sound As String

    Public Sub New()
        sound = "bark"
    End Sub

    Private Function MakeSound() As String _
                Implements IAnimalSound.MakeSound
        Return sound
    End Function
End Class

Public Module modMain
    Public Sub Main()
        Dim animalSound As IAnimalSound
        Dim pet As New Dog
        animalSound = pet
        Console.WriteLine(animalSound.MakeSound)
    End Sub
End Module
```

Example

A base class, Canine, implements the ISound interface, which defines two members, MakeSound and MakeThreateningSound. Dog inherits from Canine and reimplements only one member of ISound, MakeSound. It relies on Canine's implementation of MakeThreateningSound rather than providing its own. The code is as follows:

```vb
Public Interface ISound
    Function MakeSound() As String
    Function MakeThreateningSound() As String
End Interface

Public Class Canine : Implements ISound
    Private sound As String
    Private threatening As String

    Public Sub New()
        sound = "howl"
        threatening = "grr"
    End Sub

    Public Function MakeSound() As String _
                Implements ISound.MakeSound
        Return sound
    End Function

    Public Function MakeThreateningSound() As String _
                Implements ISound.MakeThreateningSound
        Return threatening
    End Function
End Class

Public Class Dog : Inherits Canine : Implements ISound
    Private Sound As String

    Public Sub New()
        MyBase.New()
        sound = "bark"
    End Sub

    Public Overloads Function MakeSound() As String _
                Implements ISound.MakeSound
        Return sound
    End Function
End Class

Public Module modMain
    Public Sub Main()
        Dim pet As New Dog
        Console.WriteLine(pet.MakeSound)
        Console.WriteLine(pet.MakeThreateningSound)
        Dim anim As ISound = pet
        Console.WriteLine(anim.MakeSound)
    End Sub
End Module
```

VB6 Differences

The Implements keyword is new to Visual Basic .NET. Visual Basic 6.0 required that members implementing interfaces have the same names and signatures as the interface members they were implementing.

In Visual Basic 6.0, structures (defined with the Type . . . End Type construct) were simply composite data types consisting of individual fields, and therefore their members could not implement interfaces. In Visual Basic .NET, on the other hand, structures (defined with the Structure . . . End Strucutre construct) can implement interfaces.

Visual Basic 6.0 did not allow classes to implement events defined in interfaces.

See Also

Event Statement, Function Statement, Implements Statement, Interface Statement, Property Statement, Sub Statement

Implements Statement

Indicates that a class or structure provides an implementation for one or more interfaces.

Syntax

```
Implements interfaceName [, ...]
```

Element	Description
interfaceName	The name of an interface.

Comments

A single Implements statement can be used to indicate that a class or structure implements multiple interfaces. There is no practical limit on the number of interfaces that can be implemented.

interfaceName can only be the name of an interface; it cannot be the name of a class.

A class or structure that implements an interface must also provide an implementation for each of its members. They do this by defining a member whose signature and return type correspond to that of the interface member, and including the Implements keyword in its definition.

Failing to provide an implementation for an interface member generates a compiler error.

The Implements statement can be used only in a class (defined by the Class . . . End Class construct) or structure (defined by the Structure . . . End Structure construct). It cannot be used in a standard module (defined by the Module . . . End Module construct).

A class or structure member definition indicates which member implements a particular interface member by using the Implements keyword.

A derived class automatically inherits the interface implementations of its base class; it does not have to reimplement inherited interface members. However, selected members can be reimplemented; see the Implements Keyword entry for an example.

In VB6, interface implementation was used as a means of circumventing Visual Basic's lack of inheritance. (Visual Basic 6.0 allowed you to implement classes as well as interfaces.) Inheritance and interface implementation, however, are quite different. Inheritance defines an IS

A relationship or an IS A KIND OF relationship; interface implementation defines a HAS A or CAN DO relationship (that is, a relationship defined by a contract). For example, a Dog that inherits from Animal IS an Animal; it does not have an Animal or do an Animal. A Dog that implements IDispose isn't a Disposer; it CAN Dispose. Since Visual Basic .NET does support inheritance, interface implementation should not be used instead of inheritance or as a way of circumventing single inheritance in Visual Basic .NET.

Example

The example defines a simple class, Customer, that consists of Name and Balance properties. To produce a report listing customers in descending order by balance, Customer objects are stored in a generic List(Of Customer) object. Because .NET has no intrinsic knowledge of how to compare our Customer objects, we must provide it. The example defines a BalanceDescComparer class that implements the generic IComparer(Of Customer) interface. IComparer requires that we implement a single method, Compare, which takes two arguments of type Customer. It returns a 1 if the first is to be considered greater than (i.e., come after) the second, 0 if they are equal, and –1 if the first is to be considered less than the second. An instance of BalanceDescComparer is then passed as an argument to the Sort method of the generic List object.

```vb
Public Module modMain
    Public Sub Main()
        ' Add customers to a generic list of Customer
        Dim customers As New List(Of Customer)
        Dim cust1 As New Customer("Bob", 16334.16d)
        customers.Add(cust1)
        Dim cust2 As New Customer("Bill", 14094.17d)
        customers.Add(cust2)
        Dim cust3 As New Customer("Bart", 21896.94d)
        customers.add(cust3)

        ' Sort the array using custom IComparer interface
        customers.Sort(New BalanceDescComparer)
        For Each cust As Customer In Customers
            Console.WriteLine("{0}:    {1}", cust.Name, cust.Balance)
        Next
    End Sub
End Module
Public Class Customer
    Dim custName As String
    Dim custBalance As Decimal

    Public Sub New(name As String, balance As Decimal)
        Me.custName = Name
        Me.custBalance = Balance
    End Sub

    Public Property Name() As String
        Get
            Return Me.custName
        End Get
```

```
      Set
          Me.custName = Value
      End Set
   End Property

   Public Property Balance() As Decimal
      Get
          Return Me.custBalance
      End Get
      Set
          Me.custBalance = Value
      End Set
   End Property
End Class

' Compare balances in descending order
Public Class BalanceDescComparer
   Implements IComparer(Of Customer)

   Public Function Compare(x As Customer, y As Customer) As Integer _
      Implements IComparer(Of Customer).Compare
      ' Return -1 if x > y
      If x.Balance > y.Balance Then
         Return -1
      ' Return 0 if x = y
      ElseIf x.Balance = y.Balance Then
         Return 0
      ' x must be < y, return 1
      Else
         Return 1
      End If
   End Function
End Class
```

VB6 Differences

In addition to any interfaces that a class implemented, Visual Basic 6.0 automatically defined a default interface for each class that consisted of its public members. This made it possible to define a class that implemented the interfaces of other classes. In contrast, Visual Basic .NET allows you to implement interfaces only, and not classes.

See Also

Implements Keyword, Interface Statement

Imports Statement

Allows a type or another namespace to be referenced in code without its fully qualified namespace name.

Syntax

```
Imports [ aliasName = ] namespace
```

or

```
Imports [ aliasName = ] namespace.element
```

Element	Description
aliasName	The name by which *namespace* is referenced in code in place of its fully qualified name. *aliasName* is useful to unambiguously identify a namespace if the use of unqualified type names would otherwise produce a naming conflict. If it is absent, *namespace* or *element* can be referenced without qualification.
namespace	The fully qualified name of the namespace to be imported.
element	The name of an enumeration, structure, class, or module declared in *namespace* that can be referenced without qualification.

Comments

If it is present, the Imports statement or statements must immediately follow the Option Strict statement and precede any Namespace or type definition statements.

A single Imports statement can import only one namespace. For each namespace that you want to import, use separate Imports statements. There is no limit to the number of Imports statements that can be used.

If the second syntax is used and *namespace.element* is specified, no namespaces are imported, but the members of a single enumeration, class, structure, or module within that namespace can be referenced without qualification. For example, the code

```
Imports System.Windows.Forms.MessageBoxButtons

Module modMsgBox
    Public Sub Main()
        If DialogResult.Yes = MessageBox.Show("Do you wish to continue?", _
                            "Continue", YesNo)
            DoSomething()
        End If
    End Sub

    Private Sub DoSomething()
        ' code to execute goes here
    End Sub
End Module
```

generates two compiler errors because the compiler cannot resolve the references to DialogResult and MessageBox, even though it is able to locate System.Windows.Forms.MessageBoxButtons. To resolve the problem and compile this code, we'd need either to provide fully qualified namespace names with DialogResult and MessageBox, or we'd need to import the System.Windows.Forms namespace. The following code, for example, adds an Imports statement so that the compiler can resolve the references and generate an executable:

```
Imports System.Windows.Forms.MessageBoxButtons
Imports System.Windows.Forms

Module modMsgBox
    Public Sub Main()
        If DialogResult.Yes = MessageBox.Show("Do you wish to continue?", _
                            "Continue", YesNo)
            DoSomething()
        End If
    End Sub

    Private Sub DoSomething()
        ' code to execute goes here
    End Sub
End Module
```

The Imports *namespace.element* syntax cannot be used to reference instance members of a class or structure. Instead, it can be used to reference members of an enumeration without referencing the enumeration itself, as well as to reference static members of a class or structure.

Often, references and Imports statements are confused with one another, but they're not directly related. A reference tells the compiler that it requires a particular assembly in order to early-bind to some of the types used in the code. To locate the types in that assembly, the compiler needs to be told exactly where to find them. To do this, it ordinarily requires a fully qualified namespace name. The Imports statement, however, provides a namespace that the compiler can search to resolve references that it would otherwise be unable to resolve. To put it another way, the Imports statement does not make a namespace available; adding a reference to the assembly does that. The Imports statement simply removes the requirement that references to types contain within a designated namespace be fully qualified.

A number of namespaces are imported automatically either by the Visual Basic 2005 command-line compiler or by Visual Basic projects in Visual Studio. Some of these are shown in the following table:

Project	Namespaces Automatically Imported
Command-Line Compiler	Microsoft.VisualBasic System
Visual Studio Windows Application	Microsoft.VisualBasic System System.Collections System.Collections.Generic System.Diagnostics System.Drawing System.Windows.Forms

Project	Namespaces Automatically Imported
Visual Studio Class Library	Microsoft.VisualBasic System System.Collections System.Collections.Generic System.Data System.Diagnostics
Visual Studio Windows Control Library	The same as a Visual Studio Windows Application, plus: System.Data
Visual Studio Console Application	The same as a Visual Studio Class Library project, plus the System.Console type is imported and its members can be accessed without explicitly referencing the Console class.
Visual Studio Device Application	The same as a Visual Studio Windows Application.
Visual Studio Web Control Library	The same as a Visual Studio Class Library, plus: System.Management
ASP.NET Web Site	System System.Collections System.Collections.Specialized System.Configuration System.Text System.Text.RegularExpressions System.Web System.Web.Caching System.Web.SessionState System.Web.Security system.Web.Profile System.Web.UI System.Web.UI.WebControls System.Web.UI.WebControls.WebParts System.Web.UI.HtmlControls
ASP.NET Web Service	Same as ASP.NET Web Site

Visual Studio provides an additional way besides the Imports statement to define imported namespaces. It you open the project's Properties dialog (in Solution Explorer, right-click the project and select Properties from the pop-up menu, or select <project> Properties from the main Visual Studio Project menu) and select its References tab (see Figure 8-13), you can enter or select the namespaces you'd like to import.

VB6 Differences

The Imports statement is new to Visual Basic .NET. Visual Basic 6.0 did not recognize an organization of external types into namespaces.

See Also

Namespace Statement

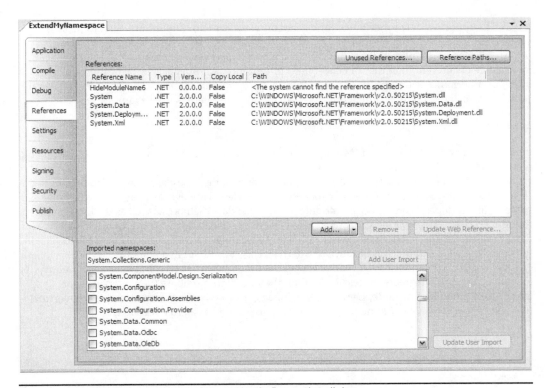

FIGURE 8-13   The References tab of the project's Properties dialog

Inherits Statement

Indicates that the current class or interface is derived from a base class and therefore inherits its members.

Syntax

```
Inherits typename
```

Element	Description
typename	The name of the class or interface from which the current class or interface is derived.

Comments

The Inherits statement can be used in either a class or interface definition (the Class . . . End Class construct or the Interface . . . End Interface construct), since only classes and interfaces can directly inherit from another type. Inherits must be the first statement immediately following the Class or Interface statement.

.NET supports single inheritance for classes only: a class can only inherit directly from a single class.

An interface can "inherit" from multiple interfaces. However, the meaning of interface inheritance is different than that of class-based inheritance. An interface is a contract, and interface inheritance is design by contract. Interfaces do not inherit base interfaces, but rather are contracts which require that other contracts also be implemented. So, for example:

```
Interface IMovement : Inherits IMotion
```

indicates that an implementor of IMovement must also implement IMotion, not that IMovement is an extension of IMotion.

Inheritance makes the members (and the functionality) of the base class available to the derived class and to instance members (i.e., clients) of the derived class. However, exactly what it is that's made available depends on the access modifier of the base class method, as well as the location of the derived class. Table 8-11 indicates what base class methods can be called from a derived class in the same assembly, from a derived class in a different assembly, from an instance of a derived class in the same assembly, and from an instance of a derived class in a different assembly.

A derived class cannot have broader access than the class from which it inherits. Similarly, its members cannot have greater accessibility than the inherited members they override. For example, in the following code, DerivedClass inherits from BaseClass and attempts to override the latter's friend GetClassName method with a public GetClassName method:

```
Public Class BaseClass
    Protected Overridable Function GetClassName() As String
        Return "BaseClass"
    End Function
End Class

Public Class DerivedClass
    Inherits BaseClass

    Public Overrides Function GetClassName() As String
        Return "DerivedClass"
    End Function
End Class
```

Access Level of Base Class Member	Derived Class in Same Assembly	Derived Class in Different Assembly	Derived Class Instance in Same Assembly	Derived Class Instance in Different Assembly
Private	No	No	No	No
Friend	Yes	No	Yes	No
Protected	Yes	Yes	No	No
Protected Friend	Yes	Yes	Yes	No
Public	Yes	Yes	Yes	Yes

TABLE 8-11   Accessibility of Base Class Methods

TABLE 8-12
Indirect Inheritance
of .NET Types

Category of Type	Indirectly Inherits From
Class	System.Object
Structure	System.ValueType
Enumeration	System.Enum
Delegate	System.Delegate or System.MulticastDelegate
Interface	none

However, because the override has broader access than the overridden method, the compiler generates error BC30266, "'Public Overrides Function GetClassName() As String' cannot override 'Protected Overridable Function GetClassName() As String' because they have different access levels."

Although only classes and interfaces can directly inherit from another class or interface, all types except interfaces indirectly inherit from a .NET base class. These types and their base classes are shown in Table 8-12.

Example

The following code defines a base class, Vehicle, with two properties: Wheels and Name. A second class, MotorVehicle, inherits from Vehicle and defines a property, Cylinders. The Cylinder, Wheels, and Name properties are all accessible through the MotorVehicle object instance.

```
Public MustInherit Class Vehicle
    Private numberOfWheels As Integer
    Private vehicleName As String

    Public Property Wheels As Integer
        Get
            Return numberOfWheels
        End Get
        Set
            numberOfWheels = Value
        End Set
    End Property

    Public Property Name As String
        Get
            Return vehicleName
        End Get
        Set
            vehicleName = Value
        End Set
    End Property
End Class

Public Class MotorVehicle
    Inherits Vehicle
```

```
    Private numberOfCylinders As Integer

    Public Property Cylinders As Integer
        Get
            Return numberOfCylinders
        End Get
        Set
            numberOfCylinders = Value
        End Set
    End Property
End Class

Public Module InheritanceTest
    Public Sub Main()
        Dim motorcycle As New Motorvehicle
        motorcycle.Name = "motorcycle"
        motorcycle.Wheels = 2
        motorcycle.Cylinders = 2
        Console.WriteLine("A {0} has {1} wheels and a {2}-cylinder engine.", _
                        motorcycle.name, _
                        motorcycle.Wheels, _
                        motorcycle.Cylinders)
    End Sub
End Module
```

VB6 Differences

The Inherits statement is new to Visual Basic .NET. Visual Basic 6.0 did not support inheritance.

See Also

Class Statement, Implements Statement, Interface Statement, MustInherit Keyword, NotInheritable Keyword

---

Input Subroutine

Reads delimited data from a sequential file and assigns it to a variable.

Member Of

Microsoft.VisualBasic.FileSystem

Syntax

```
Input(FileNumber As Integer, ByRef Value As Object)
```

Element	Description
FileNumber	The file number used in the call to the FileOpen subroutine.
Value	The variable to which the data read from the file is to be assigned. Value cannot be an array or an object variable.

Comments

Input is one of a series of related file input and output functions that works with a file number used when opening a file with the FileOpen subroutine. It is primarily intended to be used with files containing delimited written by the Write subroutine.

Input is an input function for use with sequential files only; if you attempt to use it with binary or random files, Input throws an IOException.

Once Input reads a data item, the file pointer advances to the next delimited data item. For numeric data, Input translates the string representation of a number to the data type of *Value*; for string data, it simply assigns the data it reads to *Value*. Other delimited data are translated as shown in the following table:

Data	Value
Delimiting comma or blank line	" "
#TRUE# or #FALSE#	True or False
#yyyy-mm-dd hh:mm:ss#	Date
#NULL#	DBNull

If you attempt to read past the end of the file, Input throws an EndOfStreamException.

Example

The following example writes data in a two-dimensional array to a file and then reads the data back. The file creation procedure begins by writing the upper bound of the first and second dimensions of the array before writing each element of the array itself. The code that reads the file also reads the data on the array bounds, which it uses to declare the array before reading its values.

The following is the procedure that writes the delimited data:

```
Public Sub Main()
    Const FILENAME As String = ".\Input.dat"
    Dim data(,) As Integer = {{300, 140}, {200, 120}, {100, 80}, _
                              {400, 200}, {600, 450}}
    Dim fn As Integer = FreeFile()
    Dim fileOpened As Boolean = False
    Dim bounds() As Integer = {UBound(data, 1), UBound(data, 2)}
    Try
        FileOpen(fn, FILENAME, OpenMode.Output, OpenAccess.Write)
        fileOpened = True
        Write(fn, UBound(data, 1), UBound(data, 2))
        For ctr As Integer = LBound(data, 1) To UBound(data, 1)
            Write(fn, data(ctr, 0), data(ctr, 1))
        Next
    Catch e As Exception
        Console.WriteLine(e.GetType().Name & ": " & e.Message)
    Finally
        If fileOpened Then FileClose(fn)
    End Try
End Sub
```

The following procedure then reads the data:

```
Public Sub Main()
    Const FILENAME As String = ".\Input.dat"

    Dim upper1, upper2 As Integer
    Dim arrMember As Integer
    Dim fileOpened As Boolean = False
    Dim fn As Integer = FreeFile()
    ' Open file
    Try
        FileOpen(fn, FILENAME, OpenMode.Binary, OpenAccess.Read)
        fileOpened = True
        ' Get upper bound of first dimension
        Input(fn, upper1)
        Console.WriteLine("Upper bound of first dimension is {0}", upper1)
        ' Get upper bound of second dimension
        Input(fn, upper2)
        Console.WriteLine("Upper bound of first dimension is {0}", upper1)
        Dim arr(upper1, upper2) As Integer
        For outerCtr As Integer = 0 To upper1
            For innerCtr As Integer = 0 To upper2
                Input(fn, arr(outerCtr, innerCtr))
            Next
        Next
    Catch e As Exception
        Console.WriteLine(e.GetType().Name & ": " & e.Message)
    Finally
        If fileOpened Then FileClose(fn)
    End Try
End Sub
```

VB.NET Changes

The Input subroutine in Visual Basic .NET corresponds to the Visual Basic 6.0 Input # statement.

See Also

FileClose Subroutine, FileOpen Subroutine, Write Subroutine

InputBox Function

Displays a dialog with a TextBox control that prompts the user for input.

Member Of

Microsoft.VisualBasic.Interaction

Syntax

```
InputBox(ByVal Prompt As String, Optional ByVal Title As String = "", _
        Optional ByVal DefaultResponse As String = "",
        Optional ByVal Xpos As Integer = -1, _
        Optional ByVal YPos As Integer = -1) As String
```

Element	Description
Prompt	The message or prompt to the user that appears in the dialog box. A prompt in an input box is shown in Figure 8-14.
Title	The window caption of the dialog box. A title in an input box is shown in Figure 8-14.
DefaultResponse	The text displayed in the dialog's text box when it is displayed, and the return value of the function if the user selects the OK button without entering text in the text box.
XPos	The distance in twips from the left edge of the screen to the left edge of the dialog. If omitted, the dialog is centered horizontally.
YPos	The distance in twips from the top edge of the screen to the top edge of the dialog. If omitted, the dialog is centered vertically.

Return Value

Any one of the following:

- The string entered by the user.
- *DefaultResponse* if the user makes no entry but selects the OK button.
- String.Empty if the user clicks the Cancel button.

Comments

Prompt can contain approximately 1000 characters, which should be more than adequate for virtually all purposes.

Text in *Prompt* can be broken into individual lines and blank lines can be inserted between lines of text by using the vbCrLf or ControlChars.CrLf constants.

If *Title* is omitted, the application name is used for the dialog box caption.

It is important to provide a default value. If you do not, you will be unable to distinguish between the user's pressing OK without entering text and the user's clicking the Cancel button.

You can test whether the user selected the Cancel button by comparing the InputBox function's return value with String.Empty. For example:

```
Dim prompt As String = "Enter a number: " & vbCrLf & _
                       "(Or click cancel to exit.)"
Do While True
    Dim stringNumber As String = InputBox(prompt)
    if stringNumber = String.Empty Then Exit Sub
Loop
```

FIGURE 8-14
An InputBox displaying the Prompt and Title arguments

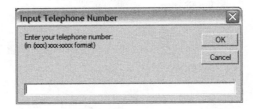

InputBox doesn't provide any data validation or data masking facilities but simply returns whatever the user has entered in the input box function's text box as a string. If Option Strict is on, you must then convert the string to the desired data type.

Since attempting to process invalid user data will generate exceptions in your application, you should validate the string returned by the InputBox function before attempting to convert it to another data type or using it.

Before attempting to convert a string returned by InputBox to another data type, you can call the following conversion validation functions:

- The IsNumeric function, to determine whether you can successfully convert the string representation of a number to an integral or floating point value. Each of the numeric data types (Byte, Decimal, Double, Integer, Long, Short, Single, SByte, UInteger, ULong, and UShort) also has a TryParse method that attempts to convert the string representation of a number of that data type. If the conversion succeeds, the method returns True; otherwise, it returns False.

- The IsDate function, to determine whether you can successfully convert the string representation of a date to a Date data type, or the Date.TryParse method, which attempts to convert the string representation of a Date to a Date and returns a Boolean value indicating whether it was able to successfully perform the conversion.

- The Boolean.TryParse method, which attempts to convert the string representation of a Boolean to a Boolean. It returns a Boolean value indicating whether it was able to successfully perform the conversion.

VB6 Differences

The Visual Basic 6.0 version of the InputBox function had a *helpfile* parameter immediately after *ypos* that allowed you to specify a filename containing help for the dialog. It was followed by a context parameter that allowed you to specify the context ID of a topic in *helpfile*. If both *helpfile* and *context* were present, the dialog included a Help button beneath the Cancel button that the user could select for information about the dialog. In Visual Basic .NET, neither of these parameters is supported, nor is it possible to include a Help button on the dialog produced by the InputBox function.

See Also

MsgBox Function

InputString Function

Returns a string value from a file opened in binary or sequential mode.

Member Of

Microsoft.VisualBasic.FileSystem

Syntax

```
InputString(ByVal FileNumber As Integer, ByVal CharCount As Integer) As String
```

Element	Description
FileNumber	The file number used in the call to the FileOpen subroutine.
CharCount	The number of characters to read.

Return Value

A String containing the next *CharCount* characters from the file pointer.

Comments

InputString is one of a series of related file input and output functions that works with a file number used when opening a file with the FileOpen subroutine. It is primarily intended to be used with files written by the Print and FilePut subroutines.

InputString is an input function for use with binary and sequential files only; it does not work with random files.

InputString reads *CountChar* characters from the current position of the file pointer. Unlike the Input function, it reads all characters, including white space characters and special characters (such as the characters in the ControlChars enumeration). When it finishes, it advances the position of the file pointer by *CountChar* characters.

According to the documentation, attempting to read data from a binary file until the EOF function returns True throws an exception. Instead, the documentation recommends that the return value of the Loc function be compared with that of the LOF function, as in the following code fragment:

```
Do While Loc(fn) < LOF(fn)
```

However, we have not experienced difficulties with the EOF function.

InputString always attempts to read *CharCount* characters from the current record pointer. If there are not *CharCount* characters remaining in the file, InputString throws an exception.

Whether it reads from a binary or a sequential file, InputString must read data that was written as string data.

Example

The example illustrates the use of the InputString function to read data on the voter registration rate for income groups in the United States during the 2004 Presidential election. The data is written to a file as strings using the FilePut subroutine, as the following code illustrates:

```
Public Sub Main()
    Const FILENAME As String = ".\InputString.dat"

    Dim incomeRange() As String = {"Under $10,000", "$10,000 to $14,999", _
                        "$15,000 to $19,999", "$20,000 to $29,999", _
                        "$30,000 to $39,999", "$40,000 to $49,999", _
                        "$50,000 to $74,999", "$75,000 to $99,999", _
                        "$100,000 to $149,999", "Over $150,000"}
    Dim voterRate() As Decimal = {49.5d, 49.0d, 53.9d, 58.1d, 62.9d, 69.8d, _
                        75.6d, 79.4d, 82.2d, 82.6d}
    Dim fn As Integer = FreeFile
    Dim fileOpened As Boolean = False
```

```
    Try
        FileOpen(fn, FILENAME, OpenMode.Binary, OpenAccess.Write)
        fileOpened = True
        For ctr As Integer = LBound(incomeRange, 1) To UBound(incomeRange, 1)
            FilePut(fn, incomeRange(ctr).PadRight(20))
            FilePut(fn, CStr(voterRate(ctr)).PadRight(6))
        Next
    Catch e As Exception
        Console.WriteLine(e.GetType().Name & ": " & e.Message)
    Finally
        If fileOpened Then FileClose(fn)
    End Try
End Sub
```

The following code then uses the InputString function to read the data from the file and then outputs it to the console:

```
Public Structure VoterRegistrationRate
    <vbFixedString(20)> Public IncomeLevel As String
    Public RegistrationRate As Decimal
End Structure

Public Sub Main()
    Const FILENAME As String = ".\InputString.dat"

    Dim regData As New VoterRegistrationRate
    Dim income, regRate As String
    Dim fn As Integer = FreeFile
    Dim fileOpened As Boolean = False
    Try
        FileOpen(fn, FILENAME, OpenMode.Binary, OpenAccess.Read)
        fileOpened = True
        Do While Not EOF(fn)
            income = InputString(fn, 20)
            regRate = InputString(fn, 6)
            regData.IncomeLevel = income
            regData.RegistrationRate = CDec(regRate)
            ShowData(regData)
        Loop
    Catch e As Exception
        Console.WriteLine(e.GetType().Name & ": " & e.Message)
    Finally
        If fileOpened Then FileClose(fn)
    End Try
End Sub

Private Sub ShowData(voterReg As VoterRegistrationRate)
    Console.WriteLine("{0}: {1}", voterReg.IncomeLevel, voterReg.RegistrationRate)
End Sub
```

VB6 Differences

Although InputString is new to Visual Basic .NET, it closely corresponds to the Input, Input$, InputB, and InputB$ functions in Visual Basic 6.0. (This set of function is unrelated to the Visual Basic 6.0 Input # statement, which wrote delimited data to a binary or sequential file.)

In Visual Basic 6.0, the Input$ and InputB$ functions returned a string, whereas the Input and InputB functions returned a variant. In Visual Basic .NET, variants are not supported, so the single version of the function, InputString, returns a string.

In Visual Basic 6.0, *FileNumber* could be preceded by an optional # symbol. In Visual Basic .NET, this syntax is not supported.

The order of parameters in the Visual Basic 6.0 and Visual Basic .NET versions of the function is reversed.

See Also

FileOpen Subroutine, FileClose Subroutine, Input Subroutine, LineInput Function

InStr Function

Indicates the starting position of a substring within a larger string.

Member Of

Microsoft.VisualBasic.Strings

Syntax

```
InStr(ByVal String1 As String, ByVal String2 As String, _
      Optional ByVal Compare As CompareMethod) As Integer
```

or

```
InStr(ByVal Start As Integer, ByVal String1 As String, _
      ByVal String2 As String, _
      Optional ByVal Compare As CompareMethod) As Integer
```

Element	Description
Start	The position of the character in *String1* to begin the search. *Start* can range from 1 to the length of *String1*. If it is 0 or less, InStr throws an ArgumentException; if it is greater than the length of *String1*, the function returns 0.
String1	The string to search.
String2	The substring to search for in *String1*.
Compare	A member of the CompareMethod enumeration indicating how characters should be compared. Possible values are CompareMethod.Binary for a binary (case sensitive) comparison and CompareMethod.Text for a text (case insensitive) comparison.

Return Value

The starting character position of *String2* within *String1*, or 0 if *String2* is not found in *String1*.

Comments

You may have noticed that the syntax for the two overloads of the InStr function doesn't list a default value, even though one is required with the use of the Optional keyword. This is because the default value is determined at runtime by the value of the Option Compare statement. For example, the InStr function in the following code

```
Option Strict On
Option Compare Text

Public Module modInStr
    Public Sub Main()
        Dim targetString As String = _
                "This is a shamefully horrendous habit, Howard!"
        Dim searchString As String = "H"
        Dim stringPos As Integer
        Do
            stringPos += 1
            stringPos = InStr(stringPos, targetString, searchString)
            If stringPos > 0 Then
                Console.WriteLine("{0} found at position {1}", _
                                searchString, stringPos)
            End If
        Loop While stringPos > 0
    End Sub
End Module
```

finds five occurrences of the string "h", as the following output shows:

```
H found at position 2
H found at position 12
H found at position 22
H found at position 33
H found at position 40
```

However, if Option Compare is changed to Binary and the code recompiled, it only finds one occurrence, as the following output shows:

```
H found at position 40
```

If the Option Compare statement is absent, its value defaults to Option Compare Binary; string comparisons are case-sensitive.

The overloaded version of the InStr function with no *Start* parameter always begins the search at the first character position in *String1*.

The return value of the InStr function actually depends on the respective values of *String1* and *String2,* as the following table shows:

Condition	Return Value
String1 is an empty string or Nothing	0
String2 is an empty string or Nothing	*Start*
String2 cannot be found in *String1*	0
String2 is found in *String1*	position of *String2* in *String1*
Start > Len(*String1*)	0

The InStr function is often used along with the Mid function to extract data from a string or to parse a string. This is illustrated in the example.

The InStr function is also used to determine whether a substring is present or absent in a string, and to take some action based on its presence or absence. For example, the following routine uses the InStr function to ensure that the user has entered hyphens in the proper positions of a social security number:

```
Private Function IsSSN(ssn As String) As Boolean
    ssn = Trim(ssn)
    ' Check total length
    If Len(ssn) <> 11 Then Return False

    ' Check for hyphens in positions 4 and 7
    If InStr(1, ssn, "-") <> 4 Then
        Return False
    ElseIf InStr(5, ssn, "-") <> 7 Then
        Return False
    End If

    ' Test As regular expression
    Return RegEx.IsMatch(ssn, "^\d{3}-\d{2}-\d{4}$")
End Function
```

The InStr function closely resembles the String.IndexOf instance function in the .NET Framework Class Library, which returns the position of the first occurrence of a substring within a string instance. The overloads of IndexOf allow you to specify either a Char or a string consisting of one or more characters to locate in the current string instance. You can specify the starting position for the search, and, unlike when using InStr, you can also specify the number of characters to search. The String class also includes an overloaded IndexOfAny instance method that allows you to search for the first occurrence of multiple Char or string values.

Example

The following code illustrates the use of the InStr and Mid functions to parse a string and extract each of its words. The string parsing is handled by a function named ExtractWords, which returns a generic List to the caller. Note that the same functionality could have been implemented far more efficiently by using the Visual Basic .NET Split function.

```
Private Function ExtractWords(ByVal targetString As String) As List(Of String)
    If targetString = String.Empty Then Return Nothing

    Dim words As New List(Of String)
    Dim searchString As String = " "
    ' Initialize positional indexes
    Dim currentPos As Integer = 0
    Dim startPos As Integer = 1

    Do
        ' locate next space character
        currentPos = Instr(startPos, targetString, searchstring)
        If currentPos > 0 Then
            words.Add(Mid(targetString, startPos, currentPos - startPos))
```

```
          ' increment starting position to pass previous word
          startPos = currentPos + 1
      End If
   Loop While currentPos > 0
   ' Add final word
   words.Add(Mid(targetString, startPos, Len(targetString) - startPos + 1))
   Return words
End Function
```

Each time the search string is found, the starting position for the next search is assigned a value one greater than the starting position. This allows the entire string to be searched from start to finish for all possible occurrences of the search string, and prevents the same search string from being found repeatedly, possibly resulting in an endless loop. Once the loop exits because no more instances of the search string are found, the routine still needs to deal with the final word, which is located from the final space to the end of the string.

The routine can then be called as follows, passing it the opening sentence of Nathaniel Hawthorne's *The Scarlet Letter*:

```
Public Sub Main()
   ' First sentence of Hawthorne's "The Scarlet Letter"
   Dim sentence As String = "A throng of bearded men, in sad-colored " & _
           "garments and gray, steeple-crowned hats, intermixed with women, " & _
           "some wearing hoods, and others bareheaded, was " & _
           "assembled in front of a wooden edifice, the door of " & _
           "which was heavily timbered with oak, and studded with " & _
           "iron spikes."
   Dim words As List(Of String) = ExtractWords(sentence)
   Console.WriteLine("Found {0} words:{1}", words.Count, vbCrLf)
   For Each word As String In words
      Console.Write("{0}{1}", word, " ")
   Next
End Sub
```

VB6 Differences

The Visual Basic 6.0 InStrB function, which returned the starting byte position of a substring, is no longer supported.

See Also

InStrRev Function, Mid Function, Option Compare Statement

InStrRev Function

Searches for a substring within a string from the end of the string to its front, and returns its position in the string.

Member Of

Microsoft.VisualBasic.Strings

Syntax

```
InStrRev(ByVal StringCheck As String, ByVal StringMatch As String, _
        Optional ByVal Start As Integer = -1, _
        Optional ByVal Compare As CompareMethod) As Integer
```

Element	Description
StringCheck	The string to search for a substring.
StringMatch	The substring to locate in *StringCheck*.
Start	The starting position of the search. The default value is –1, which indicates that the search begins at the last, or Len(*StringCheck*), character position.
Compare	A member of the CompareMethod enumeration indicating how characters should be compared. Possible values are CompareMethod.Binary for a binary (case sensitive) comparison and CompareMethod.Text for a text (case insensitive) comparison.

Return Value

The starting position of *StringMatch* in *StringCheck,* or 0 if *StringMatch* is not found in *StringCheck.*

Comments

The operation of InStrRev is identical to that of InStr, except that it begins its search from the end of a string rather than the beginning. If *StringMatch* is found within *StringCheck,* however, it returns the position of *StringMatch* from the beginning of *StringCheck,* just as the InStr function does.

Although the official documentation lists CompareMethod.Binary as the default value of the *Compare* argument, some qualification is in order. The default value of the *Compare* method is determined by the setting of the Option Compare statement, if it is present. If Option Compare is set to Text, text comparisons are case insensitive. If Option Compare is set to Binary, they are case sensitive. If an Option Compare statement is not present, the default is Option Compare Binary. In that case, the default value of the *Compare* argument is CompareMethod.Binary.

A value of –1 as the argument for *Start* is equivalent to Len(*StringCheck*). Any other negative value or a zero value throws an ArgumentException.

The return value of the InStrRev function actually depends on the respective values of *StringCheck* and *StringMatch,* as the following table shows:

Condition	Return Value
StringCheck is an empty string or Nothing	0
StringMatch is an empty string or Nothing	*Start*, or Len(*StringCheck*)
StringMatch cannot be found in *StringCheck*	0
StringMatch is found in *StringCheck*	position of *StringMatch* in *StringCheck*
Start > Len(*String1*)	0

InStrRev is often used with a string extraction function, such as the Mid function, to extract a substring from the end of a string. The example provides an illustration.

You can use the InStrRev function to search backward in a path and filename to extract particular components, such as the root filename or the directory containing a file. However, in .NET, these parsing operations are more easily performed by the shared members of the System.File.IO.Path class.

The InStrRev function closely resembles the String.LastIndexOf instance function in the .NET Framework Class Library, which returns the position of the last occurrence of a substring within a string instance. The overloads of LastIndexOf allow you to specify either a Char or a String consisting of one or more characters to locate in the current string instance. You can specify the starting position for the search, and unlike when using InStrRev, you can also specify the number of characters to search. The String class also includes an overloaded LastIndexOfAny instance method that allows you to search for the last occurrence of multiple Char or string values.

Example

The example modifies the source code shown in the InStr example to parse a string from end to beginning rather than from beginning to end:

```
Private Function ExtractWords(ByVal targetString As String) As List(Of String)
    If targetString = String.Empty Then Return Nothing

    Dim words As New List(Of String)
    Dim searchString As String = " "
    ' Initialize positional indexes
    Dim currentPos As Integer = 0
    Dim startPos As Integer = Len(targetString)

    Do
        ' locate next space character
        currentPos = InStrRev(targetString, searchstring, startPos)
        If currentPos > 0 Then
            words.Add(Mid(targetString, currentPos + 1, startPos - currentPos))
            ' increment starting position in front of previous space
            startPos = currentPos - 1
        End If
    Loop While currentPos > 0
    ' Add first word
    words.Add(Left(targetString, startPos))
    Return words
End Function
```

The call to the function must also be modified, since the contents of the List of String object can no longer be enumerated with a For Each . . . Next construct. Instead, for the words to appear in order, they must be enumerated from end to beginning using a For . . . Next construct:

```
Public Sub Main()
    ' First sentence of Hawthorne's "The Scarlet Letter"
    Dim sentence As String = "A throng of bearded men, in sad-colored " & _
            "garments and gray, steeple-crowned hats, intermixed with women, " & _
            "some wearing hoods, and others bareheaded, was " & _
            "assembled in front of a wooden edifice, the door of " & _
            "which was heavily timbered with oak, and studded with " & _
            "iron spikes."
```

```
    Dim words As List(Of String) = ExtractWords(sentence)
    Console.WriteLine("Found {0} words:{1}", words.Count, vbCrLf)
    If words.Count > 0 Then
        For ctr As Integer = words.Count - 1 To 0 Step - 1
            Console.Write("{0}{1}", words.Item(ctr), " ")
        Next
    End If
End Sub
```

See Also

InStr Function, Mid Function, Option Compare Statement

Int Function

Returns the integer portion of a number (i.e., truncates a number).

Member Of

Microsoft.VisualBasic.Conversion

Syntax

```
Function Int(ByVal Number As Byte) As Byte
Function Int(ByVal Number As Decimal) As Decimal
Function Int(ByVal Number As Double) As Double
Function Int(ByVal Number As Integer) As Integer
Function Int(ByVal Number As Long) As Long
Function Int(ByVal Number As Object) As Object
Function Int(ByVal Number As SByte) As SByte
Function Int(ByVal Number As Short) As Short
Function Int(ByVal Number As Single) As Single
Function Int(ByVal Number As UInteger) As UInteger
Function Int(ByVal Number As ULong) As ULong
Function Int(ByVal Number As UShort) As UShort
```

Element	Description
Number	A numeric expression to truncate to an integral value.

Return Value

An integral value of the same data type as *Number*.

Comments

The Int function works with all integral and floating point types, as well as variables of type Object that at runtime hold numeric or string representations of numeric data. Int will convert the string representation of a number to a numeric value regardless of the setting of Option Strict.

If *Number* is a string that cannot be converted to a number, the Int function throws an InvalidCastException.

The Int function always returns an integer value that is less than or equal to its argument. This means that positive fractional values are discarded (for example, if *Number* equals 10.99, Int returns 10.0), and negative decimal values are changed to the next smaller integer (for example, if *Number* equals –1.01, Int returns –2.0).

Int is generally viewed as a conversion function, but in fact it doesn't perform any type conversion. Instead, it is a math function: it simply truncates a numeric value to return its integer portion. The data type of the numeric value, however, remains unchanged.

Int is very similar in operation to the Visual Basic Fix function, which also returns the integer portion of a number. Both functions return a value of the same data that was passed to them as an argument. And both simply truncate the value of the number passed to them as an argument. If that number is positive or zero, they return an identical result. The difference lies in their handling of negative numbers: while Int returns the integer smaller than its argument, Fix returns the integer greater that its argument. For example, if passed the value –.01, Int return –1.0, while Fix returns 0.0.

As a truncation function, Int differs from rounding functions such as the shared and overloaded Math.Round and Decimal.Round methods, which round a floating point value either to the nearest integer or to the nearest number of decimal places. This truncation is termed *rounding toward negative infinity* and conforms to IEEE Standard 754, section 4.

The operation of the Int function is identical to the operation of the Decimal.Floor and Math.Floor methods in the .NET Framework Class Library.

Example

See the example for the Fix function.

See Also

CInt Function, Fix Function

Interface Statement

Defines an interface.

Syntax

```
[ <attrlist> ] [ accessModifier ] [ Shadows ] Interface name [( Of typelist )]
    [ Inherits interfacename[, interfacename ]]
    [ [ Default ] [ ReadOnly | WriteOnly ] Property membername ]
    [ Function membername ]
    [ Sub membername ]
    [ Event membername ]
End Interface
```

Element	Description
<attrlist>	A comma-separated list of attributes with their arguments that apply to the interface. Only attributes whose AttributeUsage attribute is AttributeTargets.All or AttributeTargets.Interface can be applied to an interface.
accessModifier	One of Public, Private, Protected, Friend, and Protected Friend. If *accessModifier* is not specified, an interface's access modifier is Friend by default; it is visible only in the assembly in which it is declared.

Element	Description
Shadows	Indicates that the interface hides an identically named programming element in a base class.
Of *typelist*	For an interface that supports generic types, the list of type parameters required by the interface.
Inherits	Specifies additional interfaces that implementers must implement as a necessary part of fulfilling the interface contract. Multiple interfaces can be specified with the Inherits keyword, but classes are not permitted. In addition, the Inherits keyword cannot specify any interface with a more restrictive access level than the interface being defined. (For example, a Protected Friend interface cannot inherit from a Friend interface.)
interfacename	The name of one or more interfaces inherited by the current interface.

For details on member definitions, see the entry for the member type.

Comments

An interface defines a contract that specifies a "can do" relationship or a "has a" relationship. It specifies the members and the member signatures that must be implemented to fulfill the contract, but the interface itself provides no implementation code.

The purpose of an interface is to define the instance members that types implementing that interface must make callable. Because of this, interface members do not have an access modifier, nor can they be shared.

By convention, interface names begin with an **I**.

Member definitions for interfaces include the member's definition (that is, its signature and return type) only; interfaces provide no implementation code, nor do they include any End or Exit statements (such as End Property or Exit Property, End Function or Exit Function, etc.).

Member definitions include no access modifiers, since an interface is necessarily a public interface. Practically, interface members have the same accessibility as the interface to which they belong.

Interfaces are implemented by a class by using the Implements statement. Each class method that implements a member of the interface must also be identified by using the Implements keyword. The signatures and return types of implementing members must match the interface definitions. However, the user of the Implements keyword removes the restriction that the interface name and the name of the implementing method also match.

If an interface inherits from one or more interfaces, the class implementing the interface must also implement all of its inherited members. (This means that inheritance, when applied to interfaces, imposes a requirement that other interfaces be implemented; it is not a mechanism for sharing implementation code.)

The Implements keywords of the members implementing inherited interface members can identify them either as members of the derived interface or base interface.

Interfaces are commonly used in the .NET Framework Class Library to implement some service or functionality that is common to a number of types but whose implementation can vary. For example, it's clear how to compare integral or floating point values, but what if you want to compare two instances of the Widget class? You can define how the comparison works, however, by implementing the IComparer interface and its single member, Compare. Then whenever two objects are compared, the .NET runtime calls the Compare method to determine whether one object is "greater" or "less" than the other or whether they are equal. Similarly, software add-ins often work by implementing particular interfaces that the application environment within which they're running can call.

Interfaces are sometimes used for versioning. Do not do that! For example, the first version of a product might define an interface named IMyInterface. The second version would define an interface named IMyInterface2 that is a superset of (inherits from) IMyInterface. For each subsequent version, there is a new interface that is a superset of the previous interface. (Needless to say, this can become as cumbersome as it is confusing after several versions have been released.) The application's class library can then be called through its interfaces. For example, developers using version 1 can write code like:

```
Dim interfaceVar As IMyInterface = New MyApplicationClass()
```

while developers using version 2 can write code like:

```
Dim interfaceVar As IMyInterface2 = New MyApplicationClass()
```

This ensures that applications developed using version 1 interfaces can run on both versions 1 and 2, although applications developed using version 2 may not necessarily run on version 1. The .NET Framework Class Library does not use interfaces in this way.

An interface, unlike the other categories of .NET types, does not implicitly inherit from any class. That means that common methods, such as GetType and ToString, that you might expect to always be callable are not available in interface types. For example, the following is a very simple interface named IDisplay that has only one member, Show:

```
Public Interface IDisplay
    Sub Show(value As Object)
End Interface
```

The interface can then be implemented as follows, in this case by a class named Display with only one member, Show, which implements IDisplay.Show:

```
Public Class Display
    Implements IDisplay

    Public Sub Show(value As Object) Implements IDisplay.Show
        Console.WriteLine(value)
    End Sub
End Class
```

We can then declare a variable to be of the interface type and instantiate it using the constructor of a class that implements the interface. The following code does that and then attempts to call the GetType method, which is a member of System.Object and therefore, we might assume, is available to all .NET types:

```
Public Module modMain
    Public Sub Main()
        Dim disp As IDisplay = New Display()
        Console.WriteLine(disp.GetType.Name)
    End Sub
End Module
```

This code, however, fails to compile because "'GetType' is not a member of 'IDisplay'." However, we can call GetType (or any method implemented by the Object class) if we first case the interface variable to an object, as the following code illustrates:

```
Public Module modMain
   Public Sub Main()
      Dim disp As IDisplay = New Display()
      Console.WriteLine(CObj(disp).GetType.Name)
   End Sub
End Module
```

Example

Most books published throughout the world are uniquely identified by an ISBN (International Standard Book Number). The ISBN, in turn, could be viewed as part of a more general system of identification codes for publications. Therefore, we could define an IIdentifier interface for publications that classes such as Book, Newspaper, Magazine, and Journal implement. The interface definition might appear as follows:

```
Public Interface IIdentifier
   ReadOnly Property Length() As Integer
   ReadOnly Property ExtraChars() As Char()
   Function Validate(identifier As String) As Boolean
End Interface.
```

We could then define a class, Book, that implements the interface by providing code that applies to ISBNs:

```
Public Class Book : Implements IIdentifier
   Private bookTitle As String
   Private ISBNLength As Integer = 10
   Private chars() As Char = {"-"c}

   Public Sub New(title As String)
      Me.bookTitle = title
   End Sub

   Public ReadOnly Property Title() As String
      Get
         Return Me.bookTitle
      End Get
   End Property

   Public ReadOnly Property ISBN() As String
      Get
         Return Me.bookID
      End Get
   End Property

   Public ReadOnly Property Length As Integer _
               Implements IIdentifier.Length
      Get
         Return ISBNLength
      End Get
   End Property
```

```
     Public ReadOnly Property ExtraChars() As Char() _
                     Implements IIdentifier.ExtraChars
        Get
             Return chars
        End Get
     End Property

     Public Function Validate(identifier As String) As Boolean _
           Implements IIdentifier.Validate
        ' check if identifier.length - extrachars = length
        ' verify checksum
        Return True
     End Function
End Class
```

A general validation program could then call the Validate function when a new instance of Book is being instantiated to check that its ISBN is valid. It wouldn't care that it was instantiating a Book object as opposed to a Newspaper object or Journal object. Instead, it would simply call the Validate method implemented by the interface, which therefore is the appropriate Validate method for an instance of the Book class.

VB.NET Changes

Visual Basic .NET as of Version 2005 supports the use of generic parameters with interfaces.

VB6 Differences

The Interface . . . End Interface statement is new to Visual Basic .NET. Although Visual Basic 6.0 allowed you to define interfaces, they were class modules (.cls files) whose members had no implementation.

In Visual Basic 6.0, the Implements statement defined the interfaces implemented by a class, as it does in Visual Basic .NET. However, the Implements keyword, which identifies the members that implement particular interface members, is new to Visual Basic 6.0. As a result, the names of class members that implemented interface members had to match.

Although Visual Basic 6.0 interfaces had no code, they did have complete skeleton definitions that included the End Statement (End Function, End Property, etc.). In Visual Basic .NET, the use of End statements is not supported.

See Also

Class Statement, Implements Keyword, Implements Statement

IPmt, NPer, and PPmt Functions

Calculates the interest payment, number of payment periods, and principal payment, respectively, for a specific period of an annuity based on periodic, fixed payments and a fixed interest rate.

Member Of

Microsoft.VisualBasic.Financial

Syntax

```
IPmt(ByVal Rate As Double, ByVal Per As Double, ByVal NPer As Double, _
    ByVal PV As Double, Optional ByVal FV As Double = 0, _
    Optional ByVal Due As DueDate = DueDate.EndOfPeriod) As Double

NPer(ByVal Rate As Double, ByVal Pmt As Double, ByVal PV As Double, _
    Optional ByVal FV As Double = 0, _
    Optional ByVal Due As DueDate = DueDate.EndOfPeriod) As Double

PPmt(ByVal Rate As Double, ByVal Per As Double, ByVal NPer As Double, _
    ByVal PV As Double, Optional ByVal FV As Double = 0, _
    Optional ByVal Due As DueDate = DueDate.EndOfPeriod) As Double
```

Element	Description
Rate	The interest rate per period, expressed as a decimal rather than a percentage. For example, an interest rate of 12 percent per year is 1 percent per month, which equals a Rate of .01.
Per	The particular payment period whose interest payment you want to retrieve. Its value can range from 1 to the value of NPer.
Pmt	The payment to be made each period.
NPer	The total number of payment periods.
PV	The present value of a series of future payments or receipts. If PV is a liability, its value should be negative. If PV is a loan, it reflects the initial loan amount. For a savings plan, the present value can be either the current level of savings or 0.
FV	The future or cash balance after the final payment is made. If omitted, a future value of 0 is assumed, and the values returned by IPmt and PPmt reflect the interest component and principal component of a loan repayment, respectively. If FV is a liability, its value should be negative. For example, for a loan, its value is typically 0. For a savings plan, its value is the savings goal.
Due	A member of the DueDate enumeration indicating whether payments are due at the beginning (DueDate.BegOfPeriod) or end (DueDate.EndOfPeriod) of the period. If omitted, the default value is DueDate.EndOfPeriod.

Return Value

A Double indicating the interest included in the payment, the number of payments required to reach the future value, and the principal repayment included in the payment, respectively.

Comments

An *annuity* is a series of equal payments or receipts (a level stream of cash inflow or outflow) that occurs at evenly spaced intervals for a fixed period of time. Mortgage payments, lease payments, and rental payments are all examples of annuities. Typically, for an ordinary annuity, the payments or receipts occur at the end of each period, while for an annuity due they occur at the beginning of each period.

Rate is expressed as a fraction. For example, an interest rate of 1 percent per month is expressed as .01.

For the IPmt and PPmt functions, *Rate* and *NPer* must be expressed in the same time interval. For example, if the interest rate is 8 percent annually and there are 60 payments spread over five years, *NPer* equals 60 and *Rate* is expressed as a monthly interest rate of .00667.

For the NPer function, *Rate* and *Pmt* must reflect the interest rate and the amount of the payment over the same time period. If *Pmt* is the payment per month, for example, then *Rate* must be expressed as the monthly interest rate.

Typically, the *PV* argument is used in the case of loans to indicate the initial loan amount.

For the *Pmt, PV,* and *FV* arguments, cash paid out is represented by a negative value, while cash received is represented by a positive value.

While the IPmt function calculates the interest payment for a particular period, the PPmt function calculates the principal payment and the Pmt function calculates the total payment. If arguments with the same values are supplied to each of the three functions, IPmt + PPmt = Pmt.

Example

The example illustrates a mortgage calculator for a loan based on a fixed interest rate. It calls the InputBox function to prompt the user for the necessary inputs (the mortgage rate, amount, and number of payments) and then calls the IPmt, PPmt, and Pmt functions to calculate the interest amount, the principal amount, and the total amount of each payment. The results are written to a text file, mortgage.txt, in the user's My Documents directory.

```
Imports System.IO

Public Class MortgageCalc
    Public Shared Sub Main()
        Dim pv As Decimal = CDec(InputBox("Total loan amount: ", _
                        "Total Amount", "0"))
        Dim nper As Integer = CInt(InputBox("Number of payment periods: ", _
                        "Mortgage Term", "360"))
        Dim rate As Decimal = CDec(InputBox("Annual interest rate as a percent: ", _
                        "Interest Rate"))
        Calculate(rate, nper, pv)
    End Sub

    Public Shared Sub Calculate(rate As Decimal, nper As Integer, pv As Decimal)
        ' Open file
        Dim fn As String = My.Computer.FileSystem.SpecialDirectories.MyDocuments & _
                        Path.DirectorySeparatorChar & "Mortgage.txt"
        Dim sw As StreamWriter = New StreamWriter(fn)
        fileOpened = True
        ' make loan amount negative
        If Math.Abs(pv) = pv Then pv = -1 * pv
        ' convert annual rate to monthly rate
        Dim monthlyRate As Decimal = (rate / 100) / 12
        ' Output amounts
        sw.WriteLine("Payments for a {0}-year loan of {1} at {2}%:", nper/12, _
                    FormatCurrency(Math.Abs(pv)), rate)
        sw.WriteLine()
        sw.WriteLine("{0,8}{1,15}{2,15}{3,15}","Payment", "Interest", "Principal", _
                    "Total Payment")
```

```
    For per As Integer = 1 to nper
        sw.WriteLine("{0,7}.{1,15:$#,##0.00}{2,15:$#,##0.00}{3,15:$#,##0.00}", _
                    per, _
                    IPmt(monthlyRate, per, nper, pv, 0, DueDate.BegOfPeriod), _
                    PPmt(monthlyRate, per, nper, pv, 0, DueDate.BegOfPeriod), _
                    Pmt(monthlyRate, nper, pv, 0, DueDate.BegOfPeriod))
    Next
    sw.Close()
    End Sub
End Class
```

See Also

FV Function, IRR Function, MIRR Function, NPer Function, NPV Function, Pmt Function, PV Function, Rate Function

IRR Function

Determines the internal rate of return for a series of periodic cash flows composed of both payments and receipts.

Member Of

Microsoft.VisualBasic.Financial

Syntax

```
IRR(ByRef ValueArray() As Double, Optional ByVal Guess As Double = 0.1) _
    As Double
```

Element	Description
ValueArray	The cash flow values. The array must include at least one payment (expressed as a negative value) and one receipt (expressed as a positive value).
Guess	An estimated internal rate of return. If omitted, an IRR of 10 percent (0.1) is assumed

Return Value

A Double specifying the internal rate of return.

Comments

The *internal rate of return* is the interest on an investment that consists of regular payments and receipts.

The order of items in *ValueArray* indicates the order of payments and receipts. The item at index 0 is interpreted as chronologically first, while the item with the greatest index value is interpreted as chronologically last. Each item should reflect a payment or a receipt for a comparable time period.

The cash flows for each period can be variable, unlike those of an annuity, which are fixed.

The function calculates the internal rate of return by iteration, starting with *Guess,* and returns a value that is accurate within .001 percent. The function will make up to 20 iterations to calculate the internal rate of return.

Example

The example calculates the internal rate of return from the annual net income of a hypothetical small business. The result returned by the function is 31.1 percent.

```
Public Sub Main()
    Dim cashFlow() As Double = {-102450.55, -30967.12, 134.85, 82930.91, _
                                121766.18, 90345.58, 125093.16}
    Dim guess As Double = .15
    Console.WriteLine("{0}%", Math.Round(IRR(cashFlow, guess)*100,1))
End Sub
```

See Also

MIRR Function

Is Keyword

Compares two object expressions, two object types, or a test expression with another expression.

Comments

The Is keyword is used in three different contexts: alone, as an operator; with the TypeOf operator; and as one of the test conditions in a Select Case statement. In all three cases, it is used in an expression that evaluates to a Boolean (True or False) value.

Visual Basic as of Version 2005 also adds the IsNot operator, which can be used alone as an operator and with the TypeOf operator. Its use is not supported in a Select Case statement. Is Not is simply a syntactic convenience that frees developers from the need to use the potentially confusing If Not . . . Is . . . construction.

Alone as a Comparison Operator

As a comparison operator, Is is used to compare two object references to determine whether they refer to the same object. For example, the code

```
Dim fil As FileInfo = New FileInfo("readme.txt")
Dim fi2 As FileInfo = fil
Console.WriteLine(fil Is fi2)
```

returns True, because fil1 and fil2 both refer to the same FileInfo object. On the other hand, the code

```
Dim fil As FileInfo = New FileInfo("readme.txt")
Dim fi2 As FileInfo = New FileInfo("readme.txt")
Console.WriteLine(fil Is fi2)
```

returns False, even though both file1 and fil2 have identical values, because they refer to differ FileInfo objects that were created independently of one another.

Because it compares two object references, Is requires that its two arguments be reference types. An attempt to use an early-bound value type as an argument generates a compiler error.

Late-bound value types (that is, variables of type Object whose runtime type is a value type) can be used with the Is keyword, although the result of the evaluation is always False.

The Is operator is equivalent to calling the Equals method of the Object class, which is inherited (but can be overridden) by all reference types. (Note that the Equals method is also inherited by the ValueType class, which overrides it to test for an equality of values rather than of references.) For example, instead of using the Is operator to test whether the fil1 and fil2 object variables are equal, we could call the two overloads of the Object.Equals method as follows:

```
Console.WriteLine(fil.Equals(fi2))
Console.WriteLine(Object.Equals(fil, fi2))
```

The Is operator is also used to test for a null object reference using the Nothing keyword. For example, the following code tests that a string array returned by a function call has been properly initialized before using it:

```
Dim stringArray() As String = GetArray()
If stringArray Is Nothing Then
    ' handle uninitialized array
Else
    ' proceed since array is initialized
End If
```

The Is keyword can also be used to test for a valid object reference or to test whether two object references are not equal. There are two methods for doing this. The first, which works with all versions of Visual Basic from Version 4.0 through Visual Basic 2005, uses the Not operator along with Is:

```
If Not objectReference1 Is objectReference2
If Not objectReference1 Is Nothing
```

The second uses the IsNot keyword, which is new to Visual Basic 2005:

```
If objectReference1 IsNot objectReference2
If objectReference1 IsNot Nothing
```

With the TypeOf Operator

The Is operator can be used with the TypeOf operator to determine:

- The type of a variable
- The runtime type of an Object variable
- Whether a variable's type is derived from another type
- Whether a variable's type implements a particular interface

For example, the following code checks whether a variable (in this case a string array) implements the IEnumerable interface before iterating its elements:

```
Dim stringArray() As String = {"one", "two", "three"}
If TypeOf stringArray Is IEnumerable Then
    For Each stringElement As String In StringArray
        Console.WriteLine(stringElement)
    Next
End If
```

The TypeOf . . . Is construct cannot be used to evaluate the type of strongly typed (that is, early-bound) value types; it can only be used to evaluate the type of reference types and late bound types (variables declared as the Object type).

The TypeOf . . . Is construct is rarely used apart from an If statement. The expression, however, does evaluate to a Boolean, which can be assigned to a variable. For example:

```
Dim derived As Boolean = (TypeOf stringArray Is Object)
Console.WriteLine(derived)
```

You can test that a type is not a particular type, is not derived from a particular type, or does not implement a particular interface by using the Not TypeOf . . . Is construct. For example:

```
If Not TypeOf obj Is Hashtable Then
```

Note that the IsNot operator is not supported with the TypeOf operator.

Comparing a Test Expression

Is can be used in the Case statement of a Select Case statement to determine whether its comparison with the test expression is true, and therefore whether its Case code block should be executed. For example, the following Select Case statement uses the Is keyword to determine whether an integer is positive, zero, or negative:

```
Dim number As Integer = -30
Select Case number
   Case Is < 0
      Console.WriteLine("Number is negative.")
   Case Is = 0
      Console.WriteLine("Number is zero.")
   Case Is > 0
      Console.WriteLine("Number is positive.")
   Case Else
      Console.WriteLine("What kind of number are we dealing with?")
End Select
```

The use of the Is keyword with the Case statement is optional.

VB.NET Changes

In addition to the Not . . . Is . . . syntax, Visual Basic .NET supports the IsNot keyword. Two object references can be compared using the . . . IsNot . . . syntax.

VB6 Differences

In Visual Basic 6.0, the use of the Is keyword in a Case expression was required whenever the comparison of a value with the test expression involved a relationship other than equality. In Visual Basic .NET, the Is keyword is optional for all comparisons.

See Also

IsNot Keyword, Nothing Keyword

IsArray Function

Indicates whether a variable or an expression is an array.

Member Of

Microsoft.VisualBasic.Information

Syntax

```
IsArray(ByVal VarName As Object) As Boolean
```

Element	Description
VarName	A variable or expression to be evaluated.

Return Value

True if *VarName* is an array; False otherwise.

Comments

If *VarName* is an empty array or a null reference (an object variable whose value is Nothing), the IsArray function throws a NullReferenceException. To eliminate the exception that would result from passing an empty array to the IsArray function, you can pass the possible array to the IsNothing function as well. For example:

```
Dim emptyArray() As String
If Not IsNothing(emptyArray) AndAlso IsArray(emptyArray) Then
    ' Perform array operations
End If
```

IsArray does not return True when passed array-like objects as arguments. For example, if passed an ArrayList object, it returns False.

IsArray does not recognize arrays stored in non-array containers. For example, in the code

```
Dim arr() As String = {"Phillies", "76ers", "Eagles"}
Dim collec As New Collection
collec.Add(arr)
Console.WriteLine(IsArray(collec))
```

IsArray returns False.

In addition to determining whether an expression is an array, you can determine the number of dimensions it has if it is an array by retrieving the value of the Array object's Rank property. It returns a one-based integer indicating the number of dimensions in an array. For example, the code

```
Dim arr2D(,) As Object = {{"Penny", .01}, {"Nickel", .05}, {"Quarter", .25}, _
                          {"Half Dollar", .50}, {"Dollar", 1.00f}}
Console.WriteLine(arr2D.Rank)
```

returns 2.

The IsArray property the .NET Framework Class Library's Type class also allows you to determine whether a particular expression is an array. To use it, you retrieve a Type object representing the type of the variable in which you're interested, and then retrieve the value of its IsArray property. For example:

```
Dim arr() As String = {"Lions", "Pistons", "Red Wings"}
Console.WriteLine(arr.GetType().IsArray)
```

VB6 Differences

In Visual Basic 6.0, the IsArray function returned True if it was passed an uninitialized array; in Visual Basic .NET, it throws a NullReferenceException.

See Also

IsNothing Function, IsReference Function, TypeName Function, VarType Function

IsDate Function

Indicates whether an expression can be converted to the Date data type.

Member Of

Microsoft.VisualBasic.Information

Syntax

```
IsDate(ByVal Expression As Object) As Boolean
```

Element	Description
Expression	Any expression that might be converted to a Date value.

Return Value

A Boolean indicating whether Expression can be converted to a Date.

Comments

Since the Date data type consists of both a date and a time value, IsDate indicates whether *expression* contains a valid date, a valid time, or both.

The utility of the IsDate function stems from the fact that only some String data can be successfully converted. Calling the IsDate function before calling a conversion function reduces the need for and the overhead of handle conversion errors in an exception handler. For example:

```
If IsDate(stringInput) Then
    todaysDate = CDate(stringInput)
Else
    ' handle invalid case
End If
```

IsDate is extremely useful in validating user date and time input. For example, the following routine asks the user to enter a date value and performs validation on the user input. The routine exits only if the user enters a valid date or an empty string, in which case the routine returns an uninitialized Date value.

```
Private Function GetDate() As Date
    Dim inputString As String
    Dim messageText As String = MESSAGE_TEXT
    Do
        inputString = InputBox(messageText)
        If IsDate(inputString) Then
            Return CDate(inputString)
        Else
            messageText = ERR_TEXT & MESSAGE_TEXT
        End If
    Loop While Not IsDate(inputString) And inputString <> String.Empty
    Return New Date
End Function
```

By default, IsDate interprets *expression* according to the locale settings of the local computer. However, you can change the culture of the current thread so that it recognizes some other date format. (This should be done with care: other code executing on the thread may not be prepared to handle its locale suddenly changing.) For example, the following code changes the culture of the current thread to British English:

```
' Get current thread
Dim thrd As Thread = Thread.CurrentThread
' Save current culture
Dim currentCulture As CultureInfo = thrd.CurrentCulture
' Format as en-gb
Try
    thrd.CurrentCulture = New CultureInfo("en-gb")
    Dim stringDate As String = "26/01/06"
    If IsDate(stringDate) Then
        Console.WriteLine(FormatDateTime(CDate(stringDate), DateFormat.LongDate))
    End If
' Restore culture
Finally
    thrd.CurrentCulture = currentCulture
End Try
```

.NET 2.0 adds a method that combines the Visual Basic IsDate and CDate functions in a single method call. The shared Date.TryParse method attempts to convert a String to a Date and, if the conversion is successful, returns True. Its syntax is:

```
TryParse(ByVal s As String, ByRef result As DateTime) As Boolean
```

where *s* is the string to convert to a Date, and *result* is the variable to which the converted Date is assigned when the function returns.

VB6 Differences

In Visual Basic 6.0, IsDate is capable of interpreting *expression* only according to the locale settings of the local computer.

See Also

CDate Function, DateSerial Function

IsDBNull Function

Indicates whether an expression evaluates to null, typically because data is missing or invalid.

Member Of

Microsoft.VisualBasic.Information

Syntax

```
IsDBNull(ByVal Expression As Object) As Boolean
```

Element	Description
Expression	An expression to evaluate.

Return Value

True if *Expression* evaluates to DBNull; False otherwise.

Comments

IsDBNull determines whether the value of an expression is equal to System.DBNull, which is used to indicate missing data. System.DBNull is a data type with a single value, indicated by System.DBNull.Value. It is particularly useful when retrieving column values from databases; DBNull indicates that a value is missing or has never been assigned.

DBNull.Value is different from an object reference whose value is Nothing and from a String whose value is String.Empty.

You would expect that any expression that includes a DBNull value would also evaluate to DBNull, since otherwise the result of the expression is based on invalid data. Although this is how Visual Basic 6.0 and VBScript handled missing data, it is not how .NET does. For example, you would expect the call to IsDBNull in the following code to evaluate to True, since addressLine1 repesents the concatenation of a valid string with a DBNull value:

```
Dim title As String = "Mr."
Dim name As Object = DBNull.Value
Dim addressLine1 As String = title & " " & name
If IsDBNull(addressLine1) Then
    Console.WriteLine("Null value")
Else
    Console.WriteLine(addressLine1)
End If
```

Instead, it evaluates to False, and the code fragment returns the string "Mr.".

Example

The example is part of a label generation program in which a main routine calls a function named AddValue, which checks whether a field value is equal to DBNull.Value and, if it is not, adds it to the label string.

```
Imports System.Data
Imports System.Data.OleDb

Public Module modMain

    Public Sub Main()
        Dim conn As New OleDbConnection
        Dim cmd As New OleDbCommand
        Dim adapter As New OleDbDataAdapter
        Dim ds As New DataSet
        Dim dt As DataTable
        Dim dbFilename As String = "C:\Databases\contacts.mdb"
        Dim label As String = String.Empty
        ' Open database connection
        conn.ConnectionString = "Provider=Microsoft.Jet.OLEDB.4.0;Data Source=" & _
                                dbFilename & ";"
        conn.Open()
        ' Define command : retrieve all records in contact table
        cmd.CommandText = "SELECT * FROM Contact"
        cmd.Connection = conn
        adapter.Selectcommand = cmd
        ' Fill dataset
        ds.Clear()
        adapter.Fill(ds, "Contact")
        ' Close connection
        conn.Close()
        ' Get table
        dt = ds.Tables("Contact")
        ' Iterate rows of table
        For Each row As DataRow In dt.Rows
            Dim labelLen As Integer
            label = String.Empty
            label += AddValue(label, row, "Title")
            label += AddValue(label, row, "FirstName")
            label += AddValue(label, row, "MiddleInitial")
            label += AddValue(label, row, "LastName")
            label += AddValue(label, row, "Suffix")
            label += vbCrLf
            label += AddValue(label, row, "Address1")
            label += AddValue(label, row, "AptNo")
            label += vbCrLf
            labelLen = Len(label)
            label += AddValue(label, row, "Address2")
            If Len(label) <> labelLen Then label += vbCrLf
            label += Addvalue(label, row, "City")
            label += AddValue(label, row, "State")
            label += AddValue(label, row, "Zip")
            OutputLabel(label)
        Next
    End Sub
```

```
    Private Function AddValue(label As String, row As DataRow, _
                             fieldName As String) As String
        If Not IsDbNull(row.Item(fieldName)) Then
            Return CStr(row.Item(fieldName)) & " "
        Else
            Return Nothing
        End If
    End function
End Module
```

VB6 Differences

The IsDBNull function is new to Visual Basic .NET. It is roughly equivalent, however, to the Visual Basic 6.0 IsNull function, which reported whether the expression passed to it as an argument contained missing or invalid data. In Visual Basic .NET, the IsNull function is not supported.

See Also

IsNothing Function

IsError Function

Indicates whether an object is an Exception class instance.

Member Of

Microsoft.VisualBasic.Information

Syntax

```
IsError(ByVal Expression As Object) As Boolean
```

Element	Description
Expression	An object.

Return Value

True if *Expression* is an Exception object; False otherwise.

Comments

The function returns True if *Expression* is an instance of the Exception class or of a class derived from Exception.

IsError is a modernized version of a compatibility function. Some legacy Visual Basic code, rather than raising an error, returned an error from a function call. Evidently the intention behind the IsError function is that it would continue to support such a scenario. For example:

```
Public Module modError
    Public Sub Main()
        Dim number1 As Integer = 10
        Dim number2 As Integer = 0
```

```
    Dim result As Object = Divide(number1, number2)
    If IsError(result) Then
        Console.WriteLine("A {0} exception occurred", result.GetType.Name)
    Else
        Console.WriteLine("The result of the division is {0}", result)
    End If
End Sub

Private Function Divide(dividend As Integer, divisor As Integer) As Object
    If divisor = 0 Then
        Return New DivideByZeroException
    Else
        Return dividend/divisor
    End If
End Function
End Module
```

Here, the Divide function returns a DivideByZeroException object if the divisor is zero; otherwise, it returns the result of the division. Two points are worth noting about this method of error handling and the ways in which it differs from structured exception handling:

- It is up to the caller to verify that the return value is valid before using it further. Often, however, the caller neglects to do that, which often leads to exceptions later in code that are more difficult to diagnose or debug.

- Since a function must return a valid value if there is not an error and an Exception object if there is, its return type must necessarily be Object rather than a strong data type.

Raising exceptions using the Throw statement, and declaring and handling exceptions in Try . . . Catch . . . Finally blocks, offers a vastly preferable means of handling errors.

VB.NET Changes

Visual Basic 6.0 included an IsError function, which returned True if the argument passed to it was a Variant whose runtime type was vbError. It was used when the return value of a function or the value of an expression evaluated to vbError. In Visual Basic .NET, the role of the function is similar, although it determines whether the argument passed to it is an instance of the Exception class or one of its derived classes.

See Also

Try . . . Catch . . . Finally Statement

IsNot Keyword

Compares two object expressions for inequality.

Comments

The IsNot keyword is identical to using the syntax

```
If Not obj1 Is obj2
```

For details on the use of the IsNot keyword, see the section "Alone as a Comparison Operator" under the entry for the Is keyword.

VB.NET Changes

The IsNot keyword is new to Visual Basic 2005.

See Also

Is Keyword, Nothing Keyword

IsNothing Function

Indicates whether an expression contains a null object reference.

Member Of

Microsoft.VisualBasic.Information

Syntax

```
IsNothing(ByVal Expression As Object) As Boolean
```

Element	Description
Expression	An Object expression.

Return Value

True if *Expression* is a reference type to which an object is not currently assigned; False otherwise.

Comments

IsNothing is a convenience function that encapsulates a code block like the following:

```
Public Shared Function IsNothing(expression As Object) As Boolean
    Return expression Is Nothing
End Function
```

IsNothing is intended to be used with reference types only. If it is used with a value type (any of the primitive data types other than String, a .NET structure, or a Visual Basic structure defined with the Structure . . . End Structure statement), it returns False. You can call the IsReference function in conjunction with the IsNothing function if you need to determine whether *Expression* is a reference type.

Strings are reference types and therefore cannot have a valid object reference. However, there is a difference between a string whose value is Nothing and a string whose value is Empty (or ""). In the former case, the string has not been assigned a value; in the latter, its value is a null string (""). This is evident from the following code:

```
Dim str As String = String.Empty
Console.WriteLine(IsNothing(str))              ' returns False

Dim nullStr As String = Nothing
Console.WriteLine(IsNothing(nullStr))          ' returns True
```

```
Dim unassignedStr As String
Console.WriteLine(IsNothing(unassignedStr))    ' returns True
```

VB6 Differences

The IsNothing function is new to Visual Basic .NET.

See Also

Is Keyword, IsReference Function

IsNumeric Function

Indicates whether an expression is numeric or can be converted to a number.

Member Of

Microsoft.VisualBasic.Information

Syntax

```
IsNumeric(ByVal Expression As Object) As Boolean
```

Element	Description
Expression	Any expression.

Return Value

True if *expression* is numeric or can be successfully converted to a number; False otherwise.

Comments

IsNumeric returns True if *Expression* is an integral or floating point data type, a Boolean, or a string representation of a number. All other values, including Date values, return False.

IsNumeric is particularly valuable when validating numeric representations of string data input by the user. If the user is supposed to input only numeric data and IsNumeric returns False, you know that the user has input invalid data and that conversion would fail.

IsNumeric is locale-aware, and recognizes localized currency symbols, thousands separators, and decimal points. By default, IsNumeric interprets currency symbols according to the locale settings of the local computer. However, IsNumeric will recognize the locale settings of the current thread, as the following code shows:

```
' Get current thread
Dim thrd As Thread = Thread.CurrentThread()
' Define current culture as en-gb
thrd.CurrentCulture = New CultureInfo("en-gb")
' Convert decimal to a formatted string
Dim decimalValue As Decimal = 1245.43d
Dim stringValue As String = Format(decimalValue, "C")
Console.WriteLine("{0} {1} number.", stringValue, _
                IIf(IsNumeric(stringValue), "is a", "is not a"))
```

Instead of calling IsNumeric before calling a numeric conversion function to convert the string representation of a number to a number, you can combine the two operations into a single method call by calling the TryParse method of the numeric data type to which you'd like to convert *Expression*. TryParse has two parameters, a string containing a representation of the number, and a by reference variable of the numeric type to which you'd like to convert the string. If the method is unable to convert the string, it returns False; if it is able to convert the string, it returns True and stores the converted number in the numeric variable.

IsNumeric evaluates whether data is numeric (that is, whether it is a number, a string representation of a number, or a value, such as a Boolean, capable of conversion to a number), not whether the data type is of *Expression* is numeric. To determine whether a data type is one of the numeric types, you can call the following method:

```
Public Shared Function IsANumber(expr As Object) As Boolean
    ' Get type object corresponding to expr
    Dim exprType As Type = expr.GetType()
    ' Determine if it's a primitive type
    If Not exprType.IsPrimitive Then
        Return False
    Else
    ' eliminate chars and Booleans
        If TypeOf(expr) Is Char Then
            Return False
        ElseIf TypeOf(expr) Is Boolean Then
            Return False
        Else
            Return True
        End If
    End If
End Function
```

The function first retrieves the Type object of the expression passed to it and calls its IsPrimitive method. IsPrimitive returns True for all numeric data types (Byte, SByte, Short, UShort, etc.), as well as for the Char and Boolean types. The remaining code simply returns False if the runtime type of *expr* is either Char or Boolean. If it is a primitive data type and is neither a Char nor a Boolean, it must be numeric, so the function returns True.

See Also

IsArray Function, IsDate Function

IsReference Function

Indicates whether an expression evaluates to a reference type.

Member Of

Microsoft.VisualBasic.Information

Syntax

```
IsReference(ByVal Expression As Object) As Boolean
```

Element	Description
Expression	Any expression.

Return Value

True if *Expression* is a reference type, False otherwise.

Comments

The Visual Basic type system recognizes reference types (types that contain a reference to their data) and value types (types that store their data directly). The first group are implicitly derived from the System.Object type (and in fact System.Object is one of the reference types), while the latter are implicitly derived from System.ValueType (which in turn is implicitly derived from System.Object). The following table lists Visual Basic .Net data types and whether they are reference or value types:

Data Type	Reference Type or Value Type
Boolean	Value type
Byte	Value type
Char	Value type
Class instance	Reference type
Date	Value type
Decimal	Value type
Double	Value type
Integer	Value type
Long	Value type
Object	Reference type (see next comment)
SByte	Value type
Short	Value type
Single	Value type
String	Reference type
Structure instance	Value type
UInteger	Value type
ULong	Value type
UShort	Value type

Whether a variable of type Object is a reference type or a value type is determined by its runtime data type. Since more than one kind of data can be assigned to an Object variable, it is possible for it to be both a reference type and a value type at different points during its lifetime. For example:

```
Public Sub Main()
    Dim generalObject As Object
    Console.WriteLine(IsReference(generalObject))              ' returns True

    generalObject = 12
    Console.WriteLine(IsReference(generalObject))              ' returns False

    generalObject = New List(Of String)
    Console.WriteLine(IsReference(generalObject))              ' returns True

    generalObject = "This is a string assigned to the object."
    Console.WriteLine(IsReference(generalObject))              ' returns True

    generalObject = False
    Console.WriteLine(IsReference(generalObject))              ' returns False

    generalobject = New Point(100, 100)
    Console.WriteLine(IsReference(generalObject))              ' returns False
End Sub
```

Calling IsReference when *Expression* is Nothing returns True for an object data type; it does not generate an exception.

The IsValueType method of the System.Type class is comparable to the IsReference function, except that it returns False instead of True if *Expression* is a reference type. For example:

```
Dim stringVar As String = "Is a string a reference type?"
Console.WriteLine(stringVar.GetType().IsValueType)            ' returns False

Dim arrValues(10) As Integer
Console.WriteLine(arrValues.GetType().IsValueType)            ' returns False

Dim floatValue As Double = 12.3445
Console.WriteLine(floatValue.GetType().IsValueType)           ' returns True
```

VB6 Differences

The function is new to Visual Basic .NET. Visual Basic 6.0 did not differentiate between reference and value types.

See Also

IsArray Function, IsNothing Function

Join Function

Concatenates an array of strings.

Member Of

Microsoft.VisualBasic.Strings

Syntax

```
Join(ByVal SourceArray() As { Object | String }, _
    Optional ByVal Delimiter As String = " ") As String
```

Element	Description
SourceArray	The one-dimensional string array whose elements are to be concatenated.
Delimiter	The character to insert between individual string elements. If none is specified, a space is inserted between substrings.

Return Value

A string formed from individual string array elements delimited by *Delimiter*.

Comments

If the elements of *SourceArray* contain non-string data, *SourceArray* must be declared as a one-dimensional array of type Object. For example, the code

```
Dim mixedArray() As Object = {100, 200, 3.1417, #02/03/2007#, True, _
                            "end of array"}
Dim mixedResult As String = Join(mixedarray, " ")
Console.WriteLine(mixedResult)
```

produces the following output:

```
100 200 3.1417 2/3/2007 True end of array
```

The function handles the conversion of non-string data to strings regardless of the setting of Option Strict.

If *Delimiter* is a zero-length string or Nothing, the strings in *SourceArray* are concatenated with no delimiter.

Delimiter can contain zero (see the previous comment), one, or more characters. For example, the code

```
Dim animals() As String = {"lions", "tigers", "bears"}
Console.WriteLine(Join(animals, ", "))
```

produces the output:

```
lions, tigers, bears
```

If individual members of an array are uninitialized, contain String.Empty values, or have been set to Nothing, Join still appends *Delimiter* to the concatenated string, even though the *SourceArray* member has no data. For example, the code

```
Dim primes(9) As String
primes(0) = "one"
primes(1) = "two"
primes(3) = "three"
primes(4) = "five"
Console.WriteLine(Join(primes, ", "))
```

produces the following output:

```
one, two, , three, five, , , , ,
```

The Join function can be used to write the elements of an array to a comma-delimited text file.

The Join function corresponds closely to the shared String.Join function in the .NET Framework Class Library. The Framework version of the function has two overloads, one of which is identical to the Visual Basic Join function except that the order of its parameters is reversed (the delimiter parameter precedes the string array). The second overload allows you to concatenate only part of an array and has four parameters: the separator character, the index of the first array member to concatentate to the returned string, the index of the last array member to concatenate to the returned string, and the string array. Unlike the Visual Basic Join function, the shared String.Join function, however, requires a strongly typed array.

See Also

Split Function

Kill Subroutine

Deletes a file.

Member Of

Microsoft.VisualBasic.FileSystem

Syntax

```
Kill(ByVal PathName As String)
```

Element	Description
PathName	The optional path and name of the file to delete.

Comments

PathName can include either an absolute path (that is, an absolute path that specifies the current drive and the path from its root directory to the file or files to be deleted, or that specifies the path from the root directory of the current drive to the file or files to be deleted) or a relative path. A relative path is interpreted as the path from the current directory.

If *PathName* does not include a path component, the Kill subroutine attempts to delete a file or files in the current directory.

The Kill subroutine can delete multiple files in a single operation. *PathName* supports the use of the * and ? wildcard characters as part of the filename specification that determines which files are deleted.

If any part of the path component of PathName is invalid, the Kill subroutine throws a DirectoryNotFoundException. If the path is valid but no files matching the file specification can be found, the Kill subroutine throws a FileNotFoundException. If Kill cannot delete the file because it has been opened by another process, the Kill subroutine throws an IOException. If Kill is unable to open the file because it is read-only, it throws an UnauthorizedAccessException.

If the user or process does not have the necessary permissions to delete the file, the Kill subroutine throws a SecurityException.

Kill deletes files without warning or prompting, and does not place deleted files in the Recycle Bin. Because of this, Kill should be used with caution.

To delete a file and place it in the Recycle Bin, you can use the one of the overloads of the My.Computer.FileSystem.DeleteFile, which can delete a single file at a time. For details, see the entry for the My.Computer.FileSystem class.

If an error occurs during a multifile deletion operation, Kill simply aborts the operation. The Message property of the UnauthorizedAccessException or IOException indicates the file that raised the exception, although it may not indicate the cause of the exception. There is no rollback in the event of an exception; any files deleted up to the point that the exception was thrown remain deleted.

Kill deletes files only; to delete a directory, use the RmDir subroutine or one of its .NET framework equivalents.

See Also

My.Computer.FileSystem.DeleteFile Method, RmDir Subroutine

LBound Function

Indicates the lower bound of a particular dimension of an array.

Member Of

Microsoft.VisualBasic.Information

Syntax

```
LBound(ByVal Array As System.Array, Optional ByVal Rank As Integer = 1) _
    As Integer
```

Element	Description
Array	The array whose lower bound is to be determined.
Rank	The one-based dimension whose lower bound is to be determined. If Rank is not specified, the function returns the lower bound for the first dimension of the array.

Return Value

The lower bound of the Rank dimension of the array.

Comments

The lower bound of an array is the index value used to access the first element of a particular dimension of the array. Most commonly, the lower bound of an array is 0.

Passing an uninitialized array to the LBound function throws an ArgumentNullException. Passing an invalid value for Rank throws a RankException.

When iterating an array, the LBound function or its .NET Framework Class Library equivalent should always be used to determine the array's lower bound. This avoids using a hard-coded value that either could be incorrect or could be subject to change.

By default, the lower bound of an array dimension is zero, and the Visual Basic 6.0 language features that allowed the lower bound of an array to be set at something other than zero have been removed from the language. This has led some programmers to always attempt to access the lower bound of an array at index zero, rather than using the value returned by the LBound function, since LBound supposedly always returns 0. (This is repeated, in fact, in the Visual Basic .NET documentation.) However, although Visual Basic language elements no longer support it, a non-zero lower bound can nevertheless be encountered in .NET code. There are two ways that this can happen:

- The array can be instantiated by calling one of the overloads of the shared Array.CreateInstance method. Its syntax is:

```
Shared Function CreateInstance(ByVal elementType As Type, _
                        ByVal lengths() As Integer, _
                        ByVal lowerBounds() As Integer) _
                        As Array
```

where *elementType* is a Type object that defines the data type of the array, *lengths* is an integer array that defines the number of elements in each dimension of the returned array, and *lowerBounds* is an integer array that defines the lower bound of each element in of the returned array. The following code illustrates the use of the CreateInstance method of the Array class, as well as the use of the LBound function to retrieve its lower bound:

```
Dim intType As Type = GetType(Integer)
Dim lengths() As Integer = {10}
Dim bounds() As Integer = {1}
Dim integerArray As Array = Array.CreateInstance(intType, lengths, bounds)
For ctr As Integer = LBound(integerArray, 1) To UBound(integerArray, 1)
    Console.WriteLine("Index {0}: Value {1}", ctr, integerArray(ctr))
Next
```

- The array can be passed to a .NET method from a COM component that supports non-zero lower array bounds.

The LBound function is equivalent to the instance GetLowerBound method of the Array class. Its syntax is:

```
GetLowerBound(ByVal dimension As Integer) As Integer
```

where *dimension* is the zero-based dimension whose lower bound is to be determined.

Example

The following code illustrates the use of the LBound function to sum the values in an array. The array itself is filled with a series of numbers input by the user and is expanded dynamically if the number of values entered by the user exceeds the upper bound of the array:

```
Public Module SumValues
    Public Sub Main()
        ' Set initial size of array to 10
        Dim Values(9) As Double
        ' Set pointer to array index
        Dim index As Integer = 0
        ' define string for input box
        Dim msg As String = "Enter a number " & vbCrLf & "(Press Cancel to Exit):"
        ' input string
        Dim userInput As String = String.Empty
        ' Loop until user cancels
        Do
            userInput = InputBox(msg, "Sum of Values", "")
            If userInput <> String.Empty AndAlso IsNumeric(userInput) Then
                Values(index) = CDbl(userInput)
                index += 1
                ' If array needs expansion, add 10 elements
                If index > UBound(Values, 1) Then
                    ReDim Preserve Values(Ubound(Values, 1) * 2)
                End If
            End If
        Loop While userInput <> String.Empty
        ' Iterate array and sum values
        Dim sum As Double
        For ctr As Integer = LBound(Values, 1) To UBound(Values, 1)
            sum += Values(ctr)
        Next
        Console.WriteLine("The sum of the values in the array is {0}", sum)
    End Sub
End Module
```

See Also

UBound Function

LCase Function

Converts a character or string to lowercase.

Member Of

Microsoft.VisualBasic.Strings

Syntax

```
LCase(ByVal Value As Char) As Char
```

or

```
LCase(ByVal Value As String) As String
```

Element	Description
Value	A single character or a string.

Return Value

Value whose uppercase characters are converted to lowercase.

Comments

If *Value* is an uppercase Char or a string that includes uppercase characters, they are converted to lowercase; other characters (such as white space, lowercase characters, special characters, and character representations of numbers) remain unchanged.

You can determine whether a Char or a particular character in a string is either upper- or lowercase and therefore is or is not in need of conversion by calling the shared Char.IsUpper and Char.IsLower methods. Their syntax is:

```
Char.IsLower(ByVal c As Char) As Boolean
Char.IsLower(ByVal s As String, ByVal index As Integer) As Boolean
Char.IsUpper(ByVal c As Char) As Boolean

Char.IsUpper(ByVal s As String, ByVal index As Integer) As Boolean
```

index is the position of the character in *s* whose case is to be determined.

Either the LCase or UCase function is sometimes used when comparing user input to a hard-coded string so that differences of casing don't affect the comparison. For example:

```
Do
    Dim userInput As String = InputBox("Enter a name, or 'exit' to quit:")
    If LCase(userInput) = "exit" Then
        Exit Do
    End If
    ' Process input
Loop
```

Note, though, that if Option Compare is set to Text, the call to the LCase function is unnecessary. String comparisons using the equal sign are affected by the setting of Option Compare, which in this case defines a case-insensitive comparison.

The .NET Framework Class Library also includes methods that allow you to convert strings or Char values to lowercase. These include the overloaded ToLower shared method of the Char class and the overloaded ToLower instance method of the String class. One overload is of each type is functionally identical to the LCase method. The other allows you to convert to lowercase using the casing rules of a particular culture. The syntax of these overloads is:

```
Char.ToLower(ByVal c As Char, ByVal culture As CultureInfo) As Char
string_instance.ToLower(ByVal culture As CultureInfo) As String
```

Example

The following example converts a title to proper case:

```
Imports System.Collections.Generic

Public Class TitleHandler
    Private Function ToProperCase(inputString As String) As String
        ' Initialize exceptions list
        Static exceptions As List(Of String) = InitializeExceptions()
```

```
        ' Lowercase title
        inputString = LCase(inputString)
        ' Split title into words
        Dim words() As String = Split(inputString, " ")
        ' Iterate words
        For ctr As Integer = 0 To UBound(words, 1)
            ' See if 2nd or later word is in exception list
            If ctr > 0 AndAlso exceptions.Contains(words(ctr)) Then
                Continue For
            Else
                Mid(words(ctr), 1, 1) = UCase(Left(words(ctr), 1))
            End If
        Next
        Return Join(words)
    End Function

    Private Function InitializeExceptions() As List(Of String)
        ' Initialize table of exceptions: words that should not be
        ' uppercased unless they're the first word in a title.
        '
        ' In a real application, these would be maintained in some external
        ' store to support extensibility
        Dim lst As New List(Of String)
        lst.Add("a")
        lst.Add("an")
        lst.Add("and")
        lst.Add("at")
        lst.Add("but")
        lst.Add("by")
        lst.add("for")
        lst.add("in")
        lst.add("into")
        lst.add("of")
        lst.add("on")
        lst.add("the")
        lst.add("to")
        Return lst
    End Function
End Class
```

For example, the following call to the ToProperCase function:

```
Public Sub Main()
    Dim th As New TitleHandler
    Dim title As String = "ALL QUIET ON THE WESTERN FRONT"
    Console.WriteLine(th.ToProperCase(title))
End Sub
```

results in the following output:

```
All Quiet on the Western Front
```

VB6 Differences

Visual Basic 6.0 supported two versions of the LCase function. The first, LCase$, accepted a string argument; the second, LCase, a variant argument. In Visual Basic .NET, the LCase$ function is not supported, and the LCase function can accept either a Char or a String as an argument.

See Also

Option Compare Statement, StrConv Function, UCase Function

Left Function

Extracts a particular number of characters from the left side of a string.

Member Of

Microsoft.VisualBasic.Strings

Syntax

```
Left(ByVal str As String, ByVal Length As Integer) As String
```

Element	Description
str	The string whose leftmost characters are to be extracted.
Length	The number of characters to extract.

Return Value

The leftmost *Length* characters of *str*.

Comments

If *Length* is 0, a zero-length string (String.Empty) is returned. If *Length* is greater than the length of *str*, the entire string is returned unchanged. If *Length* is less than 0, the Left function throws an ArgumentException.

A number of classes (particularly form and control classes) have a Left property, which creates a naming conflict with the Left function. In order to use the Left function, you should fully qualify it with its namespace name, Microsoft.VisualBasic.Strings.Left or Microsoft.VisualBasic.Left.

You can determine the length of *str* by passing it as an argument to the Visual Basic Len function or by retrieving the value of its Length property.

Instead of the Left function, you can call one of the overloads of the String.Substring method in the .NET Framework Class Library. Its syntax is:

```
stringInstance.Substring(ByVal startIndex As Integer, _
                         ByVal length As Integer) As String
```

where *startIndex* is the starting position of the substring (and must be set to 1 to duplicate the functionality of the Left function) and *length* is the number of characters to return in the substring.

VB6 Differences

Visual Basic 6.0 included four comparable string extraction functions: Left, Left$, LeftB, and LeftB$. The LeftB and LeftB$ functions were intended to work with binary data in string form. The Left$ and LeftB$ functions were intended to work with variants whose runtime type was String. Visual Basic .NET, in contrast, supports a single Left function.

See Also

Mid Function, Mid Statement, Right Function, Split Function

Len Function

Indicates the number of characters in a String or the number of bytes required to store a variable.

Member Of

Microsoft.VisualBasic.Strings

Syntax

```
Len(ByVal Expression As Boolean) As Integer
Len(ByVal Expression As Byte) As Integer
Len(ByVal Expression As Char) As Integer
Len(ByVal Expression As Date) As Integer
Len(ByVal Expression As Decimal) As Integer
Len(ByVal Expression As Double) As Integer
Len(ByVal Expression As Integer) As Integer
Len(ByVal Expression As Long) As Integer
Len(ByVal Expression As Object) As Integer
Len(ByVal Expression As SByte) As Integer
Len(ByVal Expression As Short) As Integer
Len(ByVal Expression As Single) As Integer
Len(ByVal Expression As String) As Integer
Len(ByVal Expression As UInteger) As Integer
Len(ByVal Expression As ULong) As Integer
Len(ByVal Expression As UShort) As Integer
```

Element	Description
Expression	Any expression.

Return Value

An Integer indicating the number of characters in *Expression* or, if *Expression* is not a String, the number of bytes required to store *Expression*.

Comments

If *Expression* is a String, the Len function returns the number of characters in the string. Its operation is identical to the String.Length method, with two exceptions:

- If *Expression* is an uninitialized string (its value is Nothing), the Len function returns 0, while the String.Length method throws a NullReferenceException.

- If *Expression* is an empty string (""), the Len function returns 0, while the String.Length method throws a NullReferenceException. However, the recommended method for testing for an empty string is to call the shared IsNullOrEmpty method of the String class, as follows:

```
If String.IsNullOrEmpty(thisString) Then
    ' do something for null string
Else
    ' handle string contents
End If
```

If the runtime type of *Expression* is a primitive value type (such as a Boolean, a Date, a Decimal, an Integer, or an SByte), the Len function returns the number of bytes occupied by a variable of that type in memory. The value returned for a particular data type is always the same and is shown in the following table:

Value Type	Length
Boolean	2
Byte	1
Char	2
Date	8
Decimal	8
Double	8
Integer	4
Long	8
SByte	1
Short	2
Single	4
UInteger	4
ULong	8
UShort	2

If the runtime type of *Expression* is a strongly typed object, the Len function throws an InvalidCastException.

If *Expression* is a structure, the Len function is unable to calculate its length and instead returns 0 if the structure has any members other than fields. In addition, the Len function is unable to work with structures that include fields of some of the new value types (in particular, SByte, UShort, UInteger, and ULong) and instead throws an ArgumentException.

For structures whose members are fields only, the total size of the structure is usually but not always the sum of its individual components. In some cases, fields have to be aligned on two- or four-byte boundaries, and any empty memory locations are included in the total size of the structure.

Each string field adds four bytes to the size of a structure. Even though this may not be the actual length of the string, the Len function calculates the size of the address that the string variable references, rather than the string data itself. However, if a string field as defined as a fixed-length field using the <vbFixedString> attribute, the Len function includes the size of the string data, rather than the size of its address, in the calculation. For example, the following code defines two structures, BasicBatter and FixedBatter, that are identical except that the latter structure has a fixed-length string field:

```
Public Structure FixedBatter
   Public PlayerID As Integer
   <VBFixedString(20)> Public PlayerName As String
   Public BA As Decimal
End Structure

Public Structure BasicBatter
   Public PlayerID As Integer
   Public PlayerName As String
   Public BA As Decimal
End Structure
```

The following code then creates an instance of each structure and passes it to the Len function:

```
Public Sub Main()
   Dim basic As New BasicBatter()
   Console.WriteLine("BasicBatter: " & Len(basic))

   Dim fixed As New FixedBatter()
   console.WriteLine("FixedBatter: " & Len(fixed))
End Sub
```

The output indicates that the size of the structure without a fixed-length string is 24 bytes, while the size of the structure with a fixed-length string is 40 bytes.

If *Expression* is an array, Len throws an InvalidCastException. To determine the length (number of elements) in an array, you can use either of two methods. The instance Array.Length property returns the total number of elements in an array. Its syntax is:

```
arrayInstance.Length() As Integer
```

The instance Array.GetLength method returns the number of elements in a particular dimension of an array. Its syntax is:

```
arrayInstance.GetLength(ByVal dimension As Integer) As Integer
```

For one-dimensional arrays, the Length property and the GetLength method return identical values.

VB6 Differences

Visual Basic 6.0 included a LenB function, which returned the number of bytes in a string. In Visual Basic .NET, LenB is not supported.

In Visual Basic 6.0, if the Len function was passed a variable whose design-time type was Variant, the return value reflected not the memory requirements of the design-time variable, but the amount of space required to store the data to disk. (For example, the Len function returned 1 with a Byte variable whose value was 100, but it returned 3 with a Variant whose runtime type was Byte and whose value was 100. Although the Visual Basic .NET documentation indicates that this distinction between strongly and weakly typed variables is maintained by the Len function, in fact it is not; the Len function examines only the runtime type of variables and reports the amount of storage space that they require in memory only.

See Also

LBound Function, UBound Function

Lib Keyword

A required clause in a Declare statement that defines the dynamic link library file in which an external function or subroutine resides.

Syntax

```
Lib "dllName"
```

Element	Description
dllName	The path and name of the dynamic link library file.

Comments

dllName must be a standard Windows dynamic link library file. It cannot be any of a number of other library files, such as an MFC class library file.

If *dllName* is a memory-resident DLL (such as System32.dll or advapi32.dll), *dllName* can include the root filename without a file extension or a path.

The path need not be included if the path to the DLL is defined by the local system's PATH environment variable, or if it is in the same directory as the application.

See Also

Auto Keyword, Declare Statement

LineInput Function

Reads a line from an open sequential file.

Member Of

Microsoft.VisualBasic.FileSystem

Syntax

```
LineInput(ByVal FileNumber As Integer) As String
```

Element	Description
FileNumber	The file number used in the call to the FileOpen subroutine.

Return Value

A String containing the line read.

Comments

LineInput is one of a series of related file input and output functions that works with a file number used when opening a file with the FileOpen subroutine.

Although LineInput can be used to read files written with the Print and PrintLine subroutines, it is a general-purpose file input function that can be used with any text file.

LineInput reads an entire line until it encounters any of the following:

- The end-of-line character combinarion (vbCrLf or ControlChars.CrLf)
- The carriage return character (vbCr or ControlChars.Cr)
- The end of the file

The string returned by the LineInput function does not include the end-of-line or carriage return character. This means that, if you want to write the line back to a file, you must add it back.

After it reads a line, LineInput advances the file pointer to the beginning of the next line or, if the end of the file is encountered, to the end of the file.

Attempting to read beyond the end of the file throws an EndOfStreamException. To prevent this, you should use the EOF function to check for the end of the file, as the example illustrates.

You should call the FileClose subroutine when you have finished reading from the file. It's a good idea to do so in the Finally block of an exception handler so that if an exception is thrown while the file is opened, the file is still closed. For details, see the FileClose Subroutine.

As an alternative to using LineInput to read from a text file, you can use the System.IO .StreamReader class. The following code is functionally identical to the code in the example, except that it uses the StreamReader and StreamWriter classes instead of LineInput and PrintLine to read from and write to a text file:

```
Imports System.IO

Public Module FileInput
    Const INPUTFILE As String = ".\InputFile.txt"
    Const OUTPUTFILE As String = ".\OutputFile.txt"

    Public Sub Main()
        Dim line As String
        Dim inFileOpened, outFileOpened As Boolean
        ' Open Files
        Try
            Dim inFile As StreamReader = New StreamReader(INPUTFILE)
            inFileOpened = True
```

```
        Dim outFile As StreamWriter = New StreamWriter(OUTPUTFILE, False)
        outFileOpened = True

        Do While inFile.Peek >= 0
            line = inFile.ReadLine().ToLower()
            outFile.WriteLine(line)
        Loop
    Catch e As Exception
        Console.WriteLine(e.GetType().Name & ": " & e.Message)
    Finally
        If inFileOpened Then inFile.Close()
        If outFileOpened Then outFile.Close()
    End Try
    End Sub
End Module
```

Using the StreamReader and StreamWriter class produces code that is easier to read and understand, and that is more self-contained. (It does not rely on a file number to open the file or to identify it.)

Example

The following code uses the LineInput function to read each line of a text file, converts it to lowercase, and uses the PrintLine function to write it back to a new file:

```
Public Module FileInput
    Const INPUTFILE As String = ".\InputFile.txt"
    Const OUTPUTFILE As String = ".\OutputFile.txt"

    Public Sub Main()
        Dim line As String
        ' Open Files
        Dim fin, fout As Integer
        Dim finOpened, foutOpened As Boolean
        fin = FreeFile()
        Try
            FileOpen(fin, INPUTFILE, OpenMode.Input, OpenAccess.Read)
            finOpened = True
            fout = FreeFile()
            FileOpen(fout, OUTPUTFILE, OpenMode.Output, OpenAccess.Write)
            foutOpened = True
            ' Read each line of input file
            Do
                line = LineInput(fin)
                If Not String.IsNullOrEmpty(line)
                    line = line.ToLower()
                    PrintLine(fout, line)
                End If
            Loop While Not EOF(fin)
        Catch e As Exception
            Console.WriteLine(e.GetType().Name & ": " & e.Message)
        Finally
            If finOpened Then FileClose(fin)
```

```
            If foutOpened Then FileClose(fout)
        End Try
    End Sub
End Module
```

The routine simply loops until the EOF function tells us that the end of the input file has been reached. Note that the LineInput function returns a line without the end-of-line character(s); the PrintLine subroutine automatically adds them back when it writes a line.

VB6 Differences

Visual Basic 6.0 included a Line Input or Line Input # statement that is the functional equivalent to the LineInput function, although its syntax was slightly different (its two parameters were *FileNumber* and a string variable passed by reference to the statement). Visual Basic .NET implements this statement as a function that returns the line read.

See Also

FileClose Subroutine, FileOpen Subroutine, Print Function, PrintLine Function

---

Loc Function

Indicates the current position of the file pointer.

Member Of

Microsoft.VisualBasic.FileSystem

Syntax

```
Loc(ByVal FileNumber As Integer) As Long
```

Element	Description
FileNumber	The file number used in the call to the FileOpen subroutine.

Return Value

A Long indicating the position of the file pointer.

Comments

Loc is one of a series of related file input and output functions that works with a file number used when opening a file with the FileOpen subroutine.

Loc is a zero-based function. If the file pointer is pointing to the first byte or the first record of a file, it returns 0, not 1.

The precise interpretation of the value returned by the Loc file depends on the type of file (sequential, random, or binary) represented by *FileNumber*. For binary files, it represents the byte to which the file pointer is pointing. For random files, it represents the record to which the record pointer is pointing. For sequential files, it represents the byte to which the file pointer is pointing divided by 128. However, in the case of sequential files, the function has no practical significance.

Note that Loc is a function, not a property; it reports the position of the file pointer but doesn't allow it to be set.

Example

The example reads displays the position of the record pointer in a random file before displaying the record.

```
Option Strict Off

Public Structure Fielder
    <vbFixedString(15)> Public LastName As String
    <vbFixedString(15)> Public FirstName As String
    <vbFixedString(2)> Public Position As String
    <vbFixedString(4)> Public sBA As String
    <vbFixedString(3)> Public sHR As String
    <vbFixedString(4)> Public sRBI As String
End Structure

Public Module modMain

    Public Sub Main()
        Const FILENAME As String = ".\Loc.bin"

        Dim player As New Fielder
        Dim fn As Integer = FreeFile()
        Dim fileOpened As Boolean
        Try
            FileOpen(fn, FILENAME, OpenMode.Random, OpenAccess.Read, , Len(player))
            fileOpened = True
            Seek(fn, 1)
            Do While Not EOF(fn)
                Console.WriteLine("Reading record {0}", Loc(fn))
                FileGet(fn, player, Loc(fn) + 1)
                Console.WriteLine("   {0} {1} had a career batting average of {2}.", _
                                  Trim(player.FirstName), Trim(player.LastName), _
                                  player.sBA)
                Seek(fn, loc(fn)+1)
            Loop
        Catch e As Exception
            Console.WriteLine(e.GetType().Name & ": " & e.Message)
        Finally
            If fileOpened Then FileClose(fn)
        End Try
    End Sub
End Module
```

See Also

FileClose Subroutine, FileLen Function, FileOpen Subroutine, LOF Function

Lock Subroutine

Locks all or part of a file opened using the FileOpen subroutine.

Member Of
Microsoft.VisualBasic.FileSystem

Syntax

```
Lock(ByVal FileNumber As Integer)
```

or

```
Lock(ByVal FileNumber As Integer, ByVal Record As Long)
```

or

```
Lock(ByVal FileNumber As Integer, ByVal FromRecord As Long, _
    ByVal ToRecord As Long)
```

Element	Description
FileNumber	The file number used in the call to the FileOpen subroutine.
Record	The number of a single record or byte to lock.
FromRecord	The number of the first record or byte to lock.
ToRecord	The number of the last record or byte to lock.

Comments

Lock is one of a series of related file input and output functions that works with a file number used when opening a file with the FileOpen subroutine.

Lock is for use in a networked or multiuser environment and prevents another process from accessing a file, record, or block of data until it is unlocked by a call to the Unlock subrotuine.

For each call to Lock, you should be sure to call the Unlock subroutine once your code is finished with the locked object. This means that, if you are calling Lock within a Try block, you should call Unlock in the Finally block to ensure that it executes in the event of an error.

There must be a one-to-one correlation between calls to Lock and Unlock. You can't lock an entire random file, for example, and then release the locks by calling Unlock one record at a time. If a call to Unlock does not correspond to a preceding call to Lock, Lock throws an IOException with the rather confusing error message, "The segment is already unlocked."

If *FileNumber* is used with no other arguments in the call to Lock, the entire file is locked; the file itself can be a binary, random, or sequential file.

The Lock subroutine can be called with the *Record* argument for binary and random files (but not sequential files). *Record* indicates the single record to lock for random files and the single byte to lock for binary files.

The Lock subroutine can be called with the FromRecord and ToRecord arguments for binary and random files (but not sequential files). *FromRecord* and *ToRecord* designate the range of records to lock for random files and the range of bytes to lock for binary files.

The numbering for records and bytes starts at 1, not 0.

Attempting to access a locked file or a locked block of records or bytes in a file throws an IOException.

VB6 Differences

In Visual Basic 6.0, Lock was implemented as a statement that could include the # symbol before the file number. In Visual Basic .NET, it is implemented as a subroutine, and this syntax is not supported.

In Visual Basic 6.0, the version of the Lock statement that specified *FromRecord* and *ToRecord* separated them with the To keyword. In Visual Basic .NET, a comma is used as the separator between arguments, and this syntax is not supported.

See Also

FileOpen Subroutine, Unlock Subroutine

LOF Function

Indicates the size in bytes of an open file.

Member Of

Microsoft.VisualBasic.Filesystem

Syntax

```
LOF(ByVal FileNumber As Integer) As Long
```

Element	Description
FileNumber	The file number used in the call to the FileOpen subroutine.

Return Value

A Long indicating the size of the file.

Comments

LOF is one of a series of related file input and output functions that works with a file number used when opening a file with the FileOpen subroutine.

LOF is for use with files opened using Visual Basic's "intrinsic" file handling functions only. Its rationale is that it takes into account the contents of the buffer of an open sequential file. For files that are not open or that have not been opened with the Visual Basic FileOpen subroutine, use the FileLen function or its .NET Framework equivalent, FileInfo.Length.

The LOF function is sometimes used in a comparison with the return value of the Loc function to ensure that a file input routine does not read past the end of the binary file. For a binary file, this takes the form:

```
Do While Loc(fn) < LOF(fn)
```

For a random file, it takes the form:

```
Do While Loc(fn) < LOF(fn)/Len(recordLen)
```

The example illustrates this usage.

The LOF function can be used to calculate the number of records in a random file. For example, if the record corresponds to a structure, the number of records in a file can be determined using code like the following:

```
nRecords = LOF(filenumber)/Len(structure)
```

Example

The following example reads customer records from a file and displays information about them to the console. The LOF function is used to calculate the number of records, as well as to ensure that the program does not attempt to read beyond the end of the file:

```
Option Strict Off

Public Structure Customer
    <VBFixedString(6)> Public AcctNo As String
    <VBFixedString(25)> Public Name As String
    Public Balance As Decimal
    Public PastDue As Decimal
    Public CustomerSince As Date
    Public Active As Boolean
End Structure

Public Module FileModule
    Const FILENAME As String = ".\LOF.dat"

    Dim cust As New Customer

    Public Sub Main()
        Dim fn As Integer = FreeFile()
        Dim fileOpened As Boolean
        Try
            FileOpen(fn, FILENAME, OpenMode.Random, OpenAccess.Read, , Len(cust))
            fileOpened = True
            Console.WriteLine("The file {0} has {1} records.", FILENAME, _
                            LOF(fn)/Len(cust))
            Console.WriteLine()
            Do While Loc(fn) * Len(cust) < LOF(fn)
                FileGet(fn, cust)
                Console.WriteLine("{0} has a balance of {1}, " & _
                            "of which {2} is past due.", _
                            Trim(cust.Name), FormatCurrency(cust.Balance), _
                            FormatCurrency(cust.PastDue))
            Loop
        Catch e As Exception
            Console.WriteLine(e.GetType().Name & ": " & e.Message)
        Finally
            If fileOpened Then FileClose(fn)
        End Try
    End Sub
End Module
```

See Also

FileLen Function, FileOpen Subroutine

LSet Function

Left-aligns a string and pads it with spaces to make it a specified length.

Member Of

Microsoft.VisualBasic.Strings

Syntax

```
LSet(ByVal Source As String, ByVal Length As Integer) As String
```

Element	Description
Source	The string to left-align.
Length	The desired length of the string.

Return Value

A left-aligned string with spaces appended, if necessary, to make it *Length* characters.

Comments

To some degree, this function is misnamed; it is more appropriately named PadRight, since it is designed to pad the right side of a string with spaces up to a particular length.

If the length of *Source* is less than or equal to *Length,* LSet returns *Source* with enough space characters appended to make it *Length* characters long. It is equivalent to the code:

```
result = Source & Space(Length - Len(Source))
```

If *Source* contains leading spaces, these are retained in the returned string. The function really does not left-align a string.

If the length of *Source* is greater than *Length,* it is truncated to *Length* characters. In this case, the LSet function is equivalent to

```
Left(Source, Length)
```

The LSet function is a legacy of Basic before the introduction of Visual Basic.

The String class in the .NET Framework Class Library includes a PadRight method whose operation is similar to that of LSet: it appends characters to the right of a string to pad it to a particular length. Although by default the space character is used to pad the string, one of the method's overloads allows you to specify the padding character. The behavior of the PadRight method also differs when the length of *Source* exceeds *Length;* in that case, *Source* is returned unchanged, rather than truncated to *Length* characters.

VB.NET Changes

In Visual Basic 6.0, *Source* had to be a fixed-length string.

In Visual Basic 6.0, LSet was an assignment statement that assigned a fixed-length string to a normal string. Consequently, its syntax was different, and there was no need to provide a *Length* argument.

See Also

LTrim Function, RSet Function, RTrim Function, Space Function, Trim Function

LTrim Function

Removes any leading spaces from a string.

Member Of

Microsoft.VisualBasic.Strings

Syntax

```
LTrim(ByVal str As String) As String
```

Element	Description
str	The string to be trimmed.

Return Value

str with leading spaces removed.

Comments

If *str* has no leading spaces, the function returns *str* unchanged.

The LTrim function corresponds to the instance TrimStart method of the String class, which has the syntax:

```
String.TrimStart(ParamArray trimChars() As Char) As String
```

where *trimChars* is a parameter array that defines the characters to be removed from the string. If it is Nothing, only leading white space is removed.

To remove trailing spaces, use the RTrim function.

To remove both leading and trailing spaces, use the Trim function or the String.Trim instance method. The latter is overloaded: one version removes spaces, while the other allows you to specify the character or characters to be removed.

VB6 Differences

Visual Basic 6.0 included an LTrim$ function that returned a String, while LTrim returned a Variant. In Visual Basic .NET, LTrim$ is not supported, and the LTrim function returns a String.

See Also

LTrim Function, RTrim Function

Me Keyword

Provides a reference to the class or structure instance for which the current procedure was invoked.

Comments

The Me keyword can be used in a class or a structure (that is, within a Class . . . End Class construct or a Structure.End Structure construct) to refer to an instance of the class or structure. It cannot be used in a module defined with the Module . . . End Module construct, since all code in the module is shared.

The Me keyword can be used to differentiate private variables or other instance members from parameters. For example, in the code

```
Public Class Document
    Private docType As DocumentType

    Public Sub New(docType As DocumentType)
        MyBase.New()
        Me.docType = docType
    End Sub

    Public ReadOnly Property DocumentType() As DocumentType
        Get
            Return Me.docType
        End Get
    End Property
End Class

Public Enum DocumentType As Integer
    Letter = 1
    Report = 2
    Manuscript = 3
    Notes = 4
    Receipt = 5
    Form = 6
End Enum
```

The Document class constructor has a parameter named *docType* whose value is assigned to a private variable named docType. The compiler is able to resolve this apparent ambiguity and produce our intended result because the private variable type is prefaced with the Me keyword. If we remove it, the code still compiles, but the compiler interprets the assignment statement as an assignment of a parameter value to itself, since the parameter shadows the member; as a result, it displays 0 as the value of the DocumentType property. (Note also that while we can assign a variable, property, or method the same name as a parameter, the names of type members must be unique. If we attempt to assign the name docType to both the private variable and the public property in this example, a compiler error results.)

The Me keyword can be used to reference a variable that is otherwise hidden by a local variable with more immediate scope (that is, by a local variable that shadows a second variable). For example, the following code is a portion of a class that tracks web visitors. It maintains a private variable, Counter, that counts the number of visitors to a web site over a particular period of time. A local variable, also named Counter, is used to list the last five visitors to the web site. Its initial value is one less than the value of the private Counter variable. By prefacing the Counter variable with the Me keyword, the code is able to access it even though the local Counter variable is in scope and hides it:

```
Public Class Visitors
    Private Counter As Integer
    Private From() As String

    Public Sub ShowLastVisitors()
        For counter As Integer = Me.Counter - 1 To Me.Counter - 6 Step -1
            Console.WriteLine(From(counter))
        Next
    End Sub
End Class
```

Note, though, that since we identify variables by their names, this duplication of variable names is a source of confusion that makes code less readable, less maintainable, and more error-prone.

The Me keyword can be used to invoke a member of the class or structure instance. However, its behavior differs from that of the MyClass keyword. If a method is implemented in a base class and a derived class, the compiler resolves Me as a reference to the caller and calls the caller's version of the function. For a discussion of the difference between Me and the MyClass keyword, see the entry for the MyClass Keyword.

The most common use of the Me keyword is to pass a reference to the current class or structure instance to a method, particularly an external method. For example, a class library named ReflectionLib contains a number of shared methods for reflection, including the following method, CountProperties:

```
Imports System.Reflection

Public Module ReflectionLib
    Public Function CountProperties(obj As Object) As Integer
        Dim objType As Type = CObj(obj).GetType()
        Dim flags As BindingFlags = BindingFlags.Instance Or BindingFlags.Static Or _
                                    BindingFlags.Public Or BindingFlags.NonPublic
        Dim props() As PropertyInfo = objType.GetProperties(flags)
        Return props.Length
    End Function
End Module
```

A class named classMain includes a property, PropertyCount, that reports the number of properties that the class has. To get a count of its own properties, it simply calls the ReflectionLib.CountProperties method and uses the Me keyword to pass a reference to itself:

```
Public Class classMain
    Private className As String

    Public ReadOnly Property Name() As String
        Get
            Return className
        End Get
    End Property

    Public ReadOnly Property PropertyCount() As Integer
        Get
            Return ReflectionLib.CountProperties(Me)
        End Get
    End Property
End Class
```

A client of the class can then retrieve the value of its PropertyCount property, which is 2:

```
Public Module modMain
    Public Sub Main()
        Dim cl As New ClassMain()
        Console.WriteLine(cl.PropertyCount)
    End Sub
End Module
```

VB6 Differences

In Visual Basic 6.0, the role of the Me keyword is more limited than in Visual Basic .NET. It can be used to pass a reference to the current class to a routine, and it can be used to qualify a reference to a member of a class or form.

See Also

MyBase Keyword, MyClass Keyword

Mid Function

Returns a substring that starts at a specified position in a string.

Member Of

Microsoft.VisualBasic.Strings

Syntax

```
Mid(ByVal str As String, ByVal Start As Integer, _
    Optional ByVal Length As Integer) As String
```

Element	Description
str	The string from which a substring is to be extracted.
Start	The one-based starting position of the substring in str.
Length	The number of characters to extract.

Return Value

A substring of *Length* characters extracted from the *Start* position in *str*.

Comments

If *Start* exceeds the length of *str*, the function returns a string set to Nothing. If *Start* is negative or zero, the Mid function throws an ArgumentException.

If *Length* is omitted, or if *Length* exceeds the number of characters from *Start* to the end of *str*, the function returns all characters from *Start* to the end of *str*.

If you need to determine the number of characters in a string when using the Mid function, you can use either the Len function or the String.Length instance method.

The InStr function, which indicates the position of the first occurrence of a character in a string, and the InStrRev function, which indicates the position of the last occurrence of a character in a string, are often used to determine either the value of *Start* or to calculate the value of *Length*. For an example, see the Example section of the entry for the InStr function. For example, the following code uses the InStrRev along with the Mid function to extract the last word of a sentence and to strip out its final period:

```
Private Function ExtractLastWord(sentence As String) As String
    Dim periodPosition As Integer
    Dim position As Integer = InStrRev(sentence, " ")
    If position > 0 Then
        periodPosition = InstrRev(sentence, ".")
        Return Mid(sentence, position + 1, periodPosition - position - 1)
    Else
        Return sentence
    End If
End Function
```

The Mid function extracts a substring from a string; the Mid statement is an assignment statement that replaces a portion of a string.

The Mid function is virtually identical in operation to the Substring instance method of the String class. The Substring method is overloaded as follows:

```
stringInstance.Substring(ByVal startIndex As Integer) As String
```

```
stringInstance.Substring(ByVal startIndex As Integer, ByVal length As Integer) _
                    As String
```

where *startIndex* is the zero-based starting position of the string to extract, and *length* is the number of characters to return. The first overload returns all characters from *startIndex* to the end of the string.

Example

See the example for the InStr function.

VB6 Differences

In addition to the Mid function, which returned a Variant, Visual Basic 6.0 included the Mid$, MidB, and MidB$ functions. The Mid$ and MidB$ functions returned Strings, while the MidB function, like Mid, returned a Variant. The Mid and Mid$ functions returned character strings, while the MidB and MidB$ functions returned byte strings. In Visual Basic .NET, only the Mid function, which returns a character string, is supported.

See Also

GetChar Function, Left Function, Mid Statement, Right Function

Mid Statement

Replaces a specified number of characters in a string with another string.

Syntax

```
Mid(ByRef Target As String, ByVal Start As Integer, _
    Optional ByVal Length As Integer) = StringExpression
```

Element	Description
Target	The string containing a substring to be replaced.
Start	The one-based position at which the replacement is to begin.
Length	The number of characters to replace. If omitted, all characters from *Start* to the end of *Target* are replaced if *StringExpression* has enough characters; otherwise, Len(*StringExpression*) characters are replaced from *Start* on.
StringExpression	The string to replace the specific range of characters in *Target*. If there are more characters in *StringExpression* than there are in *Target* from the *Start* position for *Length* characters, then only the first *Length* characters in *StringExpression* are used.

Comments

The syntax of the Mid statement is a bit unusual: it is really an assignment statement, in which a substring is being assigned to (and replacing) a portion of a string.

The Mid statement is different from the Mid function. The latter returns a substring from a larger string. The former replaces a portion of a string with another string.

Note that the Mid statement does not return a value and cannot be used as part of an expression. For example, the apparently innocuous line

```
Console.WriteLine("Result: {0}", Mid(Target, Start, Length) = Replacement)
```

which is intended to display the result of replacing *Length* characters in *Target* starting at position *Start*, actually returns a Boolean value because Mid is interpreted as a function rather than a statement. This type of error can be fixed by calling the Mid statement on a separate line of code:

```
Mid(Target, Start, Length) = Replacement
Console.WriteLine("Result: {0}", Target)
```

The Mid statement holds the length of *Target* (i.e., the number of characters in *Target*) constant. *Target* cannot be shortened or lengthened by the Mid statement.

If *StringExpression* is Nothing or String.Empty, the Mid statement does not throw an exception; instead, it simply leaves *Target* unchanged.

Visual Basic also includes a Replace function that replaces one or more occurrences of a substring in a longer string with another string. It also offers the advantages of a function rather than a statement; that is, it returns a value that can be used in an expression.

The Mid statement is also similar to the instance Replace method of the String class, which replaces one substring in a string with another.

Example

The example is a rather silly one that uses the Mid function to extract each character in the string representation of a number, increases its ASCII value by one, and uses this Mid statement to assign it back to the original string. The result is that each character is one digit greater than the original string.

```
Public Sub Main()
    Dim target As String = "1234567890"
    Console.WriteLine(target)
    Dim character As String
    Dim asciiCode As Integer

    For ctr As Integer = 1 to Len(target)
        ' Extract one character
        character = Mid(target, ctr, 1)
        asciiCode = Asc(character)
        If asciiCode = 57 then asciicode -= 10
        character = Chr(asciiCode + 1)
        Mid(target, ctr, 1) = character
    Next
    Console.WriteLine(target)
End Sub
```

VB6 Differences

Visual Basic 6.0 included a MidB statement, which replaced bytes rather than characters. It is not supported in Visual Basic .NET.

See Also

Mid Function, Replace Function

Minute Function

Extracts the minute component of a time value.

Member Of

Microsoft.VisualBasic.DateAndTime

Syntax

```
Minute(ByVal TimeValue As DateTime) As Integer
```

Element	Description
TimeValue	A time value.

Return Value

A number ranging from 0 to 59 reflecting the minute component of *TimeValue*.

Comments

If Option Strict is off, the compiler automatically converts a string representation of a date to a Date value before calling the Minute function. To ensure that the string can be successfully converted, you can call the IsDate function beforehand.

The DatePart function can also be used to extract the minute component of a time value. For example, the following two function calls return identical values:

```
minutes = Minute(Date.Now)

minutes = DatePart(DateInterval.Minute, Date.Now)
```

The Date data type also includes a Minute member that extracts the minute component of its Date instance. For example:

```
minutes = Date.Now.Minute
```

See Also

DatePart Function, Hour Function, Second Function

MIRR Function

Calculates the modified internal rate of return for a series of cash flow payments.

Member Of

Microsoft.VisualBasic.Financial

Syntax

```
MIRR(ByRef ValueArray() As Double, ByVal FinanceRate As Double, _
     ByVal ReinvestRate As Double) As Double
```

Element	Description
ValueArray	A one-dimensional array containing at least two cash flow values, one a payment (payments are represented by negative values) and one a receipt (receipts are represented by positive values).
FinanceRate	The interest rate paid as the cost of financing. *FinanceRate* is expressed as a decimal value (e.g., a finance rate of 8.5 percent is expressed as .085).
ReinvestRate	The interest rate received on gains from cash reinvestment. *ReinvestRate* is expressed as a decimal value (e.g., a reinvestment rate of 12.5 percent is expressed as .125).

Return Value

A Double representing the modified internal rate of return.

Comments

Unlike the internal rate of return, which assumes that cash flows are reinvested at the rate of return, the *modified internal rate of return* assumes that payments and receipts are financed at different rates. Because of this, the modified internal rate of return is often considered a more reliable tool for assessing investment opportunities.

The order of payments and receipts within *ValueArray* is interpreted as the actual order of payments and receipts. For the function to return an accurate result, they must be in the correct order.

MIRR also assumes that the payments and receipts occur at regular time intervals. If this is not the case, MIRR will return inaccurate results.

If there is not at least one negative value (payment) and one positive value (receipt) in *ValueArray,* the MIRR function throws a DivideByZeroException.

Example

An investment opportunity for a business involves $125,000 in startup costs but should generate $19, 000, $24,000, $26,000, $28,000, and $32,000 over the following five years. The modified internal rate of return is calculated as follows:

```
Public Sub Main()
    Dim values() As Double = {-125000, 19000, 24000, 26000, 28000, 32000}
    Dim financeRate As Double = .0975
    Dim reinvestRate As Double = .1225
    Console.WriteLine("The MIRR is {0:p}", _
                    MIRR(values, financeRate, reinvestRate))
End Sub
```

This produces the following output:

```
The MIRR is 5.10 %
```

See Also

IRR Function

MkDir Subroutine

Creates a directory.

Member Of

Microsoft.VisualBasic.FileSystem

Syntax

```
MkDir(ByVal Path As String)
```

Element	Description
Path	The name of the directory to create, along with an optional path.

Comments

If no drive specification is included with the Path argument, the subroutine creates the directory on the current drive. You can determine what the current drive is by using code like the following:

```
Public Function CurDrive() As Char
    Return CChar(Left(CurDir(), 1))
End Function
```

If no path is included with the *Path* argument, the subroutine creates a child directory of the current directory. You can determine what the current directory is by calling the CurDir function.

Either an absolute or a relative path can be included with the *Path* argument. A relative path is interpreted in relationship to the current directory.

If *Path* includes any intermediate directories that do not exist, they will be created as well.

If the directory to be created already exists, the MkDir throws an IOException. You can either handle this error or check whether the directory already exists before attempting to create it. To do this, you can call the shared Exists method of the System.IO.Directory class, as the following code illustrates:

```
Imports System.IO

Public Module modMain
    Public Sub Main()
        Dim filepath As String = Environment.GetFolderPath( _
                        Environment.SpecialFolder.CommonApplicationData) & _
                        Path.DirectorySeparatorChar & "MyCompanyApp"
        If Not Directory.Exists(filepath) Then
            Try
                MkDir(filepath)
            Catch
                ' Handle possible exception
            End Try
        End If
    End Sub
End Module
```

You should still be prepared to handle an exception, however. It is possible that the user is not authorized to create the directory. In addition, it is possible that another process might create the directory between the time that you check for it and the time that you call the MkDir subroutine.

You can also call the My.Computer.FileSystem.CreateDirectory method to create a new directory. Its syntax is identical to that of MkDir:

```
CreateDirectory(ByVal directory As String)
```

You can also create a directory by calling the shared CreateDirectory method of the System.IO.Directory class. The syntax of one of its overloads is very similar to that of the MkDir subroutine:

```
CreateDirectory(ByVal path As String) As DirectoryInfo
```

Unlike the Visual Basic directory creation methods, the Directory.CreateDirectory method returns a DirectoryInfo object that you can then use to perform such operations as setting the directory's attributes or setting its date/time stamp.

See Also

ChDir Subroutine, ChDrive Subroutine, CurDir Subroutine, RmDir Subroutine

Module Keyword

Indicates that an attribute applies to an entire module, rather than to an individual programming element within it.

Syntax

```
<Module:attribute(arglist)>
```

Element	Description
attribute	The attribute to be applied to the module.
arglist	The attribute's optional argument list.

Comments

Ordinarily, attributes are placed immediately before the language element to which they apply. Since there is no module element, the Module keyword is used to indicate that the attribute applies to a module. (A module is a single code file within a larger assembly.)

The Module keyword must precede any declarations in a program file; that is, it must precede any Namespace, Class, Module, Structure, Interface, and Enumeration statements. It must immediately follow any Option and Imports statements. It can either proceed or follow the Assembly keyword.

If multiple attributes are to be applied to a module or assembly, you can place them all in a single statement (i.e., a single set of angle brackets). However, each attribute that applies to a module must be preceded by the Module keyword. For example:

```
<Assembly:ClsCompliant(True), Module:CLSCompliant(True)>
```

Because Module is both a Visual Basic keyword and the name of a .NET class (in the System.Reflection namespace), attempting to define a Module object may produce a compiler error. In that case, simply bracket the type name, as follows:

```
Dim currentModule As [Module]
```

Example

See the example for the Assembly keyword.

VB6 Differences

The Module keyword is new to Visual Basic .NET.

See Also

Assembly Keyword

Module Statement

Declares a code module.

Syntax

```
[ <attrilist> ] [ access_modifier ] Module name
    [ statements ]
End Module
```

Element	Description
attrilist	A comma-separated list of attributes with their arguments that apply to the module. Only attributes whose AttributeUsage attribute is AttributeTargets.All or AttributeTargets.Class can be applied to a module. Note that an attribute whose AttributeUsage attribute is AttributeTargets.Module cannot be applied to a Visual Basic code module.
access_modifier	The access modifier, either Public (the module is publicly accessible) or Friend (the module is accessible only to types in the same assembly).
name	The module name, which must follow standard Visual Basic naming conventions and must be unique in its namespace.

Comments

The following discussion of the Module keyword consists of two sections. The first discusses topics related to the character of Visual Basic modules and to creating modules. The second covers accessing modules and their members from code outside the module.

General Comments

If *access_modifier* is not specified, a code module has Friend access by default.

Modules are defined using the Module . . . End Module construct at the namespace level; they cannot be nested within a module, a class, or a structure.

Modules can contain fields (variables and constants), properties, methods (functions and subroutines), delegates, and events. Enumerations can also be nested in a module.

Modules cannot contain nested classes, structures, or interfaces. They also cannot inherit from other classes or implement interfaces.

You may be wondering how the Module statement relates to the .NET type system. If we create the following simple module and compile it, we can see how the compiler translates it into an element in the .NET type system:

```
Public NotInheritable Module Utilities
    Public Function CurDrive() As Char
        Return CChar(Left(CurDir(), 1))
    End Function
End Module
```

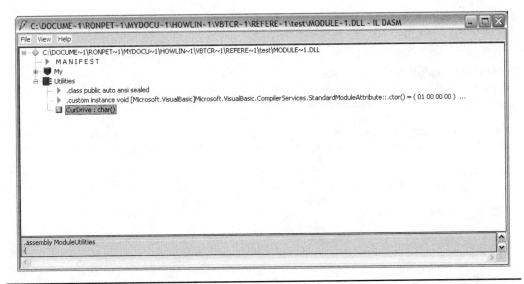

FIGURE 8-15   ILDasm displaying a Visual Basic module

As Figure 8-15 shows, the Visual Basic compiler translates the Module . . . End Module construct into a .NET class. The class is marked as NotInheritable (i.e., sealed). However, if we try to add the NotInheritable keyword to our code, a compiler error results, which suggests that all modules are not inheritable, and that this characteristic cannot be overridden. In addition, if we use ILDasm to inspect the code generated for the module's single method (see Figure 8-16), we see that the compiler has marked it with the **static** keyword, which is the same as the Shared keyword in Visual Basic .NET. If we then declare the method as Shared in our code and try to

```
Utilities::CurDrive : char()
Find  Find Next
.method public static char  CurDrive() cil managed
{
  // Code size       21 (0x15)
  .maxstack  2
  .locals init (char V_0)
  IL_0000:  call       string [Microsoft.VisualBasic]Microsoft.VisualBasic.FileSystem::CurDir()
  IL_0005:  ldc.i4.1
  IL_0006:  call       string [Microsoft.VisualBasic]Microsoft.VisualBasic.Strings::Left(string,
                                                                                          int32)
  IL_000b:  call       char [Microsoft.VisualBasic]Microsoft.VisualBasic.CompilerServices.Conver
  IL_0010:  stloc.0
  IL_0011:  br.s       IL_0013
  IL_0013:  ldloc.0
  IL_0014:  ret
} // end of method Utilities::CurDrive
```

FIGURE 8-16   ILDasm displaying information about a module's member

recompile, a compiler error results, once again suggesting that all members of modules are shared. Finally, one member that is absent from Figure 8-16 is a default constructor. So a module is a class that can't be instantiated, has no instance members, and has only shared members.

Accessing a Module and Its Members

The members of modules can be accessed by qualifying them with their namespaces and module names, or they can also be accessed by qualifying them with their namespace names alone. If the Imports statement is used to import the namespace to which the module belongs, its members can be accessed without qualification. For example, the following code illustrates a module in the MyCompany.Libraries namespace named MathLib that contains two members, Square and Cube:

```
Namespace MyCompany.Libraries
    Public Module MathLib
        Public Function Square(x As Double) As Double
            Return x ^ 2
        End Function

        Public Function Cube(x As Double) As Double
            Return x ^ 3
        End Function
    End Module
End Namespace
```

The members of the module can then be accessed in four different ways, as the following code illustrates:

```
Imports MyCompany.Libraries

Public Class ModuleTestClass
    Public Shared Sub Main()
        Dim number As Integer = 12
        Console.WriteLine(MyCompany.Libraries.MathLib.Square(number))
        Console.WriteLine(MyCompany.Libraries.Cube(number))
        number += 1
        Console.WriteLine(MathLib.Square(number))
        Console.WriteLine(Cube(number))
    End Sub
End Class
```

Executing the code produces the following output:

```
144
1728
169
2197
```

That members of modules can be accessed without qualification makes naming conflicts more likely. For example, the following code shows two modules that have an identically named GetName member that return the names of different things:

```
Namespace MyCompany.Libraries
    Public Module Accounts
```

```
    Dim custName As String
        Public Function GetName(acctNo As Integer) As String
            ' retrieve customer name from database
            Return custName
        End Function
    End Module

    Public Module Inventory
    Dim itemName As String
        Public Function GetName(sku As Integer) As String
            ' retrieve item name from database
            Return itemName
        End Function
    End Module
End Namespace
```

An unqualified call to a GetName method results in a compiler error ("'GetName' is ambiguous between declarations in Modules 'MyCompany.Libraries.Accounts' and 'MyCompany.Libraries .Inventory'.") Since both methods belong to the same namespace, they must be differentiated by qualifying them with the name of the module to which they belong.

Although modules can expose events, they can't be handled by clients by declaring an object variable using the WithEvents keyword and defining the event handler with the Handles clause, since this syntax requires an object instance, and modules cannot be objects. Instead, events declared by modules must be handled with the AddHandler and RemoveHandler constructs.

VB6 Differences

The Module statement is new to Visual Basic .NET. In Visual Basic 6.0, each code module was stored in its own .bas file. In contrast, in Visual Basic .NET, multiple code modules (as well as multiple classes, structures, enumerations, etc.) can be placed in a single file, thus necessitating a language statement to indicate where a module begins and ends.

See Also

Class Statement, Shared Keyword

Month Function

Extracts the number of the month from a given date value.

Member Of

Microsoft.VisualBasic.DateAndTime

Syntax

```
Month(ByVal DateValue As DateTime) As Integer
```

Element	Description
DateValue	A Date value from which the month number is to be retrieved.

Return Value

An Integer ranging from 1 to 12 indicating the number of the month.

Comments

If Option Strict is off, the compiler automatically converts a string representation of a date to a Date value before calling the Month function. If the conversion fails, the Month function throws an InvalidCastException. To ensure that the string can be successfully converted, you can call the IsDate function beforehand.

The DatePart function can also be used to extract the month component of a date value. For example, the following two function calls return identical values:

```
Console.WriteLine(Month(Date.Now))

Console.WriteLine(DatePart(DateInterval.Month, Date.Now))
```

The Date data type also includes a Month property that extracts the month component of its Date instance. For example:

```
mnth = Date.Now.Month
```

To return the localized name of the month, you can pass the value returned by the Month function to the MonthName function. For example:

```
Console.WriteLine(MonthName(Month(Date.Now)))
```

See Also

Day Function, MonthName Function, Year Function

MonthName Function

Returns a string with the name of a specified month.

Member Of

Microsoft.VisualBasic.DateAndTime

Syntax

```
MonthName(ByVal Month As Integer, Optional ByVal Abbreviate As Boolean = False) _
        As String
```

Element	Description
Month	The number of the month whose name is to be returned.
Abbreviate	A Boolean that indicates whether the month name is to be abbreviated or not. If omitted, its value defaults to False; the month name is not abbreviated.

Return Value

A String containing the name of the month.

Comments

Since MonthName requires the number of the month rather than a date, you can use the Month function, the DatePart function, or the Date structure's instance Month property to retrieve the number of the month that you pass to MonthName. For example:

```
Console.WriteLine(MonthName(Month(Date.Now)))
Console.WriteLine(MonthName(DatePart(DateInterval.Month, Date.Now)))
Console.WriteLine(MonthName(Date.Now.Month))
```

On systems with a 12-month calendar, *Month* can range from 1 to 12. On systems with a 13-month calendar, it can range from 1 to 13. However, on systems with a 12-month calendar, a value of 13 for Month throws an ArgumentException.

Calling the MonthName function and setting the *Abbreviate* argument to False (or not supplying a value) is equivalent to calling the Format function as follows:

```
Console.WriteLine(Format(Date.Now, "MMMM"))
```

Calling the MonthName function and setting its *Abbreviate* argument to True is equivalent to calling the Format function as follows:

```
Console.WriteLine(Format(Date.Now, "MMM"))
```

The MonthName function is localized; it returns a string containing the name of the month using the culture of the current thread.

See Also

DatePart Function, Month Function, WeekdayName Function

MsgBox Function

Displays a message box with a caption, text, buttons, and an icon.

Member Of

Microsoft.VisualBasic.Interaction

Syntax

```
MsgBox(ByVal Prompt As Object, _
       Optional ByVal Buttons As MsgBoxStyle = MsgBoxStyle.OKOnly, _
       Optional ByVal Title As Object = Nothing) _
As MsgBoxResult
```

Element	Description
Prompt	The message to display in the message box. The prompt in a message box is shown in Figure 8-17. *Prompt* is the function's single required argument.
Buttons	One or more members of the MsgBoxStyle enumeration that define the button or buttons that appear on the dialog, the icon that appears, the default button, the dialog's modality, the direction in which characters are read, and several other settings. If *Buttons* is omitted, the message box has a single OK button without an icon.
Title	The caption to appear on the dialog. The caption in a message box is shown in Figure 8-17. If *Title* is not provided, it defaults to the name of the application for which the message box is displayed.

Return Value

A member of the MsgBoxResult enumeration indicating the button selected by the user to close the dialog, as follows:

Enumeration Member	Description	Value
MsgBoxResult.Abort	The Abort button was clicked.	3
MsgBoxResult.Cancel	The Cancel button was clicked or the ESC key was pressed.	2
MsgBoxResult.Ignore	The Ignore button was clicked.	5
MsgBoxResult.No	The No button was clicked.	7
MsgBoxResult.OK	The OK button was clicked.	1
MsgBoxResult.Retry	The Retry button was clicked.	4
MsgBoxResult.Yes	The Yes button was clicked.	6

Comments

Prompt can be divided into multiple lines using the ControlChars.CrLf enumeration member or vbCrLf constant.

The *Buttons* argument actually controls six different aspects of the dialog. (These are discussed separately in the following comments.) Each set of options forms a group from which only one option should be chosen. Selecting multiple options from a single group or selecting an invalid combination of options from different groups (for example, by selecting the MsgBoxStyle.OKOnly member to display only a single button while selecting the MsgBoxStyle.DefaultButton3 member to make a non-existent third button the default selection) generates neither a compiler error nor a runtime error, although it does produce unpredictable results.

FIGURE 8-17

A message box produced by the MsgBox function

To specify multiple options, you can add them or Or them. For example:

```
result = MsgBox("Are you sure that you want to overwrite thie file?", _
                MsgBoxStyle.YesNoCancel Or MsgBoxStyle.Critical Or _
                MsgBoxStyle.DefaultButton2, _
                "Overwriting a File")
```

uses the Or operator to specify three enumeration members that define the buttons, icon, and default button on the message box.

To determine which buttons the message box displays, you can select one of the following enumeration members:

Member	Description
MsgBoxStyle.OKOnly	The OK button; this is the default value.
MsgBoxStyle.OKCancel	The OK and Cancel buttons.
MsgBoxStyle.AbortRetryIgnore	The Abort, Retry, and Ignore buttons.
MsgBoxStyle.YesNoCancel	The Yes, No, and Cancel buttons.
MsgBoxStyle.YesNo	The Yes and No buttons.
MsgBoxStyle.RetryCancel	The Retry and Cancel buttons.

In addition, you can include a help button by specifying MsgBoxStyle.MsgBoxHelp enumeration member. However, this is a holdover from Visual Basic 6.0, which allowed you to connect your message box to a help system. This feature is not supported in Visual Basic .NET, and so the help button has no effect (other, that is, than confusing the user).

To define which icon the message box displays, you can select one of the following enumeration members:

Member	Description
MsgBoxStyle.Critical	Used for a warning or error condition.
MsgBoxStyle.Exclamation	Used to convey something positive.
MsgBoxStyle.Information	Used to provide information.
MsgBoxStyle.Question	Used to prompt the user.

The four icons are shown in Figure 8-18. If none of the icon-related enumeration members is specified, no icon is displayed.

The *default button* is the button whose value is returned if the user presses the ENTER key. If a dialog has more than one button, the default button is displayed with dotted lines near its border. You can designate a particular button as the default by using one of the following MsgBoxStyle enumeration members:

Member	Description
MsgBoxStyle.DefaultButton1	The first button from the left.
MsgBoxStyle.DefaultButton2	The second button from the left.
MsgBoxStyle.DefaultButton3	The third button from the left.

FIGURE 8-18
Icons defined by
the MsgBoxStyle
enumeration

Critical   Exclamation Information   Question

Particularly when displaying warnings, it's best to make the default button the one that takes the least drastic action (and the one that can be undone most easily) in the event that the user makes a selection in error. For example, in Figure 8-19, a message box is asking the user to confirm a file deletion. The default button is the No button, since canceling the deletion is the least drastic alternative that the dialog provides.

If a message box is *application modal,* the user cannot switch away from the message box to any of the application's other windows until the message box is closed. A *system modal* message box is application modal, but it also remains the topmost window if the user switches the focus to other applications. You specify whether an a dialog is application modal or system modal (there is no modeless option) by using one of the following enumeration members:

Member	Description
MsgBoxStyle.ApplicationModal	The message box is application modal. This is the default value.
MsgBoxStyle.SystemModal	The message box is system modal.

In addition to the MsgBoxStyle.MsgBoxHelp enumeration member that was discussed earlier, there are three miscellaneous options that are not part of a group and are not mutually exclusive. They are:

Member	Description
MsgBoxStyle.MsgBoxRight	Right-aligns the text in the message box. By default, it is left-aligned.
MsgBoxStyle.MsgBoxRtlReading	For Hebrew and Arabic systems, reads text from right to left. The default (for which there is no enumeration member) is to read text from left to right.
MsgBoxStyle.MsgBoxSetForeground	Sets the message box as the foreground window. In the Windows XP family of operating systems, this enumeration member has no effect.

Unlike the InputBox function, which has parameters that allow you to position the dialog on the screen, the MsgBox function automatically centers the message box in the center of the screen; you cannot control its positioning.

FIGURE 8-19
A message box
with the No button
selected

Although message boxes are closely associated with Windows form applications, the MsgBox function is not dependent on the System.Windows.Forms library and can be called from console applications as well.

Since the MsgBox function is a modal application that suspends execution of the current process until the message box is closed, you want to make sure that you don't call the MsgBox function in a range of application types, such as ASP.NET applications, server applications, service applications, and unattended applications. Nor should you include calls to the MsgBox function in general-purpose components, unless you're certain that they'll be used entirely in applications with user interfaces. As an alternative to displaying information to the message box, you can write it to the Windows system event log or write it to an application-generated log file.

The MsgBox function corresponds to the Show method of the MessageBox class in the System.Windows.Forms namespace. With its 21 overloads, though, sorting through its syntax, particularly when using IntelliSense, to find the overload that you want to call can be far more trouble than its worth. In contrast, the MsgBox function offers an elegant simplicity that continues to make it a valuable function for the Visual Basic programmer.

VB6 Differences

The Visual Basic 6.0 version of the MsgBox function included two additional parameters, *helpfile* and *context*, that allowed you to specify a help file and a context ID within the help file that provided additional information about the message box display. If the *buttons* arguments included the vbMsgBoxHelpButton constant, a Help button appeared on the form; if the user clicked it, the message box remained opened, and an additional help window displaying the topic defined by *context* in *helpfile* was opened. In Visual Basic .NET, help is not supported with the MsgBox function, although the MsgBoxStyle.MsgBoxHelpButton enumerated constant still survives.

See Also

InputBox Function

MustInherit Keyword

Indicates that a class is an abstract base class that cannot be instantiated.

Syntax

See the syntax for the Class . . . End Class construct.

Comments

Classes defined using the MustInherit keyword cannot be instantiated. Attempting to do so generates the compiler error, "'New' cannot be used on a class that is declared 'MustInherit'."

Abstract base classes are defined for a number of reasons, including the following:

The functionality of the classes to be derived from the abstract base class in an object model is so diverse that the base class cannot provide a very meaningful implementation. For example, in an application that models organizations, the Organization class might be defined as MustInherit because the diversity of organizational types and forms makes it impossible to provide a meaningful implementation of very many members.

The base class contains significant functionality, but itself does not provide a complete implementation. Instead, it relies on derived classes to provide that implementation for particular application areas.

The abstract base class can still be used polymorphically. In other words, variables of the abstract base class type can still be declared and used to instantiate derived classes. For example:

```
Dim thisclass As AbstractClass = New DerivedClass()
```

Similarly, the abstract base class can be used as a parameter type in method calls, which restricts the argument passed to the method to an instance of a derived class.

Although you can mark a class as MustInherit so that it can't be instantiated, unless you explicitly provide one or more constructors, the Visual Basic .NET compiler will automatically provide a public constructor. For consistency, you can define a parameterless constructor as follows:

```
Protected Sub New()
```

This makes it clear that the default constructor can only be called from derived classes.

You have three choices in defining the relationship between the members of the base class and the members of any classes derived from it:

- **Overridable**   The base class can provide functionality that derived classes can either use or override.
- **NotOverridable**   The base class can provide functionality that derived classes must use. This is the default behavior.
- **MustOverride**   The base class provides no implementation, but just as when implementing an interface, derived classes must provide a method implementation with the same signature as the base class method.

If any members of a class are marked MustOverride, then the class must also be marked with the MustInherit keyword.

VB6 Differences

The MustInherit keyword is new to Visual Basic .NET. Visual Basic 6.0 did not support inheritance.

Example

See the example for the MustOverride Keyword.

See Also

Class Statement, MustOverride Keyword, NotInheritable Keyword, NotOverridable Keyword, Overridable Keyword

MustOverride Keyword

Indicates that a base class does not provide an implementation of a member, which must be overridden in a derived class in order to be used.

Syntax

```
MustOverride Function name
MustOverride Property name
MustOverride Sub name
```

Element	Description
name	The name of the function, property, or subroutine.

Comments

The MustOverride keyword defines a class member as an *abstract member*. The member provides no implementation, instead leaving the member implementation to derived classes.

MustOverride is used exclusively with Function, Sub, and Property statements defined in a class. It cannot be used with other members, nor can it be applied to structure, module, or interface members.

Function, Sub, and Property statements that are declared MustOverride include no implementation code and no End Function, End Sub, or End Property statement. (Members marked MustOverride are very much like interface members.) However, if you do include an End . . . statement, the compiler flags the first line of implementation code, the Get statement of a Property statement, the Set statement of a Property statement, or the End statement as having a syntax error, but fails to identify the source of the error as the presence of the MustOverride keyword.

Typically, MustOverride is used so that a base class member can define a member name, signature, and return value while leaving the implementation of the method up to derived classes. In a drawing program, for example, a base class named Shape might define a Draw method but leave its implementation up to individual derived classes that will better be able to draw themselves.

If MustOverride is used as a keyword, the class in which it is declared must be declared as an abstract base class using the MustInherit keyword.

If a member is declared using the MustOverride keyword, derived classes that themselves are not abstract base classes must provide an implementation that matches the member in name, signature, and return type. Properties must also have the same read-write attribute applied as the Derived class members must also be marked with the Overrides keyword. For a derived class, implementing an abstract member is very much like implementing an interface member, except that its name must be the same as that of the abstract member.

The implementation of the abstract member can be called either through a variable of the derived class or of the base class. For example, if Shape is an abstract base class and Square is a derived class, the Square.Draw method can be invoked in any of the following ways:

- The Square.Draw method can be called using a variable of type Square:

```
Dim figure As Square = New Square
figure.Draw()
```

- The Square.Draw method can be called through a variable of type Shape:

```
Dim figure As Shape = New Square()
figure.Draw()
```

- The Square object can be passed to a method expecting an argument of type Shape and its draw method can be called:

```
Dim rect As New Shape
CallDrawMethod(rect)

Private Sub CallDrawMethod(figure As Shape)
    figure.Draw()
End Sub
```

Example

The example illustrates the use of the MustInherit keyword to define an abstract base class and of the MustOverride keyword to define two abstract properties. An abstract base class named Shape defines an Area property and a Circumference property. They are abstract, since there is no general formula for calculating the area and circumference of a geometric shape; instead, the formula is dependent on the attributes of the shape itself. The abstract base class is defined as follows:

```
Public MustInherit Class Shape
    Public MustOverride ReadOnly Property Area() As Double
    Public MustOverride ReadOnly Property Circumference() As Double
End Class
```

Any derived class (unless it is also an abstract class) must then implement the members of Shape:

```
Public Class Circle : Inherits Shape
    Private radius As Double

    Public Sub New(radius As Double)
        Me.radius = radius
    End Sub

    Public Overrides ReadOnly Property Area() As Double
        Get
            Return Math.Pi * radius ^ 2
        End Get
    End Property

    Public Overrides ReadOnly Property Circumference() As Double
        Get
            Return Math.Pi * 2 * radius
        End Get
    End Property
End Class
```

The Circle class can then be used in code as follows:

```
Public Module modShape
    Public Sub Main
        Dim shape As Shape
        shape = New Circle(2.55)
        Console.WriteLine(shape.Area)
        Console.WriteLine(shape.Circumference)
    End Sub
End Module
```

VB6 Differences

The MustOverride keyword is new to Visual Basic .NET. Visual Basic 6.0 did not support inheritance.

See Also

MustInherit Keyword, NotOverridable Keyword, Overridable Keyword

MyBase Keyword

References a base class from within a derived class.

Syntax

`MyBase.`*name*

Element	Description
name	Name of a base class member.

Comments

The MyBase keyword serves as an object reference to a base class from within a derived class. It is used to invoke members of a base class from a derived class.

MyBase can be used within a class (that is, within the Class . . . End Class construct) to refer to the base class of that class. It cannot be used from client code, nor can it be used within a structure.

The use of the MyBase keyword to call inherited members not implemented by the current class is not required; the compiler will resolve method calls identically whether or not the method call is qualified with the MyBase keyword. However, use of the MyBase keyword is required under two circumstances:

- To invoke a member of the base class that the current class overrides or shadows and that is therefore hidden by the derived class implementation. Often, the method in the derived class itself needs to call the overridden or shadowed method. For instance, the following pseudocode example defines a Window class that contains the code to draw a border around itself. The Button class inherits from Window and overrides its Draw method. It contains the code to draw the button caption, but calls the Window.Draw implementation to draw the border, thus saving the need to duplicate low-level drawing code in all derived class Draw methods:

```
Class Window
    Overridable Sub Draw
        ' Draw border
    End Sub
End Class

Class Button : Inherits Window
    Overrides Sub Draw
        ' Code to draw caption
        MyBase.Draw
    End Sub
End Class
```

Without the MyBase keyword, however, this is not a straightforward method call.

- To invoke a member of the base class that is accessible but is not inherited by the derived class. Non-private constructors in particular fall into this category.

There are some restrictions on the use of the MyBase keyword:

- MyBase cannot be passed as a method argument in the same way that Me can be passed.
- MyBase cannot be used to access base class members that are not otherwise accessible. It cannot be used, for example, to access Private members or to access Friend members in a base class located in another assembly.
- MyBase cannot be used to access a shared member.
- MyBase cannot be used to access a base class member that is marked MustOverride, nor can it be used to access an interface method.
- In general, you should call the base class constructor from the constructor of a derived class using the syntax

  ```
  MyBase.New(argument_list)
  ```

The call to the base class constructor is optional for parameterless constructors but required for parameterized constructors. The call to the base class constructor must be the first executable statement in the derived class constructor.

VB6 Differences

The MyBase keyword is new to Visual Basic .NET. Visual Basic 6.0 did not support inheritance.

See Also

Me Keyword, MyClass Keyword, Overrides Keyword

MyClass Keyword

Provides a reference to the class or structure instance in which the code is currently executing as it was originally implemented.

Syntax

MyClass.*name*

Element	Description
name	The name of a class member.

Comments

Unlike the Me keyword, MyClass cannot be used by itself to represent a reference to the current class, nor can it be passed as an argument to a method.

MyClass is largely identical to Me when it is used as a qualifier for a reference call, except in one respect. When an overridden member is invoked using MyClass, the compiler resolves the method call by interpreting MyClass as a reference to the class or structure in which the method was defined. This means that, if a derived class calls an inherited method in the base class, which in turn calls an overridden method using the MyClass keyword, the base class version of the method is invoked. To put it another way, MyClass turns off virtual method calls. The example illustrates this scenario.

Example

The example illustrates the difference between the Me and the MyClass keywords when calling an overridden method from the base class. An overridable method in the base class named DisplayMethodInfo displays the string "BaseClass.DisplayMethodInfo" when it is invoked. The derived class overrides this method to display the string "DerivedClass.DisplayInfoMethod." The base class also implements to methods to call the DisplayMethodInfo function. The first, InvokeCaller, invokes DisplayMethodInfo using the Me keyword; the second, InvokeBase, uses the MyClass keyword.

```
Public Class BaseClass
    Public Overridable Sub DisplayMethodInfo()
        Console.WriteLine("BaseClass.DisplayMethodInfo")
    End Sub

    Public Sub InvokeCaller()
        Console.WriteLine("About to call Me.DisplayMethodInfo()")
        Me.DisplayMethodInfo()
    End Sub

    Public Sub InvokeBase()
        Console.WriteLine("About to call MyClass.DisplayMethodInfo()")
        MyClass.DisplayMethodInfo()
    End Sub
End Class

Public Class DerivedClass : Inherits BaseClass
    Public Overrides Sub DisplayMethodInfo()
        Console.WriteLine("DerivedClass.DisplayMethodInfo")
    End Sub
End Class

Public Module Test
    Public Sub Main()
        Dim dc As New DerivedClass
        dc.InvokeCaller()
        dc.InvokeBase()
    End Sub
End Module
```

In the code module, the derived class is instantiated and both the InvokeCaller and InvokeBase methods are called. The result is as follows:

```
About to call Me.DisplayMethodInfo()
DerivedClass.DisplayMethodInfo
About to call MyClass.DisplayMethodInfo()
BaseClass.DisplayMethodInfo
```

Since the InvokeBase method in which the MyClass keyword appears belongs to the base class, the compiler interprets MyClass as a reference to the base class and calls its version of the DisplayMethodInfo method. On the other hand, because it interprets Me as referring to the caller of the InvokeCaller method, it calls the derived class version of the DisplayMethodInfo method.

VB6 Differences

The MyClass keyword is new to Visual Basic .NET.

See Also

Me Keyword, MyBase Keyword

Namespace Statement

Indicates that all types defined until the End Namespace tag is encountered belong in the designated namespace.

Syntax

```
Namespace name
    [ componentTypes ]
End Namespace
```

Element	Description
name	The name of the namespace.
componentTypes	The elements defined within the namespace. This can consist of other namespaces, as well as classes, modules, structures, interfaces, enumerations, and delegates.

Comments

All namespaces are public. For that reason, attempting to assign an access modifier to a namespace produces a compiler error.

If a Namespace statement is nested, the inner namespace is contained by the outer namespace. The fully qualified path of the nested namespace includes the entire fully qualified path of the outer namespace.

A nested namespace can only be contained by an outer namespace; it cannot be specified within a .NET type definition construct.

In the case of an outer namespace, *name* does not necessarily specify the fully qualified namespace name. Visual Studio automatically assigns projects a "root namespace," which is defined on the Application tab of the Project Properties dialog. By default, the root namespace name is the same as the project name, and any namespaces specified by the Namespace statement are appended to the root namespace. So, for example, if a project is named MyAddOnLib and the source code defines a namespace named MyBusiness, the fully qualified namespace name will be MyAddOnLib.MyBusiness, rather than simply MyBusiness. The compiler similarly has a **/rootnamespace** switch that works identically, although it does not supply a default root namespace if none is specified.

The purpose of namespaces in .NET is to provide for a logical organization of .NET types and to prevent naming collisions among types. For instance, both System.Windows.Forms and System.Web.UI have a Control class. They can be distinguished by the namespace in which they reside.

Because the major purpose of namespaces is to allow you to organize and categorize types, you can use the Namespace statement with considerable freedom. The same namespace can be specified in different source code files and even in different assemblies. (The System namespace, for example, includes types that are found in both mscorlib.dll and System.dll.) And a single source code file can specify multiple namespaces, and can even specify the same namespace multiple times.

In order for the compiler to locate particular types, you must either indicate their fully qualified type name (complete namespace and type name) or use the Imports statement so that type names either do not need qualification, can be referenced using an alias, or can be referenced using a relative instead of a fully qualified namespace path.

If the namespace that contains your code is nested in another namespace, you can use either a single Namespace statement or nested namespace statements. For example, you can define a Utilities namespace that is nested in the MyApplication namespace as follows:

```
Namespace MyApplication
    Public Class classMain
    End Class
End Namespace

Namespace MyApplication.Utilities
    Public Class StringHandler
    End Class
End Namespace
```

The following code also produces a Utilities namespace nested in the MyApplication namespace:

```
Namespace MyApplication
    Public Class classMain
    End Class

    ' Namespae is nested in MyApplication
    Namespace Utilities
        Public Class StringHandler
        End Class
    End Namespace
End Namespace
```

Example

The following code uses Namespace statements to specify the same namespace twice in a single source code file, uses two different methods (a fully qualified namespace name and an outer and nested Namespace statement) to specify the same namespace, and also specifies a third, unrelated namespace:

```
Namespace HowlingWolfConsulting
    Namespace Libraries
        Public Class MathLib
            ' class members go here
        End Class
    End Namespace
End Namespace

Namespace System.Utilities
    Public Enum UtilityType As Integer
```

```
        Disk = 1
        Internet = 2
        Windows = 3
    End Enum
End Namespace

Namespace HowlingWolfConsulting.Libraries
    Public Class StringLib
        ' class members go here
    End Class
End Namespace

Namespace HowlingWolfConsulting.Libraries
    Public Class FileLib
        ' class members go here
    End Class
End Namespace
```

In Figure 8-20, ILDasm displays the result: the compiler has created two namespaces,
System.Utilities and HowlingWolfConsulting.Libraires. (These fully qualified namespace names
resulted from the fact that no root namespace was supplied to the compiler.)

You can define nested namespaces either with a single Namespace statement or with multiple
Namespace statement. For example, to define a class, UtilityLibrary, in the MyCompany.MyApplication
.MyLibraries namespace, the code:

```
Namespace MyCompany.MyApplication.MyLibraries
    Public Class UtilityLibrary
        ' member definitions
    End Class
End Namespace
```

FIGURE 8-20
The namespace
hierarchy produced
by the code
example

uses a single statement to indicate that the UtilityLibrary class is found in the MyLibraries namespace, which is a child namespace of the MyApplication namespace, which in turn is a child namespace of the MyCompany namespace. The following code produces identical results:

```
Namespace MyCompany
    Namespace MyApplication
        NameSpace MyLibraries
            Class UtilityLibrary
                ' member definitions
            End Class
        End Namespace
    End Namespace
End Namespace
```

VB6 Differences

The Namespace statement is not supported by Visual Basic 6.0.

See Also

Imports Statement

Narrowing Keyword

Used with the Operator statement to indicate that a custom type conversion operation defined with CType is a narrowing operation that could result in a loss of data.

Syntax

```
Public Shared Narrowing Operator CType(operand1) [ As type ]
    [ statements ]
    [ statements ]
    Return returnvalue
    [ statements ]
End Operator
```

Element	Description
operand1	The name and type of the instance whose conversion the Operator statement defines. operand1 has the general syntax: [**ByVal**] operandname [**As** operandtype] where operandname is the name by which the instance is referred in statements, and operandtype is its data type. operandtype must be the type of the class or structure in which the Operator statement is contained. If Option Strict is on, operandtype is required; otherwise, it is optional.
type	The type to which operand1 is to be converted.
returnvalue	An instance of operand1 converted to type that is to be returned to the caller.

For the complete syntax, see the entry for the Operator Statement.

Comments

Narrowing conversions involve converting from one type to a more restrictive type that could involve data loss. For example, a conversion from an Integer (a 32-bit signed integral value) to a Byte (an 8-bit unsigned integral value) involves the possibility of data loss for most of the range of the Integer. Similarly, a conversion of a base data type to a derived type is a narrowing conversion. If Option Strict is off, the compiler will attempt to perform narrowing conversions automatically. If Option Strict is on, however, an explicit conversion operator (for structures and classes, either the DirectCast, TryCast, or CType functions) must be used for all narrowing conversions.

The Operator statement with the Narrowing keyword is used to define conversions of instances of classes or structures to other types.

The Operator statement always defines a shared procedure.

The Return statement must be used to return a value to the caller.

When the CType conversion function is called to perform the conversion, an instance of *operand1* is supplied as an argument to the CType function's first parameter (the instance to be converted), and *type* is supplied as its second argument (the destination type).

Example

The following code defines a structure named Person that includes some basic information about a person, namely his or her name, age, and gender. The code also defines a narrowing operator to convert an instance of Person to a String.

```
Public Structure Person

    Public Sub New(fName As String, middleInit As String, lname As String, _
                gender As Char, birth As Date)
        Me.FirstName = fname
        Me.MiddleInitial = middleInit
        Me.LastName = lname
        Me.Gender = gender
        Me.DOB = birth
    End Sub

    Public FirstName As String
    Public MiddleInitial As String
    Public LastName As String
    Public Gender As Char
    Public DOB As Date

    Public Shared Narrowing Operator CType(per As Person) As String
        Return Trim(per.FirstName & " " & per.MiddleInitial) & " " & per.LastName
    End Operator
End Structure
```

If Option Strict is on, the following code converts an instance of Person to a String:

```
Public Module modMain
    Public Sub Main()
        Dim contact As New Person("John", "J.", "Doe", "M"c, New Date(1977, 1, 2))
        Dim contactName As String = CType(contact, String)
        Console.WriteLine(contactName)
    End Sub
End Module
```

If Option Strict is on, the call to the CType function to convert an instance of Person to a String is mandatory. Without it, the compiler generates an error, since implicit narrowing conversions are not allowed. On the other hand, if Option Strict is off, the line of code that calls the CType function can be replaced with the code:

```
Dim contactName As String = contact
```

since the compiler will attempt implicit narrowing conversions as well as implicit widening conversions.

VB.NET Changes

The Narrowing keyword is new to Visual Basic 2005.

Visual Basic 2005 is the first version of Visual Basic to support custom conversion operators.

See Also

Operator Statement, Option Strict Statement, Widening Conversion

New Keyword

Defines a class constructor, or instantiates a new object instance and invokes its class constructor.

Syntax

To define a class constructor:

```
<attributelist> [accessModifier] Shared Sub New [(Of typeparamlist)] _
        [(parameterlist)]
    [ statements ]
    [ Exit Sub]
    [ statements ]
End Sub
```

Element	Description
attributelist	A list of attributes to be applied to the function. Only attributes whose AttributeUsage attribute is AttributeTargets.All or AttributeTargets.Constructor can be applied to a constructor.
accessModifier	The constructor's accessibility, which determines where the class can be instantiated using this constructor. Possible keywords are Public (the default if accessModifier is not specified), Private, Friend, Protected, and Protected Friend. For details, see the entry for each of the access modifiers.
typeparamlist	A list of type parameters for the constructor of a generic type. For details, see the entry for the Of Keyword.
parameterlist	The constructor's parameter list, which can consist of any number of parameters. If multiple parameters are present, they are separated from one another with commas. At runtime, the arguments passed to the constructor can be referenced by their parameter names. For the syntax of an individual parameter, see the syntax for the Sub Statement.

To instantiate a new class or structure instance:

```
New name[([arglist])]
```

Element	Description
name	The name of the class or structure to instantiate.
arglist	A comma-separated list of arguments to the constructor. For the syntax of *arglist*, see the Sub Statement entry.

Comments

The following discussion treats defining constructors separately from invoking a constructor to instantiate a class or structure instance.

To Define a Constructor

A class constructor is executed automatically when a new instance of the class is created. Typically, it contains initialization code necessary to properly instantiate the class. Both classes defined with the Class . . . End Class construct and structure defined with the Structure . . . End Structure construct can define constructors.

The constructor's access modifier should reflect where your class or structure can be instantiated. This is not the same as the accessibility of the class or structure itself. Often, constructors are relatively inaccessible or even hidden from client code. A common technique for restricting access to a constructor is to make it private, to invoke it from a call to a shared method, and to return an instance of the newly created object to the caller. (You might call this a "shared factory method.") For example:

```
Public Class Viewer
    ' New inaccessible except from within class
    Private Sub New()
        ' Add whatever code is needed for instantiation
    End Sub

    Public Shared Function GetViewer() As Viewer
        Dim newView As New Viewer
        Return newView
    End Function
End Class
```

Similarly, child objects in an object hierarchy are often created by their parent objects, which return them to the caller through a public property.

Since base class constructors are not inherited by classes derived from them, a number of keywords commonly used with method declarations are not supported with constructors. These include the inheritance modifiers (MustOverride, NotOverridable, Overloads, Overrides, and Overridable) as well as Shadows.

Constructors can either be parameterless (this is sometimes called the default constructor) or parameterized—that is, the constructor can require that arguments be passed to it when the object is instantiated.

In defining a class, if you supply no constructor, a parameterless constructor is created automatically by the compiler. For example, the following code defines a class with no members:

```
Public Class EmptyClass
End Class
```

FIGURE 8-21
A class with a
default constructor

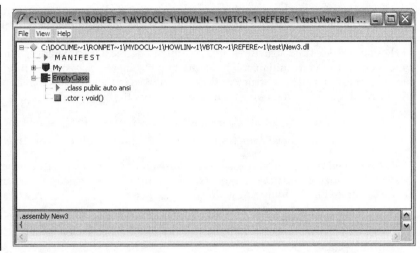

But when we examine the class using ILDasm (see Figure 8-21), we see that the class in fact has a single member, a constructor that accepts no arguments, because the compiler has automatically generated it.

If you define parameterized constructors for the class, the compiler does not automatically generate a default or parameterless constructor for it. If you want one, you must remember to add it yourself.

Typically, derived classes call their base class constructors from their own constructors. This is required for parameterized constructors, and option for default constructors. If it is present, the call to the base class' constructor must be the first executable statement in the derived class' constructor. For example, the following code shows the code for a base class, Auto, and a derived class, Sedan. The first statement in the constructor of Sedan calls the constructor of Auto:

```
Public Class Auto
    Protected Make As String
    Protected Model As String

    Public Sub New(make As String, model As String)
        Me.Make = make
        Me.Model = model
    End Sub
End Class

Public Class Sedan : Inherits Auto
    Private seats As Integer

    Public Sub New(make As String, model As String, passengers As Integer)
        MyBase.New(make,model)
        Me.seats = passengers
    End Sub
End Class
```

Unlike classes, structures can have only parameterized instance constructors. You cannot define a parameterless instance constructor for a structure, nor does the Visual Basic compiler automatically add one in the output assembly.

For both classes and structures, it is possible to define a parameterless shared constructor, which can perform any initialization required by the shared class or structure. The shared constructor for that class or structure is fired just once in the lifetime of an application under whichever of the following two circumstances occurs first:

- A shared member of the class or structure is accessed for the first time.

- The first attempt is made to create a new instance of the class or structure.

If the shared constructor is executed because an instance of a class or structure is being created, the shared constructor is executed before the class or structure's instance constructor. This is illustrated in the following code:

```
Public Class classMain

    Public Shared Sub Main()
        Dim cs As New ConstructStructure(12)
        Console.WriteLine()
'        Console.WriteLine(ConstructStructure.ReturnName)
    End Sub

End Class

Public Structure ConstructStructure
    Private Value As Integer
    Private Shared Name As String

    Public Sub New(value As Integer)
        Me.Value = value
        Console.WriteLine("Parameterized constructor")
    End Sub

    Shared Sub New()
        Console.WriteLine("Default Shared constructor")
        Name = "Structure to Test Constructors"
    End Sub

    Public Shared Function ReturnName() As String
        Return Name
    End Function
End Structure
```

The example produces the following output, which indicates that the shared constructor is invoked before the instance constructor:

```
Default Shared constructor
Parameterized constructor
```

Constructors can be overloaded. Typically, when they are, a single constructor actually performs initialization, while the remaining overloads simply call that constructor. For example, the following code defines a Contact class that has three constructors, one that expects the contact's first name to be passed as an argument, one that expects the contract's first and middle names, and one that expects the contact's first, middle, and last names. The first constructor wraps a call to the second, while the second wraps a call to the third:

```
Public Class Contact
    Private firstName As String
    Private middleInitial As String
    Private lastName As String

    Public Sub New(firstName As String)
        Me.New(firstname, String.Empty)
    End Sub

    Public Sub New(firstName As String, middleInitial As String)
        Me.New(firstname, middleInitial, String.Empty)
    End Sub

    Public Sub New(firstName As String, middleInitial As String, _
                   lastName As String)
        Me.firstName = firstName
        Me.middleInitial = middleInitial
        Me.lastName = lastName
    End Sub
End Class
```

To Create a Class or Structure Instance

The New keyword can be used with a variable declaration statement (the Dim statement, as well as the Private, Friend, Protected, and Protected Friend statements), in an assignment statement, and in some method arguments to invoke a class or structure's constructor and initialize a new instance of that class or structure.

When the New keyword is used to instantiate a class or a structure, the appropriate number and type of arguments defined by one of the class or structure's constructors must be provided, or the compiler displays the error message, "Argument not specified for parameter '*xxx*' of '*constructor_signature*'".

A class or structure can be instantiated at the same time that the variable that references it is declared. Either of the following Dim statements, for example, could instantiate a new System.Collections.Hashtable object instance:

```
Dim htable As HashTable = New Hashtable(initialCapacity)

Dim htable As New HashTable(initialCapacity)
```

A class or structure can also be instantiated separately from the variable declaration, in an assignment statement. For example, the following code declares a System.IO.FileInfo object and instantiates it in a separate line of code:

```
Dim fileInf As FileInfo
fileInf = New FileInfo(filename)
```

There is no practical difference between instantiating a variable in the same line of code as it is declared and instantiating it in separate lines.

Finally, a class constructor can be instantiated when arguments are provided to Visual Basic statements. For example, the following Throw statement instantiates the Exception object that contains exception information and provides its constructor with an error message:

```
Throw New InvalidCastException("The value you've entered is not numeric.")
```

VB.NET Changes

The use of the Of *typeparamlist* clause to support a generic parameter list is new to constructors in Visual Basic 2005.

VB6 Differences

Visual Basic 6.0 did not support constructors. Instead, it included an Initialize event that was fired shortly after an object was instantiated.

In Visual Basic 6.0, variables that were instantiated using the New keyword in an assignment statement were reinstantiated if necessary whenever the variable was referenced. As a result, a comparison statement such as

```
If thisObject Is Nothing
```

always returned False, since the statement itself caused thisObject to be reinstantiated. In contrast, in Visual Basic .NET, there is no practical difference between instantiating an object variable in its declaration or instantiating it separately.

See Also

Dim Statement, MyBase Keyword, Sub Statement

Next Keyword

Marks the end point of a loop, or directs program flow using unstructured error handling.

Comments

When used with the For . . . Next or For Each . . . Next constructs, the Next statement causes program flow to branch to the For or For Each clause, where the looping condition is evaluated. If the looping condition is met then the loop is executed again; otherwise, control resumes following the Next statement.

When it appears in an On Error Resume Next statement, it causes program flow to continue to the line immediately following the error. It is used for inline error handling.

When used with the Resume statement in an error handler, it redirects program flow out of the error handler to the statement that immediately follows the error (or if the error occurred in a called procedure, it redirects program flow to the statement that immediately follows the statement that last called out of the procedure where the error handler is defined).

See Also

For . . . Next Statement, For Each . . . Next Statement, On Error Statement, Resume Statement

Nothing Keyword

Represents the default value of any data type.

Syntax

```
name = Nothing
If name Is Nothing
If name = Nothing
```

Element	Description
name	The name of a variable to set or compare to Nothing.

Comments

When used in an assignment, the Nothing keyword sets a variable to its default value. The default value of each of the data types is shown in the following table:

Data Type	Value or Reference Type	Default Value
Array	Reference	Does not refer to a valid object
Boolean	Value	False
Byte	Value	0
Char	Value	Chr(0)
Date	Value	1/1/0001 12:00:00 AM
Double	Value	0.00
Integer	Value	0
Long	Value	0
Object	Reference	Does not refer to a valid object
SByte	Value	0
Short	Value	0
Single	Value	0.00
String	Reference	String.Empty
Type defined with Class	Reference	Does not refer to a valid object
Type defined with Structure	Value	Individual fields are initialized to their default values
UInteger	Value	0
ULong	Value	0
UShort	Value	0

You can determine whether a value type is Nothing (that is, whether it is set to its default value) by using the syntax:

```
If variableName = Nothing
```

You can determine whether a reference type is Nothing (that is, whether it references a valid object) by using the syntax:

```
If variableName Is Nothing
```

If you fail to use the correct syntax for an early bound (non-Object) data type, you'll receive a compiler error. For a late-bound Object type with Option Strict On, you must use the Is Nothing syntax regardless of the Object's runtime type. For a late-bound Object type with Option Strict off, you can use either syntax with an Object whose runtime type is a value type. But with an Object whose runtime type is a reference type, you must use the Is Nothing syntax or the .NET runtime throws an InvalidCastException.

If you need to determine whether a particular variable is a reference or data type in order to use the proper expression, you can use the IsReference function. For example:

```
If IsReference(value) Then
    If value Is Nothing Then
        ' do something
    ' handle value as a value type
    Else
        ' do something
    End If
End If
```

VB6 Differences

In Visual Basic 6.0, Nothing was used only in its more restrictive sense, that an object did not reference valid data. Nothing did not represent the default value of a data item, nor could Nothing be used with non-object data types.

See Also

Is Keyword, IsNothing Function

NotInheritable Keyword

Indicates that a class cannot serve as a base class.

Syntax

See the syntax for the Class . . . End Class construct.

Comments

An attempt to inherit from a class marked with the NotInheritable keyword generates a compiler error.

There are five major reasons for marking a class NotInheritable:

- Inheritance is unnecessary. The class is the final object in an object model's object hierarchy. Since the object model's inheritance hierarchy, public interface, and functionality are complete, there is no need to further derive from this class.

- You don't want to invest the extra time for development, testing, and maintenance that might be required to make your class extensible by third parties.

- Versioning. A sealed class can always be safely unsealed, but it is a breaking change to seal an unsealed class. Sealed classes help to maintain compatibility.

- It is safer to maintain and modify a base class. Sealed classes never induce the brittle base class problem, since there are no derived classes to break.

- Security. If a base class can be extended by third parties, then you must write it to not rely an any invariant values or conditions that are true of your implementation but not others. Polymorphism also means that any derived classes have an "is a" relationship to your base class. This has definite security implications.

By default in Visual Basic .NET, classes are inheritable. If you don't want your class to be derived from, you must use the NotInheritable keyword in the class definition.

The term *sealed* is sometimes used to describe a class that is not inheritable. *sealed* is the C# equivalent of the NotInheritable keyword.

Instead of marking entire classes NotInheritable, you can mark individual methods as NotOverridable, which allows classes to inherit from your base class but prevents them from overriding some or all of its methods. By default, methods are not overridable.

VB6 Differences

The NotInheritable keyword is new to Visual Basic .NET. Visual Basic 6.0 did not support inheritance.

See Also

Class Statement, Inherits Statement, MustInherit Keyword

NotOverridable Keyword

Indicates that a class member cannot be overridden in a derived class.

Syntax

See the syntax for the Function Statement, Property Statement, and Sub Statement.

Comments

NotOverridable is used with a class method or property to indicate that the member cannot be overridden in a derived class.

By default, methods in inheritable classes cannot be overridden unless they are marked with the Overridable keyword. To prevent a member that does not override a base class member from being overridden, you simply have to make sure that the Overrides keyword is not present; since this is the default behavior, there is no language element to prevent overriding in this situation.

The NotOverridable keyword is intended for use with methods that override base class methods. By default, these functions, which are marked with the Overrides keyword, are also Overridable. In other words, the NotOverridable keyword can only be used with class members that use the Overrides keyword to indicate that they override members of their base class. The NotOverridable keyword cannot be used with the Shared, MustOverride, or Overridable keywords.

If you implement a derived class member with the same name as a base class member marked with the NotOverridable keyword or that is not overridable, the Visual Basic compiler will automatically assume that you want to the derived class member to shadow the base class member, even if you don't add the Shadows keyword and will display a compiler warning.

Example

The following example illustrates the use of the NotOverridable keyword to prevent any possible derived classes from overriding the DerivedClass override of a method named MethodA:

```
Public Class BaseClass
    Public Overridable Sub MethodA()
        Console.WriteLine("BaseClass1.MethodA")
    End Sub
End Class

Public Class DerivedClass : Inherits BaseClass
    Public NotOverridable Overrides Sub MethodA()
        Console.WriteLine("DerivedClass.MethodA")
    End Sub
End Class
```

VB6 Differences

The NotOverridable keyword is new to Visual Basic .NET. Visual Basic 6.0 did not support inheritance or member overriding.

See Also

MustOverride Keyword, NotInheritable Keyword, Overridable Keyword, Overrides Keyword

Now Property

Returns the current system date and time.

Member Of

Microsoft.VisualBasic.DateAndTime

Syntax

```
Now() As Date
```

Return Value

A Date value representing the current system date and time.

Comments

The Now property is read-only; you can use it to retrieve the date and time, but not to set it.

As the following line from an ILDasm disassembly shows, the Now property simply wraps a call to the .NET DateTime.Now property.

```
IL_002f:  call      valuetype [mscorlib]System.DateTime
          [Microsoft.VisualBasic]Microsoft.VisualBasic.DateAndTime::get_Now()
```

To retrieve just the date or to set the date, you can use the Today property. To retrieve just the time or to set the time, you can use the TimeString property.

Example

The example prompts the user for his year of birth, extracts the current year from the Now property, and estimates the user's age.

```
Public Sub Main()
   Dim birthYear As Integer
   Dim inputString As String = InputBox("Enter your year of birth: ")
   If Not IsNumeric(inputString) Then Exit Sub

   birthYear = CInt(inputString)
   MsgBox("Your age is approximately " & Year(Now) - birthYear)
End Sub
```

See Also

TimeString Property, Today Property

NPer Function

See the entry for the IPmt, NPer, and PPmt Functions.

NPV Function

Determines the net present value of an investment based on a series of periodic cash flows.

Member Of

Microsoft.VisualBasic.Financial

Syntax

```
NPV(ByVal Rate As Double, ByRef ValueArray() As Double) As Double
```

Element	Description
Rate	The discount rate over the period of the investment, expressed as a decimal rather than a percentage (e.g., 10 percent is expressed as 0.10).
ValueArray	A one-dimensional array of Double containing cash flow values. The array must have at least two elements, one a payment (expressed as a negative value) and one a receipt (expressed as a positive value).

Return Value

A Double representing the net present value of the investment.

Comments

Net present value is the current value of a future series of payments and receipts that constitute an investment. You can compare the net present value with the amount needed for the investment. If the net present value is greater than the cost, the project will be profitable.

The NPV function interprets the order of values in *ValueArray* as a reflection of the order of payments and receipts. If the values are not in the correct sequence, the function will return inaccurate results.

The investment begins one period before the first cash flow in *ValueArray* and ends with the last cash flow in the array. The NPV function assumes that the elements in ValueArray represent cash flows for identical intervals of time (e.g., one month or one year).

Both *Rate* and the interval between the individual payments in *ValueArray* should reflect the same time unit. For example, if *ValueArray* reflects annual cash flows, *Rate* should be the annualized discount rate.

The net present value assumes that all cash flows are in the future. If the first cash flow occurs at the beginning of the first period, it must be added to the value returned by the NPV function rather than being included in *ValueArray*.

Although the NPV function requires that there be at least one negative value and one positive value in *ValueArray*, it does not throw an exception if this requirement is not met; instead, the function returns inaccurate results.

The NPV function is similar to the PV function, except that the NPV function assumes that cash flows occur at the beginning of a period and it allows variable cash flow values, whereas the PV function allows cash flows to occur either at the beginning or end of a period and assumes fixed cash flows.

Example

The startup cost of a project that is expected to return $2,000 per year over a five-year period is $7,750.00. With a discount rate of 10 percent, we can calculate the net present value of the investment with the following code:

```
Public Sub Main()
    Dim values() As Double = {-7750, 2000, 2000, 2000, 2000, 2000}
    Dim disct As Double = .10
    Console.WriteLine("The net present value is {0}", _
                    FormatCurrency(NPV(disct, values)))
End Sub
```

The result displayed to the console is:

```
The net present value is ($153.11)
```

See Also

FV Function, PV Function

Oct Function

Returns a string representing the octal (base 8) value of a number.

Member Of

Microsoft.VisualBasic.Conversion

Syntax

```
Oct(ByVal Number As { Byte | SByte | Short | UShort |
    Integer | UInteger | Long | ULong | Object } ) As String
```

Element	Description
Number	Any numeric or string expression.

Return Value

A string containing the octal representation of a number.

Comments

If *Number* is the string representation of a number, the Oct function must be able to successfully convert it to a numeric value before converting it to octal; otherwise, Oct throws an InvalidCastException. To prevent this, you can pass a string to the IsNumeric function beforehand to ensure that it can be successfully converted.

If *Number* is a floating point number (a Double, Single, or Decimal), the Oct function rounds it before converting it to a string. All positive floating point values of .5 and lower are rounded down, while positive values ending in .5 are rounded using banker's rounding. All negative floating point values greater than .5 are rounded up. Negative floating point values ending in .5 are rounded using banker's rounding.

If a string already contains the octal representation of a number, the Oct function merely returns that string unchanged, except that it strips off its identifying &O characters. For example:

```
Console.WriteLine(Oct("&O7311"))      ' Displays  "7311"
Console.WriteLine(Oct("&H7777"))      ' Displays "73567"
```

To convert the string representation of an octal number to a decimal number, you just have to pass it to an integer conversion function. For example:

```
Dim convertedOctal As Integer = CInt("&O7302")
Console.WriteLine(convertedOctal)              ' writes 3778
```

You can assign octal values to numeric variables directly by using the &O symbols in front of the octal numbers. For example:

```
Dim maxValue As Byte = &O377
Dim posValue As UInteger = &H170060
```

See Also

Hex Function

Of Keyword

Defines a type parameter of a generic class, structure, interface, delegate, or procedure.

Syntax

See the syntax for the Class, Delegate, Function, Interface, Structure, and Sub statements.

Comments

The Of keyword is used to define generic type parameters both by clients consuming a generic type and by types and members that define generic type parameters. Generic classes allow you to use a strongly typed object whose precise type is determined at compile time.

A generic type allows you to define a single type that is capable of accepting a virtually unlimited number of argument types while still being early bound. Most commonly, generic type parameters are used with collections. Ordinarily, even though collections accept parameters of type Object, they are used to hold objects of a single data type. Because generic parameters allow the type of data that a collection is to hold to be determined at compile time, there is no need to create a separate collection object to hold each type of data that might be assigned to a collection.

Though used extensively with to defined generic collections to define the data type that the collection can hold, generic parameters aren't limited to use with collections. For example, the generic System.Nullable structure has a generic parameter that is any value type capable of being assigned a value of Nothing.

The Of keyword is used with the Dim statement to define the compile-time type of a generic type. For example, the following code uses the generic List object (the generic equivalent of the ArrayList object) to store and then display a shopping list:

```
Imports System.Collections.Generic

Public Module modMain
    Public Sub Main()
        ' Define list and add items to it
        Dim shoppingList As New List(Of String)
        shoppingList.Add("Milk")
        shoppingList.Add("Goat's cheese")
        shoppingList.Add("Artichokes")
        shoppingList.Add("Eggplant")
        shoppingList.Add("Chipotle peppers")
        shoppingList.Add("Pita Bread")
        shoppingList.Sort()
        ' Display list
        For Each item As String In shoppingList
            Console.WriteLine(item)
        Next
    End Sub
End Module
```

Except for using the Of keyword to define the object type, this code is virtually identical to the code used to instantiate and use a weakly typed collection object.

The type supplied as an argument to the Of keyword can be a concrete type, or it can itself be another type parameter.

The Of keyword is also used with the Class, Delegate, Interface, and Structure statements to define a type that accepts generic parameters, as well as with the Function statement to define a routine that operates on a generic type. For example, the following code defines a generic class that wraps the generic Dictionary class:

```
Imports System.Collections.Generic

Public Class DataContainer(Of keyType As IComparable, dataType)
    Private dict As Dictionary(Of keyType, dataType)

    Public Sub New()
        dict = New Dictionary(Of keyType, dataType)
    End Sub

    Public Sub Add(ByVal key As keyType, value As dataType)
        dict.Add(key, value)
    End Sub

    Public ReadOnly Property Count() As Integer
        Get
            Return dict.Count
        End Get
    End Property

    Public Function Item(ByVal key As KeyType) As dataType
        If Not dict.ContainsKey(key) Then
            Return Nothing
        Else
            Return dict.Item(key)
        End If
    End Function
End Class
```

The following code then instantiates the class and calls its members:

```
Public Structure RegionSales
    Dim Region As String
    Dim Sales As Decimal
    Dim Year As Integer
End Structure

Public Module modMain
    Public Sub Main()
        Dim regSales As New RegionSales
        Dim container As New DataContainer(Of String, RegionSales)

        ' Add data to collection object
        regSales.Region = "NE"
        regSales.Sales = 12342558.74d
        regSales.Year = 2005
        container.Add(regSales.Region, regSales)
```

```
        regSales.Region = "SE"
        regSales.Sales = 8367143.68d
        regSales.Year = 2005
        container.Add(regSales.Region, regSales)

        regSales.Region = "MW"
        regSales.Sales = 14930162
        regSales.year = 2005
        container.Add(regSales.Region, regSales)

        ' Display number of items in collection
        Console.WriteLine("The collection has {0} items.", container.Count)

        ' Retrieve an item
        regSales = container.Item("NE")
        If regSales.Region IsNot Nothing Then
            Console.WriteLine("Sales for the {0} region in {1} were {2}.", _
                        regSales.Region, regSales.Year, _
                        FormatCurrency(regSales.Sales))
        End If
    End Sub
End Module
```

VB.NET Changes

The Of keyword and generic type parameters are new to Visual Basic 2005.

See Also

Class Statement, Delegate Statement, Dim Statement, Function Statement, Interface Statement, Structure Statement, Sub Statement

On Error Statement

Directs program flow in the event of an error using unstructured exception handling.

Syntax

```
On Error GoTo [ line | 0 | -1 ] |
```

or

```
On Error Resume Next
```

Element	Description
line	Causes program flow to proceed to the line label *line* in the event of an error. *line* must be located in the same procedure in which the On Error GoTo *line* statement is found. A line label must be placed at the beginning of a line of code, must be terminated with a colon, and must not be a Visual Basic keyword.
0	Disables any enabled error handler.

Element	Description
-1	Clears the Err object.
Resume Next	Causes program execution to proceed with the line following the line that generated the exception.

Comments

Visual Basic supports two methods for handling exceptions. The first, unstructured exception handling with the On Error statement, is a legacy of Visual Basic 6.0 and earlier versions. The second, structured exception handling with Try . . . Catch . . . Finally blocks, is common to .NET languages. Actually, there is a third kind of exception handling, though one that leaves it to users to deal with exceptions: exception handling by the .NET runtime. If there is no enabled exception handler, or if exception handling has been disabled (using the On Error GoTo 0 statement), then the .NET runtime handles the exception by displaying an error message and terminating the application.

On Error Resume Next is used either to ignore an error or to provide inline error handling. When inline error handling is used, code that is mostly likely to produce an error is usually followed immediately by an evaluation of the Err object. For example, in the OpenFile function in the following code, the call to the FileOpen subroutine is followed by an evaluation of the Err.Number property. In the event of an error, the routine gives the user three chances to enter a valid filename. If after three tries, the user fails to enter a valid name or the file cannot be opened for some other reason, the function returns a False value to the calling routine. Once the user provides a valid filename and the file is successfully opened, the function returns True to the calling routine. Note that it also passes the file number used to open the file back to the caller, since the argument was passed to the OpenFile function by reference:

```
Public Sub Main()
    Dim fileNo As Integer
    If OpenFile(fileno) Then
        DisplayDocument(fileNo)
    Else
        MsgBox("Unable to Open File. Application must close.", _
                MsgBoxStyle.OKOnly Or MsgBoxStyle.Critical, "No File")
    End If
End Sub

Private Function OpenFile(ByRef fileNo As Integer) As Boolean
    ' Enable error handler
    On Error Resume Next

    Dim filename As String = String.Empty
    Dim msg As String = "Enter the path and name of the file " & _
                    "that you'd like to display: "
    Dim errMsg As String = String.Empty
    Dim retries As Integer = 0

    fileNo = FreeFile()

    ' Try up to 3 times until filename is valid
    Do While retries < 3 And Not validFile
        ' Get user input
        filename = InputBox(CStr(IIf(retries = 0, msg, errMsg & msg)))
```

```
          ' Exit if user has not entered a filename
          If filename = String.Empty Then
             Return False
          End If
          ' Attempt to open file
          FileOpen(fileNo, filename, OpenMode.Input, OpenAccess.Read)
          ' If there's an error, increment counter and assign error message to display
          If Err.Number <> 0 Then
             retries += 1
             If Err.Number = 53 Then
                errMsg = "The filename that you've entered is invalid. " & _
                         "Please try again." & vbCrLf & vbCrLf
             ElseIf Err.Number <> 0 then
                errMsg = Err.Description & vbCrLf & vbCrLf
             End If
             ' Clear error (or we'll have to handle it again)
             Err.Clear
          Else
             ' File is open: set flag
             validFile = True
          End If
       Loop
       ' Return flag indicating whether file is open
       If validFile Then
          Return True
       Else
          Return False
       End If
    End Function
```

On Error GoTo *label* causes program execution to jump to a label named *label*. Typically, the error handler is located at the end of the routine and is preceded by an Exit statement (Exit Sub, Exit Function, Exit Procedure, etc.) to prevent the error handler from executing even if there is not an error. When the error handler has executed, the routine may terminate, or if the error occurs in a component, the handler may raise another error to pass back to the client. More common, however, is the use of the Resume statement to transfer program flow back to the line that caused the error (Resume or Resume 0), to the line following the line that caused the error (Resume Next), or to a label somewhere in the current routine (Resume *label*). The following example uses On Error GoTo *label* and Resume *label* to provide an error handler comparable to the inline error handler in the previous code example:

```
Private Function OpenFile(ByRef fileNo As Integer) As Boolean
    ' Enable error handler
    On Error GoTo ErrHand:

    Dim filename As String = String.Empty
    Dim msg As String = "Enter the path and name of the file " & _
                        "that you'd like to display: "
    Dim errMsg As String = String.Empty
    Dim validFile As Boolean
    Dim retries As Integer = 0

    fileNo = FreeFile()
    ' Get user input
```

```
GetInput:
    filename = InputBox(CStr(IIf(retries = 0, msg, errMsg & msg)))
    ' Exit if user has not entered a filename
    If filename = String.Empty Then
        Return False
    End If
    ' Attempt to open file
    FileOpen(fileNo, filename, OpenMode.Input, OpenAccess.Read)
    ' exception has not occurred, so file is open: return True
    Return True

    Exit Function
ErrHand:
    retries += 1
    if retries = 3 Then Return False

    If Err.Number = 53 Then
        errMsg = "The filename that you've entered is invalid. Please try again." _
                & vbCrLf & vbCrLf
    Else
        errMsg = Err.Description & vbCrLf & vbCrLf
    End If
    Resume GetInput:
End Function
```

On Error Goto –1 clears the Error object so that it no longer contains information about the current error. It is equivalent to calling the Clear method of the Err object. Ordinarily, the Error object is cleared when the Resume statement executes from within an error handler, or when program flow leaves an error handler either because of an Exit statement or an End statement.

An error handler is enabled from the time that it is declared in a procedure using the On Error GoTo statement until either that procedure terminates or the On Error GoTo 0 statement executes. It remains enabled if the procedure in which the handler is declared calls other procedures. For details on how executing an enabled error handler in the event of an error affects program flow if the error occurs in the procedure in which the error handler is define or in a called procedure, see the entry for the Resume Statement.

If an exception is thrown in an error handler, the runtime looks for the next higher enabled error handler in the call stack. If there is none, the runtime handles the exception and terminates the application.

You cannot use both structured exception handling and unstructured exception handling within a single member.

Except for maintaining legacy code (i.e., code originally written for Visual Basic 6.0 or earlier versions), structured exception handling should be used instead of error handling with the On Error statement. Particularly for component-based development or for error handling in an environment in which individual portions of an application are built using different languages, structured exception handling provides a uniform method of handing errors across CLS-compliant .NET languages. Unstructured exception handling, on the other hand, is unique to Visual Basic and integrates poorly with .NET exception handling.

VB6 Differences

In Visual Basic 6.0, the On Error GoTo syntax also allowed control to be transferred to a line number. In Visual Basic .NET, *line* can only be a label, and cannot be a line number.

See Also

Err Object, Resume Statement

Operator Statement

Defines either an operation or a custom conversion for a class or a structure.

Syntax

```
[ <attrlist> ] Public [ Overloads ] Shared [ Shadows ] [ Widening | Narrowing ]
Operator operatorsymbol ( operand1 [, operand2 ]) [ As [ <attrlist> ] type ]
    [ statements ]
    Return returnvalue
    [ statements ]
End Operator
```

Element	Description
<attrlist>	A list of attributes that apply to the operator. Only attributes whose AttributeUsage attribute is AttributeTargets.All or AttributeTargets.Method can be applied to an operator procedure.
Public	All operator procedures must be defined as Public.
Overloads	Indicates that this operator procedure is overloaded. The Overloads keyword is valid only if *operatorsymbol* is a binary operator and its two operands are a base class and a class derived from it. (See the entry for the Overloads keyword.) Overloads cannot be used in the same Operator statement as Shadows.
Shared	Indicates that an instance of the class or structure is not required to invoke the operator. The Shared keyword is required.
Shadows	Indicates that the operator procedure shadows an identical operator procedure in a base class. (See the entry for the Shadows keyword.) Shadows cannot be used in the same Operator statement as Overloads.
Widening	Indicates that the result of the operation is a widening conversion. See the comments for additional details.
Narrowing	Indicates that the result of the operation is a narrowing conversion. See the comments for additional details.
operatorsymbol	The operation defined by the Operator statement. Visual Basic .NET supports unary operators (+, -, IsFalse, IsTrue, Not), binary operators (+, -, *, /, \, &, ^, >>, <<, = (the comparison operator, not the assignment operator),<>, >, >=, <, <=, And, Like, Mod, Or, Xor), and conversion operators (the CType function).
operand1	The name and type of the single operand to a unary operator procedure or the left operand to a binary or conversion operator procedure. *operand1* has the syntax: `[ ByVal ] operandname [ As operandtype ]`

Element	Description
operand2	The name and type of the right operand to a binary or conversion operator procedure. *operand2* has the syntax: `[ ByVal ] operandname [ As operandtype ]`
attrlist	An optional list of attributes that apply to the return value. Only attributes whose AttributeUsage attribute is AttributeTargets.All or AttributeTargets.ReturnValue can be applied to the return value of an operator procedure.
type	The type of data returned by the operator procedure. It is optional unless Option Strict is on. Some operators must return particular kinds of data. IsTrue and IsFalse both return a Boolean.
returnvalue	The value returned by the operator procedure. It must be specified by using one or more Return statements.

Comments

Conversion operators have the more general syntax (ignoring attributes or procedure modifiers):

```
Public Shared [Widening | Narrowing] Operator CType(ByVal operand1 As type1) _
    As [ type2 ]
```

where either *type1* or *type2* must be the class or structure in which the conversion operator is defined, and *type2* is the type to which *type1* is to be converted.

Each conversion operator procedure must be defined as either a widening or a narrowing conversion. A *widening conversion* is a conversion between two data types so that data loss cannot possibly occur. It includes conversions from one data type to another data type with a greater range (such as a conversion of a Byte to an Integer or of an Integer to a Long), from a derived type to one of its base types, or from a type to an interface that it implements. In Visual Basic .NET, widening conversions are handled automatically by the compiler if Option Strict is off (its default value), but they must be handled by explicit calls to conversion functions if Option Strict is on.

A *narrowing conversion* is a conversion between two data types so that data loss might occur and the conversion might fail at runtime. It includes conversions from one data type to another data type with a smaller or non-overlapping range (such as a conversion from a UInteger to an Integer), from a base type to its derived type, or from an interface to a type that implements that interface. In Visual Basic .NET, narrowing conversions are handled automatically by the compiler if Option Strict is off (its default value), but they must be handled by explicit calls to conversion functions if Option Strict is on.

Since a widening conversion must always succeed at runtime, it must always return *type*, and it must handle all possible exceptions as well as any exceptions thrown by the procedures it calls without notifying its client.

If the Operator statement is used to define a conversion operation, that conversion can only be performed by calling the CType function. Custom conversion operators are not invoked by calls to either the DirectCast or the TryCast functions. (Widening conversions, however, can be performed automatically by the .NET runtime without calling a conversion or casting routine.)

Unary operators have the more general syntax (ignoring attributes or procedure modifiers):

```
Public Shared Operator op([ ByVal ] operand1 [ As thistype]) As [ type ]
```

where *operand1* must be the class or structure in which the unary operator is defined, and *op* is one of the following operators: **+, -, IsTrue, IsFalse**, and **Not**.

You can define a logical operator procedure for Not, but you cannot define a bitwise operator procedure for it.

If you implement the IsTrue operator, then you must also implement the IsFalse operator. The compiler will generate an error if you define an operator procedure for one without the other.

The IsTrue and IsFalse operator procedures are used by the compiler in evaluating logical conditions that use the class or structure instance for which the operators are defined in a For, If, ElseIf, or While statement or in an ElseIf clause.

In defining the IsTrue and IsFalse operators (as well as other operators that must be defined in pairs), it would be most convenient to simply define one operator fully while having the second operator call the first operator, as the following code illustrates:

```
Public Shared Operator IsFalse(obj As CustomClass) As Boolean
    Return Not CustomClass.IsTrue(obj)     ' Not valid
End Operator
```

However, operator procedures are not considered members of a class, so this code generates a compiler error. Instead, both the IsTrue and IsFalse operator procedures must be fully defined without referring to the other operator procedure.

Binary logical operators have the more general syntax (ignoring attributes or procedure modifiers):

```
Public Shared Operator op([ ByVal ] operand1 [ As type1], _
                    [ ByVal ] operand2 [ As type2]) As [ type ]
```

where either *operand1* or *operand2* must be the class or structure in which the comparison operator is defined, and *op* is one of the following operators: **+, -, *, /, \, Mod, &, ^, =, <>, >, >=, <, <=**, and **Like**.

Some binary operators must be implemented in pairs, rather than singly. If you implement the = operator, you must also implement <>, and vice versa. Similarly, you must implement both < and >, and you must implement both <= and >=.

Binary bitwise operators have the more general syntax

```
Public Shared Operator op([ ByVal ] operand1 [ As type1], _
                    [ ByVal ] operand2 [ As type2]) As [ type ]
```

where either *operand1* or *operand2* must be the class or structure in which the comparison operator is defined, and *op* is one of the following operators: **And, Or, XOr, >>**, or **<<**. And, Or, and XOr can be used both as logical operators and as bitwise operators in Visual Basic .NET. In operator procedures, however, they can only be used as logical operators.

The purpose of operator overloads is to allow consumers of a class or structure to perform operations upon its instances. Therefore, the only permitted access modifier is Public.

In client code, you can use the AndAlso operator with a class or structure if the following conditions are true:

- The class or structure has a defined And operator procedure that returns an instance of the class or structure.

- The class or structure has a defined IsFalse operator procedure.

In client code, you can use the OrElse operator with a class or structure if the following conditions are true:

- The class or structure has a defined Or operator procedure that returns an instance of the class or structure.
- The class or structure has a defined IsTrue operator procedure.

The Visual Basic .NET compiler actually implements operator procedures as special methods. The following table lists the operators and the names assigned the corresponding operator methods by the compiler:

Operator	Method Name
Widening conversion	op_Implicit
CType (Narrowing conversion)	op_Explicit
=	op_Equality
<>	op_Inequality
<	op_LessThan
>	op_GreaterThan
+	op_Addition
And	op_BitwiseAnd
Or	op_BitwiseOr
IsTrue	op_True
IsFalse	op_False
XOr	op_ExclusiveOr
/	op_Division
>=	op_GreaterThanOrEqual
<=	op_LessthanOrEqual
Mod	op_Modulus
*	op_Multiply
-	op_Subtraction
-	op_UnaryNegative
+	op_UnaryPlus
^	op_Exponent
\	op_IntegerDivision
&	op_Concatenate
>>	op_RightShift
<<	op_LeftShift
Like	op_Like

Example

Rock Paper Scissors is a popular child's game that is often played to determine who takes the first turn in some other game. The game is easily implemented using operator overloading (although it should be noted that, while this may be an interesting code example, it is not a good use of operator overloading). The following code defines a GameObject class whose Name property contains a member of the GameObject enumeration, that can have values of GameObject.Rock, GameObject.Paper, or GameObject.Scissors:

```
Public Enum DrawnObject As Integer
    Rock = 0
    Paper = 1
    Scissors = 2
End Enum

Public Class Gameobject
    Private drawnName As DrawnObject

    Public Sub New(name As DrawnObject)
        Me.drawnName = name
    End Sub

    Public ReadOnly Property Name() As DrawnObject
        Get
            Return Me.drawnName
        End Get
    End Property

' Do both players have the same object?
Public Shared Operator = (ByVal player1 As GameObject, ByVal player2 As GameObject) _
                    As Boolean
    If player1.Name = player2.Name Then
        Return True
    Else
        Return False
    End If
End Operator

' Do players have different objects?
' <> must be implemented if = is implemented
Public Shared Operator <> (ByVal player1 As GameObject, ByVal player2 As GameObject) _
                        As Boolean
    If player1.Name <> player2.Name Then
        Return True
    Else
        Return False
    End If
End Operator

' See if player1 wins (is greater)
Public Shared Operator > (ByVal player1 As GameObject, ByVal player2 As GameObject) _
                        As Boolean
    Select Case player1.Name
        Case DrawnObject.Rock
```

```
            If player2.Name = DrawnObject.Scissors Then Return True
        Case DrawnObject.Paper
            If player2.Name = DrawnObject.Rock Then Return True
        Case DrawnObject.Scissors
            If player2.Name = DrawnObject.Paper Then Return True
    End Select
    Return False
End Operator

' See if player1 loses (is less)
' < must be implemented if > is implemented
Public Shared Operator < (ByVal player1 As GameObject, ByVal player2 As GameObject) _
                    As Boolean
    Select Case player1.Name
        Case DrawnObject.Rock
            If player2.Name = DrawnObject.Paper Then Return True
        Case DrawnObject.Paper
            If player2.Name = DrawnObject.Scissors Then Return True
        Case DrawnObject.Scissors
            If player2.Name = DrawnObject.Rock Then Return True
    End Select
    Return False
End Operator
End Class
```

A tie occurs if both players have the same object. To test for this, the class defines an equals (=) operator. Because the comparison operators have to be implemented in pairs, it also has to define a not equals (<>) operator. To determine who won, the class defines the greater-than operator. Again, because it implements is greater than, the class also has to define a less-than operator.

The game can then be played using code like the following:

```
Public Module PaperRockScissors
    'Dim Objects() As String = {"Paper", "Rock", "Scissors"}
    Dim player1, player2 As GameObject

    Public Sub Main()
        Dim player1wins, player2wins As Integer
        Randomize()
        ' Loop until someone wins 2 of 3 decisions, excluding ties
        Do Until player1wins = 2 OrElse player2wins = 2
            player1 = New GameObject(CType(Int(Rnd(1)*3), DrawnObject))
            player2 = New GameObject(CType(Int(Rnd(1)*3), DrawnObject))
            If player1 <> player2 Then
                If player1 > player2 Then
                    Console.WriteLine("{0} beats {1}", player1.Name.ToString, _
                                    player2.Name.ToString)
                    player1wins += 1
                Else
                    Console.WriteLine("{0} loses to {1}", player1.Name.ToString, _
                                    player2.Name.ToString)
                    player2wins += 1
                End If
            End If
```

```
        Loop
        If player1wins = 2 Then
            Console.WriteLine("Player 1 wins")
        Else
            Console.WriteLine("Player 2 wins")
        End If
    End Sub
```

For an example of a conversion operator, see the entry for the Narrowing Keyword.

VB.NET Changes

Support for overloaded operators and for user-defined conversions is new to Visual Basic 2005. Previous versions of Visual Basic .NET did not support the Operator statement.

VB6 Differences

The Operator statement is new to Visual Basic 2005. Visual Basic 6.0 did not support operator overloading or custom type conversions with CType.

See Also

Narrowing Keyword, Option Strict Statement, Return Statement, Widening Keyword

Option Compare Statement

Defines whether string comparisons are case sensitive or insensitive.

Syntax

```
Option Compare { Binary | Text }
```

Element	Description
Binary	Indicates that string comparison should be case-sensitive.
Text	Indicates that string comparison should be case-insensitive.

Comments

The Option Compare statement controls string comparisons for the file in which it is found. If it is used, a single Option Compare statement must be placed at the beginning of the file, along with the Option Explicit and Option Strict statements, if they are present. For example:

```
Option Explicit On
Option Strict On
Option Compare Text

Imports System.Collections
Imports System.IO
```

```
Class ExampleClass
    ' class members
End Class

Module Example Library
    ' module members
End Module
```

To control string comparison for an entire project in Visual Studio .NET, use the **Option Compare** drop-down list box on the Compile tab of the project's Properties dialog.

To control string comparison for an entire assembly with the Visual Basic .NET command line compiler, use the /optioncompare:binary or /optioncompare:text switches.

If an Option Compare statement is not present, string comparisons are case sensitive (Option Compare Binary is the default setting).

The Option Compare statement affects string comparisons with the Visual Basic language elements listed in the following table:

Element	Description
= Operator	Determines whether two strings are equal.
<>Operator	Determines whether two strings are unequal.
> Operator	Determines whether one string is "greater than" another (i.e., follows it alphabetically).
< Operator	Determines whether one string is "less than" another (i.e., precedes it alphabetically).
>= Operator	Determines whether one string is greater than or equal to another.
<= Operator	Determines whether one string is less than or equal to another.
Filter function	Returns an array consisting of strings that contains a designated substring. Option Compare can be overridden by the *Compare* parameter, which allows you to define the case sensitivity of a comparison on a function-by-function basis.
InStr function, InStrRev function	Determines whether a substring can be found in a target string. Option Compare can be overridden by the *Compare* parameter, which allows you to define the case sensitivity of a comparison on a function-by-function basis.
Like Operator	Determines whether a string matches a pattern string.
Replace function	Returns a string in which one substring, if found, has been replaced with another. Option Compare can be overridden by the *Compare* parameter, which allows you to define the case sensitivity of a comparison on a function-by-function basis.
Select Case statement	Executes one of a number of blocks of code depending on the evaluation of a conditional expression.

Element	Description
Split function	Parses a string with delimiting characters into an array. Option Compare can be overridden by the *Compare* parameter, which allows you to define the case sensitivity of a comparison on a function-by-function basis.
StrComp function	Determines the relationship between two strings. Option Compare can be overridden by the Compare parameter, which allows you to define the case sensitivity of a comparison on a function-by-function basis.

Option Explicit Statement

Determines whether variables must be explicitly declared before they are used.

Syntax

```
Option Explicit [{ On | Off }]
```

Element	Description
On	Requires that variables be declared before they are used, or a compiler error results. If the Option Explicit statement is used without a qualifier, Option Explicit On is assumed.
Off	Creates a variable dynamically when its name is first encountered in code.

Comments

The Option Explicit statement determines whether variables must be declared before they are used for the file in which the statement is found. If it is used, a single Option Explicit statement must be placed at the beginning of the file, along with the Option Strict and Option Compare statements, if they are present. For an example, see the first comment for the Option Compare statement.

If an Option Explicit statement is not present, variable declaration is required (Option Explicit On is the default setting).

To define whether variables must be declared in advance in an entire project in Visual Studio .NET, use the **Option Explicit** drop-down list box on the Compile tab of the project's Properties dialog.

To require variable declaration for an entire assembly with the Visual Basic command line compiler, use the **/optionexplicit** switch. **/optionexplicit+** requires variable declaration, while **/optionexplicit-** allows variables to be used without declaration.

In web pages, Option Explicit is also on by default. However, it has to be set separately for a page and its code-behind form. For the code-behind form, it is set using the Option Explicit statement. For a web page, it is set by using the Explicit attribute of the Page directive. Possible values of the Explicit attribute are true and false. For example, the following Page directive turns Option Expicit on:

```
<%@ Page Language="VB" AutoEventWireup="false"  Explicit ="true"
    CodeFile="Default.aspx.vb" Inherits="_Default" %>
```

while the following Page directive turns it off:

```
<%@ Page Language="VB" AutoEventWireup="false"  Explicit ="false"
    CodeFile="Default.aspx.vb" Inherits="_Default" %>
```

For web pages, it is also possible to define whether Option Explicit is on or off at the machine level by using the machine.config file and at the web application level by using the web.config file. In both cases, the Option Explicit setting can be defined by adding a <compilation> tag, if it is not already present, to the <system.web> section of the file. The setting of Option Explicit is defined by the explicit attribute, as follows:

```
<compilation explicit="[true|false]" />
```

There is no reason to ever set Option Explicit off, since doing so makes source code subject to its greatest source of potential bugs, the typo. Every time that a programmer makes a error in typing a variable name or in using what he or she incorrectly *thinks* is the proper variable name, the Visual Basic compiler happily defines a new variable. Even in relatively brief programs, this quickly becomes a very serious problem. For example, in the following code, the variable *totl* is a typo that is supposed to be *total*:

```
Public Module modMain
    Public Sub Main()
        Dim values() As Double = {12.3, 18.67, 19.14, 2.168, 7.115}
        Console.WriteLine(SumValues(values))
    End Sub

    Private Function SumValues(arr() As Double) As Double
        Dim total As Double

        For Each value As Double In Arr
            total += value
        Next
        Return totl
    End Function
End Module
```

Because the variable *totl* is created dynamically by the compiler, the function returns a value of 0 to the caller if Option Explicit is off. In contrast, if Option Explicit is on, the compiler generates BC30451, "Name 'totl' is not declared.", and the error is easily diagnosed and corrected.

Setting Option Explicit on simply requires that all variables be declared before they are used, not the the variable's type need be specified. A simple declaration of the form

```
Dim d, i, s, str
```

satisfies this requirement. If the type of variables is not specified in the variable declaration, they are all created as objects.

See Also
Option Strict Statement

Option Strict Statement

Prohibits implicit narrowing conversions, weak typing, and late binding.

Syntax

```
Option Strict [{ On | Off }]
```

Element	Description
On	Prohibits implicit narrowing conversions, weak typing, and late binding. If the Option Strict statement is used with no modifier, it defaults to Option Strict On.
Off	Allows implicit narrowing conversions, weak typing, and late binding.

Comments

The Option Strict setting controls three aspects of the Visual Basic compiler's operation:

- Whether implicit narrowing conversions (that is, narrowing conversions that are handled automatically by the compiler, rather than explicitly by your code) are allowed. If Option Strict is on, only implicit widening conversions are allowed.

- Whether weakly typed variables are allowed. If Option Strict is on, all variables must not only be declared (Option Strict On implies that Option Explicit is also on), but declarations must include the As clause. In other words, setting Option Strict on makes Visual Basic a statically typed language.

- Whether late binding is permitted. If Option Strict is on, most forms of late binding are not allowed. (This is discussed further later in the Comments section.)

If an Option Strict statement is not present, Option Strict is set off by default.

To control the Option Strict setting for an entire project in Visual Studio .NET, use the **Option Strict** drop-down list box on the Compile tab of the project's Properties dialog.

To control the Option Strict setting for an entire assembly with the Visual Basic .NET command line compiler, use the /optionstrict+ setting to turn Option Strict on, /optionstrict- to turn Option Strict off, and /optionstrict:custom to have the compiler produce warnings rather than errors when strict semantics are violated.

For web pages, it is also possible to define whether Option Strict is on or off at the machine level by using the machine.config file and at the web application level by using the web.config file. In both cases, the Option Strict setting can be defined by adding a <compilation> tag, if it is not already present, to the <system.web> section of the file. The setting of Option Strict is defined by the strict attribute, as follows:

```
<compilation strict="[true|false]" />
```

If there are multiple Option Strict settings, the per-file setting takes precedence over the global setting.

If Option Strict is on, the compiler still performs widening conversions if you do not explicitly handle them in your code. A *widening conversion* is a conversion from a type (such as an Integer) to a type with a greater range (such as a Long) that cannot result in a loss of data. The compiler requires that you explicitly handle all *narrowing conversions,* or conversions from a type with a wider range to one with a narrower range, since they can result in data loss and, in most cases when this happens, a runtime error. The assumption behind Option Strict is that if you are aware of a narrowing conversion because you have to handle it yourself, you are at least aware of the possibility of data loss and a runtime exception and can either prevent it or handle it.

You typically can determine whether a type conversion will result in data loss by comparing the value to be converted with the minimum and maximum range of the target data type, which are represented by the MinValue and MaxValue fields of the following types: Byte, Char, Date, Decimal, Double, Integer, Long, SByte, Short, Single, UInteger, ULong, UShort. In the case of a conversion from an Integer to a Short, the code might appear as follows:

```
' Convert a Long named number to an Integer
If number >= Integer.MinValue And number <= Integer.MaxValue Then
    ' number is in range of integer: perform conversion
    result = CInt(number)
Else
    ' number is not in range of integer; do something else
End If
```

The prohibition of implicit narrowing conversions often produces compiler errors in unexpected places. For example, with Option Strict set on, the seemingly innocuous line of code

```
Dim retailPrice As Decimal = 12.83
```

generates error BC30512, "Option Strict On disallows implicit conversions from 'Double' to 'Decimal'." So does attempting to pass arguments to a method of types wider than the method's defined parameters. For example, with Option Strict set on, the code

```
Public Sub Main()
    Dim number As Long = 1234
    number = DoubleIt(Number)
End Sub

Public Function DoubleIt(value As Integer) As Integer
    Return value * 2
End Function
```

generates error error BC30512, "Option Strict On disallows implicit conversions from 'Long' to 'Integer'." The first type of error is fixed by adding a type identifier to the variable initialization:

```
Dim retailPrice As Decimal = 12.83d
```

The second by explicitly converting the Long to an Integer when calling the method:

```
number = DoubleIt(CInt(Number))
```

Some forms of late binding are allowed by Option Strict. In particular, you can define variables of type Object and assign them a value of a particular scalar type, you can access the scalar type's value, and you can call System.Object members for that Object type. Other forms of late binding are not allowed. As a result, the following code compiles because it simply assigns an Integer value to an Object variable and then passes that variable to the TypeName function:

```
Dim obj As Object = 30
Console.WriteLine(TypeName(obj))
```

On the other hand, the following code generates a compiler error because it calls a method of the Integer type that it does not inherit from System.Object, and therefore that involves a late-bound method call:

```
Dim obj As Object = 30
Console.WriteLine(obj.MaxValue)
```

Although Option Strict is set to off by default, you should always set it on unless you explicitly need to take advantage of late binding. There are a number of minor reasons, such as the improved performance that results from taking advantage of early binding, that make setting Option Strict to on preferable. The most compelling reason is that it makes the compiler strict about eliminating bad programming practices that could turn into unexpected, unhandled exceptions at runtime. Option Strict is a good idea because it saves you dollars in support costs and lost customers.

VB6 Differences

The Option Strict statement is new to Visual Basic .NET. There was no setting that controlled whether the Visual Basic 6.0 compiler would automatically handle only widening conversions or both widening and narrowing conversions.

See Also

Option Explicit Statement

Optional Keyword

Defines a parameter as optional; it does not have to be supplied as an argument by the caller.

Syntax

```
Optional [{ ByVal | ByRef }] name[( )] [ As type ] = default_value
```

Element	Description
ByVal	The argument is passed by value to the procedure or property. If neither ByVal nor ByRef is specified, the argument is passed by value.
name	The name by which the parameter array will be referenced in the procedure's code.
type	The parameter's data type. It is required if Option Strict is on. If Option Strict is off and the As type clause is absent, the data type of the parameter defaults to Object.
default_value	The value to be assign to the parameter if an argument is not supplied in the procedure call. A default value is required.

Comments

The Optional keyword is used with the Declare, Function, Property, and Sub statements to define an optional argument that may be omitted when invoking the procedure. However, it is rarely used with either the Declare statement or the Property statement.

If a parameter is defined as optional, all subsequent parameters in a parameter list must also be defined as optional as well.

When using positional arguments to call a function with optional parameters, you can omit intermediate arguments by including empty commas as placeholders for where the argument would otherwise go. For example, the call to the class constructor in the Example would appear as follows if no middle name was passed as an argument:

```
Dim person2 As New Person("John",, "Smith")
```

In this situation, using named arguments makes the function call both easier and more self-documenting, since the optional *middleName* argument can be ignored completely, as the following code that instantiates a Person class (shown in the example) illustrates:

```
Dim person1 As New Person(firstName := "John", lastName := "Smith")
```

An alternative to using optional parameters is to use method overloading. In the case of our example, for instance, we probably wouldn't really want the last name to be an optional parameter. But if we declare the middle name to be optional, and we decide that the middle name has to be positioned before the last name in the parameter list, we have no choice but to declare it optional. If we were to use method overloading instead, the following two class constructors would appear as follows, replacing the single one shown in the example:

```
Public Sub New(firstName As String, lastName As String)
   Me.New(firstName, string.empty, lastName)
End Sub

Public Sub New(firstName As String, middleName As String, lastName As String)
   MyBase.New
   Me.firstName = firstName
   Me.middleName = middleName
   Me.lastName = lastName
End Sub
```

Optional arguments are probably best used with methods that accept large numbers of arguments.

Although optional arguments are CLS-compliant, they are not necessarily easy to use for clients written in other languages. For instance, in C#, arguments cannot simply be omitted; some argument (usually Type.Missing) must be provided in place of the optional argument.

Example

In the following example, the constructor of the Person class illustrates the use of the Optional keyword. Invoking the constructor (or any method with optional parameters) is discussed in the Comments section.

```
Public Class Person

   Private firstName As String
   Private middleName As String
   Private lastName As String
```

```
   Public Sub New(firstName As String, Optional middleName As String = "", _
                  Optional lastName As String = "")
      Me.firstName = firstName
      Me.middleName = middleName
      me.lastName = lastName
   End Sub

   Public Function GetFullName() As String
      Return Trim(Trim(Me.firstName & " " & Me.middleName) & " " & Me.lastName)
   End Function
End Class
```

VB6 Differences

Although Visual Basic 6.0 supported optional parameters and the Optional keyword, it allowed parameters to be assigned a default value but did not require it. Instead, omitted arguments could be detected using the IsMissing function. Visual Basic .NET, on the other hand, requires a default value for each optional parameter, and the Visual Basic 6.0 IsMissing function is no longer supported.

See Also

Declare Statement, Function Statement, Property Statement, Sub Statement

Overloads Keyword

Indicates that a property or method is one of two or more properties or methods with the same name but different signatures.

Syntax

See the syntax for the Function Statement, Property Statement, and Sub Statement.

Comments

In general, an *overloaded* member is a method or property that has the same name but a different signature than another member. A signature is defined by the number, order, and types of the member's parameters. In the case of conversion operators, it is also defined by return value, and in the case of generic procedures, by the number of type parameters. A member's signature does *not* include the member's type or return value (except for a conversion operator), the names of parameters, the attributes (such as optional) of individual parameters, whether arguments are passed by value or by reference, etc.

Although the Overloads keyword can be used in this more general context, as a means of indicating that multiple members with the same name exist, its use is optional. There are, however, some restrictions: It cannot be used with constructors. If it is used, it must be used for all of the overloads of a type that share the same name. And although it can be used with member declarations in classes, interfaces, and structures, it cannot be used in modules.

The real intent of the Overloads keyword is to declare members of derived classes that overload and override members of base classes.

Overloads cannot be used along with the Shadows keyword. In fact, they are mutually exclusive: if you fail to specify the Overloads keyword in a context in which it is applicable, the property or method will shadow the corresponding property or method in its base class.

VB6 Differences

The Overloads keyword is new to Visual Basic .NET. Visual Basic 6.0 did not support inheritance or member overloading.

See Also

Function Statement, Property Statement, Shadows Keyword, Sub Statement

Overridable Keyword

Indicates that a base class member can be overridden by an identically named member in a derived class.

Syntax

See the syntax for the Function Statement, Property Statement, and Sub Statement.

Comments

The Overridable keyword is used with the Function, Property, and Sub statements in a class definition to indicate that derived classes can override them. Since by default members of a class are not overridable (with a single exception, discussed in the next comment), it is important to include the Overridable keyword if there is any possibility that you or consumers of the class may want to derive from it and override its members.

The sole exception to class members not being overridable by default is a member of a derived class that itself overrides a member of a base class. These members are overridable by default, and you cannot specify the Overridable keyword in their member definitions. If you do, Visual Basic generates compiler error BC30730, "Methods declared 'Overrides' cannot be declared 'Overridable' because they are implicitly overridable." Note that, if you do not want them to be overridden, you can specify the NotOverridable keyword in their member definitions.

Overridable cannot be used along with the MustOverride keyword (MustOverride requires that a member be overridable), the NotOverridable keyword (which is the opposite of Override), the Overrides keyword (a member that overrides a base class member is itself overridable), or the Shared keyword (overridable members must be instance members).

Example

See the example for the NotOverridable keyword.

VB6 Differences

The Overridable keyword is new to Visual Basic .NET. Visual Basic 6.0 did not support inheritance or member overriding.

See Also

Function Statement, NotOverridable Keyword, Overrides Keyword, Property Statement, Shadowing Keyword, Sub Statement

Overrides Keyword

Indicates that a derived class member overrides an identically named member in its base class.

Syntax

See the syntax for the Function Statement, Property Statement, and Sub Statement.

Comments

A derived class inherits the accessible members of its base class, and client code that calls the base class member can call the methods that the derived class inherits as if they belonged to the derived class. Often, however, the derived class requires that its members operate differently or store different information that the inherited implementation allows. When this happens, the derived class can use *method overriding*: it can indicate that it is replacing the base class implementation of a method or property with its own. This is the purpose of the Overrides keyword.

In order to override a base class member, the derived class member must meet the following conditions:

- It must have the same signature as the member it overrides. (.NET considers the signature to be the number, order, and types of parameters, but it does not consider a method's return value as part of its signature.)
- It must have the same accessibility. That is, if the base class member is Public, the derived class member must be as well.
- It must pass each of its parameters in the same way (i.e., by reference or by value) as the base class member.
- It must return the same data type.
- If a generic procedure in a base class is overridden, the derived class implementation must have the same number of type parameters, and their constraint lists must be identical.

If you implement a member in a derived class that meets the previous criteria but you fail to include the Overrides keyword, that member shadows the base class member. (See the entry for the Shadows keyword.) If you fail to include the Overrides keyword and the base class member is marked MustOverride, the Visual Basic .NET compiler generates a compiler error.

Because a member overrides a base class member, that member is called even if the derived class is referenced through a variable whose type is that of the base class. For example, the following class, BaseClass, has a single method, GetName, that uses a hard-coded string to return its class name:

```
Public Class BaseClass
    Public Overridable Function GetName() As String
        Return "BaseClass"
    End Function
End Class
```

A class named DerivedClass inherits form BaseClass and overrides its GetName method to return another hard-coded string:

```
Public Class DerivedClass : Inherits BaseClass
    Public Overrides Function GetName() As String
        Return "DerivedClass"
    End Function
End Class
```

The following client code then instantiates the DerivedClass class and calls its GetName method in three different ways, one through a variable of type DerivedClass and two through a variable of type BaseClass:

```
Public Module modMain
    Public Sub Main()
        Dim dc1 As New DerivedClass
        Console.WriteLine(dc1.GetName)

        Dim dc2 As New DerivedClass
        Dim bc1 As BaseClass = dc2
        Console.WriteLine(bc1.GetName)

        Dim bc2 As BaseClass = New DerivedClass
        Console.Writeline(bc2.GetName)
    End Sub
End Module
```

In all three cases, the derived class' GetName method is called, as the program output illustrates:

```
DerivedClass
DerivedClass
DerivedClass
```

Ordinarily, members of a class are not overridable unless they are explicitly defined using the Overridable keyword. However, members defined using the Overrides keyword that override members of their base class or classes are automatically overridable. Because of this, the Overridable and Overrides keywords cannot be applied to a single property or method definition.

Since a class constructor is not inherited, it cannot be overridden.

Example

The default implementation of the Object.ToString method, which is inherited by all classes, is equivalent to calling the Name property returned by the object's GetType() method. Because this is often less than useful, the ToString method is often overridden. The following code, for example, defines a class that overrides the ToString method to return the value of a private field:

```
Public Class InheritsFromObject
    Dim instanceName As String

    Public Sub New(name As String)
        Me.instanceName = name
    End Sub

    Public Overrides Function ToString() As String
        Return Me.instanceName
    End Function
End Class
```

```
Public Module modTest
    Public Sub Main
        Dim obj As New InheritsFromObject("This object")
        Console.WriteLine(obj.ToString())
    End Sub
End Module
```

VB6 Differences

The Overrides keyword is new to Visual Basic .NET. Visual Basic 6.0 did not support inheritance or member overriding.

See Also

Function Statement, Property Statement, Shadows Keyword, Sub Statement

ParamArray Keyword

Defines a parameter as a parameter array that represents a variable number of arguments.

Syntax

```
ParamArray name() [ As type ]
```

Element	Description
name	The name by which the parameter array will be referenced in the procedure's code.
type	The data type of the parameter array. It is required if Option Strict is on. If Option Strict is off and the As type clause is absent, the data type of the parameter array defaults to Object.

Comments

The ParamArray keyword is used with the Declare, Function, Property, and Sub statements to define a parameter array. However, it is rarely used with either the Declare or the Property statements.

The ParamArray keyword can only be used with the last argument in an argument list. *name* must be defined as a single-dimensional array. It cannot be a multidimensional array. *name* is passed by value; it cannot be passed by reference.

In some cases, you may not know at design time precisely how many arguments will be passed to a function. For example, if you're coding a routine that computes the mean for a finite set of numbers, you don't want to have to define separate functions to handle different numbers of parameters. One solution is to simply use an array, as follows:

```
Public Shared Function Average(numbers() As Decimal) As Decimal
    Dim sum As Decimal
    For Each number As Decimal In Numbers
        sum += number
    Next
    Return sum / numbers.Length
End Function
```

However, you can give clients calling your method greater flexibility by defining its argument as a parameter array:

```
Public Shared Function Average(ParamArray numbers() As Decimal) As Decimal
    Dim sum As Decimal
    For Each number As Decimal In Numbers
        sum += number
    Next
    Return sum / numbers.Length
End Function
```

If a function has a parameter defined as a parameter array, an argument can be passed to the parameter array in either of two ways. For example, the Average function in the previous code example can be called either by passing in an array containing the values to be averaged:

```
Dim numbers() As Decimal = {12d, 18d, 14.5d, 16.93d}
Console.WriteLine(MathLib.Average(numbers))
```

or it can be called by passing a comma-separated list of arguments:

```
Dim num1 As Decimal = 12.2d
Dim num2 As Decimal = 12.4d
Console.WriteLine(MathLib.Average(num1, num2))
```

There is an important difference between passing an array of values to a parameter array and passing a list of comma-separated arguments: an array is a reference type whose individual members can be modified, whereas if the individual comma-separated list of arguments consists of value types, they cannot be modified. For example, the following code modifies the previous Average method to change the value of the first element of the *numbers* array to zero:

```
Public Shared Function Average(ParamArray numbers() As Decimal) As Decimal
    Dim sum As Decimal
    For Each number As Decimal In Numbers
        sum += number
    Next
    numbers(0) = 0
    Return sum / numbers.Length
End Function
```

If the function is called using comma-delimited arguments as follows:

```
Dim number1 As Decimal = 12.2d
Dim number2 As Decimal = 12.4d
Dim number3 As Decimal = 12.6d
Console.WriteLine(MathLib.Average(number1, number2, number3))
Console.WriteLine(number1)
```

the value of *number1*, the variable that corresponds to *numbers(0)*, is unchanged when control returns to the calling routine, as the following output shows:

```
12.4
12.2
```

However, if the function is called using an array as follows:

```
Dim numbers() As Decimal = {12d, 18d, 14.5d, 16.93d}
Console.WriteLine(MathLib.Average(numbers))
Console.WriteLine(numbers(0))
```

the value of numbers(0) has been modified, as the following output illustrates:

```
15.3575
0
```

Because the parameter array is defined as an array, all of the normal Array members can be used with it, as can all of Visual Basic's array handling functions. In particular, you can determine the array's upper and lower bounds using the Array object's GetLowerBound and GetUpperBound properties, and you can determine the number of elements in the array by using the Array object's GetLength method or its Length property.

The ParamArray statement corresponds to the ParamArray attribute. In fact, if we change the function declaration to appear as follows:

```
Public Shared Function Average( <[ParamArray]> numbers() As Decimal) As Decimal
```

the function can be called and behaves just as it did using the ParamArray keyword. Note that this code brackets the ParamArray attribute to differentiate it from the ParamArray keyword.

VB6 Differences

In Visual Basic 6.0, a parameter defined using the ParamArray statement had to be of type Variant. In Visual Basic .NET, it can be any data type.

In Visual Basic 6.0, arguments could only be passed to a parameter array as an array. In Visual Basic .NET, they can be passed in either an array or a comma-separated list. As a result, Visual Basic .NET parameter arrays are considerably easier to use and more flexible than in Visual Basic 6.0.

If you want to pass an array of objects as the first element in your parameter array, you have to define the parameter array as type Object, and if you choose to pass the parameter array as a single array argument, that has to be of type Object as well. (If you pass the parameter array a series of individual arguments, they can be of any type.) The following code illustrates how to passes an array as the first element of a parameter array:

```
Public Module modMain
    Public Sub Main()
        Dim paramInfo() As String = {"First", "Second", "Third", "Fourth"}
        Dim paramArr() As Object = {paramInfo, "arg2", "arg3", "arg4"}
        DisplayParamArray(paramArr)
    End Sub

    Private Sub DisplayParamArray(ParamArray arr() As Object)
        For Each element As Object In arr
            If TypeOf element Is Array Then
                Dim subarray As Array = DirectCast(element, Array)
                For Each innerElement As Object In subarray
                    Console.WriteLine(innerElement.ToString())
                Next
```

```
        Else
            Console.WriteLine(element.ToString)
        End If
    Next
    End Sub
End Module
```

See Also

ByRef Keyword, ByVal Keyword, Declare Statement, Function Statement, Property Statement, Sub Statement

Partial Keyword

Indicates that a class or structure declaration provides only a partial definition of the type.

Syntax

See the syntax of the Class and Structure statements.

Comments

The Partial keyword allows the definition of class or a structure to be split into multiple Class . . . End Class or Structure . . . End Structure constructs, respectively, that can span multiple files. This allows code generated by a designer, for instance, to be separated from developer-created code, or user interface code to be separated from code implementing business logic or application logic.

You can divide your class or structure definition among as many Class . . . End Class or Structure . . . End Structure constructs as you want. The Class or Structure statement of at least one of the constructs, however, must include the Partial keyword or a compiler error results.

The individual definitions that form the class or structure defined using the Partial keyword must all belong to the same namespace and be included in a single assembly. (A single class cannot be split across multiple namespaces, nor can it be stored in multiple assemblies.) The compiler, however, does not necessarily enforce this requirement and display a compiler error if it is violated. In part, this is because the compiler does not require that there be at multiple portions of a definition if the Partial keyword is present. But it is also because the compiler cannot determine your intention. So if your partial class definitions don't share a single namespace or a single assembly, the Visual Basic compiler generally creates two different classes with the same name in different namespaces or in different assemblies.

The keywords assigned to the Class or Structure statement must be consistent. For example, one definition cannot be public while the other is protected, and one definition cannot be NotInheritable while the other is MustOverride.

Each members defined in a class or structure construct must have a unique signature when it is combined with the remaining individual class or structure constructs.

VB.NET Changes

The Partial keyword is new to Visual Basic 2005.

See Also

Class Statement, Structure Statement

Partition Function

Returns a string describing the range of numbers within which a particular number falls.

Member Of

Microsoft.VisualBasic.Interaction

Syntax

```
Partition(ByVal Number As Long, ByVal Start As Long, ByVal Stop As Long, _
          ByVal Interval As Long) As String
```

Element	Description
Number	The number whose range is to be determined.
Start	The starting value of the first range. It must be greater than or equal to 0.
Stop	The ending value of the last range. It must be greater than *Start*.
Interval	The interval between ranges. Note that *Interval* is an integral rather than floating point value.

Return Value

A string depicting the numeric range within which *Number* falls, in the form *lowervalue:uppervalue*.

Comments

If necessary, both *lowervalue* and *uppervalue* are padded with enough spaces so that the length of each is one space greater than *Stop*. This allows the values returned by multiple calls to the function to be displayed, as well as to be treated as intermediate results that are subsequently sorted.

The individual ranges used by the function must be uniform in size. An individual range cannot be greater or smaller than the other rangers.

If *Number* is less than *Start*, the function returns the string " : *Start - 1*".

If *Number* is greater than *Stop*, the function returns the string "*Stop + 1*: ".

Example

The Partition function is useful in generating frequency distributions. For example, the following code uses U.S. Census Bureau data (available at http://www.census.gov/hhes/www/income/medincsizeandstate.html) to calculate the distribution of median income for a family of four among 25 of the 50 states of the United States:

```
Imports System.Collections.Generic

Public Module modMain
```

```
Public Sub Main()
    ' Median household income for a family of four by state in the U.S.
    Dim income() As Long = {54338, 76369, 58187, 49790, 68310, 66664, _
                            88276, 72003, 51510, 59798, 58060, 75785, _
                            55914, 70357, 63276, 61951, 59498, 55001, _
                            51402, 64083, 85554, 85157, 68563, 73498}
    Dim result As New List(Of String)

    ' Store range to intermediate generic list
    For Each value As Long In income
        result.Add(Partition(value, 40000, 90000, 10000))
    Next
    result.Sort()
    ' Output header information
    Console.WriteLine("Median Income by State for a Family of Two " & _
                      "in the United States")
    Console.WriteLine("U.S. Census Estimate, 2004")
    Console.WriteLine()
    Console.WriteLine("Median Income      States")
    ' count similar items in list
    Dim count As Integer
    Dim currentString As String = result(0)
    For Each output As String in result
        If output = currentString Then
            count += 1
        Else
            Console.WriteLine(" {0}                 {1}", currentString, count)
            currentString = output
            count = 1
        End If
    Next
End Sub
End Module
```

The code first passes the individual data items to the Partition function, which stores the data range corresponding to each item in a generic List object, the strongly typed equivalent of an ArrayList. After sorting the list, the code then counts the number of data items with identical range values and displays the result. The output to the console appears as follows:

```
Median Income by State for a Family of Two in the United States
U.S. Census Estimate, 2004

Median Income      States
40000:49999          1
50000:59999          9
60000:69999          6
70000:79999          5
```

VB6 Differences

The Partition function is new to Visual Basic .NET.

Pmt Function

Determines the payment for an annuity based on periodic fixed payments and a fixed interest rate.

Member Of

Microsoft.VisualBasic.Financial

Syntax

```
Pmt(ByVal Rate As Double, ByVal NPer As Double, ByVal PV As Double, _
    Optional ByVal FV As Double = 0,
    Optional ByVal Due As DueDate = DueDate.EndOfPeriod) As Double
```

Element	Description
Rate	The interest rate per period, expressed as a decimal rather than a percent (e.g., an interest rate of 1 percent per month is .01).
NPer	The total number of payment periods.
PV	The present value of a series of future payments or receipts. If PV is a liability, its value should be negative.
FV	The future or cash balance after the final payment is made. If omitted, a future value of 0 is assumed, reflecting the full repayment of a loan. If FV is a liability that is not paid off, its value should be negative.
Due	A member of the DueDate enumeration indicating whether payments are due at the beginning (DueDate.BegOfPeriod) or end (DueDate.EndOfPeriod) of the period. If omitted, the default value is DueDate.EndOfPeriod.

Return Value

A Double indicating the amount of the payment.

Comments

An *annuity* is a series of equal payments or receipts (a level stream of cash inflow or outflow) that occurs at evenly spaced intervals for a fixed period of time. Mortgage payments, lease payments, and rental payments are all examples of annuities. Typically, for an ordinary annuity, the payments or receipts occur at the end of each period, while for an annuity due they occur at the beginning of each period.

Rate and *NPer* must both be expressed in the same time interval. For example, if the interest rate is 8 percent annually and there are 60 payments spread over 5 years, *NPer* equals 60 and *Rate* is expressed as a monthly interest rate of .00667.

Typically, the *PV* argument is used in the case of loans to indicate the initial loan amount.

Arguments that represent cash paid out are expressed with negative numbers; arguments that represent cash received are expressed with positive numbers.

While the Pmt function calculates the total payment for all periods in the life of the annuity, the PPmt function calculates the principal component and the IPmt function calculates the interest component for a particular payment. If arguments with the same values are supplied to each of the three functions, IPmt + PPmt = Pmt for any particular payment.

Example

See the example for the IPmt function.

See Also

IPmt Function, NPer Function, PPmt Function

PPmt Function

See the entry for the IPmt, NPer, and PPmt Functions.

Preserve Keyword

Preserves the existing data in an array when the number of elements in a dimension is modified.

Syntax

```
ReDim Preserve name(boundlist) [, name(boundlist) [, ... ] ]
```

Element	Description
name	The name of the array to be redimensioned.
boundlist	The new upper bounds of the array.

Comments

Ordinarily, an array is cleared before it is redimensioned, so that data from existing array is not copied to the redimensioned array. The Preserve keyword is used with the ReDim statement to copy existing data to the redimensioned array.

If the ReDim statement expands an array dimension, the Preserve keyword causes the data in existing members to be preserved, while new members are initialized to the default values of their data types. For example, the following code creates an integer array containing six elements and then redimensions the array by adding six more elements but preserving the value of the original six:

```
Public Sub Main()
   Dim PowerOf2() As Integer = {0, 1, 2, 4, 8, 16}
   Redim Preserve PowerOf2(PowerOf2.GetUpperBound(0) + 6)
   For Each int As Integer In PowerOf2
      Console.Write("--{0}--", int)
   Next
End Sub
```

The example produces the following output:

```
--0----1----2----4----8----16----0----0----0----0----0----0—
```

Only the last dimension of a multidimensional array can be redimensioned if the Preserve keyword is present.

If the ReDim statement shrinks an array dimension, the Preserve keyword causes the data in members that are retained to be saved. However, the data in the eliminated members is lost. For example, the following code declares an integer array with 12 elements and then shrinks the array in half:

```
Public Sub Main()
    Dim PowerOf2() As Integer = {0, 1, 2, 4, 8, 16, 32, 64, 128, 256, 512, 1024}
    Redim Preserve PowerOf2(PowerOf2.GetUpperBound(0)\2)
    For Each int As Integer In PowerOf2
        Console.Write("--{0}--", int)
    Next
End Sub
```

The console output confirms that the upper half of the array's data has been lost:

```
--0----1----2----4----8----16--
```

See Also

Dim Statement, ReDim Statement

Print, PrintLine Subroutines

Writes formatted data to a sequential file.

Member Of

Microsoft.VisualBasic.FileSystem

Syntax

```
Print(ByVal FileNumber As Integer, ByVal ParamArray Output() As Object)

PrintLine(ByVal FileNumber As Integer, ByVal ParamArray Output() As Object)
```

Element	Description
FileNumber	The file number used in the call to the FileOpen subroutine.
Output	A parameter array containing the data to be written to the file. (See the Comments section for additional detail.)

Comments

Print and PrintLine are two of a series of related file input and output routines that work with the file number used when opening a file with the FileOpen subroutine.

Print and PrintLine are general-purpose output routines for writing to a sequential file. The input routine typically used to read from files written with the Print and PrintLine subroutines is the Input subroutine or the LineInput function.

Print writes all of *Output* on a single line. In contrast, PrintLine adds a linefeed, but only after all the elements in *Output* have been written to the file. If Output contains multiple elements, they all appear on a single line.

Output is a parameter array, which means that it can be specified as either a comma-delimited set of arguments or an array. For example, the following calls to the Print subroutine are equivalent, each writing three strings separated by five spaces:

```
Dim output() As Object = {"Basic", SPC(5), "Visual Basic", SPC(5), "VBScript"}
Print(fileNo, output)

Print(fileNo, "Basic", SPC(5), "Visual Basic", SPC(5), "VBScript")
```

Output can include one or more of the following:

- A numeric expression. However, Print and PrintLine throw an ArgumentException if the expression is of type SByte, UInteger, ULong, or UShort.
- Any of the other scalar data types (i.e., String, Char, Date, Boolean). Data are written using the local system's standard date/time format, and an uninitialized date or time element is omitted. A Boolean value is translated as either True or False and is not localized.
- The SPC function, which inserts a designated number of spaces between output elements.
- The Tab function, which writes the following argument in *Output* at a particular character position.

If the element or argument following a data element or data argument in *Output* is not a call to the SPC or Tab functions, the Print or PrintLine subroutine adds enough white space to print the following data item at the next print position.

Except for writing the literal strings True and False, Print and PrintLine are locale-aware. Dates and numeric values are formatted according to the local computer's regional settings.

Output is actually optional. If it is omitted or if it is Nothing, the Print subroutine outputs nothing to the file, while the PrintLine subroutine outputs a single linefeed character combination.

You should call the FileClose subroutine when you have finished writing to the file.

Print and PrintLine are "compatibility" functions that are part of legacy Visual Basic code. In new code written to take advantage of the .NET platform, you can instead use the StreamWriter class. For an example, see the LineInput function.

Example

See the example for the LineInput function.

VB6 Differences

The Visual Basic 6.0 equivalent of the Print subroutine was the Print statement. The Print statement required that a # precede the *FileNumber* argument, a syntax not supported by Visual Basic .NET.

expression, the data item written to the file by the Visual Basic 6.0 Print statement, has to be a single scalar variable. In contrast, Visual Basic .NET can write multiple data items supplied either as separate arguments or in a parameter array.

Visual Basic 6.0 included an optional third parameter, *charpos,* that specified the position at which the next data item would be written. In Visual Basic .NET, this role is played by the Tab function.

The Visual Basic 6.0 Print statement allowed you to separate the second and third arguments (*expression,* which corresponds to Output in the Visual Basic .NET Print subroutine, and *charpos*) with either a comma or a semicolon. In Visual Basic .NET, if a the Print subroutine is supplied with a list of arguments rather than a parameter array, they must be separated by commas; the use of a semicolon is not supported.

See Also

FileClose Subroutine, FileOpen Subroutine, Input Subroutine, LineInput Function, SPC Function, Tab Function

Private Keyword

Declares a program element that is accessible only from the context in which it is declared.

Syntax

The Private keyword can be used with the following language elements:

- Type declarations: the Class, Delegate, Enum, Interface, and Structure statements
- Member declarations: the Const, Declare, Dim, Event, Function, Property, and Sub statements

For syntax, see the entry for the respective language element that the Private keyword modifies.

Comments

The Private keyword defines the least accessible program element in Visual Basic .NET. Private types or members are hidden from client code and are not part of a type's public interface. There are a number of reasons for making a type or member private:

- The data are proprietary or confidential and should not be easily accessible.
- Allowing client code direct access to the data is likely to create invalid data.
- The data are not particularly useful or usable by client code, although other data derived from them are.
- Less effort is required to ensure that the integrity of the data than if the data were to be publicly exposed.

The Private keyword can only be used to declare a member variable. It cannot be used to declare local variables.

If used to declare a type (that is, a class, delegate, enumeration, interface, or structure), that type must be nested within another a class or a structure. For example, in the following code, the Floor class is defined inside of the House class and is therefore accessible only by the House class:

```
Public Class House
    Private floors() As Floor

    Public Sub New(numFloors As Integer)
        ReDim floors(numFloors - 1)
```

```
        For ctr As Integer = 0 To numFloors - 1
            floors(ctr) = New Floor(ctr)
        Next
    End Sub

    Private Class Floor
        Private lvl As Integer

        Public Sub New(level As Integer)
            Me.lvl = level
        End Sub

        Public ReadOnly Property Level() As Integer
            Get
                Return Me.lvl
            End Get
        End Property
    End Class
End Class
```

When used to declare a type member, the Private keyword serves to make that member inaccessible from outside the class, structure, or enumeration in which it is defined. This serves to protect it from direct modification by client code.

Typically, Property statements are used to provide access to private variables. This allows data to be validated before it is assigned to the private variable, rather than allowing client code to modify it directly. It also allows a program to return values that are calculated on the fly. Both are illustrated in the following Person class, which uses a private variable, birthday, to store a date of birth:

```
Public Class Person
    Private birthDay As Date

    Public ReadOnly Property Age() As Integer
        Get
            If Not birthDay = Nothing Then
                ' Determine number of years since birthDay
                Return (DirectCast((Date.Now - birthDay), TimeSpan).Days) \ 365
            Else
                Return Nothing
            End If
        End Get
    End Property

    Public Property DateOfBirth() As Date
        Get
            Return birthDay
        End Get
        Set
            ' Throw exception is date is after now
            If value > Date.Now Then
                Throw New ArgumentException("The birth date cannot be in the future.")
            ' Throw exception if date is more than 125 years ago
            ElseIf value < New DateTime(Date.Now.Year - 125, Date.Now.Month, _
                                        Date.Now.Day) Then
```

```
             Throw New ArgumentException("The birth date is too far in the past.")
          ' assign value to birthDay
          Else
             birthDay = value
          End If
       End Set
    End Property
End Class
```

The Person class defines a private variable named birthDate that is set by the DateOfBirth property. Before assigning a value to the variable, the property's set accessor ensures that the date is not in the future or that it is not more than 125 years in the past. If either of these is the case, an ArgumentException is thrown. In addition, the class includes an Age property that returns a value calculated from the value of the birthDate variable.

A private program element can still be accessible to client code either if it is explicitly returned to the caller as the return value of a method or of a property get accessor or if it is included in a reference type such as an array that is accessible to client code. This is problematic both because it defeats the purpose of making the element private in the first place and it exposes an undocumented program element to the user.

VB6 Differences

Visual Basic 6.0 supported an Option Private Module statement that allowed a Visual Basic code module (a .bas file) to be private to the project in which it was used. In Visual Basic .NET, this statement is not supported. Its equivalent is defining a module using the Friend keyword.

See Also

Dim Statement, Friend Statement, Protected Statement, Public Statement

---

Property Statement

Defines a property procedure, which typically stores data about some attribute of a class or structure.

Syntax

```
[ <attributelist> ] [ Default ] [ accessmodifier ] _
[ propertymodifiers ] [ Shared ] [ Shadows ] [ ReadOnly | WriteOnly ] _
Property name ( [ ByVal parameterlist ] ) [ As returntype ] [ Implements implementsList ]
    [ <attributelist> ] [ accessmodifier ] Get
        [ statements ]
    End Get
    [ <attributelist> ] [ accessmodifier ] Set ( ByVal value As returntype )
        [ statements ]
    End Set
End Property
```

Element	Description
<attributelist>	A list of attributes that apply to the property. Only attributes whose AttributeUsage attribute is AttributeTargets.All or AttributeTargets.Property can be applied to a Property statement.
Default	Indicates that the property is the default member of its class, interface, or struc ture. If Default is specified, *accessmodifier* cannot be Private. A default property must have a parameter, typically an index. See the comments for the definition of a default property, as well as the entry for the Default keyword.
accessmodifier	Any of the standard access modifiers (Public, Private, Friend, Protected, and Protected Friend). If *accessmodifer* is not specified, the property is Public by default. Note that *accessmodifier* cannot be used with a property in an Interface statement
propertymodifiers	Provides overloading and overriding information about the property. Possible values are: Overloads. The property redeclares one or more properties with the same name. Since the return is not considered in overloading, it is comparatively rare to overload a property. Overrides. The property overrides a program element with the same name in the base class. Overridable. The property can be overridden by a member of a derived class. NotOverridable. The property cannot be overridden by a derived class. MustOverride. A derived class must implement this property. In that case, only a property statement with no implementation and no End Property statement is provided.
Shared	Indicates that an instance of the object or structure need not be created to access the property. The Shared keyword cannot be used with a property in an interface. Shared cannot be used with any of *propertymodifiers* except Overloads.
Shadows	Indicates that this property hides an identically named program element in a base class. Shared cannot be used with the Overloads keyword.
ReadOnly | WriteOnly	Indicates whether the property is read-only, write-only, or read-write. For a read-only property, only a Property Get statement is provided; for a write-only property, only a Property Set statement; for a read-write property, both a Property Get and a Property Set statement.
name	The name of the property. It must follow standard Visual Basic naming conventions.
paramlist	The property's parameter list, which defines the arguments passed to the property when it is accessed. See the detailed syntax that follows.

Element	Description
returntype	The property's data type. If Option Strict is On, it is required; if Option Strict is off and it is not specified, it defaults to Object. The property value can be any accessible type.
Implements *implementsList*	Indicates that the property provides the implementation of a property that belongs to an interface implemented by the class to which the property belongs. Each implement member in *implementsList* takes the form *interfacename.propertyname*.

The detailed syntax of *paramlist* is:

```
ByVal paramname[()] [ As type ],...
```

Element	Description
paramname	The name of the parameter, which is the name by which the argument passed to the property will be referenced in the property's code.
type	The data type of the parameter. It is required if Option Strict is on. If Option Strict is off and no data type is specified, it defaults to Object.

Comments

A property can be defined at the member level inside a class, interface, module, or structure. If it is defined inside an interface, it should provide no implementation, including no Property Get or Property Set statements.

The default property is a property that does not have to be explicitly referenced by name in order for its data to be retrieved and set. For example, the Item property is the Visual Basic .NET Collection object's default property. To access a particular member of a collection, you can use code like the following:

```
Dim dataItem = myCollection.Item(index)
```

or you can omit the reference to the Item property entirely:

```
Dim dataItem = myCollection(index)
```

The presence of an argument suggests that we are accessing an unnamed member of the class instance, rather than the class instance itself. The example illustrates a default property.

The syntax defined for the Property statement is actually the syntax of a Property Get statement. The Property Set statement has an additional parameter, the value to be assigned to the property. This parameter is typically named *value,* and its presence can either be implied or it can be listed explicitly as a parameter in the Property Set statement.

In addition to the access level specified in the Property statement, an access level can be specified for either the property get accessor or the property set accessor, but not for both. If an access level is defined for the individual accessor, it must be more restrictive than that defined in the Property statement. In addition, if a property is read-only or read-write, the single property get or property set accessor cannot specify the access level.

Typically, properties have no parameters, and a few properties define one parameter. (Most of these properties are collection objects that accept an index to an array or collection as an argument.) Note that, in order to define a default property, the property statement must define at least one parameter.

The property get accessor is responsible for returning a value of *returntype* to the caller. This can be done using either the Return statement or by assigning a value to a variable whose name is the same as the property name. In addition, if no defined value is returned by the Get procedure (as might happen if an Exit Property statement is executed without first assigning the property's return value to a variable whose name is the same as the property), the default value of the property is returned. This means that, in the case of a property whose value is a class instance, Nothing is returned, and a null reference exception could result. The example illustrates returning a value.

Most commonly, a property is used to provide access to a private variable. This type of property definition takes the general form:

```
Public Class PropertyClass
    Private instname As String

    Public Property Name() As String
       Get
           Return Me.instname
       End Get
       Set
           Me.instname = Value
       End Set
    End Property
End Class
```

The Property Get statement returns the private variable, while the Property Set statement assigns a value to it.

The value of a read-only property can be set at runtime rather than at design time by supplying the value to the constructor of its class or structure. For example:

```
Public Class Species
    Private speciesName As String

    Public Sub New(name As String)
       Me.speciesName = name
    End Sub

    Public ReadOnly Property Name() As String
       Get
           Return Me.speciesName
       End Get
    End Property
End Class
```

The Visual Basic compiler implements the Property statement by creating separate methods for the get accessor and the set accessor as well as creating the property itself. The property get accessor is translated into a method named get_*propertyName,* while the property set accessor is translated into a method named set_*propertyName.* For example, the following simple code,

FIGURE 8-22
The implementation of Property Get and Property Set accessors

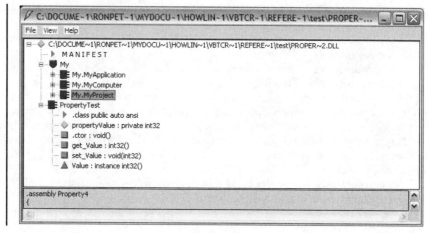

FIGURE 8-22 The implementation of Property Get and Property Set accessors

which defines a class with a single property named Value, appears as shown in Figure 8-22 when viewed in ILDasm. Note that the single property named Value is present, as are the get_Value and set_Value methods.

```
Public Class PropertyTest
    Dim propertyValue As Integer

    Public Property Value() As Integer
        Get
            Return Me.propertyValue
        End Get
        Set
            Me.propertyValue = value
        End Set
    End Property
End Class
```

So, if you use reflection to retrieve information about a class, structure, or interface, the type's member information reflects these additional special methods. You can use the Type object's IsSpecialName property to determine if a MemberInfo or MethodInfo describes a special method. It returns True for overloaded operators and property get and set accessors. The following code uses the PropertyTest class to illustrate how to exclude special members when using reflection to determine what members a type has. It lists all non-inherited members, all non-inherited methods, all non-inherited properties, and all non-inherited, normal methods:

```
Imports System.Reflection

Public Module modMain
    Const filename As String = ".\Property4.dll"
    Const notInherited As BindingFlags = BindingFlags.Instance Or _
                    BindingFlags.Public Or BindingFlags.NonPublic _
                    Or BindingFlags.Static Or BindingFlags.DeclaredOnly
    Public Sub Main()
        Dim assem As Assembly = [Assembly].LoadFrom(filename)
```

```vb
        Dim typ As Type = assem.GetType("PropertyTest")
        ListUniqueMembers(typ)
        ListAllMethods(typ)
        ListNormalMethods(typ)
        ListProperties(typ)
    End Sub

    Public Sub ListUniqueMembers(typ As Type)
        Dim members() As MemberInfo = typ.GetMembers(notInherited)
        ListMembers(members, typ, "members")
    End Sub

    Public Sub ListAllMethods(typ As Type)
        Dim methods() As MethodInfo = typ.GetMethods(notInherited)
        ListMembers(methods, typ, "methods")
    End Sub

    Public Sub ListNormalMethods(typ As Type)
        Dim output As String
        Dim ctr As Integer
        Dim methods() As MethodInfo = typ.GetMethods(notInherited)
        For Each method As MethodInfo In methods
            If Not method.IsSpecialName Then
                ctr += 1
                output &= ("    " & method.Name & vbCrLf)
            End If
        Next
        If ctr > 0 Then
            Console.WriteLine("{0} has the following methods:", typ.Name, _
                            methods.Length)
            Console.WriteLine(output)
        Else
            Console.WriteLine("{0} has no normal methods.", typ.Name)
        End If
        Console.WriteLine()
    End Sub

    Public Sub ListProperties(typ As Type)
        Dim props() As PropertyInfo = typ.GetProperties(notInherited)
        ListMembers(props, typ, "properties")
    End Sub

    Private Sub ListMembers(members As MemberInfo(), typ As Type, desc As String)
        Console.WriteLine("{0} has the following {1} {2}:", typ.Name, _
                        members.Length, desc)
        For Each mi As MemberInfo In members
            Console.WriteLine("    {0}", mi.Name)
        Next
        Console.WriteLine()
    End Sub
End Module
```

The code produces the following output:

```
PropertyTest has the following 5 members:
    get_Value
    set_Value
    .ctor
    Value
    propertyValue

PropertyTest has the following 2 methods:
    get_Value
    set_Value

PropertyTest has no normal methods.

PropertyTest has the following 1 properties:
    Value
```

Example

The following code defines a Contact class that includes a parameterized Phones property, which is the default member of the Contact class.

```
Public Enum Phones As Integer
    Business = 0
    Home = 1
    Cell = 2
End Enum

Public Class Contact
    Private contactPhone([Enum].GetValues(GetType(Phones)).Length) As String

    Public Default Property Phone(index As Phones) As String
        Get
            If index >= contactPhone.Length Then
                Exit Property
            ElseIf contactPhone(index) = String.Empty Then
                Return "(   )    -    "
            Else
                Phone = contactPhone(index)
            End If
        End Get
        Set
            If index >= contactPhone.Length Then
                Throw New IndexOutOfRangeException(index & " _
                    is not a valid value in the Phone enumeration.")
            Else
                contactPhone(index) = value
            End If
        End Set
    End Property
End Class
```

The property get accessor illustrates all three methods of returning a value: using the Return statement; assigning the return value to a variable whose name is the same as that of the property; and exiting the procedure without returning an explicit value.

VB.NET Changes

Visual Basic 2005 allows you to set an access level for either a Property Get or a Property Set statement that is different from the access level specified in the Property statement. Although previous versions of Visual Basic .NET did not support mixed accessibility for properties, Visual Basic 6.0 did.

VB6 Differences

A single Property statement is new to Visual Basic .NET. Visual Basic 6.0 had separate Property Get, Property Let, and Property Set statements. Property Get returned a value, Property Let assigned a scalar property value, and Property Set assigned an object property value.

The Visual Basic 6.0 syntax required that all arguments passed to a property accessor be expressed as a parameter. In Visual Basic .NET, the value passed to the property set accessor to set a value can be implicit.

Although VBScript had a Default keyword that allowed you to designate the default property of a class, Visual Basic 6.0 did not have a corresponding Default keyword. In contrast, Visual Basic .NET has a Default keyword but requires that the default property be parameterized.

See Also

Default Keyword, Get Statement, Set Statement

Protected Keyword

Indicates that a program element is accessible from within the class in which it is declared and from derived classes.

Syntax

The Protected keyword can be used with the following language elements:

- Type declarations: the Class, Delegate, Enum, Interface, and Structure statements
- Member declarations: the Const, Declare, Dim, Event, Function, Property, and Sub statements

For syntax, see the entry for the respective language element that the Protected keyword modifies.

Comments

Protected provides the next most restrictive accessibility after Private. Whereas the Private keyword makes a program element accessible only from the type in which it is declared, Protected makes it accessible both from the type in which it is declared and from derived types.

The Protected keyword can only be used to declare a member variable. Local variables cannot be protected. If the Protected keyword is used to declare a type (a class, delegate, enum, structure, or interface), that type must be declared inside a class, since only classes support direct inheritance.

It is also possible to declare the accessibility of a program element as Protected Friend. This indicates that the element is accessible within the class in which it is declared and to all derived types, as well as to types within the same assembly. In other words, Protected Friend offers broader, and not more restrictive, accessibility than either Protected or Friernd alone.

Note that although protected program elements are accessible from within derived classes, they are not accessible from consumers of derived classes.

In some cases, a derived class may not be able to access a protected member of its base class, and a compiler error results. This occurs when the protected method is called through a variable whose compile-time type is that of the base class rather than the derived class. For example:

```
Public Class Animal
    Protected Sub Walk()
        Console.WriteLine("Step...Step...Step...Step")
    End Sub
End Class

Public Class Dog : Inherits Animal
    Public Sub Stroll()
        Dim anim As New Animal()
        Dim dg As New Dog()
        MyBase.Walk()
        Console.WriteLine("Stop, Sniff")
        dg.Walk()
        Console.WriteLine("Stop, Sniff")
        anim.Walk()
    End Sub
End Class
```

The call to MyBase.Walk and to dg.Walk work correctly, but the call to anim.Walk fails because the static type analyzer is unable to determine that the instance whose protected member is called is actually an instance of the derived class.

Interestingly, it is possible to declare a Protected program element within a class marked NotInheritable, which means that the derived classes that are able to access the protected program element cannot be defined.

VB6 Differences

The Protected keyword is new to Visual Basic .NET.

See Also

Dim Statement, Friend Keyword, Private Keyword, Public Keyword

Public Keyword

Defines a program element that is accessible to any client able to access its assembly or type.

Syntax

The Public keyword can be used with the following Visual Basic language elements:

- Type declarations: the Class, Delegate, Enum, Interface, Module, and Structure statements
- Member declarations: the Const, Declare, Dim, Event, Function, Operator, Property, and Sub statements

For syntax, see the entry for the respective language element that the Public keyword modifies.

Comments

Ignoring any possible security constraints, the Public keyword provides unrestricted access to any program element by any code that has access to the assembly defining it, in the case of non-nested types, or the type defining it, in the case of members.

Public can be used to define the accessibility of program elements within a namespace (where it can define the accessibility of types) and at the member level (where it can define the accessibility of nested types and type members). It cannot be used to define accessibility of a program element within a method or property, since these are always local.

The accessibility of nested types and type members is restricted by the accessibility of the types that define them. For example, a Public function defined in a Friend class is accessible without restriction within the assembly within which its defining class is located.

Defining the accessibility of program elements is an important part of sound application design. Particularly for inexperienced programmers, it's tempting to simply make all program elements public, since they can be accessed from anywhere. But you should resist that temptation. In general, you should define a particular program element with the most restrictive accessibility possible given the needs of your application.

Avoid defining public fields (that is, variables that are members of classes), since these are globally accessible outside of your application, and you have no control over whether and how they are modified aside from whatever constraints (such as type checking) that are imposed by the compiler. Almost all public fields in the .NET Framework Class Library, for example, are either read-only fields (if their values are established at runtime by the class constructor) or constants.

VB6 Differences

In Visual Basic 6.0, the Global keyword, although it was deprecated, was still supported as a replacement for the Public keyword. In Visual Basic .NET, it is not supported.

See Also

Dim Statement, Friend Keyword, Private Keyword, Protected Keyword

PV Function

Calculates the present value of an annuity based on regular fixed payments in the future and a fixed interest rate.

Member Of

Microsoft.VisualBasic.Financial

Syntax

```
PV(ByVal Rate As Double, ByVal NPer As Double, ByVal Pmt As Double, _
    Optional ByVal FV As Double = 0, _
    Optional ByVal Due As DueDate = DueDate.EndOfPeriod) As Double
```

Element	Description
Rate	The interest rate per period, expressed as a decimal rather than a percentage. For example, an interest rate of 12 percent per year is 1 percent per month, which equals a *Rate* of .01.
NPer	The total number of payment periods.
Pmt	The payment to be made each period.
FV	The future or cash balance after the final payment is made. If omitted, a future value of 0 is assumed..
Due	A member of the DueDate enumeration indicating whether payments are due at the beginning (DueDate.BegOfPeriod) or end (DueDate.EndOfPeriod) of the period. If omitted, the default value is DueDate.EndOfPeriod.

Return Value

A Double representing the present value of the annuity.

Comments

An *annuity* is a series of equal payments or receipts (a level stream of cash inflow or outflow) that occurs at evenly spaced intervals for a fixed period of time. Mortgage payments, lease payments, and rental payments are all examples of annuities. Typically, for an ordinary annuity, the payments or receipts occur at the end of each period, while for an annuity due they occur at the beginning of each period.

Rate, NPer, and *Pmt* must be expressed in the same time unit for the value returned by the function to make sense. For example, if the rate is 5.75 percent per year for fixed payments of $1,458.93 per month for 30 years, the three arguments must either be expressed in terms of years (in which case the fixed payment would have to be changed to $17,507.16) or of months (in which case the rate would have to be changed to .4792 percent and the number of payments would have to be changed to 360).

FV can represent the value of a loan after repayment and is usually equal to 0. It also can represent a savings goal, in which case it is a positive integer.

Arguments that represent cash paid out are expressed with negative numbers; arguments that represent cash received are expressed with positive numbers.

See Also

FV Function. IPmt Function, NPer Function, Pmt Function, PPmt Function, Rate Function

QBColor Function

Returns an Integer representing an RGB color value.

Member Of

Microsoft.VisualBasic.Information

Syntax

```
QBColor(Color As Integer) As Integer
```

Element	Description
Color	An Integer ranging from 1 to 15, or a color constant.

Return Value

An RGB color value.

Comments

The possible values of Color are shown in the following table:

Integer	Description	Integer	Description
0	Black	8	Gray
1	Blue	9	Light Blue
2	Green	10	Light Green
3	Cyan	11	Light Cyan
4	Red	12	Light Red
5	Magenta	13	Light Magenta
6	Yellow	14	Light Yellow
7	White	15	Bright White

QBColor is a legacy function that was part of QBasic, a version of Basic from which Visual Basic was originally derived. Even in Visual Basic 6.0, it was far less flexible than the RGB function, which allowed more precise control over the color used for forms. In Visual Basic .NET, the function is virtually unused, since its return value, an integer representing an RGB color, cannot be directly converted to a System.Drawing.Color value required to set the color of forms, controls, and other interface objects. Instead, to use the QBColor function to set the background color of a form to gray, for example, code like the following is required:

```
frm.BackColor = Color.FromARGB(&HFF000000 Or QBColor(8))
```

In contrast, setting the color using the static fields of the System.Drawing.Color or the System.Drawing.SystemColors structures both is easier and produces more readable code:

```
frm.BackColor = Color.Gray
```

or

```
frm.BackColor = SystemColors.Window
```

See Also
RGB Function

RaiseEvent Statement

Fires an event defined with the Event statement.

Syntax

RaiseEvent eventname*[(* argumentList *)]*

Element	Description
eventname	The name of the event, as defined by the Event statement.
argumentList	A comma-delimited list of arguments to pass to listeners handling the event. *argumentList* must match the parameter list defined by the Event statement.

Comments

The RaiseEvent statement can be used in a property or method of a class, structure, or module to fire an event. The event must be declared using the Event statement at the member level of that class or structure. In other words, the event must be fired by a member of the same class, structure, or module in which it is declared; a derived class cannot fire events declared in its base class, nor can clients use the RaiseEvent statement to fire events declared in the classes or structures that they've instantiated.

Because derived classes cannot fire events declared in base classes, it's a good idea to declare a protected On*eventname* method in the base class that fires the event. Because it's protected, it is callable only by derived classes. For example:

```
Protected Sub OnBaseClassEvent(sender As Object, e As EventArgs)
    RaiseEvent BaseClassEvent(sender, e)
End Sub
```

Although events can be raised by a module, they must be shared events (although the Shared keyword cannot be used in the Event statement defining the event). The event handlers for such events must be associated with the event in clients by the AddHandler and RemoveHandler statements. In the following code, for example, the CheckStockPrice function in a module fires a StockDecline event if a stock that it's monitoring has declined by 5 percent or more during the day:

```
Imports System.Collections.Generic

Public Class StockDeclineEventArgs : Inherits EventArgs
    Dim stockSymbol As String
    Dim priceStart As Decimal
    Dim priceNow As Decimal
```

```vb
    Friend Sub New(symbol As String, openPrice As Decimal, currentPrice As Decimal)
        Me.stockSymbol = symbol
        Me.priceStart = openPrice
        Me.priceNow = currentPrice
    End Sub

    Public ReadOnly Property Symbol As String
        Get
            Return Me.stockSymbol
        End Get
    End Property

    Public ReadOnly Property PercentLost As Decimal
        Get
            Return (Me.priceNow - Me.priceStart)/Me.priceStart * 100
        End Get
    End Property

    Public ReadOnly Property OpeningPrice As Decimal
        Get
            Return Me.priceStart
        End Get
    End Property

    Public ReadOnly Property CurrentPrice As Decimal
        Get
            Return Me.priceNow
        End Get
    End Property
End Class

<HideModuleName> Public Module StockTrackTools

    Public Event StockDecline(ByVal sender As Object, _
                              ByVal e As StockDeclineEventArgs)

    Public Function CheckStockPrice(symbol As String, price As Decimal) As Decimal
        Static dict As New Dictionary(Of String, Decimal)
        If Not dict.ContainsKey(symbol) Then
            dict.Add(symbol, price)
            Return 0
        Else
            Dim startPrice As Decimal = dict.Item(symbol)
            Dim pctChange As Decimal = (price - startPrice) / startPrice * 100
            If pctChange <= -5.0 Then
                RaiseEvent StockDecline(Nothing, New StockDeclineEventArgs( _
                        symbol, dict.Item(symbol), price))
            End If
            Return pctChange
        End If
    End Function
End Module
```

The event is handled in the client by using the AddHandler statement to define an event handler:

```
Public Module ModClient
    Public Sub Main
        AddHandler StockDecline, AddressOf StockFallEvent
        Console.WriteLine("VWID: 100, {0}%", CheckStockPrice("VWID", 100))
        Console.WriteLine("VWID: 102, {0}%", CheckStockPrice("VWID", 102))
        Console.WriteLine("VWID: 106, {0}%", CheckStockPrice("VWID", 106))
        Console.WriteLine("VWID: 100, {0}%", CheckStockPrice("VWID", 100))
        Console.WriteLine("VWID: 99, {0}%", CheckStockPrice("VWID", 99))
        Console.WriteLine("VWID: 94, {0}%", CheckStockPrice("VWID", 94))
        RemoveHandler StockDecline, AddressOf StockFallEvent
    End Sub

    Public Sub StockFallEvent(sender As Object, e As StockDeclineEventArgs)
        Console.WriteLine()
        Console.WriteLine("   ALERT: {0} has declined by {1}!", _
                          e.Symbol, Math.Abs(e.PercentLost))
        Console.WriteLine()
    End Sub
End Module
```

The typical signature of a .NET event is

```
eventname(Byval sender As Object, ByVal e As EventArgs)
```

This means that, when RaiseEvent is called, the most common argument passed to the *sender* parameter is Me. In addition, if *e* is either an EventArgs object, an object derived from EventArgs that has no non-default members, or an object derived from EventArgs whose non-default members are defined by its class constructor, the EventArgs object can be created at the same time that it is instantiated. In this case, the call to RaiseEvent takes the form:

```
RaiseEvent eventname(Me, New EventArgs())
```

If the RaiseEvent statement is used to raise an instance (or non-shared) event in a class constructor, client event handlers may not be able to catch the event. This is the case because the constructor is still in the process of executing and the class is still in the process of being instantiated, which means that listeners have still not been established. If an event needs to be raised in the constructor of the class or structure in which the event is declared, it should be a Shared event.

When the RaiseEvent statement is used to raise an instance event, it means that every variable that holds a reference to that object instance, as well as the class instance itself, can receive notification of the event. When RaiseEvent is used to raise a shared event, all consumers of a class regardless of class instance can receive event notifications, as can the class itself.

Events raised by the RaiseEvent statement can be associated with an event handler either by the combination of the WithEvents and Handles keywords for events defined in classes, or by the AddHandler and RemoveHandler statements, which can be used for all events.

By default, the RaiseEvent statement causes the synchronous execution of registered event handlers. That is, each event handler is executed synchronously in the order in which it connected to the event, and a subsequent handler is executed only after the preceding event handler has finished execution. This default behavior can be overridden by defining an event using the Event statement along with the Custom keyword, which causes the RaiseEvent accessor to be executed when the RaiseEvent statement is executed.

Example

See the examples for the AddHandler Statement and Custom Keyword for events raised using the RaiseEvent statement.

VB6 Differences

In Visual Basic 6.0, only classes could raise events. In Visual Basic .NET, classes, structures (the equivalent of Visual Basic 6.0 user-defined types), and modules can raise events.

In Visual Basic 6.0, event handlers were always executed synchronously. In Visual Basic .NET, their order and mode of execution can be controlled by defining a custom event handler using the Custom keyword and a custom RaiseEvent procedure in the Event statement.

See Also

AddHandler Statement, Event Statement, Handles Keyword, RemoveHandler Statement, WithEvents Keyword

Randomize Subroutine

Initializes the random number generator.

Member Of

Microsoft.VisualBasic.VBMath

Syntax

```
Randomize([ Number As Double ])
```

Element	Description
Number	A seed value used to initialize the Rnd function's random number generator. If omitted, a value returned by the system timer is used.

Comments

The Randomize subroutine is used to provide a seed value to the random number generator. The *seed value* is supplied to an algorithm that uses it to generate a series of pseudo-random numbers.

You can use the random number generator without initializing it with a call to the Randomize subroutine. In that case, however, the Rnd function generates the same sequence of pseudo-random numbers.

To generate the same sequence of pseudo-random numbers each time you use the random number generator, you can use code like the following:

```
Rnd(-1)
Randomize(number)                    ' Number is any Double
For ctr As Integer = 1 to 10
   Console.WriteLine(Rnd())
Next
```

Example

See the example for the Rnd function.

See Also

Rnd Function

Rate Function

Calculates the interest rate per period for an annuity.

Member Of

Microsoft.VisualBasic.Financial

Syntax

```
Rate(ByVal NPer As Double, ByVal Pmt As Double, ByVal PV As Double, _
     Optional ByVal FV As Double = 0, _
     Optional ByVal Due As DueDate = DueDate.EndOfPeriod, _
     Optional ByVal Guess As Double = 0.1) As Double
```

Element	Description
NPer	The number of periods over which the payments are spread.
Pmt	The amount of the payment per period.
PV	The present value of a series of future payments or receipts. In the case of a loan, its value represents the loan amount. If PV is a liability such as a loan, its value should be positive, since it represents cash received for which subsequent payments will be made.
FV	The future value or cash balance of the annuity, or its value at the end of the payments term. FV defaults to 0, reflecting the repayment of a loan. If FV is a liability that is not paid off, its value should be negative.
Due	A member of the DueDate enumeration indicating whether payments are due at the beginning (DueDate.BegOfPeriod) or end (DueDate.EndOfPeriod) of each period. If omitted, the default value is DueDate.EndOfPeriod.
Guess	An estimate of the value to be returned by the Rate function. If omitted, 0.1 (an interest rate of 10 percent) is assumed.

Return Value

A Double indicating the interest rate per period.

Comments

An *annuity* is a series of equal payments or receipts (a level stream of cash inflow or outflow) that occurs at evenly spaced intervals for a fixed period of time. Mortgage payments, lease payments, and rental payments are all examples of annuities, as are savings plans. Typically, for an ordinary annuity, the payments or receipts occur at the end of each period, while for an annuity due they occur at the beginning of each period.

Rate is expressed as a decimal (e.g., 0.10 instead of 10 percent) and reflects the interest rate for the same unit of time reflected by *NPer*. If *NPer* is the number of monthly payments, for example, the value returned by the Rate function reflects the interest rate per month.

For the *Pmt*, *PV*, and *FV* arguments, cash paid out is represented by a negative value, while cash received is represented by a positive value.

The value returned by the Rate function is calculated through iteration starting with *Guess* as a best estimate. The function will attempt up to 20 iterations before failing.

Example

Often, you'll be told that some expensive purchase can be paid off in *x* easy payments. You can use the Rate function to determine what the interest rate is on those "easy monthly payments." The example is a kind of rate calculator that calculates the interest rate based on a fixed payment over time.

```
Public Module RateCalculator
    Public Sub Main()
        Dim FV, PV, NPer, Pmt, interestRate As Double
        Dim inputString As String
        Dim title As String = "Rate Calculator"
        Dim result As MsgBoxResult
        Do
            inputString = InputBox("Enter the Number of Payments: ", title, "60")
            If Not IsNumeric(inputString) Then
                MsgBox("Number of payments is not a number." & vbCrLf & _
                        "Assuming a value of 60.")
                NPer = 60
            Else
                NPer = CInt(inputString)
            End If

            inputString = InputBox("Enter the Payment Amount: ", title, "0")
            If Not IsNumeric(inputString) Then
                MsgBox("Payment amount is not a number. Assuming 0.")
                Pmt = 0
            Else
                Pmt = -CDbl(inputString)
            End If

            inputString = InputBox("Enter the Loan Value: ", title, "0")
            If Not IsNumeric(inputString) Then
                MsgBox("Loan amount is not a number. Assuming 0.")
                PV = 0
            Else
                PV = CDbl(inputString)
            End If

            inputString = InputBox("Balance after loan repayment: " & vbCrLf & _
                                "(Typically, this value is 0.)", title, "0")
            If Not IsNumeric(inputString) Then
                MsgBox("Balance after repayment is not a number. Assuming 0")
                FV = 0
            Else
                FV = CDbl(inputString)
            End If
```

```
               ' Calculate rate
               Try
                   interestRate = Rate(NPer, Pmt, PV, FV, DueDate.BegOfPeriod, 0.1)
                   MsgBox("The interest rate is " & FormatPercent(interestRate, 2, _
                   TriState.True))
               Catch e As Exception
                   MsgBox("Unable to compute interest rate.")
                   MsgBox(e.Gettype.Name & ": " & e.Message)
                   MsgBox("FV: " & FV & "   PV: " & PV & "   NPer: " & NPER & _
                        "  PMT: " & Pmt)
               End Try
               result = MsgBox("Calculate another interest rate?", _
                              MsgBoxStyle.YesNo Or MsgBoxStyle.Question)
          Loop while result = MsgBoxResult.Yes
     End Sub
End Module
```

See Also

FV Function, IPmt Function, NPer Function, Pmt Function, PPmt Function, PV Function

---

ReadOnly Keyword

Indicates that the value of a variable or property can be retrieved but not assigned.

Syntax

See the syntax for the Dim and Property statements.

Comments

The ReadOnly keyword is used with the Dim and Property statements to define a variable and a property, respectively, whose value can be read but not written.

Although constants and read-only variables are both read-only, there is a significant difference between them. The value of a constant is known at design time and is part of the constant's declaration. Though the value of a read-only variable may be known at design time, most commonly it is known only at runtime. To put it another way, constants are now and forever; they are never written to, and are eternal. Read-only variables are more accurately described as "write once" variables.

You can assign the value of a read-only variable at the same time as you declare the variable, as in the following code:

```
     Private ReadOnly value1 As Integer = 10
```

But you can also assign the value of a read-only variable in the constructor of the class or subroutine to which it belongs:

```
Public Class ReadOnlyVar
     Private ReadOnly value1 As Integer

     Public Sub New()
        value1 = 20
     End Sub

     ' rest of code for class
End Class
```

The ReadOnly keyword can only be used to define member variables and properties. It cannot be used to define local variables.

Even if a reference type is declared to be read-only, the value of individual members (in the case of a class) or elements (in the case of an array) can be changed. For example, the following code defines a class, Number, that is declared as a read-only object instance in another class named Startup. Number has two members, an Integer property and a read-only Boolean property named IsEven whose underlying private variable, even, is calculated whenever the Value property is set. A read-only instance of number is created in the Startup class, which indicates whether the Number object instance holds an even or odd value, increments its Value property by 3, and indicates whether that value is even or odd:

```
Public Class Number
    Dim number As Integer
    Dim even As Boolean

    Public Sub New(value As Integer)
        Me.Value = value
    End Sub

    Public Property Value() As Integer
        Get
            Return Me.Number
        End Get
        Set
            Me.number = Value
            Me.even = (value / 2 = value \ 2)
        End Set
    End Property

    Public ReadOnly Property IsEven() As Boolean
        Get
            Return Me.even
        End Get
    End Property
End Class

Public Class Startup
    Private startupValue As Integer
    Private ReadOnly num As New Number(startupValue)

    Public Sub New(value As Integer)
        Me.startupValue = value
    End Sub

    Public Shared Sub Main()
        Dim input As Integer = CInt(InputBox("Enter an integer: "))
        Dim su As New Startup(input)
        su.Execute()
    End Sub
```

```
    Private Sub Execute()
        Console.WriteLine(num.IsEven)
        num.Value += 3
        Console.WriteLine(num.IsEven)
    End Sub
End Class
```

If the user inputs the number 12, the output from the program indicates that the value of the read-only object's two properties have changed:

```
True
False
```

Creating a variable of a read-only reference type is very much like passing a reference type by value: the object or array itself cannot be replaced, although its individual members or elements can.

VB6 Differences

The ReadOnly keyword is new to Visual Basic .NET.

See Also

Dim Statement, Property Statement, WriteOnly Keyword

ReDim Statement

Resizes an array.

Syntax

```
ReDim [ Preserve ] name(boundlist) [, name(boundlist) [, ... ] ]
```

Element	Description
Preserve	Keyword indicating that existing array elements are to be preserved after the array is redimensioned; for details, see the entry for the Preserve keyword.
name	The name of the array to be redimensioned. It must have been declared previously with the Dim statement.

boundlist	The bounds of the redimensioned array. For a one-dimensional array, this can take the form
	
	`arrayName(upperbounds)`
	
	or
	
	`arrayName(0 To upperbounds)`
	
	If multiple dimensions are present, they are separated by commas. The number of dimensions must match that of the original array. Since Visual Basic arrays are zero-based, the upper bound of an array is one less than its number of elements.

Comments

In order to resize an array using the ReDim statement, it must already have been declared using the Dim statement. This is true even if Option Explicit is off.

The ReDim statement can only be used within a procedure; it cannot be used at member level (i.e., within a class, structure, or module, but outside of a procedure). However, the array variable itself can be declared at member level or can be passed as an argument to the procedure containing ReDim.

By default, resizing an array causes all data in the original array to be lost. The Preserve keyword causes data in elements of the array that also exist in the resized array to be preserved.

You can use a single ReDim statement to resize more than one dimension of a multidimensional array if you don't specify the Preserve keyword. For example, the following code resizes both dimensions of a two-dimensional array:

```
Dim contactArray(25, 5) As String
' statements
Redim contactArray(50, 10)
```

If you do use the ReDim statement with the Preserve keyword to resize an array, you can only resize its last dimension. If you resize more than one dimension, the the ReDim statement throws an ArrayTypeMismatchException at runtime.

If the Dim statement is used to declare an array as an Array data type, as in the following code:

```
Dim arr As Array = Array.CreateInstance(GetType(Integer), 10)
```

the ReDim statement is unable to resize it.

ReDim works by creating a new array, copying the existing elements from the old array to the new one if the Preserve keyword is present, and then replacing the old array with the new one. This means that, if you pass the array by value to a procedure in which the array is resized, the original array is restored when control returns to the caller. For example, in the following code, the upper bound of an array is changed from 7 to 14 in the ExpandArray procedure and the Preserve keyword is not used, but the original array is still preserved when control returns to the Main procedure:

```
Public Class TestReDim
    Public Shared Sub Main()
        Dim numbers() As Integer = {1, 2, 4, 8, 16, 32, 64, 128}
        Console.WriteLine("Before expanding the array:")
        DisplayArray(numbers)
        ExpandArray(numbers)
        Console.WriteLine("After expanding the array:")
        DisplayArray(numbers)
    End Sub

    Private Shared Sub DisplayArray(ByVal numbers() As Integer)
        For ctr As Integer = numbers.GetLowerBound(0) To numbers.GetUpperBound(0)
            Console.Write("    ")
            if ctr < numbers.GetUpperBound(0) Then
                Console.Write("{0}, ", numbers(ctr))
            Else
                Console.WriteLine(numbers(ctr))
            End If
```

```
        Next
    End Sub

    Private Shared Sub ExpandArray(ByVal arr() As Integer)
        ReDim arr(arr.GetUpperBound(0) * 2)
        Console.WriteLine("In the ExpandArray procedure:")
        DisplayArray(arr)
    End Sub
End Class
```

The code produces the following output:

```
Before expanding the array:
    1,   2,  4,  8, 16, 32, 64, 128
In the ExpandArray procedure:
    0,   0,  0,  0,  0,  0,  0,   0,  0,  0,  0,  0,  0,  0,  0
After expanding the array:
    1,   2,  4,  8, 16, 32, 64, 128
```

This means that, in order to resize an array in a called procedure and have the changes reflected when control leaves the procedure, the array must be passed by reference rather than by value. In the case of the example, the declaration of the ExpandArray procedure would have to be changed to the following:

```
Private Shared Sub ExpandArray(ByRef arr() As Integer)
```

Frequently, you have no idea at design time how many elements may be stored to a particular array. In that case, you can resize the array as needed when the current array reaches capacity. However, resizing an array involves a performance hit, particularly if the array is large. Rather than resizing the array one element at a time, it should be resized by a number of elements sufficient to meet additional short-term data storage requirements. A counter should then be used to keep track of which unused array element is the next one to be assigned a value. The example illustrates this scenario.

Example

The example creates an array to hold a series of numbers entered by the user. It initially allocates 11 elements to the array, and it doubles its size whenever all existing elements are have been assigned values:

```
Public Class TestReDim
    Dim bound As Integer = 10
    Dim inputNumbers(bound) As Integer

    Public Shared Sub Main()
        Dim test As New TestReDim
        test.GetInput(test.inputNumbers)
    End Sub

    Private Sub GetInput(ByVal arr() As Integer)
        Dim ctr As Integer = 0          ' Position in the array to get next number
        Dim input As String
```

```
    ' Get user input
    Do While True
        input = InputBox("Enter an integer: " & vbCrLf & _
                "(Press Cancel to exit.)")
        If Input = String.Empty OrElse Not IsNumeric(input) Then Exit Do
        inputNumbers(ctr) = CInt(input)
        ' Determine if all array elements have numbers
        If ctr = inputNumbers.GetUpperBound(0) Then
            ReDim Preserve inputNumbers(inputNumbers.Length * 2 - 1)
        End If
        ctr += 1
    Loop
    ' Iterate array to get sum
    Dim total As Long
    For number As Integer = inputNumbers.GetLowerBound(0) To ctr - 1
        total += inputNumbers(number)
    Next
    Console.WriteLine("The {0} numbers entered total {1} with a mean of {2}.", _
                    ctr, total, total / ctr)
    End Sub
End Class
```

VB6 Differences

In Visual Basic 6.0, an array variable could be declared with the ReDim statement and then subsequently resized with a ReDim statement. For example:

```
ReDim vars(10) As Integer
vars(10) = 100
ReDim Preserve vars(20)
```

In Visual Basic .NET, the ReDim statement can only be used to resize an existing array. Attempting to declare an array with the ReDim statement generates compiler error BC30451, "Name '*varname*' is not declared."

In Visual Basic 6.0, the ReDim statement could include an As clause to define the array's data type. If ReDim was used to declare the array, the array could be of any Visual Basic data type. If ReDim was used to resize the array, the type of the array had to be the same as the originally declared type. In Visual Basic .NET, the As clause is not supported.

In Visual Basic 6.0, arrays could be resized using the ReDim statement only if they were declared with the ReDim statement or if their bounds were not specified when they were declared. For example, the following array could be resized:

```
Dim intArray() As Integer
ReDim intArray(20)
```

while the following array could not be:

```
Dim intArray(10) As Integer
ReDim intArray(20)
```

In Visual Basic .NET, all arrays other than those declared as type Array can be resized using the ReDim statement.

In Visual Basic 6.0, the ReDim statement allowed you to redefine both the lower bound and the upper bound of an array. Since you cannot explicitly define the lower bound of an array using Visual Basic language elements alone, this usage is not supported in Visual Basic .NET.

See Also

Dim Statement, Preserve Keyword

Rem Statement

Indicates a comment in source code.

Syntax

```
Rem text
' text
'''<xmlTag>
```

Comments

The Rem statement is almost never used in Visual Basic programming. Instead, use the ' symbol.

The comment symbol applies only to the line of code on which it appears. This means, for example, that you cannot use a single comment symbol to "comment out" a line along with all of its continuation lines.

Use comments in your code judiciously and sparsely. Overly commented code often tends to restate the obvious, becomes stale more easily, and as a result is often completely ignored. Use naming conventions to express the syntax of your code; use comments to express its semantics (why it was implemented that way).

Comments are ignored when an application is built and do not appear in the final assembly.

If you use Visual Studio, you can have Visual Studio create a special XML documentation file during the build process that contains comments from your code. Although this and the conventional method of documenting code are not strictly incompatible, it's difficult to combine them.

To generate XML documentation, the **Generate XML Documentation File** box on the Build tab of the Project Properties dialog must be checked (it is by default). You can then apply a recommended set of tags (each of which has a designated syntax) in your code, as well as use your own tags, as long as the result is well-formed XML. XML tags apply to the language element that they immediately precede. When you build the project, Visual Studio creates a special *projectName*.xml file that contains the comments. For DLLs, if the XML file resides n the same directory as the DLL, Visual Studio uses the text in the <comment> tag for IntelliSense help with individual members that are defined in the file.

VB6 Differences

In Visual Basic 6.0, if a line included a comment symbol and ended with a line continuation, that line and all subsequent continuation lines were interpreted as comments. In Visual Basic .NET, the comment symbol applies to only a single line.

RemoveHandler Statement

Deactivates an event handler defined using the AddHandler statement.

Syntax

```
RemoveHandler event, AddressOf eventhandler
```

Element	Description
event	The name of an event, in the form *className.event*.
eventhandler	The name of the procedure responsible for handling *event*.

Comments

The RemoveHandler statement disables event handlers added using the AddHandler statement. It cannot be used to deactivate an event handler for an object declared using the WithEvents keyword and whose event handler is defined using the Handles keyword.

In contrast to the Handles statement, which allows you connect an event with an event handler for the lifetime of an application, combination of the AddHandler and RemoveHandler statements allow you to define an event handler dynamically for a duration of your choice. This is an excellent alternative for applications or components in which the code that should handle an event is based on conditions that can only be determined at runtime.

Although structures and modules can raise events, the WithEvents keyword cannot be used to define event handlers to respond to them. The AddHandler and RemoveEvent statements provide the only way in which a client can handle events raised by a structure or module.

Custom events defined using the Custom keyword in the Event statement (see the entry for the Event Statement) require that the RemoveHandler statement be used.

Example

See the example for the AddHandler statement.

VB6 Differences

The RemoveHandler statement does not exist in Visual Basic 6.0.

See Also

AddHandler Statement, Handles Statement, WithEvents Keyword

Rename Subroutine

Renames a file or directory.

Member Of

Microsoft.VisualBasic.FileSystem

Syntax

```
Rename(ByVal oldPath As String, ByVal newPath As String)
```

Element	Description
oldPath	An absolute or relative path to the directory or file to be renamed. If *oldPath* is a relative path, it is interpreted in relationship to the current directory. *oldPath* must name a single file or directory, and it cannot contain wildcard characters. If it does, an ArgumentException is thrown. *oldPath* must also exist; if it doesn't, a FileNotFoundException is thrown.
newPath	The new name of the file or directory. *newPath* must not already exist, or an IOException is thrown. *newpath* is always interpreted as consisting of either an absolute or relative path component, along with a filename if *oldpath* includes a filename.

Comments

Although this subroutine is new to Visual Basic .NET, it strongly resembles a "compatibility" function that is reminiscent of the days of DOS, when renaming commands often did double duty by renaming file system objects, moving them, or doing both simultaneously.

The typical syntax of renaming methods and statements assumes that *newPath,* the argument that contains the new name and/or the new location of the file or directory, is to be interpreted relative to the directory in which *oldpath* resides, if an absolute path is not specified. For example, if you enter the command line statement

```
Rename "C:\Documents\Introduction.Doc" "Chapter01.Doc"
```

in a console window, Introduction.Doc is renamed to Chapter01.Doc, but it is not moved. Not so the Rename subroutine. If *newPath* does not specify an absolute path, it interprets *newPath* as a path relative to the current directory. For example, if the current directory is "C:\Program Files\MyApplication", the method call

```
Rename("C:\Documents\Introduction.Doc", "Chapter01.Doc")
```

renames the file and moves it to the MyApplication subdirectory. This makes it very easy for the operation of the Rename subroutine to have consequences not intended by the developer and not desired by the user. To avoid this, you should always specify absolute paths in both *oldPath* and *newPath* in order to remove any possible ambiguity.

Although Rename can move a file or directory from one drive to another, it cannot rename files or directories when moving them from one drive to another. An attempt to move *oldPath* from one drive to another and rename it throws an IOException. If *oldPath* is a file, it must not be open or an IOException is thrown.

Instead of using the Visual Basic Rename subroutine, you can instead call the My.Computer .FileSystem.RenameFile method if you want to rename a file and the My.Computer.FileSystem .MoveFile method if you would like to move one. (For details, see Chapter 9.) Similarly, if you want to rename a directory, you can call the My.Computer.FileSystem.RenameDirectory method, while you can call the My.Computer.FileSystem.MoveDirectory method to move one. The .NET Framework Class Library also has a number of move methods in the System.IO namespace.

These include the static Directory.Move method, the instance DirectoryInfo.MoveTo method, and the instance File.Move method.

VB6 Differences

The Rename subroutine is new to Visual Basic .NET. It is equivalent to the Name statement in Visual Basic 6.0.

See Also

ChDir Subroutine, ChDrive Subroutine, CurDir Function, Kill Subroutine, MkDir Subroutine

Replace Function

Replaces a substring with another string a specified number of times.

Member Of

Microsoft.VisualBasic.Strings

Syntax

```
Replace(ByVal Expression As String, ByVal Find As String, _
        ByVal Replacement As String, Optional ByVal Start As Integer = 1, _
        Optional ByVal Count As Integer = -1, _
        Optional ByVal Compare As CompareMethod = CompareMethod.Binary) _
        As String
```

Element	Description
Expression	A string containing the substring to be replaced.
Find	The substring to replace in Expression.
Replacement	The string to replace Find.
Start	The starting position in Expression at which to begin the search for Find, as well as the first character position in the returned substring. If omitted, the beginning of the string is assumed. If Start less than or equal to zero, an ArgumentException is thrown.
Count	The number of occurrences of Find that are to be replaced with Replacement. If omitted, all occurrences are replaced.
Compare	A CompareMethod constant indicating whether the comparison of Find with Expression is case sensitive (CompareMethod.Binary) or insensitive (CompareMethod.Text).

Return Value

A String in which the first Count instances of Find have been replaced by Replacement.

Comments

The default value of the *Compare* argument is determined by the value of the Option Compare setting. If there is no Option Compare setting, binary is the default, and the comparison is case-sensitive.

The following table shows the return value of Replace given various combinations of arguments that are equal to String.Empty, Nothing, or 0:

Argument Name	Argument Value	Return Value
Expression	String.Empty	String.Empty
Find	String.Empty	*Expression*
Replacement	String.Empty	*Expression* with *Find* removed
Start	*Start* > Len(*Expression*)	String.Empty
Count	0	*Expression*

The return value is *Expression* from its *Start* position to its end with the first *Count* occurrences of *Find* replaced by *Replacement*. That *Start* marks the starting position of the string to return, rather than the starting position at which to replace *Find* by *Replacement*, makes the Replace function less useful than it otherwise might be. For example, it is not possible to use the Replace function along with any other Visual Basic .NET string handling functions to replace one or more substrings starting from the end of *Expression*.

The *Start* parameter is problematic, since it serves a dual purpose: it both indicates where the search for *Find* is to start and determines the starting position position of the returned substring.

An alternative to the Replace function is the Replace method of the String class. The Replace method has two overloads which allow you to replace all occurrences of a single character in a string with another character, or to replace all occurrences of a substring with another substring. You cannot determine the starting position of the replacement, nor can you determine how many replacements are made.

See Also

InStr Function, InStrRev Function, Left Function, Mid Statement, Right Function

Reset Subroutine

Closes all files opened with the FileOpen subroutine.

Member Of

Microsoft.VisualBasic.FileSystem

Syntax

```
Reset()
```

Comments

A call to Reset is equivalent to separate calls to the FileClose subroutine.

Before closing each file, the Reset subroutine flushes its buffer so that no data loss occurs.

See Also

FileClose Subroutine, FileOpen Subroutine

Resume Statement

Defines program flow in the event of an error or in an error handler.

Syntax

```
Resume
Resume Next
Resume label
```

Element	Description
Resume	When used in an error handler, returns program control to the statement where the error occurred. If the error occurs in a called routine, returns program control to the statement in the procedure containing the error handler that called out of the procedure. An endless loop results if the error is not corrected by the error handler.
Resume Next	When used with the On Error statement (On Error Resume Next), indicates that when it is the active error handler, errors in the same procedure as the statement should be ignored and execution should proceed with the statement immediately following the error.
	When used in an error handler, returns program control to the statement immediately following the error. If the error occurs in a called routine (or if an error occurs in a called routine when On Error Resume Next defines the error handler), returns program control to the line in the procedure containing the error handler that called out of the procedure.
Resume *label*	When used in an error handler, indicates that program control should return to *label*, which is either a line label (an arbitrary label followed by a colon) or a line number (a number followed by a colon).

Comments

Resume can only be used with the On Error statement or in an error handling routine. If it appears outside of an error handling routine, it generates a compiler error.

Unstructured exception handling with On Error and Resume cannot be combined with structured exception handling with Try . . . Catch . . . Finally . . . End Try.

We strongly recommend the use of structure exception handling with Try . . . Catch . . . Finally . . . End Try rather than exception handling using the Err object and the On Error and Resume statements.

VB6 Differences

In Visual Basic 6.0, Resume (with no additional arguments) and Resume 0 were identical. In Visual Basic .NET, Resume 0 is not supported.

See Also

Error Object, On Error Statement, Try Statement

Return Statement

Immediately transfers program flow from a function, subroutine, property get procedure, property set procedure, or operator procedure to its caller.

Syntax

In a subroutine or property set procedure:

```
Return
```

In a function, property get procedure, or operator procedure:

```
Return expr
```

Element	Description
expr	The return value of the function, property get procedure, or operator procedure.

Comments

In a subroutine or property set procedure, the Return statement is equivalent to the Exit Sub statement and Exit Property statement, respectively; it immediately transfers control from the subroutine to the Finally block of the current structured exception handler or, if there is none, to the caller. Code that follows the Return statement does not execute.

In a function, property get procedure, or operator procedure, Return causes an immediate exit from the procedure and also defines its return value.

When used in a function, the Return statement is equivalent to the following code:

```
functionName = valueToAssign
Exit Function
```

In a function, procedure, property get procedure, or property set procedure, the Return statement is optional. If it is not present, program flow will terminate with the End Function, End Procedure, End Set, or End Get statement and control will return to the caller. In the case of the Function statement, the function's return value should have been assigned to a variable whose name is the same as the function before the End Function statement.

In an operator procedure, the use of the Return statement is required unless the operator procedure does nothing but throw an exception.

Unlike previous versions of Visual Basic .NET, the compiler checks to make sure that all code paths within a function, property get, or operator procedure return a valid value to the caller. If not, it issues a warning like the following: "Function '<name>' doesn't return a value on all code paths. A null reference exception could occur at run time when the result is used."

VB.NET Changes

Because versions of Visual Basic .NET before Visual Basic 2005 did not support operator overloading, they did not support the Return statement with overloaded operators.

VB6 Differences

In Visual Basic 6.0, the Return statement was used to return control from a subprocedure (a block of code within a procedure) that was called by the GoSub statement. (Neither GoSub nor Return could not transfer control outside of the procedure in which they were found.) Visual Basic .NET does not support this usage.

See Also

Exit Statement, Function Statement, Get Statement, Property Statement, Set Statement, Sub Statement

RGB Function

Returns an Integer representing an RGB color value.

Member Of

Microsoft.VisualBasic.Information

Syntax

```
RGB(Red As Integer, Green As Integer, Blue As Integer) As Integer
```

Element	Description
Red	The value of the red color component. Although it is an Integer, its value can only range from 0 to 255.
Green	The value of the green color component. Although it is an Integer, its value can only range from 0 to 255.
Blue	The value of the blue color component. Although it is an Integer, its value can only range from 0 to 255.

Return Value

An RGB color value.

Comments

In Visual Basic 6.0, the RGB function was the major method for defining the color of the BackColor and ForeColor properties of a Windows form. In Visual Basic .NET, however, those properties are of type Color, and attempting to assign the value returned by the RGB function to them generates a compiler error (error BC30311, "Value of type 'Integer' cannot be converted to 'System.Drawing.Color'.").

While the RGB function returns an integer representing the RGB color, a Color object is derived from an ARGB color value. An ARGB color value is an RGB color with an added value, A, that represents the color's opacity. Like the RGB values, the value of A can range from 0 to 255. A value of 0 indicates that the color is transparent, while a value of 255 indicates that it is opaque.

You can convert an ARGB value to a Color object by using the overloaded Color.FromArgb method. One overload has a single parameter, an ARGB value. However, if you supply the value returned by the RGB function to it when assigning a Color object to a form color property, an ArgumentException results. The reason is that you are assigning the property a transparent color, which is not supported as a background color by Windows forms and controls. Instead, if you want to continue to use the RGB function, the best solution is to yourself add the opacity value to this overload of the ARGB function. The closer the value is to 255, the more opaque the color. The opacity value is represented by the high-order byte of the high-order word of the Integer value. For example:

```
frm.BackColor = Color.FromARGB(&HFF000000 Or RGB(128, 128, 128)
```

sets the background color to gray.

In comparison to the RGB function, the Color structure and SystemColor structures produce more readable code and are far easier to use. They, rather than the RGB function, should be used when working with colors in .NET.

See Also

QBColor Function

Right Function

Extracts a particular number of characters from the right side of a string.

Member Of

Microsoft.VisualBasic.Strings

Syntax

```
Right(ByVal str As String, ByVal Length As Integer) As String
```

Element	Description
str	The string whose rightmost characters are to be extracted.
Length	The number of characters to extract.

Return Value

The rightmost *Length* characters of *str*.

Comments

If *Length* is 0, a zero-length string (String.Empty) is returned. If *Length* is greater than the length of *str*, the entire string is returned unchanged. If *Length* is less than 0, an ArgumentException is thrown.

A number of classes (particularly form and control classes) have a Right property, which creates a naming conflict with the Right function. In order to use the Right function, you should fully qualify it with its namespace name, Microsoft.VisualBasic.Strings.Right or Microsoft .VisualBasic.Right.

You can determine the length of *str* by passing it as an argument to the Visual Basic Len function or by retrieving the value of its Length property before calling the Right function.

The String class in the .NET Framework Class Library lacks a direct replacement for the Right function, since Substring, its major substring extraction method, invariably counts the position of the first character to be extracted from the start of the string. It is easy, however, to create an equivalent of the Right function by subtracting the a character position from the right end of the string from the total length of the string:

```
Dim newString As String = str1.Substring(str1.Length - rightPosition)
```

Calling one of the overloads of the Substring method in this way allows you to extract a particular number of characters starting from a character position calculated at the right end of the string.

VB6 Differences

Visual Basic 6.0 included four comparable string extraction functions: Right, Right$, RightB, and RightB$. The RightB and RightB$ functions were intended to work with binary data in string form. The Right$ and RightB$ functions were intended to work with variants whose runtime type was String. Visual Basic .NET, in contrast, supports a single Right function.

See Also

Left Function, Mid Function, Mid Statement, Split Function

RmDir Subroutine

Deletes a directory.

Member Of

Microsoft.VisualBasic.FileSystem

Syntax

```
RmDir(ByVal Path As String)
```

Element	Description
Path	The directory or folder to delete.

Comments

Path can designate the drive on which the directory resides. If it does not, the current drive is assumed.

Path can specify either an absolute path (i.e., a fully qualified path from the root directory of a drive to the directory to be deleted) or a relative path. A relative path is interpreted as a path from the current directory.

If *Path* is String.Empty, an ArgumentException is thrown. If *Path* is a path to a non-existent directory, the subroutine throws a DirectoryNotFoundException.

The subroutine throws an IOException under any of the following conditions:

- The directory to be deleted is the current directory.
- The directory to be deleted contains files.
- The directory to be deleted contains one or more subdirectories.

To use RmDir to delete a directory that is not empty, you must first recursively retrieve the names of subdirectories, use Kill to delete their files, and them use RmDir to remove them. Though this is not difficult, it does involve reinventing the wheel, since other Visual Basic and .NET methods can perform these operations automatically.

RmDir deletes the directory specified by *Path*; it does not move it to the Recycle Bin.

The My.Computer.FileSystem.DeleteDirectory method offers much more flexibility when deleting a directory. Its four overloads allow you to control the following:

- What the method should do if the directory to be deleted contains either files or directories. Options are DirectoryDeleteOption.DeleteAllContents to delete the directory with its contents, and DirectoryDeleteOption.ThrowIfDirectoryNonEmpty to throw an IOException. The latter constant reproduces the behavior of the RmDir subroutine.

- What information to display during the deletion process. Options are UIOption.AllDialogs to display both progress dialogs and error dialogs, and UIOption.OnlyErrorDialogs to display only error dialogs. There are no dialogs associated with the RmDir subroutine.

- Whether the deleted directory and its contents should be moved to the Recycle Bin. Options are RecycleOption.DeletePermanently to simply delete the directory (the default value), and RecycleOption.SendToRecycleBin to place it in the Recycle Bin.

- What the method should do besides canceling the operation if the user clicks the Cancel button on a UI dialog during the delete operation. Options are UICancelOption.DoNothing and UICancelOption.ThrowException. The RmDir subroutine does not allow the deletion operation to be cancelled by the user.

You can also delete a directory using the shared Directory.Delete method. One overload allows you to delete an empty directory, while a second allows you to specify whether the method should recursively delete any subdirectories and their files. You can also call the instance DirectoryInfo.Delete method, which has the same two overloads as the Directory.Delete method.

See Also

ChDir Subroutine, CurDir Function, MkDir Subroutine,
My.Computer.FileSystem.DeleteDirectory Method

Rnd Function

Generates a random number.

Member Of

Microsoft.VisualBasic.VBMath

Syntax

`Rnd[(number)] As Single`

Element	Description
number	A seed value.

Return Value

A random number that is greater than or equal to 0 but less than 1.

Comments

The Rnd function, used together with or independently of the Randomize subroutine, generates a pseudo-random number.

The Rnd function returns a *pseudo-random number,* rather than a truly random number, because a known algorithm is used to generate a number based on a seed value, which means both that the sequence of random numbers can be controlled and that, with a knowledge of the algorithm and the seed value, the value of a particular random number can be determined in advance.

The affect of the value of *seed* on the value returned by the Rnd function is as follows:

Value	Description
< 0	The same number each time, using *number* as the seed value.
> 0	The next pseudo-random number in the current sequence.
0	The most recently generated pseudo-random number.
Not supplied	The next pseudo-random number in the current sequence (the same as if *number* > 0).

To generate a pseudo-random number that ranges from 0 to a maximum value, use the following formula:

```
CInt(Int(Rnd(number) * max_value + 1))
```

More generally, to generate a pseudo-random number with a particular minimum value and a particular maximum value, use the following formula:

```
CInt(Int((max_value - min_value + 1) * Rnd() + min_value))
```

To generate the same sequence of pseudo-random numbers each time you use the random number generator, you can use code like the following:

```
Rnd(-1)
Randomize(number)              ' Number is any Double
For ctr As Integer = 1 to 10
   Console.WriteLine(Rnd())
Next
```

The Rnd function is particularly useful for generating random numbers used to determine outcomes in games applications, as well as for using random numbers for testing numeric values in applications.

Because the combination of the Randomize statement and the Rnd function use a known algorithm for generating random numbers, they should never be used for generating random numbers for use in cryptography. To generate truly random numbers, call either the GetBytes or the GetNonZeroBytes method of the System.Security.Cryptography.RNGCryptoServiceProvider class.

Example

The following is the source code for a Dealer class that deals cards for a card game, and uses the Rnd function to generate a random number for each card to determine its order in the shuffled deck:

```
' Represents an individual card
Public Class Card
    Public Suit As Suit
    Public FaceValue As String
End Class

' Enum for the four card suits
Public Enum Suit As Integer
    Hearts = 0
    Diamonds = 1
    Spades = 2
    Clubs = 3
End Enum

Public Class Dealer
    Private deck(51) As SortTuple
    Dim ptr As Integer              ' Next card to deal (at top of deck)

    ' Tuple used for sorting cards
    Private Class SortTuple
      Implements IComparable

      Friend Key As Double
      Friend Card As Card

      Friend Function CompareTo(obj As Object) As Integer _
                            Implements IComparable.CompareTo
        If Not TypeOf obj Is SortTuple Then Throw New ArgumentException()
        Dim crd As SortTuple = DirectCast(obj, SortTuple)
        If Me.Key > crd.Key Then
           Return 1
        ElseIf Me.Key = crd.Key Then
           Return 0
        Else
           Return -1
        End If
      End Function
    End Class
```

```vbnet
Public Sub New()
    ' Initialize deck
    For ctr As Integer = 0 To 51
        Dim suit As Suit = DirectCast(ctr \ 13, Suit)
        Dim face As String = Cstr((Ctr + CInt(suit) * 1) Mod 14)
        Dim crd As New Card
        crd.Suit = suit
        crd.FaceValue = ConvertToCard(face)
        Dim tuple As New SortTuple
        tuple.Card = crd
        deck(ctr) = tuple
    Next
End Sub

Public Sub Shuffle()
    Randomize
    For Each crd As SortTuple In deck
        crd.Key = Rnd(1)
    Next
    Array.Sort(deck)
    ptr = 51
End Sub

Public Function Deal() As Card
    Dim cardToReturn As Card = deck(ptr).Card
    ptr -= 1
    If ptr < 0 Then Me.Shuffle
    Return cardToReturn
End Function

' Converts an integer to a card's face value
Private Function ConvertToCard(cardValue As Integer) As String
    ' Returns "2" to "10"
    If cardValue >= 1 And CardValue <= 9 Then
        Return CStr(cardValue + 1)
    ' Handles "A" and "J" through "K"
    Else
        Select Case cardValue
            Case 0
                Return "A"
            Case 10
                Return "J"
            Case 11
                Return "Q"
            Case 12
                Return "K"
        End Select
    End If
End Function
End Class
```

See Also

Randomize Subroutine

RSet Function

Right-aligns a string and prepends spaces to it to make it a specified length.

Member Of

Microsoft.VisualBasic.Strings

Syntax

```
RSet(ByVal Source As String, ByVal Length As Integer) As String
```

Element	Description
Source	The string to right-align.
Length	The desired length of the string.

Return Value

A right-aligned string with spaces prepended, if necessary, to make it *Length* characters.

Comments

To some degree, this function is misnamed; it is more appropriately named PadLeft, since it is designed to pad the left side of a string with spaces up to a particular length.

If the length of *Source* is less than or equal to *Length*, RSet returns *Source* with enough space characters prepended to make it *Length* characters long. It is equivalent to the code:

```
result = Space(Length - Len(Source)) & Source
```

If *Source* contains trailing spaces, these are retained in the returned string. The function really does not right-align a string.

If the length of *Source* is greater than *Length*, *Source* is truncated to *Length* characters. In this case, the RSet function is equivalent to

```
Left(Source, Length)
```

In this case, the behavior of the RSet and LSet functions is identical. The RSet function is a legacy of Basic before Visual Basic.

The String class in the .NET Framework Class Library includes a PadLeft method whose operation is similar to that of RSet: it appends characters to the right of a string to pad it to a particular length. Although by default the space character is used to pad the string, one of the method's overloads allows you to specify the padding character. The behavior of the PadLeft method also differs when the length of *Source* exceeds *Length*; in that case, *Source* is returned unchanged, rather than truncated to *Length* characters.

VB.NET Changes

In Visual Basic 6.0, *Source* had to be a fixed-length string.

In Visual Basic 6.0, RSet was an assignment statement that assigned a fixed-length string to a normal string. Consequently, its syntax was different, and there was no need to provide a *Length* argument.

See Also

LSet Function, LTrim Function, RTrim Function, Space Function, Trim Function

RTrim Function

Removes any trailing spaces from a string.

Member Of

Microsoft.VisualBasic.Strings

Syntax

```
RTrim(ByVal str As String) As String
```

Element	Description
str	The string to be trimmed.

Return Value

str with trailing spaces removed.

Comments

If *str* has no trailing spaces, the function returns *str* unchanged.

The RTrim function corresponds to the instance TrimEnd method of the String class, which has the syntax:

```
String.TrimEnd(ParamArray trimChars() As Char) As String
```

where *trimChars* is a parameter array that defines the characters to be removed from the string. If it is Nothing, only trailing white space is removed.

It is extremely easy for trailing spaces to appear at the end of a string, particularly a string that has been input by a user. These extra spaces cause comparisons that would otherwise be True to become False. This can be prevented by calling the RTrim function before comparing strings for equality.

To remove leading spaces, use the LTrim function.

To remove both leading and trailing spaces, use the Trim function or the String.Trim instance method. The latter is overloaded: one version removes spaces, while the other allows you to specify the character or characters to be removed.

VB6 Differences

Visual Basic 6.0 included an RTrim$ function that returned a String, while RTrim returned a Variant. In Visual Basic .NET, RTrim$ is not supported, and the RTrim function returns a String.

See Also

LTrim Function, Trim Function

SaveSetting Subroutine

Creates or saves a registry value.

Member Of

Microsoft.VisualBasic.Interaction

Syntax

```
SaveSetting(ByVal AppName As String, ByVal Section As String, _
          ByVal Key As String, ByVal Setting As String)
```

Element	Description
AppName	A string describing a relative registry path from HKEY_CURRENT_USER\Software\VB and VBA Program Settings to the key named *section*.
Section	A string describing a relative registry path from the *AppName* key to the key that contains *Key* (which is, incidentally, not a key).
Key	A named value whose fully qualified path is HKEY_CURRENT_USER\Software\VB and VBA Program Settings*AppName**Section*.
Setting	The value to be assigned to the named value *Key*.

Comments

The SaveSetting subroutine was introduced in Visual Basic 4.0 and worked with both the 16- and 32-bit versions of Visual Basic. In the 16-bit version, it saved configuration information to an initialization file; in the 32-bit version, it saved configuration information to the registry. The result is a confusing use of parameter names that reflects a usage more appropriate for initialization files than the registry. For instance, the *Key* parameter specifies not the name of a registry key, as one might naturally suppose, but a named value.

   Like the other registry settings that are a part of the Visual Basic language, SaveSetting does not work with the entire registry, but only with the subkeys of HKEY_CURRENT_USER\Software\VB and VBA Program Settings. The subroutine is not intended as a general-purpose utility for creating and saving registry values. Instead, it is intended to be used by an application to save its private data to the registry.

   AppName is described in the documentation as "the name of the application or project to which the setting applies." This assumes that there is a single registry key named *AppName*, and that its name corresponds to the name of a Visual Basic project or application. There is nothing, however, to enforce this rule. In fact, *AppName* can consist of one or more registry keys.

Section is described in the documentation as "the name of the section in which the key setting is being saved." However, neither the word "section" nor the phrase "key section" have any meaning when applied to the registry. In fact, *Section* can consist of a relative path that includes one or more registry keys.

AppName and *Section* in fact together describe a relative path that begins with HKEY_CURRENT_USER\Software\VB and VBA Program Settings and ends with the key that has a named value named *Key*. Neither argument should begin with the registry path delimiter. For example, if the program is to delete a value named WindowState in the HKEY_CURRENT_USER \Software\VB and VBA Program Settings\MyCompany\MyApplication\UserSettings \Windows key, *AppName* and *Section* have any of the following values:

AppName	Section
MyCompany	MyApplication\UserSettings\Windows
MyCompany\MyApplication	UserSettings\Windows
MyCompany\MyApplication\UserSettings	Windows

SaveSetting does not allow you to assign the default or unnamed value of a registry key. If you attempt to provide an empty string as the value of the *Key* argument, an ArgumentException is thrown.

The registry supports a number of data types, the most common of which are REG_DWORD (Integer data), REG_BINARY (binary data), REG_SZ (null-terminated string data), REG_EXPAND_SZ (string data with embedded environment variables), and REG_MULTI_SZ (null-terminated string arrays). The only data type supported by the SaveSetting subroutine, however, is REG_SZ. If you attempt to save REG_MULTI_SZ data, SaveSetting truncates it before the first terminating null. If you attempt to save REG_EXPAND_SZ data, the string will be accurately saved, but you must expand its environment strings yourself by calling the ExpandEnvironmentVariables method of the Environment class before using the string.

The function is intended to save user configuration settings, and not application configuration settings, to the registry. (Application configuration settings are saved to the subkeys of HKEY_LOCAL_MACHINE.) This means that you should not rely on the necessary registry keys and values being populated either by an installation program or by your application's first use. Nor should you use SaveSetting to write information to the registry for services, which run continuously on a system whether or not a user is logged on.

The Visual Basic registry functions are badly underpowered and of very limited utility. Rather than use them, you should use either the registry classes in the Microsoft.Win32 namespace or the My.Computer.Registry object.

See Also

DeleteSetting Function, GetAllSettings Function, GetSetting Function, My.Computer.Registry Class

ScriptEngine Property

Returns the string "VB".

Member Of

Microsoft.VisualBasic.Globals

Syntax

```
Public ReadOnly Property ScriptEngine() As String
```

Return Value

The string "VB".

Comments

Typically, the documentation indicates that the ScriptEngine property indicates either the scripting or programming language in use or the runtime in use. In fact, however, it does neither. The runtime in use is the .NET Common Language Runtime. And the fact that if the property is retrieved from C# code (see the example) it still returns "VB" indicates that the property simply returns the fixed string "VB" regardless of the caller. This in turn means that it only indicates that the Visual Basic implementation of the ScriptEngine property (as opposed to the JScript or VBScript implementation) has been called.

The property's original intent was to allow code that could run as either VBScript or Visual Basic .NET to determine which was the scripting engine so that code execution could branch accordingly if particular language constructs were supported in one environment but not the other.

Example

The following C# code retrieves the value of the ScriptEngine property and displays it to the console:

```
using Microsoft.VisualBasic;
using System;

public class EngineCS
{
    public static void Main()
    {
        Console.WriteLine(Globals.ScriptEngine);
    }
}
```

The result is:

```
VB
```

which indicates that the version of the property in the Visual Basic runtime library has been retrieved, rather than that the script engine is Visual Basic.

VB6 Differences

The property is new to Visual Basic .NET. The ScriptEngine function, however, was implemented in VBScript.

See Also

ScriptEngineBuildVersion Property, ScriptEngineMajorVersion Property, ScriptEngineMinorVersion Property,

---

ScriptEngineBuildVersion Property

Returns the build number of the .NET runtime currently in use.

Member Of

Microsoft.VisualBasic.Globals

Syntax

```
ReadOnly Public Property ScriptEngineBuildVersion As Integer
```

Return Value

An Integer indicating the build number.

Comments

Versions of software typically have the form *mm.nn.bbbb,* where *mm* is the major version, *nn* is the minor version, and *bbbb* is the build version.

In general, the build version is rarely used in application programming. It is most commonly used to indicate patches or interim releases.

VB6 Differences

The property is new to Visual Basic .NET. The ScriptEngineBuildVersion function, however, was implemented in VBScript.

See Also

ScriptEngine Property, ScriptEngineMajorVersion Property, ScriptEngineMinorVersion Property

---

ScriptEngineMajorVersion Property

Indicates the major version number of the .NET runtime.

Member Of

Microsoft.VisualBasic.Globals

Syntax

```
ReadOnly Public Property ScriptEngineMajorVersion As Integer
```

Return Value

An Integer indicating the major version number.

Comments

Versions are typically identified by a series of integers separated by periods, in the following format:

```
<major_version>.<minor_version>.<build>.
```

The major versions reported by .NET are as follows:

.NET Version	ScriptEngineMajorVersion Value
.NET 1.0 and 1.1	7
.NET 2.0	8

You can use the ScriptEngineMajorVersion property, possibly along with the ScriptEngineMinorVersion property, to determine whether the platform on which an application or component is running provides the required functionality.

When using version numbers to test for a baseline version (a minimum version required for an application or component to run successfully), a common mistake is to test for equality with the baseline version. For example, the code

```
If ScriptEngineMajorVersion = 8 Then
    ' Load startup window
Else
    MsgBox("This application requires .NET 2.0.")
    Exit Sub
End If
```

will run only under .NET 2.0, and not under subsequent major releases. Instead, the code should test to make sure that the major version number is at least (that is to say, is equal to or greater than) the baseline version. The preceding code should instead read:

```
If ScriptEngineMajorVersion >= 8 Then
    ' Load startup window
Else
    MsgBox("This application requires .NET 2.0.")
    Exit Sub
End If
```

You can use the ScriptEngineMajorVersion property to provide separate blocks of code to implement your application's functionality. For example, the SByte data type is new to Visual Basic 2005. In previous versions, it was a type in the System namespace and so was recognized by Visual Basic, although Visual Basic itself provided little support for signed bytes. An application using the SByte data type might include code like the following:

```
Dim sbyt As System.SByte
If ScriptEngineMajorVersion >= 8 Then
    sbyt = 12
Else
    sbyt = Convert.ToSByte(12)
End If
```

Note that this conditional evaluation must occur at runtime (using the If statement, for example) rather than at compile time (using the #If statement), since it returns the runtime version of the script engine.

VB6 Differences

The property is new to Visual Basic .NET. However, it is identical to the ScriptEngineMajorVersion function found in VBScript.

See Also

ScriptEngine Property, ScriptEngineMinorVersion Property

ScriptEngineMinorVersion Property

Indicates the minor version number of the .NET runtime.

Member Of

Microsoft.VisualBasic.Globals

Syntax

```
ReadOnly Public Property ScriptEngineMinorVersion As Integer
```

Property Value

An Integer indicating the minor version number.

Comments

Versions of software typically have the form *mm.nn.bbbb*, where *mm* is the major version, *nn* is the minor version, and *bbbb* is the build version.

A minor version number of 0 indicates a major release of Visual Basic. A minor version number that is non-zero indicates an interim release.

Depending on the version of Visual Basic and the .NET runtime with which an application is running, the ScriptEngineMinorVersion returns the following values:

Visual Basic, .NET Runtime	ScriptEngineMinorVersion
Visual Basic for .NET 1.0. .NET 1.0	0
Visual Basic for .NET 1.1, .NET 1.1	10
Visual Basic 2005, .NET 2.0	0

The minor version number is typically used in code when testing whether a .NET feature introduced in an interim release is present in the current runtime. However, a common mistake is to test for equality with a particular major and minor version. For example, the code

```
If ScriptEngineMajorVersion = 7 And ScriptEngineMinorVersion = 10 Then
    ' Access .NET 1.1 member
```

```
Else
   MsgBox("This application requires .NET 1.1.")
   Exit Sub
End If
```

will run only under .NET 1.1, and not under any other version. Instead, the code should include two tests: one to determine whether a particular major version along with a particular baseline minor version or a later minor version is present, and a second to determine whether the major version present is greater than the baseline major version. If either of these conditions is true, the code path associated with the "new" version can execute. For example, the preceding code should be modified to read:

```
If (ScriptEngineMajorVersion = 7 And ScriptEngineMinorVersion >= 10) Or _
    ScriptEngineMajorVersion > 7 Then
   ' Access .NET 1.1 member
Else
   MsgBox("This application requires .NET 1.1 or later.")
   Exit Sub
End If
```

The evaluation of version information should occur in the runtime environment, rather than the compile-time environment. In other words, you should not use the #If conditional compiler constant to evaluate the version number. Instead, you should use the If construct.

VB6 Differences

The property is new to Visual Basic .NET. However, it is identical to the ScriptEngineMinorVersion function found in VBScript.

See Also

ScriptEngine Property, ScriptEngineBuildVersion Property, ScriptEngineMajorVersion Property

Second Function

Extracts the number of seconds from a time value.

Member Of

Microsoft.VisualBasic.DateAndTime

Syntax

```
Second(ByVal TimeValue As Date) As Integer
```

Element	Description
TimeValue	A time value.

Return Value

A number ranging from 0 to 59 reflecting the second component of *TimeValue*.

Comments

If Option Strict is off, the compiler automatically converts a string representation of a date to a Date value before calling the Second function. To ensure that the string can be successfully converted, you can call the IsDate function beforehand.

The DatePart function can also be used to extract the second component of a time value. For example, the following two function calls return identical values:

```
seconds = Second(Date.Now)

seconds = DatePart(DateInterval.Second, Date.Now)
```

The Date data type also includes a Second member that extracts the second component of its Date instance. For example:

```
seconds = Date.Now.Second
```

See Also

DatePart Function, Hour Function, Minute Function

Seek Function

Gets or sets the position of the file pointer in a file opened using the FileOpen subroutine.

Member Of

Microsoft.VisualBasic.FileSystem

Syntax

The first overload retrieves the position of the file pointer:

```
Seek(ByVal FileNumber As Integer) As Long
```

The second overload sets the position of the file pointer:

```
Seek(ByVal FileNumber As Integer, ByVal Position As Long)
```

Element	Description
FileNumber	The file number used in the call to the FileOpen subroutine.
Position	An integer ranging from 1 to 2,147,483,647 that indicates the position to which the file pointer should be moved.

Return Value

For the first overload of the Seek function, an integer ranging from 1 to 2,147,483,647 that indicates the current position of the file pointer. The second overload has no return value.

Comments

Seek is one of a series of related file input and output functions that works with a file number used when opening a file with the FileOpen subroutine.

Seek can be used to get or set the position of the file pointer, which determines where the next read or write operation occurs.

The meaning of *Position* or of the return value of the Seek function depends on the mode in which the file indicated by *FileNumber* was opened. For random files, it indicates the record at which the file pointer is positioned. For binary and sequential files, it indicates the byte at which the file pointer is positioned.

If Seek is used to position the record pointer beyond the end of the file or beyond the last record, an exception is not thrown. However, the next attempt to read from the file throws an exception. Therefore, it is always important to check for the end of the file after the file pointer has been positioned using Seek. The example provides an illustration.

If the *RecordNumber* argument is used in the next read operation with the FileGet and FileGetObject subroutines or in the next write operation with the FilePut or FilePutObject subroutines, it overrides the positioning of the file pointer established by the call to the Seek function.

Example

The following code prompts the user to enter the number of the record to retrieve and uses the Seek function to position the record pointer. If this positions the record pointer at the end of the file, a message is displayed; otherwise, the record is retrieved and its contents displayed.

```
Public Structure Book
    <vbFixedString(35)> Dim Title As String
    <vbFixedString(25)> Dim Author As String
    <vbFixedString(20)> Dim Publisher As String
End Structure

Public Module modMain
    Private Const FILENAME As String = ".\Bookfile.dat"

    Public Sub Main()
        Dim recno As Integer
        Dim inputString As String = InputBox("Enter record number to retrieve: ")
        If Not IsNumeric(inputString) Then Exit Sub

        recno = CInt(inputString)

        Dim fileNo As Integer = FreeFile()
        FileOpen(fileNo, FILENAME, OpenMode.Random)
        ' Position record pointer
        Try
            Seek(fileNo, recno)
            If Not EOF(fileNo) Then
                Dim bk As Book
                FileGet(fileNo, bk)
                Console.WriteLine("{0}, written by {1}, and published by {2}", _
                            RTrim(bk.Title), RTrim(bk.Author), _
                            RTrim(bk.Publisher))
```

```
        Else
            Console.WriteLine("The record number was not found.")
        End If
    Catch ex As Exception
        Console.WriteLine(ex.Gettype.Name)
    End Try
   End Sub
End Module
```

See Also

EOF Function, FileOpen Subroutine, Loc Function, LOF Function

Select Case Statement

Executes one of a variable number of blocks of code, depending on the evaluation of a test expression.

Syntax

```
Select [ Case ] testExpression
    [ Case expressionList
        [ statements ]
        [ Exit Case ]
        [ statements ]]
    [ Case Else
        [ elseStatements ] ]
End Select
```

Element	Description
testExpression	An expression to be evaluated to determine which of the following Case statement blocks to execute. It must evaluate to one of the elementary data types (Boolean, Byte, Char, Date, Double, Decimal, Integer, Long, SByte, Short, Single, String, UInteger, ULong, and UShort) or an Object whose runtime type is one of the elementary data types.
expressionList	A list of expression clauses representing match values for *testExpression*. If *testExpression* matches any of the values in *expressionList,* the Case statement block is executed. If multiple values are present. Individual expression clauses are separated from one another by commas.
statements	The statements that are executed if testExpression results in the values in expressionList.
elseStatements	The statements to execute if *testExpression* results in none of the values in any of the other Case *expressionList* clauses and therefore if no other case statement is executed.

The individual expression clauses in *expressionList* can have the following format, as shown in this table:

Expression Clause	Description
expression	The Case construct is executed if the evaluation of *testExpression* results in *expression*.
expression1 To *expression2*	The Case construct is executed if the evaluation of *testExpression* results in a value that is greater than or equal to *expression1* and less than or equal to *expression2*.
expression1, expression2, . . .	The Case construct is executed if the evaluation of *testExpression* results in *expression1* or *expression2*, etc.
[Is] *comparisonoperator expression*	*comparisonoperator* is a standard comparison operator (=, <>, >, >=, <, or <=). The Case construct is executed if the comparison of *testExpression* with *expression* is true. Note that Is is not the standard Visual Basic Is operator, which is used to compare object references.

Comments

If the evaluation of *testExpression* results in a value in *expressionList*, the code in that Case block is executed, and program flow then proceeds to the End Selected statement and exits the Case construct. If multiple Case blocks are True, only the code in the first Case block to be encountered is executed, and the remaining Case blocks as well as the Else block are skipped.

The Select Case . . . End Select construct can include as many Case statements as needed. However, the Select Case construct is typically used if three or more values of *testExpression* are to be evaluated. If only two values of *testExpression* are evaluated, the If . . . Else . . . End If construct provides a more readable choice.

While the expressions in *expressionList* need not be of the same data type as *testExpression*, they must be implicitly convertible to the data type of *expressionList* if Option Strict is off. If Option Strict is on, they also must not involve narrowing conversions.

If *expressionList* involves string comparison, the Option Compare setting determines whether it is case sensitive (the default value if no Option Compare statement is present) or case insensitive.

Any custom operator procedures or conversion operators defined using the Operator statement are ignored when evaluating *expressionList*.

If *expressionList* includes multiple expressions, only the first true expression will be evaluated; subsequent expressions will be skipped. For example, in the Case statement

```
Case Is >= GetValue1(), Is = GetValue2()
```

the call to the GetValue2 method is skipped if the call to GetValue1 returns value greater than or equal to *testExpression*. Where multiple expressions involve calls to methods or properties, this short-circuiting behavior can produce undesirable results.

One or more Exit Case statements can be used to prematurely exit a Case block. See the entry for the Case keyword for the additional description of the Case clause's syntax and usage.

Depending on *testExpression*, it may be important to include a Case Else construct to handle values of *testExpression* not handled by other Case statements. This is particularly true under any of the following conditions:

- *testExpression* is based on data input by the user.
- *testExpression* evaluates a member of an enumeration, which is capable of changing in versions of a class library.
- *testExpression* evaluates data extracted from a database or from the file system.
- Any other circumstance—even not obvious ones—under which *testExpression* might produce an unexpected value or a value that the existing Case blocks are not prepared to handle.

If Select Case statements are nested, the inner Select Case . . . End Select construct must be entirely contained within an outer Case . . . End Case construct.

The Select Case statement is in part a replacement for nested If statements or a series of ElseIf statements; Select Case typically produces more readable code than two or more ElseIf statements. However, there is a difference between the Select Case and the If statement: each Case statement in a Select Case statement must evaluate a single expression defined by *testExpression*, whereas the expressions evaluated by each If and ElseIf statement can be independent of one another. In the latter case, the Select Case statement cannot replace nested If statements or multiple ElseIf statements.

Example

The following example illustrates the use of the Select Case statement to return a letter grade from a test score: The user inputs a test score, and the Select Case statement is used to determine which letter grade corresponds to that score.

```
Imports System.Diagnostics

Public Module Grader
    Public Sub Main()
        Dim inputScore As String

        inputScore = InputBox("Enter the student's grade: ", "Test Score")
        If inputScore = String.Empty OrElse Not IsNumeric(inputScore) Then Exit Sub
        Console.WriteLine(GetScore(inputScore))
    End Sub

    Private Function GetScore(inputScore As String) As String
        Dim letterGrade As String = String.Empty
        Select Case CInt(inputScore)
            Case Is <= 64
                letterGrade = "F"
            Case 65 To 74
                letterGrade = "D"
            Case 74 To 83
                letterGrade = "C"
            Case 84 To 90
                letterGrade = "B"
            Case 91 To 98
                letterGrade = "A"
```

```
            Case Is >= 99
                letterGrade = "A+"
            Case Else
                letterGrade = "Unknown"
                Debug.Assert(False, "Invalid input score: " & inputScore)
        End Select
        Return letterGrade
    End Function
End Module
```

See Also

Case Keyword, Choose Function, If Statement, IIf Function

Set Statement

Defines a property set accessor, which is used to assign a value to a property.

Syntax

```
[ <attrlist> ] [<accessmodifier>] Set([ByVal value [As datatype]])
    [ statements ]
    [ Exit Property ]
    [ statements ]
End Set
```

Element	Description
attrlist	A list of attributes to be applied to the property set accessor. Only attributes whose AttributeUsage attribute is AttributeTargets.All or AttributeTargets.Property can be applied to a Set statement.
accessmodifier	An optional access modifier (possible values are Private, Friend, Protected, or Protected Friend) if access to the property set accessor is more restrictive than the access defined in the Property statement.
value	The value to be assigned to the property.
datatype	The data type of *value*. Typically, it is omitted. If present, it must correspond to the data type of the property declared in the Property statement or a compiler error results.
statements	The code that executes when the property value is retrieved.

Comments

The Property Set statement is contained within a Property . . . End Property statement that defines the name of the property, its return type, its parameter list (if it has one), whether it is the default property, and whether it is read-write, write-only, or read-only (in which case a Set statement is not allowed). The Set statement cannot be overloaded; there can only be one Set statement for a read-write or write-only property.

Attempting to provide a Set statement for a read-only property generates a compiler error.

The property set accessor can have a different, more restrictive access level than the property construct as a whole. If it is assigned the same or a less restrictive access level, a compiler error results.

The property stub for a read-write or write-only property that is automatically generated by Visual Studio includes the *value* parameter and the data type of *value*, as follows:

```
Property name() As datatype
    Get

    End Get
    Set(ByVal value As datatype)

    End Set
End Property
```

However, the value parameter can also be implicit and need not be stated explicitly, and the data type of *value*, since it must be the same as the data type of the property, can also be omitted regardless of the setting of Option Strict. (The documentation incorrectly states that the set accessor's data type must be explicitly declared if Option Strict is on.) The following is also a legal stub for a Property statement that is identical to the preceding stub:

```
Property name() As datatype
    Get

    End Get
    Set

    End Set
End Property
```

Typically, the set accessor assigns a value to a private variable that is used to hold the property value. When used in this way, the property set accessor serves as a single access point to otherwise protected data, which allows it to be used for such things as data validation or checking user credentials. The example for the Get statement illustrates this pattern of using a property set accessor as a gateway that provides access to private instance data.

Example

See the example for the Get Statement.

VB.NET Changes

As of Visual Basic 2005, a property can have mixed access levels. The Property . . . End Property construct defines either the least restrictive access or the access level that applies to the property get and property set accessors, if both are present. The Set statement (or the Get statement) can then define a different, more restrictive access level.

VB6 Differences

Visual Basic 6.0 supported separate Property Get, Property Let, and Property Set statements. In contrast, Visual Basic .NET supports a single Property . . . End Property statement, which in turn can contain a Get statement and a Set statement. The functionality of both the Property Let and the Property Set statement has been merged into the single Set statement, leaving the Property

Let statement with no equivalent in Visual Basic .NET. Overall, the syntax of the Property statement in Visual Basic .NET is far more straightforward than its Visual Basic 6.0 counterpart.

The Set statement in Visual Basic 6.0, which assigned an object reference to an object variable, is not supported in Visual Basic .NET.

See Also

Get Statement, Property Statement

SetAttr Subroutine

Sets the attributes of a file or directory.

Syntax

```
SetAttr(ByVal PathName As String, ByVal Attributes As FileAttribute)
```

Element	Description
PathName	The path to the file or directory whose attributes are to be set.
Attributes	A bitmask containing more or more members of the FileAttribute enumeration that defines the attributes to set for the file or directory.

Comments

Although the documentation only mentions using the SetAttr function to set file attributes, it can be used to set the attributes of directories as well.

PathName can provide either an absolute path or a relative path. If an absolute path does not provide a drive specification, the current drive is assumed. A relative path is interpreted as the path from the current directory.

The members of the FileAttribute enumeration or a corresponding intrinsic Visual Basic constant that can be used with the SetAttr function are listed in the following table:

FileAttribute Member	Constant	Description
Normal	vbNormal	No attributes set (the default).
ReadOnly	vbReadOnly	A read-only file.
Hidden	vbHidden	A hidden file.
System	vbSystem	A system file.
Archive	vbArchive	A file has changed since the last backup.

The FileAttribute enumeration actually includes two additional members, FileAttribute.Volume (which indicates a volume label), and FileAttribute.Directory (which indicates a directory). These flags can be returned by the GetAttr function. However, SetAttr will throw an ArgumentException if passed these flags.

Since members of the FlagsAttribute enumeration are not mutually exclusive, you can Or them together to set two or more attributes. For example, the following code sets the System, Hidden, and ReadOnly attributes:

```
Dim attrib As FileAttribute = FileAttribute.Hidden Or FileAttribute.System Or _
                              FileAttribute.ReadOnly
SetAttr(fn, attrib)
```

Although individual attributes can be ORed together, it makes no sense to Or any other attribute with the FileAttribute.Normal attribute, since it represents the absence of any set attributes.

The SetAttr function clears existing attributes and sets only those specified by the Attributes argument. Typically, you want to preserve existing attributes while setting new ones. The example provides a method that allows you to do this.

According to the documentation, attempting to set the attributes of an open file generates a runtime exception. However, this does not appear to be the case.

Instead of the SetAttr function, you can use the read-write Attributes property of the System.IO.FileInfo class. To set the property value, you provide it with one or more members of the System.IO.FileAttributes enumeration that define the attributes you'd like to set.

Example

The following code sets new file attributes while preserving existing ones:

```
Public Shared Sub AddFileAttribute(pathname As String, _
                                   attributes As FileAttribute)
    Dim existingAttributes As FileAttribute
    Try
        If attributes <> FileAttribute.Normal Then
            existingAttributes = GetAttr(pathname)
            If (existingAttributes And FileAttribute.Directory) = _
                              FileAttribute.Directory Then
                existingAttributes = existingAttributes And _
                              (Not FileAttribute.Directory)
            End If
            attributes = attributes Or existingAttributes
        End If
        SetAttr(pathname, attributes)
    Catch e As Exception
        Throw New ArgumentException("Unable to set file attributes", e)
    End Try
End Sub
```

The major complication of the code is that when you retrieve the file attributes for a directory, its FileAttribute.Directory attribute is set. However, including the FileAttribute.Directory value in the *attributes* argument throws an ArgumentException, since this attribute can only be set by the file system itself. Therefore, it must be removed from the FileAttribute value returned by the SetAttr function. The statement

```
existingAttributes = existingAttributes And (Not FileAttribute.Directory)
```

does that. Note that, if the *attributes* argument is FileAttribute.Normal, the existing attributes are not retrieved, and the call to the SetAttr subroutine simply clears all existing attributes.

See Also

GetAttr Function

Shadows Keyword

Indicates that a program element redeclares and hides an identically named element in a base class.

Syntax

See the syntax for each of the statements that the Shadows keyword modifies.

Comments

In Visual Basic, you can have a number of options for defining the relationship between a program element in a base class and a program element in a derived class:

- **Inheritance**   The derived class does not implement the base class element. When the derived class element is called, the base class element is called instead.

- **Overriding**   The derived class provides a different implementation of the base class element, but one whose signature is identical to that of the base class element. When the derived class element is called, it executes instead of the base class element.

- **Overloading**   The derived class provides an implementation with the same name but a different signature as the base class. The derived class member is invoked when the signature of a method call matches its overloaded version.

- **Shadowing**   The derived class defines a program element with the same name as a base class; it need not be the same type of program element (for example, a property can shadow a method), nor need it have the same signature as the base class element. The base class element (the shadowed element) is inaccessible from the derived class; only the derived class element is accessible.

The Shadows keyword is used to define this last relationship, and can be used with the Class, Const, Declare, Delegate, Dim, Enum, Event, Function, Interface, Property, Structure, and Sub statements. The Shadows keyword can only appear at member level in a Class statement. It cannot be used to define a program element in a namespace, nor can it be used inside a method body to define a local variable. In addition, the Shadows keyword can only be used inside a class definition; it cannot be used at member level in a structure, interface, or module.

Shadows cannot be used with the Overloads or Overrides keywords, nor can it be used with the Shared keyword. However, because overriding and shadowing express different base class-derived class relationships, Shadows can be used to shadow a base class member that is marked NotOverridable.

If Shadows is used with the Dim statement to define fields in a class, only a single field can be defined with a Dim statement.

The Shadows keyword only considers the name of a base class program element. It allows you to hide it by defining any kind of element with any signature. For example, in the following code, a base class defines a method, MemberA, that a derived class shadows with a read-only property:

```
Public Class BaseClass
    Public Function MemberA() As String
        Return "MemberA"
    End Function
End Class
```

```
Public Class DerivedClass : Inherits BaseClass
    Public Shadows ReadOnly Property MemberA() As Integer
        Get
            Return Asc("A")
        End Get
    End Property
End Class

Public Module modMain
    Public Sub Main()
        Dim dc As New DerivedClass
        Console.WriteLine(dc.MemberA)
    End Sub
End Module
```

The call to MemberA in the module is resolved as a call to the DerivedClass object's property get accessor, which returns an integer representing the ASCII code for the letter "A".

On occasion, third-party documentation describes Shadows as the default behavior. Since this is not quite accurate, it is a source of needless confusion. If the relationship between the base class and derived class member is not defined explicitly, the compiler will interpret the relationship as one of shadowing. When this happens, the compiler displays a warning message to alert you that a base class member is being shadowed, in case that is not your intent.

If the shadowing element is inaccessible from the context in which it is called, then the shadowed element in the base class is called instead. For example, if the shadowing property MemberA from the preceding code example were declared as a Private property rather than a Public one, attempt to invoke MemberA from a client with code like the following:

```
Dim dc As New DerivedClass
Console.WriteLine(dc.MemberA)
```

invokes the base class MemberA method. The shadowed element in the base class can still be accessed from its derived class by prefacing the name of the program element with the MyBase keyword.

The shadowed element is still accessible from the derived class or a derived class instance through an object declared with the type of the base class. For example, assuming the same definitions of BaseClass and DerivedClass as previously, the following client code accesses the shadowed MemberA method:

```
Dim dc As New DerivedClass
Dim bc As BaseClass = dc
Console.WriteLine(bc.MemberA)        ' displays "MemberA"
```

Note that this differs from the behavior of a derived class member defined using the Overrides keyword. For example, in the following code:

```
Public Class BaseClass
    Public Overridable Function MemberA() As String
        Return "MemberA"
    End Function
End Class
```

```
Public Class DerivedClass : Inherits BaseClass
    Public Overrides Function MemberA() As String
        Return "A"
    End Function
End Class

Public Module modMain
    Public Sub Main()
        Dim dc As New DerivedClass
        Console.WriteLine(dc.MemberA)            ' displays "A"

        Dim bc As BaseClass = dc
        Console.WriteLine(bc.MemberA)            ' displays "A"
    End Sub
End Module
```

both calls to the MemberA method in the Main procedure end up calling the derived class implementation of MemberA.

VB6 Differences

The Shadows keyword is new to Visual Basic .NET.

See Also

Overloads Keyword, Overrides Keyword

Shared Keyword

Declares a program element that is associated with a class or structure, and not with a particular instance of that class or structure.

Syntax

See the syntax for the Dim, Event, Function, Operator, Property, and Sub statements.

Comments

Shared is used with the Dim, Event, Function, Operator, Property, and Sub statements to indicate that a member of a class, structure, or module is not an instance member but rather is shared among all instances of a class or structure in an application. This means that an object does not have to be instantiated to access the member. For example, the Empty property of the String class, which can be used to return an empty string to compare with a string variable, can be accessed as follows:

```
If Me.thisStringVar = String.Empty Then
    ' String is empty; do something
```

Shared cannot be used with the Overrides, Overridable, NotOverridable, MustOverride, or Static keyword.

In Visual Basic, you can access a shared member either using an instance of the class or structure or using the name of the class or structure. In the former case, however, the Visual Basic compiler displays the warning message, "Access of shared member or nested type through an instance; qualifying expression will not be evaluated." Typically, this will work as expected, unless the shared member is accessed through an expression that evaluates to an instance of the class or structure that contains the shared member. For example, if the class SharedClass has a method named SharedMethod, then the code

```
Dim shClass As New SharedClass()
shClass.SharedMethod()
```

will work as expected. However, if the ReturnSharedInst method of the AnotherClass class returns an instance of SharedClass, then the code:

```
Dim anClass As New anClass
anClass.ReturnSharedInst().SharedMethod()
```

will not work as expected, However, the code

```
Dim anClass As New anClass
Dim shClass2 As SharedClass = anClass.ReturnSharedInst()
shClass2.SharedMethod()
```

will work as expected.

In addition to creating program elements on a per-instance basis and on a per-application basis, you can also define program elements on a per-thread basis. This requires that you use the ThreadStatic attribute along with the Shared keyword. For example, the following code is virtually identical to the code in the example, except that it counts the number of instances of the PerThreadMember class that are created on a per-thread rather than a per-application basis:

```
Imports System.Threading

Public Class PerThreadMember
    <ThreadStatic> Private Shared instancesCreated As Integer = 0

    Public Sub New()
        instancesCreated += 1
    End Sub

    Public Shared ReadOnly Property InstanceCount() As Integer
        Get
            Return instancesCreated
        End Get
    End Property
End Class

Public Module modThreaded
    Public Sub Main()
        Dim secondThread As New Thread(AddressOf Thread2Proc)
        secondThread.Start()
        Dim inst1 As New PerThreadMember
        Console.WriteLine("Main Thread: " & _
                "There are {0} instances of the PerThreadMember class", _
                PerThreadMember.InstanceCount)
        Thread.Sleep(250)
```

```
        Dim inst2 As New PerThreadMember
        Console.WriteLine("Main Thread: " & _
                "There are {0} instances of the PerThreadMember class", _
                PerThreadMember.InstanceCount)
        Thread.Sleep(250)
        Dim inst3 As New PerThreadMember
        Console.WriteLine("Main Thread: " & _
                "There are {0} instances of the PerThreadMember class", _
                PerThreadMember.InstanceCount)
    End Sub

    Public Sub Thread2Proc()
        Dim inst1 As New PerThreadMember
        Console.WriteLine("Thread 2: " & _
                "There are {0} instances of the PerThreadMember class", _
                PerThreadMember.InstanceCount)
        Thread.Sleep(150)
        Dim inst2 As New PerThreadMember
        Console.WriteLine("Thread 2: " & _
                "There are {0} instances of the PerThreadMember class", _
                PerThreadMember.InstanceCount)
        Thread.Sleep(150)
        Dim inst3 As New PerThreadMember
        Console.WriteLine("Thread 2: " & _
                "There are {0} instances of the PerThreadMember class", _
                PerThreadMember.InstanceCount)
    End Sub
End Module
```

Example

The example illustrates the use of a shared variable, instancesCreated, to count the number of times an instance of the SharedMember class was instantiated in an application. The class is then instantiated four times from a module, and the value of the instancesCreated variable is displayed after the third and the final instance have been created.

```
Public Class SharedMember
    Public Sub New
        instancesCreated += 1
    End Sub

    Private Shared instancesCreated As Integer = 0

    Public Shared ReadOnly Property InstanceCount() As Integer
        Get
            Return instancesCreated
        End Get
    End Property
End Class


Public Module modMain
    Public Sub Main()
        Dim inst1 As New SharedMember
```

```
        Dim inst2 As New SharedMember
        Dim inst3 As New SharedMember
        Console.WriteLine(SharedMember.InstanceCount)      ' Displays 3
        dim inst4 As New SharedMember
        Console.Writeline(SharedMember.InstanceCount)      ' Displays 4
    End Sub
End Module
```

VB6 Differences

The Shared keyword is new to Visual Basic .NET.

See Also

Dim Statement, Event Statement, Function Statement, Operator Statement, Property Statement, Sub Statement, Static Keyword

Shell Function

Runs an executable program.

Member Of

Microsoft.VisualBasic.Interaction

Syntax

```
Shell(ByVal Pathname As String, _
      Optional ByVal Style As AppWinStyle = AppWinStyle.MinimizedFocus, _
      Optional ByVal Wait As Boolean = False, _
      Optional ByVal Timeout As Integer = -1) As Integer
```

Element	Description
Pathname	The path and filename of the program to execute, along with any command-line arguments and switches.
Style	A member of the AppWinStyle enumeration indicating the style of the window in which the program is to run. Possible values are AppWinStyle.Hide, AppWinStyle.NormalFocus, AppWinStyle.MinimizedFocus, AppWinStyle.MaximizedFocus, AppWinStyle.NormalNoFocus, and AppWinStyle.MinimizedNoFocus. The default value is AppWinStyle.MinimizedFocus, which runs the application in an iconized window that has the focus.
Wait	A Boolean value indicating whether the program is to run synchronously or asynchronously. By default, *wait* is False, and the program runs asynchronously; execution of Visual Basic code proceeds immediately after the call to the Shell function.
Timeout	If *Wait* is True and the application runs synchronously, the number of milliseconds to wait for the application to complete. If the program has not terminated in *Timeout* milliseconds, control returns to the Visual Basic application. The default value is –1, which indicates that there is no timeout.

Return Value

An integer containing the process ID, or 0.

Comments

The Shell function is able to launch executable (.exe) files and batch (.bat or .cmd) files.

Pathname can include either an absolute or a relative path to the executable. A relative path is interpreted in relationship to the current directory. If no path is included, the Shell function attempts to locate the executable file in the directories indicated by the Path environment variable.

If the path and filename component of *Pathname* includes spaces, they should be enclosed in quotation marks. For example, if the Shell function is to launch Microsoft Word, which is located in the C:\Program Files\Microsoft Office\OFFICE11 directory, the *Pathname* argument containing the path to Word can be defined as in either of the following ways:

```
' String literal with double quotation marks
Dim pathname as string = _
    """C:\Program Files\Microsoft Office\OFFICE11\winword.exe"""
shell(pathname)

' String literal with double quotation marks along with file to load
Dim pathname As String = _
    """C:\Program Files\Microsoft Office\OFFICE11\winword.exe"" "
c:\temp\shelltest.doc"
    Shell(pathname)

' Chr(34) used to form quotation marks around path that includes spaces
Dim pathname As String = chr(34) & _
        "C:\Program Files\Microsoft Office\OFFICE11\winword.exe" _
        & chr(34)
shell(pathname)
' Chr(34) used to form quotation marks around path that includes spaces,
' along with name of file to open
Dim pathname As String = Chr(34) & _
        "C:\Program Files\Microsoft Office\OFFICE11\winword.exe" & chr(34) _
        & " c:\temp\shelltest.doc"
shell(pathname)
```

Of course, if the path or name of the file to execute contains spaces, it should also be delimited with quotation marks.

If the Shell function is unable to launch *PathName* because it is not executable, it throws a FileNotFoundException. If you're handling the exception and re-throwing it to a client, you'll want to throw an exception of a different type in order to avoid confusing the user, as the following code fragment illustrates:

```
Try
    Shell(path)
Catch e As FileNotFoundException
    ' File exists but is not executable
    If File.Exists(path) Then
        Throw New ArgumentException("The path argument is not an executable file", _
                        e)
```

```
        ' The file does not exist
    Else
        Throw
    End If
' Handle other exceptions
End Try
```

One of the most common questions that programmers asked about the Shell function in Visual Basic 6.0 was how to detect that an application launched by the function had terminated. In Visual Basic .NET, this is easily done by setting *Wait* to True. This launches the program synchronously, so that, when control returns to Visual Basic, the program has both executed and terminated, or the attempt to run it has timed out. If you launch the program asynchronously, it is also easy to determine when the process has terminated, as the example shows.

If *Wait* is True, you should generally override the default *Timeout* value of –1. Otherwise, if your application is unable to launch *Pathname*, or if the program relies on the user to terminate it, control might never return to your application.

The Shell function returns the process ID for a process that is launched asynchronously (that is, if *Wait* is False). It returns 0 for a process that it launched synchronously, since control returns to the application only when the process has terminated (in which case the process ID would be invalid) or when the function call times out (in which case a process ID has never been assigned).

For programs launched asynchronously, the process ID can be used in a call to the AppActivate subroutine to give the launched program's window the focus.

The process ID can also be used to retrieve a Process object that corresponds to the launched application process by passing it to the Process object's shared GetProcessById method. The Process object can then be used to retrieve information about the process, such as the name and handle of its main window, whether it is still running and whether its user interface is responding, and when it started and ended. The properties and methods of the Process object also give you some control over the process. You can set the EnableRaisingEvents property to True to handle the Process object's Exiting event, as the example illustrates. You can also terminate the process.

Note that, if the Shell function's return value is the process ID of the process launched by the Shell function and that process in turn launches another process or accesses some component, the latter process or component is inaccessible from the Shell function. The most common example of this is rundll32.exe, which calls a supported entry point in a Windows dynamic link library. For example, the following code opens the Control Panel's Display Properties dialog and returns a process ID:

```
procID = Shell("rundll32.exe shell32.dll,Control_RunDLL Desk.cpl,,1")
```

However, the process ID returned by the Shell function is that of rundll32, and not of the process that corresponds to the Display Properties dialog.

Example

The following code uses the Shell function to launch Notepad asynchronously, and then uses the GetProcessById method to retrieve Notepad's Process object and display information on several of its properties. The code illustrates two ways to determine whether a process is still running: by examining the value of the Process object's HasExited property, and by setting the value of its EnableRaisingEvents property to True and handling the object's Exited event.

```
Imports System.Diagnostics
Imports System.Threading

Public Module modMain
    Public WithEvents proc As Process

    Public Sub Main()
        Dim procID As Integer = Shell("Notepad.exe", AppWinStyle.NormalFocus, False)
        proc = Process.GetProcessById(procID)
        If proc IsNot Nothing Then
            If Not proc.HasExited Then
                Thread.Sleep(500)
                proc.EnableRaisingEvents = True
                Console.WriteLine("Process Name: {0}", proc.ProcessName)
                Console.Writeline("Window Title: {0}", proc.MainWindowTitle)
                Console.WriteLine("Has Exited: {0}", proc.HasExited)
                Console.WriteLine("Responding: {0}", proc.Responding)
                Thread.Sleep(1000)
                proc.CloseMainWindow()
                Console.WriteLine()
            End If
            proc.CloseMainWindow()
            Thread.Sleep(500)
            Console.WriteLine("Has Exited: {0}", proc.HasExited)
        End If
    End Sub

    Public Sub Notepad_Exiting(sender As Object, e As EventArgs) _
                              Handles proc.Exited
        Console.WriteLine("{0} exited at {1}.", proc.ProcessName, _
                                            FormatDatetime(proc.ExitTime))
    End Sub
End Module
```

VB6 Differences

The optional *Wait* and *Timeout* parameters are new to Visual Basic .NET.

See Also

AppActivate Subroutine

SLN Function

Calculates the straight-line depreciation of an asset in a single period.

Member Of

Microsoft.VisualBasic.Financial

Syntax

```
SLN(ByVal Cost As Double, ByVal Salvage As Double, _
    ByVal Life As Double) As Double
```

Element	Description
Cost	The initial cost or value of the asset.
Salvage	The value of the asset at the end of its useful life.
Life	The length of the useful life of the asset.

Return Value

A Double indicating the total amount of depreciation in any period.

Comments

Four major depreciation methods are available:

- The single-declining balance method, which assumes a constant rate of depreciation of an asset in each period. The single-declining balance method is performed by supplying a value of 1 for the *Factor* argument of the DDB function.

- The double-declining balance method, which uses a variable rate of acceleration that varies inversely with year. In other words, the rate of depreciation is greater in the early period of an asset's useful life than in the later period. The double-declining balance method is performed by supplying a value of 2 for the *Factor* argument of the DDB function.

- The sum-of-the-years digits depreciation method, which calculates depreciation at an accelerated rate using the sum of the years digits.

- The straight-line method, which depreciates an asset by a constant value in each period. This is the method used by the SLN function.

All three arguments to the function must be expressed as positive numbers.

The value returned by the function reflects the depreciation in the same time period expressed by *Life*. For example, if *Life* reflects the life of an asset measured in years, the value returned by the function reflects the amount by which an asset depreciates for each year of its life.

In calculating the depreciation per period, the SLN function uses the following simple formula:

```
(cost - salvage) / life
```

See Also

DDB Function, SYD Function

Space Function

Returns a string consisting of a specified number of spaces.

Member Of

Microsoft.VisualBasic.Strings

Syntax

```
Space(ByVal Number As Integer) As String
```

Element	Description
Number	The number of spaces in the newly created string.

Return Value

A String consisting of *number* spaces.

Comments

The Space function creates a string of *number* length that is filled with space characters.
    If *Number* is 0, the function returns a null string, as the following code shows:

```
Dim String0 As String = Space(0)
Console.WriteLine(String0 = String.Empty)          ' Displays True
```

If *Number* is negative, an ArgumentException is thrown.
    The Space function is particularly useful in three areas:

- For clearing existing data in fixed-length strings.
- For formatting output. For example, the following function centers a string in a column whose total width is known:

```
Private Function CenterTitle(Title As String, totalLength As Integer) As String
    Return Space(CInt((totalLength - Title.Length)/2)) + Title
End Function
```

- For creating space-filled string buffers to pass to Win32 API functions. The example provides an illustration.

You can also initialize a string with a particular number of characters other than space characters, or initialize it with a particular sequence of characters, by calling one of the overloaded constructors of the String class. For example, the following constructor returns a string filled with 10 "*" characters:

```
Dim checkAmount As String = New String("*"c, 10)
```

You can also achieve the same result by calling the Visual Basic StrDup. The following call to StrDup, for example, also returns a string filled with 10 "*" characters:

```
Dim checkAmount As String = StrDup(10, "*"c)
```

Example

The following example illustrates the use of the Space function to create a string buffer for use in a call to the Win32 GetUserNameEx function, which returns the name of the user who owns the current thread. The function includes an lpNameBuffer variable, which is passed by reference to the function. It is filled with spaces, and a value indicating its size is assigned to the nSize variable, which is also passed by reference to the function. When the function returns, nSize indicates the number of characters written to the buffer, including a final terminating null character. The code then extracts these characters (except for the final terminating null) and displays them to the console.

```
Friend Enum EXTENDED_NAME_FORMAT
    NameUnknown = 0
    NameFullyQualifiedDN = 1
    NameSamCompatible = 2
    NameDisplay = 3
    NameUniqueId = 6
    NameCanonical = 7
    NameUserPrincipal = 8
    NameCanonicalEx = 9
    NameServicePrincipal = 10
End Enum

Public Module SpaceAPI
    Private Declare Function GetUserNameEx Lib "secur32.dll" _
            Alias "GetUserNameExA" ( _
            ByVal NameFormat As EXTENDED_NAME_FORMAT, _
            ByVal lpNameBuffer As String, ByRef nSize As Integer) As Integer

    Public Sub Main()
        Dim NameFormat As EXTENDED_NAME_FORMAT = EXTENDED_NAME_FORMAT.NameSamCompatible
        Dim lpNameBuffer As String = Space(256)
        Dim nSize As Integer = Len(lpNameBuffer)
        Dim retVal As Integer

        retVal = GetUserNameEx(NameFormat, lpNameBuffer, nSize)
        If retVal > 0 Then
            Console.WriteLine("The current user is {0}", Left(lpNameBuffer, nSize - 1))
        Else
            If Err.LastDLLError = 1332 Then
                Console.WriteLine("No mapped {0} name format.", NameFormat.ToString)
            Else
                Console.WriteLine("Error {0} in call to GetUserNameEx", Err.LastDLLError)
            End If
        End If
    End Sub
End Module
```

VB6 Changes

Visual Basic 6.0 included a Space function, which returned a Variant, and a Space$ function, which returned a String. In Visual Basic .NET, the Space function returns a String, and Space$ is not supported.

See Also

SPC Function, StrDup Function

SPC Function

Inserts a designated number of spaces between expressions in a Print or PrintLine function.

Member Of

Microsoft.VisualBasic.FileSystem

Syntax

```
SPC(ByVal Count As Short) As SPCInfo
```

Element	Description
Count	The number of spaces to insert.

Return Value

An undocumented SPCInfo structure representing spaces to be inserted between expressions in an output line.

Comments

The SPC function inserts spaces between expressions that are output using the Print and PrintLine subroutines. Attempting to use the function in any other context generates a compiler error.

The precise number of spaces and positioning of output data depends on the output line width. By default, output line width is unlimited, and *Count* indicates the exact number of spaces to be inserted between items. If the line width for an output file has been set by a call to the FileWidth subroutine, however, the print position of the data item following the call to the SPC function is calculated as follows:

- If *Count* is less than the line width, the next print position immediately follows *Count* spaces.
- If *Count* is greater than the line width, the next print position is calculated using the following formula:

  ```
  currentprintposition + (Count Mod width)
  ```

If the difference between the current print position and the output line width is less than *Count*, the SPC function inserts a line break and adds spaces according to the following formula:

```
Count - (width - currentposition)
```

Typically, *Count* is an expression that calculates the number of spaces after a data field so that individual columns are aligned. The example illustrates this usage.

Example

The following code iterates an array to write four columns per line to a data file. Each column is 15 columns wide. The SPC function is used to align the columns by calculating the difference between 15 and the length of the output string.

```
Public Module modMain
    Public Sub Main()
        Dim teams(,) As String = {{"Anaheim", "Mighty Ducks", "Hockey", "NHL"}, _
                                  {"Detroit", "Pistons", "Basketball", "NBA"}, _
                                  {"New England", "Patriots", "Football", "NFL"}, _
                                  {"San Francisco", "Giants", "Baseball", "NL"}}
        ' Open File
        Dim fileNo As Integer = FreeFile
        Dim fileOpened As Boolean
        Try
            FileOpen(fileNo, ".\SportsInfo.txt", OpenMode.Output)
            fileOpened = True
            ' Write data to file
            For teamCtr As Integer = teams.GetLowerBound(0) To _
                                sportsTeams.GetUpperBound(0)
                For itemCtr As Integer = sportsTeams.GetLowerBound(1) To _
                                    sportsTeams.GetUpperBound(1)
                    Print(fileNo, sportsTeams(teamCtr, itemCtr), _
                            SPC(CShort(15 - (sportsTeams(teamCtr, itemCtr).Length))))
                Next
                PrintLine(fileNo, "")
            Next
        Catch e As Exception
            Console.WriteLine(e.GetType().Name & ": " & e.Message)
        Finally
            ' Close file
            If fileOpened Then FileClose(fileNo)
        End Try
    End Sub
End Module
```

VB6 Differences

In Visual Basic 6.0, the SPC function returned a String; in Visual Basic .NET, it returns an instance of a SpcInfo structure. The difference, however, is transparent, since the return value of the SPC function is not manipulated directly in code.

In Visual Basic 6.0, the SPC function could also be used to insert spaces in the output of a Debug.Print statement. In Visual Basic .NET, the Debug.Print statement is not supported.

See Also

FileWidth Subroutine, Print, PrintLine Subroutines, Tab Function

Split Function

Returns a one-dimensional array of strings extracted from a single delimited string.

Member Of

Microsoft.VisualBasic.Strings

Syntax

```
Split(ByVal Expression As String, Optional ByVal Delimiter As String = " ", _
    Optional ByVal Limit As Integer = -1, _
    Optional ByVal Compare As CompareMethod = CompareMethod.Binary) _
    As String()
```

Element	Description
Expression	A delimited string from which substrings are to be extracted.
Delimiter	A single character that delimits the substrings in Expression. If the argument is omitted, the space character is used as the delimiter.
Limit	The maximum number of substrings to return. The default value, –1, indicates that all substrings should be included in the returned array. Otherwise, the function returns an array whose upper bound is *Limit* – 1.
Compare	A member of the CompareMethod enumeration indicating whether the comparison of *Delimiter* with the characters in *Expression* is case-sensitive or case-insensitive.

Return Value

A String array containing the individual substrings in *Expression.*

Comments

If *Expression* is an empty string, the Split function returns a single-element array with an empty string. If *Delimiter* cannot be found in *Expression,* the function returns a single-element array with *Expression* unchanged.

If Limit is –1 (the default value), or if *Limit* is equal to or greater than the number of delimited strings in Expression, Split places each delimited substring in a separate array element. For example, the code

```
Dim rodentString As String = "squirrel chipmunk raccoon capibara"
Dim rodents As String() = Split(rodentString, " ", -1)
For ctr As Integer = rodents.GetLowerBound(0) To rodents.GetUpperBound(0)
    Console.WriteLine("String at position {0}: {1}", ctr, rodents(ctr))
Next
```

displays the following output:

```
String at position 0: squirrel
String at position 1: chipmunk
String at position 2: raccoon
String at position 3: capibara
```

The output is identical if we set the value of the *Limit* argument in the call to the Split function to 4 or greater.

If *Limit* is not –1 and is less than the number of delimited strings in *Expression*, the Split function returns delimited strings in array elements 0 through *Limit – 2*. Rather than placing delimited substrings in as many array elements as possible, the function includes any remaining portion of *Expression* in last element. For example, we can modify the prior code fragment, which used the default value of *Limit* and returned a one-dimensional array with four elements, by setting the value of Limit to 3:

```
Dim rodentString As String = "squirrel chipmunk raccoon capibara"
Dim rodents As String() = Split(rodentString, " ", 3)
For ctr As Integer = rodents.GetLowerBound(0) To rodents.GetUpperBound(0)
   Console.WriteLine("String at position {0}: {1}", ctr, rodents(ctr))
Next
```

The output is:

```
String at position 0: squirrel
String at position 1: chipmunk
String at position 2: raccoon capibara
```

If *Expression* contains side-by-side delimiters, an empty string is included in the array. For example, the code

```
Dim rodentString As String = "gopher,hamster,,guinea pig,gerbil"
Dim rodents As String() = Split(rodentString, ",")
For ctr As Integer = rodents.GetLowerBound(0) To rodents.GetUpperBound(0)
   Console.WriteLine("String at position {0}: {1}", ctr, rodents(ctr))
Next
```

produces the following output:

```
String at position 0: gopher
String at position 1: hamster
String at position 2:
String at position 3: guinea pig
String at position 4: gerbil
```

The default value of the *Compare* argument is determined by the value of the Option Compare setting. If there is no Option Compare setting, binary is the default, and the comparison is case-sensitive.

An obvious application of the *Limit* argument is to match the number of elements in an array that has already been dimensioned. For example:

```
Dim marsupialString As String = "opossum kangaroo koala wombat"
Dim marsupials(3) As String
marsupials = Split(marsupialString, " ", marsupials.GetLength(0))
```

When using the Split function, you may want to determine how many elements delimited string contains in order to preallocate an array or supply a non-default Limit *argument*. You can determine the number of substrings using the following code:

```
Private Function CountDelimitedElements(str As String, _
              Optional delimiter As String = " ") As Integer
```

```
    Dim pos As Integer = 1
    Dim ctr As Integer = 0
    Do
        pos = Instr(pos, str, delimiter, CompareMethod.Text)
        If pos > 0 Then
            pos += 1
            ctr += 1
        End If
    Loop While pos > 0
    Return ctr + 1
End Function
```

See Also

Join Function, Option Compare Statement

Static Keyword

Indicates that a local variable remains in existence and retains a value after the procedure in which it is declared has terminated.

Syntax

See the syntax for the Dim statement.

Comments

Since the Static keyword is used in local variable declarations, it can only appear in a Dim statement inside a method body (a function or a subroutine) or a property get or set accessor.

Because its value persists between procedure calls, static variables are particularly useful as counters: each call to the procedure in which the static variable is declared increments the static counter variable.

Like any local variable, a static variable is accessible only within the member in which it is declared or, if it is declared in a block construct within a member, only within the block in which it is declared. However, unlike other local variables, its lifetime is the lifetime of the application in which it is declared.

There are some restrictions on the use of the Static keyword. First, the Static keyword cannot appear in the same variable declaration as the ReadOnly, Shadows, or Shared keywords. Second, it cannot be used to declare local variables in a member of a structure (i.e., a type defined using the Structure . . . End Structure construct).

In some programming languages that support static local variables, it is necessary to ensure that the declaration of the static variable can be executed only once in order to prevent it from being reinitialized to its default value. Typically, an If statement is used for this purpose. This is not true of Visual Basic, however. (In fact, defining a static variable in an If statement gives it block scope, which makes it inaccessible from the rest of the procedure in which it is declared.) Instead, variable declarations that use the Static keyword are executed only once, when the procedure is first executed.

If a static variable requires explicit initialization, it should be initialized in the Static statement rather than in a separate assignment statement. Otherwise, unless that assignment statement appears in a conditional statement such as an If statement, its value will be reset.

There occasionally is some confusion about the difference between the C# **static** keyword and the Visual Basic Static keyword. The C# **static** keyword corresponds directly to the Visual Basic .NET Shared keyword. If used in a variable declaration, it defines a variable that has a single value per application, regardless of how many instances of its defining type are created in that application. In addition, it is referenced using the name of the class or module to which it belongs. (For details, see the entry for the Shared keyword.) In contrast, the Visual Basic Static keyword defines a local instance variable (and not a variable with a single application-wide value) whose lifetime is the lifetime of the application, but which is accessible only from within the procedure or the code block in which it is declared.

You can implement the functionality of a Static variable by simply declaring a variable at member level, so that its lifetime is the lifetime of the application. It can then be used in a procedure or a block structure in the same way as a static variable. For example, the following definition of the HitCounter class that uses a Static variable:

```
Public Class HitCounter
   Public Function Increment() As Integer
      Static counter As Integer = 0

      counter += 1
      Return counter
   End Function
End Class
```

could be replaced by the following code, which defines a Private variable at member level:

```
Public Class HitCounter
   Private counter As Integer = 0

   Public Function Increment() As Integer
      counter += 1
      Return counter
   End Function
End Class
```

The difference is that the Static keyword allows you to have the most restrictive accessibility possible; the *counter* variable can be modified only in the Increment method. Defining the variable as private, on the other hand, makes it accessible throughout the class and allows its value to be modified either deliberately or inadvertently outside of the Increment method.

Example

The following code defines a BankAccount class with a RecordTransaction method that applies deposits and debits to the account balance. A static variable, balance, is used to store the account balance, which the method then returns to the caller:

```
Public Class BankAccount
   Public Sub New(openingBalance As Decimal)
      RecordTransaction(openingBalance)
   End Sub

   Public Function Deposit(depositAmount As Decimal) As Decimal
      Return RecordTransaction(depositAmount)
   End Function
```

```
    Public Function Debit(debitAmount As Decimal) As Decimal
        Return RecordTransaction(-debitAmount)
    End Function

    Private Function RecordTransaction(amount As Decimal) As Decimal
        Static balance As Decimal = 0
        balance += amount
        Return balance
    End Function
End Class
```

The following code then instantiates the BankAccount class and records one deposit and one debit:

```
Public Module UseChecking
    Public Sub Main()
        Dim credit, debit As Decimal
        Dim openingBalance As Decimal = 1721.39d
        Dim checking As New BankAccount(openingBalance)

        Console.WriteLine("The account's opening balance is {0}", openingBalance)

        credit = 162.75d
        Console.WriteLine("The balance after a deposit of {0} is {1}", _
                          credit, checking.Deposit(credit))

        debit = 106.92d
        Console.WriteLine("The balance after a debit of {0} is {1}", _
                          debit, checking.Debit(debit))
    End Sub
End Module
```

The output from the program appears as follows:

```
The account's opening balance is 1721.39
The balance after a deposit of 162.75 is 1884.14
The balance after a debit of 106.92 is 1777.22
```

VB6 Differences

In Visual Basic 6.0, the Static keyword could be used with the Function and Sub statements to indicate that all local variables declared within the function or procedure, respectively, were static. In Visual Basic .NET, this usage is not supported, and the Static keyword can only be used to declare individual variables.

See Also

Dim Statement, Shared Keyword

Step Keyword

Used in For . . . Next statement to define how much the loop counter is incremented.

Syntax

```
[Step step]
```

Element	Description
step	A numeric expression.

Comments

Step is an optional part of the For . . . Next statement. If it is omitted, the loop counter is incremented by 1 at the beginning of each pass through the loop.

The step value can be either positive or negative. If it is positive, the loop counter is incremented by the step value after each iteration of the loop. If it is negative, the loop counter is decremented by the step value.

The loop does not execute at all if the step value is negative but the loop's end value is greater than its start value, or if the step value is positive but the loop's start value is less than its end value.

See Also

For . . . Next Statement

Stop Statement

Suspends program execution.

Syntax

```
Stop
```

Comments

In the Visual Studio design-time environment, the Stop statement is equivalent to setting a breakpoint. It suspends execution, preserves the state of the running application, and transfers control to the IDE's debugger.

In the Windows runtime environment, the Stop statement suspends program execution, preserves the state of the running application, and displays a system modal dialog like the one shown in Figure 8-23. If the user selects the Debug button, he or she is offered a choice of debuggers to load.

If you use the Stop statement instead of setting breakpoints, make sure that you remove them all from your code before building the release version unless you want users to see the dialog shown in Figure 8-23.

See Also

End Statement

FIGURE 8-23
The dialog
produced by the
Stop statement at
runtime

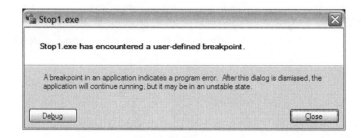

Str Function

Converts a number to a String.

Member Of

Microsoft.VisualBasic.Conversion

Syntax

```
Str(ByVal Number As Object) As String
```

Element	Description
Number	The number to be converted to a String.

Return Value

The string representation of *Number*.

Comments

Number can be any numeric type (including SByte, UShort, UInteger, and UInteger), or an Object whose runtime type is either a numeric type or a string contraining a representation of a number. If none of these is the case, the Str function throws an InvalidCastException. You can prevent this and ensure that Number is a valid argument by calling the IsNumeric function before calling the Str function.

The Str function always adds a leading space for the sign of *Number*. In the case of negative numbers, it is replaced by the - unary operator. In the case of positive numbers, the leading space is retained.

The Str function is not locale-aware. The only decimal separator that it recognizes is the period (.).

Str is a legacy function inherited from Basic before Visual Basic. To handle numeric-to-string conversion, use the CStr function or the ToString method of the numeric type.

VB6 Differences

Visual Basic 6.0 included both a Chr$ function and a Chr function. The former returned a String, while the latter returned a Variant. In Visual Basic .NET, the Chr function returns a String, and Chr$ is not supported.

See Also

CStr Function, Format Function, Val Function

StrComp Function

Returns the result of a string comparison.

Member Of

Microsoft.VisualBasic.Strings

Syntax

```
StrComp(ByVal String1 As String, ByVal String2 As String, _
        <Microsoft.VisualBasic.OptionCompareAttribute> _
        Optional ByVal Compare As CompareMethod _
        ) As Integer
```

Element	Description
String1	The string to be compared with String2.
String2	The string to be compared with String1.
Compare	A member of the CompareMethod enumeration indicating whether the comparison is case-sensitive (CompareMethod.Binary) or case-insensitive (CompareMethod.Text).

Return Value

–1 if *String1* < *String2*, 0 if *String1* = *String2*, and 1 if *String1* > *String2*.

Comments

The comparison indicates which string precedes the other in an ascending sort.

The default value of the *Compare* argument is determined by the value of the Option Compare setting. If there is no Option Compare setting, CompareMethod.Binary is the default, and the comparison is case-sensitive.

You can also perform string comparison using the standard Visual Basic comparison operators.

The StrComp function corresponds to two of the overloads of the shared Compare method of the String class. The first is

```
String.Compare(strA, strB)
```

which performs a case-sensitive comparison on two strings. The second is

```
String.Compare(strA, strB, ignoreCase)
```

where *ignoreCase* is a Boolean specifying whether the comparison should be case-insensitive. The method's return value is interpreted exactly like that of the StrComp function.

The interpretation of the value returned by the StrComp function is identical to that of the CompareTo method of the IComparable interface, which is used to define custom comparisons between objects of the same type. This allows us to define the CompareTo method by simply calling the StrComp function if we wish to compare two objects based on a string property. For example, the following code compares and orders object instances based on the value of their Name property:

```
Public Class Item
    Implements IComparable

    Private itemName As String

    Public Sub New(name As String)
        Me.itemName = name
    End Sub

    Public Property Name() As String
        Get
            Return Me.itemName
        End Get
        Set
            Me.itemName = Value
        End Set
    End Property

    Public Function CompareTo(ByVal obj As Object) As Integer _
                        Implements IComparable.CompareTo
        If Not TypeOf obj Is Item Then
            Throw New ArgumentException("Argument is not of type Item.")
        End If
        Dim item2 As Item = DirectCast(obj, Item)
        Return StrComp(Me.Name, item2.Name)
    End Function
End Class
```

See Also

Option Compare Statement

StrConv Function

Performs any of a variety of supported string conversions.

Member Of

Microsoft.VisualBasic.Strings

Syntax

```
StrConv(ByVal str As String, _
        ByVal Conversion As Microsoft.VisualBasic.VbStrConv, _
        Optional ByVal LocaleID As Integer) As String
```

Element	Description
str	A string to be converted to another string.
Conversion	The type of conversion to perform on *str*, as defined by a member of the VbStrConv enumeration.
LocaleID	The locale identifier to use for the conversion. The default value is the local system's locale ID.

Return Value

The converted string.

Comments

The StrConv function performs the following conversions:

VbStrConv Enumeration Member	Conversion
None	None (returns *str* unchanged)
LinguisticCasing	To uppercase or lowercase using linguistic casing. (Can be combined with the LowerCase or UpperCase members to indicate that linguistic casing rather than the default casing defined by the system should be used. (Linguistic casing allows accurate case conversion for Turkic and some other locales.)
UpperCase	To uppercase.
LowerCase	To lowercase.
ProperCase	To proper case (converts the first letter of each word without exception to uppercase).
Wide	Narrow (half-width) characters to wide (full-width) characters. The constant applies to Asian locales only.
Narrow	Wide (full-width) characters to narrow (half-width) characters. The constant applies to Asian locales only.
Katakana	From Hiragana to Katakana. The constant applies to Japanese only.
Hiragana	From Katakana to Hiragana. The constant applies to Japanese only.
SimplifiedChinese	From Traditional Chinese to Simplified Chinese. The constant applies to Asian locales only.
TraditionalChinese	From Simplified Chinese to Traditional Chinese. The constant applies to Asian locales only.

The vbStrConv.ProperCase constant causes the StrConv function to capitalize the first letter of a string, as well as the string that follows any of the following characters:

- Null (vbNullChar, ControlChars.NullChar, or Chr(0))
- Horizontal tab (vbTab, ControlChars.Tab, or Chr(9))

- Carriage return (vbCr, ControlChars, Cr, or Chr(13))
- Carriage return and line feed (vbCrLf, vbNewLine, ControlChars.CrLf, or ControlChars.NewLine)
- Form feed (vbFormFeed, ControlChars.FormFeed, or Chr(12))
- Vertical tab (vbVerticalTab, ControlChars.VerticalTab, or Chr(11))
- Quotation mark (vbQuote or Chr(34))

Proper casing will capitalize even words that would normally not be capitalized. For instance, "I had the time of my life" is converted to "I Had The Time Of My Life".

The locale ID is an integer that represents a combination of language and country or region. A list of locale IDs is available in "Locale ID (LCID) Chart" topic in the Visual Studio .NET documentation. Most commonly, the locale is identified by a string that consists of language and region code (such as en-us for English in the United States). The following function can be used to convert a locale code to a locale ID:

```
Public Function GetLocaleIdFromCode(localeCode As String) As Integer
    Try
        Dim ci As New CultureInfo(localeCode)
        Return ci.LCID
    Catch
        Return CultureInfo.CurrentCulture.LCID
    End Try
End Function
```

VB6 Differences

In Visual Basic 6.0, the *Conversion* argument of the StrConv function supported a vbUnicode constant for conversion from ANSI to Unicode, and a vbFromUnicode constant for conversion from Unicode to ANSI. In Visual Basic .NET, these arguments (as well as the constants that represent them) are not supported.

See Also

CStr Function, LCase Function, UCase Function

StrDup Function

Creates a string consisting of a particular character repeated a specified number of times.

Member Of

Microsoft.VisualBasic.Strings

Syntax

```
StrDup(ByVal Number As Integer, ByVal Character As { Char | String }) As String

StrDup(ByVal Number As Integer, ByVal Character As Object) As Object
```

Element	Description
Number	The number of times to duplicate Character. *Number* also defines the length of the returned String.
Character	The character to be duplicated in the returned String. If *Character* is an Object, its runtime type must be either Char or String.

Return Value

A String consisting of the *Character* character repeated *Number* times.

Comments

If *Number* is 0, the function returns an empty string, as the following code shows:

```
Dim duplicatedString As String = StrDup(0, "*"c)
Console.WriteLine(duplicatedString = String.Empty)' Displays True
```

If *Number* is negative, an ArgumentException is thrown.

If Character is a string that contains more than one character, only its first character duplicated in the returned string. For example, the following code

```
Dim XOString As String = StrDup(10, "XOXOXOXO")
Console.WriteLine(XOString)
```

returns "XXXXXXXXXX".

The Space function is a specialized variation of the StrDup function. It is equivalent to:

```
StrDup(number, " ")
```

where *number* is the number of spaces to include in the space.

You can also initialize a string filled with a particular number of characters by calling one of the overloaded constructors of the String class. For example, the following constructor returns a string filled with 30 "-" characters:

```
Dim dashedLine As New String("-"c, 30)
Console.WriteLine(dashedLine)
```

VB6 Differences

The StrDup function is new to Visual Basic .NET.

See Also

Space Function

StrReverse Function

Returns a string in which the order of characters is the reverse of a source string.

Member Of

Microsoft.VisualBasic.Strings

Syntax

```
StrReverse(ByVal Expression As String) As String
```

Element	Description
Expression	The String whose character order is to be reversed.

Return Value

A String whose characters appear in reverse order from those in *Expression.*

Comments

If *Expression* is an empty string, the function returns an empty string.

Passing the string returned by StrReverse to the StrReverse function once again returns the original string. For example:

```
Public Module ReverseString
    Public Sub Main()
        Dim word As String = "natures"
        Dim newWord As String = StrReverse(word)
        Console.WriteLine(newWord)              ' Displays "serutan"
        word = StrReverse(newWord)
        Console.WriteLine(word)                 ' Displays "natures"
    End Sub
End Module
```

This makes it possible to reverse the string, to perform string manipulation on it from left to right, and then to reverse it to its original order.

See Also

InStrRev Function

Structure Keyword

Constrains a generic type parameter by requiring that the argument passed to it be a value type. For details, see the discussion of the As keyword.

Syntax

See the syntax of the As keyword.

Comments

A generic parameter can be constrained by value type by using the Structure keyword or by reference type by using the Class keyword. If neither keyword is used, the generic parameter is not constrained by type.

The Structure keyword is unrelated to the Structure statement.

Example

See the example for the As Keyword.

VB.NET Changes

The Structure keyword is new as of Visual Basic 2005.

VB6 Differences

The Structure keyword is new to Visual Basic .NET; Visual Basic 6.0 did not support generic types.

See Also

As Keyword, Of Keyword, Structure Keyword

Structure Statement

Defines a structure, a value type that is one of the five basic .NET types.

Syntax

```
[ <attrlist> ] [ accessModifier ] [ Shadows ] _
Structure name [( Of typelist )]
    [ Implements interfacenames ]
        variabledeclarations
    [ proceduredeclarations ]
End Structure
```

Element	Description
attrlist	An attribute that can be applied to a structure. Only attributes whose AttributeUsage attribute is AttributeTargets.All or AttributeTargets.Struct can be applied to a structure.
accessModifier	The accessibility of the structure. Possible keywords are Public, Private, Friend, Protected, and Protected Friend. If *accessModifier* is not specified, the structure has Friend access. The Private modifier can only be used for structures defined inside another class or structure; the Protected and Protected Friend modifiers can only be used for structures defined inside another class. For details, see the entry for each of the access modifiers.
Shadows	Indicates that the current structure hides an identically named programming element or a set of overloaded elements in a base class. For details, see the entry for the Shadows Keyword.
name	The name of the structure. It must follow standard Visual Basic naming conventions and be unique within the namespace in which the structure is defined.

Element	Description
typelist	The list of parameters for the structure. *typelist* is used when defining a generic structure and takes the general form *(Of* value *[As* constraintlist*])* where *value* is a placeholder for the runtime type of the generic structure, and *constraintlist* is a one or more predefined conditions that the runtime type of the generic structure must satisfy. For details, see the entry for the As Keyword.
interfacenames	The name of one or more interfaces implemented by the current structure. If multiple interfaces are specified, their names are separated by commas. If the structure does implement any interfaces, it must provide an implementation for each interface member. (See the Interface Statement for details.)
variabledeclarations	At least one or more Dim or Event statements declaring instance variables and events, which define the data members of the structure. At least one instance variable or event is required by the Structure . . . End Structure construct. (Constants can also be defined, although they don't satisfy this requirement.) If an access modifier is not specified with a particular variable declaration, it is public by default.
proceduredeclarations	Optional definitions of zero, one, or more functions, subroutines (including event handlers), properties, and operators. Together, these define the method of the structure. If a procedure declaration does not have an access modifier, it is public by default. Note that the subroutines can include constructors, although parameterless constructors cannot be defined.

Comments

The Structure . . . End Structure construct defines a .NET structure, which is a value type. In contrast, the Class . . . End Class construct defines a .NET class, which is a reference type. For some of the differences between classes and structures, see the sidebar "Classes and Structures" in the entry for the Class Statement.

Structures implicitly inherit SystemValueType and, unlike classes, may not inherit from any other type.

Structures can be declared at the namespace level or at the member level (that is, inside another class or structure). They cannot, however, be declared at the procedure level.

Variables declared in structures using the Dim statement without an access modifier are public by default.

There are two major restrictions on non-local variables defined in structures:

- The variable declaration cannot also initialize the variable. For example, the code:

```
Public Structure IllegalStructure
    Dim ctr As Integer = 1              ' Illegal initialization
End Structure
```

is illegal because it both declares and initializes the *ctr* variable.

- The size of an array cannot be specified. For example, the code

```
Public Structure IllegalStructure
    Dim names(10) As String            ' Illegal to declare initial size
End Structure
```

generates a compiler error because it is illegal to declare an array's initial size.

These restrictions do not apply to local variables defined in a method, property, or operator belonging to a structure.

If any constants are defined in a structure, they are shared members of the structure. However, the Shared keyword is not used when declaring them.

Structures can contain one or more constructors, which are named New in Visual Basic code and are executed whenever a new instance of the structure is created using the New keyword. Any constructor you define for a structure must be parameterized; you cannot define a default or parameterless constructor for a structure. In addition, it is typical in classes to call the base class constructor. In the case of a structure, this generates a compiler error.

Although Structures inherit a Finalize method from the ValueType class, the .NET runtime does not garbage collect structure instances. As a result, the Finalize method is never called by the .NET runtime.

Because all structures are implicitly derived from the System.ValueType class, the following members of the System.ValueType class can be called as if they were members of the current structure:

- **Equals method**   Returns a Boolean indicating whether two structure instances have identical field values. Its syntax is:

```
Equals(obj As Object)
```

This implementation of Equals overrides that of System.Object, and individual value types can in turn override this implementation.

- **GetHashCode method**   Returns a hash code used by a Hashtable object to store and retrieve instances of the class. The ValueType class overrides the GetHashCode method in System.Object, and individual structures can also override the implementation in the ValueType class. The GetHashCode method should return an integer that is based on the value of one or more of the structure's instance members that serves to uniquely identify it from similar structure instances with different values.

- **GetType method**   Returns a Type object that represents the current class. The GetType method cannot be overridden.

- **ToString method**   Returns the fully qualified name of the structure. Individual structures often override this method. For instance, the intrinsic Visual Basic value types (such as Boolean or Integer) override it to return a string containing the instance's value.

A structure can include both shared and instance members. Shared members belong to the structure as a whole, rather than to individual class instances. A shared variable, for example, has a single value across all instances of a structure in an application. Instance members, on the other hand, belong to individual instances of a structure. An instance variable, for example, can have a different value in each structure instance in a particular application.

A structure can be instantiated either with or without using the New keyword. For example, the following two statements both instantiate a structured named TestStruct:

```
Dim var1 As TestStruct
Dim var2 As New TestStruct()
```

When the structure is instantiated, all fields are automatically initialized to their default values. However, if a structure has a parameterized constructor, it can only be invoked using the New keyword.

Shared members of a structure can be accessed without instantiating that structure. For example, the following code defines a structure named Counter with a shared fields named MinValue and MaxValue, and shows code that instantiates the structure and accesses its instance and shared members:

```
Public Structure Counter
    Dim Value As Integer
    Const MaxValue As Integer = 10
    Const MinValue As Integer = 0
End Structure

Public Module modMain
    Public Sub Main()
        Dim ctr As Integer = CInt(InputBox("Enter an integer:"))
        Dim votes As Counter
        If ctr <= Counter.MaxValue And ctr >= Counter.MinValue Then
            votes.Value = ctr
            Console.WriteLine(votes.Value)
        Else
            Console.WriteLine("The value is out of range.")
        End If
    End Sub
End Module
```

Events raised by structures cannot be handled using the WithEvents and Handles keywords. Instead, they must be handled dynamically using the AddHandler and RemoveHandler statements. For an example, see the AddHandler statement.

In some cases, particularly when passing a structure to a Win32 API function, you may need to ensure that the physical layout of the structure conforms to that expected by the Win32 function. You can use the <StructLayout> attribute, possibly combined with the <FieldOffset> attribute, to do this. For example, the following code uses the <StructLayout> attribute in the definition of a SHELLEXECUTEINFO structure, which is passed to the ShellExecuteEx function in order to launch a program capable of opening a text file:

```
Imports System.Runtime.InteropServices

<StructLayout(LayoutKind.Sequential)> Friend Structure SHELLEXECUTEINFO
    Dim cbSize As Integer
    Dim fMask As Integer
    Dim hwnd As Integer
    Dim lpVerb As String
    Dim lpFile As String
    Dim lpParameters As String
    Dim lpDirectory As String
    Dim nShow As Integer
    Dim hInstApp As Integer
    ' fields
    Dim lpIDList As Integer
    Dim lpClass As String
```

```
        Dim hkeyClass As Integer
        Dim dwHotKey As Integer
        Dim hIcon As Integer
        Dim hProcess As Integer
End Structure

Public Module RunProgram
    Private Declare Function ShellExecuteEx Lib "shell32.dll" _
                    (ByRef lpExecInfo As SHELLEXECUTEINFO) As Integer
    Private Const SEE_MASK_NOCLOSEPROCESS As Integer = &H40
    Private Const SW_RESTORE As Integer = 9

    Public Sub Main()
        Dim shExec As SHELLEXECUTEINFO
        shExec.cbSize = Len(shExec)
        shExec.fMask = SEE_MASK_NOCLOSEPROCESS
        shExec.lpVerb = "open"
        shExec.lpfile = "StructDesc.txt" & Chr(0)
        Dim retVal As Integer = ShellExecuteEx(shExec)
        Console.WriteLine(retVal)
    End Sub
End Module
```

VB6 Differences

The Structure . . . End Structure statement is new to Visual Basic .NET. Its rough equivalent in Visual Basic 6.0 was the Type . . . End Type statement. In Visual Basic 6.0, structures were known as user-defined types.

The Visual Basic 6.0 user-defined type is a much simpler data type that is simply the sum of its member fields. As a result, its members could be manipulated directly in memory. Visual Basic .NET, on the other hand, a structure is a more complex data type. The layout of its member fields is not guaranteed, nor are they intended to be manipulated directly.

In Visual Basic 6.0, using either the Dim statement or an access modifier to define the structure's fields generated a compiler error. In Visual Basic .NET, one or both is required.

In Visual Basic 6.0, user-defined types contained instance fields only. In Visual Basic .NET, structures can contain both shared and instance fields, as well as methods.

Sub Statement

Defines a subroutine (a procedure that does not return a value).

Syntax

```
[ <attributelist> ] [ accessmodifier ] [ proceduremodifiers ] _
[ Shared ] [ Shadows ] Sub name [ (Of typeparamlist) ] [ (parameterlist) ] _
[ Implements implementsList | Handles eventlist ]
        [ statements ]
        [ Exit Sub ]
        [ statements ]
[ End Sub ]
```

Element	Description
attributelist	A list of attributes to be applied to the subroutine. Only attributes whose AttributeUsage attribute is AttributeTargets.All or AttributeTargets.Method can be applied to a Sub statement.
accessmodifier	The subroutine's accessibility. Possible keywords are Public, Private, Friend, Protected, and Protected Friend. For details, see the entry for each of the access modifiers. If *accessModifier* is not specified, the subroutine is Public by default. If the Sub statement appears in an interface definition, *accessmodifier* cannot be used, since subroutines defined in interfaces must be public.
proceduremodifiers	One or more of the following modifiers: Overloads, which indicates this is one of two or more identically named subroutines with different signatures; Overrides, which indicates that this subroutine overrides an identically named programming element in a base class; Overridable, which indicates that this subroutine can be overridden by an identically named subroutine in a derived class; NotOverridable, which indicates that a derived class cannot override this subroutine; and MustOverride, which indicates that a derived class must override the subroutine. By default, subroutines are NotOverridable.
Shared	Indicates that the subroutine can be called without creating an instance of the type in which it is defined. The Shared keyword cannot be used with the Sub statement in interface definitions (since interfaces by definition define public instance members) or in modules (since they can only define shared members). Shared cannot be used with the Overrides, Overridable, NotOverridable, and MustOverride keywords.
Shadows	Indicates that the subroutine hides an identically named programming element in a base class. For details, see the entry for the Shadows Keyword. Shadows cannot be used along with Overloads.
name	The name of the subroutine. It must follow standard Visual Basic naming conventions.
typeparamlist	A list of type parameters for a generic subroutine. For details, see the entry for the Of Keyword.
paramlist	The subroutine's parameter list, which can consist of zero, one, or more parameters. If multiple parameters are present, they are separated from one another with commas. At runtime, the arguments passed to the subroutine can be referenced by their parameter names. The syntax of a single parameter is shown at the end of the Syntax section.
implementsList	A comma-separated list of interface methods, in the form *interfacename.methodname* . . . , which defines the function as implementing a particular interface method. If *implementsList* is present, the function's containing class, structure, or interface must also implement that interface (it must have an Implements statement), and the function must have the same signature as the interface member for which it provides an implementation.

paramlist can be zero, one, or more parameters, each separated from one another by commas. A single parameter has the syntax:

```
[ <attribute_list> ] [ Optional ] [{ ByVal | ByRef }] [ ParamArray ] _
argument_name[( )] [ As argument_type ] [ = default_value ]
```

Element	Description
attribute_list	A comma-separated list of attributes that apply to the parameter. Only attributes whose AttributeUsage attribute is AttributeTargets.All or AttributeTargets.Parameter can be applied to a subroutine parameter.
Optional	Indicates that an argument need not be supplied when calling the subroutine. All parameters that follow an optional parameter must also be optional or a compiler error results. For details on optional arguments, see the entry for the Optional keyword.
ByVal	Indicates that the argument is passed by value to the subroutine. When control returns to the caller, the value of its original argument is not modified. If ByVal or ByRef is not explicitly specified, the argument is passed by value.
ByRef	Indicates that the argument is passed by reference to the subroutine. When control returns to the caller, any modifications made by the subroutine to the value of the argument are reflected in its value.
ParamArray	Indicates that the argument is an optional parameter array whose size is not known at design time. If present, it must be the last parameter is *paramlist*. For details on the user of parameter arrays, see the entry for the ParamArray Keyword.
argument_name	The name of the parameter. The argument passed to the function by the caller is referenced by this name within the subroutine.
argument_type	The data type of the argument. It can be any data type recognized by the .NET framework.
default_value	The default value to be assigned to optional arguments.

Comments

Subroutines are useful only to the degree that your code can call them. Therefore, separate sections discuss declaring a subroutine and calling it.

Declaring Subroutines

The Sub statement can be used to define a function (that is, a procedure that does not return a value) in a class, structure, interface, or module. However, a subroutine cannot be defined within a member of any of those types. In addition, the Sub statement can be used with the Delegate statement to define the signature of the delegate.

The Overrides keyword cannot be used with a subroutine defined in an interface or in a module. The Overrides keyword cannot be used with a method in an interface because interfaces provide no code implementation. It cannot be used with a method in a module because instance members and not shared members can be overridden, and a module can have only shared members.

Unless they are explicitly declared otherwise, subroutines in base classes are not overridable, which in turn means that the attempt to override them using the Overrides keyword generates a compiler error (error BC31086: "'Public Overrides Sub <sub signature>' cannot override 'Public Sub <sub signature>' because it is not declared 'Overridable'"). As a result, if there is any possibility that your class can legitimately be used as a base class from which other classes derive, you should define its methods as Overridable.

The Overloads keyword cannot be used with a subroutine defined in a module.

Generally, the End Sub construct is used to end the subroutine definition. However, subroutines that provide no code implementation but simply define signatures do not have an End Sub statement. This is true of the subroutines defined using the Delegate statement, subroutines in external DLL routines, subroutines defined in interface statements, and subroutines defined as MustOverride.

The *implementsList* syntax effectively frees you from having to assign a subroutine the same name as the interface methods that it implements. However, you'll find that it is still helpful (and self-documenting) to give the subroutine a name that is reasonably close to that of the interface method it implements.

Use self-documenting names that describe the purpose of the parameter. Not only will the subroutine signature appear in Object Browser and IntelliSense, but callers of the function can call it more easily using named arguments.

Any number of Exit Sub statements can occur within the body of a Sub . . . End Sub construct to exit the subroutine body prematurely. Typically, the Exit Sub statement is placed within an If statement to transfer control outside of the function body if some condition exists.

The constructor, which is called when an instance of a class or structure is first created, is implemented in Visual Basic .NET as a subroutine named New. For classes, if you do not define a parameterless or default constructor, the compiler will provide one. You can instead define your own parameterless constructor if you want, as well as any number of parameterized constructors. For structures, you cannot define a default or parameterless constructor, although you can define overloaded parameterized constructors. For example, the following code defines an overloaded parameterized constructor:

```
Public Class Item
    Private itemName As String
    Private itemCategory As ItemCategory

    Public Sub New(name As String)
       Me.itemName = name
    End Sub

    Public Sub New(name As String, category As ItemCategory)
       Me.itemName = name
       Me.itemCategory = category
    End Sub

    Public ReadOnly Property Name() As String
       Get
           Return Me.itemName
       End Get
    End Property
```

```
    Public Property Category() As ItemCategory
        Get
            Return Me.itemCategory
        End Get
        Set
            Me.itemCategory = Value
        End Set
    End Property
End Class
```

Note the use of the constructor to assign a value to a read-only property.

If you define one or more parameterized constructors, the Visual Basic compiler does not automatically create a parameterless constructor. If you want one, you have to provide it yourself.

By providing constructors with access modifiers that are more restrictive than the access modifier applied to a the class or structure they belong to, you can make the class or structure instance broadly accessible while allowing it to be instantiated only within a particular class or structure or within a particular assembly.

Calling Functions

If a subroutine has a parameter list, arguments can usually be passed to it either positionally (by specifying the argument in the order in which it occurs in the subroutine declaration) or by name (by assigning the parameter name the value of the argument). For example, if a class named Person is defined in part as follows:

```
Public Class Person

    Private firstName As String
    Private middleName As String
    Private lastName As String

    Public Sub New(firstName As String, middleName As String , lastName As String)
        Me.firstName = firstName
        Me.middleName = middleName
        me.lastName = lastName
    End Sub
End Class
```

its constructor can be invoked using positional arguments as follows:

```
Dim person2 As New Person("John", "J.", "Smith")
```

or it can be invoked using named arguments as follows:

```
Dim person1 As New Person(firstName := "John", lastName := "Smith", _
                          middleName := "J.")
```

Named arguments can be passed to the subroutine in any order.

If a subroutine takes an argument by reference and you would prefer that the value not be modified, you can do any of three things. For example, the following subroutine, SquareIt, squares a number that is passed to it by reference:

```
Public Sub SquareIt(ByRef number As Integer)
    number = CInt(number ^ 2)
End Sub
```

Ordinarily, you would call the subroutine as follows:

```
Dim number As Integer = 12
SquareIt(number)
Console.WriteLine("The value of number is now {0}", number)
```

However, to pass an argument by value rather than by reference, you can do the following:

- Override the by reference argument by enclosing it in parentheses. If it is the only argument to the function, enclose it in double parentheses. For example, the following code passes its argument to the SquareIt subroutine by value rather than by reference:

```
SquareIt((number))
```

  The result is that *number* is unchanged when the subroutine completes and control returns to the caller.

- Pass a literal value to the subroutine. For example:

```
SquareIt(12)
```

  Often, this is not possible, since the literal value to pass to the function is not known at design time.

- Make a copy of the variable that you can then pass to the subroutine. For example, in the following code, a new variable, *duplicateNumber,* is assigned the value of *number* and then passed as an argument:

```
Dim duplicateNumber As Integer = number
SquareIt(duplicateNumber)
```

  This value can then be discarded when control returns to the caller. This method only works for value types, however. For reference types, you can make a copy of a class instance by calling the MemberwiseClone method if you are calling a method from within the class itself or one of its derived classes. (MethodwiseClone is a protected method.)

Passing an argument to a subroutine by value does not necessarily mean that it cannot be modified by the subroutine. If the argument is a reference type, property and field values can be modified, and if the argument is an array (which is also a reference type), individual array elements can be modified. For details, see the entry for the ByRef Keyword.

VB.NET Changes

The use of the Of *typeparamlist* clause to support a generic parameter list is new to Visual Basic 2005.

VB6 Differences

Probably the most significant difference between subroutines in Visual Basic 6.0 and in Visual Basic .NET functions is that the default method of passing arguments in the former is by reference, and in the latter is by value.

In Visual Basic 6.0, methods had to be named after the interface members that they implemented. In Visual Basic .NET, the Implements *implementsList* clause removes this requirement and leaves you free to name method implementations as you choose.

In Visual Basic 6.0, parameter arrays had to be of type Variant, whereas in Visual Basic .NET they can be strongly typed. In addition, the argument supplied to the parameter array parameter had to be an array, whereas in Visual Basic .NET it can also be a list of comma-separated values.

In Visual Basic 6.0, optional parameters defined using the Optional keyword could have a default value, although it was not required. When a function was called, it was usually possible to detect omitted arguments by using the IsMissing function. In Visual Basic .NET, a default value is required, and the IsMissing function is not supported.

In Visual Basic 6.0, the only way for a function to return a value to the caller was to assign the function's return value to an automatically instantiated variable whose name was the same as that of the function. Although Visual Basic .NET supports this syntax, it adds the Return statement.

See Also

Delegate Statement, Exit Statement, Function Statement, New Keyword, NotOverridable Keyword, Optional Keyword, ParamArray Keyword

Switch Function

Returns the result of evaluating an expression that is paired with the first expression in a list to evaluate to True.

Member Of

Microsoft.VisualBasic.Interaction

Syntax

```
Switch(ByVal ParamArray VarExpr() As Object) As Object
```

Element	Description
VarExpr	A parameter array containing paired lists of expressions to evaluate and the expressions that are associated with them.

Return Value

The result of evaluating the expression that is paired with the first expression in *VarExpr* to evaluate to True.

Comments

The Switch function can be seen as an extension of the IIf function. Whereas the IIf function evaluates a single expression, the Switch function can evaluate a variable number of expressions.

The expressions to be evaluated in *VarExpr* have even indexes, while their corresponding expressions have odd indexes. For example, the first expression to evaluate is at index 0, while the corresponding expression whose result is to be returned by the function if the first expression is True is found at index 1. The total number of elements in *VarExpr* must be even or an ArgumentException is thrown.

The expressions in *VarExpr* are evaluated from lowest index position to highest index position. The first expression with an even index to return True causes the Switch function to evaluate the corresponding expression with an odd index and to return the result.

Since *VarExpr* is a parameter array, it can be passed either as comma-delmited arguments or as a single array. For example, the following code fragment creates an array and passes it to the Switch function:

```
Dim parmArray() As Object = { x + 1 = y, 10, x + 2 = y, 20, x + 3 = y, 30}
Dim retVal As Integer = CInt(Switch(parmArray))
```

The following code represents an equivalent function call using comma-delimited arguments:

```
Dim retVal As Integer = CInt(Switch(x + 1 = y, x * 1, x + 2 = y, x * 2, _
                              x + 3 = y, x * 3))
```

Each expression in *VarExpr* is always evaluated. This occurs even if an expression has already evaluated to True, and even if the result of an expression is not to be returned by the function. If the expressions include method calls, this could severely degrade application performance. And each of the expressions is capable of throwing an exception when it is evaluated, making it important to handle the call to the Switch function in a Try . . . Catch block.

The elements of all expressions included in *VarExpr* must be defined as accessible at the time *VarExpr* is declared, or either a compiler error or a run-time error results.

If you import the System.Diagnostics namespace, your code may fail to compile because of a naming conflict, since System.Diagnostics includes a Switch class. In that case, either alias the System.Diagnostics namespace, as in:

```
Imports Diag = System.Diagnostics
```

or provide a fully qualified namespace path to the Switch function, as in:

```
retVal = Microsoft.VisualBasic.Switch(...
```

Example

The following code fragment illustrates the use of the Switch statement to display the access modifier for a method in the Visual Basic Strings class. A method can have any of five access modifiers: Private, Public, Friend, Protected, and Protected Friend.

```
Dim strng As Type = ass.GetType("Microsoft.VisualBasic.Strings")
For Each method As MethodInfo In strng.GetMethods(BindingFlags.DeclaredOnly _
            Or BindingFlags.Instance Or BindingFlags.Static _
            Or BindingFlags.Public Or BindingFlags.NonPublic)
    Dim access() As Object = { method.IsPublic, "Public", _
                               method.IsPrivate, "Private", _
                               method.IsFamilyAndAssembly, "Protected Friend", _
                               method.IsFamily, "Protected", _
                               method.IsAssembly, "Friend"}

    Dim outputLine As String
    outputLine = CStr(Switch(access)) & " " & method.Name
    Console.WriteLine(outputLine)
Next
```

VB6 Differences

In Visual Basic 6.0, *VarExpr* is not defined as a parameter array and therefore accepts only comma-delimited arguments. In Visual Basic .NET, an array as well as comma-delimited arguments can be passed to the function.

See Also

Choose Function, If Statement, IIf Function, Select Case Statement

SYD Function

Calculates the sum-of-years digits depreciation of an asset for a specified period.

Member Of

Microsoft.VisualBasic.Financial

Syntax

```
SYD(ByVal Cost As Double, ByVal Salvage As Double, ByVal Life As Double, _
    ByVal Period As Double) As Double
```

Element	Description
Cost	The initial cost or value of the asset.
Salvage	The value of the asset at the end of its useful life.
Life	The length of the useful life of the asset.
Period	The period for which the asset's depreciation is to be calculated.

Return Value

A Double indicating the depreciation for *Period*.

Comments

Four major depreciation methods are available: the straight-line method, which is handled by the SLN function; the single-declining balance method, which is handled by the DDB function with a value of 1 for its *Factor* argument; the double-declining balance method, which is handled by the DDB function with a value of 2 for its *Factor* argument; and the sum-of-the-years digits depreciation method, which calculates depreciation at an accelerated rate based on the sum of the digits that represent years in the useful life of the asset.

The sum-of-the-years digits can be calculated using the formula:

```
Sum = Life / 2 * ( Life + 1 )
```

or simply by summing the digits in an asset's useful life. For example, the sum-of-the-years digits of an asset whose useful life is 3 years is 6 (3 + 2 + 1).

The formula for calculating sum-of-the-years digits depreciation in any period is:

```
RemainingSumOfYears / SumOfYearsDigits * ( Cost - Salvage )
```

All three arguments to the function must be expressed as positive numbers. *Life* and *Period* must represent the same time unit. For instance, if an asset's life is measured in years, the periods over which its depreciation is measured must be expressed in years as well.

Example

The following code compares the amount of depreciation per period using the single-declining balance, double-declining balance, and sum-of-years digits depreciation methods. The asset has an initial cost of $15,000, a salvage value of $1,000, and a life of five years.

```
Public Sub Main()
   Dim life As Integer = 5
   Dim cost As Double = 15000
   Dim salvage As Double = 1000
Dim ddbal, sdbal, sydbal As Double
Console.WriteLine("Period        Single Declining        Double Declining      " & _
             "Sum-of-Years")
Console.WriteLine("                     Balance                Balance            " & _
             "Digits")
Console.WriteLine()
   For period As Integer = 1 to life
       sdbal = DDB(cost, salvage, life, period, 1)
       ddbal = DDB(cost, salvage, life, period, 2)
       sydbal = SYD(cost, salvage, life, period)
       Console.WriteLine("{0,5}.        {1,10:C}           {2,10:C}         {3,10:C}", _
                   period, sdbal, ddbal, sydbal)
   Next
End Sub
```

The output from the program is:

Period	Single Declining Balance	Double Declining Balance	Sum-of-Years Digits
1.	$3,000.00	$6,000.00	$4,666.67
2.	$2,400.00	$3,600.00	$3,733.33
3.	$1,920.00	$2,160.00	$2,800.00
4.	$1,536.00	$1,296.00	$1,866.67
5.	$1,228.80	$777.60	$933.33

See Also

DDB Function, SLN Function

SyncLock Statement

Prevents multiple threads from executing the same code block simultaneously.

Syntax

```
SyncLock lockObject
    [ statements ]
End SyncLock
```

Element	Description
lockObject	An object expression that controls access to the code block. *lockObject* must be a reference type.
statements	The statements to be executed when the lock is acquired.

Comments

The SyncLock statement implements a critical section: a block of code that can be executed only by one thread at a time. When a thread acquires the lock on the section, other threads are locked out of it until the first thread leaves it. In that way, a particular block of code in a multithreaded application can be executed serially by multiple threads.

When each thread reaches the SyncLock statement, *lockObject* is evaluated. If the thread can acquire an exclusive lock on the object returned by the expression, it enters the SyncLock block and executes *statements*. Otherwise, it suspends execution until it is able to acquire an exclusive lock on *lockObject*.

lockObject can be any arbitrary object expression; choosing a reliable lock object is up to the developer. The most secure pattern involves defining a private lock object within the class that the class instance locks. For security reasons, it is generally not a good idea for *lockObject* to be related to the object for which the lock is established. This could allow hostile, low-privilege code to obtain the lock object, create a new thread, and lock the object from that thread, thereby creating a denial-of-service attack.

lockObject can be either a shared object (to safeguard code, resources, or data that is shared among threads in all instances of a class) or an instance object (to safeguard code, resources, or data that is shared among all threads in a single class instance).

lockObject cannot be Nothing; the object must be instantiated before code within the SyncLock block is executed. In addition, while *statements* are executing, *lockObject* must remain unchanged.

Code cannot branch into *statements* from outside of the SyncLock block.

Since the SyncLock statement locks out threads while a single thread has exclusive access to the code in the SyncLock block, you may wonder how robust the statement is. In particular, in any poorly implemented scheme for preventing resource contention, the following is possible:

Thread A	Thread B
Evaluates SyncLock statement.	Performs some action.
Acquires exclusive lock.	Evaluates SyncLock statement.
Executes code in SyncLock block.	Waits for lock to be released.
Code in SyncLock block throws an exception.	Waits for lock to be released.
Thread terminates without releasing lock.	Waits for lock to be released.

In this case, the application hangs, since once thread has terminated because of an exception, while the other is waiting for the lock held by the first thread to be released. Since SyncLock doesn't allow explicit unlocking, you may suspect that this is a danger. In fact, however, it is not. As the following output from ILDasm shows, the SyncLock statement is implemented by using the .NET System.Threading.Monitor class. Its Enter method is called when entering the block, but its Exit method, which releases the lock, is called in a Finally block:

```
IL_0019:   call void [mscorlib]System.Threading.Monitor::Enter(object)
   .try
   {
IL_001e:   ldstr "{0} entered SyncLock block at {1}"
IL_0023:   ldarg.1
...
IL_0054:   leave.s IL_005d
   } // end .try
   finally
   {
IL_0056:   ldloc.0
IL_0057:   call void [mscorlib]System.Threading.Monitor::Exit(object)
IL_005c:   endfinally
   } // end handler
```

In other words, whether or not an exception is thrown, the Finally block always executes and releases the lock.

In addition to the Monitor class, which the SyncLock statement wraps, a number of other synchronization objects, including mutexes and semaphores, are available in the .NET Framework Class Library's System.Threading namespace.

Example

The example illustrates the use of the SyncLock statement to ensure that only one of a class instance's two threads is able to execute a block of code at the same time. Me (a reference to the current object) is used as the lock expression. The SyncLock block simply displays the name of the thread that is executing in the block, then causes the thread to sleep for 2000 milliseconds, or two seconds. This means that, if the lock works successfully, the second thread should be able to access the SyncLock block's code no earlier than two seconds after the first thread entered accessed it. The code is:

```
Imports System.Threading

Public Class App
   Private name As String

   Public Shared Sub Main()
      Dim mainThread As New App("MainThread")
      mainThread.MainProc()
   End Sub

   Public Sub New(name As String)
      Me.name = name
   End Sub
```

```
' Procedure for worker thread to execute
Public Sub WorkerProc()
    Thread.Sleep(100)
    Console.WriteLine("WorkerThread about to call CriticalProc procedure.")
    CriticalProc("WorkerThread")
    Console.WriteLine("WorkerThread returned from CriticalProc procedure.")
End Sub

Public Sub MainProc
    Dim workerThread As New Thread(AddressOf WorkerProc)
    workerThread.Start()
    Console.WriteLine("{0} about to call CriticalProc procedure.", Me.name)
    CriticalProc(Me.name)
    Console.WriteLine("{0} returned from CriticalProc procedure.", Me.name)
End Sub

Public Sub CriticalProc(enteringThread As String)
    Console.WriteLine("{0} entered CriticalProc at {1}", enteringThread, _
                    FormatDateTime(Date.Now, DateFormat.LongTime))
    SyncLock Me
        Console.WriteLine("{0} entered SyncLock block at {1}", enteringThread, _
                        FormatDateTime(Date.Now, DateFormat.LongTime))
        Thread.Sleep(2000)
        Console.WriteLine("{0} about to leave SyncLock block at {1}", _
                        enteringThread, _
                        FormatDateTime(Date.Now, DateFormat.LongTime))
    End SyncLock
    Console.WriteLine("{0} leaving CriticalProc at {1}", enteringThread, _
                    FormatDateTime(Date.Now, DateFormat.LongTime))
End Sub
End Class
```

The output produced by running the code is:

```
MainThread about to call CriticalProc procedure.
MainThread entered CriticalProc at 8:04:59 PM
MainThread entered SyncLock block at 8:04:59 PM
WorkerThread about to call CriticalProc procedure.
WorkerThread entered CriticalProc at 8:04:59 PM
MainThread about to leave SyncLock block at 8:05:01 PM
WorkerThread entered SyncLock block at 8:05:01 PM
MainThread leaving CriticalProc at 8:05:01 PM
MainThread returned from CriticalProc procedure.
WorkerThread about to leave SyncLock block at 8:05:03 PM
WorkerThread leaving CriticalProc at 8:05:03 PM
WorkerThread returned from CriticalProc procedure.
```

VB6 Differences

The SyncLock statement is new to Visual Basic .NET.

SystemTypeName Function

Returns the name of the .NET type that corresponds to a Visual Basic data type.

Member Of

Microsoft.VisualBasic.Information

Syntax

```
SystemTypeName(ByVal VbName As String) As String
```

Element	Description
VbName	The name of an "intrinsic" Visual Basic data type.

Return Value

A String containing the fully qualified name of the type corresponding to *VbName*.

Comments

For each of the intrinsic Visual Basic data types, the SystemTypeName function returns the string shown in the following table:

Visual Basic Data Type	SystemTypeName Return Value
Boolean	System.Boolean
Byte	System.Byte
Char	System.Char
Date	System.DateTime
Decimal	System.Decimal
Double	System.Double
Integer	System.Int32
Long	System.Int64
Object	System.Object
SByte	System.SByte
Short	System.UInt16
Single	System.Single
String	System.String
UInteger	System.UInt32
ULong	System.UInt64
UShort	System.UInt16

To determine the .NET data type of a particular variable, you can pass it to the Visual Basic TypeName function before calling the SystemTypeName function. For example:

```
Dim number As Double = 12.542
Dim sysType As String = SystemTypeName(TypeName(number))
Console.WriteLine(sysType)              ' Displays "System.Double"
```

You can also determine the .NET data type of a variable with less code, and without the namespace name included in the string, by using the GetType method, as shown in the following code:

```
Dim sysTypeName As String = number.GetType().Name
Console.WriteLine(sysTypeName)          ' Displays "System.Double"
```

If VbName is not the name of an intrinsic Visual Basic data type, the SystemTypeName function returns Nothing. This occurs under the following conditions:

- VbName is the name of a .NET type, such as Exception or ArrayList.
- VbName is the name of a type defined by the developer using the Class . . . End Class construct.
- VbName is the name of a structure defined by the developer using the Structure . . . End Structure construct.
- VbName simply does not correspond to any Visual Basic, .NET, or application type.

VB6 Differences

The SystemTypeName function is new to Visual Basic .NET.

See Also

TypeName Function, VbTypeName Function

Tab Function

Positions the insertion point for file output to a particular column when using the Print or PrintLine function.

Member Of

Microsoft.VisualBasic.FileSystem

Syntax

```
TAB( [ ByVal Column As Short ] ) As TABInfo
```

Element	Description
Column	The column number at which to output the next expression in a list. If omitted, the next expression is output at the beginning of the next print zone.

Return Value

A TabInfo structure whose Column field determines the column position at which the next expression is to be output.

Comments

The Tab function is placed between expressions in the Print, PrintLine, and WriteLine subroutines and is responsible for determining the column at which the expression that follows it is output. Attempting to use the function in any other context generates a compiler error.

The line and column on which the expression following the Tab function is output depends on the value of *Column,* the column of the current print position, and the output line width (which can be set by a call to the FileWidth subroutine):

- If *Column* is less than 1, the print position becomes the first column.

- If the current print position is greater than *Column* (that is, if the desired print position has already been passed), the print position skips to *Column* on the next output line.

- If *Column* is greater than the current print position (that is, the desired print position has not yet been reached) but less than the output line width (or if the output line width is unlimited, which is its default value), the print position advances to *Column.*

- If *Column* exceeds the output line width, the next print position is calculated using the formula:

  ```
  Column Mod width
  ```

Example

The following code uses the Tab function to align the columns in a text file that contains population data on the world's ten largest cities:

```
Public Module modMain
   Public Sub Main()
      Dim largestCities() As String = {"1,Bombay,India,12778721", _
                                       "2,Karachi,Pakistan,12207254", _
                                       "3,Delhi,India,11055365", _
                                       "4,Shanghai,China,10840516", _
                                       "5,Moscow,Russia,10375688", _
                                       "6,Seoul,Korea,10147972", _
                                       "7,Sao Paulo,Brazil,10136978", _
                                       "8,Istanbul,Turkey,10121565", _
                                       "9,Lima,Peru,8866160", _
                                       "10,Mexico City,Mexico,8548639"}
      ' Open File
      Dim fileNo As Integer = FreeFile
      Dim fileOpened As Boolean = False
      Try
         FileOpen(fileNo, ".\LargestCities.txt", OpenMode.Output)
         fileOpened = True
         ' Write data to file
         Print(fileNo, "Rank", Tab(8), "City Name", Tab(21), "Country", _
               Tab(30), "Population (est. 2005)")
         PrintLine(fileNo, "")
         PrintLine(fileNo, "")
```

```
            For Each largestCity As String In largestCities
                Dim extraSpace As Short = 0
                Dim cityInfo() As String = Split(largestCity, ",")
                extraSpace = CShort(8 - Len(cityInfo(3)))
                Print(fileNo, cityInfo(0), Tab(8), cityInfo(1), Tab(21), cityInfo(2), _
                    Tab(CShort(30 + extraSpace)), _
                    FormatNumber(cityInfo(3), 0, TriState.False, TriState.False, _
                        TriState.True))
                PrintLine(fileNo, "")
            Next
        Catch e As Exception
            Console.WriteLine(e.GetType().Name & ": " & e.Message)
        Finally
            ' Close file
            If fileOpened Then FileClose(fileNo)
        End Try
    End Sub
End Module
```

VB6 Differences

In Visual Basic 6.0, the Tab function returned an Integer indicating the column number; in Visual Basic .NET, it returns an instance of a TabInfo structure. The difference, however, is transparent, since the return value of the Tab function is not manipulated directly in code.

See Also

FileWidth Subroutine, Print, PrintLine Subroutines, SPC Function, WriteLine Subroutine

Throw Statement

Throws an exception.

Syntax

```
Throw [ expression ]
```

Element	Description
expression	An Exception object or an object derived from Exception that contains information about the exception.

Comments

If all of the information about the exception to be thrown can be provided to one of the exception object's constructors, the exception object is typically instantiated at the same time that it is called. For example, the following code instantiates and throws a FormatException if the data input by the user is not numeric:

```
Public Class UserInput
    Public Shared Function GetInteger() As Integer
        Dim inputString As String = InputBox("Enter an integer: ")
```

```
      If Not IsNumeric(inputString) Then
         Throw New FormatException("The input data is not numeric.")
      Else
         Return CInt(inputString)
      End If
   End Function
End Class
```

Ordinarily, the Throw statement requires *expression* as an argument. If Throw is used in a Catch block, however, *expression* can be omitted, in which case the Throw statement simply rethrows the current exception. All values of the current exception are preserved, including any inner exception objects stored to the current exception object. In addition, the call stack it preserved; re-throwing an exception does not change the call stack to the routine in which the exception was re-thrown.

When deciding which class of exception to throw, you can either choose an existing exception class from the .NET Framework Class Library, or you can create your own exception class. The example illustrates both approaches.

If you choose to create your own exception class, it should inherit from Exception or one of its derived classes. You can then supplement the functionality of the base class with whatever properties are needed to provide useful information about the exception.

Exceptions thrown with the Throw statement can be handled using unstructured exception handling (error handling with the On Error GoTo statement) or, preferably, with structured exception handling (error handling with Try . . . Catch . . . Finally . . . End Try blocks).

Example

The following code illustrates the use of use of the InvalidCastException class as well as the creation of a new exception class derived from Exception to throw exceptions when validating numeric data entry:

```
' Create custom exception class
Public Class InvalidNumberException
   Inherits Exception

   Dim invalidNumber As Double

   Public Sub New()
      MyBase.New("The number is not even.")
   End Sub

   Public Property Number() As Double
      Get
         Return Me.invalidNumber
      End Get
      Set
         Me.invalidNumber = Value
      End Set
   End Property
End Class
```

```
Public Class UserInput
    Public Function GetEvenNumber() As Integer
        Dim inputString As String
        Dim inputNumber As Integer

        ' Get user input
        inputString = InputBox("Enter an even number: ")
        If inputString = String.Empty Then Exit Function

        ' Throw exception if string cannot be converted to a number
        If Not IsNumeric(inputString) Then _
            Throw New InvalidCastException("Unable to convert '" & _
                                          inputString & "' to an integer")

        ' Throw exception if number is not even
        inputNumber = CInt(inputString)
        If Not inputNumber Mod 2 = 0 Then
            Dim ex As New InvalidNumberException()
            ex.Number = inputNumber
            Throw ex
        End If
        ' Return even number
        Return inputNumber
    End Function
End Class
```

VB6 Differences

The Throw statement is new to Visual Basic .NET. In Visual Basic 6.0, The Err.Raise method was used to raise errors.

See Also

Try Statement

TimeOfDay Property

Sets or gets the current time of day on the local computer.

Member Of

Microsoft.VisualBasic.DateAndTime

Syntax

```
TimeOfDay() As Date
```

Return Value

A Date value representing the time on the local system.

Comments

The date component of the Date value returned by the TimeOfDay property is set to its default or uninitialized value, which is 1/1/0001.

If the TimeOfDay property is used to set the system time, any date component of the Date Value is ignored.

Unless there's a compelling reason to do so, your application should not set the time on the user's local system.

If your application does set the local system time, it's generally a good idea to save the local system's current time beforehand, in the event that you have to restore it. The following code, for example, restores the current time in the event that an error occurs when setting the time:

```
Private Sub SetSystemTime()
    Dim originalTime As Date = TimeOfDay
    Try
        Dim timeString As String = InputBox("Enter time (hh:mm:ss): ")
        If IsDate(timeString) Then TimeOfDay = CDate(timeString)
    Catch
        Console.WriteLine("In error handler...")
        TimeOfDay = originalTime
    End Try
End Sub
```

VB6 Differences

The TimeOfDay property is new to Visual Basic .NET. It corresponds to the Time and Time$ functions, which could be used to retrieve the current system time in Visual Basic 6.0, and to the Time statement, which could be used to set the system time in Visual Basic 6.0. None of these language elements are supported by Visual Basic .NET.

See Also

DateString Property, Now Property, TimeString Property. Today Property

Timer Property

Returns the number of seconds elapsed since midnight.

Member Of

Microsoft.VisualBasic.DateAndTime

Syntax

```
Timer As Double
```

Return Value

A Double indicating the time elapsed since midnight.

Comments

The integral component of the function's return value indicates the number of whole seconds that have elapsed since midnight; the fractional component indicates the fractional portions of a second.

The Timer function is often used to time code execution in an attempt to measure application performance, as in the following code:

```
Dim startTime, endTime As Double
startTime = Timer
' perform some processing
endTime = Timer
Console.WriteLine("Elapsed time: {0} seconds", endTime - startTime)
```

Although the Timer property returns a value that appears to be accurate to the hundred-thousandths of a second, in fact its resolution depends on the system clock. On Windows XP, that means that its resolution is approximately one-hundredth of a second. In other words, an elapsed time of 1 to 9 milliseconds can appear to the Timer property to represent the same time. This means that the Timer property is at best able only to grossly measure performance.

If timing performance is important, a more accurate alternative is the Environment.TickCount property, which offers resolution of approximately one millisecond. The property returns the number of milliseconds that have elapsed since the system started. For example, the following code measures the execution time of a loop that iterates ten million times:

```
Dim starttime, endtime As Integer
starttime = Environment.TickCount
For ctr As Integer = 0 to 10000000
Next
endtime = Environment.TickCount
Console.WriteLine("Elapsed time is {0} milliseconds", endtime - starttime)
```

If timing performance is critically important, you can use the multimedia timer functions in the Win32 API. These functions have less than one microsecond accuracy. For an overview of the API, see the article "Using Timers to Evaluate Code Performance" at http://www.howlingwolfconsulting.com/PreviousArticles.html.

The .NET Framework provides Timer classes in the System.Threading, System.Windows.Forms, and System.Timers namespaces. If you import any of these and attempt to retrieve the value of the Timer property, the Visual Basic compiler will be unable to resolve your reference. You must then either alias one of the other namespaces (see the entry for the Imports Statement) or qualify the use of the Timer property with its namespace name.

See Also

Now Property

TimeSerial Function

Forms a time value out of individual time components.

Member Of

Microsoft.VisualBasic.DateAndTime

Syntax

```
TimeSerial(ByVal Hour As Integer, ByVal Minute As Integer, _
          ByVal Second As Integer) As DateTime
```

Element	Description
Hour	An integer expression from 0 through 23 representing the hour.
Minute	An integer expression from 0 through 59 representing the minute.
Second	An integer expression from 0 through 59 representing the second.

Return Value

A Date representing the specified time value, with the date set to 1/1/0001.

Comments

As a means of assigning a time, the following three statements are all equivalent:

```
Dim timeValue As Date = TimeSerial(12, 56, 03)
Dim timeValue As Date = #12:56:03#
Dim timeValue As Date = CDate("12:56:03")
```

The advantage of TimeSerial (although this is true as well of the CDate function) is that it can evaluate dynamic expressions or variables, whereas the middle assignment statement requires a literal expression.

Values of *Hour, Minute,* and *Second* that are outside of the specified range typically do not cause the function to throw an exception. Instead, either positive or negative values outside of the specified range are added to the next highest time value. For example:

```
Console.WriteLine(TimeSerial(12,-45, 15))        ' returns 11:15:15 AM
Console.WriteLine(TimeSerial(10, -32, -19))      ' returns 9:27:41 AM
Console.WriteLine(TimeSerial(23, 75, 92))        ' returns 1/2/0001 12:16:32 AM
```

In the last line of code, the sum of the excess minute value and the hour value exceeded the upper range of the hour value, which caused the date to increment by one day.

If the addition of the out-of-range time units to the date causes the date to exceed Date.MaxValue, an OverflowException is thrown. If the addition of the negative time units to the date causes the date to fall before Date.MinValue, an ArgumentOutOfRangeException is thrown.

See Also

CDate Function, DateSerial Function

TimeString Property

Gets or sets the current system time.

Member Of

Microsoft.VisualBasic.DateAndTime

Syntax

```
TimeString As String
```

Return Value

The string representation of the current system time.

Comments

The property returns the time in a string with an invariant 24-hour format of "HH:MM:SS". The format does not change even if the local system's regional settings are changed.

The property is somewhat more flexible if a time string is being assigned to it to set the time. It accepts any time that is recognized as a valid time representation by the IsDate function, which in turn means that you should call the function to validate the time string before attempting to set the TimeString property.

You should consider carefully whether it's actually necessary to set the system date.

You can instead retrieve the time from the Visual Basic TimeOfDay property. You can also retrieve it from the Date structure's Now property. Its string representation can then be formatted as you'd like by passing it to the Format function or the FormatDateTime function.

VB6 Differences

The TimeString property is new to Visual Basic .NET; it replaces the Visual Basic 6.0 Time and Time$ functions (which returned a string representation of the current system time) and the Time statement (which allowed the time to be set). None of these language elements are supported by Visual Basic .NET.

See Also

DateString Property

TimeValue Function

Converts the formatted string representation of a date or a date and time to a Date with a time value.

Member Of

Microsoft.VisualBasic.DateAndTime

Syntax

```
TimeValue(ByVal StringTime As String) As DateTime
```

Element	Description
StringTime	The string representation of a time or a date and time.

Return Value

A Date value whose time component is converted from *StringTime* and whose date component is 1/1/0001.

Comments

If *StringTime* includes a date component, TimeValue fails to include it in the returned Date value; instead, the Date value returned by the function always has a date of 1/1/0001, which represents an uninitialized date value.

Even though TimeValue discards the date component of *StringTime,* it throws an InvalidCastException if an invalid date component is present.

TimeValue is capable of converting any string for which the IsDate function returns True, and is capable of recognizing a time string expressed in any valid format.

There are a number of alternate ways to convert the string representation of a time to a Date value. Visual Basic provides one in the CDate conversion function; in fact, the CDate function is identical in operation to the DateValue function. The Date data type itself includes the shared Parse and TryParse methods, and the Convert class includes the shared ToDateTime method. There appears to be little reason to select TimeValue in preference to any of these other conversion methods.

VB6 Differences

In Visual Basic 6.0, the date component of the Date value returned by the function was set to 12/30/1899; in Visual Basic .NET, it is set to 1/1/0001.

See Also

CDate Function

Today Property

Gets or sets the date component of the system date.

Member Of

Microsoft.VisualBasic.DateAndTime

Syntax

```
Today As Date
```

Return Value

A Date value containing the date component of the current system time.

Comments

When the Today property is used to retrieve the system date, it returns the date component and sets the time component to 12:00:00 AM. When it is used to set the system date, any time component is ignored. Setting the date without setting the time, however, seems like a rather odd thing to do.

You should consider carefully whether it's actually necessary to set the system date.

Visual Basic .NET provides a number of other language elements that allows you to retrieve or set the system date and time. In addition to the Today property, these include the DateString property (sets or retrieves the system date using the string representation of a date), the Now property (retrieves the system date and time as a Date value), the TimeOfDay property (sets or retrieves the system time as a Date value), and the TimeString property (sets or retrieves the system time using the string representation of a time).

You can also retrieve the current date (with its time component set to 0:00:00) from the Today property of the DateTime structure.

VB6 Differences

The Today property is new to Visual Basic .NET.

See Also

Now Property

Trim Function

Removes both leading and trailing spaces from a string.

Member Of

Microsoft.VisualBasic.Strings

Syntax

```
Trim(ByVal str As String) As String
```

Element	Description
str	The string to be trimmed.

Return Value

str with any leading and trailing spaces removed.

Comments

If *str* has no leading or trailing spaces, the function returns *str* unchanged.

The Trim function corresponds to the parameterless Trim method of the String class. Another overload of the String.Trim method allows you to specify the character or characters to be removed.

To remove only leading spaces, using the LTrim function; to remove only trailing spaces, use the RTrim function.

VB6 Differences

Visual Basic 6.0 included a Trim$ function that returned a String, while Trim returned a Variant. In Visual Basic .NET, Trim$ is not supported, and the Trim function returns a String.

See Also

LTrim Function, RTrim Function

Try . . . Catch . . . Finally Statement

Provides a handler for runtime exceptions.

Syntax

```
Try
    [ tryStatements ]
[ Exit Try ]
...
 [ Catch [ exception As type ] [ When expression ]
    [ catchStatements ] ]
[ Exit Try ]
...
[ Finally
    [ finallyStatements ] ]
End Try
```

Element	Description
tryStatements	The block of statements for which an exception is handled by the corresponding Catch block.
Exit Try	Unconditional branching statement. The Finally block, if one is present, is executed, and then program execution continues with the statement immediately following the End Try statement. Exit Try can be placed in the Try and Catch blocks, but not in the Finally block.
Catch	The beginning of the block of statements to execute in the event an exception is thrown. An exception handler can have multiple Catch statements. Although the Catch block is optional, an exception handler must have either a Catch block or a Finally block.
exception	The name of the exception class instance as it is referenced in the exception handler. Although *exception* is optional, no information about the exception can be made available to the Catch block if it is not present.
type	The type of the exception class instance handled by this Catch block. It must be the System.Exception class or a class derived from it. If *exception* is specified, the As *type* clause must be present regardless of the setting of Option Strict or a compiler error results.
When *expression*	A filter condition that, when it evaluates to True, causes the Catch block to execute. The expression must implicitly convert to Boolean.
catchStatements	The statements to execute if the Catch block handles the exception.
Finally	The beginning of the block of statements to execute after the Try block and/or the Catch block. In other words, regardless of whether or not an exception is thrown, the Finally block always executes. The Finally block is optional, although either it or a Catch block must be present.
finallyStatements	The statements to execute before leaving the exception handler.

Comments

Only the first Catch statement to be true is executed. If multiple Catch statements are used to catch exceptions of various types, they must be ordered from most specific to most generic (or from the last derived class to the base class). This is because the evaluation of *exception* As *type* will evaluate to True if the current exception object either is or is derived from *type*. For example, consider the following code:

```
Dim sr As StreamReader
Try
    Dim fn As String = InputBox("Enter path and name of file:")
    sr = New StreamReader(fn)
    Dim text As String = sr.ReadToEnd
Catch e As Exception                ' WRONG ORDER: should follow IOException
    MsgBox("An unknown error has occurred. The text of the error message is: " & _
            vbCrLf & e.Message)
Catch e As IOException              ' WRONG ORDER: should precede Exception
    MsgBox("There was a problem opening the file. The text of the error message " & _
            " is: " & vbCrLf & e.Message)
Finally
    If Not sr Is Nothing Then
        sr.Close()
    End If
End Try
```

If the file to be opened cannot be found, the IOException handler never executes, since IOException is derived from Exception, the base class of all exception objects. Since IOException is of type Exception, the first Catch block will execute, and the condition for any subsequent Catch blocks will never be evaluated. The compiler does display a warning when this happens (BC42029, "'Catch' block never reached, because 'System.IO.IOException' inherits from 'System.Exception'.")

Assigning a local variable name to the exception class in the Catch statement by using the *exception* As *type* syntax makes the exception object's properties and methods available in the Catch block. At a minimum, any exception class instance has the following members, which are inherited from System.Exception:

- **Data property** Returns an IDictionary object providing additional information about the exception. The documentation for particular exception types should indicate whether the data property is used; most commonly, it is not. You can determine whether data has been stored to the collection with the code:

```
If ex.Data.Keys.Count > 0 Then
```

where *ex* is the local variable represent the exception object. You can iterate the individual DictionaryEntry objects in the IDictionary collection using code like the following:

```
Catch ex As Exception
    ' Data is returned by Data property
    If ex.Data.Keys.Count > 0 Then
        For Each dict As DictionaryEntry In ex.Data
            Console.WriteLine("{0}: {1}", dict.Key, dict.Value)
        Next
    End If
```

- **GetBaseException method** Returns the innermost exception object in the chain of exceptions. If there is no innermost exception, it returns Nothing.

- **HelpLink property** Returns a String containing help about the exception. It can be either a uniform resource name (URN) or uniform resource locator (URL). Its default value is String.Empty.

- **InnerException property** Often, the exception passed back to an exception handler is just one of a series handled by the called method. The InnerException property returns the Exception object that preceded the current exception and by implication caused it to be thrown. You can determine whether any inner exceptions are present and, if there are, retrieve information on all of the exceptions in the chain by using code like the following:

```
Catch ex As Exception
    If ex.InnerException IsNot Nothing Then
        Dim exc As Exception = ex
        Do While exc IsNot Nothing
            Console.WriteLine(exc.GetType.Name & ": " & exc.Message)
            exc = exc.InnerException
        Loop
    End If
```

- **Message property** Returns a String that (hopefully) provides a meaningful description of the exception.

- **Source property** Returns a String containing the name of the application or component in which the exception was thrown.

- **StackTrace property** Returns a String that depicts the call stack at the time the exception was thrown. The most recent method call appears first.

- **TargetSite property** Returns a MethodBase object containing information about the method in which the exception was thrown. You should check that the property value is not Nothing before attempting to access the MethodBase object's members.

The When *expression* filter allows a Catch block to be executed only if *expression* is True. For example, an exception handler might define two Catch blocks to handle IOExceptions, one for file-related exceptions and one for directory-related exceptions:

```
Catch e As IOException When e.Message.Contains("File")
    Console.WriteLine("File-related exception")
    ' Handle file-related exception
Catch e As IOException When e.Message.Contains("Directory")
    ' Handle directory-related exception
    Console.WriteLine("Directory-related exception")
```

If there is no Catch block that provides a handler for the type of exception that was thrown, a standard system exception dialog is displayed and the .NET runtime terminates the application. This makes it important to supplement handlers for specific exception types with a generic exception handler to catch unexpected exceptions.

Once an exception handler is defined, it remains enabled as long any statements inside the Try block remain to be executed, and even if they are not currently executing (as is the case, for instance, when a method call is made from within the Try block). If an exception occurs in a called method that does not have an exception handler, the .NET runtime searches the call stack for a method that does have an enabled exception handler and executes it. When the handler terminates, program flow continues with the statement immediately following the End Try statement. The following code illustrates this:

```
Public Class classMain
    Public Shared Sub Main()
        Try
            Dim exampleClass As New classMain
            exampleClass.ExecuteAMethod()
            Console.WriteLine("Returned from the ExecuteException call.")
        Catch e As Exception
            Console.WriteLine("In exception handler in Main().")
        End Try
        Console.WriteLine("About to exit Main().")
    End Sub

    Private Sub ExecuteAMethod()
        Console.WriteLine("About to throw an exception.")
        Throw New Exception("An unidentified exception.")
        Console.WriteLine("In ExecuteException after the exception.")
    End Sub
End Class
```

The code produces the following output:

```
About to throw an exception.
In exception handler in Main().
About to exit Main().
```

The important thing to note is that once the exception is thrown, control leaves the called method and never returns to it.

Exception handlers can be nested, so that multiple handlers are enabled at a particular time. This is common when a method call is made from within a Try block, and the called method also provides an exception handler. For example:

```
Public Class classMain
    Public Shared Sub Main()
        Try
            CallAMethod
        Catch

        Finally

        End Try
    End Sub

    Public Sub CallAMethod
        Try

        Catch
```

```
        Finally

        End Try
    End Sub
End Class
```

In this case, if an exception occurs in an inner exception handler, its Catch block is executed. If an exception occurs in its Catch block, the Try block of the next enabled error handler is executed, etc. An exception handler can be nested inside the Catch block, as follows:

```
Try
. . .
Catch
    Try
        . . .
    Catch
        . . .
    Finally
        . . .
    End Try
Finally
    . . .
End Try
```

This allows an exception handler to catch an exception thrown in the outer exception hanlder, which is a relatively common occurrence. Otherwise, if an exception in the exception handler is unhandled, the .NET runtime handles the exception just as if there were no exception handler in place.

If an exception occurs in the exception handler and there is no nested exception handler, the Finally block nevertheless executes.

The Try, Catch, and Finally blocks are all block constructs, which means that any variables defined in them are local to those blocks. This means that if you want variables to be available in more than one block, you must define it outside of the Try . . . Catch . . . Finally construct.

VB6 Differences

The Try . . . Catch . . . Finally construct is new to Visual Basic .NET. Visual Basic 6.0 supports unstructured error handling, which is still supported, although not recommended, in Visual Basic .NET.

See Also

Throw Statement

TryCast Function

Performs type conversion based on inheritance or interface implementation, but does not throw an exception if the conversion fails.

Syntax

```
TryCast(expression, type)
```

Element	Description
expression	An expression that evaluates to an instance of a value or reference type.
type	The type to which to convert *expression*.

Return Value

expression converted to *type* or Nothing if the conversion fails.

Comments

TryCast is comparable to the DirectCast function, except that rather than throwing an exception if the conversion of *expression* to an instance of *type* fails, it returns Nothing. *expression* must evaluate to an instance of a reference type object or structure instance that derives from *type* (if type is a class) or implements *type* (if type is an interface), or is a base class to *type* or an interface that *type* implants. This differs from the DirectCast function, which does not require that *expression* be a reference type. TryCast recognizes implicit inheritance relationships. You can, for instance, use TryCast to convert an ArrayList to an Object and vice versa.

Like the other Visual Basic .NET conversion functions, TryCast is implemented directly by the compiler, rather than in a .NET class library like Microsoft.VisualBasic.dll. The conversion itself can fail and cause TryCast to return Nothing for either of two reasons. The first is that the object instance and the target type are not related to each other through inheritance or interface implementation. The second is that the operation requires a narrowing conversion (a conversion from a base type to a derived type) that would result in a loss of information.

In many cases, the call to the TryCast function generates a compiler error if it is apparent at compile time that no conversion to *type* exists. Note that TryCast is not affected by the presence or absence of a defined implicit or explicit conversion operator. Although TryCast can be used for widening conversions (conversions from a derived type to a base type or from an instance of a class implementing an interface to an interface), these conversions can also be performed without using a conversion function. It is most useful for narrowing conversions (conversions from a base type to a derived type or from an interface to a type implementing that interface), particularly since, if Option Strict is on, such conversions cannot be made implicitly.

VB.NET Changes

The TryCast function is new to Visual Basic 2005.

See Also

CObj Function, CType Function, Option Strict Statement, TryCast Function

TypeName Function

Returns a String indicating the data type of a variable or expression.

Member Of

Microsoft.VisualBasic.Information

Syntax

```
TypeName(ByVal VarName As Object) As String
```

Element	Description
VarName	An expression whose data type is to be determined.

Return Value

A String indicating the data type of *VarName*.

Comments

Although the documentation focuses on *VarName* as a variable name, it can be any expression. In fact, the function can sometimes be useful in indicating the return type of an expression. For example, the code

```
Console.WriteLine(TypeName(2 + 1.34))          ' displays Double
```

indicates that the value returned when evaluating the expression is a Double.

According to the documentation, if Option Strict is off, *VarName* can be a variable of any data type except a structure. In fact, regardless of the setting of Option Strict, the TypeName function can successfully handle structures.

If *VarName* is an array, a set of parentheses are appended to the returned type name. For example, the code

```
Dim arr1 As Array = Array.CreateInstance(GetType(String), 10)
Console.WriteLine(TypeName(arr1))

Dim stringArray(10) As String
Console.Writeline(TypeName(stringArray))
```

displays the following:

```
String()
String()
```

If *VarName* is a generic type, the TypeName function correctly reports its name and generic parameters. For example:

```
Dim sl As New SortedList(Of String, String)
Console.WriteLine(TypeName(sl))
```

displays

```
SortedList(Of String,String)
```

If *VarName* is a valid object reference, the TypeName function returns the name of its runtime type. If *VarName* is a reference type that has not been assigned a valid object reference, an uninitialized array, or an uninitialized string, the TypeName function returns the string "Nothing".

Approximately the same result as a call to the TypeName function is obtained by retrieving a Type object's name by calling the *varName*.GetType().Name property. The major difference is that TypeName returns the name of an "intrinsic" Visual Basic .NET type, while the Type object's Name property returns the corresponding name of its .NET data type.

VB6 Differences

In Visual Basic 6.0, the TypeName function returned "String" if passed an uninitialized or empty string. In Visual Basic 2005, the TypeName function returns "Nothing" if passed an empty string.

See Also

VarType Function

UBound Function

Indicates the upper bound of a particular dimension of an array.

Member Of

Microsoft.VisualBasic.Information

Syntax

```
UBound(ByVal Array As System.Array, Optional ByVal Rank As Integer = 1) _
     As Integer
```

Element	Description
Array	The array whose upper bound is to be determined.
Rank	The one-based dimension whose upper bound is to be determined. If *Rank* is not specified, the function returns the upper bound for the first dimension of the array.

Return Value

The upper bound of the *Rank* dimension of the array.

Comments

The *upper bound* of an array is the index value used to access the last element of a particular dimension of the array.

Passing an uninitialized array to the UBound function throws an ArgumentNullException. Passing an invalid value for *Rank* throws a RankException.

When iterating an array, the UBound function or its .NET Framework Class Library equivalent should always be used to determine the array's upper bound. This avoids using a hard-coded value that either could be incorrect or could be subject to change.

The UBound function is equivalent to the instance GetUpperBound method of the Array class. Its syntax is:

```
GetUpperBound(ByVal dimension As Integer) As Integer
```

where *dimension* is the zero-based dimension whose upper bound is to be determined.

You should not assume that the total number of elements in an array is one greater than the value returned by the UBound function, since this assumes that the lower bound of the array is 0. Instead, you can determine the number of elements in a particular dimension using the formula

```
elements = UBound(array) - Lbound(array) + 1
```

Even better, you can call the instance GetLength method of the Array class, which returns the number of elements in a particular dimension of an array. Its syntax is:

```
array.GetLength(ByVal dimension As Integer) As Integer
```

where *dimension* is the zero-based dimension of the array whose number of elements is to be determined. The following code illustrates these two methods of determining how many elements are in a particular dimension of an array:

```
Public Sub Main()
    Dim numbers() As Decimal = {17.5d, 19.98d, 14.23d, 18.55d, 121.39d, 17.45d}
    Console.WriteLine("Number of elements in array using UBound and LBound: {0}", _
                    UBound(numbers) - LBound(numbers) + 1)       ' Displays 6
    Console.WriteLine("Number of elements in array using GetLength: {0}", _
                    numbers.GetLength(0))                        ' Displays 6
End Sub
```

Example

See the example for the LBound function.

See Also

LBound Function

UCase Function

Converts a character or the characters in a string to uppercase.

Member Of

Microsoft.VisualBasic.Strings

Syntax

```
UCase(ByVal Value As Char) As Char
```

or

```
UCase(ByVal Value As String) As String
```

Element	Description
Value	A single character or a string.

Return Value

Value whose lowercase characters are converted to uppercase.

Comments

If *Value* is a lowercase Char or a string that includes lowercase characters, they are converted to uppercase; other characters (such as white space, uppercase characters, special characters, and character representations of numbers) remain unchanged.

You can determine whether a Char or a particular character in a string is either upper- or lowercase and therefore is or is not in need of conversion by calling the shared Char.IsUpper and Char.IsLower methods. Their syntax is:

```
Char.IsLower(ByVal c As Char) As Boolean
Char.IsLower(ByVal s As String, ByVal index As Integer) As Boolean

Char.IsUpper(ByVal c As Char) As Boolean
Char.IsUpper(ByVal s As String, ByVal index As Integer) As Boolean
```

index is the position of the character in *s* whose case is to be determined.

Either the LCase or the UCase function can be used when comparing user input to a hard-coded string so that differences of casing don't affect the comparison. For example:

```
Do
    Dim userInput As String = InputBox("Enter a name, or 'exit' to quit:")
    If UCase(userInput) = "exit" Then
        Exit Do
    End If
    ' Process input
Loop
```

Note, though, that if Option Compare is set to Text, the call to the UCase function is unnecessary, since string comparisons using the equal sign are affected by the setting of Option Compare.

The .NET Framework Class Library also includes methods that allow you to convert strings or Char values to uppercase. These include the overloaded ToUpper shared method of the Char class and the overloaded ToUpper instance method of the String class. One overload of each type is functionally identical to the LCase method. The other allows you to convert to lowercase using the casing rules of a particular culture. The syntax of these overloads is:

```
Char.ToUpper(ByVal c As Char, ByVal culture As CultureInfo) As Char
string_instance.ToLower(ByVal culture As CultureInfo) As String
```

Example

See the example for the LCase function.

VB6 Differences

Visual Basic 6.0 supported two versions of the UCase function. The first, UCase$, accepted a string argument; the second, UCase, a variant argument. In Visual Basic .NET, the UCase$ function is not supported, and the UCase function can accept either a Char or a String as an argument.

See Also

Option Compare Statement, LCase Function, StrConv Function

Unicode Keyword

Used in the Declare statement to indicate that the .NET runtime should marshal all strings passed to and from external library routines as Unicode strings.

Syntax

See the syntax for the Declare statement.

Comments

Since Ansi is the default behavior, calling the Unicode versions of external library routines requires the use of the Unicode keyword or of the Auto keyword (.NET decides at runtime which version to call).

Unicode corresponds to setting the CharSet property of the DllImport attribute to CharSet.Unicode.

If the Unicode keyword is used, the Declare statement must exactly specify the name of the external DLL routine to be called either in the Lib clause or in the body of the Declare statement itself. Calling a routine that has a mangled name only by its unmangled alias (that is, by its general name, without the "A" or "W" suffix to indicate the Ansi or wide-character version of the routine) produces a runtime exception in Visual Basic .NET. This differs from the behavior of C#, in which the ExactSpelling property of the DllImport attribute is False by default so that the .NET runtime first attempts to locate a mangled version of a Unicode function (such as MessageBoxW), followed by an unmangled version (such as MessageBox).

There tends to be a good deal of confusion about the use of the Unicode keyword. In particular, it does not allow you to call Ansi versions of functions and seamlessly handle Unicode/Ansi string conversion.

Example

The code example consists of two short routines. The first is a standard call to the Unicode versions of two functions in the Win32 API, GetSystemDirectory and MessageBox. In both cases, the Alias clause specifies the mangled name of the function as it exists in the DLL. The following code uses the Declare statement very much like the previous versions of Visual Basic and corresponds directly to the examples for the Ansi keyword:

```
Public Module UnicodeTest

    Public Declare Unicode Function MessageBox Lib "User32.dll" _
        Alias "MessageBoxW" _
        (ByVal hWnd As IntPtr, ByVal lpText As String, _
        byVal lpCaption As String, ByVal uType As UShort) As Short

    Private Declare Unicode Function GetSystemDirectory Lib "kernel32.dll" _
        Alias "GetSystemDirectoryW" _
        (ByVal lpBuffer As String, ByVal nSize As Integer) As Integer
```

```
    Private Const MB_OK As Integer = &H0&
    Private Const MAX_LEN As Integer = 256

    Public Sub Main()
        Dim caption As String = "System Directory"
        Dim message As String
        Dim buffer As String = Space(MAX_LEN)
        Dim retChars As Integer

        retChars = GetSystemDirectory(buffer, Len(buffer))
        message = Left(buffer, retChars)

        MessageBox(Nothing, message, caption, MB_OK)
    End Sub
End Module
```

In contrast, the following code uses the <DllImport> attribute rather than the Declare statement to provide the .NET runtime with details about the two Win32 routines, and sets the attribute's ExactSpelling property to False so that .NET dynamically resolves the precise name of the function to be called at runtime:

```
Imports System.Runtime.InteropServices
Imports System.Text

Public Module UnicodeTest

    <DllImport("User32.dll", EntryPoint:="MessageBox", ExactSpelling:=False, _
            CharSet:=CharSet.Unicode)> _
    Private Function MessageBox (ByVal hWnd As IntPtr, ByVal lpText As String, _
        byVal lpCaption As String, ByVal uType As UShort) As Short
    End Function

    <DllImport("Kernel32.dll", EntryPoint:="GetSystemDirectory", ExactSpelling:=False, _
            CharSet:=CharSet.Unicode)> _
    Private Function GetSystemDirectory(ByVal lpBuffer As StringBuilder, _
            ByVal nSize As Integer) As Integer
    End Function

    Const MB_OK As Integer = &H0
    Const MAX_PATH As Integer = 260

    Public Sub Main()
        Dim caption As String = "System Directory"
        Dim buffer As New StringBuilder(MAX_PATH)

        GetSystemDirectory(buffer, MAX_PATH)
        MessageBox(Nothing, buffer.ToString(), caption, MB_OK)
    End Sub
End Module
```

VB6 Differences

The Unicode keyword is new to Visual Basic .NET.

See Also

Ansi Keyword, Auto Keyword, Declare Statement

Unlock Subroutine

Unlocks the part of a file locked using the Lock subroutine.

Member Of

Microsoft.VisualBasic.FileSystem

Syntax

```
Unlock(ByVal FileNumber As Integer)
```

or

```
Unlock(ByVal FileNumber As Integer, ByVal Record As Long)
```

or

```
Unlock(ByVal FileNumber As Integer, ByVal FromRecord As Long, _
     ByVal ToRecord As Long)
```

Element	Description
FileNumber	The file number used in the call to the FileOpen subroutine.
Record	The number of a single record or byte to unlock.
FromRecord	The number of the first record or byte to unlock.
ToRecord	The number of the last record or byte to unlock.

Comments

Unlock is one of a series of related file input and output functions that works with a file number used when opening a file with the FileOpen subroutine. Unlock is for use in a networked or multiuser environment and allows another process from to access a file, record, or block of data that was previously locked by a call to the Lock subroutine.

Each call to Lock should have a corresponding call to Unlock once your code is finished with the locked object. This means that, if you are calling Lock within a Try block, you should call Unlock in the Finally block to ensure that it executes in the event of an error.

There must be a one-to-one correlation between calls to Lock and Unlock. You can't lock an entire random file, for example, and then release the locks by calling Unlock one record at a time. If a call to Unlock does not correspond to a preceding call to Lock, .NET throws an IOException with the rather confusing error message, "The segment is already unlocked."

The Unlock subroutine can be called with the *Record* argument for binary and random files (but not sequential files). The Unlock subroutine can be called with the FromRecord and ToRecord arguments for binary and random files (but not sequential files). *FromRecord* and *ToRecord* designate the range of records to unlock for random files and the range of bytes to unlock for binary files.

The numbering for records and bytes starts at 1, not 0.

VB6 Differences

In Visual Basic 6.0, Unlock was implemented as a statement that could include the # symbol before *FileNumber.* In Visual Basic .NET, it is implemented as a subroutine, and this syntax is not supported.

In Visual Basic 6.0, the version of the Unlock statement that specified *FromRecord* and *ToRecord* separated them with the To keyword. In Visual Basic .NET, a comma is used as the separator between arguments, and this syntax is not supported.

See Also

FileOpen Subroutine, Lock Subroutine

Using Statement

Provides for an unmanaged system resource to be released.

Syntax

```
Using { resourceList / resourceExpression }
[ statements ]
End Using
```

Element	Description
resourceList	One or more system resources controlled by the Using block. Multiple resources are separated by commas.
resourceExpression	A variable or expression that refers to the resource the Using block controls. If *resourceExpression* is used, the resource must be acquired outside of the using block.
statements	The code to execute in the Using block.
End Using	Terminates the Using block and releases the resources it controls.

Each *resource* in *resourceList* has the syntax:

```
resourceName As New resourceType [ ( [ arglist ] ) ]
```

or

```
resourceName As resourceType = resourceExpression
```

Element	Description
resourceName	A variable that refers to the system resource.
resourceType	The data type of the resource. A resource handled by the Using block must implement the IDisposable interface.

Element	Description
arglist	The list of arguments to be passed to the *resourceType* class constructor. Multiple arguments are separated by commas.
resourceExpression	A variable or expression that refers to the system resource that the using block will handle. It is instantiated outside of the Using block and must implement the IDisposable interface.

Comments

Either resourceList or resourceExpression is required.

Because system resources such as ADO.NET connection objects or system drawing objects are expensive, it is a good idea to dispose of them as soon as your code has finished using them. In addition, it is also important to make sure that they are properly disposed of in the event an exception is thrown. Typically, without the Using statement, this is done in a Try . . . Catch . . . Finally block with code like the following:

```
Public Sub Main()
    Dim conn As New OleDbConnection("Provider=Microsoft.Jet.OLEDB.4.0;" & _
                "Data Source=C:\Program Files\Databases\grocertogo.mdb")
        Dim cmd As New OleDbCommand
        Dim dr As OleDbDataReader

        Try
            conn.Open
            cmd.CommandText = "Select * From Customers"
            cmd.CommandType = CommandType.Text
            cmd.Connection = conn
            dr = cmd.ExecuteReader()
            If dr.HasRows Then
                Do While dr.Read()
                    ' Get first and last name of customer
                    Console.WriteLine(CStr(dr.Item(1)) & " " & CStr(dr.Item(2)))
                Loop
            Else
                Console.WriteLine("The table has no rows.")
            End If
        Catch e As Exception
            Console.WriteLine(e.GetType().Name & ": " & e.Message)
        Finally
            Dim disp As IDisposable
            If typeof conn is IDisposable Then
                disp = conn
                disp.Dispose()
            End If
        End Try
    End Sub
```

The connection object is opened in the Try block, but the Finally block is responsible for calling its Dispose method to release the resource. The Using statement is a convenience feature that translates code within the Using block into this Try . . . Finally construct.

Example

The following code illustrates the use of the Using statement to manage an ADO.NET
OleDbConnection object. The code is the equivalent of the code implemented with a Try . . .
Catch . . . Finally block in the Comments section.

```
Public Sub Main()
    Dim conn As New OleDbConnection("Provider=Microsoft.Jet.OLEDB.4.0;" & _
                    "Data Source=C:\Program Files\Databases\grocertogo.mdb")
    Dim cmd As New OleDbCommand
    Dim dr As OleDbDataReader

    Using conn
        conn.Open
        cmd.CommandText = "Select * From Customers"
        cmd.CommandType = CommandType.Text
        cmd.Connection = conn
        dr = cmd.ExecuteReader()
        If dr.HasRows Then
            Do While dr.Read()
                ' Get first and last name of customer
                Console.WriteLine(CStr(dr.Item(1)) & " " & CStr(dr.Item(2)))
            Loop
        Else
            Console.WriteLine("The table has no rows.")
        End If
    End Using
End Sub
```

VB.NET Changes

The Using statement is new to Visual Basic 2005.

See Also

Try . . . Catch . . . Finally Statement

Val Function

Converts the string representation of a number to a numeric value.

Member Of

Microsoft.VisualBasic.Conversion

Syntax

The Val function is overloaded as follows:

```
Val(ByVal InputStr As String) As Double

Val(ByVal Expression As Object) As Double

Val(ByVal Expression As Char) As Integer
```

Element	Description
Expression or *InputStr*	Any valid String expression, Char expression, or Object expression capable of conversion to a String.

Return Value

Expression or *InputStr* converted to a number.

Comments

If *Expression* is a Char, Val returns its numeric representation if it is capable of conversion to a number; otherwise, it returns 0. For example:

```
Console.WriteLine(Val("c"c))          ' returns 0
Console.WriteLine(Val("1"c))          ' returns 1
Console.WriteLine(Val("-"c))          ' returns 0
Console.WriteLine(Val("9"c))          ' returns 9
```

If *Expression* is an Object, it must be capable of conversion to a String in order to be handled by the Val function.

If Expression is a String or an Object converted to a String, Val parses the string on a character-by-character basis and converts characters to numbers until it either runs out of characters to parse or it encounters a character it cannot convert. It then returns the number whose string representation it was able to convert. If it was unable to convert any of the string, it returns 0. For example:

```
Console.WriteLine(Val("913.3"))       ' returns 913.3
Console.WriteLine(Val("131AC57"))     ' returns 131
Console.WriteLine(Val("-132.23"))     ' returns -132.23
Console.WriteLine(Val("+1203.22"))    ' returns 1203.22
Console.WriteLine(Val("A0545"))       ' returns 0
```

Unlike the numeric conversion functions available either in the Visual Basic language or in the .NET Framework, the Val function does not recognize currency symbols or thousands separators. The only non-numeric symbols that it recognizes are the positive sign, the negative sign, and the thousands separator. If any other symbols are present, the function returns 0. For example:

```
Console.WriteLine(Val("$1034.51"))    ' returns 0
Console.WriteLine(Val("1,032.54"))    ' returns 0
```

Because of its idiosyncrasies as a numeric conversion function, there is no real point in calling the IsNumeric function to determine whether an expression can be converted to a number before calling Val. Many expressions that can be converted to numbers cannot be converted by Val, while many others that cannot be converted to numbers can be partially converted by Val.

Val is a legacy function that Visual Basic inherited from Basic. If you want to convert an expression to a numeric value, use one of those conversion functions. They perform accurately and allow you to control the destination numeric data type.

See Also

Str Function

VarType Function

Returns a member of the VariantType enumeration indicating the data type of an expression.

Member Of

Microsoft.VisualBasic.Information

Syntax

```
VarType(ByVal VarName As Object) As VariantType
```

Element	Description
VarName	A variable name or expression.

Return Value

A member of the VariantType enumeration indicating the data type of *VarName*.

Comments

The function returns one or more members of the VariantType enumeration shown in the following table:

VariantType Member	Constant Value	Comments
Array	8192	Can be combined with another member to reflect the array type (e.g., 8195 represents an integer array).
Boolean	11	Visual Basic Boolean or .NET System.Boolean.
Byte	17	Visual Basic Byte or .NET System.Byte.
Char	18	Visual Basic Char or .NET System.Char.
Currency	6	A Visual Basic 6.0 or COM Cuurrency data type.
Date	7	Visual Basic Date or .NET DateTime.
Decimal	14	Visual Basic Decimal or .NET System.Decimal.
Double	5	Visual Basic Double or .NET System.Double.
Empty	0	Visual Basic .NET Empty.
Error	10	An exception object derived from System.Exception.
Integer	3	A Visual Basic Integer or .NET System.Int32.
Long	20	A Visual Basic Long or .NET System.Int64.
Null	1	A Visual Basic 6.0 Null data type.

VariantType Member	Constant Value	Comments
Object	9	Any class instance or nstance of a generic type, as well as a Visual Basic or .NET Object expression, an uninitialized array, and an object reference that is Nothing.
Short	2	A Visual Basic Short or .NET System.Int16.
ntblSingle	4	A Visual Basic Single or .NET System.Single.
String	8	A Visual Basic String or .NET System.String.
UserDefinedType	36	The data types new to Visual Basic 2005 (SByte, UShort, UInteger, ULong), as well as a structure instance.
Variant	12	A Visual Basic 6.0 or COM Cuurrency data type.

Although the documentation focuses on *VarName* as a variable name, it can be any expression. In fact, the function can sometimes be useful in indicating the return type of an expression. For example, the code

```
Console.WriteLine(Vartype(Math.Pi * 3 ^ 2).ToString)
```

indicates that the value returned when evaluating the expression is a Double.

The function has not been updated to handle the new data types in Visual Basic 2005. Instead, for the SByte, UInteger, ULong, and UShort types, the function returns VariantType.UserDefinedType.

Typically, you can convert the VariantType value returned by the VarType function to a string by calling the VariantType enumeration member's ToString value. However, since the VariantType enumeration is not marked with the Flags attribute, this does not work if the expression is an array, since its value is the sum of VariantType.Array and another value. The string representations of the VariantType member names can be extracted using code like the following:

```
Dim arr(10) As String
Dim varEnum As VariantType = VarType(arr)
If (varEnum And VariantType.Array) = VariantType.Array Then
   Console.Write("Array, ")
   varEnum = varEnum And (Not VariantType.Array)
   Console.WriteLine(varEnum.ToString)
End If
```

VarType is a compatibility function that is increasingly showing signs of its age. Calling an object or structure instance's GetType method and working with the Type object that it returns provides a far more flexible method of determining the type of a variable or expression at runtime.

See Also

TypeName Function

vbFixedArray Attribute

Indicates the number of elements in an array in cases where a fixed-length array is needed.

Namespace

Microsoft.VisualBasic

Syntax

```
<vbFixedArrayAttribute(ByVal UpperBound1 As Integer)>
```

or

```
<vbFixedArrayAttribute(ByVal UpperBound1 As Integer, _
                       ByVal UpperBound2 As Integer)>
```

Element	Description
UpperBound1	The upper bound of the array's first dimension.
UpperBound2	The upper bound of the array's second dimension.

Comments

The vbFixedArray attribute is used with the Dim statement to define a fixed array in a structure or in module-level code. Most commonly, it is used with a Dim statement when defining a field in a Structure . . . End Structure construct.

The attribute correspond to the Microsoft.VisualBasic.vbFixedArrayAttribute class, which has the following members:

Member	Description
Bounds property	Read-only. Returns an Integer array. The index of each element in the array indicates the dimension whose bounds that member specifies. The value of this property is set by the constructor, which is executed when the attribute is used in code.
Length	Read-only. Returns an integer indicating the number of elements in the array.

The vbFixedArray attribute is designed to address a limitation of the Visual Basic Structure construct, which does not permit the upper bound of an array to be specified in its field definitions. For example, the code

```
Structure ContactHistory
    Dim ID As Integer
    Dim Dates(3) As Date              ' invalid
    Dim Comments(3) As String         ' invalid
End Structure
```

generates compiler error BC31043 ("Arrays declared as structure members cannot be declared with an initial size.") This differs from arrays in Visual Basic 6.0 user-defined types and also makes it difficult to use the structure with language elements that expect structures with fixed-length arrays, such as some file input/output functions. Instead, the vbFixedArray attribute can be used in this situation to define the upper bound of the array:

```
Structure ContactHistory
    Dim ID As Integer
    <vbFixedArray(3)> Dim Dates() As Date
    <vbFixedArray(3)> Dim Comments() As String
End Structure
```

The vbFixedArray attribute does not actually fix the size of the array or prevent its bounds from being changed. For example, client code can still modify the upper bounds of the arrays in the ContactHistory structure despite the use of the vbFixedArray attribute, as the following code shows:

```
Dim contact As ContactHistory
ReDim contact.Dates(10)
Console.WriteLine(UBound(contact.Dates, 1))          ' Displays 10
```

Instead, the attribute is informational and can be used by the compiler to allocate storage space for an array when its size is otherwise unknown. This means that, in order for the attribute to work as intended, you must initialize the array as defined by the vbFixedArray attribute and subsequently not resize it with the ReDim statement.

The vbFixedArray attribute can also be used to define the size of arrays used in calls to Win32 API functions that expect fixed-length arrays.

Example

The following example uses the vbFixedArray and vbFixedString attributes to define an array and string fields that are written to a file using the FilePut subroutine and read from the file using the FileGet subroutine.

```
Structure ContactHistory
    Dim ID As Integer
    <vbFixedArray(2)> Dim Dates() As Date
    <vbFixedString(50)> Dim Comment0 As String
    <vbFixedString(50)> Dim Comment1 As String
    <vbFixedString(50)> Dim Comment2 As String
End Structure

Public Module modMain
    Private Const filename As String = ".\ContactHistory.dat"
    Private Const array_bound As Integer = 2

    Public Sub Main()
        ' Initialize structure and provide with contact information
        Dim contact(1) As ContactHistory
        ReDim contact(0).Dates(array_bound)
        contact(0).ID = 1
        contact(0).Dates(0) = #03/28/2006#
        contact(0).Comment0 = ("Met potential customer at a trade show.")
        contact(0).Comment0 = contact(0).Comment0.PadRight(50)
        contact(0).Dates(1) = #04/12/2006#
        contact(0).Comment1 = ("Followed up with a telephone call.").Padright(50)
        contact(0).Dates(2) = #04/18/2006#
```

```
    contact(0).Comment2 = ("Customer placed first order.").Padright(50)
    ReDim contact(1).Dates(array_bound)
    contact(1).ID = 2
    contact(1).Dates(0) = #03/30/2006#
    contact(1).Comment0 = ("Met with customer to discuss fall in sales.")
    contact(1).Comment0 = contact(1).Comment0.PadRight(50)
    contact(1).Dates(1) = #04/01/2006#
    contact(1).Comment1 = ("Drafted proposal to regain account.").PadRight(50)
    contact(1).Dates(2) = #04/03/2006#
    contact(1).Comment2 = ("Discussed proposal with customer representatives.")
    contact(1).Comment2 = contact(1).Comment2.PadRight(50)


    ' Write to a file
    Dim fileNo As Integer = FreeFile()
    Dim fileOpened As Boolean = False
    Try
        FileOpen(fileNo, filename, OpenMode.Binary)
        fileOpened = True
        For Each record As ContactHistory In contact
            FilePut(fileNo, record)
        Next
    Catch e As Exception
        Console.WriteLine(e.GetType().Name & ": " & e.Message)
    Finally
        If fileOpened Then FileClose(fileNo)
        fileOpened = False
    End Try


    ' Read data
    fileNo = FreeFile()
    Try
        FileOpen(fileNo, filename, OpenMode.Binary)
        fileOpened = True
        Dim rcd As ContactHistory
        ReDim rcd.Dates(array_bound)
        Do While Not EOF(fileNo)
            FileGet(fileno, rcd)
            Console.WriteLine("Customer ID: {0}", rcd.ID)
            Console.WriteLine("   On {0}: {1}", FormatDateTime(rcd.Dates(0)), _
                            rcd.Comment0)
        Loop
    Catch e As Exception
        Console.WriteLine(e.GetType().Name & ": " & e.Message)
    Finally
        If fileOpened Then FileClose(fileNo)
    End Try
    End Sub
End Module
```

VB6 Differences

The vbFixedArray attribute is new to Visual Basic .NET; Visual Basic 6.0 did not support attributes.

See Also

Dim Statement, vbFixedString Attribute

vbFixedString Attribute

Indicates that a string should be treated as if its length is fixed.

Namespace

Microsoft.VisualBasic.vbFixedStringAttribute

Syntax

```
<vbFixedString(ByVal length As Integer)>
```

Element	Description
length	The length of the string.

Comments

The vbFixedString attribute is used with the Dim statement to indicate that a non-local string should be treated as a fixed-length string.

The attribute correspond to the Microsoft.VisualBasic.vbFixedStringAttribute class, which has only a single non-inherited member:

Member	Description
Length	Read-only. Indicates the length of the fixed-length string. Its value is supplied by the vbFixedString attribute argument.

Most commonly, the vbFixedString attribute is used to define a fixed-length string inside a structure so that the data from a structure instance can subsequently be written to and read from a file. It is also used to define fixed-length strings that serve as string buffers when calling Win32 API functions. In both cases, the precise length of the string must be known at compile time so that the resources needed to handle the data can be properly allocated.

The vbFixedString attribute does not actually fix the size of a string or prevent modification to its length. For example, the following code:

```
Public Module Fixed
    <vbFixedString(10)> Dim tenChars As String

    Public Sub Main()
        tenChars = "This string is longer than ten characters."
        Console.WriteLine("The string's length is {0}. Its content is:", _
                        tenChars.Length)
        Console.WriteLine("   {0}", tenChars)
    End Sub
End Module
```

produces the following output, which indicates that the length of a string variable can be changed:

```
The string's length is 42. Its content is:
    This string is longer than ten characters.
```

Instead, the attribute is informational, and can be used by the compiler to allocate storage space for a string when its size might otherwise be unknown. This means that, in order for the attribute to work as intended, you must ensure that you do not change the length of string.

Example

See the example for the vbFixedArray attribute.

VB6 Differences

The vbFixedString attribute is new to Visual Basic .NET; Visual Basic 6.0 did not support attributes. Instead, fixed-length strings were defined in Visual Basic 6.0 using syntax like:

```
Dim fixedString As String * stringLength
```

In Visual Basic .NET, however, this syntax is not supported.

See Also

Dim Statement, vbFixedArray Attribute

VbTypeName Function

Returns the name of the "intrinsic" Visual Basic data type that corresponds to a type in .NET's Common Type System.

Member Of

Microsoft.VisualBasic.Information

Syntax

```
VbTypeName(ByVal UrtName As String) As String
```

Element	Description
UrtName	The name of a .NET data type. It can include the type's namespace.

Return Value

A String indicating the Visual Basic type name for *UrtName*.

Comments

The following table lists the names of .NET data types and the names of their corresponding Visual Basic .NET data types:

.NET Data Type	VbTypeName Return Value
Boolean, System.Boolean	Boolean
Byte, System.Byte	Byte
Char, System.Char	Char
DateTime, System.DateTime	Date
Decimal, System.Decimal	Decimal
Double, System.Double	Double
Int16, System.Int16	Short
Int32, System.Int32	Integer
Int64, System.Int64	Long
Object, System.Object	Object
SByte, System.SByte	SByte
Single, System.Single	Single
String, System.String	String
UInt16, System.UInt16	UShort
UInt32, System.UInt32	UInteger
UInt64, System.UInt64	ULong

If *UrtName* is a .NET type that does not correspond to an intrinsic Visual Basic .NET data type, or if *UrtName* cannot be identified as a .NET type, the function returns Nothing.

You can determine whether a particular variable corresponds to an intrinsic Visual Basic .NET data type by using code like the following:

```
Dim title As String = "All Is Quiet on the Western Front"
Console.WriteLine(VbTypeName(title.GetType().Name))    ' Displays "String"
```

VB6 Differences

The VbTypeName function is new to Visual Basic .NET.

See Also

SystemTypeName Function, TypeName Function

Weekday Function

Returns an Integer whose value represents the day of the week.

Member Of

Microsoft.VisualBasic.DateAndTime

Syntax

```
Weekday(ByVal DateValue As DateTime, _
        Optional ByVal DayOfWeek As FirstDayOfWeek = FirstDayOfWeek.Sunday _
) As Integer
```

Element	Description
DateValue	The date whose position in the week you wish to determine.
DayOfWeek	A FirstDayOfWeek constant indicating which day begins the week.

Return Value

An Integer ranging from 1 to 7 indicating the ordinal position of *DateValue* in the week.

Comments

The function determines the ordinal position of *DateValue* in the week in which *DateValue* falls. A value of 1 indicates that DateValue falls on the first day of the week, a 2 indicates that it falls on the second day of the week, etc.

The *DayOfWeek* argument specifies which day begins the week. Possible values are FirstDayOfWeek.System (use the first day of the week as specified in the system's regional settings), FirstDayOfWeek.Sunday (the default value), FirstDayOfWeek.Monday, FirstDayOfWeek.Tuesday, FirstDayOfWeek.Wednesday, FirstDayOfWeek.Thursday, FirstDayOfWeek.Friday, and FirstDayOfWeek.Saturday.

If you use the Weekday function to determine the day on which a particular date falls, the function's return value is interpreted in relationship to it. For example, a value of 1 indicates that *DateValue* falls on the *DayOfWeek*, 2 indicates that it falls on the day after the DayOfWeek, etc. The Weekday function uses the calendar defined by the local system's regional settings.

An ArgumentException is thrown if the *DayOfWeek* argument is outside the range of a valid member of the FirstDayOfWeek enumeration.

Example

If a work week runs from Monday through Friday, you can use the Workday function to determine whether a particular holiday falls during the work week as follows:

```
Dim holiday As Date = #01/01/2006#
If Weekday(holiday, FirstDayOfWeek.Monday) <= 5 Then
   Console.WriteLine("The holiday on {0}, is during the work week.", _
                    FormatDateTime(holiday, DateFormat.LongDate))
Else
   Console.WriteLine("The holiday on {0}, occurs during the weekend.", _
                    FormatDateTime(holiday, DateFormat.LongDate))
End If
```

See Also

WeekdayName Function

WeekdayName Function

Indicates the name of a weekday.

Member Of

Microsoft.VisualBasic.DateAndTime

Syntax

```
WeekdayName(ByVal Weekday As Integer, _
    Optional ByVal Abbreviate As Boolean = False, _
    Optional ByVal FirstDayOfWeekValue As FirstDayOfWeek = FirstDayOfWeek.System _
) As String
```

Element	Description
Weekday	An integer indicating the ordinal position of the weekday.
Abbreviate	A Boolean value indicating whether the weekday name should be abbreviated. Its default value is False.
FirstDayOfWeekValue	A FirstDayOfWeek constant indicating which day begins the week. If not specified, the first day of the week is defined by the local system's regional settings.

Return Value

The name of the day of the week.

Comments

The WeekdayName function is designed to work with the Weekday function. The value returned by the Weekday function can be supplied as the *Weekday* argument of the WeekdayName function. When used in this way, the WeekdayName function returns the name of the day corresponding to a particular date. For example, the code call

```
Dim birthday As Date = #07/28/1993#
Console.WriteLine(WeekdayName(Weekday(birthday), True))
```

returns "Wed", indicating that the date fell on a Wednesday.

The *DayOfWeek* argument specifies which day begins the week. Possible values are FirstDayOfWeek.System (use the first day of the week as specified in the system's regional settings), FirstDayOfWeek.Sunday (the default value), FirstDayOfWeek.Monday, FirstDayOfWeek.Tuesday, FirstDayOfWeek.Wednesday, FirstDayOfWeek.Thursday, FirstDayOfWeek.Friday, and FirstDayOfWeek.Saturday.

An ArgumentException is thrown if the *DayOfWeek* argument is outside the range of a valid member of the FirstDayOfWeek enumeration.

Example

The Russian Revolution of 1905 began with a massacre in front of the Winter Palace on January 9. However, at the time, Russia used the Julian rather than the Gregorian calendar. We can still calculate the day of the week on which the event occurred using the following code:

```
Dim historicalDate As New DateTime(1905, 1, 9, New JulianCalendar())
Dim dayOfWeek As Integer = Weekday(historicalDate, FirstDayOfWeek.System)
Console.WriteLine(WeekdayName(dayOfWeek, False, FirstDayOfWeek.System))
```

The function returns Sunday, indicating that the event occurred on a Sunday.

See Also

MonthName Function, Weekday Function

While . . . End While Construct

Executes a loop until a condition becomes False.

Syntax

```
While condition
    [ statements ]
    [ Continue While ]
    [ Exit While ]
    [ statements ]
End While
```

Element	Description
condition	An expression that evaluates to True or False.
statements	Statements to execute while *condition* is True.
Continue While	Causes program flow to return to the beginning of the While construct.
Exit While	Causes program flow to immediately exit the While construct.

Comments

While . . . End While evaluates *condition*. If *condition* is False at the outset, the loop never executes. If it is True, *condition* is evaluated again each time at the beginning of the loop, and execution proceeds to the statement after the End While statement once it is False.

The While . . . End While construct is identical in operation to the Do While . . . Loop construct, which is one of the four looping structure that can be built with the Do statement.

The Exit While statement causes an unconditional transfer of control from the loop. When Exit While is encountered, program flow jumps to the first statement immediately after the End While statement.

The Continue statement causes an unconditional transfer of control to the beginning of the loop, which in turn causes *condition* to be re-evaluated.

There can be multiple Exit While and Continue While statements within the body of a loop. Typically, they are statements within If . . . End If or Select Case constructs that redirect program flow if some condition is True or False.

Once program flow enters the While loop, some code within the body of the loop must either change *condition* from True to False or cause program flow to leave the loop. Most commonly, the value of *condition* changes.

VB.NET Changes

The Continue While statement is new to Visual Basic 2005.

VB6 Differences

Instead of End While, the Visual Basic 6.0 keyword that marked the end of the While construct was Wend.

In Visual Basic 6.0, the Exit While statement is not supported.

See Also

Do Statement

Widening Keyword

Used with the Operator statement to indicate that a custom type conversion operation defined with CType is a widening operation that can be handled automatically by the .NET runtime.

Syntax

```
Public Shared Widening Operator CType(operand1) [ As type ]
    [ statements ]
    [ statements ]
    Return returnvalue
    [ statements ]
End Operator
```

Element	Description
operand1	The name and type of the instance whose conversion the Operator statement defines. *operand1* has the general syntax: [**ByVal**] operandName [**As** operandType] where *operandName* is the name by which the instance is referred in *statements*, and *operandType* is its data type. *operandType* must be the type of the class or structure in which the Operator statement is contained. If Option Strict is on, *operandType* is required; otherwise, it is optional.
type	The type to which *operand1* is to be converted.
returnvalue	An instance of *operand1* converted to *type* that is to be returned to the caller.

For the complete syntax, see the entry for the Operator Statement.

Comments

Widening conversions involve converting from one type to a less restrictive type so that data loss will not occur. For example, a conversion from an Integer (a 32-bit signed integral value) to a Long (a 64-bit signed integral value) involves no possibility of data loss, since the range of the former is entirely a subset of the latter. Similarly, a conversion of a derived type to a base type is a narrowing conversion. Regardless of the setting of Option Strict, the compiler will attempt to perform narrowing conversions implicitly if they are not handled explicitly.

The Operator statement with the Widening keyword is used to define conversions of instances of classes or structures to other types. The Operator statement always defines a shared procedure.

The Return statement must be used to return a value to the caller.

When the CType conversion function is called to perform the conversion, an instance of *operand1* is supplied as an argument to the CType function's first parameter (the instance to be converted), and *type* is supplied as its second argument (the destination type).

Example

See the example for the Narrowing keyword.

VB.NET Changes

The Widening keyword is new to Visual Basic 2005.

Visual Basic 2005 is the first version of Visual Basic to support custom conversion operators.

See Also

Narrowing Keyword, Operator Statement

With . . . End With Construct

Executes a series of statements using a common reference to a class or structure instance.

Syntax

```
With object
    [ statements ]
End With
```

Element	Description
object	An instance of a class or structure whose members are can be accessed without using a qualified object reference in *statements*.
statements	The body of statements to execute that do not have to use a qualified object reference to access the members of *object*.

Comments

The With . . . End With construct allows you to designate an object whose members you wish to access, and then allows you to access those members without having to provide an object reference. With is used when a block of code focuses exclusively or almost exclusively on working with the fields, properties, and methods of an object.

In the With block, any reference to a member of *object* does not have to be qualified with the name of object. Instead, it is indicated simply by a period. For example the following code uses the With construct to access the properties of a Form object without having to repeatedly reference the object variable:

```
Dim frm as New Form
With frm
    .BackColor = Color.Gray
    .ForeColor = Color.Red
    .Text = "The With Statement"
    .Enabled = True
    .Topmost = True
    .MinimizeBox = False
    .ShowDialog()
End With
```

The With . . . End With construct is not a program flow structure. It simply makes it possible to refer to an object's members without having to qualify each member with its object name. It provides a kind of shorthand for the following code, which is equivalent to the code in the preceding comment:

```
Dim frm as New Form
frm.BackColor = Color.Gray
frm.ForeColor = Color.Red
frm.Text = "The With Statement"
frm.Enabled = True
frm.Topmost = True
frm.MinimizeBox = False
frm.ShowDialog()
```

Not every statement in *statements* has to refer to a member of object. For example, the following code uses the With statement to avoid having to provide qualified references to a Form object, but it also uses qualified references to a Font object in the With construct:

```
Dim frm as New Form
With frm
    .BackColor = Color.Gray
    .ForeColor = Color.Red
    Dim fnt As Font = .Font
    MsgBox(fnt.Name)
    .Text = "The With Statement"
    .Enabled = True
    .Topmost = True
    .MinimizeBox = False
    .ShowDialog()
End With
```

With statements can be nested. All unqualified references in the outer With block must refer to a member of the outer object, while all unqualified references in the inner With block must refer to a member of the inner object. For example:

```
Private Sub Form1_Load(ByVal sender As System.Object, _
                       ByVal e As System.EventArgs) Handles MyBase.Load
    With Me
        .BackColor = Color.Gray
        .ForeColor = Color.Red
        .Text = "The With Statement"
        .Enabled = True
        .TopMost = True
        .MinimizeBox = False
        For Each ctrl As Control In .Controls
            With ctrl
                .BackColor = SystemColors.Window
                .AutoSize = False
                .Cursor = Cursors.Hand
            End With
        Next
    End With
End Sub
```

However, any reference in the inner With construct to the object of the outer With construct must be qualified.

You cannot reassign the value of *object* within the With block. This can only be done outside of the With block. You also cannot transfer control from the outside to the inside of a With construct, nor can you transfer control from inside a With construct to outside of the construct before all the code in the construct has executed.

WithEvents Keyword

Used with the Dim statement to indicate that a variable can handle events raised by a class instance.

Syntax

See the syntax for the Dim statement.

Comments

The variable defined in the statement that uses the WithEvents keyword must be a reference type. In other words, events raised by structures cannot be handled by variables defined using WithEvents.

The WithEvents keyword cannot be used in a local variable definition. Any variable that receives event notifications must have module-level scope. The WithEvents keyword also cannot be used in an array declaration, nor can it be used to declare an object variable of type Object.

Along with the WithEvents keyword to indicate that a variable is to receive event notifications, you must define an event handler using the Handles keyword.

If the object instance that corresponds to a variable declared using the WithEvents keyword does not raise events, a compiler error results.

Example

See the example for the Handles Keyword.

See Also

Dim Statement, Event Statement, Handles Keyword

Write, WriteLine Subroutines

Writes data to a sequential file.

Member Of

Microsoft.VisualBasic.FileSystem

Syntax

```
Write(ByVal FileNumber As Integer, ByVal ParamArray Output As Object)
```

or

```
WriteLine(ByVal FileNumber As Integer, ByVal ParamArray Output() As Object)
```

Element	Description
FileNumber	The file number used in the call to the FileOpen subroutine.
Output	An array or a comma-delimited list of data to be written to the file.

Comments

The Write and WriteLine subroutines are members of the series of related file input and output functions that work with the file number used when opening a file with the FileOpen subroutine.

Write and WriteLine write formatted data to a sequential file, and delimit each item of data written with a comma. The input routines typically used to read from files written with the Write and WriteLine subroutines are the Input subroutine and the LineInput function.

Write writes all of *Output* on a single line. In contrast, WriteLine adds a linefeed, but only after all the elements in *Output* have been written to the file. If *Output* contains multiple elements, they all appear on a single line and are delimited with commas.

Output is a parameter array, which means that it can be specified as either a comma-delimited set of arguments or an array. For example, the following calls to the WriteLine subroutine are equivalent, each writing a date, a Boolean, a string, and a numeric value:

```
Dim output() As Object = { Date.Now, True, "Comment", 12.14}
WriteLine(fn, output)

WriteLine(fn, Date.Now, True, "Comment", 12.14)
```

Output can include one or more of the following:

- A numeric value. However, *Output* cannot include any of the "new" Visual Basic integral data types (SByte, UInteger, ULong, or UShort) or an ArgumentException is thrown. Localized decimal separators are replaced by the period.

- A Boolean value, which appears as either #TRUE# or #FALSE#.

- A Date value, which formatted as #2005-12-20 02:38:20#.
- A Char value, which is not formatted.
- A String value, which is delimited with quotation marks.

Output is actually optional. If it is omitted or is Nothing, the Write subroutine outputs a single comma to the file, while the WriteLine subroutine outputs a comma followed by a linefeed character combination.

You should call the FileClose subroutine when you have finished writing to the file.

Write and WriteLine are "compatibility" functions that are part of legacy Visual Basic code.

Example

The following code uses the WriteLine subroutine to write check information to a file:

```
Public Module Checking
    Private Const filename As String = ".\CheckFile.dat"

    Public Sub Main()
        Dim fn As Integer = FreeFile
        Dim fileOpened As Boolean
        Try
            FileOpen(fn, filename, OpenMode.Append)
            fileOpened = True
            ' Write check data in Check number, date, payee, amount format
            WriteLine(fn, 1603, Date.Now, "Ace Plumbing", 253.52)
            WriteLine(fn, 1604, Date.Now, "My Corner Grocery", 64.29)
            WriteLine(fn, 1605, Date.Now, "Books, Books, and More Books", 32.19)
        Catch e As Exception
            Console.WriteLine(e.GetType().Name & ": " & e.Message)
        Finally
            If fileOpened Then FileClose(fn)
        End Try
    End Sub
End Module
```

The output file appears as follows after the program has executed:

```
1603,#2005-12-20 02:55:03#,"Ace Plumbing",253.52
1604,#2005-12-20 02:55:03#,"My Corner Grocery",64.29
1605,#2005-12-20 02:55:03#,"Books, Books, and More Books",32.19
```

VB6 Differences

In Visual Basic 6.0, the Write statement allowed an optional # symbol to precede *FileNumber*. In Visual Basic .NET, this syntax is not supported.

In Visual Basic 6.0, *Output* had to be a comma-delimited list of values. In Visual Basic .NET, it can also be an array.

See Also

FileOpen Subroutine, Print, PrintLine Subroutines

WriteOnly Keyword

Used in a Property statement to indicate that the value of the property can be set but not retrieved.

Syntax

See the syntax for the Property statement.

Comments

Write-only properties are far less common than either read-write or read-only properties. They are typically used to allow sensitive information, such as passwords, social security numbers, or credit card numbers, to be set but not viewed.

VB6 Differences

The WriteOnly keyword is new to Visual Basic .NET. In Visual Basic 6.0, a write-only property was indicated by the absence of a Property Get construct.

See Also

Property Statement, ReadOnly Keyword

Year Function

Extracts the year from a given date value.

Member Of

Microsoft.VisualBasic.DateAndTime

Syntax

```
Year(ByVal DateValue As Date) As Integer
```

Element	Description
DateValue	A Date value whose year is to be extracted.

Return Value

An Integer ranging from 1 to 9999 indicating the year of *DateValue*.

Comments

If Option Strict is off, the compiler automatically converts a string representation of a date to a Date value before calling the Year function. To ensure that the string can be successfully converted, you can call the IsDate function beforehand.

The DatePart function can also be used to extract the year component of a time value. For example, the following two function calls return identical values:

```
Console.WriteLine(Year(Date.Now))
```

```
Console.WriteLine(DatePart(DateInterval.Yesr, Date.Now))
```

The Date data type also includes a Year property that extracts the year component of its Date instance. For example:

```
Dim currentYear As Integer = Date.Now.Year
```

See Also
Day Function, Month Function

CHAPTER

My Namespace Reference

The My Namespace, which is new to Visual Basic .NET 2005, provides a set of classes and their members that are designed to accomplish two purposes:

- To make selected portions of the framework easier to use. Much of the Computer class, which allows programmatic access to hardware and system software available on the local system, is of this character.

- To provide convenient access to project or application resources. For example, the My.Resources class, which makes string and other resources easily available from program code, and the My.WebServices class, which makes web services to which a project has added a reference available, attempt to accomplish this goal.

The My namespace is designed to be extensible. Adding new classes in the My namespace is simply a matter of creating a new class whose namespace name is My, declaring the members you want to make available, and making the compiled class library available to your project. However, many of the existing classes in the My namespace—including the Application, Computer, Settings, and User classes—are designed to be extensible. Developing namespace extensions for Visual Basic 2005, however, is beyond the scope of this reference.

The following sections provide a quick reference to the classes and members of the My namespace.

Application Class

The My.Application class is available in Windows client applications. It includes a number of shared methods that provide information about the application and permit access to the application's log. It corresponds to the Microsoft.VisualBasic.ApplicationServices.ApplicationBase class in Microsoft.VisualBasic.dll.

ApplicationContext Property

Returns the application context for the current thread of a Windows forms application.

```
My.Application.ApplicationContext As System.Windows.Forms.ApplicationContext
```

The property is available only in Windows forms applications.

The ApplicationContext object returned by the property provides both contextual information about the current thread and a set of methods. Its members follow.

Dispose Method
Releases the resources used by the application context.

```
My.Application.ApplicationContext.Dispose()
My.Application.ApplicationContext.Dispose(disposing As Boolean)
```

ExitThread Method
Terminates the current thread's message loop, closes all windows on the thread, and terminates the thread.

```
My.Application.ApplicationContext.ExitThread()
```

MainForm Property
Gets or sets the main application form.

```
My.Application.ApplicationContext.MainForm As Form
```

Tag Property
Gets or sets an object that contains supplementary data about the application context.

```
My.Application.ApplicationContext.Tag As Object
```

ChangeCulture Method
Changes the culture of the current thread.

```
My.Application.ChangeCulture(ByVal cultureName As String)
```

cultureName follows the RFC 1766 standard, in which a culture name takes the form *<languagecode2>-<country/regioncode2>*, in which *languagecode2* is a two-letter language code and *country/regioncode2* is a two-letter country/region code. For example, en-us is the culture name for English in the United States of America, and fr-fr is the culture name for French in France. For example:

```
Dim amount As Decimal = 12.23d
My.Application.ChangeCulture("fr-fr")
Console.WriteLine(FormatCurrency(amount))
```

The ChangeCulture method is equivalent to setting the current thread object's CuttentCulture property with a CultureInfo object initialized with the *cultureName* string.

ChangeUICulture Method
Changes the culture that the current thread uses for retrieving culture-specific resources.

```
My.Application.ChangeUICulture(ByVal cultureName As String)
```

cultureName follows the RFC 1766 standard, which is described in the entry for the ChangeCulture method.

The ChangeUICulture method is equivalent to assigning a CultureInfo object initialized with the cultureName string to the current thread object's CurrentUICulture property.

CommandLineArgs Property

Returns a string collection consisting of command-line arguments passed to the application when it was launched.

```
My.Application.CommandLineArgs As ReadOnlyCollection(Of String)
```

Each member of the ReadOnlyCollection consists of an argument that follows the name of the executable. An argument is interpreted as a single string delimited by quotation marks, or as a string that is delimited from surrounding arguments by a space. The following code iterates the collection returned by the CommandLineArgs property to display each argument to the console:

```
For Each arg As String In My.Application.CommandLineArgs
    Console.WriteLine(arg)
Next
```

The CommandLineArgs property differs from the Command function, which returns a single string containing all command-line arguments.

Culture Property

Returns a CultureInfo object representing the cultural settings used by the current thread.

```
My.Application.Culture As System.Globalization.CultureInfo
```

Retrieving the value of the Culture property is equivalent to the following code:

```
Dim culture As CultureInfo = Thread.CurrentThread.CurrentCulture
```

Deployment Property

Returns an ApplicationDeployment object, which is used to support click-once deployment and on-demand downloads of files.

```
My.Application.Deployment As System.Deployment.Application.ApplicationDeployment
```

Instantiating an ApplicationDeployment instance in your code requires that a reference to the System.Deployment.dll assembly be added to a project. You can then instantiate the ApplicationDeployment object as follows:

```
Dim deployment As ApplicationDeployment = My.Application.Deployment
```

DoEvents Method

```
My.Application.DoEvents()
```

The DoEvents method is the equivalent of the Visual Basic 6.0 DoEvents function.

GetEnvironmentVariable Method

Retrieves the value of a named environment variable.

```
My.Application.GetEnvironmentVariable(ByVal name As String) As String
```

where *name* is the case-insensitive name of an environment variable. The method returns the value of the environment variable. However, if *name* does not exist in the environment table, the method throws an ArgumentException.

The System.Environment class in the .NET Framework has a similar shared GetEnvironmentVariable method. One of its overloads is identical to the Visual Basic method, while the second allows you to specify the specific environment table from which to retrieve the variable's value. The Environment class also has a shared GetEnvironmentVariables method that returns an IDictionary object containing DictionaryEntry objects, each of which represents an environment variable and its value.

Info Property

Returns a Microsoft.VisualBasic.AplicationServices.AssemblyInfo object that provides information about the application's assembly.

```
My.Application.Info As AssemblyInfo
```

The members of the AssemblyInfo class follow.

AssemblyName Property

Returns a String representing the name of the assembly. It can be set on the Application tab of the project's Properties dialog in Visual Studio.

CompanyName Property

Returns a String containing the name of the company associated with the application. By default, Visual Studio sets it to String.Empty. It can be set using the Assembly Information dialog, which is available by selecting the Assembly Information button on the Application tab of the project's Properties dialog.

Copyright Property

Returns a String containing the copyright notice associated with the application. By default, Visual Studio sets it to "Copyright © <currentYear>". It can be changed using the Assembly Information dialog, which is available by selecting the Assembly Information button on the Application tab of the project's Properties dialog.

Description Property

Returns a String that describes the application. By default, Visual Studio sets it to String.Empty. It can be set using the Assembly Information dialog, which is available by selecting the Assembly Information button on the Application tab of the project's Properties dialog.

DirectoryPath Property

Returns a String containing the path and name of the application directory.

LoadedAssemblies Property

Returns a read-only collection of Assembly objects representing the assemblies loaded by the application.

ProductName Property

Returns a String containing the application's product name. By default, Visual Studio sets it to the name of the project. It can be set using the Assembly Information dialog, which is available by selecting the Assembly Information button on the Application tab of the project's Properties dialog.

StackTrace Property

Returns a String containing current stack trace information, similar to the information returned by the StackTrace property of an Exception object when an exception is thrown.

Title Property

Returns a String containing the title associated with the application. By default, Visual Studio sets it to the name of the project. It can be set using the Assembly Information dialog, which is available by selecting the Assembly Information button on the Application tab of the project's Properties dialog.

Trademark Property

Returns a String containing the trademark notice associated with the application. By default, Visual Studio sets it to String.Empty. It can be set using the Assembly Information dialog, which is available by selecting the Assembly Information button on the Application tab of the project's Properties dialog.

Version Property

Returns a System.Version object containing version information for the assembly. By default, Visual Studio sets it to 1.0.0.0. It can be set using the Assembly Information dialog, which is available by selecting the Assembly Information button on the Application tab of the project's Properties dialog.

WorkingSet Property

Returns a Long with the amount of physical memory mapped to the process context.

IsNetworkDeployed Property

Returns a Boolean indicating whether the application was deployed from a network using ClickOnce.

```
My.Application.IsNetworkDeployed As Boolean
```

The IsNetworkDeployed property wraps the shared IsNetworkDeployed property of the System.Deployment.Application.ApplicationDeployment class.

Log Property

Returns a Log object that allows information to be written to application logs from a client application.

```
My.Application.Log As Microsoft.VisualBasic.Logging.Log
```

The name and location of the application's log file can be found using the code:

```
Dim logFile As String = My.Application.Log.DefaultFileLogWriter.FullLogFileName
```

The members of the Log class follow.

DefaultFileLogWriter Property

Returns the FileLogTraceListener object that represents the listener to which log output is sent.

```
My.Application.Log.DefaultFileLogWriter As FileLogTraceListener
```

You can determine the name and location of the application's log file with the following code:

```
Dim logFile As String = My.Application.Log.DefaultFileLogWriter.FullLogFileName
```

TraceSource Property

Returns the TraceSource object that allows trace messages to be written.

```
My.Application.Log.TraceSource As TraceSource
```

WriteEntry Method

Writes a message to the application's log listeners. The method has the following overloads:

```
Sub WriteEntry(message As String)
Sub WriteEntry(message As String, severity As TraceEventType)
Sub WriteEntry(message As String, severity As TraceEventType, id As Integer)
```

message is the text to be written to the log. *severity* is a member of the TraceEventType enumeration indicating the message's severity or purpose; common values are TraceEventType.Information (which is the default value), TraceEventType.Warning, TraceEventType.Error, and TraceEventType.Critical). *id* is an arbitrary identifier of the log entry; if omitted, its value is determined by the value of the *severity* argument.

WriteException Method

Writes exception information to the application's log listeners. The method has the following overloads:

```
Sub WriteException(ex As Exception)
Sub WriteException(ex As Exception, severity As TraceEventType, _
                   additionalInfo As String)
Sub WriteException(ex As Exception, severity As TraceEventType, _
                   additionalInfo As String, id As Integer)
```

exception is the Exception object whose Message property is to be written to the log. *severity* is a member of the TraceEventType enumeration indicating the message's severity or purpose; its default value is TraceEventType.Error, indicating a recoverable error. *additionalInfo* provides additional information about the exception. *id* is an arbitrary identifier of the log entry; if omitted, its value is determined by the value of the *severity* argument. The WriteException method is typically called from a Catch block.

Main Method

Provides the application entry point for a Windows forms application. The method launches the application's main form, as defined by the MainForm property of the My.Application .ApplicationContext object.

```
My.Application.Main(args() As String)
```

where *args* is a parameter array containing command-line arguments that are passed to the application on the command line or by the My.Application.Run method. This method is available only in Windows applications.

MinimumSplashScreenDisplayTime Property

Gets or sets the minimum amount of time in milliseconds during which a splash screen is displayed.

```
My.Application.MinimumSplashScreenDisplayTime As Integer
```

If program initialization completes in less time than the value defined by the MinimumSplashScreenDisplayTime property, the splash screen continues to be displayed until the minimum time has elapsed. The setting has no effect if program initialization takes longer than the minimum amount of time specified by the property. This property is available only in Windows forms applications.

NetworkAvailabilityChanged Event

Fired when the network availability changes.

```
MyApplication.NetworkAvailabilityChanged(sender As Object, _
                              e As NetworkAvailabilityEventArgs)
```

sender is the object that fired the event. The NetworkAvailabilityEventArgs class has one member that it does not inherit from System.EventArgs: the IsAvailable property, which indicates the current status of the network.

The event is available only from Windows forms applications. The event handler can be created and edited in Visual Studio by selecting the Application tab of the project's Properties dialog and clicking the View Application Events button, which opens the ApplicationEvents.vb file.

OpenForms Property

Returns a collection of all open forms in a Windows application.

```
My.Application.OpenForms As System.Windows.Forms.FormCollection
```

You can retrieve forms from the collection either by zero-based ordinal position or by form name. The FormCollection returned by the OpenForms property differs from the forms stored in the My.Forms object, since the latter includes all forms defined in a Windows application. The FormCollection returned by the OpenForms property corresponds to the collection returned by the global Forms property in Visual Basic 6.0.

The OpenForms property is available only in Windows applications.

Run Method

Sets up and starts the Visual Basic Application object.

```
My.Application.Run(commandLine As String)
```

commandLine consists of any command-line arguments or switches to be passed to the application.

SaveMySettingsOnExit Property

Gets or sets a value indicating whether the application saves user settings on exit.

```
My.Application.SaveMySettingsOnExit As Boolean
```

By default, its value is True; any user settings are saved on exit, and an explicit call to the My.Settings.Save method is not necessary. The particular settings to be saved are defined by the user-scoped properties in the My.Settings object. The property is available only for Windows forms applications. All other applications that make use of the My.Settings object and want to save settings must call the My.Settings.Save method directly.

Shutdown Event

Fired when the application shuts down.

```
My.Application.Shutdown(sender As Object, e As EventArgs)
```

The event is available only from Windows forms applications. The event handler can be created and edited in Visual Studio by selecting the Application tab of the project's Properties dialog and clicking the View Application Events button, which opens the ApplicationEvents.vb file.

SplashScreen Property

Gets or sets the application's splash screen.

```
My.Application.SplashScreen As Form
```

The property is available only in Windows forms applications.

Startup Event

Fired when the application starts.

```
My.Application.Startup(sender As Object, e As StartupEventHandler)
```

sender is the object that fired the event. The StartupEventArgs class has two members that it does not inherit from System.EventArgs: Cancel, which indicates whether application startup should be canceled, and CommandLine, which returns a ReadOnlyCollection(Of String) containing the command-line arguments with which the application was launched.

The event is available only from Windows forms applications. The event handler can be created and edited in Visual Studio by selecting the Application tab of the project's Properties dialog and clicking the View Application Events button, which opens the ApplicationEvents.vb file.

StartupNextInstance Event

Fired when an attempt is made to launch a second instance of a running single-instance application.

```
My.Application.StartupNextInstance(sender As Object, _
                              e As StartupNextInstanceEventArgs)
```

sender is the object that fired the event. The StartupNextInstanceEventArgs class has two members that it does not inherit from System.EventArgs: the BringToForeground property, which indicates whether the first application instance should be brought to the foreground when the event handler exists; and the CommandLine property, which returns a ReadOnlyCollection(Of String) containing the command-line arguments with which the second instance of the application was launched.

The event is available only from Windows forms applications. The event handler can be created and edited in Visual Studio by selecting the Application tab of the project's Properties dialog and clicking the View Application Events button, which opens the ApplicationEvents.vb file.

UICulture Property

Returns a System.Globalization.CultureInfo object representing the culture of the current thread.

```
My.Application.UICulture As System.Globalization.UICulture
```

Retrieving the property value is equivalent to retrieving the value of a Thread object's CurrentUICulture property. The CurrentUICulture property of a Thread object is read-write, however, while the CurrentUICulture property of the My.Application object is read-only.

UnhandledException Event

Fired when an exception is not caught by an event handler.

```
My.Application.UnhandledExceptionEvent(sender As Object, _
                                 e As UnhandledExceptionEventArgs)
```

sender is the object that fired the event. The UnhandledExceptionEventArgs class has two members that it does not inherit from System.EventArgs: the Exception property, which returns the unhandled exception that was thrown; and ExitApplication, which indicates whether the application should exit when the event handler has completed execution.

The event is available only from Windows forms applications. The event handler can be created and edited in Visual Studio by selecting the Application tab of the project's Properties dialog and clicking the View Application Events button, which opens the ApplicationEvents.vb file.

Computer Class

The My.Computer class represents the hardware and software resources available on the local computer. For the most part, the functionality that My.Computer makes available is implemented in the .NET Framework Class Library; the My.Computer class serves as a wrapper that makes access to the functionality in the .NET class library easier or more convenient.

The My.Computer class has the following members.

Audio Property

Returns a Microsoft.VisualBasic.Devices.Audio object that allows control of a computer's sound system.

```
My.Computer.Audio As Microsoft.VisualBasic.Devices.Audio
```

The members of the Audio class follow.

Play Method

Plays a .wav file. The method has the following overloads:

```
My.Computer.Audio.Play(location As String)
My.Computer.Audio.Play(data As Byte(), playMode As AudioPlayMode)
My.Computer.Audio.Play(stream As Stream, playMode As AudioPlayMode)
My.Computer.Audio.Play(location As String, playMode As AudioPlayMode)
```

where *location* is the filename of the sound file, along with its optional path, *data* is a Byte array that contains the sound file, *stream* is a System.IO.Stream object that provides the file's contents, and *playMode* is a member of the AudioPlayMode enumeration that plays the .wav file asynchronously (AudioPlayMode.Background), synchronously (AudioPlayMode.WaitToComplete), or asynchronously and repeatedly (AudioPlayMode.BackgroundLoop).

PlaySystemSound Method

Plays a system sound. Its syntax is:

```
My.Computer.Audio.PlaySystemSound(systemSound As System.Media.SystemSound)
```

where *systemSound* is a SystemSound object returned by one of the five shared properties (Asterisk, Beep, Exclamation, Hand, and Question) of the System.Media.SystemSounds class. For example, the following code plays the Exclamation sound:

```
My.Computer.Audio.PlaySystemSound(SystemSounds.Exclamation)
```

System sounds are defined by the Sound and Audio Devices applet in the Control Panel.

Stop Method

Stops a sound playing in the background. Its syntax is:

```
My.Computer.Audio.Stop()
```

Stop works only for sounds played by the Play method, and only if they are played in the background (with a *playMode* value of AudioPlayMode.Background or AudioPlayMode.BackgroundLoop).

Clipboard Property

Returns a Microsoft.VisualBasic.MyServices.ClipboardProxy object that allows programmatic access to the Clipboard.

```
My.Computer.Clipboard As Microsoft.VisualBasic.MyServices.ClipboardProxy
```

The ClipboardProxy class includes the following members.

Clear Method

Clears the contents of the Clipboard. Its syntax is:

```
My.Computer.Clipboard.Clear()
```

ContainsAudio Method

Indicates whether the Clipboard contains WaveAudio data (data from a .wav file). Its syntax is:

```
My.Computer.Clipboard.ContainsAudio() As Boolean
```

ContainsData Method

Indicates whether the Clipboard contains data that is in a particular format or that can be converted to a particular format. Its syntax is:

```
My.Computer.Clipboard.ContainsData(format As String) As Boolean
```

where *format* is a predefined string returned by one of the shared fields of the System.Windows .Forms.DataFormats class that indicates the desired format. For example, DataFormats fields include Bitmap, CommaSeparatedValue, Dib, Dif, EnhancedMetafile, FileDrop, and Html, among many others.

ContainsFileDropList Method

Indicates whether data on the Clipboard is in the FileDrop format or can be converted to the FileDrop format.

```
My.Computer.Clipboard.ContainsFileDropList() As Boolean
```

The FileDropList format is used to represent a file dragged during drag-and-drop operations.

ContainsImage Method

Indicates whether the data on the Clipboard is or can be converted to a bitmap.

```
My.Computer.Clipboard.ContainsImage() As Boolean
```

ContainsText Method

Indicates whether there is text on the Clipboard.

```
My.Computer.Clipboard.ContainsText() As Boolean
My.Computer.Clipboard.ContainsText(format As TextDataFormat)
```

where *format* is a member of the TextDataFormat enumeration that defines the kind of text. Possible values are TextDataFormat.CommaSeparatedValue, TextDataFormat.Html, TextDataFormat.Rtf, TextDataFormat.Text (ANSI text), and TextDataFormat.UnicodeText.

GetAudioStream Method

Retrieves audio data from the Clipboard. Its syntax is:

```
My.Computer.Clipboard.GetAudioStream() As Stream
```

GetData Method

Retrieves data in a specified format from the Clipboard. Its syntax is:

```
My.Computer.Clipboard.GetData(format As String) As Object
```

where *format* is a predefined string returned by one of the shared fields of the System.Windows .Forms.DataFormats class that indicates the desired format. For example, DataFormats fields include Bitmap, CommaSeparatedValue, Dib, Dif, EnhancedMetafile, FileDrop, and Html, among many others.

GetDataObject Method

Retrieves the data currently on the Clipboard. Its syntax is:

```
My.Computer.Clipboard.GetDataObject() As System.Windows.Forms.IDataObject
```

If no data is on the Clipboard, the method returns Nothing. Since the method returns the contents of the Clipboard regardless of its format, the members of the IDataObject interface allow you to determine what type of data was on the Clipboard and to manipulate it. The most common implementation of IDataObject is the System.Windows.Forms.DataObject class. Once you've retrieved the Clipboard data, you can do the following:

- Call the GetFormats method to retrieve an array of formats in which the data is available. The method is overloaded; a parameterless method returns all formats in which data is available, while a method with a Boolean parameter named *autoConvert* specifies whether the returned array should include all available formats (the default value) or only those in which data is actually stored.

- Call the overloaded GetDataPresent method to determine whether a particular format is available. One overload has a single argument, *format,* that is a predefined string returned by one of the shared fields of the System.Windows.Forms.DataFormats class. A second has a single argument, *format,* that is a Type object representing the type of data. A third overload has string argument, *format,* and a Boolean, *autoConvert,* that indicates whether the function should return True if data is stored on the Clipboard in *format* or can be converted to *format,* or only if it is actually stored on the Clipboard in *format.*

- Retrieve data from the Clipboard by calling the GetData method. The method has three overloads that parallel those of the GetDataPresent method.

GetFileDropList Method

Retrieves a collection of filenames involved in drag-and-drop operations from the Clipboard. Its syntax is:

```
My.Computer.Clipboard.GetFileDropList() As _
            System.Collections.Specialized.StringCollection
```

If there is no data in FileDropList format on the Clipboard, the method returns Nothing. The number of items in the StringCollection object returned by the method is available from its Count property. The collection can be iterated using For Each or For Each . . . Next, and its data can be retrieved by its ordinal position in the collection by using the Item property.

GetImage Method

Retrieves an image from the Clipboard. Its syntax is:

```
My.Computer.Clipboard.GetImage() As System.Drawing.lmage
```

If an image is not on the Clipboard, the method returns Nothing.

GetText Method

Retrieves text from the Clipboard. Its syntax is:

```
My.Computer.Clipboard.GetText() As String
My.Computer.Clipboard.GetText(format As As System.Windows.Forms.TextDataFormat) _
                     As String
```

where *format* is a member of the TextDataFormat enumeration that defines the kind of text. Possible values are TextDataFormat.CommaSeparatedValue, TextDataFormat.Html, TextDataFormat.Rtf, TextDataFormat.Text (ANSI text), and TextDataFormat.UnicodeText. If there is no text data on the Clipboard, the first overload returns Nothing. If there is no data in *format* on the Clipboard, the second overload returns Nothing.

SetAudio Method

Writes audio data to the Clipboard. Its syntax is:

```
My.Computer.Clipboard.SetAudio(audioBytes As Byte())
My.Computer.Clipboard.SetAudio(audioStream As System.IO.Stream)
```

where *audioBytes* is a Byte array containing the waveform data, and *audioStream* is a stream containing the waveform data.

SetData Method

Writes data to the Clipboard. Its syntax is:

```
My.Computer.Clipboard.SetFormat(format As String, data As Object)
```

format is a string specifying the data format; it can be a predefined string returned by one of the shared fields of the System.Windows.Forms.DataFormats class that indicates the desired format, or it can specify a custom format. *data* contains the data to be written to the Clipboard.

SetDataObject Method

Writes data to the Clipboard using a DataObject. Its syntax is:

```
My.Computer.Clipboard.SetDataObject(data As System.Windows.Forms.DataObject)
```

where *data* is a DataObject class instance containing the data to be written to the Clipboard. For example, the following code uses a DataObject instance to write the string "This data belongs on the Clipboard." to the Clipboard, and then retrieves it using the GetText method:

```
Imports System.Windows.Forms

Public Module Clipbrd
    Public Sub Main()
        ' Define string to store and to retreive data
        Dim stringToWrite As String = "This data belongs on the Clipboard."
        Dim stringToRead As String
        ' Clear Clipboard before writing data
        My.Computer.Clipboard.Clear()
        ' Assign string to data object and place on Clipboard
        Dim data As DataObject = New DataObject(DataFormats.Text, stringToWrite)
        My.Computer.Clipboard.SetDataObject(data)

        ' Retrieve data from Clipboard
        If My.Computer.Clipboard.ContainsText() Then
            stringToRead = My.Computer.Clipboard.GetText()
            Console.WriteLine("The text on the Clipboard: {0}", stringToRead)
        Else
            Console.WriteLine("There is no text on the Clipboard.")
        End If
    End Sub
End Module
```

SetFileDropList Method
Writes a collection of strings containing filenames to the Clipboard. Its syntax is:

```
My.Computer.Clipboard.SetFileDropList( _
            filePaths As System.Collections.Specialized.StringCollection)
```

where *filePaths* is a string collection containing the paths and filenames of files. Strings can be added to the StringCollection object by calling its Add method, which has a single parameter, the string value to be added to the collection.

SetImage Method
Writes an image to the Clipboard. Its syntax is:

```
My.Computer.Clipboard.SetImage(image As System.Drawing.Image)
```

where *image* is a Bitmap object to be written to the Clipboard.

SetText Method
Writes text to the Clipboard. The method is overloaded as follows:

```
My.Computer.Clipboard.SetText(text As String)
My.Computer.Clipboard.SetText(text As String, _
                        format As System.Windows.Forms.TextDataFormat)
```

where *text* is the text data to be placed on the Clipboard, and *format* is a member of the TextDataFormat enumeration that specifies the format of the text. Possible values of *format* are TextDataFormat.CommaSeparatedValue, TextDataFormat.Html, TextDataFormat.Rtf, TextDataFormat.Text (ANSI text), and TextDataFormat.UnicodeText (the default value).

Clock Property

Returns a Microsoft.VisualBasic.Devices.Clock object that provides information on the system time and Universal Coordinated Time.

```
My.Computer.Clock As Microsoft.VisualBasic.Devices.Clock
```

The Clock class includes the following properties.

GmtTime Property

Returns a Date value that expresses the local system's date and time as Universal Coordinated Time (or Greenwich Mean Time).

```
My.Computer.Clock.GmtTime As Date
```

LocalTime Property

Returns a Date value that expresses the local system's date and time.

```
My.Computer.Clock.LocalTime As Date
```

TickCount Property

Returns the millisecond count from the system timer.

```
My.Computer.Clock.TickCount As Integer
```

The TickCount property returns the number of milliseconds that have elapsed since the system last booted or the TickCount value was last reinitialized. (When the value of the TickCount property reaches Integer.MaxValue, it is reset to Integer.MinValue.)

FileSystem Property

Returns a Microsoft.VisualBasic.MyServices.FileSystemProxy object that represents the file system on the local system.

```
My.Computer.FileSystem As Microsoft.VisualBasic.MyServices.FileSystemProxy
```

The FileSystemProxy class includes the following members.

CombinePath Method

Combines two paths into a properly formatted path.

```
My.Computer.FileSystem.CombinePath(baseDirectory As String, _
                        relativePath As String) As String
```

CombinePath is a string manipulation function that assumes two strings, *baseDirectory* and *relativePath*, represent valid path names and can be combined. It determines whether they are absolute or relative path names, adds any necessary path separators, and returns the result. If either *baseDirectory* or *relativePath* begins with the path separator or a drive name followed by the path separator, it is interpreted as an absolute path. If *relativePath* is interpreted as an absolute path, then none of *baseDirectory* appears in the returned string. If *baseDirectory* and *relativePath* are interpreted as relative paths, then the method appends the combination of *baseDirectory* and *relativeDirectory* to the full path to the current directory.

CopyDirectory Method

Copies a directory, along with its files, child directories, and their files, to another directory. The method is overloaded as follows:

```
My.Computer.FileSystem.CopyDirectory(sourceDirectoryName As String, _
                                     destinationDirectoryName As String)
My.Computer.FileSystem.CopyDirectory(sourceDirectoryName As String, _
                                     destinationDirectoryName As String, _
                                     overWrite As Boolean)
My.Computer.FileSystem.CopyDirectory(sourceDirectoryName As String, _
                                     destinationDirectoryName As String, _
                                     showUI As UIOption)
My.Computer.FileSystem.CopyDirectory(sourceDirectoryName As String, _
                                     destinationDirectoryName As String, _
                                     showUI As UIOption, _
                                     onUserCancel As UICancelOption)
```

sourceDirectoryName is the directory to be copied; it can include either an absolute or a relative path (which is interpreted as the path from the current directory). *destinationDirectoryName* is the name of the destination directory to which *sourceDirectoryName* is to be copied. If a multidirectory path is specified in *destinationDirectoryName*, the last directory is the directory to which *sourceDirectoryName* is to be copied. If *destinationDirectoryName* is a relative path, it is interpreted in relation to the current directory. *overwrite* determines whether files are overwritten if they already exist; by default, its value is False, which causes an IOException to be thrown if any files would be overwritten as a result of the copy operation. (Overwriting directories, however, does not throw an exception.) *showUI* determines whether a user interface displays only error dialogs (UIOption.OnlyErrorDialogs, the default value) or whether a progress dialog is also displayed (UIOption.AllDialogs). If *showUI* is UIOption.AllDialogs, *onUserCancel* determines how to respond to the user's clicking the Cancel button; possible values are UICancelOption .ThrowException (the default) and UICancelOption.DoNothing.

CopyFile Method

Copies a single file. The method is overloaded as follows:

```
My.Computer.FileSystem.CopyFile(sourceDirectoryName As String, _
                                destinationDirectoryName As String)
My.Computer.FileSystem.CopyFile(sourceDirectoryName As String, _
                                destinationDirectoryName As String, _
                                overWrite As Boolean)
My.Computer.FileSystem.CopyFile(sourceDirectoryName As String, _
                                destinationDirectoryName As String, _
                                showUI As UIOption)
My.Computer.FileSystem.CopyFile(sourceDirectoryName As String, _
                                destinationDirectoryName As String, _
                                showUI As UIOption, _
                                onUserCancel As UICancelOption)
```

sourceDirectoryName is the file to be copied. *destinationDirectoryName* is the name of the destination file. *overwrite* determines whether files are overwritten if they already exist; by default, its value is False, and an IOException is thrown if the destination file would be overwritten as a result of the copy operation. *showUI* determines whether a user interface displays only error dialogs (UIOption.OnlyErrorDialogs, the default value) or whether a progress dialog is also displayed (UIOption.AllDialogs). If *showUI* is UIOption.AllDialogs, *onUserCancel* determines how to respond to the user's clicking the Cancel button; possible values are UICancelOption.ThrowException (the default) and UICancelOption.DoNothing.

If either *sourceDirectoryName* or *destinationDirectoryName* contains a relative path, it is interpreted in relation to the current directory. If the source and destination directories are the same, the file must be given a different name in the *destinationDirectoryName* argument so that the copied file can be renamed. Unless *destinationDirectoryName* ends in a path separator character, the last path or filename element is interpreted as the filename, which allows the copied file to be renamed. To avoid confusion and the possibility of error, you should provide fully qualified filenames when using the CopyFile method.

CreateDirectory Method
Creates a directory.

```
My.Computer.FileSystem.CreateDirectory(directory As String)
```

directory can include either a relative path (in which case it is interpreted in relation to the current directory) or an absolute path. If *directory* already exists, the method does not throw an exception.

CurrentDirectory Property
Returns a fully qualified path to the current directory.

```
My.Computer.FileSystem.CurrentDirectory As String
```

DeleteDirectory Method
Deletes a directory. The method is overloaded as follows:

```
My.Computer.FileSystem.DeleteDirectory(directory As String, _
                    onDirectoryNotEmpty As DeleteDirectoryOption)
My.Computer.FileSystem.DeleteDirectory(directory As String, showUI As UIOption, _
                    recycle As RecycleOption)
My.Computer.FileSystem.DeleteDirectory(directory As String, showUI As UIOption, _
                    recycle As RecycleOption, onUserCancel As UICancelOption)
```

directory is an absolute or relative path to the directory to be deleted; if a relative path, it is interpreted in relation to the current directory. *onDirectoryNotEmpty* defines how the method should behave if the directory contains subdirectories or files; possible values are DeleteDirectoryOption.DeleteAllContents (the default value) or DeleteDirectoryOption .ThrowIfDirectoryNonEmpty (which throws an IOException). *showUI* determines whether a user interface displays only error dialogs (UIOption.OnlyErrorDialogs, the default value) or whether a progress dialog is also displayed (UIOption.AllDialogs). If *showUI* is UIOption.AllDialogs, *onUserCancel* determines how to respond to the user's clicking the Cancel button; possible values are UICancelOption.ThrowException (the default) and UICancelOption.DoNothing. Finally, *recycle* determines whether the deleted file is placed in the Recycle Bin (RecycleOption .SendtoRecycleBin) or permanently deleted (RecycleOption.DeletePermanently, the default value).

DeleteFile Method

Deletes a single file. The method has the following overloads:

```
My.Computer.FileSystem.DeleteFile(file As String)
My.Computer.FileSystem.DeleteFile(file As String, showUI As UIOption, _
                    recycle As RecycleOption)
My.Computer.FileSystem.DeleteFile(file As String, showUI As UIOption, _
                    recycle As RecycleOption, onUserCancel As UICancelOption)
```

file is an optional path along with the name of the file; if *file* includes a relative path, it is interpreted in relation to the current directory. *showUI* determines whether a dialog is used only to display exception information (UIOption.OnlyErrorDialogs, the default value) or whether a progress dialog is also displayed (UIOption.AllDialogs). If *showUI* is UIOption.AllDialogs, *onUserCancel* determines how to respond to the user's clicking the Cancel button; possible values are UICancelOption.ThrowException (the default) and UICancelOption.DoNothing. Finally, *recycle* determines whether the deleted file is placed in the Recycle Bin (RecycleOption.SendtoRecycleBin) or permanently deleted (RecycleOption.DeletePermanently, the default value).

DirectoryExists Method

Determines whether a particular directory exists.

```
My.Computer.FileSystem.DirectoryExists(directory As String) As Boolean
```

directory can be either a relative path (in which case it's interpreted in relation to the current directory) or an absolute path.

Drives Property

Returns a collection of DriveInfo objects representing drives available on a system, including mapped network drives.

```
My.Computer.FileSystem.Drives As _
            System.Collections.ObjectModel.ReadOnlyCollection(Of DriveInfo)
```

Each System.IO.DriveInfo object returned in the read-only collection provides information about a drive. Its Name property provides the name of the drive (such as "C:\"). The following code illustrates how to iterate the collection:

```
Imports System.Collections.ObjectModel
Imports System.IO

Public Module IterateDrives
    Public Sub Main()
        Dim drives As ReadOnlyCollection(Of DriveInfo)
```

```
        drives = My.Computer.FileSystem.Drives
        For Each drive As DriveInfo In drives
            Console.WriteLine(drive.Name)
        Next
    End Sub
End Module
```

FileExists Method

Determines whether a particular file exists.

```
My.Computer.FileSystem.FileExists(file As String) As Boolean
```

file can be either a relative path (in which case it's interpreted in relation to the current directory) or an absolute path.

FindInFiles Method

Returns a read-only collection of strings with the names of files that contain the specified text. The method is overloaded as follows:

```
My.Computer.FileSystem.FindInFiles(directory As String, containsText As String, _
            ignoreCase As Boolean, _
            searchType As SearchOption) As ReadOnlyCollection(Of String)
My.Computer.FileSystem.FindInFiles(directory As String, containsText As String, _
            ignoreCase As Boolean, _
            searchType As SearchOption, _
            ParamArray fileWildcards As String() ) As ReadOnlyCollection(Of String)
```

directory specifies the directory to be searched and can be either an absolute or a relative path; a relative path is interpreted in relation to the current directory. *containsText* defines the string to search for in the files in *directory*. *ignoreCase* determines whether the search is case-insensitive (*ignoreCase* is True) or case-sensitive. *searchType* determines whether subdirectories of *directory* are also searched for *containsText*; possible values are SearchOption.SearchTopLevelOnly or SearchOption.SearchAllSubDirectories. The first overload searches all files in *directory*; the second overload allows you to specify *fileWildcards,* a string array of file specifications that defines the files to be searched.

The following code illustrates the use of the FindInFiles method to search all Visual Basic source code files (*.vb files) in the current directory for the string "Class":

```
Imports Microsoft.VisualBasic.FileIO
Imports System.Collections.ObjectModel

Public Module FileFind
    Public Sub Main()
        Dim filespec() As String = {"*.vb"}
        Dim matches As ReadOnlyCollection(Of String)
        matches = My.Computer.FileSystem.FindInFiles(".", "Class", False, _
                SearchOption.SearchTopLevelOnly, filespec)
        If matches.Count > 0 Then
            Console.WriteLine("'Class' found in:")
```

```
        For Each filename As String In matches
            Console.WriteLine("   " & filename)
        Next
    Else
        Console.WriteLine("No matches found.")
    End If
  End Sub
End Module
```

GetDirectories Method

Returns a string collection containing the names of subdirectories belonging to a particular directory. The method is overloaded as follows:

```
My.Computer.FileSystem.GetDirectories(directory As String) _
        As ReadOnlyCollection(Of String)
My.Computer.FileSystem.GetDirectories(directory As String, _
        searchType As SearchOption, ParamArray fileWildcards As String() ) _
        As ReadOnlyCollection(Of String)
```

directory is an absolute or relative path to the directory whose subdirectories are to be returned by the method; a relative path is interpreted in relation to the current directory. *searchType* determines whether only subdirectories of *directory* are searched, or whether all nested subdirectories of *directory* are searched; possible values are SearchOption.SearchTopLevelOnly (the default) or SearchOption.SearchAllSubDirectories. The first overload returns the names of all the subdirectories in *directory*; the second overload allows you to specify *fileWildcards,* a string array of file specifications that defines the subdirectories to be returned.

Each directory name in the ReadOnlyCollection(Of String) object returned by the method includes the directory's fully qualified path.

GetDirectoryInfo Method

Returns a System.IO.DirectoryInfo object containing information about a particular directory.

```
My.Computer.FileSystem.DirectoryInfo(directory As String) As DirectoryInfo
```

directory is a relative (in relation to the current directory) or absolute path to the directory whose information is to be retrieved.

GetDriveInfo Method

Returns a System.IO.DriveInfo object containing information about a particular drive.

```
My.Computer.FileSystem.DriveInfo(drive As String) As System.IO.DriveInfo
```

drive is the drive whose DriveInfo object is to be returned. If *drive* is a file system path, the method first extracts its drive component if one is present; if one is not present, the method throws an ArgumentException.

GetFileInfo Method

Returns a System.IO.FileInfo object containing information about a particular file.

```
My.Computer.FileSystem.FileInfo(file As String) As System.IO.FileInfo
```

file is a relative (in relation to the current directory) or absolute path to the file whose information is to be retrieved.

GetFiles Method

Returns a string collection containing the names of subdirectories belonging to a particular directory. The method is overloaded as follows:

```
My.Computer.FileSystem.GetFiles(directory As String) _
        As ReadOnlyCollection(Of String)
My.Computer.FileSystem.GetFiles(directory As String, _
        searchType As SearchOption, ParamArray fileWildcards As String() ) _
        As ReadOnlyCollection(Of String)
```

directory is an absolute or relative path to the directory whose files are to be returned by the method; a relative path is interpreted in relation to the current directory. *searchType* determines whether only files in *directory* are returned, or whether files in all nested subdirectories of *directory* are also returned; possible values are SearchOption.SearchTopLevelOnly (the default) or SearchOption.SearchAllSubDirectories. The first overload returns the names of all the files in *directory*; the second overload allows you to specify *fileWildcards,* a string array of file specifications that defines the files to be returned.

Each filename in the ReadOnlyCollection(Of String) object returned by the method includes the file's fully qualified path.

GetName Method

Returns the name of the last path component (a directory or filename) in a directory path.

```
My.Computer.FileSystem.GetName(path As String) As String
```

path is any file directory path or filename. GetName is purely a parsing function; it extracts the last path component from *path* but does not verify that any part of *path* exists in the file system.

GetParentPath Method

Returns all but the last path component (a directory or filename) in a directory path.

```
My.Computer.FileSystem.GetParentPath(path As String) As String
```

path is any file directory path or filename. GetParentPath is purely a parsing function; it removes the last path component from *path* and returns the remaining string. For example, the method returns String.Empty if path is equal to "." (the symbol for the current directory). The method also does not verify that any part of *path* exists in the file system.

GetTempFileName Method

Creates a uniquely named zero-length temporary file and returns its fully qualified path and filename.

```
My.Computer.FileSystem.GetTempFileName() As String
```

Typically, the file is created in the user's temporary directory. While the .NET runtime creates the file, it is your responsibility to close it and delete it once you've finished working with it.

MoveDirectory Method

Moves a directory, along with its files, child directories, and their files, to another directory. The method is overloaded as follows:

```
My.Computer.FileSystem.MoveDirectory(sourceDirectoryName As String, _
                                     destinationDirectoryName As String)
My.Computer.FileSystem.MoveDirectory(sourceDirectoryName As String, _
                                     destinationDirectoryName As String, _
                                     overWrite As Boolean)
My.Computer.FileSystem.MoveDirectory(sourceDirectoryName As String, _
                                     destinationDirectoryName As String, _
                                     showUI As UIOption)
My.Computer.FileSystem.MoveDirectory(sourceDirectoryName As String, _
                                     destinationDirectoryName As String, _
                                     showUI As UIOption, _
                                     onUserCancel As UICancelOption)
```

sourceDirectoryName is the directory to be moved; it can include either an absolute or a relative path (which is interpreted as the path from the current directory). *destinationDirectoryName* is the name of the destination directory to which *sourceDirectoryName* is to be moved. If a multidirectory path is specified in *destinationDirectoryName*, the last directory is the directory to which *sourceDirectoryName* is to be moved. If *destinationDirectoryName* is a relative path, it is interpreted in relation to the current directory. *overwrite* determines whether files are overwritten if they already exist; by default, its value is False, which causes an IOException to be thrown if any files would be overwritten as a result of the move operation. (Overwriting directories, however, does not throw an exception.) *showUI* determines whether a user interface displays only error dialogs (UIOption.OnlyErrorDialogs, the default value) or whether a progress dialog is also displayed (UIOption.AllDialogs). If *showUI* is UIOption.AllDialogs, *onUserCancel* determines how to respond to the user's clicking the Cancel button; possible values are UICancelOption .ThrowException (the default) and UICancelOption.DoNothing.

MoveFile Method

Moves a single file. The method is overloaded as follows:

```
My.Computer.FileSystem.MoveFile(sourceDirectoryName As String, _
                                destinationDirectoryName As String)
My.Computer.FileSystem.MoveFile(sourceDirectoryName As String, _
                                destinationDirectoryName As String, _
                                overWrite As Boolean)
My.Computer.FileSystem.MoveFile(sourceDirectoryName As String, _
                                destinationDirectoryName As String, _
                                showUI As UIOption)
My.Computer.FileSystem.MoveFile(sourceDirectoryName As String, _
                                destinationDirectoryName As String, _
                                showUI As UIOption, _
                                onUserCancel As UICancelOption)
```

sourceDirectoryName is the file to be moved. *destinationDirectoryName* is the name of the destination file. *overwrite* determines whether the destination file is overwritten if it already exists; by default, its value is False, and an IOException is thrown if the file would be overwritten as a result of the move operation. *showUI* determines whether a user interface displays only error dialogs (UIOption.OnlyErrorDialogs, the default value) or whether a progress dialog is also displayed (UIOption.AllDialogs). If *showUI* is UIOption.AllDialogs, *onUserCancel* determines how to respond to the user's clicking the Cancel button; possible values are UICancelOption .ThrowException (the default) and UICancelOption.DoNothing.

If either *sourceDirectoryName* or *destinationDirectoryName* contains a relative path, it is interpreted in relation to the current directory. To avoid confusion and the possibility of error, you should provide fully qualified filenames when using the MoveFile method. If the source and destination directories are the same, the file must be given a different name in the *destinationDirectoryName* argument so that the "moved" file can be renamed.

OpenTextFieldParser Method

Instantiates a Microsoft.VisualBasic.FileIO.TextFieldParser object, which can be used to parse structured text files, including fixed-width and delimited text files. The method is overloaded as follows:

```
My.Computer.FileSystem.OpenTextFieldParser(file As String) As TextFieldParser
My.Computer.FileSystem.OpenTextFieldParser(file As String, _
                    ParamArray fieldWidths As Integer() ) As TextFieldParser
My.Computer.FileSystem.OpenTextFieldParser(file As String, _
                    ParamArray delimiters As String() ) As TextFieldParser
```

file specifies the file to open; it can include a relative path (which is interpreted in relation to the current directory) or an absolute path. *fieldwidths* specifies the widths of the fields in the file, and *delimiters* indicates which characters are used to delimit data in the file.

Some of the more useful members of the TextFieldParser class include:

- The Close method, which closes the TextFieldParser object instance
- The read-only EndOfData property, which returns True if the file pointer is positioned at the end of the file
- The PeekChars method, which reads a designated number of characters without moving the file pointer
- The ReadFields method, which reads all data on the current line, returns a string array, and moves the file pointer to the beginning of the next line
- The ReadLine method, which returns a string containing the contents of the current line and advances the file pointer to the beginning of the next line
- The ReadToEnd method, which reads the contents of the file from the current cursor position to the end of the file

OpenTextFileReader Method

Opens a System.IO.StreamReader object to read from a text file. The method is overloaded as follows:

```
My.Computer.FileSystem.OpenTextFileReader(file As String) As StreamReader
My.Computer.FileSystem.OpenTextFileReader(file As String, _
                    encoding As System.Text.Encoding) As StreamReader
```

file is the name of the file to open; it can include either a relative path (which is interpreted in relation to the current directory) or an absolute path. *encoding* specifies the file's character encoding. Possible values are Encoding.ASCII (the default), Encoding.UTF7, Encoding.UTF8, Encoding.Unicode, and Encoding UTF32.

OpenTextFileWriter Method

Opens a System.IO.StreamWriter object to write to a text file. The method is overloaded as follows:

```
My.Computer.FileSystem.OpenTextFileWriter(file As String, _
                    append As Boolean) As StreamWriter
My.Computer.FileSystem.OpenTextFileWriter(file As String, append As Boolean, _
                    encoding As System.Text.Encoding) As StreamWriter
```

file is the name of the file to open; it can include either a relative path (which is interpreted in relation to the current directory) or an absolute path. *append* indicates whether the write operations will append to the file or not. *encoding* specifies the file's character encoding. Possible values are Encoding.ASCII (the default), Encoding.UTF7, Encoding.UTF8, Encoding.Unicode, and Encoding UTF32.

ReadAllBytes Method

Reads the entire contents of a file and returns them as a Byte array.

```
My.Computer.FileSystem.ReadAllBytes(file As String) As Byte()
```

file is the name of the file to open; it can include either a relative path (which is interpreted in relation to the current directory) or an absolute path. The ReadAllBytes method is typically used to read from a binary file.

ReadAllText Method

Reads the entire contents of a text file and returns it as a String. The method is overloaded as follows:

```
My.Computer.FileSystem.ReadAllText(file As String) As String
My.Computer.FileSystem.ReadAllText(file As String, encoding As Encoding) As String
```

file is the name of the file to open; it can include either a relative path (which is interpreted in relation to the current directory) or an absolute path. *encoding* specifies the file's character encoding. Possible values are Encoding.ASCII (the default), Encoding.UTF7, Encoding.UTF8, Encoding.Unicode, and Encoding.UTF32.

RenameDirectory Method

Renames a single directory.

```
My.Computer.FileSystem.RenameDirectory(directory As String, newName As String)
```

directory is the name of the directory to rename; it can include either a relative path (which is interpreted in relation to the current directory) or an absolute path. *newName* is the name to be given to the directory.

The MoveDirectory method can also be used to rename a directory. The RenameDirectory method, however, cannot be used to move a directory.

RenameFile Method
Renames a single file.

```
My.Computer.FileSystem.RenameFile(file As String, newName As String)
```

file is the name of the file to rename; it can include either a relative path (which is interpreted in relation to the current directory) or an absolute path. *newName* is the name to be given to the file.

The MoveFile method can also be used to rename a directory. The RenameFile method, however, cannot be used to move a file.

SpecialDirectories Property
Returns a Microsoft.VisualBasic.MyServices.SpecialDirectoriesProxy object that can be used to retrieve the physical path of special Windows directories.

```
My.Computer.FileSystem.SpecialDirectories As SpecialDirectoriesProxy
```

The SpecialDirectoriesProxy class has nine shared properties that return special Windows file system paths, as shown in the following table:

Property Name	Directory
AllUsersApplicationData	The application data directory for all users (typically \Documents and Settings\All Users\ApplicationData).
CurrentUserApplicationData	The application directory for the current user (typically \Documents and Settings\<current user>\ApplicationData).
Desktop	The user's desktop directory (typically \Documents and Settings\<current user>\Desktop).
MyDocuments	The user's My Documents directory (typically \Documents and Settings\<current user>\My Documents).
MyMusic	The user's My Music directory (typically \Documents and Settings\<current user>\My Documents\My Music).
MyPictures	The user's My Pictures directory (typically \Documents and Settings\<current user>\My Documents\My Pictures).
ProgramFiles	The program files installation directory (typically \Program Files).
Programs	The directory in which Program menu items are stored (typically \ Documents and Settings\<current user>\Start Menu\Programs).
Temp	The directory for storing the user's temporary files (typically \ Documents and Settings\<current user>\Local Settings\Temp).

WriteAllBytes Method
Writes data to a binary file.

```
My.Computer.FileSystem.WriteAllBytes(file As String, data As As Byte(), _
                                     append As Boolean)
```

file is the name of the file to write to; it can include either a relative path (which is interpreted in relation to the current directory) or an absolute path. *data* is a Byte array containing the data to be written to the file. *append* indicates whether data should be appended to the end of the file or whether the method should overwrite any existing content.

WriteAllText Method

Writes text to a file. The method is overloaded as follows:

```
My.Computer.FileSystem.WriteAllText(file As String, text As String, _
                                    append As Boolean)
My.Computer.FileSystem.WriteAllText(file As String, text As String, _
                                    append As Boolean, encoding As Encoding)
```

file is the name of the file to write to; it can include either a relative path (which is interpreted in relation to the current directory) or an absolute path. *text* is the text to be written to the file. *append* indicates whether the text should be appended to the end of the file or whether it should overwrite any existing content. *encoding* specifies the file's character encoding. Possible values are Encoding.ASCII (the default), Encoding.UTF7, Encoding.UTF8, Encoding.Unicode, and Encoding UTF32.

Info Property

Returns a Microsoft.VisualBasic.Devices.ComputerInfo object instance that contains information about the local system.

```
My.Computer.Info As Microsoft.VisualBasic.Devices.ComputerInfo
```

The method has the following eight shared, read-only properties.

AvailablePhysicalMemory Property

Returns the total amount of free physical memory available on the local system.

```
My.Computer.Info.AvailablePhysicalMemory As ULong
```

AvailableVirtualMemory Property

Returns the total amount of virtual memory available to user-mode code in the current process that is neither reserved nor committed.

```
My.Computer.Info.AvailableVirtualMemory As ULong
```

The total amount of virtual memory available to user-mode code in the current process is provided by the TotalVirtualMemory property.

InstalledUICulture Property

Returns a System.Globalization.CultureInfo object representing the UI culture installed with the operating system.

```
My.Computer.Info.InstalledUICulture As System.Globalization.CultureInfo
```

OSFullName Property
Returns the full name of the operating system (e.g., Microsoft Windows XP Professional).

```
My.Computer.Info.OSFullName As String
```

OSPlatform Property
Returns the operating system's platform identifier (Unix, Win32NT, Win32S, Win32Windows, or WinCE), which indicates in which family of operating systems it belongs.

```
My.Computer.Info.OSPlatform As String
```

OSVersion Property
Returns the computer's operating system version.

```
My.Computer.Info.OSVersion As String
```

The string takes the form *major.minor.build.revision,* where *major* and *minor* are the *major* and *minor* version numbers, respectively, *build* is the build number, and *revision* is the revision number.

TotalPhysicalMemory Property
Returns the total amount of physical memory available on the local system.

```
My.Computer.Info.TotalPhysicalMemory As ULong
```

TotalVirtualMemory Property
Returns the total amount of virtual memory available to user-mode code in the current process.

```
My.Computer.Info.TotalVirtualMemory As ULong
```

On most Win32 systems, its value is either 2GB or 3GB.

Keyboard Property
Returns a Microsoft.VisualBasic.Devices.Keyboard object that represents the system keyboard.

```
My.Computer.Keyboard As Microsoft.VisualBasic.Devices.Keyboard
```

Typically, the keyboard properties are used in keyboard event handlers, such as the KeyDown, KeyPress, and KeyUp events of the System.Windows.Forms class. The Keyboard class has the following properties, all of which are read-only.

AltKeyDown Property
Indicates whether the ALT key is depressed.

```
My.Computer.Keyboard.AltKeyDown As Boolean
```

CapsLock Property
Indicates whether Caps Lock is on because the CAPS LOCK key has been pressed.

```
My.Computer.Keyboard.CapsLock As Boolean
```

CtrlKeyDown Property
Indicates whether the CTRL key is depressed.

```
My.Computer.Keyboard.CtrlKeyDown As Boolean
```

NumLock Property
Indicates whether the NUMLOCK key is on.

```
My.Computer.Keyboard.NumLock As Boolean
```

ScrollLock Property
Indicates whether the SCROLLLOCK key is on.

```
My.Computer.Keyboard.ScrollLock As Boolean
```

SendKeys Method
Sends keystrokes to the active window. The method is overloaded as follows:

```
My.Computer.Keyboard.SendKeys(keys As String)
My.Computer.Keyboard.SendKeys(keys, wait As Boolean)
```

keys defines the keystrokes to send to the active window. *wait* indicates whether the sending application should wait for keystrokes to be processed before continuing; its default value is True. The following table lists the characters to use to signify special keys:

Special Key	Character(s)
ALT	%
BACKSPACE	{BACKSPACE} or {BS}
BREAK	{BREAK}
CAPS LOCK	{CAPSLOCK}
CTRL	^
DELETE	{DELETE} or {DEL}
DOWN ARROW	{DOWN}
END	{END}
ENTER	{ENTER}
ESC	{ESCAPE} or {ESC}
Help	{HELP}
HOME	{HOME}
INS	{INSERT}
LEFT ARROW	{LEFT}
NUM LOCK	{NUMLOCK}
PAGE DOWN	{PGDN}

Special Key	Character(s)
PAGE UP	{PGUP}
RIGHT ARROW	{RIGHT}
SCROLL LOCK	{SCROLLOCK}
SHIFT	+
TAB	{TAB}
UP ARROW	{UP}

In addition, repeated keystrokes can be sent to a window by bracketing the key character or key character code along with a space and the number of repeated keystrokes. For example, {ENTER 10} repeats the ENTER key ten times.

The SendKeys method with *wait* set to False is equivalent to the System.Windows.Forms .SendKeys.Send method; the SendKeys method with *wait* set to True is equivalent to the System .Windows.Forms.SendKeys.SendWait method.

In order for the SendKeys method to work, the receiving application must be a Windows application that processes Windows messages. If it is not, an InvalidOperationException is thrown.

ShiftKeyDown Property

Indicates whether the SHIFT key is depressed.

```
My.Computer.Keyboard.ShiftKeyDown As Boolean
```

Mouse Property

Returns a Microsoft.VisualBasic.Devices.Mouse object representing the system mouse.

```
My.Computer.Mouse As Microsoft.VisualBasic.Devices.Mouse
```

The Mouse class has three read-only properties.

ButtonsSwapped Property

Indicates whether the functionality of the left and right mouse buttons has been swapped.

```
My.Computer.Mouse.ButtonsSwapped As Boolean
```

WheelExists Property

Indicates whether the mouse has a scroll wheel.

```
My.Computer.Mouse.WheelExists As Boolean
```

WheelScrollLines Property

Indicates how much to scroll when the mouse wheel is rotated one notch.

```
My.Computer.Mouse.WheelScrollLines As Integer
```

If the mouse does not have a scroll wheel, an attempt to access the WheelScrollLines property raises an exception. To prevent it, only call the WheelScrollLines property if the WheelExists property is True.

Name Property

Returns the computer name.

```
My.Computer.Name As String
```

The computer name can be set or read through the user interface by selecting the Computer Name tab of the My Computer properties dialog.

Ports Property

Returns a Microsoft.VisualBasic.Devices.Ports object that represents a computer's serial ports.

```
My.Computer.Ports As Microsoft.VisualBasic.Devices.Ports
```

The Ports class has the following members.

OpenSerialPort Method

Opens a serial port and returns a SerialPort object representing that port.

```
My.Computer.Ports.OpenSerialPort(portName As String) As SerialPort
My.Computer.Ports.OpenSerialPort(portName As String, _
                            baudRate As Integer) As SerialPort
My.Computer.Ports.OpenSerialPort(portName As String, baudRate As Integer, _
                            parity As Parity) As SerialPort
My.Computer.Ports.OpenSerialPort(portName As String, baudRate As Integer, _
                            parity As Parity, dataBits As Integer) _
                            As SerialPort
My.Computer.Ports.OpenSerialPort(portName As String, baudRate As Integer, _
                            parity As Parity, dataBits As Integer, _
                            stopBits As StopBits) As SerialPort
```

portName is the name of the port to open and must be one of the strings returned by the SerialPortNames property. The remaining settings are typically set by a device driver and can also be set in the Control Panel. *baudrate* specifies the baud rate. *parity* specifies the parity and can be Parity.Even, Parity.Mark (the parity bit is set to 1), Parity.None, Parity.Odd, or Parity.Space (the parity bit is set to 0). *dataBits* specifies the number of data bits. *stopbits* specifies the number of stop bits and can be StopBits.None, StopBits.One, StopBits.OnePointFive, or StopBits.Two.

SerialPortNames Property

Returns a collection containing the names of the computer's serial ports.

```
My.Computer.Ports.SerialPortNames As ReadOnlyCollection(Of String)
```

The following code displays the names of a system's serial ports:

```
Imports System.Collections.ObjectModel

Public Module PortsTest
    Public Sub Main()
        Dim ports As ReadOnlyCollection(Of String) = _
                    My.Computer.Ports.SerialPortNames
        For Each port As String In ports
```

```
        Console.WriteLine(port)
    Next
  End Sub
End Module
```

Registry Property

Returns a RegistryProxy object that provides access to the system registry.

```
My.Computer.Registry As Microsoft.VisualBasic.MyServices.RegistryProxy
```

The RegistryProxy class has the following members.

ClassesRoot Property

Returns a RegistryKey object that provides access to HKEY_CLASSES_ROOT.

```
My.Computer.Registry.ClassesRoot As Microsoft.Win32.RegistryKey
```

CurrentConfig Property

Returns a RegistryKey object that provides access to HKEY_CURRENT_CONFIG.

```
My.Computer.Registry.CurrentConfig As Microsoft.Win32.RegistryKey
```

CurrentUser Property

Returns a RegistryKey object that provides access to HKEY_CURRENT_USER.

```
My.Computer.Registry.CurrentUser As Microsoft.Win32.RegistryKey
```

DynData Property

Returns a RegistryKey object that provides access to HKEY_DYN_DATA on Windows 95 and Windows 98 systems.

```
My.Computer.Registry.DynData As Microsoft.Win32.RegistryKey
```

In systems such as Windows NT, Windows 2000, and Windows XP that lack an HKEY_DYN_DATA branch of the registry, attempting to access any members of the returned RegistryKey instance other than the Name property throws an IOException.

GetValue Method

Retrieves data from the registry.

```
My.Computer.Registry.GetValue(keyName As String, valueName As String, _
                    defaultValue As Object) As Object
```

keyName is a complete path from a top-level key to the registry key. The top-level registry key name (such as HKEY_CLASSES_ROOT or HKEY_CURRENT_USER) should be included in the string. *valueName* is the name of the value, or String.Empty for a key's default value. *defaultValue* is the value to return if *valueName* cannot be found.

The runtime type of the value returned by the method reflects the data type retrieved from the registry. For string (REG_SZ and REG_EXPAND_SZ) data, the method returns a String. For string array (REG_MULTI_SZ) data, it returns a String array. For integer (REG_DWORD) data, it returns an Integer. For binary (REG_BINARY) data, it returns a Byte array.

The following example reads a registry value and then calls a routine named DisplayRegistryData that handles each of the major registry data types and displays its value to the console:

```
Public Module RegistryTest

    Public Sub Main()
        Dim value As Object
        value =
My.Computer.Registry.GetValue("HKEY_CLASSES_ROOT\wrifile\DefaultIcon", _
                                            String.Empty, String.Empty)
        DisplayRegistryData(value)
    End Sub

    Private Sub DisplayRegistryData(data As Object)
        If TypeOf data Is String Then
            Console.WriteLine(data)
        ElseIf TypeOf data Is Integer Then
            Console.WriteLine("Integer data: " & CInt(data))
        ElseIf TypeOf data Is String() Then
            Console.WriteLine("String array: ")
            Dim dataArray() As String = DirectCast(data, Array)
            For ctr As Integer = LBound(data, 1) To UBound(data, 1)
                Console.WriteLine("   " & data(ctr))
            Next
        ElseIf typeOf data Is Byte() Then
            Console.WriteLine("Binary data: ")
            For ctr As Integer = LBound(data, 1) To UBound(data, 1)
                Console.Write("   " & Hex(data(ctr)) & " ")
            Next
        Else
            Console.WriteLine("Unknown data type...")
        End If
    End Sub
End Module
```

LocalMachine Property

Returns a RegistryKey object that provides access to HKEY_LOCAL_MACHINE.

```
My.Computer.Registry.LocalMachine As Microsoft.Win32.RegistryKey
```

PerformanceData Property

Returns a RegistryKey object that provides access to HKEY_PERFORMANCE_DATA on Windows NT, Windows 2000, and Windows XP systems.

```
My.Computer.Registry.PerformanceData As Microsoft.Win32.RegistryKey
```

On Windows 95 and Windows 98 systems, which lack an HKEY_PERFORMANCE_DATA registry key, attempting to access any members of the returned RegistryKey instance other than the Name property throws an IOException.

SetValue Method

Writes a value to the registry. The method is overloaded as follows:

```
My.Computer.Registry.SetValue(keyName As String, valueName As String, _
                              value As Object)
My.Computer.Registry.SetValue(keyName As String, valueName As String, _
                              value As Object, valueKind As RegistryValueKind)
```

keyName is the fully qualified path from the top-level registry key to the registry key containing *valueName*. If the beginning portion of *keyName* is a valid registry path, any remaining keys that do not exist will be created. *valueName* is the name of the value entry, or String.Empty for the default value. If *valueName* does not exist, the method creates it. *value* is the data to be written to the registry. The first overload writes it as String (REG_SZ) data. The second overload allows you to specify the registry data type; possible values are RegistryValueKind.Binary (REG_BINARY), RegistryValueKind.DWord (REG_DWORD), RegistryValueKind.ExpandString (REG_EXPAND_SZ), RegistryValueKind.MultiString (REG_EXPAND_SZ), RegistryValueKind.QWord (REG_QWord), and RegistryValueKind.String (REG_SZ).

Users Property

Returns a RegistryKey object that provides access to HKEY_USERS.

```
My.Computer.Registry.Users As Microsoft.Win32.RegistryKey
```

Screen Property

Returns a Screen object that represents the computer's primary display device.

```
My.Computer.Screen As System.Windows.Forms.Screen
```

The Screen class has the following members.

AllScreens Property

A shared property that returns an array of all Screen objects on the system.

```
My.Computer.Screen.AllScreens As System.Windows.Forms.Screen()
```

You can iterate the array and call the properties or methods of the Screen object for each object in the array.

BitsPerPixel Property

Returns the number of bits of memory used to hold one pixel of data.

```
My.Computer.Screen.BitsPerPixel As Integer
```

Bounds Property

Returns the bounds of the display.

```
My.Computer.Screen.Bounds As System.Drawing.Rectangle
```

The following code fragment uses the Bounds property to display the screen resolution:

```
Dim bnds As Rectangle = My.Computer.Screen.Bounds
Console.WriteLine("Bounds: " & bnds.Width & " by " & bnds.Height)
```

DeviceName Property

Displays the name of the primary display device.

```
My.Computer.Screen.DeviceName As String
```

FromControl Method

A shared method that returns the Screen object for the display device that contains the largest portion of a specified control indicated by *control*:

```
My.Computer.Screen.FromControl(control As System.Windows.Forms.Control) As Screen
```

The method is intended for use in multidisplay environments.

FromHandle Method

A shared method that returns the Screen object for the display device that contains the largest portion of the object with a specified handle, *hwnd*:

```
My.Computer.Screen.FromHandle(hwnd As IntPtr) As Screen
```

The method is intended for use in multidisplay environments.

FromPoint Method

A shared method that returns the Screen object for the display device that contains a particular coordinate, *point*:

```
My.Computer.Screen.FromPoint(point As System.Drawing.Point) As Screen
```

The method is intended for use in multidisplay environments.

FromRectangle Method

A shared method that returns the Screen object for the display device that contains a particular coordinate, *point*:

```
My.Computer.Screen.FromRectangle(rect As System.Drawing.Rectangle) As Screen
```

The method is intended for use in multidisplay environments.

GetBounds Method

A shared method that retrieves the bounds of the display device that displays a particular coordinate or that displays the largest part of a particular control or rectangular area. The method is intended for use in a multidisplay environment and is overloaded as follows:

```
My.Computer.Screen.GetBounds(ctl As System.Windows.Forms.Control) _
                         As System.Drawing.Rectangle
My.Computer.Screen.GetBounds(pt As System.Drawing.Point) _
                         As System.Drawing.Rectangle
```

```
My.Computer.Screen.GetBounds(rect As System.Drawing.Rectangle) _
                     As System.Drawing.Rectangle
```

GetWorkingArea Method

A shared method that returns the working area of a display device that displays a particular coordinate or that displays the largest part of a particular control or rectangular area. The method is intended for use in a multidisplay environment and is overloaded as follows:

```
My.Computer.Screen.GetWorkingArea(ctl As System.Windows.Forms.Control) _
                     As System.Drawing.Rectangle
My.Computer.Screen.GetWorkingArea(pt As System.Drawing.Point) _
                     As System.Drawing.Rectangle
My.Computer.Screen.GetWorkingArea(rect As System.Drawing.Rectangle) _
                     As System.Drawing.Rectangle
```

Primary Property

Indicates whether a particular display device is the primary display.

```
My.Computer.Screen.Primary As Boolean
```

PrimaryScreen Property

A shared property that returns the system's primary display device.

```
My.Computer.Screen.PrimaryScreen As System.Windows.Forms.Screen
```

WorkingArea Property

Returns the working area of the display.

```
My.Computer.Screen.WorkingArea As System.Drawing.Rectangle
```

The working area of a display is the desktop area, excluding taskbars, docked windows, and docked toolbars.

Forms Class

The My.Forms class provides access to all the forms available in an application by name. Each form is represented by a property whose name is the same as the Name property of the form it returns:

```
My.Forms.<propertyName> As System.Windows.Forms.Form
```

The My.Forms class differs from the collection returned by the My.Application.OpenForms method, since the former includes all forms, while the latter includes only open forms. The My.Forms class is available only in Windows applications.

MySettings Class

See the section "Settings Class" later in this chapter.

Request Class

Makes the ASP.NET System.Web.HttpRequest object, which contains information about a client request, available to a web page or an ASP.NET web service.

Resources Class

The My.Resources class is intended to make retrieval of application resources easier. Although the class provides two properties to control and manage application resources, other properties are added at runtime depending on whether resources are stored with the project or not. Each resource file included with a project corresponds to an identically named property of the My.Resource class. For example, if a project includes a resource file named Icons.resx, assigning one of its icons to the application window's Icon property can be done with the following code:

```
Me.Icon = My.Resources.Icons.AppIcon
```

In addition to the properties that are added dynamically to reflect a project's specific resources, the My.Resources class has the following permanent members:

Culture Property

Returns a System.Globalization.CultureInfo object representing the culture of the application's current thread.

```
My.Namespace.Culture As System.Globalization.CultureInfo
```

ResourceManager Property

Returns a System.ResourceManager object that can be used to retrieve culture-specific resources and provide default data when a localized resource cannot be found.

```
My.Namespace.ResourceManager As System.Resources.ResourceManager
```

Some of the more important members of the ResourceManager class follow.

GetObject Method

Returns the value of a specified object resource. The method is overloaded as follows:

```
GetObject(name As String) As Object
GetObject(name As String, culture As CultureInfo) As Object
```

where *name* is the name of the resource, and *culture* represents the culture for which the resource is localized.

GetString Method

Returns the value of a specified string resource. The method is overloaded as follows:

```
GetString(name As String) As String
GetString(name As String, culture As CultureInfo) As String
```

where *name* is the name of the string resource, and *culture* represents the culture for which the string resource is localized.

Response Class

Makes the ASP.NET System.Web.HttpResponse object, which contains information about and controls the server's response to a client request, available to a web page or an ASP.NET web service.

Settings Class

The MySettings class is intended to make retrieval of user and application settings from application and user configuration files easier. Although My.Settings provides a basic set of properties (notably the Default property), the major functionality of the class is derived dynamically at runtime, when the .NET runtime reads the application's application and user configuration files. The former file is named *app.config* and is located in the application directory. The latter is named *user.config* and is located in a subdirectory of the user's application data directory. Each value defined with a **<setting>** in the **<MySettings.Settings>** section of either the **<applicationSettings>** or **<userSettings>** sections becomes a property of the My.Settings class.

The My.Settings class integrates with Visual Studio, which provides a Settings tab in a project's properties dialog, as shown in Figure 9-1. The dialog allows you to define the property's name, data type, scope (whether the value of the property is application-wide or varies by user), and value.

The My.Settings class is particularly useful for avoiding hard-coded values whose change may require that a program be recompiled. For example, ADO.NET connection strings are often hard-coded to include the name of the database server, which can vary depending on the version of SQL Server installed on the system. Similarly, file locations are not always immutable, and hard-coding a filename and path can break an application when the location of the file changes. In addition, hard-coding user-specific or security-sensitive information into your code is always problematic; these values can best be placed in a configuration file.

The following code illustrates the use of the My.Settings class to store an OleDb connection string that populates a drop-down combo box with a list of customer names:

```
Private Sub Form1_Load(ByVal sender As System.Object, _
                       ByVal e As System.EventArgs) Handles MyBase.Load
    Dim conn As OleDbConnection
    Try
        conn = New OleDbConnection(My.Settings.ConnectionString)
        conn.Open()
    Catch ex As Exception
        Console.WriteLine(ex.GetType.Name & ": " & ex.Message)
        MsgBox("Unable to open database connection. Application must terminate", _
               MsgBoxStyle.Critical Or MsgBoxStyle.ApplicationModal, _
               "Database Error")
        Exit Sub
    End Try
    Try
        Dim cmd As New OleDbCommand("Select CompanyName From Customers")
        cmd.Connection = conn
        Dim dr As OleDbDataReader
        dr = cmd.ExecuteReader()
        Do While dr.Read
            ComboBox1.Items.Add(dr.GetString(0))
```

```
        Loop
    Catch ex As Exception
        MsgBox("Unable to open Customer database", MsgBoxStyle.Critical, _
            "Database Error")
    Finally
        conn.Close()
    End Try
End Sub
```

The My.Settings class is extensible. While the default provider reads to and writes from .NET configuration files, you can define your own Settings provider that reads and writes settings from some other medium. Extending the My.Settings class, however, is beyond the scope of this book.

In addition to the properties that are defined in configuration files or other input/output medium, the My.Settings class includes the following members.

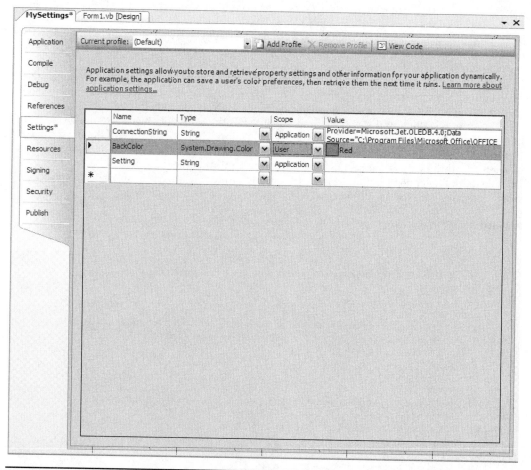

FIGURE 9-1   The Settings tab of the Project Properties dialog

Context Property

Provides contextual information about custom properties that the settings provider can use in handling the properties.

```
My.Settings.Context As System.Configuration.SettingsContext
```

Default Property

Returns the default Settings object instance.

```
My.MySettings.Default As Settings
```

The Default property is useful for assigning an object reference to a variable that can receive event notifications. For example:

```
Dim WithEvents settings As My.MySettings       ' module-level declaration
. . .
settings = My.MySettings.Default               ' instantiate in Form_Load
```

Note that Default is a property of My.MySettings, rather than My.Settings. Although the feature is not implemented, My.MySettings was intended to serve as a container object for multiple settings. My.MySettings.Default returns the object represented by My.Settings.

GetPreviousVersion Method

Returns the value of a property for the previous version of the application.

```
My.Settings.GetPreviousVersion(propertyName As String) As Object.
```

propertyName is the property whose value from a previous version is to be returned.

Initialize Method

Initializes a customized version of the My.Settings class by defining a context handler, custom properties, and a custom provider capable of handling those properties.

```
My.Settings.Initialize(context As System.Configuration.SettingsContext, _
        properties As System.Configuration.SettingsPropertyCollection, _
        providers As System.Configuration.SettingsProviderCollection)
```

context defines a settings context that handles custom properties. *properties* defines the custom settings that will be accessible from the Settings class, and *providers* defines the setting providers capable of reading and writing those settings. The method need be called only if you're customizing the My.Settings class to support media other than .NET configuration files.

IsSynchronized Property

Indicates whether access to the SettingsPropertyValue collection that represents the My.Settings class is thread-safe.

```
My.Settings.IsSychronized As Boolean
```

Item Property

Gets or sets the value of a particular custom property.

```
My.Settings.Item(propertyName As String) As Object
```

propertyName is the name of the property. If *propertyName* is not a custom property of My.Settings, a SettingsPropertyNotFoundException is thrown. In a property assignment, if the runtime type of the expression assigned to the property is incorrect, a SettingsPropertyWrongTypeException exception is thrown.

Properties Property

Returns a collection of System.Configuration.SettingsProperty objects that provide information about each of the custom properties in the collection.

```
My.Settings.Properties As System.Configuration.SettingsPropertyCollection
```

The following code uses the Properties property to retrieve the SettingsPropertyCollection and display information about each custom property in an application:

```
For Each prop As SettingsProperty In My.Settings.Properties
    Console.WriteLine("{0} ({1}): {2}", prop.Name, prop.PropertyType.Name, _
                      prop.DefaultValue)
Next
```

PropertyChanged Event

Fired after the value of a settings property has changed.

```
Public Event PropertyChanged(sender As Object, e As PropertyChangedEventArgs)
```

sender is the My.Settings object instance whose property was changed, and *e* is a PropertyChangedEventArgs instance whose PropertyName property indicates the name of the property that has changed. For example, the following code in a form's module-level code and in its Load event handler declare and instantiate a variable to receive My.Settings event notifications:

```
' Variable declaration at module level
Dim WithEvents settings As My.MySettings

' Variable instantiation in Form_Load
settings = My.MySettings.Default
```

The following code then handles the PropertyChanged event and displays the name of the property that has changed to the Immediate Window:

```
Private Sub PropertyChanged(ByVal sender As Object, _
                            ByVal e As PropertyChangedEventArgs) _
                            Handles settings.PropertyChanged
    If TypeOf sender Is My.MySettings Then
        Dim settings As My.MySettings = DirectCast(sender, My.MySettings)
```

```
        Debug.WriteLine(e.PropertyName & " has changed to " & _
            settings.PropertyValues.Item(e.PropertyName).PropertyValue.ToString)
    End If
End Sub
```

PropertyValues Property

Returns a collection of System.Configuration.SettingsPropertyValue objects that represent individual custom property values.

```
My.Settings.PropertyValues As System.Configuration.SettingsPropertyValueCollection
```

The Property property of an individual SettingsPropertyValue instance returns a SettingsProperty object, the same object stored in the collection returned by the My.Settings.Properties property.

Providers Property

Returns the collection of settings providers currently used by My.Settings.

```
My.Settings.Providers As System.Configuration.SettingsProviderCollection
```

Settings providers are responsible for reading and writing settings from a particular medium, such as a configuration file, an initialization file, or the registry.

Reload Method

Refreshes the settings property values from persistent storage.

```
My.Settings.Reload()
```

The method clears all cached property values, reloads their original saved values, and raises the PropertyChanged event for every member of the Properties collection.

Reset Method

Restores any user configuration settings to their default values.

```
My.Settings.Reset()
```

The default value of all user settings is defined in the app.config file, while individual user settings are stored in the user.config file in the user's application directory. Reset also raises the PropertyChanged event for each user property whose value is restored.

Save Method

Saves the current value of all application and user settings.

```
My.Settings.Save()
```

In the default implementation of My.Settings, the Save method saves only user settings. A call to the Save method is only necessary if your application needs to immediately save user settings data. The Save method is called and the values of custom property settings committed to configuration files when the application terminates.

SettingChanging Event

Fired before a particular property value changes and allows the change to be canceled.

```
Public Event SettingChanging(sender As Object, e As SettingChangingEventArgs)
```

sender is the My.Settings object instance whose property is to change, and *e* is a
SettingChangingEventArgs instance. Its SettingName property indicates the name of the
property that is to change, and its NewValue property returns an object representing the
property's new value. Its Cancel property, if set to True, cancels the change. The following
code, for example, displays the old and new property values in the Immediate Window:

```
Private Sub PropertyChanging(sender As Object, e As SettingChangingEventArgs)
    If TypeOf sender Is My.MySettings Then
        Dim settings As My.MySettings = DirectCast(sender, My.MySettings)
        Debug.WriteLine(e.SettingName & " is changing from " & _
            settings.PropertyValues.Item(e.SettingName).PropertyValue.ToString _
            & " to " & e.NewValue.ToString)
    End If
End Sub
```

SettingsKey Property

The SettingsKey property was intended to return the name of the current set of application and
user settings, since Visual Basic was to support multiple named sets. The feature is not implemented
in Visual Basic 2005, however, and the property returns String.Empty.

```
My.Settings.SettingsKey As String
```

SettingsLoaded Event

Fired when settings are loaded by a provider.

```
Public Event SettingsLoaded(sender As Object, e As SettingsLoadedEventArgs)
```

sender is the My.Settings object instance whose settings are loaded, and *e* is a
SettingLoadedEventArgs instance. Its Provider property returns the SettingsProvider
object that is loading the settings.

SettingsSaving Event

Fired when settings are about to be saved and allows the save operation to be canceled.

```
Public Event SettingsSaving(sender As Object, e As CancelEventArgs)
```

sender is the My.Settings object instance whose settings are loaded, and *e* is a CancelEventArgs
instance. Setting its Cancel property to True cancels the save operation.

Synchronized Method

Returns a synchronized Settings object.

```
My.Settings.Synchronized(settingsBase As SettingsBase) As SettingsBase
```

settingsBase is a Settings object instance. For example:

```
Dim setting As SettingsBase = My.Settings.Synchronized(My.MySettings.Default)
```

Upgrade Method

Attempts to migrate user settings from a previous version to a new version of an application.

```
My.Settings.Upgrade(context As SettingsContext, _
                    properties As SettingsPropertyCollection)
```

User Class

The My.User class provides access to settings that identify the current user and control the current application user's permissions.

CurrentPrincipal Property

Gets or sets the current user's security context.

```
My.User.CurrentPrincipal As IPrincipal
```

You can assign an object that implements the IPrincipal interface to the CurrentPrincipal property to implement a custom authentication routine. The IPrincipal interface includes the following members.

Identity Property

Returns the identity of the current principal, which represents the user on whose behalf the code is running.

```
My.User.CurrentPrincipal.Identity As IIdentity
```

The IIdentity interface has three read-only properties: Name (the name of the user on whose behalf the code is running), IsAuthenticated (a Boolean indicating whether the user has been authenticated), and AuthenticationType (the type of authentication used to identify the user).

IsInRole Method

Indicates whether the current principal belongs to a particular role.

```
My.User.CurrentPrincipal.IsInRole(role As String) As Boolean
```

The IsInRole property is also available from the My.User object.

InitializeWithWindowsUser Method

Initializes the My.User object by setting the current thread's principal to the Windows user that started the application.

```
My.User.InitializeWithWindowsUser()
```

In Windows Forms applications, the InitializeWithWindowsUser method is called by the .NET runtime, making the My.User object automatically available. In other types of applications, the My.User object must be initialized either by calling the InitializeWithWindowsUser method or by assigning an object that implements IPrincipal to the My.User.CurrentUser property.

IsAuthenticated Property

Indicates whether the user has been authenticated.

```
My.User.IsAuthenticated As Boolean
```

IsInRole Method

Indicates whether the current user belongs to a particular role. The method is overloaded as follows:

```
My.User.IsInRole(role As BuiltInRole) As Boolean
My.User.IsInRole(role As String) As Boolean
```

The BuiltInRole enumeration includes BuiltInRole.AccountOperator, BuiltInRole.Administrator, BuiltInRole.BackupOperator, BuiltInRole.Guest, BuiltInRole.PowerUser, BuiltInRole.PrintOperator, BuiltInRole.Replicator, BuiltInRole.SystemOperator, and BuiltInRole.User.

Name Property

Returns the name of the current user.

```
My.User.Name As String
```

The principal responsible for authenticating the user controls the format of the user name. Ordinarily, using Windows authentication, the user name has the format *DOMAIN_NAME\ Username*.

WebServices Class

The My.WebServices class represents web services to which references have been added in a project. The name of each such web service corresponds to a property of the My.WebServices class. The property returns a System.Web.Description.Service class instance that represents that web service and also makes its web methods available:

```
My.WebServices.serviceName As System.Web.Description.Service
```

For example, if a web service named GreetingService has a method named SayGreeting, the following code uses the My.WebServices object to invoke the method:

```
Console.WriteLine(My.WebServices.GreetingService.SayGreeting(Date.Now)
```

Each web method available from the My.WebServices object has two versions, one that executes synchronously and one that executes asynchronously. The previous code executes the synchronous version. The asynchronous version has the string "Async" appended to the method name. For example, the following code executes the SayGreeting web method asynchronously:

```
Console.WriteLine(My.WebServices.GreetingService.SayGreetingAsync(Date.Now)
```

What's New in
Visual Basic 2005

Visual Basic 2005 includes new features in three major areas: features that are available on the .NET platform and that are supported by Visual Basic .NET (such as support for generics), features that were available in C# and are now implemented in Visual Basic (operating and conversion overloading, language support for resource disposal), and extensions to Visual Basic aimed at enhancing its ease of development (the My namespace, as well as assorted language enhancements). This section provides a brief overview of those new features.

Generic Classes

Most applications use collection objects as containers for storing a particular type of data. Rarely is a particular collection object used to store disparate types of data. Yet, until Visual Basic 2005 and .NET 2.0 that's precisely what collection objects were designed to do. Aside from arrays, which can be strongly typed at compile time to hold a particular data type, the Visual Basic Collection class and the classes in the .NET System.Collections and System.Collections .Specialized namespaces all are designed to hold data of any type. Because of this, developers using collections to hold strongly typed data often had to perform additional type checking to make sure that only data of an appropriate type found its way into the collection.

If You're New to Visual Basic .NET

This appendix surveys only the new features introduced in Visual Basic 2005; it does not cover the features introduced in Visual Basic .NET 2002, the first release of Visual Basic .NET, which was dramatically different in a number of ways from the previous versions of Visual Basic. If you've used Visual Basic 6.0 but are new to Visual Basic .NET, be sure to read the first seven chapters of this book, which offer a fast-paced introduction to Visual Basic .NET programming. In addition, the language elements documented in Chapter 8 include a section "VB6 Differences," that discusses how a particular language element differs from the Visual Basic 6.0 implementation.

Generic classes directly address this problem. Generic classes are collection objects that are designed to store data of a particular type. However, they are not specialized objects—that is, you won't find a generic class for storing strings, another for storing unsigned 16-bit integers, and so on. Instead, each generic class is capable of storing data of any type. At compile time, you specify the data type that an instance of the generic type will store. At runtime, an instance of the generic class stores strongly typed data.

Although generic collection classes are the most commonly used, they are not the only generic (or parameterized) types. For example, the .NET Framework includes Nullable(Of T), which represents a value type that can be assigned a null, and the generic ArraySegment structure, which provides a wrapper that delimits a predefined subset of an array. Generic classes are useful whenever the functionality that that class provides is applicable to a number of types, but only one particular type is passed as an argument in any particular application.

The .NET Framework Class Library provides a set of generic classes in the System.Collections .Generic and System.Collections.ObjectModel namespaces. For example, you will find a generic List class (which corresponds to the ArrayList class), a generic ReadOnlyCollection class, a generic Dictionary class, and a generic Queue class, among others. But you are not confined to using the generic classes that are predefined in the .NET Framework Class Library; you can also create your own custom generic classes. The .NET Framework Class Library also includes several generic classes designed to serve as base classes for custom generic types that you might develop.

The following code uses a generic Dictionary class to store employee records for an HR birthday/date of hire anniversary tracker:

```vb
Imports System.Collections.Generic

Public Structure Employee
    Dim Name As String
    Dim HireDate As Date
    Dim BirthDate As Date
End Structure

Public Module TestGenericClass
    Public Sub Main()
        ' Create employee object
        Dim employees As New Dictionary(of String, Employee)
        Dim dateToFind As Date
        Dim input As String
        InitializeData(employees)

        input = InputBox("Enter date to search for birthday/hiring anniversaries: ")
        If input = String.Empty Or Not IsDate(input) Then Exit Sub

        dateToFind = CDate(input)
        For Each employee As KeyValuePair(of String, Employee) In employees
            ' Check birthday
            If Month(employee.Value.BirthDate) = Month(dateToFind) AndAlso _
                Day(employee.Value.BirthDate) = Day(dateToFind) Then
                Console.WriteLine("{0:MMMM d} is the bithday of {1}.", _
                            dateToFind, employee.Key)
            End If
```

```
         If Month(employee.Value.HireDate) = Month(dateToFind) AndAlso _
             Day(employee.Value.HireDate) = Day(dateToFind) Then
             Console.WriteLine("{0:MMMM d} is the hiring anniversary of {1}.", _
                               dateToFind, employee.Key)
         End If
     Next
 End Sub

 Private Sub InitializeData(employees As Dictionary(Of String, Employee))
     Dim emp As New Employee
     emp.Name = "Sandra Smith"
     emp.HireDate = #1/2/2003#
     emp.BirthDate = #7/12/1977#
     employees.Add(emp.Name, emp)
     emp.Name = "John Brown"
     emp.HireDate = #8/18/1999#
     emp.BirthDate = #3/16/1964#
     employees.Add(emp.Name, emp)
     emp.Name = "Richard Jones"
     emp.HireDate = #3/1/1987#
     emp.BirthDate = #11/12/1955#
     employees.Add(emp.Name, emp)
 End Sub
End Module
```

The generic Dictionary object is declared to hold string keys and values of type Employee. It is then passed to the InitializeData method, where it is populated with data. Note that, in the parameter list of the InitializeData method, we must specify the runtime type of Dictionary keys and values that the generic Dictionary class has to handle.

Once the data is initialized, a dialog box asks the user what date to look for among employee birthdays and hire dates, and lists the employees who were born or hired on that date. It does this by iterating the generic dictionary object. Each iteration returns a generic KeyValuePair object that has two members, Key and Value, whose types match that of the generic Dictionary object.

Generic classes are discussed in Chapter 7.

The My Namespace

Many Visual Basic programmers found the transition from Visual Basic 6.0 to Visual Basic .NET 2002 and Visual Basic .NET 2003 a bit daunting. Not only did Visual Basic language elements change significantly, but some of the language features were moved into the .NET Framework Class Library, with its thousands of types and tens of thousands of members. To ease the process of transition, as well as to provide a set of types and methods that would be more or less familiar to Visual Basic 6.0 programmers moving to .NET, the My namespace has been added to Visual Basic 2005.

The My namespace contains a number of objects:

- My.Application, which provides access to a diverse number of application settings, such as command-line arguments, environmental variables, the culture of the current thread, and the application log.

- My.Computer, which provides access to selected hardware and software resources on the local computer. Hardware devices include the system's audio devices, mouse, keyboard, and serial ports, while software objects include the Clipboard and the system registry.

- My.Forms, which allows Windows forms applications to easily retrieve each form in an application.

- My.Request, which provides access to user request information in an ASP.NET application.

- My.Resources, which provides access to resources, such as localized strings, images, and icons that have been included with the application.

- My.Response, which provides access to the IIS server's response to a user request in an ASP.NET application.

- My.Settings, which provides access to configuration files to save application and configuration settings.

- My.User, which provides access to the current user's name and permissions.

- My.WebServices, which provides access to the methods implemented by each web service for which a reference has been added to the application project.

The objects in the My namespace are instantiated dynamically at runtime. As a result, precisely what objects and which members are available depends on the namespace and the type of application. Windows forms applications, for example, include a My.Application object that by default is an instance of the WindowsFormsApplicationBase class, while console applications include a My.Application object that by default is an instance of the ConsoleApplicationBase class. Although both derive from the ApplicationBase class, they contain different members. The My.Forms object is available only in Windows forms applications, while the My.Response and My.Request objects are available only in ASP.NET applications.

In part, the My namespace is designed to wrap features of the .NET Framework Class Library. For example, the Application object's Culture property, which returns the application's current culture, wraps code like the following:

```
Dim thrd As Thread = Thread.CurrentThread
Dim culture As CultureInfo = thrd.CurrentCulture
```

Similarly, the My.Computer.Registry property returns a RegistryProxy object that wraps the registry classes in the Microsoft.Win32 namespace.

Other members of the objects in the My namespace are designed to make Visual Basic 6.0–like functionality available in Visual Basic 2005. For example, the My.Application.FileSystem object is strikingly reminiscent of the FileSystemObject class in the Microsoft Scripting Runtime Library. Both include methods for parsing file paths, navigating the file system and iterating or retrieving directories and files, and reading from and writing to text files (which were referred to as TextStream objects in the scripting runtime and are known as TextReader and TextWriter objects in the My.Computer object hierarchy).

Some of the functionality features available in the My namespace are unique, and some wrap a series of relatively complex .NET framework classes and methods in a way that makes them far more accessible and easy to use. For example, the My.Computer.FileSystem.FindInFiles method searches some portion of the file system for files with particular content. It is equivalent to launching a search using Windows Explorer and is otherwise unavailable through the .NET Framework Class Library. The My.Settings object does such a good job of simplifying access to application and user settings in configuration files that it provides a simple, easy-to-remember, easy-to-use object model that bears almost no resemblance to the corresponding types and methods in the .NET Framework Class Library.

The My namespace is documented in Chapter 9.

New Data Types

Versions 1.0 and 1.1 of the .NET Framework Class Library included four integral data types (System.SByte, System.UInt16, System.UInt32, and System.UInt64) that did not directly correspond to Visual Basic .NET data types. That made working with these data types awkward. For instance, instantiating an unsigned 32-bit integer required code like the following:

```
Dim number As UInt32 = Convert.ToUInt32(9)
```

Similarly, a comparison of the unsigned integer with a "standard" Visual Basic integer required the use of a .NET conversion method to convert the unsigned integer to a data type that the Visual Basic compiler supported and therefore knew how to compare with other numbers. For example:

```
If Convert.ToInt32(number) = CInt(inputString) Then
```

Visual Basic 2005 adds support for these four integral data types, which now correspond to the following "intrinsic" data types in Visual Basic:

- SByte, a signed 8-bit integer, which corresponds to the System.SByte class
- UShort, an unsigned 16-bit integer, which corresponds to the System.UInt16 class
- UInteger, an unsigned 32-bit integer, which corresponds to the System.UInt32 class
- ULong, an unsigned 64-bit integer, which corresponds to the System.UInt64 class

Because they are intrinsic Visual Basic data types, Visual Basic allows you to instantiate and compare values of these data types just as you would any other data types. For example, rather than having to instantiate the variable by calling the Convert.ToUInt32 method, we can use the code:

```
Dim number As Integer = 12ui
```

(ui is the type code for the UInteger data type, much as d is the type code for the Decimal data type). Similarly, we can now compare the UInteger named number with an Integer without having to call a .NET conversion function:

```
If number = CInt(inputString) Then
```

The new data types are discussed in Chapter 2 as well as in Appendix F and Appendix G.

Operator Overloading and Conversion

One of the features available in many programming languages and supported by the .NET platform from its inception is operator overloading—the ability to define custom operators whose behavior differs depending on the data that is supplied to them as operands.

Actually, Visual Basic has always included several overloaded operators. The + sign, for example, adds two values if provided with numeric data but concatenates two values if provided with string data. What Visual Basic lacked was the ability to define custom overloaded operators.

Visual Basic 2005 adds the ability to overload operators, as well as to define custom conversions using the CType function. The following operators (some of which must be overloaded as matched pairs) can be overloaded: = and <> as comparison operators, which must be overloaded as a pair; < and >, which must be overloaded as a pair; <= and >=, which must be overloaded as a pair; IsTrue and IsFalse, which are used in evaluating conditions using AndAlso and OrElse and must be overloaded as a pair; + as both a unary and binary operator; – as both a unary and binary operator; *; \; /; Mod; &; >>; <<; And as a logical operator; Not as a logical operator; Or as a logical operator; XOr as a logical operator; and Like.

For example, we could define a structure named Automobile that holds information on the model and year of an automobile. We could determine whether their model years are equal by using code like:

```
If auto1.Year = auto2.Year Then
```

but we can also use operator overloading to accomplish the same thing. The following code provides a brief example:

```
Public Structure Automobile
    Dim Model As String
    Dim Year As Short

    Public Sub New(model As String, year As Short)
        Me.Model = model
        Me.Year = year
    End Sub

    Public Shared Operator = (auto1 As Automobile, auto2 As Automobile) As Boolean
        Return (auto1.Year = auto2.Year)
    End Operator

    Public Shared Operator <> (auto1 As Automobile, auto2 As Automobile) As Boolean
        Return (auto1.Year <> auto2.Year)
    End Operator
End Structure
```

The syntax of custom conversion operators is very similar, except that there is only a single argument, an instance of the class or structure declared in the Class or Structure statement to which the Operator statement belongs. The return value is the type to which the argument is to be converted. In addition, all conversion operators must indicate whether a conversion is widening (the target data type can accommodate all possible data of the source data type) or narrowing (the target data type cannot accommodate all possible values of the source data type).

The use of the Widening or Narrowing keywords controls which conversions the compiler will attempt to perform implicitly. If Option Strict is on, it implicitly performs only widening conversions.

Operator overloading and custom conversion operations are discussed in Appendix C.

Custom Events

Since Visual Basic .NET 2002, Visual Basic has had AddHandler and RemoveHandler statements that allow you to dynamically define an event handler and then dynamically remove it or even remove it and replace it with a new one. In Visual Basic 2005, an event source can define a custom event that, when an event is dynamically added or removed by a sink, or when the event is raised, causes the event source to execute custom code. It is possible, for example, to use this feature to handle events asynchronously, or to provide event notifications only to some sinks and not to others according to some criteria.

Syntactically, custom events are an extension of the standard Event statement. But whereas the Event statement typically has the syntax:

```
Event eventName (sender As Object, e As EventArgs)
```

custom events have an expanded syntax:

```
Custom Event eventName As delegateName
    AddHandler(value As delegateName)
        [ code to execute when a sink adds a handler ]
    End AddHandler
    RemoveHandler(value As delegateName)
        [ code to execute when a sink removes a handler ]
    End RemoveHandler
    RasieEvent(delegatesignature)
        [ code to execute when source raises event ]
    End RaiseEvent
End Event
```

For a discussion of custom events, see the entry for the Event statement in Chapter 7.

Miscellaneous Language Changes

Visual Basic 2005 also includes a number of smaller language changes, from support for differences in the accessibility of property get and property set accessors to a new operator, IsNot. Most of these language changes are discussed in Chapter 8.

Different Accessibility of Property Statements

In Visual Basic .NET 2002 and Visual Basic .NET 2003, the Property statement defined the accessibility of a property as public, private, friend, or protected. For read-write properties, this accessibility applied to both property set and property get accessors.

In Visual Basic 2005, the Property statement must be used to define the *least* restrictive access level. Then either the property get accessor or the property set accessor (but not both) can have a more restrictive access level. Most commonly, this feature will probably be used to make property set accessors, which set the value of a property, more restrictive than property get accessors, which retrieve the value of a property. For example, it is possible to declare a property whose value can be set only within the class (the property set accessor is declared to be private) but whose value can be retrieved without restriction (the Property statement declares the property to be public).

The Using Statement

From its inception, C# included a **using** statement that allowed resources to be released without extensive coding. The C# compiler would translate the using statement into a **try** block that used the resources and a **finally** block that released them. Since the **finally** block executes whether or not an exception occurs, the resources are always released.

Visual Basic programmers were expected to write this code by hand. To release an ADO.NET Connection object, for instance, a Visual Basic programmer was expected to write code that conformed to the following pattern:

```
Dim conn As New SqlConnection(My.Settings.ConnectionString)
Try
    conn.Open()
    ' execute database code
Finally
    Dim disp As IDisposable
    If TypeOf conn Is IDisposable Then
        disp = conn
        disp.Dispose()
    End If
End Try
```

The problem was that many Visual Basic programmers did not know about the pattern, or about the need to handle resource disposal themselves.

This issue is addressed in Visual Basic 2005, which includes a Using statement that the compiler will use to generate code that follows the basic pattern just shown. For example, the following code disposes of a SqlConnection object:

```
Dim conn As New SqlConnection(My.Settings.ConnectionString)
Using conn
    ' execute database code
End Using
```

Continue Statement

While Visual Basic has always made it easy to evaluate an expression and, depending on its value, to immediately exit a loop, it has not made a return to the top of the loop as easy. Exiting the loop is just a matter of including an Exit Do, Exit For, or Exit While statement in the appropriate place. Skipping the remaining code and returning to the top of the loop, however, requires the use of labels and GoTo statements. The following code illustrates this. It indicates whether a number is even or odd. If a number is even, it returns to the beginning of the loop to process the next number. If the number is odd, it also indicates whether it is divisible by 3, 5, or 7:

```
Public Sub Main()
    For ctr As Integer = 1 to 100
        If ctr Mod 2 = 1 Then
            Console.Write("{0} is odd", ctr)
```

```
        Else
            Console.WriteLine("{0} is even.", ctr)
            GoTo EndOfLoop
        End If
        If ctr Mod 3 = 0 Then
            Console.Write(" and it is divisible by 3")
        End If
        If ctr Mod 5 = 0 Then
            Console.Write(" and it is divisible by 5")
        End If
        If ctr Mod 7 = 0 Then
            Console.Write(" and it is divisible by 7")
        End If
        Console.WriteLine()
EndOfLoop:
    Next
End Sub
```

Visual Basic 2005 adds a Continue Do, Continue For, and Continue While statement that can be used in Do, For, and While loops, respectively, and transfers control to the beginning of the loop. Using the Continue statement, we can rewrite our example as follows:

```
    Public Sub Main()
        For ctr As Integer = 1 to 100
            If ctr Mod 2 = 1 Then
                Console.Write("{0} is odd", ctr)
            Else
                Console.WriteLine("{0} is even.", ctr)
                Continue For
            End If
            If ctr Mod 3 = 0 Then
                Console.Write(" and it is divisible by 3")
            End If
            If ctr Mod 5 = 0 Then
                Console.Write(" and it is divisible by 5")
            End If
            If ctr Mod 7 = 0 Then
                Console.Write(" and it is divisible by 7")
            End If
            Console.WriteLine()
        Next
    End Sub
```

Global Keyword and Naming Collisions

Particularly when using third-party libraries, there are sometimes name collisions between the namespaces and types in the .NET Framework Class Library and the third-party library that are difficult to resolve. (For details, see the entry for the Global keyword in Chapter 8.) The Global keyword can be used to qualify a namespace reference to the .NET Framework Class Library.

Partial Classes

One of the characteristics of the code produced by the Visual Studio IDE in Visual Basic .NET 2002 and Visual Basic 2003 was that an abundance of designer-generated code was intermixed with developer code in any project, which made it difficult to work with developer code. More than occasionally, some of the designer code would be accidentally deleted, with the inevitable result that the designer no longer worked.

The Partial statement offers a solution to this problem. It allows a single class or structure definition to be split into multiple Class . . . End Class or Structure . . . End Structure blocks, as long as they share the same type name and the same fully qualified namespace location.

In addition to segregating designer-generated code from developer code, partial classes can be useful in a team environment where individual developers are responsible for coding designated portions of a class.

Conversions and the TryCast Method

In Visual Basic 2002, the language finally became fully object-oriented. One of the features of object-oriented programming, of course, is polymorphism: a particular object can take on many forms. At the same time, the Option Strict statement was introduced in the language. Although it is off by default, many spokespeople in the Visual Basic community advocated setting it on instead, and many developers complied.

Because of these two factors, Visual Basic programmers spend much more time converting one object instance to another than they did when programming in Visual Basic 6.0. To perform the conversion from an instance of a derived class to an instance of its base class, two methods are available. The first, which is really not optimized for conversions between base and derived classes or between interfaces and interface implementations, is the CType function. (It is this function that uses custom conversion operators defined with the Operator statement when performing conversions between types.) The second is the DirectCast function, which converts an object instance of one type to an object instance of another type if they share an inheritance relationship or an interface implementation relationship. Such conversions can fail because the source and destination types never share a relationship based on inheritance or interface implementation. The conversion from a base type to a derived type can also fail if the base type is not a derived type. (Each instance of a derived type is an instance of the base type. But each instance of a base type is not an instance of a derived type.) If DirectCast is unable to perform the conversion for either reason, it throws an InvalidCastException.

TryCast performs the same conversions as DirectCast but does not throw an exception if they fail. Instead, it performs the conversion if it can, and returns Nothing if the conversion fails. Of course, you have to check to make sure that TryCast returned a valid object reference. Otherwise, you'll just have to handle a NullReferenceException later in your code instead of the InvalidCastException thrown by DirectCast.

The IsNot Operator

The Is operator makes it easy to evaluate two object references for equality, or to determine if an object is equal to nothing:

```
If myObject Is yourObject Then Console.WriteLine("The same object!")

If myObject Is Nothing Then Console.WriteLine("Nothing.")
```

However, many Visual Basic programmers had a more difficult time with the syntax of statements that tested for object inequality or that tested to make sure that an object had a valid object reference:

```
If Not myObject Is yourObject Then Console.WriteLine("Different objects!")
If Not myObject Is Nothing Then Console.WriteLine("Valid object reference.")
```

To make these latter tests more comprehensible and readable, Visual Basic 2005 introduces the IsNot operator, which can replace the more awkward Not . . . Is construct:

```
If myObject IsNot yourObject Then Console.WriteLine("Different objects!")
If myObject IsNot Nothing Then Console.WriteLine("Valid object reference.")
```

However, the IsNot operator cannot be used with the TypeOf operator, which attempts to determine whether a variable is of a particular data type. The following is illegal and generates a compiler error:

```
If TypeOf myVariable IsNot ArrayList Then       ' Illegal: compiler error
```

The Lower Bounds of an Array

One of the language changes in Visual Basic .NET that most seemed to upset Visual Basic programmers was the ostensible inability to declare the lower bounds of an array. In Visual Basic 6.0, it was possible to define the default lower bounds of all arrays as either 0 or 1, and it was also possible to set the lower bound of a particular array using syntax like:

```
Dim myArray(1 To 10) As Integer
```

Visual Basic .NET removed the ability to define the lower bound of an array using a Visual Basic language element. (It can still be done using one of the overloads of the Array.CreateInstance method.) Visual Basic .NET also made it illegal to specify the lower bound of an array or to include the To keyword in the array definition. In Visual Basic .NET 2002 and Visual Basic .NET 2003, there are only two valid ways to declare an array. One is as an uninitialized array:

```
Dim myArray()
```

The other is as an array whose upper bound is specified:

```
Dim myArray(10)
```

Since arrays in .NET are zero-based, this declaration creates an array with 11 elements.

Visual Basic 2005 restores the old syntax that was supported by Visual Basic 6.0 but removed from the previous .NET versions of Visual Basic:

```
Dim myArray(0 To 10)
```

However, it still does not allow the lower bound of an array to be set at anything other than 0. Attempting to do so generates compiler error BC32059, "Array lower bounds can be only '0'."

Changes in the Visual Basic Command-Line Compiler

If you're used to using the Visual Basic command-line compiler, you may not even notice two changes that can save you quite a bit of time and typing. First, the previous versions of the compiler automatically referenced one of the two most important .NET assemblies, mscorlib.dll, but did not reference the other, system.dll. The Visual Basic 2005 command-line compiler now does reference it automatically. In the past you had to use command-line syntax like:

```
vbc /t:library MyClassLibrary.vb /r:system.dll
```

With Visual Basic 2005, since system.dll is referenced automatically, the program can be compiled with the command:

```
vbc /t:library MyClassLibrary.vb
```

Second, in previous versions of Visual Basic, the compiler did not automatically import any namespaces, including the Microsoft.VisualBasic namespace. For example, attempting to compile the following code with the Visual Basic .NET 2003 command-line compiler generates five different compiler errors:

```
Public Module modMain
    Public Sub Main()
        Dim number As UInt32 = 9ui
        Dim inputString As String = InputBox("Guess my number (between 1 and 10): ")
        If Not IsNumeric(inputString) Then Exit Sub
        If number = CInt(inputString) Then
            Console.WriteLine("You guessed right!")
        Else
            Console.WriteLine("Wrong!")
        End If
    End Sub
End Module
```

The reason is that the Microsoft.VisualBasic and System namespaces are not imported by the compiler. As a result, the compiler cannot resolve our references to UInt32, InputBox, IsNumeric, and our two references to Console. In Visual Basic 2005, these namespaces are automatically imported, and the program compiles them without any problems.

The Visual Basic command-line compiler is documented in Appendix E.

Language Elements
by Category

Often, when you know that a particular language element exists but you can't quite remember its name, it helps to be able to look at a list of language elements by category. That is precisely the purpose of this appendix. Where appropriate, a single element is included in multiple categories. You can use the list to locate that language element that you want before you look up detailed information about it in Chapter 8.

Array Handling

Element	Description
Collection class	A container whose members can be accessed by name/key or by ordinal position.
Erase statement	Erases the contents of array variables and releases their memory.
Filter function	Returns a filtered string array whose elements match a particular substring search criteria.
Join function	Concatenates a string from an array of strings.
LBound function	Indicates the lower bound of a particular dimension of an array.
Preserve keyword	Preserves the existing data in an array when the number of elements in a dimension is modified.
ReDim statement	Resizes an array.
Split function	Returns a one-dimensional array of strings extracted from a single delimited string.
UBound function	Indicates the upper bound of a particular dimension of an array.
vbFixedArray attribute	Indicates the number of elements in an array in cases where a fixed-length array is needed.

Attributes

Element	Description
Assembly keyword	Indicates that an attribute applies to an entire assembly, not to individual programming elements in it.
Module keyword	Indicates that an attribute applies to an entire module, not to individual programming elements in it.

COM Programming

Element	Description
ComClass attribute	Exposes a class as a COM object.
CreateObject function	Creates a COM object.
GetObject function	Returns a reference to a COM object.

Compiler Statements

Element	Description
#Const directive	Defines a conditional compiler constant.
#If . . . Then . . . #End If directive	Evaluates a conditional compiler constant and, if true, includes the following code block in the compiled application.

Date and Time

Element	Description
Clock property (My.Computer class)	Provides information on the system time and Universal Coordinated Time.
DateAdd function	Adds a number of date or time units to a date.
DateDiff function	Indicates the time interval between two date values.
DatePart function	Extracts a particular component from a date or time.
DateSerial function	Forms a date out of individual date components.
DateString property	Gets or sets the current system date.
DateValue function	Converts the formatted string representation of a date to a Date value.
Day function	Extracts the day of the month from a particular date value.
FileDateTime function	Indicates the date and time when a file was created or last modified.
FormatDateTime function	Returns a formatted string representation of a date/time value.

Element	Description
Hour function	Returns the hour component of a time value based on a 24-hour clock.
IsDate function	Indicates whether an expression can be converted to the Date data type.
Minute function	Extracts the minute component of a time value.
Month function	Extracts the number of the month from a given date value.
MonthName function	Returns a string with the name of a specified month.
Now property	Returns the current system date and time.
Second function	Extracts the second component of a time value.
TimeOfDay property	Sets or gets the current time of day on the local computer.
Timer function	Returns the number of seconds elapsed since midnight.
TimeSerial function	Returns a Date with a time value representing a specified hour, minute, and second.
TimeString property	Gets or sets the current system time.
TimeValue function	Converts the formatted string representation of a date or a date and time to a Date with a time value.
Today property	Gets or sets the current system date.
Weekday function	Returns an Integer whose value represents the day of the week.
WeekdayName function	Indicates the name of a weekday.
Year function	Extracts the year from a given date value.

Debugging

Element	Description
Stop statement	Suspends program execution and transfers control to a debugger.

Design-Time Environment

Element	Description
#Region directive	Defines a block of code for special handling in a design-time environment.

Documentation

Element	Description
' symbol	Defines the beginning of a comment.
''' symbols	Defines a line that contains an XML comment.
Rem statement	Defines the beginning of a comment.

Error Handling and Debugging

Unstructured Exception Handling

Element	Description
Erl function	Returns the line number on which an error occurred.
Err function	Provides access to the Err object.
Err object	Provides information about errors
Error statement	Raises an error.
ErrorToString function	Converts a standard Visual Basic error number to its corresponding error message.
IsError function	Indicates whether an expression is an Exception.
Next keyword	Directs program flow using unstructured error handling.
On Error statement	Directs program flow in the event of an error.
Resume statement	Defines program flow in the event of an error or in an error handler.
Stop statement	Suspends program execution.

Structured Exception Handling

Element	Description
Throw statement	Throws an exception.
Try . . . Catch . . . Finally statement	Provides a handler for runtime exceptions.

Event-Driven Programming

Element	Description
AddHandler statement	Dynamically defines an event handler.
Custom keyword	Used with an Event statement to indicate the presence of custom code that executes when an event handler is added or removed or when an event is raised.
DoEvents method (My.Application class)	Processes all Windows messages currently in the message queue.
Event statement	Defines a custom event.
RaiseEvent statement	Fires an event defined with the Event statement.
RemoveHandler statement	Deactivates an event handler defined using the AddHandler statement.
WithEvents keyword	Used with the Dim statement to indicate that a variable can handle events raised by a class instance.

File System

Element	Description
ChDir subroutine	Changes the current directory.
ChDrive subroutine	Changes the current drive.
CombinePath method (My.Computer.FileSystem property)	Combines two paths into a properly formatted path.
CopyDirectory method (My.Computer.FileSystem property)	Copies a directory, along with its files, child directories, and their files, to another directory.
CopyFile method (My.Computer.FileSystem property)	Copies a single file.
CreateDirectory method(My.Computer.FileSystem property)	Creates a directory.
CurDir function	Returns the current directory of a particular drive or of the application's default drive.
CurrentDirectory property (My.Computer.FileSystem property)	Returns a fully qualified path to the current directory.
DeleteDirectory method (My.Computer.FileSystem property)	Deletes a directory.
DeleteFile method (My.Computer.FileSystem property)	Deletes a single file.
Dir function	Returns the name of a file system object matching a particular file specification.
DirectoryExists method (My.Computer.FileSystem property)	Determines whether a particular directory exists.
Drives property (My.Computer.FileSystem property)	Returns a collection of DriveInfo objects representing drives available on a system.
EOF function	Indicates whether the end of a file opened for random or sequential input has been reached.
FileAttr function	Indicates the file mode in which a file was opened by the FileOpen function.
FileClose function	Closes one or more files opened using the FileOpen function.
FileCopy subroutine	Copies a file.
FileDateTime function	Indicates the date and time when a file was created or last modified.
FileGet function	Reads data from an open file into a variable.
FileGetObject function	Reads data from an open file into a variable of type Object.
FileLen function	Reports the size of a file in bytes.
FileOpen function	Opens a binary, random, or sequential file for input or output.
FilePut function	Writes data to a binary or random file.

Element	Description
FilePutObject function	Writes data to a binary or random file.
FileWidth subroutine	Defines the maximum size of a line when writing to a sequential file.
FindInFiles method (My.Computer.FileSystem property)	Returns a collection of filenames that contain specified text.
FreeFile function	Returns the next available file number for use with the FileOpen function.
GetAttr function	Retrieves information about a file system object's attributes.
GetDirectories method (My.Computer.FileSystem property)	Returns the names of subdirectories belonging to a particular directory.
GetDirectoryInfo method (My.Computer.FileSystem property)	Returns information about a particular directory.
GetDriveInfo method (My.Computer.FileSystem property)	Returns information about a particular drive.
GetFiles method (My.Computer.FileSystem property)	Returns the names of subdirectories belonging to a particular directory.
GetName method (My.Computer.FileSystem property)	Returns the name of the last path component (a directory or filename) in a directory path.
GetParentPath method (My.Computer.FileSystem property)	Returns all but the last path component (a directory or filename) in a directory path.
GetTempFileName method (My.Computer.FileSystem property)	Creates a uniquely named zero-length temporary file and returns its fully qualified path and filename.
Kill subroutine	Deletes a file.
Input subroutine	Reads data from a binary or sequential file and assigns it to a variable.
InputString function	Returns a String value from a file opened in binary or input mode.
LineInput function	Reads a line from an open sequential file.
Loc function	Indicates the current position of the file pointer.
Lock subroutine	Locks all or part of a file opened using the FileOpen subroutine.
LOF function	Indicates the size in bytes of an open file.
MkDir subroutine	Creates a directory.
MoveDirectory method (My.Computer.FileSystem property)	Moves a directory, along with its files, child directories, and their files, to another directory.
MoveFile method (My.Computer.FileSystem property)	Moves a single file.
OpenTextFieldParser method (My.Computer.FileSystem property)	Parses structured text files, including fixed-width and delimited text files.
OpenTextFileReader method (My.Computer.FileSystem property)	Opens a StreamReader object to read from a text file.
OpenTextFileWriter method (My.Computer.FileSystem property)	Opens a StreamWriter object to write to a text file.

Element	Description
Print, PrintLine subroutines	Write formatted data to a sequential file.
ReadAllText method (My.Computer.FileSystem property)	Reads the entire contents of a text file.
Rename subroutine	Renames a file or directory.
RenameDirectory method (My.Computer.FileSystem property)	Renames a single directory.
Reset subroutine	Closes all files opened using the FileOpen subroutine.
RmDir subroutine	Deletes a directory.
Seek function	Gets or sets the position of the file pointer in a file opened using the FileOpen subroutine.
SetAttr function	Sets the attributes of a file or directory.
SPC function	Inserts a designated number of spaces between expressions in a Print or PrintLine function.
SpecialDirectories property (My.Computer.FileSystem property)	Retrieves the physical path of a special Windows directory.
Tab function	Positions the insertion point for file output to a particular column when using the Print or PrintLine function.
Unlock subroutine	Unlocks the part of a file locked using the Lock subroutine.
Write, WriteLine subroutines	Write data to a sequential file.
WriteAllBytes method (My.Computer.FileSystem property)	Writes data to a binary file.
WriteAllText method (My.Computer.FileSystem property)	Writes text to a file.

Financial

Element	Description
DDB function	Calculates the depreciation of an asset for a specific time period.
FV function	Calculates the future value of an annuity based on periodic fixed payments and a fixed interest rate.
IPmt function	Calculates the interest payment for a specific period of an annuity based on periodic, fixed payments and a fixed interest rate.
IRR function	Determines the internal rate of return for a series of periodic cash flows composed of both payments and receipts.
MIRR function	Calculates the modified internal rate of return for a series of cash flow payments.
NPer function	Calculates the number of periods for an annuity based on fixed periodic payments at a fixed interest rate.
NPV function	Determines the net present value of an investment based on a series of periodic cash flows.

Element	Description
Pmt function	Determines the payment for an annuity based on periodic fixed payments and a fixed interest rate.
PPmt function	Calculates the principal payment for a specific period of an annuity based on periodic fixed payments and a fixed interest rate.
PV function	Calculates the present value of an annuity based on regular fixed payments in the future and a fixed interest rate.
Rate function	Calculates the interest rate per period for an annuity.
SLN function	Calculates the straight-line depreciation of an asset in a single period.
SYD function	Calculates the sum-of-years digits depreciation of an asset for a specified period.

General Programming

Element	Description
Alias keyword	Defines the actual name of an external method or subroutine when it will be invoked by some other name.
Ansi keyword	Indicates that any strings passed to and returned by external DLL routines should be marshaled as ANSI strings.
AppActivate subroutine	Gives the focus to a particular application window based on its caption or task ID.
ApplicationContext property (My.Computer class)	Returns the application context for the current thread of a Windows forms application.
Audio property (My.Computer class)	Allows control of a computer's sound system.
Auto keyword	Resolves the way in which the runtime searches for an external function or subroutine name at runtime.
ByRef keyword	Indicates that an argument is passed by reference to a called method.
ByVal keyword	Indicates that an argument is passed by value to a called method.
Call statement	Invokes a function, procedure, or external DLL routine.
CallByName function	At runtime, invokes a method or accesses a property's set or get accessor dynamically by its name.
Clipboard property (My.Computer class)	Allows programmatic access to the Clipboard.
Declare statement	Defines an external routine located in a Windows dynamic link library.
DeleteSetting subroutine	Deletes a key or value from the registry.
End statement	Abruptly terminates program execution, or marks the end of a code block begun with a Visual Basic language statement.
Enum statement	Declares an enumeration and defines its members.
Exit statement	Prematurely exits a Visual Basic programming construct.
Function statement	Defines a procedure that returns a value.

Element	Description
GetAllSettings function	Retrieves all the values belonging to a designated registry key.
GetSetting function	Retrieves a value from the registry.
HideModuleName attribute	Allows a member of a Visual Basic module to be accessed without referring to its containing module.
If . . . ElseIf . . . Else . . . End If statement	Conditionally executes a block of statements based on the evaluation of a logical (True or False) condition.
IIf function	Evaluates either of two expressions and returns the result, depending on whether a conditional expression is True or False.
Imports statement	Allows a type or another namespace to be referenced in code without its fully qualified namespace name.
Is keyword	Compares two object expressions, two object types, or a test expression with another expression.
IsDBNull function	Indicates whether an expression evaluates to null, typically because data is missing or invalid.
Keyboard property (My.Computer class)	Includes properties that indicate whether special keyboard keys are pressed.
Len function	Indicates the number of characters in a string, the number of bytes occupied by a variable in memory, or the number of bytes required to store a variable in a file.
Lib keyword	Defines the dynamic link library file in which an external function or subroutine resides.
Module statement	Declares a code module.
Mouse property (My.Computer class)	Provides access to properties of the system mouse.
Name property (My.Computer class)	Returns the computer name.
Option Compare statement	Defines whether string comparisons are case sensitive or insensitive.
Option Explicit statement	Determines whether variables must be explicitly declared before they are used.
Option Strict statement	Prohibits implicit narrowing conversions.
Optional keyword	Defines a parameter as optional.
ParamArray keyword	Defines a parameter array that represents a variable number of arguments.
Ports property (My.Computer class)	Provides access to a system's serial ports.
QBColor function	Returns an Integer representing an RGB color value.
ReadOnly keyword	Indicates that the value of a variable or property can be retrieved but not assigned.
Registry property (My.Computer class)	Provides access to the system registry.
Rem statement	Defines the beginning of a comment.
RGB function	Returns an Integer representing an RGB color value.
SaveSetting subroutine	Creates or saves a registry value.
Screen property (My.Computer class)	Provides access to a computer's display devices.

Element	Description
Settings class (My.Settings)	Allows access to application and user configuration settings.
Shared keyword	Declares a program element that is associated with a class or structure, and not with a particular instance of that class or structure.
Sub statement	Defines a procedure that does not return a value.
Switch function	Returns the result of evaluating an expression that is paired with the first expression in a list to evaluate to True.
SyncLock statement	Prevents multiple threads from executing the same code block simultaneously.
SystemTypeName function	Returns the name of the .NET type that corresponds to a Visual Basic data type.
Unicode keyword	Indicates that any strings passed to and returned by external DLL routines should be marshaled as Unicode strings.
With statement	Executes a series of statements using a common reference to a class or structure instance.

Generic Classes

Element	Description
As keyword	Introduces a constraint on a generic type parameter.
Class keyword	Constrains a generic type parameter by requiring that the argument passed to it be a reference type.
Of keyword	Defines a type parameter of a generic class, structure, interface, delegate, or procedure.
Structure keyword	Constrains a generic type parameter by requiring that the argument passed to it be a value type.

Information

Element	Description
Info property (My.Application class)	Provides information about the application's assembly.
Info property (My.Computer class)	Provides information about the operating system version, physical memory, and system locale.
Rem statement	Defines the beginning of a comment.
ScriptEngine property	Returns the string "VB".
ScriptEngineBuildVersion property	Returns the build number of the .NET runtime currently in use.
ScriptEngineMinorVersion property	Indicates the minor version number of the .NET runtime.
Shell function	Runs an executable program.
SystemTypeName function	Returns the name of the .NET type that corresponds to a Visual Basic data type.

Interaction

Element	Description
Beep subroutine	Sounds a tone on the computer's speaker.
Choose function	Returns one of many values based on an index value.
Command function	Returns any command-line arguments used when launching a Visual Basic executable.
CommandLineArgs property (My.Application class)	Returns a string collection consisting of command-line arguments passed to the application when it was launched.
Deployment property (My.Application class)	Returns an ApplicationDeployment object, which is used to support click-once deployment and on-demand downloads of files.
Environ function	Returns the value of an operating system environment variable.
GetEnvironmentVariable method (My.Application class)	Retrieves the value of a named environment variable.
InputBox function	Displays a dialog with a TextBox control that prompts for user input.
IsNetworkDeployed property (My.Application class)	Returns a Boolean indicating whether the application was deployed from a network using ClickOnce.
Log property (My.Application class)	Returns a Log object that allows information to be written to application logs from a client application.
MsgBox function	Displays a message box with a caption, text, buttons, and an icon.
Shell function	Runs an executable program.

Internet Programming

Element	Description
My.Request class	Provides information about the client requesting a web page.
My.Response class	Provides access to the output stream sent in response to a client request.
My.WebServices class	Provides access to the web services and web methods referenced by a project.

Math and Numeric Operations

Element	Description
Fix function	Returns the integer portion of a number.
Hex function	Returns a string representing the hexadecimal value of a number.
Int function	Returns the integer portion of a number (i.e., truncates a number).
Octal function	Returns a string representing the octal (base 8) value of a number.
Operator statement	Defines an operation for either a class or a structure.
Partition function	Returns a string describing the range of numbers within which a particular number falls.
Randomize subroutine	Initializes the random number generator.

Object-Oriented Programming

Element	Description
AddHandler statement	Dynamically defines an event handler.
As keyword	Begins an As clause, which constrains the legal types that may be stored in a variable or argument, returned by a function or property, or used as a generic type parameter.
Assembly keyword	Indicates that an attribute applies to an entire assembly, rather than to individual elements within it.
Class statement	Defines a class.
Collection class	A container whose members can be accessed by name/key or by ordinal position.
Default keyword	Identifies a property as the default property of a class.
Delegate statement	Defines a delegate.
Get statement	Defines a property get accessor, which is used to retrieve the value of a property.
Global keyword	Qualifies a .NET Framework Class Library reference to make it unambiguous.
Handles keyword	Indicates that a procedure handles one or more events raised by an object.
Implements keyword	Indicates that a particular member of a class or structure provides the concrete implementation of a particular interface member.
Implements statement	Indicates that a class or structure provides an implementation for one or more interfaces.
Inherits statement	Indicates that the current class or interface is derived from a base class and therefore inherits its members.
Interface statement	Defines an interface.
Is keyword	Compares two object expressions or two object types.
Is Not keyword	Compares two object expressions for inequality.
IsNothing function	Indicates whether an expression contains a null object reference.
IsReference function	Indicates whether an expression evaluates to a reference type.
Me keyword	Provides a reference to the class or structure instance in which the code is currently executing.
Module keyword	Indicates that an attribute applies to an entire module, rather than to an individual programming element within it.
MustInherit keyword	Defines an abstract base class that cannot be instantiated.
MustOverride keyword	Indicates that a base class does not provide an implementation of a member, which must be overridden in a derived class in order to be used.
MyBase keyword	References a base class from within its derived class.
MyClass keyword	Provides a reference to the class or structure instance in which the code is currently executing as it was originally implemented.
Namespace statement	Defines a namespace.

Element	Description
Narrowing keyword	Indicates that a custom type conversion operation defined with CType is a narrowing conversion that could result in a loss of data.
New keyword	Instantiates a new object instance and invokes its class constructor, or defines the constructor of a class or structure.
NotInheritable keyword	Marks a class as sealed.
NotOverridable keyword	Indicates that a class member cannot be overridden in a derived class.
Of keyword	Defines a type parameter of a generic class, structure, interface, delegate, or procedure.
Operator statement	Defines either an operation or a custom conversion for a class or a structure.
Overloads keyword	Indicates that a property or method is one of two or more properties or methods with the same name but different signatures.
Overridable keyword	Indicates that a base class member can be overridden by an identically named member in a derived class.
Overrides keyword	Indicates that a derived class member overrides an identically named member in its base class.
Partial keyword	Indicates that a class or structure declaration provides only a partial definition of the type.
Property statement	Defines a property procedure, which typically allows access to some attribute of a class or structure.
Protected keyword	Indicates that a program element is accessible from within the class in which it is declared and from derived classes.
Set statement	Defines a property set accessor, which is used to assign a value to a property.
Shadows keyword	Indicates that a program element redeclares and hides an identically named element in a base class.
Structure statement	Defines a structure, a value type that is one of the five basic .NET types.
Using statement	Provides for a system resource to be released.
Widening keyword	Used with the Operator statement to indicate that a custom type conversion operation defined with CType is a widening operation that can be handled automatically by the .NET runtime.
WriteOnly keyword	Indicates that the value of a property can be set but not retrieved.

Program Structure and Flow

Element	Description
Call statement	Calls a function, subroutine, class method, or external dynamic link library routine.
Case keyword	Defines the individual values against which a Select Case statement's expression is evaluated.
Continue statement	Transfers control within a looping structure to the beginning of the loop.

Element	Description
Do . . . Loop statement	Repeats a block of statements while an expression is true or until it becomes true.
Exit statement	Prematurely exits a Visual Basic programming construct.
For Each . . . Next statement	Executes a series of statements for each member of an array or a collection.
For . . . Next statement	Executes a series of statements a number of times that depends on the value of a loop counter.
GoTo statement	Unconditionally transfers control to a label within a function or subroutine.
If . . . ElseIf . . . Else...End If statement	Conditionally executes a block of statements based on the evaluation of a logical (True or False) condition.
Next keyword	Marks the end point of a loop.
Return statement	Returns control from a called procedure, function, property, or operator, and optionally returns a value.
Select Case statement	Executes one of a number of blocks of code depending on the evaluation of a test expression.
Step keyword	Defines by how much the loop counter of a For . . . Next construct is incremented.
Stop statement	Suspends program execution.
SyncLock statement	Prevents multiple threads from executing the same code block simultaneously.
While statement	Executes a loop until a condition becomes False.

Regionalization and Internationalization

Element	Description
ChangeCulture method (My.Application class)	Changes the culture of the current thread.
ChangeUICulture method (My.Application class)	Changes the culture that the current thread uses for retrieving culture-specific resources.
Culture property (My.Application class)	Returns a CultureInfo object representing the cultural settings used by the current thread.
Culture property (My.Resources class)	Returns a CultureInfo object representing the cultural settings used by the current thread.
ResourceManager property (My.Resources class)	Returns a ResourceManager object that can retrieve culture-specific resources.
UICulture property (My.Application class)	Returns a System.Globalization.CultureInfo object representing the culture of the current thread.

Security

Element	Description
CurrentPrincipal property (My.User class)	Gets or sets the current user's security context.
InitializeWithWindowsUser method (My.User class)	Initializes the My.User object.
IsAuthenticated property (My.User class)	Indicates whether the user has been authenticated.
IsInRole method (My.User class)	Indicates whether the current user belongs to a particular role.
Name property (My.User class)	Returns the name of the current user.

String Manipulation

Element	Description
Asc, AscW functions	Returns the character code that represents a character.
Chr, ChrW functions	Returns the character that corresponds to a character code.
CombinePath method (My.Computer.FileSystem property)	Combines two file system paths into a properly formatted path.
Filter function	Returns a filtered string array whose elements match a particular substring search criteria.
Format function	Returns a formatted string.
FormatCurrency function	Returns a string formatted as a currency value.
FormatDateTime function	Returns a formatted string representation of a date/time value.
FormatNumber function	Returns a formatted string representation of a number.
GetChar function	Retrieves a Char representing a single character from a string.
GetName method (My.Computer.FileSystem property)	Returns the name of the last path component (a directory or filename) in a directory path.
GetParentPath method (My.Computer.FileSystem property)	Returns all but the last path component (a directory or filename) in a directory path.
InStr function	Indicates the starting position of a substring within a larger string.
InStrRev function	Searches for a substring within a string from the end of the string to its front, and returns its position in the string.
Join function	Concatenates a string from an array of strings.
LCase function	Converts a character or the characters in a string to lowercase.
Left function	Extracts a particular number of characters from the left side of a string.
Len function	Reports the number of characters in a string.
LSet function	Left-aligns a string and pads it with spaces to make it a specified length.

Element	Description
LTrim function	Removes any leading spaces from a string.
Mid function	Returns a substring that starts at a specified position in a string.
Mid statement	Replaces a specified number of characters in a string with another string.
Option Compare statement	Defines whether string comparisons are case sensitive or insensitive.
Replace function	Replaces a substring with another string a specified number of times.
Right function	Extracts a particular number of characters from the right side of a string.
RSet function	Right-aligns a string and prepends spaces to it to make it a specified length.
RTrim function	Removes any trailing spaces from a string.
Space function	Returns a string consisting of a specified number of spaces.
SPC function	Inserts a designated number of spaces between expressions in a Print or PrintLine function.
Split function	Returns a one-dimensional array of strings extracted from a single delimited string.
StrComp function	Returns the result of a string comparison.
StrConv function	Performs any of a variety of supported string conversions.
StrDup function	Creates a string consisting of a particular character repeated a specified number of times.
StrReverse function	Returns a string in which the order of characters is the reverse of a source string.
UCase function	Converts a character or the characters in a string to uppercase.

Type System and Type Conversion

Element	Description
Asc, AscW functions	Returns the character code that represents a character.
CBool function	Converts an expression to a Boolean.
CByte function	Converts an expression to a Byte.
CChar function	Converts an expression to a Char.
CDate function	Converts an expression to a Date.
CDbl function	Converts an expression to a Double.
CDec function	Converts an expression to a Decimal.
CInt function	Converts an expression to an Integer.
CLng function	Converts an expression to a Long.
CObj function	Converts any data type to an Object.
CSByte function	Converts an expression to an SByte, or signed byte.
CShort function	Converts an expression to a Short.
CSng function	Converts an expression to a Single.

Element	Description
CStr function	Converts an expression to a String.
CType function	Converts from one .NET type to another.
CUInt function	Converts an expression to a UInteger.
CULng function	Converts an expression to a ULong.
CUShort function	Converts an expression to a UShort.
DirectCast function	Performs type conversion based on inheritance or interface implementation.
Format function	Returns a formatted string.
IsArray function	Indicates whether a variable or an expression is an array.
IsDate function	Indicates whether an expression can be converted to the Date data type.
IsReference function	Indicates whether an expression evaluates to a reference type.
Narrowing keyword	Indicates that a custom type conversion operation defined with CType is a narrowing operation that could result in a loss of data.
Nothing keyword	Represents the default value of any data type.
Operator statement	Defines either a custom conversion for a class or a structure.
Option Strict statement	Prohibits implicit narrowing conversions.
Str function	Converts a number to a string.
SystemTypeName function	Returns the name of the .NET type that corresponds to a Visual Basic data type.
TryCast function	Performs type conversion based on inheritance or interface implementation, but does not throw an exception if the conversion fails.
TypeName function	Returns a String indicating the data type of a variable or expression.
Val function	Converts the string representation of a number to a numeric value.
VarType function	Returns a member of the VariantType enumeration indicating the data type of an expression.
VbTypeName function	Returns the name of the "intrinsic" Visual Basic data type that corresponds to a type in .NET's Common Type System.

Variable and Constant Declaration and Initialization

Element	Description
As keyword	Begins an As clause, which constrains the legal types that may be stored in a variable or argument, returned by a function or property, or used as a generic type parameter.
Const statement	Declares a constant.
Dim statement	Declares one or more variables.
Erase statement	Erases the contents of array variables and releases their memory.
Friend keyword	Limits the accessibility of a programming element to the assembly in which it is declared.

Element	Description
New keyword	Instantiates a new object and invokes its class constructor.
Nothing keyword	Represents the default value of any data type.
Option Explicit statement	Determines whether variables must be explicitly declared before they are used.
Private keyword	Declares a program element that is accessible only within the context within which it is declared.
Protected keyword	Indicates that a program element is accessible from within the class in which it is declared and from derived classes.
Public keyword	Defines a program element that is accessible to any client able to access its assembly or type.
ReDim statement	Resizes an array.
Shared keyword	Declares a program element that is associated with a class or structure, and not with a particular instance of that class or structure.
Static keyword	Defines a local variable remains in existence and retains a value after the procedure in which it is declared has terminated.

Windows Forms Programming

Element	Description
DoEvents method (My.Application class)	Processes all Windows messages currently in the message queue.
Forms class (My.Forms)	Provides access to a Windows forms application's forms.
Main method (My.Application class)	Provides the application entry point for a Windows forms application.
MinimumSplashScreenDisplayTime property (My.Application class)	Gets or sets the minimum amount of time in milliseconds during which a splash screen is displayed.
NetworkAvailabilityChanged event (My.Application class)	Fired when network availability changes.
OpenForms property (My.Application class)	Returns a collection of all open forms in a Windows application.
Run method (My.Application class)	Sets up and starts the Visual Basic Application object.
SaveMySettingsOnExit property (My.Application class)	Gets or sets a value indicating whether the application saves user settings on exit.
Shutdown event	Fired when the application shuts down.
SplashScreen property (My.Application class)	Gets or sets the application's splash screen.
Startup event (My.Application class)	Fired when the application starts.
StartupNextInstance event (My.Application class)	Fired when an attempt is made to launch a second instance of a running single-instance application.
UnhandledExceptionEvent	Fired when an exception is not caught by an event handler.

Operators

I n addition to its arithmetic and assignment operators, Visual Basic .NET includes operators for comparison, string concatenation, and logical and bitwise operations. This appendix documents them, along with a miscellaneous category that includes the AddressOf and GetType operators. A section also discusses the order of precedence, which determines the order in which operations are performed. Finally, in Visual Basic 2005, Visual Basic .NET for the first time supports operator overloading. The final section of this appendix discusses how it works.

Arithmetic Operators

Visual Basic supports the standard arithmetic operators (addition, subtraction, multiplication, division, modular arithmetic, exponentiation) and also adds an integer division operator. Arithmetic operations share a number of common characteristics:

- If an arithmetic operation is attempted with a string representation of a number, Visual Basic's behavior depends on the setting of Option Strict. If Option Strict is off, the compiler converts the string to a Double before performing the operation. If Option Strict is on, the compiler generates an error.

- If an arithmetic operation is attempted with an expression whose value is Nothing, Visual Basic's behavior depends on the setting of Option Strict. If Option Strict is off, the compiler converts Nothing to an Integer with a value of 0 and performs the operation. If Option Strict is on, the compiler generates an error.

- The data type of the value that results from an arithmetic operation requiring two operands is that of the operand that has the greater range. (Numeric types in order of range, from least to greatest, are SByte, Byte, Short, UShort, Integer, UInteger, Long, ULong, Decimal, Single, and Double.) For example, the addition of a Single and a Double returns a Double value, because the Double data type has the greater range. There are two exceptions: exponentiation using the ^ operator, which always returns a Double; and floating point division using the / operator, which usually returns a Double.

The arithmetic operators supported by Visual Basic .NET follow.

+

+ is a unary operator, although it is rarely used in this way. Its most common usage is as an addition operator: it adds two numeric operands. Its syntax is:

```
expression1 + expression2
```

The + operator can also be used for concatenating two strings.

-

The minus sign is the unary operator and subtraction operator: as a unary operator, it reverses the sign of a numeric value; as a subtraction operator, it subtracts two numeric values. As a unary operator, its syntax is:

```
-expression1
```

As a subtraction operator, its syntax is:

```
expression1 - expression2
```

The data type of the value resulting from a unary operation is the same as that of the original expression (unless an overflow exception is thrown).

*

The asterisk is the multiplication operator: it multiplies two numeric operands. Its syntax is:

```
expression1 * expression2
```

Unlike some other numeric operations, multiplication does not cast its result to a wider available type in the event of an overflow. As a result, your code should be prepared to handle an OverflowException if there is a chance that the product of a multiplication might exceed the range of the wider data type used in the multiplication.

/

The slash is the floating-point division operator: it divides a dividend by a divisor and returns a floating-point quotient. Its syntax is:

```
expression1 / expression2
```

If either the divisor or the dividend is a Single and the other value is not a Double, the quotient is a Single. If either the divisor or the dividend is of type Decimal and the other value is neither a Single nor a Double, the quotient is a Decimal. Otherwise, the quotient is a Double.

A DivideByZeroException is thrown if the divisor is a Decimal equal to 0. In all other cases of division by zero, an integral divisor equal to 0 is converted to a Double, or the divisor is already either a Single or a Double. In this case, the division returns either PositiveInfinity or NegativeInfinity, depending on the sign of the dividend.

\

The backslash is the integer division operator; it divides an integral dividend by an integral divisor and returns an integral quotient. Any remainder is discarded. Its syntax is:

```
expression1 \ expression2
```

If Option Strict is off, any floating-point value is converted to a Long before the division is performed. If Option Strict is on, then a compiler error results.

If the value of the divisor is 0 (or Nothing), a DivideByZeroException is thrown.

Mod

Mod is the modulus division operator: it performs a division and returns the remainder. Its syntax is:

```
expression1 Mod expression2
```

If division by 0 occurs with an integral data type, a DivideByZeroException is thrown. If division by 0 occurs with a floating point data type, the result is NaN (Not a Number) rather than an exception.

^

The caret is the exponentiation operator: it raises a number to the power of a second number. Its syntax is:

```
expression1 ^ expression2
```

Both *expression1* and *expression2* are converted to Doubles before performing the exponentiation. The result is therefore a Double.

Assignment Operators

Visual Basic 6.0 had a single assignment operator. In Visual Basic .NET 1.0 and 1.1, there are seven additional assignment operators, one for each of the arithmetic operations and one for string concatenation. Visual Basic .NET 1.1 added two more assignment operators for bit shift operations. Each of these nine additional assignment operators has the form

```
lvalue <operator> expression
```

where *<operator>* is one of the assignment operators, *lvalue* is an expression referring to the location to which the assignment is to be made and is typically a variable, writable property, or array element, and *expression* is the value that determines by how much the operator modifies *lvalue*. For example, the statement

```
counter += 3
```

increments the variable counter by 3 and stores the result back to counter, while

```
binValue <<= 2
```

shifts the integer binValue two bits to the left, effectively multiplying its value by 8.

Visual Basic .NET supports the assignment operators shown next.

=

Assigns the result of the expression of the right side of the operator to the variable, array element, or non-read-only property on its left side.

The assignment operator can also be used to initialize a variable at the same time as it is declared, as in the statement

```
Dim counter As Integer = 1
```

Note that = is also a comparison operator. (It is analogous to the == operator in C, C++, and C#.)

+=

Increments an *lvalue* by a given amount and assigns the result back to it.

-=

Decrements a variable or property value by a given amount and assigns the result back to it.

*=

Multiplies the value of a variable or property by a given amount and assigns the result back to it.

/=

Divides a variable or property value by a given amount and assigns the result back to it. Note that if Option Strict is on, the variable or property must be a Double, or it must be explicitly converted to a Double.

\=

Performs integer division on the value of a variable or property and assigns the result back to it.

^=

Raises the value of a variable or property to a given power and assigns the result back to it.

&=

Concatenates the value of the reference of the left hand–side expression with another string value and assigns the result back to the referent of the left hand–side expression.

<<=

Shifts the value of a variable or property to the left by a given number of bits and assigns the result back to the variable or property.

>>=

Shifts the value of a variable or property to the right by a given number of bits and assigns the result back to the variable or property.

Concatenation Operators

A concatenation operator concatenates two string values and returns the resulting string. If Option Strict is on and either of the two operands is not a string, Visual Basic automatically performs any widening conversion, but generates a runtime error for any narrowing conversion. If Option Strict is off, Visual Basic attempts to perform any necessary conversions automatically. A null value is treated as an empty string. The concatenation operators follow.

&

Concatenates two strings. The setting of Option Strict does not affect the & operator, since it treats as widening conversions all non-string to string conversions. Unlike the other concatenation operator, +, & is unambiguous: it only serves as a concatenation operator.

+

Concatenates two strings. The + also serves as the addition operator, which can make its use as a concatenation operator in code that includes arithmetic operations ambiguous. If Option Strict is on, + concatenates strings only and does not convert non-strings to strings before performing concatenation, as does the & operator. With Option Strict off, + functions virtually identically to the & operator.

Comparison Operators

Comparison operators evaluate two expressions of the form

```
expression1 <operator> expression2
```

and return either a True, a False, or a Null. (A Null results only if one or both of the expressions is Null.) Typically, comparison operators are used in conditional statements, such as If and Do While statements. The comparison operators supported by Visual Basic .NET follow.

<

The less-than operator, < returns True if *expression1* is less than *expression2*, and False otherwise.

<=

The less-than or equal-to operator, <= returns True if *expression1* is less than or equal to *expression2*, and False otherwise. In VB6 and earlier versions, =< was also acceptable as the less-than or equal-to operator; in Visual Basic .NET, it generates a compiler error.

>

The greater-than operator, > returns True if *expression1* is greater than *expression2*, and False otherwise.

>=

The greater-than or equal-to operator, >= returns True if *expression1* is greater than or equal to *expression2*, and False otherwise. In VB6 and earlier versions, => was also acceptable as the greater-than or equal-to operator; in Visual Basic .NET, it generates a compiler error.

The equality operator, = returns True if *expression1* is equal to *expression2*. Note that = is also an assignment operator.

<>

The inequality operator, <> returns True if *expression1* is not equal to *expression2,* and False otherwise. In VB6 and earlier versions, >< was also acceptable as the inequality operator; in Visual Basic .NET, it generates a compiler error.

In floating point comparisons of a Single with a Double, the Single is converted to a Double before the comparison. Similarly, when a Decimal is compared with a Single or Double, it is converted to a Single or Double before the comparison.

String comparison is determined by the setting of Option Compare. If it is set to Text, the comparison is not case sensitive, and sort order is based on the local system's locale. If it is set to Binary, the comparison is case sensitive, and sort order is based on the code page.

The setting of Option Strict also determines the data types that can be used in the comparison. If this option is off, Visual Basic converts strings to their numeric representations before performing a numeric comparison, and comparisons with Object types are permitted if the object at runtime is not a reference type other than String. If on, Object types cannot be compared, and strings are not converted for numeric comparisons.

Regardless of the setting of Option Strict, the previous comparison operators can never be used to compare two reference types other than Strings. For this purpose, use the Is operator.

Visual Basic also supports a number of specialized comparison operators.

Is

Compares two object references to determine whether they reference the same object instance. Its syntax is:

```
expression1 Is expression2
```

The Is operator is also used with the TypeOf operator to determine whether an object instance is of a particular type or implements a particular interface. To test whether two object variables refer to different object instances, use the IsNot operator.

IsNot

Compares two object variables to determine whether they reference different object instances. Its syntax is:

```
expression1 IsNot expression2
```

The IsNot operator is the opposite of Is. It was introduced in .NET 2.0 to avoid awkward and potentially confusing statements such as:

```
Not (expression1 Is expression2)
```

Like

Compares a string, *expression1,* with a pattern, *expression2.* The result is True if the string matches the pattern and False otherwise. Its syntax is:

```
expression1 Like expression2
```

TypeOf

Compares an object reference to a data type. It is always used along with the Is operator. Its syntax is:

```
TypeOf object1 Is typename
```

If *typename* names a structure, the operation returns True if *object1* is of the named type, False if it is not. If *typename* names a class, the operation returns True if *object1* is an instance of the *typename* class. (Instances of classes derived from the named class are themselves instances of the named class.) If *typename* names an interface, the operation returns True if *object1* implements that interface. (An object which inherits from a class that implements an interface itself implements the interface.)

Logical (Boolean) Operators

Visual Basic .NET supports the following Boolean operators, which evaluate either one or two logical expressions to produce an expression whose value is either True or False. The Boolean operators follow.

And

And is a logical conjunction operator; that is, it returns True if both operands are True, and False otherwise. Its syntax is

```
operand1 And operand2
```

The result is shown here:

Operand1	Operand2	And	Or	Xor
True	True	True	True	False
True	False	False	True	True
False	True	False	True	True
False	False	False	False	False

AndAlso

The short-circuiting logical conjunction operator, AndAlso is identical to And, except that, if the result of the operation is known solely based on the evaluation of *operand1, operand2* is not evaluated. Its syntax is:

```
operand1 AndAlso operand2
```

The result is shown in the following table:

Operand1	Operand2	Result
True	True	True
True	False	False
False	<not evaluated>	False

Or

Or is the logical disjunction operator; that is, it returns True if either operand is True, and False otherwise. Its syntax is:

```
operand1 Or operand2
```

OrElse

The short-circuiting logical disjunction operator, OrElse is identical to Or, except that *operand2* is not evaluated if the result is known solely by evaluating *operand1*. The syntax of OrElse is:

```
operand1 OrElse operand2
```

The result is shown in the following table:

Operand1	Operand2	Result
True	<not evaluated>	True
False	True	True
False	False	False

XOr

Xor is the logical exclusion operator; that is, it returns True if the operands differ, and False otherwise. Its syntax is:

```
operand1 XOr operand2
```

Not

Not is the logical negation operator; that is, it reverses the value of a logical expression. Its syntax is:

```
Not operand1
```

The result is shown in the following table:

Operand	Result
True	False
False	True

Logical Operators Not Present in Visual Basic .NET

Visual Basic 6.0 and earlier versions supported these two logical operators that are not present in Visual Basic .NET:

- Eqv, the logical equivalence operator. It returns True if both expressions have the same value and False if they don't. Since its result is the reverse of the XOr operator, it can be simulated in Visual Basic .NET by using a statement like

```
Not (expression1 XOr expression2)
```

- Imp, the logical implication operator. The following shows the result of using the Imp operator:

Expression1	Expression2	Result
True	True	True
True	False	False
False	True	True
False	False	True

The effect of the Imp operator can be simulated in Visual Basic .NET by using a statement like

```
(Not expression1) Or expression2
```

Visual Basic .NET 2.0 also adds two new logical operators that are called by the .NET runtime to determine whether short-circuiting should occur in AndAlso and OrElse operations:

- IsTrue is called directly by the .NET runtime when the first operation in an OrElse operation is evaluated to determine whether short-circuiting should occur.
- IsFalse is called directly by the .NET runtime when the first operand in an AndAlso operation is evaluated to determine whether short-circuiting should occur.

Both operators evaluate a single operand and return a Boolean. You need to implement them in a class or structure under the following conditions:

- You've implemented an overloaded Or operator that returns an instance of your class or structure, and you want to be able to take advantage of short-circuiting with the OrElse operator as well. (See the "Operator Overloading" section later in this appendix for a discussion of operator overloading.)
- You've implemented either the IsTrue or the IsFalse operator for your class or structure. IsTrue and IsFalse are operator pairs; if you implement one, you must implement the other.

The example in the "Operator Overloading" section illustrates the use of IsTrue and IsFalse.

Binary (Bitwise) Operators

In addition to serving as logical operators, the And, Or, XOr, and Not operators serve as bitwise operators when used with numeric expressions. That is, rather than evaluating the numeric value as a whole, they perform a bit-by-bit operation on two integral values (or one integral value, in the case of the Not bitwise operator) and return an integer result.

Bitwise operations are performed on the integral data types only. If a floating point type is used, Visual Basic converts it to Long before performing the operation if Option Strict is off; typically, this produces a compiler warning. Since changing a floating point value to a Long is a narrowing conversion, a compiler error results if Option Strict is on.

The value returned by the bitwise operation corresponds to the widest type used in the operation. If integers of different sizes are used in the operation, the bitwise operator assumes that the bits not present in the shorter word are equal to 0.

In addition to And, Or, XOr, and Not as bitwise operators, Visual Basic .NET has two bit shift operators that were added in .NET 1.1: Their syntax is:

```
expression <operator> shift
```

where *expression* is an integer whose bits are to be shifted, and *shift* is the number of positions the bits in *expression* are to be shifted. The result of the operation is an integer of the same type as *expression*. Bits dropped from one end of the integer are not recycled to the other end; instead, they are simply discarded.

The bit shift operators supported by Visual Basic .NET follow.

<<

Shifts bits a designated number of bits to the left.

>>

Shifts bits a designated number of bits to the right.

Shift Operations and Signed Integers

Care must be taken in performing shift operations on signed integers whose value is negative. The leftmost bit of a signed integer is the sign bit, and a left shift operation removes it. If you want to preserve the sign bit after a shift operation, then you need to use code like the following:

```
Dim negValue As Integer = -1024
' Save state of sign bit
Dim signBit As Integer = negValue And &H80000000
negValue = negValue << 2
' Clear sign bit
negValue = negValue And &H7FFFFFFF
' Restore sign bit
negValue = negValue Or signBit
```

Miscellaneous Operators

Visual Basic includes two special purpose operators that return the address of a function, procedure, or property and a Type object representing a particular data type. These operators follow.

AddressOf

Creates a delegate that points to a particular function or procedure.

GetType

Returns a .NET System.Type object representing a particular type. Its syntax is

```
GetType(typename)
```

where *typename* is the name of the Type, which can be a Visual Basic .NET data type (in which case it returns a Type object representing the corresponding .NET data type), a type defined the .NET Framework Class Library, a type defined in the application, or a type defined in any other library that's accessible to the application. The Type object allows you to retrieve information about the type and its members.

If you want to retrieve a Type object from an instance of that type, you can use the instance's GetType method. For instance,

```
Dim firstName As String = "John"
Dim firstNameType As Type = firstName.GetType()
```

Order of Precedence

The order of precedence determines the order in which operations in an expression are performed. For instance, without a clearly defined order of precedence, the expression

```
2 * 4 + 3
```

could produce a result of either 11 or 14, depending on whether the multiplication or the addition is performed first.

The order of precedence in Visual Basic .NET expressions is the following:

1. Arithmetic operations are performed before comparison, logical, and bitwise operations. Arithmetic operations have the following order of precedence:

   a. Exponentiation

   b. Unary negation, unary plus

   c. Multiplication and division

   d. Integer division

   e. Modular arithmetic

   f. Addition, subtraction, and string concatenation using +

   g. String concatenation using &

   h. Bit shift operations

2. Comparison operations are performed after arithmetic operations but before logical and bitwise operations. All comparison operators have equal precedence.

3. Logical and bitwise operations are performed after arithmetic and comparison operations. Logical and bitwise operations have the following order of precedence:

   a. Not

   b. And, AndAlso

   c. Or, OrElse, XOr

If multiple operations within an expression have the same order of precedence, they are evaluated from left to right.

Parentheses can be used to change the order of precedence. The operations within parentheses are evaluated together at their order of precedence. For example, in the expression

```
a * b * d + e
```

a, b, and d are multiplied together, and e is added to the result. However, in the expression

```
a * b * (d + e)
```

a and b are multiplied together and then multiplied by the result of adding d and e, since the parentheses override the order of precedence and cause the expression (d + e) to be evaluated as a single expression in the second multiplication.

If parentheses are nested, they are performed from inner parentheses to outer parentheses. If multiple operations are defined within parentheses, the rules of precedence apply, and operations at the same order of precedence are performed from left to right.

Operator Overloading

A feature introduced for the first time in Visual Basic .NET 2.0 is operator overloading, which provides custom definitions that allow particular operators to work with your types.

For instance, ordinarily it makes no sense to add one instance of a class to another, or to ask whether one instance of the class is greater than another. You can, however, provide a definition for an operator that permits it to perform an operation on two instances of your class.

You define a custom operator for your class by including an operator procedure within your class or structure definition. The operator procedure has the following rules:

- It is defined by the Operator . . . End Operator construct.

- It must be a public shared procedure defined with the Public and Shared keywords.

- Its parameter list must consist of one operand for a unary operator and two operands otherwise. One operand must be of the same type as the class or structure in which the overloaded operator is defined. If you overload the binary shift operators, their second operand must also be of type Integer.

- Operands must be passed by value. The ByRef, Optional, and ParamArray keywords cannot be used in the definition.

- The data type of the value returned by the operator procedure must be defined using the As clause if Option Strict is on. If Option Strict is off, the compiler produces a warning, and a return value of type Object is assumed.

- The actual return value of the operator procedure must be defined using one or more Return statements in the operator procedure's code.

- If the operation involves conversion of the class instance, you can specify whether the conversion performed is a widening or narrowing conversion. This means that the use of the operator will be affected by the setting of Option Strict.

- In some cases, if you define one operator, you must define its corresponding operator. These operator sets are = and <>, > and <, >= and <=, and IsTrue and IsFalse.

- And, Or, XOr, and Not can be overloaded as logical operators, but not as bitwise operators. Note that this is contrary to the documentation, which states the opposite.

- AndAlso cannot be defined as an overloaded operator, though it can be used instead of the overloaded And operator. In order to use it, the And operator must return an instance of the class or structure in which it is defined, and the IsFalse operator must also be defined.

- OrElse cannot be defined as an overloaded operator, though it can be used instead of the overloaded Or operator. In order to use it, the Or operator must return an instance of the class or structure in which it is defined, and the IsTrue operator must also be defined.

- A number of operators cannot be overloaded. These include all of the assignment operators other than =, Is, IsNot, AddressOf, GetType, and TypeOf.

There are also a number of other restrictions. For details, see the entries for the Narrowing Keyword, Operator Statement, and Widening Keyword in Chapter 8.

To illustrate, imagine that we have a structure named Package that represents a packaged food product. Our structure has three members, Size, Price, and ByWeight. We want to be able to compare the unit cost of one package with another to determine which is cheaper and which is more expensive. For this purpose, we can overload the >, <, >=, and <= operators. In addition, we've defined the Or operator to return the package sold by weight or the cheapest of two packages sold by weight. As part of implementing Or, we've also implemented the IsTrue operator to return True for a package sold by weight (i.e., whose ByWeight property is True). The code for the Package structure is:

```
Public Structure Package
    Private ounces As Single
    Private cost As Decimal
    Private fWeight As Boolean

    Public Sub New(oz As Single, pr As Decimal)
        ounces = oz
        cost = pr
        fWeight = True
    End Sub

    Public Sub New(lbs As Integer, oz As Single, pr As Decimal)
        ounces = lbs * 16 + oz
        cost = pr
        fWeight = True
    End Sub

    Public Property ByWeight() As Boolean
        Get
            Return fWeight
        End Get
```

```
      Set
          fWeight = Value
      End Set
  End Property

  Public ReadOnly Property Price() As Decimal
      Get
          Return cost
      End Get
  End Property

  Public ReadOnly Property Size() As Single
      Get
          Return ounces
      End Get
  End Property

  Public Shared Operator = (operand1 As Package, operand2 As Package) As Boolean
      If operand1.Price / operand1.Size = operand2.Price / operand2.Size Then
          Return True
      Else
          Return False
      End If
  End Operator

  Public Shared Operator <> (operand1 As Package, operand2 As Package) As Boolean
      Return Not (operand1 = operand2)
  End Operator

  Public Shared Operator > (operand1 As Package, operand2 As Package) As Boolean
      If operand1.Price / operand1.Size > operand2.Price / operand2.Size Then
          Return True
      Else
          Return False
      End If
  End Operator

  Public Shared Operator >= (operand1 As Package, operand2 As Package) As Boolean
      If operand1.Price / operand1.Size >= operand2.Price / operand2.Size Then
          Return True
      Else
          Return False
      End If
  End Operator

  Public Shared Operator < (operand1 As Package, operand2 As Package) As Boolean
      If operand1.Price / operand1.Size < operand2.Price / operand2.Size Then
          Return True
      Else
          Return False
      End If
  End Operator
```

```vb
    Public Shared Operator <= (operand1 As Package, operand2 As Package) As Boolean
        If operand1.Price / operand1.Size <= operand2.Price / operand2.Size Then
            Return True
        Else
            Return False
        End If
    End Operator

    Public Shared Operator Or (op1 As Package, op2 As Package) As Package
        If op1.ByWeight And op2.ByWeight Then
            If op1 < op2 Then
                Return op1
            Else
                Return op2
            End If
        Else
            If op1.ByWeight Then
                Return op1
            ElseIf op2.ByWeight Then
                Return op2
            Else
                Return Nothing
            End If
        End If
    End Operator

    Public Shared Operator IsTrue(Byval op1 As Package) As Boolean
        If op1.ByWeight Then
            Return True
        Else
            Return False
        End If
    End Operator

    Public Shared Operator IsFalse(ByVal op1 As Package) As Boolean
        If op1.ByWeight Then
            Return False
        Else
            Return True
        End If
    End Operator
End Structure

Public Module modTest
    Public Sub Main()
        Dim smTomatoes As Package = New Package(12, .33d)
        Dim medTomatoes As Package = New Package(24, .50d)

        smTomatoes.ByWeight = False
        medTomatoes.ByWeight = True

        If smTomatoes Or medTomatoes Then Console.WRiteLine(smTomatoes.Size)
        If smTomatoes OrElse medTomatoes Then Console.WriteLine(smTomatoes.Size)
'        Console.WriteLine(medTomatoes < smTomatoes)
'        Console.WriteLine(Package.op_LessThan(medTomatoes, smTomatoes))
    End Sub
End Module
```

We find that the medTomatoes package is indeed less expensive than the smTomatoes package.

Not all .NET languages support operator overloading. (In fact, in the two previous releases of the .NET platform, C# supported operator overloading, while Visual Basic did not.) To make overloaded operators available to other languages that do not support them, Visual Basic automatically defines shared methods that perform the same function as the overloaded operators. The names that it assigns to them are shown in the following table:

Operator	Function Name
+ (unary operator)	op_UnaryPlus
+ (addition operator)	op_Addition
- (unary operator)	op_UnaryNegation
− (subtraction operator)	op_Subtraction
*	op_Multiply
^	op_Exponent
/	op_Division
Mod	op_Modulus
\	op_IntegerDivision
&	op_Concatenate
= (comparison operator)	op_Equality
>	op_GreaterThan
<	op_LessThan
>=	op_GreaterThanOrEqual
<=	op_LessThanOrEqual
<>	op_Inequality
Like	op_Like
= (assignment operator)	op_Assign
And	op_BitwiseAnd
Or	op_BitwiseOr
XOr	op_ExclusiveOr
Not	op_OnesComplement
<<	op_LeftShift
>>	op_RightShift

So to continue our example, we could also call our overloaded is-less-than operator from a module that consumes the Package structure with the following code:

```
Console.WriteLine(Package.op_LessThan(medTomatoes, smTomatoes))
```

Constants and Enumerations

The Microsoft.VisualBasic namespace defines a number of intrinsic constants, as well as several enumerations. This appendix documents them.

Visual Basic Constants

Visual Basic's constants are all defined as static, read-only fields of the Constants class in the Microsoft.VisualBasic namespace. They are globally available to the compiler without the need to instantiate an instance of the Constants class.

All but four of the constants were available in Visual Basic 6.0, where many of the constants (such as vbArray, vbTrue, and vbUnicode) were part of enumerations. Otherwise, the constants have not been expanded to support new Visual Basic .NET features, such as its greater number of available data types.

Interestingly, in Visual Basic 2005, the values of many of the constants, rather than being defined as numeric literals, are now defined as members of a Visual Basic .NET enumeration.

The constants supported by Visual Basic are listed in the following table:

Constant Name	Data Type	Value	Comments
vbAbort	MsgBoxResult	Abort	Return value of the MsgBox function
vbAbortRetryIgnore	MsgBoxStyle	DefaultButton1, OKOnly, AbortRetryIgnore	Defines the buttons on the MsgBox dialog
vbApplicationModal	MsgBoxStyle	ApplicationModal	Defines an application modal dialog
vbArchive	FileAttribute	Archive	Used with the Dir, GetAttr, and SetAttr functions
vbArray	VariantType	Array	Used by the VarType function
vbBack	String	Chr(8)	Same as ControlChars.Back

Constant Name	Data Type	Value	Comments
vbBinaryCompare	CompareMethod	Binary	Controls how some string manipulation functions handle casing and sort order
vbBoolean	VariantType	Boolean	Used by the VarType function
vbByte	VariantType	Byte	Used by the VarType function
vbCancel	MsgBoxResult	Cancel	Return value of the MsgBox function
vbCr	String	Chr(13)	Same as ControlCharsCr
vbCritical	MsgBoxStyle	DefaultButton1, OKOnly, Critical	Defines the icon on the MsgBox dialog
vbCrLf	String	Chr(13) & Chr(10)	Same as ControlChars.CrLf
vbCurrency	VariantType	Currency	Used by the VarType function
vbDate	VariantType	Date	Used by the VarType function
vbDecimal	VariantType	Decimal	Used by the VarType function
vbDefaultButton1	MsgBoxStyle	ApplicationModal	Defines the MsgBox dialog's default button
vbDefaultButton2	MsgBoxStyle	DefaultButton1, OKOnly, DefaultButton2	Defines the MsgBox dialog's default button
vbDefaultButton3	MsgBoxStyle	DefaultButton1, OKOnly, DefaultButton3	Defines the MsgBox dialog's default button
vbDirectory	FileAttribute	Directory	Used with the Dir, GetAttr, and SetAttr functions
vbDouble	VariantType	Double	Used by the VarType function
vbEmpty	VariantType	Empty	Used by the VarType function
vbExclamation	MsgBoxStyle	DefaultButton1, OKOnly, Exclamation	Defines the icon on the MsgBox dialog
vbFalse	TriState	False	Used with the FormatCurrency, FormatNumber, and FormatPercent functions
vbFirstFourDays	FirstWeekOfYear	FirstFourDays	Used with the DateDiff and DatePart functions
vbFirstFullWeek	FirstWeekOfYear	FirstFullWeek	Used with the DateDiff and DatePart functions
vbFirstJan1	FirstWeekOfYear	Jan1	Used with the DateDiff and DatePart functions
vbFormFeed	String	Chr(12)	Same as ControlChars.FormFeed
vbFriday	FirstDayOfWeek	Friday	Used with a number of date/time functions to define the first day of the week

Constant Name	Data Type	Value	Comments
vbGeneralDate	DateFormat	GeneralDate	Used with the FormatDateTime function; this is the default value.
vbGet	CallType	Get	Used with the CallByName function
vbHidden	FileAttribute	Hidden	Used with the Dir, GetAttr, and SetAttr functions
vbHide	AppWinStyle	Hide	Used with the Shell function
vbHiragana	VbStrConv	Hiragana	Used with the StrConv function
vbIgnore	MsgBoxResult	Ignore	Return value of the MsgBox function
vbInformation	MsgBoxStyle	DefaultButton1, OKOnly, Information	Defines the icon on the MsgBox dialog
vbInteger	VariantType	Integer	Used by the VarType function
vbKatakana	VbStrConv	Katakana	Used with the StrConv function
vbLet	CallType	Let	Used with the CallByName function
vbLf	String	Chr(10)	Same as ControlChars.Lf
vbLinguisticCasing	VbStrConv	LinguisticCasing	Not a VB6 constant. Used with the StrConv function
vbLong	VariantType	Long	Used by the VarType function
vbLongDate	DateFormat	LongDate	Used with the FormatDateTime function
vbLongTime	DateFormat	LongTime	Used with the FormatDateTime function
vbLowerCase	VbStrConv	LowerCase	Used with the StrConv function
vbMaximizedFocus	AppWinStyle	MaximizedFocus	Used with the Shell function
vbMethod	CallType	Method	Used with the CallByName function
vbMinimizedFocus	AppWinStyle	MinimizedFocus	Used with the Shell function. Default value of the Style argument
vbMinimizedNoFocus	AppWinStyle	MinimizedNoFocus	Used with the Shell function
vbMonday	FirstDayOfWeek	Monday	Used with a number of date/time functions to define the first day of the week
vbMsgBoxHelp	MsgBoxStyle	DefaultButton1, OKOnly, MsgBoxHelp	Displays a Help button on the MsgBox dialog
vbMsgBoxRight	MsgBoxStyle	DefaultButton1, OKOnly, MsgBoxRight	Text is right-aligned
vbMsgBoxRtlReading	MsgBoxStyle	DefaultButton1, OKOnly, MsgBoxRtlReading	Text is read from right to left (Hebrew and Arabic systems)

Constant Name	Data Type	Value	Comments
vbMsgBoxSetForeground	MsgBoxStyle	DefaultButton1, OKOnly, MsgBoxSetForeground	Non-modal MsgBox dialog
vbNarrow	VbStrConv	Narrow	Used with the StrConv function
vbNewLine	String	Chr(13) & Chr(10)	Same as ControlChars.NewLIne
vbNo	MsgBoxResult	No	Return value of the MsgBox function
vbNormal	FileAttribute	Normal	Used with the Dir, GetAttr, and SetAttr functions
vbNormalFocus	AppWinStyle	NormalFocus	Used with the Shell function
vbNormalNoFocus	AppWinStyle	NormalNoFocus	Used with the Shell function
vbNull	VariantType	Null	Used by the VarType function
vbNullChar	String	Chr(0)	Same as ControlChars.NullChar
vbNullString	Object	Nothing	
vbObject	VariantType	Object	Used by the VarType function
vbObjectError	Integer	&H80040000	The base error number used by COM objects to generate an error number to return to their consumers
vbOK	MsgBoxResult	OK	Return value of the MsgBox function
vbOKCancel	MsgBoxStyle	DefaultButton1, OKOnly, OKCancel	Defines the buttons on the MsgBox dialog
vbOKOnly	MsgBoxStyle	ApplicationModal	Defines the buttons on the MsgBox dialog
vbProperCase	VbStrConv	ProperCase	Used with the StrConv function
vbQuestion	MsgBoxStyle	DefaultButton1, OKOnly, Question	Defines the icon on the MsgBox dialog
vbReadOnly	FileAttribute	ReadOnly	Used with the Dir, GetAttr, and SetAttr functions
vbRetry	MsgBoxResult	Retry	Return value of the MsgBox function
vbRetryCancel	MsgBoxStyle	DefaultButton1, OKOnly, RetryCancel	Defines the buttons on the MsgBox dialog
vbSaturday	FirstDayOfWeek	Saturday	Used with a number of date/time functions to define the first day of the week
vbSet	CallType	Set	Used with the CallByName function
vbShortDate	DateFormat	ShortDate	Used with the FormatDateTime function
vbShortTime	DateFormat	ShortTime	Used with the FormatDateTime function

Constant Name	Data Type	Value	Comments
vbSimplifiedChinese	VbStrConv	SimplifiedChinese	Not a VB6 constant. Used with the StrConv function
vbSingle	VariantType	Single	Used by the VarType function
vbString	VariantType	String	Used by the VarType function
vbSunday	FirstDayOfWeek	Sunday	Used with a number of date/time functions to define the first day of the week
vbSystem	FileAttribute	System	Used with the Dir, GetAttr, and SetAttr functions
vbSystemModal	MsgBoxStyle	DefaultButton1, OKOnly, SystemModal	Defines a system modal dialog
vbTab	String	Chr(9)	Same as ControlChars.Tab
vbTextCompare	CompareMethod	Text	Controls how some string manipulation functions handle casing and sort order
vbThursday	FirstDayOfWeek	Thursday	Used with a number of date/time functions to define the first day of the week
vbTraditionalChinese	VbStrConv	TraditionalChinese	Not a VB6 constant. Used with the StrConv function
vbTrue	TriState	True	Used with the FormatCurrency, FormatNumber, and FormatPercent functions
vbTuesday	FirstDayOfWeek	Tuesday	Used with a number of date/time functions to define the first day of the week
vbUpperCase	VbStrConv	UpperCase	Used with the StrConv function
vbUseDefault	TriState	UseDefault	Used with the FormatCurrency, FormatNumber, and FormatPercent functions
vbUserDefinedType	VariantType	UserDefinedType	Used by the VarType function
vbUseSystem	FirstWeekOfYear	System	Used with the DateDiff and DatePart functions
vbUseSystemDayOfWeek	FirstDayOfWeek	System	Used with a number of date/time functions to define the first day of the week
vbVariant	VariantType	Variant	Used by the VarType function
vbVerticalTab	String	Chr(11)	Same as ControlChars.VerticalTab
vbVolume	FileAttribute	Volume	Used with the Dir, GetAttr, and SetAttr functions
vbWednesday	FirstDayOfWeek	Wednesday	Used with a number of date/time functions to define the first day of the week

Constant Name	Data Type	Value	Comments
vbWide	VbStrConv	Wide	Used with the StrConv function
vbYes	MsgBoxResult	Yes	Return value of the MsgBox function
vbYesNo	MsgBoxStyle	DefaultButton1, OKOnly, YesNo	Defines the buttons on the MsgBox dialog
vbYesNoCancel	MsgBoxStyle	DefaultButton1, OKOnly, YesNoCancel	Defines the buttons on the MsgBox dialog

ControlChars Shared Fields

Visual Basic includes a ControlChars class that duplicates many of the control character constants defined by the Microsoft.VisualBasic.Constants class. Each member of the ControlChars class is a shared, read-only field. Unlike the members of the Constants class, however, the members of the ControlChars class are not globally available. Instead, they can only be accessed as shared members of the ControlChars class, as in the following code fragment:

```
Dim msg As String = "File has not been saved." & ControlChars.CrLf & _
                    "Are you sure you want to exit without saving your work?"
```

The constants of the ControlChars class are:

Constant Name	Data Type	Field Value	VB Constant
Back	Char	Chr(8)	vbBack
Cr	Char	Chr(13)	vbCr
CrLf	String	Chr(13)Chr(10)	vbCrLf
FormFeed	Char	Chr(12)	vbFormFeed
Lf	Char	Chr(10)	vbLf
NewLine	String	Chr(13)Chr(10)	vbNewLine
NullChar	Char	Chr(0)	vbNullChar
Quote	Char	Chr(34)	
Tab	Char	Chr(9)	vbTab
VerticalTab	Char	Chr(11)	vbVerticalTab

Visual Basic Enumerations

The Microsoft.VisualBasic namespace includes many of the same enumerations found in Visual Basic 6.0 and earlier versions, although it also adds some new enumerations (such as OpenAccess, OpenMode, and OpenShare) that replace integer arguments used in Visual Basic 6.0. The following sections document the enumerations defined by Visual Basic.

AppWinStyle Enumeration

Used with the *Style* argument of the Shell function to determine how an application window opened by the function call is to be displayed. It corresponds directly to the VbAppWinStyle enumeration in Visual Basic 6.0.

Members of the AppWinStyle enumeration are:

```
Public Enum AppWinStyle
   Hide = 0
   NormalFocus = 1
   MinimizedFocus = 2
   MaximizedFocus = 3        ' The default value
   NormalNoFocus = 4
   MinimizedNoFocus = 6
End Enum
```

AudioPlayMode Enumeration

Supplied as the *playmode* argument of the My.Computer.Audio.Play method to control how the sound is played. The enumeration, which is new to Visual Basic 2005, is defined as:

```
Public Enum AudioPlayMode
   WaitToComplete = 0    ' Play sound and wait for completion
   Background = 1        ' Play sound in background; default value
   BackgroundLoop = 2    ' Play sound in background until Stop method called
End Enum
```

CallType Enumeration

Used with the *UseCallType* argument of the CallByName function to define the type of procedure called by the function. It corresponds directly to the VbCallType enumeration in Visual Basic 6.0.

Members of the CallType enumeration are:

```
Public Enum CallType
   Method = 1        ' Method, function, or subroutine
   Get = 2           ' Property Get procedure
   Let = 4           ' Obsolete; same as Get
   Set = 8           ' Property Set procedure
End Enum
```

CompareMethod Enumeration

Used by a number of string manipulation functions (Filter, InStr, InStrRev, Replace, Split, and StrComp) to control how the function handles casing and sort order. It resembles the VbCompareMethod enumeration in Visual Basic 6.0, except that it lacks the latter's vbDatabaseCompare member. For details on its use, see the entry for each of the functions that use the CompareMethod enumeration in Chapter 7.

The definition of the CompareMethod enumeration is:

```
Public Enum CompareMethod
   Binary = 0        ' Case-sensitive comparison
   Text = 1          ' Case-insensitive comparison
End Enum
```

Note that a member of the CompareMethod enumeration cannot be used with the Option Compare statement at the beginning of a Visual Basic module.

DateFormat Enumeration

Used with the *NamedFormat* argument of the FormatDateTime function to determine the format in which a date or time is displayed. It corresponds exactly to the VbDateTimeFormat enumeration in Visual Basic 6.0. It is defined as follows:

```
Public Enum DateFormat
    GeneralDate = 0                    ' Default value
    LongDate = 1
    ShortDate = 2
    LongTime = 3
    ShortTime = 4
End Enum
```

DateInterval Enumeration

Used with the DateAdd, DateDiff, and DatePart functions to indicate the units of time with which the functions are working. There is no corresponding Visual Basic 6.0 enumeration; in Visual Basic 6.0, these functions relied on a one- to four-character string as an argument. The enumeration is defined as follows:

```
Public Enum DateInterval
    Year = 0
    Quarter = 1
    Month = 2
    DayOfYear = 3
    Day = 4
    WeekOfYear = 5
    Weekday = 6
    Hour = 7
    Minute = 8
    Second = 9
End Enum
```

DueDate Enumeration

Used with the Pmt and PPmt functions to define whether a payment falls at the beginning or end of a date period. The enumeration is new to Visual Basic .NET; in Visual Basic 6.0, the due date parameter was represented by a numeric value. The definition of the DueDate enumeration is:

```
Public Enum DueDate
    EndOfPeriod = 0                    ' Default value
    BegOfPeriod = 1
End Enum
```

FileAttribute Enumeration

Used with the Dir, GetAttr, and SetAttr functions to indicate the attributes of a file or directory. The enumeration corresponds closely to the VbFileAttribute enumeration, except that it is missing the latter's Alias member.

The definition of the FileAttribute enumeration is:

```
Public Enum FileAttribute
    Normal = 0
```

```
    ReadOnly = 1
    Hidden = 2
    System = 4
    Volume = 8
    Directory = 16
    Archive = 32
End Enum
```

Members of the FileAttribute enumeration are not necessarily mutually exclusive. FileAttribute.Volume must appear alone, without any other enumerated members, but the remaining members of the FileAttribute enumeration can appear in various combinations. For details, see the entries for the Dir, GetAttr, and SetAttr functions in Chapter 8.

FirstDayOfWeek Enumeration

Used with the DateDiff, DatePart, Weekday, and WeekdayName functions to indicate the first day of the week. It is similar to the VbDayOfWeek enumeration in Visual Basic 6.0. It is defined as follows:

```
Public Enum FirstDayOfWeek
    System = 0           ' Default for WeekdayName function
    Sunday = 1           ' Default for DateDiff, DatePart, Weekday functions
    Monday = 2
    Tuesday = 3
    Wednesday = 4
    Thursday = 5
    Friday = 6
    Saturday = 7
End Enum
```

FirstWeekOfYear Enumeration

Used with the DateDiff and DatePart functions to define which week is to be considered the first week of the year. It is similar to the VbFirstWeekOfYear enumeration in Visual Basic 6.0. Its definition is:

```
Public Enum FirstWeekOfYear
    System = 0
    Jan1 = 1             ' Default value
    FirstFourDays = 2
    FirstFullWeek = 3
End Enum
```

MsgBoxResult Enumeration

Provides constants that represent the button selected by the user to close the message box displayed by the MsgBox function. It is identical to the VbMsgBoxResult enumeration in Visual Basic 6.0. The MsgBoxResult enumeration is defined as follows:

```
Public Enum MsgBoxResult
    OK = 1
    Cancel = 2
    Abort = 3
```

```
    Retry = 4
    Ignore = 5
    Yes = 6
    No = 7
End Enum
```

MsgBoxStyle Enumeration

Used by the MsgBox function to define the appearance and style of the message box. Enumerated members as a whole are not mutually exclusive, although the members for the most part fall into groups, each of which consists of mutually exclusive members. A group of constants defines each of the following:

- The command buttons that can appear on the MsgBox dialog
- The dialog's icon
- The default button, which is automatically selected if the user presses the ENTER key
- The dialog's modality (nonmodal, application-modal, system-modal)
- Text alignment

Note that multiple members share a common value, 0. These are the default members of their group.

The MsgBoxStyle enumeration has the following definition:

```
Public Enum MsgBoxStyle
    OKOnly = 0                      ' Button constant; default value
    OKCancel = 1                    ' Button constant
    AbortRetryIgnore = 2            ' Button constant
    YesNoCancel = 3                 ' Button constant
    YesNo = 4                       ' Button constant
    RetryCancel = 5                 ' Button constant
    Critical = 16                   ' Icon constant
    Question = 32                   ' Icon constant
    Exclamation = 48                ' Icon constant
    Information = 64                ' Icon constant
    DefaultButton1 = 0              ' Default button constant; default value
    DefaultButton2 = 256            ' Default button constant
    DefaultButton3 = 512            ' Default button constant
    ApplicationModal = 0            ' Application-modal dialog; default value
    SystemModal = 4096              ' System-modal dialog
    MsgBoxHelp = 16384              ' Display help button
    MsgBoxRight = 524288            ' Right-align text in messagebox
    MsgBoxRtlReading = 1048576      ' Read text from right to left
    MsgBoxSetForeground = 65536     ' Non-modal dialog in the foreground
End Enum
```

OpenAccess Enumeration

Used with the FileOpen function to determine the access mode for a file. Valid values depend on the value of the OpenMode enumeration. For example, files opened for input can only be opened with OpenAccess.Default or OpenAccess.Write, while files opened for output can only be opened with OpenAccess.Default or OpenAccess.Read. The enumeration is new to Visual Basic .NET. It is defined as:

```
Public Enum OpenAccess
    Default = -1            ' Default value
    Read = 1
    ReadWrite = 3
    Write = 2
End Enum
```

OpenMode Enumeration

Used by the FileAttr and FileOpen functions to determine the mode in which a file is opened. The enumeration, which is defined as follows, is new to Visual Basic .NET:

```
Public Enum OpenMode
    Input = 1
    Output = 2
    Random = 4
    Append = 8
    Binary = 32
End Enum
```

In Visual Basic 6.0, the mode in which a file was opened was defined by a set of Long integers.

OpenShare Enumeration

Used with the FileOpen function to determine the access that other users or processes have to an open file. The enumeration is new to Visual Basic .NET. Its definition is:

```
Public Enum OpenShare
    Default = -1            ' The default value
    Shared = 3
    LockRead = 2
    LockReadWrite = 0
    LockWrite = 1
End Enum
```

TriState Enumeration

Used with the FormatCurrency, FormatNumber, and FormatPercent functions to determine how formatted output should appear. It is identical to the VbTriState enumeration in Visual Basic 6.0. The definition of the TriState enumeration is:

```
Public Enum TriState
    False = 0
    True = -1
    UseDefault = -2          ' Use system-defined value; the default value
End Enum
```

VariantType Enumeration

The VariantType enumeration defines the possible return values of the VarType function, which indicates the data type of a variable. It corresponds to the Visual Basic 6.0 VbVarType enumeration. For details on the VarType function and its handling of Visual Basic .NET data types, see Chapter 8.

The VariantType enumeration is defined as follows:

```
Public Enum VariantType
    Empty = 0
    Null = 1
    Short = 2
    Integer = 3
    Single = 4
    Double = 5
    Currency = 6
    Date = 7
    String = 8
    Object = 9
    Error = 10
    Boolean = 11
    Variant = 12
    DataObject = 13
    Decimal = 14
    Byte = 17
    Char = 18
    Long = 20
    UserDefinedType = 36
    Array = 8192
End Enum
```

Enumeration members are not mutually exclusive. An array of integers, for instance, returns a value of 8195, or VariantType.Integer Or VariantType.Array.

VbStrConv Enumeration

Used with the StrConv function to define how a string is to be converted. It is similar to the VbStrConv enumeration in Visual Basic 6.0, except that some members (vbFromUnicode and vbUnicode) have been removed, and others (New, SimplifiedChinese, TraditionalChinese, LinguisticCasing) have been added. The enumeration is defined as follows:

```
Public Enum VbStrConv
    None = 0
    UpperCase = 1
    LowerCase = 2
    ProperCase = 3
    Wide = 4             ' Single-byte Asian characters to double-byte
    Narrow = 8           ' Double-byte Asian characters to single-byte
    Katakana = 16
    Hiragana = 32
    SimplifiedChinese = 256
    TraditionalChinese = 512
    LinguisticCasing = 1024
End Enum
```

The Visual Basic
Command-Line Compiler

Like previous releases, Version 2.0 of the .NET platform includes *vbc.exe*, a full-featured command-line compiler for Visual Basic .NET. This means that, if you want to occasionally or completely forgo Visual Studio or a similar tool as a development editor, you can instead write Visual Basic code using a text editor like Notepad or WordPad and compile it from the command line. When using this method, you define options to the compiler using command-line switches. In this appendix, we'll examine the syntax required by the command line compiler.

Compiling a Program

A simple program compilation requires that the compiler be provided with four items of information, three of which have default values and are therefore optional:

- The file or files to be compiled. Files to be compiled are listed without a command-line switch, and multiple files are separated by a space.

- The type of output file. To specify the project type, the compiler uses the **/target** (or **/t**) switch. Possible values are **exe** for a console application (the default output if the **/target** switch is omitted), **winexe** for a Windows application, **library** for a class library (DLL), and **module** for a module that can eventually be compiled into an assembly.

- References to any assemblies required by the program. These assemblies are defined by the **/references** (or **/r**) switch, followed by the path and filenames (including the .DLL file extensions) of referenced assemblies. Multiple assemblies should be separated from one another by commas. By default, the compiler automatically references mscorlib.dll and Microsoft.VisualBasic.dll. All other assemblies must be explicitly referenced.

- The name of the output file, which is defined by the **/out** switch followed by output filename. This can be either the relative or absolute path from the current directory. It defaults to the same root filename as the first file specified on the command line.

Instead of specifying an exact filename, the standard wildcard characters, * and ?, can be used to include source code files in an assembly. The compiler will apply the file specification

The Order of Command-Line Switches and Arguments

The Visual Basic .NET compiler for the most part doesn't care about the order of command-line arguments and switches, as long as the syntax is valid. It does, however, care about the position of the **/out** switch, if you use one. It must immediately follow the list of files to compile.

Paths and Filenames with Spaces

When specifying paths and filenames as command-line options, place quotation marks around paths and filenames that contains spaces.

only to the current directory. If wildcard characters are used, the **/out** switch should also be used to control the name of the output file, since otherwise the compiler will give the output file the same root filename as the first file it includes in the compilation process.

The following are fairly typical examples of compiler syntax:

```
vbc displayinfo.vb

vbc addonlib.vb /t:library /r:system.dll

vbc displayinfo.vb lib\addonlib.vb /t:winexe
/r:system.dll,system.windows.forms.dll,system.data.dll

vbc addonlib.vb /out:UtilityLibrary.dll /t:library /r:system.windows.forms.dll
```

The following sections list the command-line switches supported by Visual Basic .NET.

Input File Switches

The source code files to be compiled into an assembly do not require switches but simply are listed on the command line and, if there is more than one file, separated by spaces. In addition, Visual Basic uses a number of switches to define additional input files.

Switch	Description
/addmodule:\<file>	Includes a .netmodule file (a file compiled with the **/module** switch) in the assembly. After compiling source code files written in different languages to modules, you can then use the **/addmodule** switch to compile them into a single assembly. **\<file>** must include the file extension in addition to the filename. Only a single file can be specified with an **/addmodule** switch; if you want to include multiple module files, you must use a separate **/addmodule** switch for each. If a relative path is specified as part of **\<file>**, it is interpreted as the path from the current directory. In addition to one or more modules, at least one source code file must be included in the build. If building an executable, a source code file must also contain the application entry point.

Switch	Description
`/libpath:<path_list>`	A semicolon-delimited list of directories to search for referenced assemblies that are not found in the current directory or the .NET system directory.
`/noconfig`	Instructs the compiler not to include the VBC.RSP response file. By default, it is included for each compilation. This response file adds references to the most common .NET assemblies (like System.dll, System.Data.dll, System.Windows.Forms.dll, and System.Web.dll) and imports the System and Microsoft.VisualBasic namespaces. For information on response files, see the later section "Response Files."
`/recurse:<wildcard>`	Includes all files that meet the file specifications and reside in the directory identified by <wildcard> and its subdirectories. **<wildcard>** recognizes the standard wildcard characters. In addition, it should include a path other than that of the source code files whose names were used as command-line arguments, or the compiler will generate errors when it attempts to compile files residing in those directories twice. If **<wildcard>** includes a relative path, it is interpreted as the path from the current directory.
`/reference:<file_list>` or `/r:<file_list>`	Adds a reference to an assembly. This is identical to adding a reference to a project in Visual Studio. Multiple assembly files are separated from one another by commas, and the file assembly's file extension must be included. Paths are unnecessary for assemblies registered in the global assembly cache (GAC). Otherwise, a path should be provided, or the **/libpath** switch should be used to specify where to search for referenced assemblies. If a relative path is provided, it is interpreted as the path from the directory that contains the first source code file.

Referencing Assemblies and Importing Namespaces

When using the Visual Basic .NET command-line compiler with .NET versions 1.0 and 1.1, you had to include references to *mscorlib.dll* and *Microsoft.VisualBasic.dll* if you used any types and members of those assemblies. In addition, the compiler did not automatically import any namespaces, so unless you added your own Imports statements, all types had to be referenced with their fully qualified names.

In contrast, the Visual Basic 2005 command-line compiler automatically adds references to both *mscorlib.dll* and *Microsoft.VisualBasic.dll* to every project; you don't have to use the **/r** switch to add references to them. In addition, it automatically imports the Microsoft.VisualBasic and System namespaces; you don't have to use an Imports statement in your source code or an **/imports** switch at the command line to import them.

Output File Switches

The following switches allow you to control the output generated by the compiler.

Switch	Description
/doc[+|-]	Indicates whether an XML documentation file should be generated as part of the compilation process. + generates the file; − suppresses it. The default setting is −, for off; an XML documentation file is not created.
/doc:<file>	Turns on the XML documentation feature as if you were also compiling with the **/doc**+ switch, and defines its output filename. <file> should include a file extension and can include an optional path. A relative path is interpreted as the path from the current directory.
/out:<file>	Defines the output filename; a file extension need not be included as part of <file>. If omitted, the filename defaults to the root filename of the first source code file. If no path is specified, the file will be placed in the same directory as the first source code file. If a relative path is specified, it is interpreted as the path from the directory that contains the first source code file. The **/out** switch, if used, must immediately follow the list of files to compile.
/target:<target> or /t:<target>	Indicates the type of file to output. Valid values for *target* are **exe** (a console application, the default value), **winexe** (a Windows application), library (a .NET assembly or DLL), and **module** (a .NET module file, with a file extension of .netmodule). A .NET module can later be linked into an assembly by using the **/addmodule** switch. (Using modules in this way, you can combine code written in multiple languages into a single assembly.)

Resource Switches

A number of switches control how resources are handled during the compilation process.

Switch	Description
/linkresource:<resinfo> or /linkres:<resinfo>	Establishes a link to a managed resource file in the output assembly's manifest, but does not embed it in the output file. **<resinfo>** has the syntax **filename[,identifier[,public | private]]**, where *filename* is the optional path and filename of the .NET Framework resource file, *identifier* is the name by which the resource will be referenced in code, and **public** or **private** indicates whether the resource will be marked as public or private in the assembly manifest. .NET Framework resource files are created by the Resource File Generator (Resgen.exe) or by the Visual Studio environment.
/resource:<resinfo> or /res:<resinfo>	Embeds a managed resource file in the output file. **<resinfo>** has the syntax **filename[,identifier[,public | private]]**, where *filename* is the optional path and filename of the .NET Framework resource file, *identifier* is the name by which the resource will be referenced in code, and **public** or **private** indicates whether the resource will be marked as public or private in the assembly manifest.

Switch	Description
`/win32icon:<file>`	Includes an icon (.ico) file in the output file as the application's default icon. **\<file\>** must be the name of an .ico file, along with an optional path. If a relative path is provided, it is interpreted as the path from the project directory.
`/Win32resource:<file>`	Includes a Win32 resource (.res) file in the compiled output. **\<file\>** must be the name of a .res file, along with an optional path. If a relative path is provided, it is interpreted as the path from the project directory. Win32 resource files can contain icons, bitmaps, and strings and are created with the Resource Compiler (RC.exe).

Information and Help

A number of command-line switches control the information displayed by the compiler. This includes the following switches, whose functions range from displaying help to suppressing the banner ordinarily displayed when the compiler begins execution.

Switch	Description

`/help`
or
`/?`
	Displays the compiler's help.

`/nologo`	Suppresses the display of the compiler's copyright banner.
`/quiet`	Quiet output mode; the compiler displays information primarily about error messages. **/quiet** is the default and the opposite of **/verbose**.
`/verbose`	Displays verbose messages. The compiler displays additional and more detailed information, particularly about the compilation process.

Visual Basic Language

A number of compiler options can be used to control the precise operation of the Visual Basic compiler. For example, rather than placing the Option Strict On statement in each source code file, you can simply use a compiler switch to set Option Strict On for the compilation process as a whole. The following switches are supported by the compiler control language settings.

Switch	Description

`/define:<symbol_list>`
or
`/d:<symbol_list>`
	Defines a global conditional compiler constant. It is the equivalent of using the #Const statement in each file of a project, and it frees you from the need to actually make changes to conditional compiler constants in source code. **\<symbol_list\>** has the syntax **symbol=value[,symbol=value...]**.

`/imports:<import_list>`	Declares global imports. **\<import_list\>** is a comma-separated list of namespaces. The switch is equivalent to including Imports statements with the specified namespaces in each source code file of a project.

`/optioncompare:binary`
or
`/optioncompare:text`
	Defines the Option Compare setting for all source code files in a project. Binary means that string comparison is case sensitive; text, that it is case insensitive. If the switch is not specified, **binary** is the default.

Switch	Description
`/optionexplicit[+|-]`	Requires variable declaration. The switch is the equivalent of including the Option Explicit statement in each source code file of a project. Like the Visual Basic editor, the compiler automatically sets Option Explicit on.
`/optionstrict[+|-]`	Sets Option Strict for all source code files in the project. The switch is the equivalent of including the Option Strict statement in each source code file of a project. Like the Visual Basic editor, the compiler automatically sets Option Strict off.
`/rootnamespace:<string>`	Specifies the root namespace for all types declared in the project. It is the equivalent of the Root namespace text box in the Application tab of the Project Properties dialog. If you then use Namespace statements to define namespaces in your code, the compiler interprets them as children of the root namespace.

Debugging Code Generation

The following switches define some of the code internals produced by the compiler, as well as the availability of debugging information.

Switch	Description

`debug[+|-]`
or
`/debug:full`
or
`/debug:pdbonly`
	Determines whether the compiler includes debugging symbols and information in the output file, and generates a .pdb file containing debugging information. The default is **/debug–**; no debugging information is put in the output file. **/debug:full** is equivalent to /debug+ and allows you to attach a debugger to the running program. **/debug:pdbonly** allows source code debugging only when the program is started in the debugger.

`optimize[+|-]`	Enables or suppresses compiler optimizations. By default, optimizations are enabled.
`removeintchecks[+|-]`	Removes integer checks for conditions such as overflows and division by zero. The default setting is off (–); integer checks are enabled.

Errors and Warnings

You can configure whether or not the compiler produces warnings, as well as whether warnings cause the compilation process to fail.

Switch	Description
`/nowarn:[<number_list>]`	Disables some or all compiler warnings. By default, all warnings are displayed. `/nowarn` with no argument suppresses all warnings, while **<number_list>** is a comma-separated list that indicates the specific warnings to be disabled. For example, to suppress warning BC42104, "Variable '<name>' is used before it has been assigned a value. A null reference exception could result at runtime.", use the syntax: `/nowarn:42104`

Switch	Description
`/warnaserror[+|-]` and `/warnaserror:[<number_list>]`	Determines whether warnings are treated as errors and cause compilation to fail. The default is off (–). Turning the switch on but not providing a second switch with *<number_list>* treats all warnings as errors. *<number_list>* is an optional comma-delimited list of compiler error codes. Individual error codes should include the numeric portion of the error code and exclude its alphanumeric portion. When compilation fails because a warning has been treated as an error, the compiler displays the usual message but notes that the warning is treated as an error.

Miscellaneous and Advanced Settings

The following switches are less frequently used. Many are of interest primarily to advanced Visual Basic developers.

Switch	Description
`/baseaddress:<number>`	The base address at which the .NET runtime should load a DLL. When multiple DLLs are loaded, assigning them nonoverlapping base addresses can improve performance. *<number>* must be a hexadecimal number with the format **0xhhhhhhhh**, where h is a hexadecimal digit.
`/bugreport:<file>`	During the compilation process, prompts for information about a bug and stores it as well as other project information (such as a copy of all source code files) in *<file>*. The bug report is sent using the **/errorreport** switch.
`/codepage:<number>`	Indicates the code page the compiler should use when reading all source files to be compiled. The switch is only needed when reading source files saved in something other than the current code page.
`/delaysign[+|-]`	Used with the **/keycontainer** and **/keyfile** switches to indicate whether an assembly should be delay-signed. Delay signing means that only the public portion of a strong name key is stored in the assembly, and space is reserved for later storage of the private key. The default is – for a fully signed assembly.
`/errorreport:<string>`	Specifies whether to send reports on internal compiler errors. Possible values for *<string>* are prompt, send, or none. The default is none.
`/filealign:<number>`	Specifies the boundary alignment for the code and data sections of a portable executable file, the file format in which .Net assemblies are written. Valid values of *<number>* are 512, 1024, 2048, 4096, and 8192. Ordinarily, this option is not used, and the compiler chooses the boundary alignment value. It can be used to produce smaller executables and DLLs for systems with memory constraints.

Switch	Description
`/keycontainer:<string>`	Specifies a key container filename to give an assembly or module a strong name.
`/keyfile:<file>`	Specifies the name and location of a key file to give a module or assembly a strong name. Strong-name key files are generated with the Strong Name tool (Sn.exe).

`/main:<class>`
or
`/m:<class>`
	For executables, indicates the class or module that contains the entry point, Sub Main. **<class>** can also be a class that inherits from System.Windows.Forms.Form. Without it, the compiler searches all files and modules for a valid entry point. It can be used to compile Windows Forms applications at the command line that have been created in the Visual Studio development environment, as well as to eliminate ambiguity when two classes or modules contain a procedure named Main.

`/netcf`	Builds an output file targeted at the .NET Compact Framework. Designed to be used with the **/sdkpath** switch, it causes compiler errors to be generated when a number of language elements (such as the End statement) and features (such as late binding) are encountered in code.
`/nostdlib`	Causes the compiler to not reference mscorlib.dll, system.dll, and Microsoft.VisualBasic.dll. It is used in targeting very restricted compact platforms.
`/platform:<string>`	Defines the platforms on which the compiled assembly runs. Possible values for **<string>** are **x86**, **x64**, **Itanium**, or **anycpu**. The default value is **anycpu**.
`/sdkpath:<path>`	Indicates where the .NET Framework libraries (particularly mscorlib.dll and Microsoft.VisualBasic.dll) reside. It is intended to be used with **/netcf** to indicate the location of special versions of the .NET framework that have been developed to support particular devices.
`unify:<assembly_name>`	Suppresses warnings that result from a mismatch between the versions of referenced assemblies.
`/utf8output[+|-]`	Displays compiler output (messages, warnings, errors, etc.) using UTF8 character encoding. In some international and regional configurations, this is required to display compiler output correctly. The default value is – (off); compiler output is not displayed using UTF8 encoding.

Response Files

In addition to specifying all compiler settings on the command line, it is possible to include them in one or more files and have the files, which are known as response files, included in the compilation process. In fact, unless the **/noconfig** switch is used when compiling, the compiler automatically includes one response file, vbc.rsp. The command-line syntax for including an additional response file in the compilation process is:

Symbol	Description
@<file>	Includes command-line settings from **<file>**

To include more than one response file, simply include multiple @*<file>* clauses, each separated from the next by a space.

The response file itself contains the names and optionally the paths of source code files to include in the compilation, as well as switches and their arguments that would otherwise have to be entered on the command line. Comments can be included in response files; the comment symbol is #. A single line can include multiple switches and compiler options or arguments. However, a single switch with its options must be entirely contained on one line; it cannot span multiple lines.

The compiler processes command options as it encounters them. This means that a switch may be reversed or canceled by a later switch.

Conversions Reference

If you've chosen to set Option Strict on (the recommended setting), Visual Basic will continue to handle widening conversions (such as a conversion of an Integer to a Long) for you automatically. Implicit narrowing conversions, however, are no longer allowed; you have to handle those conversions yourself using a conversion function. Late binding also generates a compiler error, again requiring that you use early binding and, in many cases, explicit type conversion. Because of the increased importance of type conversion with Option Strict set to on, this appendix documents the conversion functions available to convert from a data type to any other data type.

When converting between numeric types, there are two categories of conversions:

- **Widening conversions** These involve the conversion of a value from one numeric type to another numeric type with a larger range of legal values (such as, for example, the conversion of a Short to an Integer). Such conversions can be made implicitly even if Option Strict is on, and never involve a loss of data.

- **Narrowing conversions** These involve the conversion of a value from one numeric type to another numeric type with a smaller range of legal values (such as, for example, the conversion of a Long to an Integer). In other words, the range of values of the source data type is not entirely a subset of the range of values of the destination data type. Narrowing conversions must be handled explicitly if Option Strict is on. If data is lost as a result of the conversion, an OverflowException is thrown.

Visual Basic does not support typecasting using a C- or C#-like syntax. However, Visual Basic itself, along with the .NET framework, offers a rich array of conversion functions. These include the following:

- Intrinsic Visual Basic conversion functions, such as CBool, CByte, CInt, CStr, and CType. Most of these functions in turn wrap calls to methods of the Microsoft.VisualBasic.CompilerServices.Conversions class.

- The members of the System.Convert class.

- The methods of the IConvertible interface, which is implemented by each of the .NET data types as well as by the System.Convert class. These methods all require an IFormatProvider implementation as an argument, though Nothing can be passed as an argument instead. Since the conversion methods can only be called from an instance of the interface, using this method to convert a Boolean to an Integer, for example, requires code like the following:

```
Public Class Conversion
    Public Shared Sub Main()

        Dim conv As IConvertible

        Dim flag As Boolean = True
        conv = flag
        Dim num As Integer = conv.ToInt32(Nothing)
        Console.WriteLine(num)
    End Sub
End Class
```

- The members of the source type. For example, each data type has a ToString method that, in the case of most data types, converts its value to a string. (For most reference types, though, the ToString method returns the name of the type.) And the Decimal data type has a number of methods to convert a decimal to another data type.
- The members of the destination type. In particular, the Parse and TryParse methods attempt to convert a string representation to the destination data type.

Floating Point to Integer Conversions

All of the conversion functions that convert a floating point to an integral value use Banker's rounding if the floating point number contains a fractional component. This means that fractional components that are midway between two integral numbers are rounded to the nearest even number. Using Banker's rounding, for example, 12.5 is rounded down to 12, but 13.5 is rounded up to 14.

The table for each data type shows the methods available to convert Visual Basic's intrinsic data types to that type. Only the members of the IConvertible interface are not shown, since they are in any event duplicated by the methods of the Convert class.

Boolean

Table F-1 shows the methods available to convert each of the supported VB data types to a Boolean. More common, however, is conversion of a Boolean to a numeric or integral value. In such conversions, a Boolean with a value of False is converted to 0 and a Boolean with a value of True is converted to –1. For the methods available to convert a Boolean to another data type, see the table in the section devoted to that type.

Data Type	Methods	Comments
Boolean	CBool, Convert.ToBoolean	Returns the Boolean value passed as an argument unchanged.
Byte	CBool, Convert.ToBoolean	Positive values convert to True, zero values convert to False.
Char		Not supported.
Date		Not supported.
Double	CBool, Convert.ToBoolean	Non-zero values convert to True, zero values convert to False.
Decimal	CBool, Convert.ToBoolean	Non-zero values convert to True, zero values convert to False.
Integer	CBool, Convert.ToBoolean	Non-zero values convert to True, zero values convert to False.
Long	CBool, Convert.ToBoolean	Non-zero values convert to True, zero values convert to False.
Object	CBool, Convert.ToBoolean, CType	Must be a supported object type, such as a string, a number, or a Boolean. Null object references (objects that equal Nothing) convert to False; all others throw an InvalidCastException.
SByte	CBool, Convert.ToBoolean	Non-zero values convert to True, zero values convert to False.
Short	CBool, Convert.ToBoolean	Non-zero values convert to True, zero values convert to False.
Single	CBool, Convert.ToBoolean	Non-zero values convert to True, zero values convert to False.
String	CBool, Convert.ToBoolean, Boolean.Parse, Boolean.TryParse	Strings equal to a case-insensitive version of Boolean.TrueString convert to True. All other strings convert to False if using CBool and Convert.ToBoolean. Parse and TryParse recognize only Boolean.TrueString and Boolean.FalseString as valid values, and Parse otherwise throws a FormatException.
UInteger	CBool, Convert.ToBoolean	Positive values convert to True, zero values convert to False.
ULong	CBool, Convert.ToBoolean	Positive values convert to True, zero values convert to False.
UShort	CBool, Convert.ToBoolean	Positive values convert to True, zero values convert to False.

TABLE F-1   Converting Data to a Boolean

Byte

Table F-2 shows the methods available to convert each of the supported VB data types to a Byte. For successful conversion, however, numeric values must lie within the legal range of a Byte (i.e., 0 to 255). If they are not (that is, in the case of narrowing conversions where data would be lost, or in the case of an attempt to convert a negative number), the call to the conversion method throws an exception.

Data Type	Methods	Comments
Boolean	CByte, Convert.ToByte	CByte converts True to 255, Convert.ToByte converts True to 1. Both convert False to 0.
Byte	CByte, Convert.ToByte	Returns the Byte value passed as an argument unchanged.
Char	Convert.ToByte	Narrowing conversion. Converts a Char to its one-byte character code.
Date		Not supported.
Double	CByte, Convert.ToByte	Narrowing conversion. Fractional numbers are rounded to integers before conversion; this means that a negative Double from slightly less than 0 to –0.5 converts to 0. Attempting to convert Double.Nan, Double.PositiveInfinity, or Double.NegativeInfinity throws an OverflowException.
Decimal	CByte, Convert.ToByte, Decimal.ToByte	Narrowing conversion. Fractional numbers are rounded to integers before conversion.
Integer	CByte, Convert.ToByte	Narrowing conversion.
Long	CByte, Convert.ToByte	Narrowing conversion.
Object	CByte, Convert.ToByte, CType	Must be a supported object type, such as a string, a number, or a Boolean. Null object references (objects that equal Nothing) convert to 0. Otherwise, an exception is thrown.
SByte	CByte, Convert.ToByte	Narrowing conversion.
Short	CByte, Convert.ToByte	Narrowing conversion.
Single	CByte, Convert.ToByte	Narrowing conversion. Fractional numbers are rounded to integers before conversion; this means that a negative Double from slightly less than 0 to –0.5 converts to 0. Attempting to convert Single.Nan, Single.PositiveInfinity, or Single.NegativeInfinity throws an OverflowException.

TABLE F-2   Converting Data to a Byte

Data Type	Methods	Comments
String	CByte, Convert.ToByte, Byte.Parse, Byte.TryParse	Converts string representations of Byte values from "0" to "255" to Byte values. If a fractional value is present, CByte rounds it to the nearest integer before converting, while Convert.ToByte throws an exception.
UInteger	CByte, Convert.ToByte	Narrowing conversion
ULong	CByte, Convert.ToByte	Narrowing conversion.
UShort	CByte, Convert.ToByte	Narrowing conversion.

TABLE F-2   Converting Data to a Byte *(continued)*

For information on converting a Byte to another data type, see the conversion table for the data type to which you wish to convert the Byte.

Char

Table F-3 shows the methods available to convert each of the supported VB data types to a Char. Note that CChar, the intrinsic Visual Basic function, is not available for all valid conversions.

Data Type	Methods	Comments
Boolean		Not supported.
Byte	CChar, Convert.ToChar	Interprets a Byte value as a single-byte character code.
Char	CChar, Convert.ToChar	Returns the Char value passed as an argument unchanged.
Date		Not supported.
Decimal		Not supported.
Double		Not supported.
Integer	Convert.ToChar	Interprets an Integer in the range of 0 to 65,535 as a Unicode UTF-16 character code.
Long	Convert.ToChar	Interprets a Long in the range of 0 to 65,535 as a Unicode UTF-16 character code.
Object	CChar, CType, Convert.ToChar	Must be a supported object type, such as a string or Byte. Null object references (objects that equal Nothing) convert to a Char whose code is 0. Otherwise, an exception is thrown.

TABLE F-3   Converting Data to a Char

Data Type	Methods	Comments
SByte	Convert.ToChar	Interprets a signed byte in the range of 0 to 127 as a Unicode UTF-16 character code.
Short	Convert.ToChar	Interprets a Short in the range of 0 to 32,767 as a Unicode UTF-16 character code.
Single		Not supported.
String	CChar, Convert.ToChar, Char.Parse, Char.TryParse	CChar converts the first character of a string to a Char. Convert.ToChar requires that a string's length be one character, which it converts to a Char.
UInteger	Convert.ToChar	Interprets an unsigned integer in the range of 0 to 65,535 as a UTF-16 Unicode character code.
ULong	Convert.ToChar	Interprets an unsigned long integer in the range of 0 to 65,535 as a UTF-16 Unicode character code.
UShort	Convert.ToChar	Interprets an unsigned short integer as a UTF-16 Unicode character code.

TABLE F-3   Converting Data to a Char *(continued)*

For information on converting a Char to another data type, see the conversion table for the data type to which you wish to convert the Char.

Date

The Date is one of the more restrictive data types in terms of conversions. You can use either the CDate function or the shared Convert.ToDateTime method to convert either Date values (in which case the method simply returns the Date value passed to it as an argument unchanged), String representations of dates, or Objects whose values are either dates or string representations of dates. You can also use the Date.Parse and Date.TryParse methods to convert a string representation of a date or time to a Date value.

For information on converting a Date to another data type, see the conversion table for the data type to which you wish to convert the Date.

Decimal

Table F-4 shows the methods available to convert each of the supported VB data types to a Decimal. For information on converting a Decimal to another data type, see the conversion table for the data type to which you wish to convert the Decimal.

Data Type	Methods	Comments
Boolean	CDec, Convert.ToDecimal	Converts False to 0. CDec converts True to −1, Convert.ToDecimal converts it to 1.
Byte	CDec, Convert.ToDecimal	Widening conversion.
Char		Not supported.
Date		Not supported.
Decimal	CDec, Convert.ToDecimal	Returns a Decimal value unchanged.
Double	CDec, Convert.ToDecimal	Narrowing conversion.
Integer	CDec, Convert.ToDecimal	Widening conversion.
Long	CDec, Convert.ToDecimal	Widening conversion.
Object	CDec, CType, Convert.ToDecimal	Must be a supported object type. Null object references (objects that equal Nothing) convert to 0. Otherwise, an exception is thrown.
SByte	CDec, Convert.ToDecimal	Widening conversion.
Short	CDec, Convert.ToDecimal	Widening conversion.
Single	CDec, Convert.ToDecimal	Narrowing conversion.
String	CDec, Convert.ToDecimal. Decimal.Parse, Decimal.TryParse	Converts the string representation of a number to a Decimal value.
UInteger	CDec, Convert.ToDecimal	Widening conversion.
ULong	CDec, Convert.ToDecimal	Widening conversion.
UShort	CDec, Convert.ToDecimal	Widening conversion.

TABLE F-4   Converting Data to a Decimal

Double

Table F-5 shows the methods available to convert each of the supported VB data types to a Double. For information on converting a Double to another data type, see the conversion table for the data type to which you wish to convert the Double.

Integer

Table F-6 shows the methods available to convert each of the supported VB data types to an Integer. For information on converting an Integer to another data type, see the conversion table for the data type to which you wish to convert the Integer.

Data Type	Methods	Comments
Boolean	CDbl, Convert.ToDouble	Converts False to 0. CDbl converts True to −1, Convert.ToDouble converts it to 1.
Byte	CDbl, Convert.ToDouble	Widening conversion.
Char		Not supported.
Date		Not supported.
Decimal	CDbl, Convert.ToDouble, Decimal.ToDouble	Widening conversion. Some conversions may involve a loss of precision.
Double	CDbl, Convert.ToDouble	Returns a Double value unchanged.
Integer	CDbl, Convert.ToDouble	Widening conversion.
Long	CDbl, Convert.ToDouble	Widening conversion. Some conversions may involve a loss of precision.
Object	CDbl, CType, Convert.ToDouble	Must be a supported object type. Null object references (objects that equal Nothing) convert to 0. Otherwise, an exception is thrown.
SByte	CDbl, Convert.ToDouble	Widening conversion.
Short	CDbl, Convert.ToDouble	Widening conversion.
Single	CDbl, Convert.ToDouble	Widening conversion.
String	CDbl, Convert.ToDouble, Double.Parse, Double.TryParse	The string must represent a number.
UInteger	CDbl, Convert.ToDouble	Widening conversion.
ULong	CDbl, Convert.ToDouble	Widening conversion. Some conversions may involve a loss of precision.
UShort	CDbl, Convert.ToDouble	Widening conversion.

TABLE F-5   Converting Data to a Double

Data Type	Methods	Comments
Boolean	CInt, Convert.ToInt32	Converts False to 0. CInt converts True to −1, Convert.ToInt32 converts it to 1.
Byte	CInt, Convert.ToInt32	Widening conversion.
Char	Convert.ToInt32	Widening conversion.
Date		Not supported.
Decimal	CInt, Convert.ToInt32, Decimal.ToInt32	Narrowing conversion. Any fractional component is rounded before conversion.

TABLE F-6   Converting Data to an Integer

Data Type	Methods	Comments
Double	CInt, Convert.ToInt32	Narrowing conversion. Any fractional component is rounded before conversion. Attempting to convert Double.Nan, Double.PositiveInfinity, or Double.NegativeInfinity throws an OverflowException.
Integer	CInt, Convert.ToInt32	Returns the Integer value unchanged.
Long	CInt, Convert.ToInt32	Narrowing conversion.
Object	CInt, CType, Convert.ToInt32	Must be a supported object type. Null object references (objects that equal Nothing) convert to 0. Otherwise, an exception is thrown.
SByte	CInt, Convert.ToInt32	Widening conversion.
Short	CInt, Convert.ToInt32	Widening conversion.
Single	CInt, Convert.ToInt32	Narrowing conversion. Any fractional component is rounded before conversion. Attempting to convert Single.Nan, Single.PositiveInfinity, or Single.NegativeInfinity throws an OverflowException.
String	CInt, Convert.ToInt32, Integer.Parse, Integer.TryParse	The string must be a numeric representation.
UInteger	CInt, Convert.ToInt32	Narrowing conversion.
ULong	CInt, Convert.ToInt32	Narrowing conversion.
UShort	CInt, Convert.ToInt32	Widening conversion

TABLE F-6   Converting Data to an Integer *(continued)*

Long

Table F-7 shows the methods available to convert each of the supported VB data types to a Long. For information on converting a Long to another data type, see the conversion table for the data type to which you wish to convert the Long.

Object

Several functions (CObj, CType, and Convert.ChangeType) can convert a strongly typed variable to a variable of type Object. The result, however, is simply the creation of an object variable with the same data type and no data loss. More common is the use of the object conversion functions to cast a derived class to its base class or an instance of a class or structure to its implemented interface (termed an upcast). Less common is the use of the object conversion functions to cast an interface or a base class to a derived class or an implementing class (termed a downcast). The latter is considered a narrowing conversion and can throw an InvalidCastException.

Data Type	Methods	Comments
Boolean	CLng, Convert.ToInt64	Converts False to 0. CLng converts True to −1, Convert.ToInt64 converts it to 1.
Byte	CLng, Convert.ToInt64	Widening conversion.
Char	Convert.ToInt64	Widening conversion.
Date		Not supported.
Decimal	CLng, Convert.ToInt64, Decimal.ToInt64	Narrowing conversion. Any fractional component is rounded before conversion.
Double	CLng, Convert.ToInt64	Narrowing conversion. Any fractional component is rounded before conversion. Attempting to convert Double.Nan, Double.PositiveInfinity, or Double.NegativeInfinity throws an OverflowException.
Integer	CLng, Convert.ToInt64	Widening conversion.
Long	CLng, Convert.ToInt64	Returns the Long value unchanged.
Object	CLng, CType, Convert.ToInt64	Must be a supported object type. Null object references (objects that equal Nothing) convert to 0. Otherwise, an exception is thrown.
SByte	CLng, Convert.ToInt64	Widening conversion.
Short	CLng, Convert.ToInt64	Widening conversion.
Single	CLng, Convert.ToInt64	Narrowing conversion. Any fractional component is rounded before conversion. Attempting to convert Single.Nan, Single.PositiveInfinity, or Single.NegativeInfinity throws an OverflowException.
String	CLng, Convert.ToInt64, Long.Parse, Long.TryParse	The string must be a numeric representation.
UInteger	CLng, Convert.ToInt64	Widening conversion.
ULong	CLng, Convert.ToInt64	Narrowing conversion.
UShort	CLng, Convert.ToInt64	Widening conversion.

TABLE F-7   Converting Data to a Long

SByte

Table F-8 shows the methods available to convert each of the supported VB data types to an SByte. For information on converting an SByte to another data type, see the conversion table for the data type to which you wish to convert the SByte.

Data Type	Methods	Comments
Boolean	CSByte, Convert.ToSByte	Converts False to 0. CSByte converts True to −1, Convert.ToSByte converts it to 1.
Byte	CSByte, Convert.ToSByte	Narrowing conversion.
Char	Convert.ToSByte	Narrowing conversion.
Date		Not supported.
Decimal	CSByte, Convert.ToSByte, Decimal.ToSByte	Narrowing conversion. Any fractional component is rounded before conversion.
Double	CSByte, Convert.ToSByte	Narrowing conversion. Any fractional component is rounded before conversion. Attempting to convert Double.Nan, Double.PositiveInfinity, or Double.NegativeInfinity throws an OverflowException.
Integer	CSByte, Convert.ToSByte	Narrowing conversion.
Long	CSByte, Convert.ToSByte	Narrowing conversion.
Object	CSByte, CType, Convert.ToSByte	Must be a supported object type. Null object references (objects that equal Nothing) convert to 0. Otherwise, an exception is thrown.
SByte	CSByte, Convert.ToSByte	Returns the SByte value unchanged.
Short	CSByte, Convert.ToSByte	Narrowing conversion.
Single	CSByte, Convert.ToSByte	Narrowing conversion. Any fractional component is rounded before conversion. Attempting to convert Single.Nan, Single.PositiveInfinity, or Single.NegativeInfinity throws an OverflowException.
String	CSByte, Convert.ToSByte, SByte.Parse, SByte.TryParse	The string must be a numeric representation.
UInteger	CSByte, Convert.ToSByte	Narrowing conversion.
ULong	CSByte, Convert.ToSByte	Narrowing conversion.
UShort	CSByte, Convert.ToSByte	Narrowing conversion.

TABLE F-8   Converting Data to an SByte

Short

Table F-9 shows the methods available to convert each of the supported VB data types to a Short. For information on converting a Short to another data type, see the conversion table for the data type to which you wish to convert the Short.

Data Type	Methods	Comments
Boolean	CShort, Convert.ToInt16	Converts False to 0. CShort converts True to –1, Convert.ToInt16 converts it to 1.
Byte	CShort, Convert.ToInt16	Widening conversion.
Char	Convert.ToInt16	Converts a Char to a Short representing its character code.
Date		Not supported.
Decimal	CShort, Convert.ToInt16, Decimal.ToInt16	Narrowing conversion. Any fractional component is rounded before conversion.
Double	CShort, Convert.ToInt16	Narrowing conversion. Any fractional component is rounded before conversion. Attempting to convert Double.Nan, Double.PositiveInfinity, or Double.NegativeInfinity throws an OverflowException.
Integer	CShort, Convert.ToInt16	Narrowing conversion.
Long	CShort, Convert.ToInt16	Narrowing conversion.
Object	CShort, CType, Convert.ToInt16	Must be a supported object type. Null object references (objects that equal Nothing) convert to 0. Otherwise, an exception is thrown.
SByte	CShort, Convert.ToInt16	Widening conversion.
Short	CShort, Convert.ToInt16	Returns the Short value unchanged.
Single	CShort, Convert.ToInt16	Narrowing conversion. Any fractional component is rounded before conversion. Attempting to convert Single.Nan, Single.PositiveInfinity, or Single.NegativeInfinity throws an OverflowException.
String	CShort, Convert.ToInt16, Short.Parse, Short.TryParse	The string must be a numeric representation.
UInteger	CShort, Convert.ToInt16	Narrowing conversion.
ULong	CShort, Convert.ToInt16	Narrowing conversion.
UShort	CShort, Convert.ToInt16	Narrowing conversion.

TABLE F-9   Converting Data to a Short

Single

Table F-10 shows the methods available to convert each of the supported VB data types to a Single. For information on converting a Single to another data type, see the conversion table for the data type to which you wish to convert the Single.

Data Type	Methods	Comments
Boolean	CSng, Convert.ToSingle	Converts False to 0. CSng converts True to −1, Convert.ToSingle converts it to 1.
Byte	CSng, Convert.ToSingle	Widening conversion.
Char		Not supported.
Date		Not supported.
Decimal	CSng, Convert.ToSingle, Decimal.ToSingle	Widening conversion. Some conversions may involve a loss of precision.
Double	CSng, Convert.ToSingle	Numbers outside of the range of Single are converted to either Single.PositiveInfinity or Single.NegativeInfinity.
Integer	CSng, Convert.ToSingle	Widening conversion. Some conversions may involve a loss of precision.
Long	CSng, Convert.ToSingle	Widening conversion. Some conversions may involve a loss of precision.
Object	CSng, CType, Convert.ToSingle	Must be a supported object type. Null object references (objects that equal Nothing) convert to 0. Otherwise, an exception is thrown.
SByte	CSng, Convert.ToSingle	Widening conversion.
Short	CSng, Convert.ToSingle	Widening conversion.
Single	CSng, Convert.ToSingle	Returns the Single value unchanged.
String	CSng, Convert.ToSingle, Single.Parse, Single.TryParse	The string must represent a number.
UInteger	CSng, Convert.ToSingle	Widening conversion. Some conversions may involve a loss of precision.
ULong	CSng, Convert.ToSingle	Widening conversion. Some conversions may involve a loss of precision.
UShort	CSng, Convert.ToSingle	Widening conversion.

TABLE F-10   Converting Data to a Single

String

Table F-11 shows the methods available to convert each of the supported VB data types to a String. For information on converting a String to another data type, see the conversion table for the data type to which you wish to convert the String.

Data Type	Methods	Comments
Boolean	CStr, Convert.ToString, Boolean.ToString	Converts True to Boolean.TrueString, False to Boolean.FalseString.
Byte	CStr, Convert.ToString, Byte.ToString	Narrowing conversion.
Char	CStr, Convert.ToString, Char.ToString	Widening conversion.
Date	CStr, Convert.ToString, Date.ToString	Narrowing conversion.
Decimal	CStr, Convert.ToString, Decimal.ToString	Narrowing conversion.
Double	CStr, Convert.ToString, Double.ToString	Narrowing conversion. Double.Nan converts to "NaN", Double.PositiveInfinity to "Infinity", Double.NegativeInfinity to "-Infinity".
Integer	CStr, Convert.ToString, Integer.ToString	Narrowing conversion.
Long	CStr, Convert.ToString, Long.ToString	Narrowing conversion.
Object	CStr, CType, Convert.ToString	Must be a supported object type. Null object references (objects that equal Nothing) convert to Nothing. Otherwise, an exception is thrown.
SByte	CStr, Convert.ToString, SByte.ToString	Narrowing conversion.
Short	CStr, Convert.ToString, Short.ToString	Narrowing conversion.
Single	CStr, Convert.ToString, Single.ToString	Narrowing conversion. Single.Nan converts to "NaN", Single.PositiveInfinity converts to "Infinity", and Single.NegativeInfinity converts to "-Infinity".
String	CStr, Convert.ToString, String.ToString	Returns the original string value unchanged.
UInteger	CStr, Convert.ToString, UInteger.ToString	Narrowing conversion.
ULong	CStr, Convert.ToString, ULong.ToString	Narrowing conversion.
UShort	CStr, Convert.ToString, UShort.ToString	Narrowing conversion.

TABLE F-11   Converting Data to a String

UInteger

Table F-12 shows the methods available to convert each of the supported VB data types to a UInteger. For information on converting an Integer to another data type, see the conversion table for the data type to which you wish to convert the UInteger.

Data Type	Methods	Comments
Boolean	CUInt, Convert.ToUInt32	Converts False to 0. CUInt converts True to UInteger.MaxValue (which has the same bit pattern as −1), Convert.ToUInt32 converts it to 1.
Byte	CUInt, Convert.ToUInt32	Widening conversion.
Char	Convert.ToUInt32	Widening conversion. Converts a Char to its numeric character code.
Date		Not supported.
Decimal	CUInt, Convert.ToUInt32, Decimal.ToUInt32	Narrowing conversion. Any fractional component is rounded before conversion.
Double	CUInt, Convert.ToUInt32	Narrowing conversion. Any fractional component is rounded before conversion. Attempting to convert Double.Nan, Double.PositiveInfinity, or Double.NegativeInfinity throws an OverflowException.
Integer	CUInt, Convert.ToUInt32	Narrowing conversion.
Long	CUInt, Convert.ToUInt32	Narrowing conversion.
Object	CInt, CType, Convert.ToInt32	Must be a supported object type. Null object references (objects that equal Nothing) convert to 0. Otherwise, an exception is thrown.
SByte	CUInt, Convert.ToUInt32	Narrowing conversion.
Short	CUInt, Convert.ToUInt32	Narrowing conversion.
Single	CUInt, Convert.ToUInt32	Narrowing conversion. Any fractional component is rounded before conversion. Attempting to convert Single.Nan, Single.PositiveInfinity, or Single.NegativeInfinity throws an OverflowException.
String	CUInt, Convert.ToUInt32, UInteger.Parse, UInteger.TryParse	The string must be a numeric representation.
UInteger	CUInt, Convert.ToUInt32	Returns the original unsigned integer (UInteger) unchanged.
ULong	CUInt, Convert.ToUInt32	Narrowing conversion.
UShort	CUInt, Convert.ToUInt32	Widening conversion.

TABLE F-12   Converting Data to a UInteger

ULong

Table F-13 shows the methods available to convert each of the supported VB data types to a ULong. For information on converting a ULong to another data type, see the conversion table for the data type to which you wish to convert the ULong.

Data Type	Methods	Comments
Boolean	CULng, Convert.ToUInt64	Converts False to 0. CULng converts True to ULong.MaxValue (which has the same bit pattern as −1), Convert.ToInt64 converts it to 1.
Byte	CULng, Convert.ToUInt64	Widening conversion.
Char	Convert.ToInt64	Narrowing conversion.
Date		Not supported.
Decimal	CULng, Convert.ToUInt64, Decimal.ToInt64	Narrowing conversion. Any fractional component is rounded before conversion.
Double	CULng, Convert.ToUInt64	Narrowing conversion. Any fractional component is rounded before conversion. Attempting to convert Double.Nan, Double.PositiveInfinity, or Double.NegativeInfinity throws an OverflowException.
Integer	CULng, Convert.ToUInt64	Narrowing conversion.
Long	CULng, Convert.ToUInt64	Narrowing conversion.
Object	CULng, CType, Convert.ToUInt64	Must be a supported object type. Null object references (objects that equal Nothing) convert to 0. Otherwise, an exception is thrown.
SByte	CULng, Convert.ToUInt64	Narrowing conversion.
Short	CULng, Convert.ToUInt64	Narrowing conversion.
Single	CULng, Convert.ToUInt64	Narrowing conversion. Any fractional component is rounded before conversion. Attempting to convert Single.Nan, Single.PositiveInfinity, or Single.NegativeInfinity throws an OverflowException.
String	CULng, Convert.ToUInt64, ULong.Parse, ULong.TryParse	The string must be a numeric representation.
UInteger	CULng, Convert.ToUInt64	Widening conversion.
ULong	CULng, Convert.ToUInt64	Returns the original value unchanged.
UShort	CULng, Convert.ToUInt64	Widening conversion.

TABLE F-13   Converting Data to a ULong

UShort

Table F-14 shows the methods available to convert each of the supported VB data types to a UShort. For information on converting an unsigned Short to another data type, see the conversion table for the data type to which you wish to convert the UShort.

Data Type	Methods	Comments
Boolean	CUShort, Convert.ToUInt16	Converts False to 0. CUShort converts True to UShort.MaxValue, Convert.ToInt16 converts it to 1.
Byte	CUShort, Convert.ToUInt16	Widening conversion.
Char	Convert.ToUInt16	Widening conversion. Converts a Char to a UShort representing its character code.
Date		Not supported.
Decimal	CUShort, Convert.ToUInt16, Decimal.ToUInt16	Narrowing conversion. Any fractional component is rounded before conversion.
Double	CUShort, Convert.ToUInt16	Narrowing conversion. Any fractional component is rounded before conversion. Attempting to convert Double.Nan, Double.PositiveInfinity, or Double.NegativeInfinity throws an OverflowException.
Integer	CUShort, Convert.ToUInt16	Narrowing conversion.
Long	CUShort, Convert.ToUInt16	Narrowing conversion.
Object	CUShort, CType, Convert.ToUInt16	Must be a supported object type. Null object references (objects that equal Nothing) convert to 0. Otherwise, an exception is thrown.
SByte	CUShort, Convert.ToUInt16	Narrowing conversion.
Short	CUShort, Convert.ToUInt16	Narrowing conversion.
Single	CUShort, Convert.ToUInt16	Narrowing conversion. Any fractional component is rounded before conversion. Attempting to convert Single.Nan, Single.PositiveInfinity, or Single.NegativeInfinity throws an OverflowException.
String	CUShort, Convert.ToUInt16, UShort.Parse, UShort.TryParse	The string must be a numeric representation.
UInteger	CUShort, Convert.ToUInt16	Narrowing conversion.
ULong	CUShort, Convert.ToUInt16	Narrowing conversion.
UShort	CUShort, Convert.ToUInt16	Returns the UShort value unchanged.

TABLE F-14   Converting Data to a UShort

.NET Data Type Reference

In Visual Basic 6.0 and earlier versions, a *data type* is simply a template that defines the structure and organization of data. Although Visual Basic .NET's data types (like any data types) also perform this function, they correspond directly to .NET data types. As standard .NET types, data types have members (constructors, fields, properties, and methods) that are either shared (that is, they can be called by referencing the type without creating an instance of the type) or instance (that is, they can be called from an instance of the type). For example, the following code illustrates a call to a shared member, the Concat method of the String class:

```
Dim arr() As String = {"One ", "Two ", "Three ", "Four ", "Five"}
Dim out As String = String.Concat(arr)
Console.WriteLine(out)
```

Because data types are .NET types, they are derived from other .NET classes and therefore share a common set of members that they inherit from their base class. The next section will discuss that common set of members.

The Object Class and Inherited Members

All reference types in .NET inherit indirectly from the System.Object class, and therefore inherit all of its members. All value types inherit indirectly from the System.ValueType class, which in turn inherits indirectly from System.Object and overrides some of its members, while it does not add any unique members. In other words, each data type inherits a number of members from System.Object that can be called directly from your code. In addition, the Object class itself is a data type in Visual Basic .NET.

Equals Method

The behavior of the Equals method depends on whether the System.Object implementation or the System.ValueType implementation is called. (That is, System.ValueType overrides the implementation of System.Object, giving the Equals method a different behavior for value types than for reference types.) The syntax of Equals is:

```
Function Equals(obj As Object) As Boolean
Shared Function Equals(objA As Object, objB As Object) As Boolean
```

The first overload compares the current object with a second one, while the second overload is a shared method that compares the two object instances passed to it as arguments. For reference types, Equals returns True if both objects reference the same object instance and False otherwise. For value types, Equals returns True if both value types have the same value and False otherwise.

GetHashCode Method

The GetHashCode method returns the hash code for the object. The hash code is used internally by a Hashtable object for ordering the items stored in a hash table.

```
Function GetHashCode() As Integer
```

GetType Method

The GetType method returns a System.Type object that contains information about the runtime data type of a variable. Its behavior is identical for both reference types and value types. Its syntax is:

```
Function GetType() As Type
```

ReferenceEquals Method

Determines whether two objects reference a common object instance.

```
Shared Function ReferenceEquals(objA As Object, objB As Object) As Boolean
```

Note that, because the method is shared, it is not inherited by classes derived from Object.

ToString Method

The ToString method is overridden by System.ValueType, so its behavior differs depending on whether the method is called on a reference type or a value type. For a reference type, it is equivalent to retrieving the value of the type's FullName property; that is, it provides the fully qualified namespace and type name of the type. For a value type, it returns the value that the instance of the value type contains. Its syntax is:

```
Function ToString() As String
```

Boolean

When working with values of type Boolean, you can call the members of the System.Boolean structure in the Framework Class Library. Its unique members are listed in the following sections.

FalseString Field

```
Shared ReadOnly FalseString As String
```

Returns the string representation of a False value. Its value is "False".

TrueString Field

```
Shared ReadOnly TrueString As String
```

Returns the string representation of a True value. Its value is "True".

CompareTo Method

```
Function CompareTo(value As Boolean) As Integer
Function CompareTo(obj As Object) As Integer
```

Compares a Boolean instance with a Boolean argument. *value* and *obj* are variables of type Boolean and Object, respectively, that have Boolean values. The function returns 0 if they are equal, –1 if the instance is "less than" the argument (i.e., the instance is False and the argument True), and 1 if the instance is "greater than" the argument (i.e., the instance is True and the argument False). If *value* or *obj* is not a Boolean value, an ArgumentException is thrown.

Equals Method

```
Function Equals(obj As Boolean) As Boolean
Function Equals(obj As Object) As Boolean
```

Determines whether two Boolean values are equal. *obj* is a Boolean value or an object with a Boolean value. If *obj* is not a Boolean value, the method returns False.

GetTypeCode Method

```
GetTypeCode() As TypeCode
```

Returns the Boolean's type code, which is System.TypeCode.Boolean, or 3.

Parse Method

```
Shared Function Parse(value As String)
```

Converts a string passed to it as an argument to its Boolean equivalent. *value* is a string that must correspond to an uppercase, lowercase, or mixed-case variation of Boolean.FalseString or Boolean.TrueString. If it does not, a FormatException is thrown.

ToString Method

```
Function ToString() As String
Function ToString(provider As IFormatProvider) As String
```

Converts a Boolean value to TrueString or FalseString, depending on its value. In its second overload, *provider* is an object implementing the IFormatProvider interface that ordinarily controls formatting, though it has no effect when used with a Boolean.

TryParse Method

```
Shared Function TryParse(value As String, ByRef result As Boolean) As Boolean
```

Converts a string to its Boolean equivalent. *value* is the string to be converted to a Boolean, and *result* is a Boolean variable that, when the function returns, contains the result of the conversion. Because the function's return value indicates whether the conversion succeeded, the method requires less error handling than Parse. Note that, if the conversion fails, *result* is set to False; rather than accessing a possibly incorrect Boolean value, you should first check the method's return value to make sure that the conversion succeeded.

Char

When working with values of type Char, you can call the members of the System.Char structure in the Framework Class Library:

MaxValue Field

```
Public Const MaxValue As Char
```

A shared, read-only field that returns the maximum value of the Char type. Its value is &HFFFF.

MinValue Field

```
Public Const MaxValue As Char
```

A shared, read-only field that returns the minimum value of the Char type. Its value is 0.

CompareTo Method

```
Function CompareTo(value As Char) As Integer
Function CompareTo(value As Object) As Integer
```

Compares a Char instance with a Char argument. *value* is a Char value or an Object with a Char value. The function returns 0 if the instance and *value* are equal, –1 if the instance is less than the argument, and 1 if the instance is greater than the argument. If *value* is not a Char, an ArgumentException is thrown.

ConvertFromUtf32 Method

```
Shared Function ConvertFromUtf32(utf32 As Integer) As String
```

Converts a 32-bit Unicode code represented by *utf32* to a String containing a Char or surrogate pair of Char objects.

ConvertToUtf32 Method

```
Shared Function ConvertToUtf32(highSurrogate As Char, _
                               lowSurrogate As Char) As Integer
Shared Function ConvertToUtf32(s As String, index As Integer) As Integer
```

Converts a UTF16-encoded value to a Unicode code value. *highSurrogate* is a Char containing a high surrogate character (a character code from &HD800 to &HDBFF), *lowSurrogate* is a Char containing a low surrogate character (a character code from &HDC00 to &HDFFF), *s* is a String containing a surrogate pair, and *index* is the position in *s* at which the surrogate pair begins. If *highSurrogate* and *lowSurrogate* are outside the valid range, or if *index* doesn't point to the beginning of a surrogate pair, an ArgumentOutOfRangeException is thrown.

Equals Method

```
Function Equals(obj As Char) As Boolean
Function Equals(obj As Object) As Boolean
```

Determines whether two Char values are equal. *obj* is a Char value or an object with a Char value. If *obj* is not a Char, the method returns False.

GetNumericValue Method

```
Shared Function GetNumericValue(c As Char) As Double
Shared Function GetNumericValue(s As String, index As Integer) As Double
```

Converts a numeric Unicode character to a Double. *c* is a Char value, *s* is a String containing a numeric Unicode character, and *index* is the position of the numeric character in *s*. If *c* is not a Char, or if *index* points to a Unicode code point without a numeric value, the method returns –1 instead of throwing an exception.

GetTypeCode Method

```
Function GetTypeCode() As TypeCode
```

Returns the Char's type code, which is System.TypeCode.Char, or 4.

GetUnicodeCategory Method

```
Shared Function GetUnicodeCategory(c As Char) As UnicodeCategory
Shared Function GetUnicodeCategory(s As String, _
                            index As Integer) As UnicodeCategory
```

Indicates the category of a Unicode character *c* or the Char at *index* position in the string *s*.

Char.Is<someCharType> Method

Each of these shared overloaded methods determines the category or type to which a particular Char belongs; they all have a common syntax:

```
Shared Function Is<someChartype>(c As Char) As Boolean
Shared Function Is<someCharType>(s As String, index As Integer) As Boolean
```

where *c* is the Char whose type is to be determined, or the *index* position in a String *s* indicates the Char whose type is to be determined. The methods are:

Member Name	Description
IsControl	Indicates whether a character is a control character.
IsDigit	Indicates whether a character is a decimal digit.
IsHighSurrogate	Indicates whether a character is a high surrogate.
IsLetter	Indicates whether a character is an alphabetic letter.
IsLetterOrDigit	Indicates whether a character is an alphabetic letter or a decimal digit.
IsLower	Indicates whether a character is a lowercase letter.
IsLowSurrogate	Indicates whether a character is a low surrogate.
IsNumber	Indicates whether a character is a number.
IsPunctuation	Indicates whether a character is a punctuation symbol.

Member Name	Description
IsSeparator	Indicates whether a character is a valid separator character (i.e., a space separator, line separator, or paragraph separator).
IsSurrogate	Indicates whether a character is a surrogate.
IsSurrogatePair	The first overload of the method has non-standard syntax: Shared Function IsSurrogatePair(_ *highSurrogate* As Char, _ *lowSurrogate* As Char) As Boolean Indicates whether two Char objects indicated by *highSurrogate* and *lowSurrogate* or starting at *index* position in String *s* form a surrogate pair.
IsSymbol	Indicates whether a character is a symbol (such as a math symbol or a currency symbol).
IsUpper	Indicates whether a character is an uppercase letter.
IsWhiteSpace	Indicates whether a character is a space separator.

Parse Method

```
Shared Function Parse(s As String) As Char
```

Converts a one-character string to its Char equivalent. If *s* is Nothing or a multicharacter string, a FormatException is thrown.

ToLower Method

```
Shared Function ToLower(c As Char) As Char
Shared Function ToLower(c As char, culture As CultureInfo) As Char
```

Converts a Char value to its lowercase equivalent. *c* is the character to convert to lowercase, and *culture* is a CultureInfo object that includes culture-specific case rules.

ToLowerInvariant Method

```
Shared Function ToLowerInvariant(c As Char) As Char
```

Converts a Char value, *c*, to its lowercase equivalent using the invariant culture.

ToUpper Method

```
Shared Function ToUpper(c As Char) As Char
Shared Function ToUpper(c As char, culture As CultureInfo) As Char
```

Converts a Char value to its uppercase equivalent. *c* is the character to convert to uppercase, and *culture* is a CultureInfo object that includes culture-specific case rules.

ToUpperInvariant Method

```
Shared Function ToUpperInvariant(c As Char) As Char
```

Converts a Char value, *c*, to its uppercase equivalent using the invariant culture.

ToString Method

```
Function ToString() As String
Shared Function ToString(c As Char) As String
Function ToString(provider As IFormatProvider) As String
```

Converts a Char to its String equivalent. *c* is a Char value, and *provider* is an object implementing IFormatProvider that defines a custom format for the output string.

TryParse Method

```
Shared Function TryParse(s As String, ByRef result As Char) As Boolean
```

Converts a one-character string to its Char equivalent. s is a String to be converted, and *result* is a Char variable that, when the function returns, contains the result of the conversion. Because the return value of the function indicates whether the conversion succeeded, the method call requires less error handling than the Parse method.

Date

The Visual Basic Date data type corresponds to the .NET DateTime data type. Its unique members are listed in the following sections.

New Method (Constructor)

```
Sub New(ticks As Long)
Sub New(ticks As Long, kind As DateTimeKind)
Sub New(year As Integer, month As Integer, day As Integer)
Sub New(year As Integer, month As Integer, day As Integer, calendar As Calendar)
Sub New(year As Integer, month As Integer, day As Integer, hour As Integer, _
        minute As Integer, second As Integer)
Sub New(year As Integer, month As Integer, day As Integer, hour As Integer, _
        minute As Integer, second As Integer, calendar As Calendar)
Sub New(year As Integer, month As Integer, day As Integer, hour As Integer, _
        minute As Integer, second As Integer, kind As DateTimeKind)
Sub New(year As Integer, month As Integer, day As Integer, hour As Integer, _
        minute As Integer, second As Integer, millisecond As Integer)
Sub New(year As Integer, month As Integer, day As Integer, hour As Integer, _
        minute As Integer, second As Integer, millisecond As Integer, _
        calendar As Calendar)
Sub New(year As Integer, month As Integer, day As Integer, hour As Integer, _
        minute As Integer, second As Integer, millisecond As Integer, _
        kind As DateTimeKind)
Sub New(year As Integer, month As Integer, day As Integer, hour As Integer, _
        minute As Integer, second As Integer, millisecond As Integer, _
        calendar As Calendar, kind As DateTimeKind)
```

Instantiates a new Date instance with the date defined by arguments supplied to the constructor. In alphabetical order, these parameters are as follows:

- *calendar* is a class derived from System.Globalization.Calendar indicating the calendar in which the date is expressed.
- *day* is an Integer ranging from 1 to 31 representing the day of the date.

- *hour* is an Integer ranging from 0 to 23 representing the hour of the day.
- *kind* is a member of the DateTimeKind enumeration that allows you to specify whether the time value is local time, UTC time, or an unspecified time.
- *milliseconds* is an Integer ranging from 0 to 9999 representing the number of milliseconds in the time.
- *minute* is an Integer ranging from 0 to 59 representing the minute of the hour.
- *month* is an Integer ranging from 1 to 12 representing the month of the date.
- *second* is an Integer ranging from 0 to 59 representing the second of the minute.
- *ticks*, which expresses the date and time in ticks since midnight (0:00:00) of January 1, 0001; there are 10 million ticks per second.
- *year* is an Integer representing the year of the date.

MaxValue Field

```
Public Const MaxValue As Date
```

Returns the latest valid date. Its value is 11:59:59 PM on 12/31/9999.

MinValue Field

```
Public Const MinValue As Date
```

Returns the earliest valid date. Its value is 12:00:00 AM on 01/01/0001.

Date Property

```
ReadOnly Property Date As Date
```

Returns the date component of a Date instance without the time.

Day Property

```
ReadOnly Property Day As Integer
```

Returns the day of the month represented by a Date instance.

DayOfWeek Property

```
ReadOnly Property DayOfWeek As DayOfWeek
```

Returns a member of the DayOfWeek enumeration indicating the day of the week of a Date instance.

DayOfYear Property

```
ReadOnly Property DayOfYear As Integer
```

Returns the day of the year represented by the instance.

Hour Property

```
ReadOnly Property Hour As Integer
```

Returns the hour component of a Date value.

Kind Property

```
ReadOnly Property Kind As DateTimeKind
```

Indicates whether the date value is local time, coordinated universal time (UTC), or unspecified.

Millisecond Property

```
ReadOnly Property Millisecond As Integer
```

Returns the millisecond component of a Date value.

Minute Property

```
ReadOnly Property Minute As Integer
```

Returns the minute component of a Date value.

Month Property

```
ReadOnly Property Month As Integer
```

Returns the month component of a Date value.

Now Property

```
Shared ReadOnly Property Now As Date
```

Returns the current system date and time.

Second Property

```
ReadOnly Property Second As Integer
```

Returns the seconds component of a Date value.

Ticks Property

```
ReadOnly Property Ticks As Long
```

Returns the number of ticks that represent the Date value.

TimeOfDay Property

```
ReadOnly Property TimeOfDay
```

Returns the time component of a Date instance.

Today Property

```
Shared ReadOnly Property Today As Date
```

Returns the current system date.

UtcNow Property

```
Shared ReadOnly Property UtcNow As Date
```

Returns the current coordinated universal time (UTC).

Year Property

```
ReadOnly Property Year As Integer
```

Returns the year component of a Date instance.

Add Method

```
Function Add(value As TimeSpan) As Date
```

Adds the number of units specified in a TimeSpan structure represented by *value* to a date value.

AddDays Method

```
Function AddDays(value As Double) As Date
```

Adds or subtracts whole or fractional days from a date. *value* specifies the number of days to add (if it is positive) or subtract (if it is negative).

AddHours Method

```
Function AddHours(value As Double) As Date
```

Adds or subtracts whole or fractional hours from a date. *value* specifies the number of hours to add (if it is positive) or subtract (if it is negative).

AddMilliseconds Method

```
Function AddMilliseconds(value As Double) As Date
```

Adds or subtracts whole or fractional milliseconds from a date.

AddMinutes Method

```
Function AddMinutes(value As Double) As Date
```

Adds or subtracts whole or fractional minutes from a date. *value* specifies the number of minutes to add (if it is positive) or subtract (if it is negative).

AddMonths Method

```
Function AddMonths(value As Double) As Date
```

Adds or subtracts whole months or fractional portions of a month from a date. *value* specifies the number of months to add (if it is positive) or subtract (if it is negative).

AddSeconds Method

```
Function AddSeconds(value As Double) As Date
```

Adds or subtracts whole or fractional seconds from a date. *value* specifies the number of seconds to add (if it is positive) or subtract (if it is negative).

AddTicks Method

```
Function AddTicks(value As Long) As Date
```

Adds or subtracts a number of ticks from a date. *value* specifies the number 100-nanosecond ticks to add (if it is positive) or subtract (if it is negative).

AddYears Method

```
Function AddYears(value As Integer) As Date
```

Adds or subtracts a number of years from a date. *value* specifies the number of years to add (if it is positive) or subtract (if it is negative).

Compare Method

```
Shared Function Compare(t1 As Date, t2 As Date) As Integer
```

Indicates the relationship between two dates, *t1* and *t2*. The method returns a negative value if *t1* is earlier than *t2*, 0 if they are equal, and a positive value if *t1* is later than *t2*.

CompareTo Method

```
Function CompareTo(value As Date) As Integer
Function CompareTo(value As Object) As Integer
```

Compares the value of a Date instance with a Date argument. *value* is either a Date value or an Object with a Date value. The function returns 0 if the Date instance and *value* are equal, −1 if the instance is earlier than *value*, and 1 if the instance is later than *value*. If *value* is not a Date value, an ArgumentException is thrown.

DaysInMonth Method

```
Shared Function DaysInMonth(year As Integer, month As Integer) As Integer
```

A shared method that indicates the number of days in a particular month (indicated by *month*) of a particular year (indicated by *year*).

Equals Method

```
Function Equals(value As Date) As Boolean
Function Equals(value As Object) As Boolean
Shared Function Equals(t1 As Date, t2 As Date) As Boolean
Shared Function Equals(objA As Object, objB As Object) As Boolean
```

Determines whether two Date values are equal. *value* is either a Date value or an Object with a date value that is compared to the value of the Date instance. *t1* and *t2* are Date values, and *objA* and *objB* are Objects with date values.

FromBinary Method

```
Shared Function Date.FromBinary(dateData As Long)
```

Returns a date based on the number of ticks specified by the lower 62 bits of *dateData* and a DateTimeKind value in the upper 2 bits of *dateData*. It is equivalent to supplying *ticks* and *kind* arguments to one of the overloads of the Date constructor.

FromFileTime Method

```
Shared Function FromFileTime(fileTime As Long) As Date
```

Returns a Date value that corresponds to a particular FILETIME value represented by *filetime*. (FILETIME is a 64-bit structure used by Windows to represent the number of 100-nanosecond intervals since January 1, 1601.)

FromFileTimeUtc Method

```
Shared Function FromFileTimeUtc(fileTime As Long) As Date
```

Returns a Date value that corresponds to a particular FILETIME value represented by *fileTime* adjusted to coordinated universal time.

FromOADate Method

```
Shared Function FromOADate(d As Double) As Date
```

Returns a Date value corresponding to an OLE Automation date, where *d* is a Double containing a date in OLE Automation format.

GetDateTypeFormats Method

```
Function GetDateTimeFormats() As String()
Function GetDateTimeFormats(format As Char) As String()
Function GetDateTimeFormats(provider As IFormatProvider) As String()
Function GetDateTimeFormats(format As Char, _
                           provider As IFormatProvider) As String()
```

Returns a String array containing all of the date formats for a particular date. *format* is a Char representing a format, and *provider* is an IFormatProvider implementation that defines culture-specific formatting information.

GetTypeCode Method

```
Function GetTypeCode() As TypeCode
```

Returns the Date's type code, which is System.TypeCode.DateTime, or 16.

IsDaylightSavingTime Method

```
Function IsDaylightSavingTime() As Boolean
```

Indicates whether the Date instance is within the range of daylight saving time if its DateTimeKind is Local or Unspecified.

IsLeapYear Method

```
Shared Function IsLeapYear(year As Integer) As Boolean
```

Indicates whether a particular year indicated by *year* is a leap year.

op_Addition Method

```
Shared Operator op_Addition(d As Date, t As TimeSpan) As Date
```

Defines the addition operation for Date values, which allows the + operator to be used with dates as follows:

```
Dim dat As Date = #01/03/2001#
Dim ts As Timespan = New Timespan(2,0,0,0)
Dim newDat As Date = dat + ts
```

op_Equality Method

```
Shared Function op_Equality(d1 As Date, d2 As Date) As Boolean
```

Defines the equality comparison operation for Date values, which allows the = comparison operator to be used with dates, as in the following code:

```
Dim dat1 As Date = #01/03/2001#
Dim dat2 As Date = #01/03/2004#
Dim dat3 As Date = #01/03/2001#

Console.WriteLine(dat1 = dat2)
Console.WriteLine(dat1 = dat3)
```

op_GreaterThan Method

```
Shared Function op_GreaterThan(t1 As Date, t2 As Date) As Boolean
```

Defines the greater-than comparison operation for Date values, which allows the > operator to be used to determine if a date, *t1*, is greater than another date, *t2*.

op_GreaterThanOrEqual Method

```
Shared Function op_GreaterThanOrEqual(t1 As Date, t2 As Date) As Boolean
```

Defines the greater-than or equal comparison operation for Date values, which allows the => operator to be used to determine if a date, *t1*, is greater than or equal to another date, *t2*.

op_Inequality Method

```
Shared Function op_Inequality(t1 As Date, t2 As Date) As Boolean
```

Defines the inequality operation for Date values, which allows the <> operator to be used to determine if two dates, *t1* and *t2*, are not equal to one another.

op_LessThan Method

```
Shared Function op_LessThan(t1 As Date, t2 As Date) As Boolean
```

Defines the less-than comparison operation for Date values, which allows the < operator to be used to determine if a date, *t1*, is less than another date, *t2*.

op_LessThanOrEqual Method

```
Shared Function op_LessThanOrEqual(t1 As Date, t2 As Date) As Boolean
```

Defines the less-than or equal comparison operation for Date values, which allows the <= operator to be used to determine if a date, *t1*, is less than or equal to another date, *t2*.

op_Subtraction Method

```
Shared Function op_Subtraction(d1 As Date, d2 As Date) As TimeSpan
Shared Function op_Subtraction(d As Date, t As TimeSpan) As Date
```

Defines the subtraction operation for Date values, which allows the - operator to be used with dates. One date, *d2*, can be subtracted from another date, *d1*, or a time span, *t*, can be subtracted from a date, *d*.

Parse Method

```
Shared Function Parse(s As String) As Date
Shared Function Parse(s As String, provider As IFormatProvider) As Date
Shared Function Parse(s As String, provider As IFormatProvider, _
                      styles As DateTimeStyles) As Date
```

Converts the String representation of a Date, *s*, to a Date Value. *provider* is an object implementing IFormatProvider that provides culture-specific formatting information about *s*, and *styles* is a member of the DateTimeStyles enumeration that controls how *s* is parsed.

ParseExact Method

```
Shared Function ParseExact(s As String, format As String, _
                           provider As IFormatProvider) As Date
Shared Function ParseExact(s As String, format As String, _
                           provider As IFormatProvider, _
                           style As DateTimeStyles) As Date
Shared Function ParseExact(s As String, formats As String(), _
                           provider As IFormatProvider, _
                           style As DateTimeStyles) As Date
```

Converts the String representation of a Date that exactly matches a format specifier to a Date value. *s* is the string representation of a date, *format* is a String and *formats()* a String array containing expected formats, *provider* is an object implementing IFormatProvider that provides culture-specific formatting information about *s*, and *styles* is a member of the DateTimeStyles enumeration that controls how *s* is parsed.

SpecifyKind Method

```
Shared Function SpecifyKind(value As Date, kind As DateTimeKind) As Date
```

Returns a date of a specified type from a particular date. *value* is a Date value, and *kind* is a member of the DateTimeKind enumeration that designates the type of date and time to return.

Subtract Method

```
Function Subtract(value As TimeSpan) As Date
Function Subtract(value As Date) As TimeSpan
```

Subtracts either a time span (represented by *value* in the first overload) or a date (represented by *value* in the second overload) from a date instance.

ToBinary Method

```
Function ToBinary() As Long
```

Serializes a Date value to a Long whose lower 62 bits contain date/time data and upper 2 bits contain DateTimeKind information.

ToFileTime Method

```
Function ToFileTime() As Long
```

Converts a Date value to a local Windows file time value (a FILETIME structure).

ToFileTimeUtc Method

```
Function ToFileTimeUtc() As Long
```

Converts a Date value to a Windows file time value (a FILETIME structure) ignoring the local time zone.

ToLocalTime Method

```
Function ToLocalTime() As Date
```

Converts a UTC time value to local time.

ToLongDateString Method

```
Function ToLongDateString() As String
```

Converts a Date value to its long date string representation.

ToLongTimeString Method

```
Function ToLongTimeString() As String
```

Converts a Date value to its long time string representation.

ToOADate Method

```
Function ToOADate() As Double
```

Converts a Date value to its OLE Automation equivalent.

ToShortDateString Method

```
Function ToShortDateString() As String
```

Converts a Date value to its short date string representation.

ToShortTimeString Method

```
Function ToShortTimeString() As String
```

Converts a Date value to its short time string representation.

ToString Method

```
Function ToString() As String
FunctionToString(provider As IFormatProvider) As String
dateVar.ToString(format As String) As String
dateVar.ToString(format As String, provider As IFormatProvider) As String
```

Converts a date instance to its string representation. *provider* is an IFormatProvider implementation containing culture-specific formatting information, and *format* is a String containing formatting information.

ToUniversalTime Method

```
Function ToUniversalTime() As Date
```

Converts a local time value to coordinated universal time (UTC).

TryParse Method

```
Shared Function TryParse(s As String, result As Date) As Boolean
Shared Function TryParse(s As String, provider As IFormatProvider, _
                  styles As DateTimeStyles, result As Date) As Boolean
```

Converts the string representation of a date/time to a Date value. *s* is the string representation of a date or time, *provider* is an IFormatProvider implementation with culture-specific formatting information, *styles* is member of the DateTimeStyles enumeration that contains information about the formatting of *s*, and *result* is the Date value to which *s* is converted. The method's return value indicates whether the conversion succeeded.

TryParseExact Method

```
Shared Function TryParseExact(s As String, format As String, _
                     provider As IFormatProvider, _
                     style As DateTimeStyles, result As Date) As Boolean
Shared Function TryParseExact(s As String, formats() As String, _
                     provider As IFormatProvider, _
                     style As DateTimeStyles, result As Date) As Boolean
```

Attempts to convert the string representation of a date that exactly matches a format string to a Date value and returns a Boolean indicating whether the conversion succeeded. *s* is the string representation of a date, *format* is a format string and *formats()* an array of format strings specifying the formats that *s* must match, *provider* is an IFormatProvider implementation containing culture-specific formatting information, *style* is member of the DateTimeStyles enumeration that contains information about the formatting of *s*, and *result* is the Date value to which *s* is converted.

Decimal

When working with values of type Decimal, you can call the members of the System.Decimal structure in the Framework Class Library. Its unique members are shown in the following sections.

New Method (Constructor)

You can initialize a Decimal value by passing its constructor a value of any of the following types: Double, Integer, Long, Single, UInteger, and ULong. In addition, two overloads of the constructor are based on the physical layout of the Decimal data type. The second overload is more accessible:

```
Sub New(bits() As Integer)
Sub New(lo As Integer, mid As Integer, hi As Integer, isNegative As
boolean, _
        scale As Byte)
```

The parameters are as follows:

- *bits* is a four-element array. Its parameters correspond to directly those of the Decimal's second overloaded constructor, as discussed in the next item.

- *lo* contains the lower 32-bits of the value to be assigned to the Decimal; it is equivalent to *bits*(0).

- *mid* contains the middle 32-bits of the value to be assigned to the Decimal; it is equivalent to *bits*(1).

- *hi* contains the upper 32-bits of the value to be assigned to the Decimal; it is equivalent to *bits*(2).

- *isNegative* indicates whether the Decimal value is negative (True) or positive (False). It is equivalent to bit 31 (0 is positive, 1 is negative) of *bits*(3).

- *scale* defines the Decimal value's exponent and ranges from 0 to 28. It corresponds to bits 16–23 of *bits*(3).

MaxValue Field

```
Shared ReadOnly MaxValue As Decimal
```

Returns the largest possible Decimal value. It can be used before converting to a Decimal to determine whether a value is out of the Decimal's range.

MinusOne Field

```
Shared ReadOnly MinusOne As Decimal
```

Represents the value –1.

MinValue Field

```
Shared ReadOnly MinValue As Decimal
```

Returns the smallest possible Decimal value. It can be used before converting to a Decimal to determine whether a value is out of the Decimal's range.

One Field

```
Shared ReadOnly One As Decimal
```

Represents the value 1.

Zero Field

```
Shared ReadOnly Zero As Decimal
```

Represents the value 0.

Add Method

```
Shared Function Add(d1 As Decimal, d2 As Decimal) As Decimal
```

Adds two decimal values.

Ceiling Method

```
Shared Function Ceiling(d As Decimal) As Decimal
```

Returns the smallest integral value that is greater than the argument.

Compare Method

```
Shared Function Compare(d1 As Decimal, d2 As Decimal) As Integer
```

Indicates the relationship of two Decimal values. It returns a negative value if *d1* is less than *d2*, 0 if they are equal, and a positive value if *d1* is greater than *d2*.

CompareTo Method

```
Function CompareTo(value As [ Decimal | Object ]) As Integer
```

Compares the value of the Decimal instance with a Decimal argument and returns 0 if the Decimal instance and *value* are equal, –1 if the instance is less than *value*, and 1 if the instance is greater than *value*. An ArgumentException is thrown if *value* is not a Decimal.

Divide Method

```
Shared Function Divide(d1 As Decimal, d2 As Decimal) As Decimal
```

Divides two decimal values passed as arguments.

Equals Method

```
Function Equals(value As Decimal) As [Decimal | Object]) As Boolean
Shared Function Equals(d1 As Decimal, d2 As Decimal) As Boolean
```

Determines whether two Decimal values are equal.

Floor Method

```
Shared Function Floor(d As Decimal) As Decimal
```

Returns the largest integral value that is less or equal to the argument.

FromOACurrency Method

```
Shared Function FromOACurrecy(cy As Long) As Decimal
```

Converts an OLE Automation Currency value (a value of the Currency data type in Visual Basic 6.0) to a Decimal value.

GetBits Method

```
Shared Function GetBits(d As Decimal) As Integer()
```

Converts a Decimal value to its binary representation and returns an Integer array with four elements that correspond to the four elements in *bits*() in one of the Decimal type's overloaded constructors.

GetTypeCode Method

```
Function GetTypeCode() As System.TypeCode
```

Returns the Decimal's type code, which is TypeCode.Decimal, or 15.

Multiply Method

```
Shared Function Multiply(d1 As Decimal, d2 As Decimal) As Decimal
```

Multiples two decimal values.

Negate Method

```
Shared Function Negate(d As Decimal) As Decimal
```

Multiplies a Decimal value by –1.

Overloaded Operators

For languages that don't support overloaded operators or particular operators (such as ++ or --), the Decimal type implements operator procedures as method calls, all of which begin with the prefix op_ and the name of the operation (e.g., op_Addition, op_Decrement). The operations supported are: Addition (adds two Decimals and returns a Decimal), Decrement (decrements a Decimal by one and returns a Decimal), Division (divides two Decimals and returns a Decimal), Equality (compares two Decimal values for equality and returns a Boolean), GreaterThan (returns a Boolean indicating whether a first Decimal value is greater than a second), GreaterThanOrEqual (returns a Boolean indicating whether a first Decimal value is greater than or equal to a second), Implicit (defines widening conversions from a type to a Decimal), Increment (increments a Decimal by one and returns a Decimal), InEquality (compares two Decimal values for inequality and returns a Boolean), LessThan (returns a Boolean indicating whether a first Decimal value is less than a second), LessThanOrEqual (returns a Boolean indicating whether a first Decimal value is less than or equal to a second), Modulus (divides two Decimal values and returns a Decimal whose value is the remainder), Multiply (multiplies two Decimals and returns a Decimal), Subtraction (subtracts a Decimal from a first Decimal and returns a Decimal), UnaryNegation (negates a Decimal value and returns it as a Decimal), and UnaryPlus (returns a Decimal value unchanged).

In addition, the op_Explicit method defines the narrowing conversions that can be performed with a Decimal (see Appendix F), but only two of its overloads (that take a Single argument and Double argument and convert it to a Decimal) can be called directly from Visual Basic code; the remaining overloads cannot be resolved by the Visual Basic compiler because it does not consider return types in overload resolution.

Parse and TryParse Methods

```
Shared Function Parse(s As String) As Decimal
Shared Function TryParse(s As String, ByRef result As Decimal) As Boolean
Shared Function Parse(s As String, provider As IFormatProvider) As Decimal
```

```
Shared Function Parse(s As String, style As NumberStyles) As Decimal
Shared Function Parse(s As String, style As NumberStyles, _
                      provider As IFormatProvider) As Decimal
Shared Function TryParse(s As String, style As NumberStyles, _
                         provider As IFormatProvider, ByRef result As Decimal) _
                  As Boolean
```

Converts the String representation of a number to its Decimal equivalent. *s* is the string to be converted, *result* is string converted to a Decimal, *provider* is an object implementing the IFormatProvider interface that provides culture-specific formatting information about *s*, and *styles* is a member of the NumberStyles enumeration that controls how *s* is parsed. Parse throws an exception if it is unable to convert the string; TryParse returns False.

Remainder Method

```
Decimal.Remainder(d1 As Decimal, d2 As Decimal) As Decimal
```

Returns the remainder from a division. Its operation is identical to the Mod operator.

Round Method

```
Decimal.Round(d As Decimal) As Decimal
Decimal.Round(d As Decimal, decimals As Integer) As Decimal
Decimal.Round(d As Decimal, mode As MidpointRounding) As Decimal
```

Rounds a Decimal value. *d* is a Decimal value, *decimals* is an Integer indicating the number of decimal positions to which to round, and *mode* controls how midpoint values (like 0.5) are rounded.

Subtract Method

```
Shared Function Decimal.Subtract(d1 As Decimal, d2 As Decimal) As Decimal
```

Subtracts two Decimal values.

ToOACurrency Method

```
Shared Function Decimal.ToOACurrency(value As Decimal) As Long
```

Converts a Decimal to an OLE Automation Currency data type (the Currency data type in VB 6.0). It can be used in working with COM components using COM interop.

Truncate Method

```
Shared Function Decimal.Truncate(d As Decimal) As Decimal
```

Discards any fractional component of a Decimal value.

Type Conversion Methods

In addition to the casting operators, op_Explicit and op_Implicit, the Decimal type supports a number of conversion methods that convert a Decimal value to a value of another data type.

These include the following integer conversion methods, which truncate any fractional component of the Decimal and convert it to an integral type if it is in that integer type's range.

```
Shared Function Decimal.ToByte(value As Decimal) As Byte
Shared Function Decimal.ToInt16(value As Decimal) As Short
Shared Function Decimal.ToInt32(d As Decimal) As Integer
Shared Function Decimal.ToInt64(d As Decimal) As Long
Shared Function Decimal.ToSByte(value As Decimal) As SByte
Shared Function Decimal.ToUInt16(value As Decimal) As UShort
Shared Function Decimal.ToUInt32(d As Decimal) As UInteger
Shared Function Decimal.ToUInt64(d As Decimal) As ULong
```

The Decimal type also includes the following floating point conversion methods, which perform widening conversions but, if a Decimal value has a fractional component, typically suffer from rounding error, since the Double and Single types have less precision than the Decimal:

```
Shared Function Decimal.ToDouble(d As Decimal) As Double
Shared Function Decimal.ToSingle(d As Decimal) As Single
```

ToString Method

The Decimal also supports another conversion method that converts a Decimal value to its string representation:

```
Function Decimal.ToString() As String
Function Decimal.ToString(format As String) As String
Function Decimal.ToString(provider As IFormatProvider) As String
Function Decimal.ToString(format As String, _
                          provider As IFormatProvider) As String
```

format is a String specifying the format of the returned string, and *provider* is an IFormatProvider implementation that supplies culture-specific formatting information.

Double and Single

The System.Double and System.Single structures have identical members. The Double or Single data type in the syntax statements is indicated by the notation <float>, which stands for the type whose member is called.

Epsilon Field

```
Shared ReadOnly Epsilon As <float>
```

A constant that represents the smallest possible positive value of a floating point number. For a Double, its value is 4.94065645841247^{-324}; for a Single, 1.401298^{-45}. It can be used in comparisons for near equality to determine whether the difference between two values is likely attributable to lack of precision.

MaxValue Field

```
Shared ReadOnly MaxValue As <float>
```

Returns the largest possible floating point value. For a Double, its value is 1.79769313486232^{308}; for a Single, 3.402823^{38}.

MinValue Field

```
Shared ReadOnly MinValue As <float>
```

A constant that represents the largest possible negative value of a floating point number. For a Double, its value is -1.79769313486232^{308}; for a Single, -3.402823^{38}.

NaN Field

```
Shared ReadOnly NaN As <float>
```

A constant that represents a value that is not a number. It results from an operation that is undefined, such as division of zero by zero. A NaN value can be evaluated with the IsNan method.

NegativeInfinity Field

```
Shared ReadOnly NegativeInfinity As <float>
```

A constant that represents negative infinity. It results from dividing a negative number by zero or when the result of an operation is less than MinValue.

PositiveInfinity Field

```
Shared ReadOnly PositiveInfinity As <float>
```

A constant that represents positive infinity. It results from dividing a positive number by zero or when the result of an operation is greater than MaxValue.

CompareTo Method

```
Function CompareTo(value As <float>) As Integer
Function CompareTo(value As <Object>) As Integer
```

Compares a *<float>* with a value of the same type and returns 0 if the instance and *value* are equal, –1 if the instance is less than the argument, and 1 if the instance is greater than the argument. In .NET 2.0, the method attempts to convert *value* to the same type as *floatVar* before performing the comparison.

Equals Method

```
Function Equals(obj As <float>) As Boolean
Function Equals(obj As <Object>) As Boolean
Shared Function Equals(objA As <float>, objB As <float>) As Boolean
```

Determines whether two floating point values are equal. However, due to rounding error, it is likely that the test for equality with two equal values will return False. Typically, equality with floating point values is determined by taking their difference and comparing it with a small quantity, like ten times epsilon.

GetTypeCode Method

```
Function GetTypeCode() As System.TypeCode
```

Returns the Double's type code, which is TypeCode.Double, or 14, or the Single's type code, which is TypeCode.Single, or 13.

IsInfinity Method

```
Shared Function IsInfinity(d As <float>) As Boolean
Shared Function IsInfinity(f As Single) As Boolean
```

Returns True if *d* or *f* evaluates to positive or negative infinity.

IsNan Method

```
Shared Function IsNan(d As Double) As Boolean
Shared Function IsNan(f As Single) As Boolean
```

Returns True if *d* or *f* evaluates to Nan.

IsNegativeInfinity Method

```
Shared Function IsNegativeInfinity(d As Double) As Boolean
Shared Function IsNegativeInfinity(f As Single) As Boolean
```

Returns True if *d* or *f* evaluates to NegativeInfinity.

IsPositiveInfinity Method

```
Shared Function IsPositiveInfinity(d As Double) As Boolean
Shared Function IsPositiveInfinity(f As Single) As Boolean
```

Returns True if *d* or *f* evaluates to PositiveInfinity.

Parse and TryParse Methods

```
Shared Function Parse(s As String) As <float>
Shared Function TryParse(s As String, ByRef result As <float>) As Boolean
Shared Function Parse(s As String, provider As IFormatProvider) As <float>
Shared Function Parse(s As String, style As NumberStyles) As <float>
Shared Function Parse(s As String, style As NumberStyles, _
                      provider As IFormatProvider) As <float>
Shared Function TryParse(s As String, style As NumberStyles, _
                         provider As IFormatProvider, ByRef result As <float>) _
                         As Boolean
```

Converts the String representation of a number to its floating point equivalent. *s* is the string to be converted, *result* is string converted to a *<float>*, *provider* is an object implementing the IFormatProvider interface that provides culture-specific formatting information about *s*, and *style* is a member of the NumberStyles enumeration that controls how *s* is parsed. Parse throws an exception if it is unable to convert the string; TryParse returns False.

ToString Method

```
Function <float>.ToString() As String
Function <float>.ToString(format As String) As String
Function <float>.ToString(provider As IFormatProvider) As String
Function <float>.ToString(format As String, _
                         provider As IFormatProvider) As String
```

Converts a floating point value to its string representation.

Integral Data Types

Visual Basic supports eight different integer data types. Four are signed: the SByte, Short (or System.Int16), Integer (or System.Int32), and Long (or System.Int64). Four are unsigned: Byte, UShort (or System.UInt16), UInteger (or System.UInt32), and ULong (or System.UInt64). The integral data type in the syntax statements is indicated by the notation <int>, which stands for the integer type whose member is called.

MaxValue Field

```
Shared ReadOnly MaxValue As <int>
```

Returns the largest possible integral value. Its values are: Byte, 255; Integer, 2,147,483,647; Long, 9,223,372,036,854,775,807; SByte, 127; Short, 32,767; UInteger, 4,294,967,295; ULong, 18,446,744,073,709,551,615; UShort, 65,535.

MinValue Field

```
Shared ReadOnly MinValue As <int>
```

Returns the smallest possible integral value. Its values are: SByte, –128; Short, –32,768; Integer, –21,474,83,648; Long, –9,223,372,036,854,775,808. The minimum value of all the unsigned data types (Byte, UShort, UInteger, and ULong) is 0.

Equals Method

```
Function Equals(obj As <int>) As Boolean
Function Equals(obj As <Object>) As Boolean
Shared Function Equals(objA As Object, objB As Object) As Boolean
```

Determines whether two integer values are equal. If *obj* is not of the same integral type, the method automatically converts it. However, the method will then return True only if a narrowing conversion was performed and the values are equal.

GetTypeCode Method

```
Function GetTypeCode() As System.TypeCode
```

Returns the integer's type code, as follows: System.TypeCode.Byte (6) for a Byte; System.TypeCode.Int32 (9) for an Integer; System.TypeCode.Int64 (11) for a Long; System.TypeCode.Int16 (7) for a Short; System.TypeCode.SByte (5) for an SByte;

System.TypeCode.UInt16 (8) for a UInteger; System.TypeCode.ULong (10) for a ULong; and System.TypeCode.UShort (12) for a UShort.

Parse and TryParse Methods

```
Shared Function Parse(s As String) As <int>
Shared Function TryParse(s As String, ByRef result As <int>) As Boolean
Shared Function Parse(s As String, provider As IFormatProvider) As <int>
Shared Function Parse(s As String, style As NumberStyles) As <int>
Shared Function Parse(s As String, style As NumberStyles, _
                    provider As IFormatProvider) As <int>
Shared Function TryParse(s As String, style As NumberStyles, _
                    provider As IFormatProvider, ByRef result As <int>) _
                    As Boolean
```

Converts the String representation of a number to its integer equivalent. *s* is the string to be converted, *result* is string converted to a *<float>*, *provider* is an object implementing the IFormatProvider interface that provides culture-specific formatting information about *s*, and *styles* is a member of the NumberStyles enumeration that controls how *s* is parsed. Parse throws an exception if it is unable to convert the string; TryParse returns False.

ToString Method

```
Function <int>.ToString() As String
Function <int>.ToString(format As String) As String
Function <int>.ToString(provider As IFormatProvider) As String
Function <int>.ToString(format As String, _
                                provider As IFormatProvider) As String
```

Converts an integer value to its string representation.

String

In comparison to Visual Basic 6.0, the String data type is enormously enhanced, since in addition to containing string data itself, it includes members that also provide much of the functionality needed to work with strings. The Visual Basic String data type corresponds to the System.String type, whose unique members are shown in the following sections.

New Method (Constructor)

```
Sub New(value() As Char)
Sub New(c As Char, count As Integer)
Sub New(value() As Char, startIndex As Integer, length As Integer)
```

value() is an array of Char values. *c* is a Char value representing a single character to be repeated, and *count* is an integer that defines the number of times *c* is to be repeated in the string. *startIndex* is the beginning position in *value* from which characters are to be extracted to form the string, and *length* is the number of characters to extract.

Empty Field

```
Shared ReadOnly Empty As String
```

Represents an empty string.

Chars Property

```
ReadOnly Default Property Chars(index As Integer) As Char
```

Returns the character at a particular position in the string. *index* indicates the zero-based character position of the character to return.

Length Property

```
ReadOnly Property Length As Integer
```

Returns the number of UTF16 characters in a string.

Clone Method

```
Function Clone() As Object
```

Returns a reference to the current string instance.

Compare Method

```
Shared Function Compare(strA As String, strB As String) As Integer
Shared Function Compare(strA As String, strB As String, _
                        ignoreCase As Boolean) As Integer
Shared Function Compare(strA As String, strB As String, _
                        comparisonType As StringComparison) As Integer
Shared Function Compare(strA As String, strB As String, _
                        ignoreCase As Boolean, culture As CultureInfo) _
                        As Integer
Shared Function Compare(strA As String, indexA As Integer, strB As String, _
                        indexB As Integer, length As Integer) As Integer
Shared Function Compare(strA As String, indexA As Integer, strB As String, _
                        indexB As Integer, length As Integer, _
                        ignoreCase As Boolean) As Integer
Shared Function Compare(strA As String, indexA As Integer, strB As String, _
                        indexB As Integer, length As Integer, _
                        comparisonType As StringComparison) As Integer
Shared Function Compare(strA As String, indexA As Integer, strB As String, _
                        indexB As Integer, length As Integer, _
                        ignoreCase As Boolean, culture As CultureInfo) As Integer
```

Indicates the relationship of two strings. It returns a negative value if *strA* is shorter than or precedes *strB*, 0 if they are equivalent or zero-length, and a positive value if *strA* is longer than or follows *strB*. *indexA* and *indexB* are the starting positions in *strA* and *strB*, respectively, for a substring comparison; *ignoreCase* is a Boolean indicating whether the comparison should be case-insensitive; *comparisonType* is a member of the StringComparison enumeration that specifies culture, case, and ordering rules for the comparison; *culture* is a CultureInfo instance with culture-specific comparison information; and *length* is the number of characters to compare in *strA* and *strB* for a substring comparison.

CompareOrdinal Method

```
Shared Function CompareOrdinal(strA As String, strB As String) As Integer
Shared Function CompareOrdinal(strA As String, indexA As Integer, _
                               strB As String, indexB As Integer, _
                               length As Integer) As Integer
```

Performs a character-by-character comparison of the character codes in two strings or substrings. *strA* and *strB* are the two strings to be compared, *indexA* and *index B* are the starting positions of the substring to compare in the first and second string, respectively, and *length* is the number of characters to compare. The method returns a negative value if *strA* is shorter than or precedes *strB*, 0 if they are equivalent or both zero-length, and a positive value if *strA* is longer than or follows *strB*.

CompareTo Method

```
Function CompareTo(value As Object) As Integer
Function CompareTo(strB As String) As Integer
```

Compares a String instance with a String argument represented either by *value* or *strB*. The function returns 0 if they are equal, –1 if the instance is shorter than or precedes the argument, and 1 if the instance is longer than or follows the argument. If *value* or *strB* is not a String value, an ArgumentException is thrown.

Concat Method

```
Shared Function Concat(arg0 As Object) As String
Shared Function Concat(ParamArray args() As Object) As String
Shared Function Concat(ParamArray values() As String) As String
Shared Function Concat(arg0 As Object, arg1 As Object) As String
Shared Function Concat(str0 As String, str1 As String) As String
Shared Function Concat(arg0 As Object, arg1 As Object, arg2 As Object) As String
Shared Function Concat(str0 As String, str1 As String, str2 As String) As String
Shared Function Concat(arg0 As Object, arg1 As Object, arg2 As Object, _
                       arg3 As Object) As String
Shared Function Concat(str0 As String, str1 As String, str2 As String, _
                       str3 As String) As String
```

Concatenates two or more strings. Overloads with arguments of type Object convert the object value to its string representation before performing the concatenation.

Contains Method

```
Function Contains(value As String) As Boolean
```

Indicates whether a substring specified by *value* exists within the string instance.

Copy Method

```
Shared Function Copy(str As String) As String
```

Creates a new String instance with the same value as *str*.

CopyTo Method

```
Sub CopyTo(sourceIndex As Integer, destination() As Char, _
           destinationIndex As Integer, count As Integer)
```

Copies a portion of a String instance to a designated position in a Char array, where *sourceIndex* is the one-based position in the string instance from which to begin the copy operation. *destination* is an array of Char; *destinationIndex* is the ordinal position in *destination* at which to begin the copy operation. *length* is the number of characters to copy. The destination array must be properly dimensioned for the copy operation to succeed or the method throws an ArgumentOutOfRangeException.

EndsWith Method

```
Function EndsWith(value As String) As Boolean
Function EndsWith(value As String, comparisonType As StringComparison) As Boolean
Function EndsWith(value As String, ignoreCase As Boolean, _
          culture As CultureInfo) As Boolean
```

Indicates whether the end of a String instance matches *value*. *ignoreCase* and *comparisonType* define how the comparison is made. *culture* is a CultureInfo object that defines culture-specific rules of comparison; it can also be set equal to Nothing.

Equals Method

```
Function Equals(obj As Object) As Boolean
Function Equals(value As String) As Boolean
Shared Function Equals(objA As Object, objB As Object) As Boolean
Shared Function Equals(a As String, b As String) As Boolean
Function Equals(value As String, _
    comparisonType As StringComparison) As Boolean
Shared Function Equals(a As String, b As String, _
    comparisonType As StringComparison) As Boolean
```

Indicates whether two strings or a string instance and an argument have the same value. *comparisonType* is a member of the StringComparison enumeration that defines how culture and case affect the comparison.

Format Method

```
Shared Function Format(format As String, arg0 As Object)  As String
Shared Function Format(format As String, ParamArray args() As Object) As String
Shared Function Format(provider As IFormatProvider, format As String, _
                  ParamArray args()As Object)  As String
```

```
Shared Function Format(format As String, arg0 As Object, _
                       arg1 As Object)  As String
Shared Function Format(format As String, arg0 As Object, _
                       arg1 As Object, arg2 As Object)  As String
```

Outputs a formatted string. *format* is a string containing format information; *arg0, arg1,* and *arg2* are Objects; and *args()* is an array of Objects containing data to be included in the output string. *provider* is an IFormatProvider implementation supplying culture-specific formatting information.

GetEnumerator Method

```
Function GetEnumerator() As CharEnumerator
```

Returns a CharEnumerator object that can be used to iterate a collection.

GetTypeCode Method

```
Function GetTypeCode() As TypeCode
```

Returns the String's type code, which is System.TypeCode.String, or 18.

IndexOf Method

```
Function IndexOf(value As Char) As Integer
Function IndexOf(value As String) As Integer
Function IndexOf(value As Char, startIndex As Integer) As Integer
Function IndexOf(value As String, startIndex As Integer) As Integer
Function IndexOf(value As String, comparisonType As StringComparison) As Integer
Function IndexOf(value As Char, startIndex As Integer, _
                 count As Integer) As Integer
Function IndexOf(value As String, startIndex As Integer, _
                 count As Integer) As Integer
Function IndexOf(value As String, startIndex As Integer, _
                 comparisonType As StringComparison) As Integer
Function IndexOf(value As String, startIndex As Integer, count As Integer, _
                 comparisonType As StringComparison) As Integer
```

Identifies the starting position of a Char or String in a string instance. *value* is either a string or Char to find, *startIndex* is the zero-based starting position of the search in the string instance, *count* is the number of characters in the instance to search, and *comparisonType* is a member of the StringComparison enumeration that defines how culture and case affect the comparison. The method returns the zero-based index position at which *value* starts, or −1 if *value* is not found.

IndexOfAny Method

```
Function IndexOfAny(anyOf() As Char) As Integer
Function IndexOfAny(anyOf() As Char, startIndex As Integer) As Integer
Function IndexOfAny(anyOf() As Char, startIndex As Integer, _
                    count As Integer) As Integer
```

Identifies the zero-based position in a string instance of any one of a number of characters in a Char array. *anyOf* is the Char array, *startIndex* is the zero-based starting position of the search, and *count* is the number of characters to search. The method returns the zero-based index position at which the first of any of the characters in *anyOf* is found, or –1 if none is not found.

Insert Method

```
Function Insert(startIndex As Integer, value As String) As String
```

Inserts a substring into a string and returns the resulting string. *startIndex* is the zero-based position at which to insert the substring, and *value* is the substring to insert.

Intern Method

```
Shared Function Intern(str As String) As String
```

Interns *str*, or returns a reference to an existing interned string. To conserve resources, the CLR maintains the *intern pool*, a table of all literal strings declared in a program. The Intern method allows you to retrieve strings from and place strings in the pool.

IsInterned Method

```
Shared Function IsInterned(str As String) As String
```

Returns a reference to *str* if it is in the intern pool (see the description of the Intern method), or Nothing if *str* is not interned.

IsNormalized Method

```
Function String.IsNormalized() As Boolean
Function String.IsNormalized(normalizationForm As NormalizationForm) As Boolean
```

Indicates whether a Unicode string is in normal form C (the default) or some other designated form indicated by *normalizationForm*.

IsNullOrEmpty Method

```
Shared Function IsNullOrEmpty(value As String)
```

Indicates whether the value of a string expression is Nothing or an empty string.

Join Method

```
Shared Function Join(separator As String, value() As String) As String
Shared Function Join(separator As String, value() As String, _
                     startIndex As Integer, count As Integer) As String
```

Concatenates a string array, *value*, using a particular separator character, *separator*. *startIndex* is the starting index in *value* at which to begin the concatenated string, and *count* is the number of elements in *value* to concatenate.

LastIndexOf Method

```
Function LastIndexOf(value As Char) As Integer
Function LastIndexOf(value As String) As Integer
Function LastIndexOf(value As Char, startIndex As Integer) As Integer
Function LastIndexOf(value As String, startIndex As Integer) As Integer
Function LastIndexOf(value As String, _
                    comparisonType As StringComparison) As Integer
Function LastIndexOf(value As Char, startIndex As Integer, _
                    count As Integer) As Integer
Function LastIndexOf(value As String, startIndex As Integer, _
                    count As Integer) As Integer
Function LastIndexOf(value As String, startIndex As Integer, _
                    comparisonType As StringComparison) As Integer
Function LastIndexOf(value As String, startIndex As Integer, _
                    count As Integer, comparisonType As StringComparison) _
                    As Integer
```

Returns the zero-based index position in a string at which the last occurrence of a particular character or substring is found, or –1 if the character or substring is not found. *value* is the character or substring to search for, *startindex* is the zero-based position at which to start the search, *count* is the number of character positions to search, and *comparisonType* is a member of the StringComparison enumeration that defines how culture and case affect the comparison.

LastIndexOfAny Method

```
Function LastIndexOfAny(anyOf() As Char) As Integer
Function LastIndexOfAny(anyOf() As Char, startIndex As Integer) As Integer
Function LastIndexOfAny(anyOf() As Char, startIndex As Integer, _
                       count As Integer) As Integer
```

Identifies the position in a string of the last occurrence of any one of a number of characters in a Char array. *anyOf* is the Char array, *startIndex* is the zero-based starting position of the search, and *count* is the number of characters to search. The method returns the zero-based index position at which the last of any of the characters in *anyOf* is found, or –1 if none is not found.

Normalize Method

```
Function Normalize() As String
Function Normalize(normalizationForm As NormalizationForm) As String
```

Returns a string whose textual value is the same as the original string instance but whose binary representation is Unicode normal form C (in the case of the first overload) or the normalization form defined by *normalizationForm*.

Overloaded Operators

For languages that don't support overloaded operators, the String type implements two operator procedures as method calls. The operations supported are: op_Equality (determines whether two string instances are equal by comparing their value) and op_Inequality (determines whether two string instances have different values).

PadLeft Method

```
Function PadLeft(totalWidth As Integer) As String
Function PadLeft(totalWidth As Integer, paddingChar As Char) As String
```

Right-aligns a string by padding its left side with spaces or another character, *paddingChar*. *totalWidth* is the total length of the resulting string, including padding characters.

PadRight Method

```
Function PadRight(totalWidth As Integer) As String
Function PadRight(totalWidth As Integer, paddingChar As Char) As String
```

Left-aligns a string by padding its right side with spaces or another character, *paddingChar*. *totalWidth* is the total length of the resulting string, including padding characters.

Remove Method

```
Function Remove(startIndex As Integer) As String
Function Remove(startIndex As Integer, count As Integer)
```

Removes a range of characters from a string starting at the zero-based *startIndex* position and continuing either to the end of the string or for *count* characters.

Replace Method

```
Function Replace(oldChar As Char, newChar As Char) As String
Function Replace(oldValue As String, newValue As String) As String
```

Replaces all occurrences of a single Char, *oldChar*, with another Char, *newChar*, or replaces all occurrences of a substring, *oldValue*, with another substring, *newValue*.

Split Method

```
Function Split(ParamArray separator() As Char) As String()
Function Split(separator() As Char, count As Integer) As String()
Function Split(separator() As Char, options As StringSplitOptions) As String()
Function Split(separator() As String, options As StringSplitOptions) As String()
Function Split(separator() As Char, count As Integer, _
               options As StringSplitOptions) As String()
Function Split(separator() As String, count As Integer, _
               options As StringSplitOptions) As String()
```

Returns a string array from a string instance by separating it at each character or substring in *separator*. Both *omitEmptyEntries* and *options* indicate whether empty elements should be omitted from the returned string array, and *count* determines the maximum number of elements to return.

StartsWith Method

```
Function StartsWith(value As String) As Boolean
Function StartsWith(value As String, _
                    comparisonType As StringComparison) As Boolean
Function StartsWith(value As String, ignoreCase As Boolean, _
                    culture As CultureInfo) As Boolean
```

Determines whether a string instance starts with a particular substring specified by *value*. *ignoreCase* determines whether the comparison should be case insensitive, *comparisonType* defines how culture and case affect the comparison, and *culture* defines the culture to be used for the comparison.

Substring Method

```
Function Substring(startIndex As Integer) As String
Function Substring(startIndex As Integer, length As Integer) As String
```

Returns a substring from a string instance starting at the zero-based *startIndex* position and continuing either to the end of the string or for *length* characters.

ToCharArray Method

```
Function ToCharArray() As Char()
Function ToCharArray(startIndex As Integer, length As Integer) As Char()
```

Returns a character array containing the individual characters in a string instance. Either all characters are included, or only those characters from the zero-based *startIndex* position for *length* characters.

ToLower, ToLowerInvariant Methods

```
Function ToLower() As String
Function ToLower(culture As CultureInfo) As String
Function ToLowerInvariant() As String
```

Converts the characters in a string to lowercase using the casing rules of the current culture (in the case of ToLower with no arguments), the culture specified by the *culture* argument, or the invariant culture (the ToLowerInvariant method).

ToString Method

```
Function ToString() As String
Function ToString(provider As IFormatProvider) As String
```

Returns a string instance unchanged. *provider* has no effect on the operation of the method.

ToUpper, ToUpperInvariant Methods

```
Function ToUpper() As String
Function ToUpper(culture As CultureInfo) As String
Function ToUpperInvariant() As String
```

Converts the characters in a string to uppercase using the casing rules of the current culture (in the case of ToUpper with no arguments), the culture specified by the *culture* argument, or the invariant culture (the ToUpperInvariant method).

Trim Method

```
Function Trim() As String
Function Trim(trimChars() As Char) As String
```

Returns a string with all leading and trailing spaces removed, or with all leading and trailing characters included in the *trimChars* array removed.

TrimEnd Method

```
Function TrimEnd(ParamArray trimChars() As Char) As String
```

Removes all occurrences of a set of characters designated by *trimChars* from the end of a string.

TrimStart Method

```
Function TrimStart(ParamArray trimChars() As Char) As String
```

Removes all occurrences of a set of characters designated by *trimChars* from the beginning of a string.

Language Elements Removed from Visual Basic .NET

A long with its addition of new features, Visual Basic .NET represents an attempt to streamline and rationalize the Visual Basic language, as well as to integrate it with .NET and the .NET Framework Class Library. One reflection of this is the fact that the Visual Basic type system now simply wraps the .NET Common Type System. Another is that a number of language elements present in Visual Basic 6.0 and earlier versions have been removed. There are a number of reasons for the removal of language elements:

- The functionality was sufficiently important to relocate outside of the Visual Basic language and in the .NET Framework Class Library. For instance, many of the math and financial functions previously available in Visual Basic 6.0 and earlier versions are now members of the System.Math class.

- A number of language elements, such as the Visual Basic file access statements, were considered representative of an older style of procedural programming that is not appropriate in an object-oriented, event-driven runtime environment.

- Some language elements, such as the GoSub statement, were antiquated and little used.

- Some language elements had little to do with Visual Basic and much more to do with general application programming. Many of these elements, such as many of Visual Basic's mathematical functions, were moved to the System namespace of the .NET Framework Class Library.

This appendix lists the language elements removed from Visual Basic in the initial release of Visual Basic .NET. It defines Visual Basic 6.0 rather broadly, to include not only the VBA library and the language elements implemented by the Visual Basic compiler, but also the types and type members available in the Microsoft Scripting Runtime. In each case, it also lists a replacement element or work-around, if one exists.

Language Element	Description	Replacement
Abs function	Returns the absolute value of a number	System.Math.Abs method
Array function	Initializes an array	Array initialization statement
Atn function	Returns the angle whose tangent is a specified number	System.Math.Atan method
Calendar property	Returns or sets a value (vbCalGreg or vbCalHijri) that specifies the type of calendar to use with a project	The Calendar property of the CultureInfo.DateTimeFormat class in the System.Globalization namespace
CCur function	Converts an expression to a Currency data type	None
Close statement	Closes a file opened with the Open statement	FileClose subroutine
Cos function	Returns the cosine of a specified angle	System.Math.Cos method
CVDate function	Returns a variant whose runtime type is Date	CDate function
CVErr function	Returns a variant whose runtime type is Error that contains an application-defined error number	None
Date statement	Sets the system date	DateString property
Debug object	Provides access to program debugging methods in the design-time environment	System.Diagnostics.Debug class
Debug.Assert method	Suspends program execution and transfers control to the Immediate window if an expression evaluates to False	Assert method of the System.Diagnostics.Debug class
Debug.Print method	Writes output to the Immediate window	Write, WriteIf, WriteLine, and WriteLineIf methods of the System.Diagnostics.Debug class
Def... statements (DefBool, DefByte, DefInt, etc.)	Defines a default data type for variables whose names start with a particular letter or range of letters	None
Dictionary object (Microsoft Scripting Runtime)	Stores a collection of name/value pairs	In the System.Collections namespace, the Hashtable class and IDictionary interface; in the System.Collections.Generic namespace, the Generic Dictionary class
DoEvents subroutine	Pauses to read from a project's message queue	My.Application.DoEvents method; DoEvents method of the Application object in the System.Windows.Forms namespace

Language Element	Description	Replacement
Drive object (Microsoft Scripting Runtime)	Provides information about a system drive	System.IO.DriveInfo class
Drives object (Microsoft Scripting Runtime)	A collection object containing Drive objects	Drives property of My.Computer.FileSystem class, which returns a ReadOnlyCollection(Of System.IO.DriveInfo) objects; GetDrive method of DriveInfo class, which returns an array of DriveInfo objects
End Type statement	Ends a user-defined type definition	End Structure statement
Eqv operator	Logical equivalence operator	Not (*expression1* XOr *expression2*)
Error, Error$ functions	Returns a description that corresponds to an error code	ErrorToString function; Message property of the System.Exception class or any class derived from it
Exp function	Returns the antilogarithm of a number	System.Math.Exp method
File object (Microsoft Scripting Runtime)	Provides information about a file	System.IO.File and System.IO.FileInfo classes.
Files object (Microsoft Scripting Runtime)	A collection object containing File objects	An array of FileInfo objects returned by the GetFiles method of the DirectoryInfo object
FileSystemObject object	Provides information about a file system and access	FileSystemProxy class of the Microsoft.VisualBasic.CompilerServices namespace, accessible through the My.Computer.FileSystem property
Folder object (Microsoft Scripting Runtime)	Provides information about a directory	System.IO.Directory and System.IO.DirectoryInfo classes
Folders object (Microsoft Scripting Runtime)	A collection object containing Folder objects	GetDirectory method of the DirectoryInfo class, which returns an array of DirectoryInfo objects
Get statement	Stores data from a file to a variable	FileGet, FileGetObject subroutines
Global statement	Defines a public program element	Public keyword
GoSub statement	Passes execution to a subroutine within a procedure	None
IMEStatus function	Indicates the character set used by the Input Method Editor for Far Eastern versions of Windows	ImeMode property of a number of user interface elements
Imp operator	Logical implication operator	(Not *expression1*) Or *expression2*
Initialize event	Event fired when an object is first used	None. (A rough equivalent is the class constructor, defined in Visual Basic .NET by the New subroutine. The constructor executes when an object is instantiated using the New keyword.)
Input statement	Reads delimited data from a sequential file	Input subroutine

Language Element	Description	Replacement
IsEmpty function	Determines if a variant variable has been initialized	None
IsMissing function	Determines whether an optional argument has been passed to a procedure	None. (In Visual Basic .NET, optional arguments must be assigned a default value.)
IsNull function	Determines whether an expression contains any Null data, which usually indicates missing data	None
IsObject function	Indicates whether a variable contains an object reference	None. IsReference provides similar (although not identical) functionality in Visual Basic .NET
Line Input statement	Reads a line from an open sequential file	LineInput function
Load statement	Loads a form or control into memory	In Visual Basic .NET, forms and controls are loaded by instantiating them using the New keyword.
LoadResData function	Loads a resource from a resource (.RES) file included with a project	GetObject method of the System.Resources.ResourceManager class. If necessary, an equivalent Support.LoadResData method is available in the Microsoft.VisualBasic.Compatibility.VB6 namespace (found in the Microsoft.VisualBasic.Compatibility.dll assembly)
LoadResPicture function	Assigns an image to the Picture property of a form or control	NET provides a number of methods for handling image and icon resources, including the GetObject method of the Sustem.Resources.ResourceManager class. If necessary, an equivalent Support.LoadResPicture method is available in the Microsoft.VisualBasic.Compatibility.VB6 namespace (found in the Microsoft.VisualBasic.Compatibility.dll assembly)
LoadResString function	Retrieves a string from a resource (.RES) file	.NET provides a number of methods for handling string resources, including the GetString method of the Sustem.Resources.ResourceManager class. If necessary, however, an equivalent Support.LoadResString method is available in the Microsoft.VisualBasic.Compatibility.VB6 namespace (found in the Microsoft.VisualBasic.Compatibility.dll assembly)
Lock statement	Locks all or part of a file	Lock subroutine

Language Element	Description	Replacement
Log function	Returns the natural logarithm of a number	System.Math.Log method
Name statement	Renames a file or directory	Rename subroutine
ObjPtr function	Returns a pointer to an object	None
Open statement	Opens a file	FileOpen subroutine
Option Base statement	Defines the default lower bound of an array	None
Option Private Module statement	Restricts the accessibility of a VBA code module to the project in which the module appears	Though Option Private Module is available only in a hosted VBA environment, a rough Visual Basic .NET equivalent is the Module statement with the Friend access modifier.
Print statement	Writes formatted data to a file	Print, PrintLine subroutines
Property Get statement	Defines a property get accessor	Get statement nested in a Property statement
Property Let statement	Defines a property set accessor	Set statement nested in a Property statement
Property Set statement	Defines a property set accessor that assigns an object reference to a property	Set statement nested in a Property statement
Put statement	Writes the value of a variable to a file	FilePut, FilePutObject subroutines
Return statement	Returns from a GoSub call	None. The Return statement in Visual Basic .NET transfers control from a function or subroutine.
Round function	Rounds a number	System.Math.Round method
Seek statement	Positions the file or record pointer	Seek function
SendKeys statement	Simulates keyboard input	My.Computer.Keyboard.SendKeys method, System.Windows.Forms.SendKeys class
Set statement	Assigns an object reference to a variable	None; no statement is needed for an object assignment. (The Set statement in Visual Basic .NET serves as a property set accessor.)
Sgn function	Indicates the sign of a number	System.Math.Sign method
Sin function	Returns the sine of an angle	System.Math.Sin method
Sqr function	Calculates the square root of a number	System.Math.Sqrt method
String function	Creates a string consisting of a particular character repeated a specified number of times	StrDup function

Language Element	Description	Replacement
StrPtr function	Returns a pointer to a string buffer	None
Tan function	Computes the tangent of an angle	System.Math.Tan method
Terminate event	Fired when the last reference to an object is removed from memory	Equivalent to the class destructor (Finalize and Dispose)
TextStream object (Microsoft Scripting Runtime)	Represents a read or write stream to a text file	System.IO.StreamReader, System.IO.StreamWriter classes
Time function	Returns the current system time	TimeOfDay property, TimeString property
Time statement	Sets the current system time	TimeOfDay property, TimeString property
Type statement	Defines a user-defined type	Structure statement
Unload statement	Unloads a form or a dynamically loaded control	System.Windows.Forms.Form.Close method
Unlock statement	Removes a lock placed with the Lock statement	Unlock subroutine
VarPtr function	Returns a pointer to a variable	None
Wend statement	Ends a While block	End While statement
Width statement	Defines the number of characters in an output line	FileWidth subroutine
Write statement	Writes structured data to a file	Write, WriteLine subroutines

Index